The Guru's Guide to SQL Server Architecture and Internals

The Guru's Guide to SQL Server Architecture and Internals

Ken Henderson

✦✦Addison-Wesley

Boston • San Francisco • New York • Toronto • Montreal
London • Munich • Paris • Madrid
Capetown • Sydney • Tokyo • Singapore • Mexico City

The publisher offers discounts on this book when ordered in quantity for bulk purchases and special sales. For more information, please contact:

U.S. Corporate and Government Sales
(800) 382-3419
corpsales@pearsontechgroup.com

For sales outside of the U.S., please contact:

International Sales
(317) 581-3793
international@pearsontechgroup.com

Visit Addison-Wesley on the Web: www.awprofessional.com

Library of Congress Cataloging-in-Publication Data

Henderson, Ken.
    The Guru's guide to SQL server architecture and internals / Ken Henderson.
      p. cm.
    ISBN 0-201-70047-6 (Paperback : alk. paper)
    1. SQL server. 2. Client/server computing.   3. Debugging in computer science—Computer programs.
  I. Title.

QA76.9.C55H44 2003
005.75'85—dc22

                                2003015828

ISBN: 0-201-70047-6
Text printed on recycled paper
1 2 3 4 5 6 7 8 9 10—CRS—0706050403
First printing, October 2003

For D

Contents

List of Exercises

Foreword

When I first started programming computers, I wrote many programs before taking the time to understand the instruction set of the system I was developing on. I got most of these programs working, but debugging complex issues was a painstaking process. As the sophistication of the programs evolved, I eventually hit a wall. When I stepped back and learned the instruction set and underlying architecture of the system, an amazing thing happened: I was able to break through the wall, and I became much more proficient. Frustration and complexity melted away, and, armed with a deep knowledge of the system, I was able to do things that were impossible before.

You've no doubt experienced something similar. Maybe it was while programming computers. Perhaps it was in learning to play a musical instrument—after a short time, you could play scales or simple melodies. However, to truly master an instrument to the point where you can improvise freely requires deep knowledge in both musical theory and proficiency in the instrument. This is the difference between surface knowledge (having the ability to use something) and deep knowledge (knowing how something really works so that you can master it and synthesize new knowledge based on your deep understanding).

Ken Henderson has invested tremendous effort in unlocking the secrets of Microsoft SQL Server, having recently written *The Guru's Guide to Transact-SQL* (Addison-Wesley, 2000) and *The Guru's Guide to SQL Server Stored Procedures, XML, and HTML* (Addison-Wesley, 2002). Ken is one of those people who seek deep knowledge. He isn't satisfied in knowing how to operate something—he needs to know how something operates. In his research for *The Guru's Guide to SQL Server Architecture and Internals*, Ken learned how SQL Server operates, from the ground up—and that is how he presents it.

Part I, Foundations, describes the fundamental substrate on which SQL Server is built. By discussing various Windows services and facilities, this section helps familiarize readers with how SQL Server (or any other high-performance Windows application) communicates with Windows.

Part II, Subsystems, Components, and Technologies, delves into the architecture of SQL Server's core relational engine. Ken discusses the User Mode Scheduler (UMS), a base component of SQL Server that allows it to efficiently scale to thousands of users and process tens of thousands of transactions per second. A highlight of this section is the chapter on the query processor. Ken offers an incredibly clear description of how a query is transformed from SQL text (supplied by an application or user) through parsing, normalization, optimization, and ultimate conversion into a series of physical operators that the execution engine runs to solve the query. Throughout this section Ken describes many of the optimizer's inputs, plan choices, and execution strategies. He also offers a number of "under the cover" tips for how you can peer into this complex portion of the product to determine why the optimizer may have chosen a particular plan to solve your complex query.

Part III, Data Services, discusses the various ways you can interact with SQL Server's core data engine. In this section Ken describes SQL Server's XML facilities and how Data Transformation Services (DTS) can be used to transform and move data into and out of SQL Server. The recently released Notification Services, which can be used to create highly scaled event- and subscription-based data services, is also covered. Finally, Ken describes the various replication technologies supported by SQL Server in great detail.

One obligation in writing a foreword for a book is to provide guidance about who should read it. In this instance, the recommendation is clear: This book is for anyone interested in furthering their existing knowledge of SQL Server into deep knowledge. Some people are naturally inclined to explore any new subject in a deep way. If you are someone who is not satisfied in knowing that something works, but rather you need to know how and why it works, Ken's book will quench your thirst. Perhaps you find that your knowledge of SQL Server, built over a period of time by using the product, no longer offers you explanations to complex issues and questions you face. Ken's book will take you beyond Books Online and into the inner workings of the product. Maybe you simply want to know how SQL Server, a complex and high-performance application, was designed and constructed. Again, *The Guru's Guide to SQL Server Architecture and Internals* will meet your needs.

I can pretty much guarantee that anyone who uses SQL Server on a regular basis (even those located in Redmond working on SQL Server) can learn something new by reading this book.

David Campbell
June 2003

David Campbell joined Microsoft in 1994 as a developer on the core storage engine of Microsoft SQL Server. He has been with the SQL Server team since then and is currently the Product Unit Manager of the Relational Server team.

Historical Perspective

It is hard to believe that it has been ten years since I was offered a job to work at Microsoft to support its new SQL Server Windows NT product. I never thought I would find myself or our product in the position we are today. My previous experience was as a C programmer and database developer on UNIX systems mainly working with Oracle and Ingres. My perception of Microsoft was purely as a desktop company. The only database I had even seen on a PC was dBase. As I contemplated the job offer, I was naturally skeptical. How could Microsoft even create a product that could compete with the biggest names in the database industry? Fortunately for me, Andrea Stoppani, the director of SQL Support for Microsoft in 1993, convinced me that not only would Microsoft and SQL Server be successful but also that I would find a rewarding career with Microsoft because I would have an opportunity like never before: to train, learn, debug, and dig into the internal "nuts and bolts" of a relational database engine.

Ten years later, that promise has held true. In my role as an escalation engineer at Microsoft, I've had to train, learn, debug, and dig into the internal mechanics of the engine that drives SQL Server. Because of that gained knowledge, I've been asked to advise and provide feedback and insight to the development team with each new release. Through these years, I've witnessed an evolution and revolution with this product, from the early years of supporting SQL Server 4.20 for OS/2 when customers on single processor machines were limited to 16MB of RAM to the enterprise-ready, TPC record-breaking SQL Server 2000 Enterprise Server running on a machine with 64CPUs and 512GB of RAM.

The engine itself has clearly evolved from its early origin. The storage engine and query processor for SQL Server 4.20 through SQL Server 6.5 were all based on the original architectural design that came from the port of the Sybase engine on OS/2. During these years, remarkable changes and additions were performed to make the engine run faster and become a reliable, affordable platform for many users looking to deploy database systems. However, these efforts ultimately reached their limits. This is why SQL Server 7.0 was so significant. Microsoft attracted some of the leading developers in the database industry to design and implement a new architecture for the engine, a foundation to build on for years to come.

The changes and evolution have not just been with the SQL Server engine. In fact, in my early years of supporting SQL Server, the engine was the primary focus of the job because the product was pretty much the engine, sqlservr.exe. The development community back then focused its efforts on Visual Basic or C applications using DB-Library communicating over named pipes or IPX/SPX. ODBC was just an idea on Kyle Geiger's computer. Today, it is more common for Microsoft support engineers to deal with multitiered Web-based applications supporting online business retail applications with thousands of users all communicating over TCP/IP. The mind-set of supporting "just the engine" no longer applies. The SQL Server product has expanded to include a rich framework of data services including Multi-Server Job Scheduling, Data Replication, XML, Data Transformation Services, and Notification Services.

As I reflect on the changes to the engine and the core additions that have made it such a popular product, I think about the common questions I get from customers and other Microsoft employees: "How can I learn more about what makes SQL Server so powerful? How can I gain expert knowledge of some of the internals of the SQL Server engine in order to maximize the usage of the product?" My answer is always, "Think like a programmer." To be more specific, "Think like a Windows programmer."

I have learned the importance of gaining a solid understanding of the foundation of technology that the engine uses to perform its work. This includes a range of Windows programming topics such as processes, threads, synchronization, asynchronous I/O, dynamic linked libraries, virtual memory, networking, and COM. Regardless of the various SQL Server releases over the years, learning these topics has been essential to my understanding of the internals of the product. Learning these topics takes much more than just reading about them. You must apply the knowledge and truly understand the meaning behind the concepts. Don't just read about what structure exception handling is—understand why it has become an important feature for the SQL Server engine to use. Part I of this book can help guide you toward that goal. It provides concise, comprehensible coverage of Windows programming fundamentals. But don't just read those chapters. Go through the examples and be sure you understand the answers to the questions in each chapter. Once you master a solid knowledge of these concepts, you will have the right foundation and frame of mind to understand Part II of this book, which covers the internals of the core components that make up the SQL Server engine. Armed with this information, you will be able to broaden and round your skills by understanding the technologies covered in Part III that complement the engine and provide the complete database services product that SQL Server has become.

SQL Server has grown as a technology and as a force in the database industry. The number of high-quality books on this product alone is a leading indicator. When I started at Microsoft in 1993, there were no books on Microsoft SQL Server (and only one was produced within the next year). Today you can search the Web or go to your local bookstore and find dozens of books dedicated to this product ranging from topics on performance tuning to database administration to XML. The development of this book is a testament to the product's success. The book seeks to expand the knowledge of important topics about SQL Server in order to broaden the level of expertise worldwide. With knowledge there is power, and this book is about empowering SQL Server users, developers, and administrators to get the most out of the product.

Bob Ward
June 2003

Bob Ward joined Microsoft in 1993 as a support engineer for Microsoft SQL Server. He is currently an escalation engineer in SQL Server Support.

Preface

I grew up on a farm in America's heartland. From the time I was eight years old until I left home for college, I lived in a small wood-frame house in rural Oklahoma with my parents and sisters. I experienced life as a bona fide country boy with all its attendant wholesomeness, adventure, and isolation.

I came up in a time when running water and electricity were already commonplace, even in rural Oklahoma, so I have no horror stories to relate about the lack of basic accoutrements or outhouses or dirt floors. I did, however, milk five cows every day before I went to school; I bailed hay in the summer and cut firewood in the fall; and my sisters and I helped our parents plant and harvest a large truck garden every spring and summer. I fed chickens, hogs, and various other creatures, and I delivered my share of baby calves and slaughtered perhaps more than my share of feeder steers.

My parents' motivation for moving to the country was never quite clear to me. My dad's work as a government engineer afforded us a comfortable life in suburbia that didn't seem to be in need of such a major overhaul. Nevertheless, during my ninth year on earth, my parents uprooted us and took us to a life that we city dwellers had never even dreamt of. Prior to that time, I'd never seen a live cow except on television, nor had I ever ridden a horse. We pulled up stakes and went to the country, and all that changed.

I still remember my mother sitting us down the day before we moved and telling us that leaving the city was a chance to learn some wonderful new aspects of life, to gain perspective, to see things through different eyes than most people ever had the chance to. She countered our litany of complaints and misgivings with enthusiasm and reassurance that not only would everything work out, it would actually be for the best. She believed that every experience was a chance to learn something. Like Thoreau, she wanted to suck the very marrow out of life. She decided early on that we would get the most out of our time on the farm, and she did everything in her power to make sure that happened. I didn't really understand the import of all she said back then—I did not want to move—but I understand now.

Without a doubt, moving to the country *was* a wonderful opportunity to learn life's lessons. They were all right there in nature: in the rivers, in the trees, and in the cycle of living and dying so evident all around us. For a boy of eight, there was no better place to learn. Exploring the woods, rafting down the creek, fishing in the pond, pulling fresh fruit from a tree and eating it unwashed—every day was an adventure, a time of exploration to learn more about the observable world. I learned what life had to teach in ways I never could have had we stayed in the city, and I'll always be thankful for that.

My mother went to great lengths to make sure our education did not suffer as a result of our being transplanted to the sticks. She started a personal library for each of us and tried to infuse in us all the same love for reading that she'd had her whole life. When the county wouldn't open a library anywhere near us, she convinced the library to start up a summer bookmobile program. Bookmobile Day, as it came to be known, was a joyous occasion, a time when a rambunctious pack of little kids raced each other up the quarter-mile jaunt to the old country church where the mobile library parked. Inside the converted RV, the walls were lined with books, and the air-conditioned coolness was a wonderful respite from the hot Oklahoma sun. We would stay until they kicked us out, each time leaving with an armload of books to be returned on the next Bookmobile Day.

It was during this time that I first began to explore the mysteries of life itself. I wanted to know where it all came from, how it all worked. I read voraciously, my eight-year-old mind gobbling up every science book and every electronics book I could get my hands on. I wanted to know the secret of it all; I wanted to know what the basic essence of everything was. I wanted to know how life, how the world—how everything—worked. I wanted to understand what literally made the world go 'round.

It was in those days that I came across my first physics books and realized that I was on to something. I had found a trail that might lead me to the understanding I sought. I read about gravity and magnetism, about strong and weak particles. I formed a mind model of how the universe worked. I gained an understanding—however imperfect it might have been—of how everything interoperated, how it was designed, and how reality as I understood it came down to just a handful of fundamental concepts that I could readily see at work in the natural world around me. I came to know a basic "system" of life, a framework that could explain pretty much everything that existed. Suddenly, the country, nature, and the world as I knew it began to make sense.

Since that time, I have approached almost everything I've learned with the same raw curiosity. I want to know how it works; I want to understand it holistically. I work hard not to settle for cursory explanations or shallow understanding. I am driven to know precisely how something is put together and how its component parts interoperate and interrelate. I believe this is the only real way to master something, to truly grasp its *raison d'être*.

That philosophy was the genesis of this book. I wrote it to pass on what I have learned about how SQL Server and its fundamental technologies are designed, how they work, and how they interoperate. I wrote it because I enjoy exploring SQL Server. I have covered how to use and program SQL Server in previous books; I wrote this book to detail how SQL Server is put together from an architectural standpoint. By doing so, it's my hope that I can pass on to you the same wonderment, the same love for technology and for all things SQL Server that I have.

It's my belief that the road to true mastery of SQL Server or any other technology begins with exploring its design. Knowing how to put a technology to practical use is certainly important, but that begins with understanding how it works and how it was intended to be used. Being intimately familiar with how SQL Server is designed will make you a better SQL Server practitioner. It will take you to heights that otherwise would have been unreachable.

I said goodbye to that sandy-haired boy running barefoot through the backwoods of rural Oklahoma long ago. I live in the city now, but the country lives in me still. My mind often drifts back to moonlit walks in the field, the open sky, the wonderment of all that was and all that could be. I still recall the smell of fresh alfalfa on the evening breeze, the unfettered joy of rolling headlong down golden hills, the abandonment of all of life's cares for that one rapturous moment. I miss the adventure and the oneness with life that I came to know back then. I grow wistful for the echo of the crow in the distance; I miss twilight in the forest. I miss the tire swing over the pond and the taste of fresh corn pulled ripe from the stalk.

As I've said, although I left the country, the country never really left me. The same is true of my insatiable desire to explore and understand all that I can about the world around me and the things that pique my interest. Although I've moved around a bit and changed jobs from time to time, the sense of adventure that drove me to explore the strange new place I found myself in at the age of eight is with me still. I have spent my life since those days on one journey after another, exploring one new world after another in hopes of learning all that I possibly can. I am still on my quest to learn all that I can about SQL Server. I've been working with the technology since 1990, and still there's plenty left to be discovered. Here's hoping that you'll join me as I retrace my path through the technology, exploring new places and discovering sights yet unseen. And here's hoping that you will enjoy the trip as much as I have.

Ken Henderson
March 11, 2003

Acknowledgments

Every book I've written has literally had an entire army of people behind it that helped make it come to pass. This book is no exception. I will begin by thanking the many SQL Server MVPs and industry experts who reviewed this book and gave me a wealth of constructive feedback on it. I'm especially grateful to Greg Linwood, Tony Rogerson, Allan Mitchell, Darren Green, Aaron Bertrand, T. K. Dinesh, and Wayne Snyder. This wouldn't be the book that it is without your contributions.

I would also like to thank my friends at Microsoft who reviewed the manuscript and helped me turn out a better book than I otherwise could have, particularly Bart Duncan, Robert Dorr, Keith Elmore, Bob Ward, Diane Larsen, Christa Carpentiere, Dick Dievendorff, and those on the SQL Server development team who reviewed the text. I'd also like to thank Vern Ameen of Microsoft for first believing in me and the value I would bring to the company. Thanks, Vern—your confidence in me will not be forgotten. I'd like to thank Ron Soukup, also formerly of Microsoft and the original "father" of SQL Server, for his belief in me and his support of my work. Ron, the talk we had shortly after you left the company made all the difference—thank you again for it.

From a personal standpoint, I'd like to thank my friends John Cochran and Lorraine Beaudette, who reviewed several portions of the manuscript and encouraged me to keep the edge on it when I was sorely tempted to round it off. Your support of my work and your personal friendship over the years are worth more to me than you will ever know.

My friend Neil Coy has, as always, been both a source of inspiration and a steadfast mentor throughout this project. I don't think anyone who ever met Neil wasn't influenced by him in some positive way, and I am certainly in his debt. This book has benefited from his influence, as have all my books. There are a few constants in my life that I've come to depend on. One of them is my close kinship with Neil Coy. Neil, you're a coder's coder. Thanks for all you taught me all those years ago and for all you continue to teach.

I would be remiss if I didn't also pause to thank the wonderful people at Addison-Wesley who helped make this book possible. My editor, Karen Gettman, has been a real trooper throughout the whole project. Thanks for keeping me on track, Karen. Emily Frey, Karin Hansen, and Curt Johnson have also been a tremendous help in making this project come to pass. The production team, Elizabeth Ryan of Addison-Wesley, Kim Arney Mulcahy, Monica Groth Farrar, and Chrysta Meadowbrooke, have also been wonderful to work with. I will single out Chrysta here for special recognition: Chrysta, you're the best copyeditor I've ever worked with—keep up the excellent work. And I'd like to also thank Carter Shanklin, who originally brought me to Addison-Wesley, and Michael Slaughter and Mary O'Brien, my former editors, who are largely responsible for the success we've had thus far.

Lastly, I'd like to thank my wife. Simply put, she is a saint. She has made this and every other book I've written possible. Her superhuman abilities as a mother help me get past the natural guilt that comes from being away from my kids for months at a time while I struggle along in my office cranking out my latest book. She makes the whip that Capote talks about a little more bearable. And she makes all the late nights and bleary-eyed mornings somehow worth it.

Introduction

One day I started writing, not knowing that I had chained myself for life
to a noble but merciless master. When God hands you a gift, he hands
you a whip; and the whip is intended solely for self-flagellation. . . .
I'm here alone in my dark madness, all by myself with my deck
of cards—and, of course, the whip God gave me.

—Truman Capote[1]

I wrote this book to get inside SQL Server. I wanted to see what we could learn about the product and the technologies on which it's based through the use of a freely downloadable debugger, a few well-placed xprocs, and a lot of tenacity. The book you're reading is the result of that experiment.

In my two previous SQL Server books, I focused more on the pragmatic aspects of SQL Server—how to program it and how to make practical use of its many features. As the title suggests, this book focuses more on the architectural design of the product. Here, we dwell on the technical underpinnings of the product more than on how to use it. It's my belief that understanding how the product works will make you a better SQL Server practitioner. You will use the product better and leverage its many features more successfully in your work because you will have a deeper understanding of how those features work and how they were intended to be used.

About Books Online

As with my previous books, one of the design goals of this book was to avoid needlessly repeating the information in Books Online. This necessitated

---

1. Capote, Truman. *Music for Chameleons* (reprint edition). New York: Vintage Books, 1994, pp. xi and xix.

omitting certain subjects that you might expect to find in a book like this. For example, I had originally planned to include an overview chapter that covered the architectural layout of the product from a high-level point of view. I had also planned to have a chapter on the architecture of the storage engine. However, on rereading the coverage of these subjects in Books Online (see the topic SQL Server Architecture Overview and the subtopics it links) and in other sources, I didn't feel I could improve on it substantially.

My purpose isn't to fill these pages with information that is already readily available to you; it is to pick up where the product documentation (and other books and whitepapers) leave off and take the discussion to the next level. As such, in this book I assume that you've read through Books Online and that you understand the basic concepts it relates.

About WinDbg

This book features a good deal of work with WinDbg, Microsoft's freely downloadable symbolic debugger. You may be wondering why we need a debugger to explore SQL Server in the first place. After all, we obviously aren't going to "debug" SQL Server, and we certainly don't have source code for it, so we won't be stepping through code as is typically the case with a debugger.

The reason we use a debugger is that it gives us the ability to look under the hood of a running process in ways no other tool can. A debugger lets us see the threads currently running inside the process, their current call stacks, the state of virtual memory and heaps within the process, and various other important process-wide and thread-specific data. It lets us set breakpoints, view registers, and see when DLLs are loaded by the process or rebased by Windows. It lets us pause execution, dump memory regions, and save and restore the complete process state. In short, a debugger provides a kind of "X-ray" facility—a tool that lets us peer inside a process and see what's really going on within it. In this case, the object of our interest is SQL Server, but the basic debugging skills you'll learn in this book could be used to investigate any Win32 application. One of the chief goals of this book is to equip you with some basic coding and debugging skills so that you can continue the exploration of SQL Server on your own.

If we are to truly get inside the product and understand how it works, using a debugger is a must. Trying to understand the internal workings of a technology by merely reading about it in books or whitepapers is like trying to learn about a foreign country without actually visiting it—there's no substitute for just going there.

Given that WinDbg is freely downloadable from the Microsoft Web site, has the features we need, and is relatively easy to use, it seems the obvious choice. A symbolic debugger, it can use the symbols that ship with SQL Server and that are publicly available over the Internet, so it's a suitable choice for exploring the inner workings and architectural design of the product.

About the Fundamentals

You'll notice an emphasis in this book on understanding the technologies behind SQL Server in order to understand how it works. I spend several chapters going through the fundamentals of processes and threads, memory management, Windows I/O, networking, and several other topics. To the uninitiated, these topics may seem only tangentially related at best. After all, why do you need to know about asynchronous I/O to understand SQL Server? You need to know something about it and the other fundamental technologies on which SQL Server is based in order to have a proper frame of reference and to gain a deep understanding of how the product itself works. You need to understand the fundamental Windows concepts on which SQL Server, a complex Windows application, is based for the same reason that a medical student needs to understand basic biology in order to get into medical school: Without this fundamental knowledge, you lack the perspective and foundation necessary to properly root and ground the more advanced concepts you will be attempting to learn. Humans learn by association—by associating new data with knowledge already acquired. Without a solid grounding in the fundamentals of Windows application design, you lack the basic knowledge required to systematically associate the details of how a complex Windows application such as SQL Server works.

To be sure, you can gain a superficial idea of how SQL Server works (for example, by reading that it makes use of scatter-gather I/O) without really understanding what the details mean. If you *really* want to master the product—if you really want to know it literally inside-out—you have to have some understanding of the technologies from which it's composed. Knowing how scatter-gather I/O works will give you immediate insight into why SQL Server uses it and why it enhances performance. The same is true for virtual memory, thread synchronization, networking, and the many other foundational topics we explore in this book. Not only are they relevant; having a basic understanding of them is *essential* to truly understanding SQL Server. Without a basic understanding of the fundamental technologies on which SQL Server is based—Win32 processes and threads, virtual memory, asynchronous I/O, COM, Windows networking, and various others—you have neither the tools nor the frame of reference to truly grasp how the product works or to master how to use it.

I fully realize that not every reader will be interested in the Windows technologies and APIs behind SQL Server's functionality. That's okay. If the nitty-gritty details of the Win32 APIs, how to use them, and how applications such as SQL Server typically employ them don't interest you, feel free to skip the Foundations section (Part I) of this book. There's still plenty of useful information in the rest of the book, and you don't have to understand every detail of every API to benefit from it.

About the "How-To"

I've tried very hard to provide the architectural details behind how the various components of SQL Server work without neglecting the discussion of how to apply them in practical use. I am still a coder at heart, and there is still plenty of "how-to" information in this book. At last count, there were some 900 source code files slated for inclusion on the book's CD. That's more than either of my last two books, both of which were very focused on putting SQL Server to practical use, as I've said.

In terms of the central topic of all three of my SQL Server books— namely, getting the most out of the product—I've attempted to elevate the discussion to an exploration of the architectural design behind the product without leaving behind my core reader base. Regardless of whether you came to this book expecting the mother lode of code and practical use information that you typically find in my books or you agree with me that understanding how the product works is key to using it effectively, I hope you won't be disappointed with what you find here.

About the Breadth of Topics

You will notice that this book covers a wide range of product features and technologies. It is not limited merely to the functionality provided within sqlservr.exe—it tries to cover the entire product. It's my opinion that a book that purports to discuss the internal workings and architectural design of a complex product such as SQL Server should cover *the whole product*, not just the functionality that resides within the core executable or product features that have been in place for many years. The world of SQL Server is a lot bigger than just a single executable. Prior to the 7.0 release of the product, I suppose you could get away with just covering the functionality provided by the main executable, but that's no longer the case and hasn't been for years. The product has matured and has broadened substantially with each new release.

This book isn't titled *The Guru's Guide to sqlservr.exe*—it's about all of SQL Server and how its many component pieces work and fit together. So, you'll see coverage in this book of what might seem like fringe SQL Server technologies such as Full Text Search, Notification Services, and SQLXML. We'll explore replication, DTS, and a host of other SQL Server technologies that are not implemented in the main SQL Server executable. Of necessity, I can't cover every feature in the product or even as many as I'd like. The book would take ten years to write and would be 5,000 pages long. However, I've tried to strike a balance between covering topics in the depth that people have come to expect from my books and exploring a sufficient breadth of features and technologies such that you can get a good feel for the overall design and architecture of SQL Server as a product.

About C++

I'm fully aware that many SQL Server people are more comfortable in Visual Basic than in any C or C++ dialect. I used C and C++ to cover Windows programming fundamentals and elsewhere in the book for a couple of reasons.

First, the Win32 API itself is written in C. Although whole books have been written on accessing the Win32 API from VB, it has been my experience that this ranges from clunky to outright impossible in some circumstances, depending on the API function in question. The Win32 API was originally written in C, and therefore C and C++ are the purest and most direct methods of accessing it. Any other approach—be it from VB, Delphi, C#, or some other language or tool—adds a layer of indirection that can cloud the discussion.

Second, I used C++ because I happen to believe that the language is not that hard to learn and that most VB people are more than capable of developing basic C++ programming skills and effectively reading C++ code, regardless of whether they believe that themselves. There seems to be a natural aversion or fear of all things C++ among those in the VB community. It's my belief that these concerns are largely unfounded and that they needlessly limit people's ability to really understand Windows and complex

Windows apps such as SQL Server. My advice: Even if you don't know C++ and feel you're out of your depth when reading through C++ code, don't be afraid of it. Work through the examples in this book, follow the instructions I provide, and see where your exploration leads you. Pick up an introductory book on the language if it suits you. You may find that the language isn't nearly as hard to get around in as you thought, and you may benefit—perhaps immensely—from the experience.

All that said, C++ is far from the only language used in this book. I know that no one language is used by everyone so I've tried to keep the book balanced in terms of the language tools used. A good deal of the example code used throughout the book is some flavor of Visual Basic—VB6, VBScript, or VB.NET. In the ODSOLE chapter, for example, I show you how to build COM objects in VB6. In the SQLXML chapter, I show you how to access SQLXML using VBScript. And in the Notification Services chapter, I show you how to implement a subscription management application using VB.NET. There's also a healthy helping of C#, Delphi, CMD files, and even a discussion or two of assembly language. And, of course, there's a wealth of Transact-SQL code throughout the book. Regardless of your preferred language(s), you should find code of interest to you in this book.

About Visual C++ 6.0

Some of you may question the decision to use Visual C++ 6.0 for most of the C++ code examples in this book. I chose VC6 over Visual Studio .NET for two reasons: (1) having been around considerably longer, VC6 is much more pervasive, and (2) Visual Studio .NET (both the 2001 and the 2003 releases) will automatically upgrade VC6 projects when they are first opened. So, regardless of whether you have Visual Studio 6 or Visual Studio .NET, the C++ projects on the CD accompanying this book should open just fine for you. You should be able to compile and run them without incident. Also, when teaching basic Windows concepts such as thread synchronization and memory management, I do not use any version-specific features, so there's no advantage to using Visual Studio .NET over VC6.

About the Terms and Knowledge Measures

Readers of my previous books may notice a significant amount of "supplementary" material in several of the chapters. You'll likely notice the term definitions that precede some of the chapter discussions and the knowledge measures at the end of each discussion. Don't worry: I still hate filler material and have gone to great lengths to avoid unnecessary screen shots, summaries, and other devices commonly used to lengthen technical books.

Though I personally don't like putting together term definition tables, knowledge measures, and the like and have avoided them in previous books, a growing number of readers have asked for additions such as these in order to make my books more suitable for classroom use. Several of my previous books are regularly used in classroom settings even though, admittedly, those books do not lend themselves well to it. Therefore, I've finally decided to try to do something about that. If you do not find these sections particularly useful, feel free to skip over them. All of the data contained in the term definitions is also in the chapter text—you won't miss anything by skipping them. That said, you may find that having a basic understanding of some of the terms and concepts before we get into them in depth may be useful to you. It really comes down to your individual preferences.

I have intentionally not included the answers to the questions in the knowledge measure sections in order to get a feel for how much they are used. Again, this is an adaptation intended to make the book more usable in classroom scenarios. I may or may not continue it in future books, depending on how useful it proves to be. If you want the answers to the knowledge measure questions, e-mail me at khen@khen.com, and I'll provide them.

About SQL Server Versions

This book targets the latest release of SQL Server currently available, SQL Server 2000. Throughout the book, when you see a reference to SQL Server, you can assume that it definitely applies to SQL Server 2000 and probably to other releases as well. I rarely mention SQL Server's version number because I've found it to be a little cumbersome. That said, when in doubt, assume what you read in this book applies to SQL Server 2000.

About Master Programming

With the sheer volume of code and code-related discussions in this book, it might appear to some that I'm trying to turn you into a master programmer rather than a master SQL Server practitioner. Nothing could be further from the truth. In order to really address that concern, let's first define what a master programmer is.

To begin with, a master programmer is someone who likely codes for a living. You cannot develop expert-level coding skills and keep them sharp by merely studying other people's code or reading programming books. You have to get in there and get your hands dirty, and you have to keep doing it. Technology changes and software engineering evolves quickly enough that there's simply no substitute for coding every day.

Second, a master programmer is someone who doesn't just know how to churn out source code. A person I worked with once suggested that the defining characteristic of an expert coder is great typing skill! I laughed out loud at that assertion because being an expert coder has nothing to do with typing—I know expert coders who don't type well at all. That notion reminds me of what Truman Capote said when asked about Jack Kerouac's work: "That isn't writing at all, it's typing."[2] Just as good writing amounts to a lot more than typing, so does expert-level coding. Cranking out reams of source code does not a master programmer make. In fact, there's a paucity and efficacy about the code of the programming masters that often accomplishes an astonishing amount of work with a surprisingly small amount of code. The idea isn't to write lots of code; it is to write *good* code. It's a question of quality versus quantity.

Third, a master programmer is well rounded. A master programmer knows a number of languages and works on multiple operating systems and platforms. He does not use one language at the expense of all others regardless of the problem. He uses the right tool for the job and constantly seeks to broaden his horizons and immerse himself in the art and science of computer language mastery. A master programmer is not a "jack of all trades and master of none" but maintains expert-level skills in several areas at once.

Fourth, an expert programmer masters the operating system environment and fundamental technologies with which he works just as much as he masters programming languages. He knows that simply mastering the language with which he happens to be working on a particular project is not enough; he must also know a good deal about the operating system and the foundational components with which he will construct applications. Whether this is COM or EJB, Windows or Linux, the master programmer knows that he must also have expert-level knowledge of the environment in which his code will run and the components from which it will be constructed in order to produce software that is robust, efficient, and extensible.

---

2. Capote, Truman. As quoted in *New Republic*, Feb. 9, 1959.

Fifth, a master programmer keeps up with the technology and developments in software engineering. A master programmer can tell you the difference between the decorator design pattern and the façade design pattern. He can tell you why COM is preferable to plain DLL use and about the advantages the .NET Framework offers over COM. He can tell you where Java fits in the grand scheme of things and how it compares to other languages. You can mention the term "refactoring" to him without getting a blank stare, and he can describe the relationship between eXtreme Programming and Aspect-Oriented Programming. He may not work every day with these concepts and technologies, but he stays current enough with the industry in which he works to understand them conceptually, to be able to explain the relationships between them, and to be able to discuss them articulately.

Sixth, a master programmer is well read. He knows who Martin Fowler is. He reads Kent Beck, and he's well versed in Erich Gamma's work. He reads both technology-specific books as well as those related to software engineering as a discipline. He reads Steve McConnell, and he also reads Donald Knuth. He knows who Jon Bentley is, and he also knows Brian Kernighan's work. He is well versed in Grady Booch's work and also reads Charles Petzold. In a day and age in which technology and the engineering required to master and put it to practical use seem to evolve at the speed of light, one can't read too much or stay too current with the latest developments in the industry. A master programmer knows this and dedicates himself to a lifelong course of continuing education.

So, with this in mind, I hope it's obvious that I'm not trying to turn anyone into a master programmer. This book isn't about software development; it's about SQL Server. To the extent that I delve into subjects seemingly more related to coding than to SQL Server, there is a method to the madness: I am trying to help develop basic coding and debugging skills in those who may lack them so that they can better understand how and why SQL Server is designed the way it is and so that they can continue the exploration of SQL Server on their own. The whole thrust of this book is about gaining as deep an understanding of SQL Server as possible so that we can put it to better use in the real world.

About
the Author

Ken Henderson is a husband and father who lives in Dallas, Texas. He is the author of seven previous books and a long-time software developer, consultant, and conference speaker. He is also an avid Mavericks fan and spends his spare time playing games with his kids, watching sports, and playing music. Henderson's Web site is http://www.khen.com, and he may be reached via e-mail at khen@khen.com.

Foundations

Overview

That which is borne of loneliness and from the heart cannot be defended
against the judgment of a committee of sycophants.

—Raymond Chandler[1]

I'll begin by touching on each of the major subjects covered in this book and give a brief overview of each chapter. This will give you a high-level view of what the book itself is about and what we'll be talking about in the chapters ahead.

Chapter Overview

Chapter 2: Windows Architectural Overview

In this chapter, we'll talk about how Windows works from an architectural standpoint. We'll discuss the various components of Windows and how Windows applications are constructed. You'll learn about DLLs, virtual memory, CPU nuances, and a variety of other Windows elements that affect how complex Windows applications such as SQL Server behave.

Chapter 3: Processes and Threads

This chapter covers Windows' process and threading architecture. You'll learn what a process is, how it differs from a thread, and how SQL Server behaves itself as a process. You'll learn about Windows' scheduler and how threads are scheduled for execution, and you'll explore thread synchronization in depth. You'll work through several C++ applications and xprocs that

---

1. Chandler, Raymond. "Writers in Hollywood." *Atlantic Monthly*, November 1945.

demonstrate how processes and threads work under Windows and how this applies to SQL Server. Starting in this chapter and continuing throughout the Foundations section, we'll build a series of applications that search text files for strings. We'll create several different versions of a text search application—each one employing different Windows foundational concepts—so that you can readily see how the various Windows technologies are typically used in real applications. We'll pick up where this chapter leaves off when we discuss SQL Server's User Mode Scheduler (UMS) later in the book (Chapter 10).

Chapter 4: Memory Fundamentals

In this chapter, you'll learn about Windows' memory management. You'll learn about the difference between virtual memory and physical memory, as well as the difference between virtual memory and heaps. You'll learn how Windows apportions memory to applications and how it translates virtual memory addresses into physical memory addresses. We'll continue the text file search theme started in the previous chapter and build several applications that illustrate how Windows applications can make use of the memory management facilities provided by the operating system. You'll gain insight into how SQL Server makes use of some of these facilities by building apps that feature them. We'll build on the concepts taught in this chapter when we get to SQL Server Memory Management (Chapter 11) later in the book.

Chapter 5: I/O Fundamentals

We'll take a tour of Windows' foundational I/O facilities in this chapter. We'll continue the text file search theme and build applications that make use of synchronous I/O, asynchronous I/O, nonbuffered file I/O, scatter-gather I/O, and file I/O using memory-mapped files. You'll gain insight into how SQL Server makes use of Windows' I/O facilities by seeing them at work in real applications. In SQL Server as a Server (Chapter 9), we'll discuss how SQL Server makes use of these concepts.

Chapter 6: Networking

In this chapter, we'll explore Windows' networking application programming interfaces (APIs). You'll learn about Windows sockets and named pipes, as well as the RPC API. We'll continue our exploration of text search applications and build applications that make use of Windows' networking APIs to communicate with one another and process input and output. You'll also gain some insight into how SQL Server makes use of Windows' networking facilities. We'll build on the information in this chapter when we discuss how SQL Server employs the various networking APIs in Chapter 9.

Chapter 7: COM

We'll explore the basics of Microsoft's Component Object Model (COM) technology and discuss how COM is used by SQL Server. You'll learn about threading models, interfaces, marshaling, reference counting, and many other COM concepts. We'll talk about how Windows applications typically make use of COM, and we'll talk about some of the ways in which SQL Server uses it. This chapter will provide the background you'll need to work through the ODSOLE chapter later in the book.

Chapter 8: XML

In this chapter, you'll learn about the eXtensible Markup Language (XML). You'll learn how to construct your own XML documents and how HTML and XML fundamentally differ. You'll learn about attributes, elements, and schemas, and you'll learn to apply XML style sheets to transform your data. This chapter will provide the background and foundational information you'll need to work through Chapter 18 (SQLXML) later in the book.

Chapter 9: SQL Server as a Server

We'll discuss how SQL Server behaves as a Windows server application in this chapter. We'll pull together several of the concepts discussed earlier in the book and show how they're employed by SQL Server. For example, we'll show how SQL Server uses the Windows networking APIs to listen for new connections and schedule them for processing via UMS. We'll talk about the DLLs imported by SQL Server and what they're used for, and we'll talk about where SQL Server fits in the general taxonomy of Windows applications.

Chapter 10: User Mode Scheduler

In this chapter, we'll investigate how SQL Server schedules work to be done using worker threads and fibers. You'll learn how SQL Server's scheduler compares to Windows' scheduler, and you'll learn how SQL Server makes use of Windows scheduling facilities and synchronization objects. By delving into UMS, you'll develop great insight into how SQL Server carries out client requests.

Chapter 11: SQL Server Memory Management

We'll build on the earlier discussion of Windows memory management fundamentals and show how the concepts we learned are applied by SQL Server to manage its memory. You'll learn about the BPool and the MemToLeave regions, about how Address Windowing Extensions (AWE) fits into the whole picture, and how SQL Server attempts to balance high performance with efficient resource utilization.

Chapter 12: Query Processor

In this chapter, we'll document how the SQL Server query processor works internally and how it processes and optimizes queries. You'll learn about the four major stages of query optimization and how each one affects the overall optimization process. You'll learn how indexes, statistics, and constraints are used by the optimizer to generate efficient execution plans, and you'll learn how to structure queries for maximum performance.

Chapter 13: Transactions

The Transactions chapter examines SQL Server transactions in depth. We'll write several Transact-SQL queries that make use of transactions, then explore how they work and how SQL Server's transaction management constructs work in general. You'll learn how to avoid common errors and how to properly use SQL Server's transaction management facilities in your own applications.

Chapter 14: Cursors

In this chapter, we'll explore how SQL Server cursors work. You'll learn about the different types of cursors, how to use them, and how to avoid common mistakes. We'll talk about how transactions and cursors interrelate and how you can avoid common concurrency and performance issues caused by cursor misuse.

Chapter 15: ODSOLE

We'll explore how you can make use of COM objects from within Transact-SQL via SQL Server's Open Data Services Object Linking and Embedding (ODSOLE) facility. You'll learn about the sp_OA extended procedures, how to use them, and when not to use them. You'll build several interesting COM objects for use within Transact-SQL including a bevy of financial functions, array functions, and string manipulation functions. You'll likely find much of the sample code in this chapter to be very useful.

Chapter 16: Full-Text Search

In this chapter, we'll explore SQL Server's Full-Text Search (FTS) facility. You'll learn how it works and how it is designed. You'll explore FTS queries and how to make use of FTS in your own code.

Chapter 17: Server Federations

You'll learn about distributed partitioned views and how they relate to server federations in this chapter. You'll dig into a few execution plans and delve into how partitioned views affect performance and scalability.

Chapter 18: SQLXML

In this chapter, you'll explore the many aspects of SQL Server's XML technology. You'll learn about FOR XML, OPENXML(), sp_xml_preparedocument, updategrams, templates, the SQLXML managed classes, and so on. We'll build on the XML fundamentals we explored in Chapter 8 and explore how SQL Server exposes a powerful collection of XML-enabled features and how to make use of those features in your own applications.

Chapter 19: Notification Services

In this chapter, you'll get to explore SQL Server's Notification Services technology. You'll learn about how it is designed and how the typical Notification Services application is architected. You'll see how easy the Notification Services platform makes building and deploying notification-oriented applications that are fully functional, very powerful, and scalable. You'll finish up the chapter by building a Notification Services application of your own and a subscription management application using VB.NET.

Chapter 20: Data Transformation Services

You'll explore SQL Server's Data Transformation Services (DTS) in this chapter. We'll talk about how DTS is designed, the fundamental components that make up DTS packages, and the ways you can leverage them to build data transformation applications that are powerful and flexible. We'll build a number of packages that explore the many features and facilities of DTS. You'll finish up with a project that teaches you how to access and control DTS packages via Automation.

Chapter 21: Snapshot Replication

In this chapter, you'll explore snapshot replication. You'll learn how data typically moves between a publisher and a subscriber in snapshot replication and how you can track exactly what is moved between them. You'll learn about the distribution database and how the Snapshot Agent facilitates the replication process.

Chapter 22: Transactional Replication

As with the previous chapter, this chapter is dedicated to replication. In this case, we'll discuss transactional replication and the ways it differs from snapshot replication and merge replication. You'll learn how the Log Reader Agent reads the transaction log and sends changes to subscribers by way of the distribution database. You'll learn about immediate and queued updating subscribers, and you'll see how they work internally.

Chapter 23: Merge Replication

As the title suggests, you'll explore merge replication in this chapter. You'll set up several subscriptions, then watch as they participate in a generic merge replication scenario. You'll learn about generations and conflict resolvers, and you'll see how merge provides a flexible (yet complex) data replication facility.

Chapter 24: Finding Undocumented Features

In this chapter, you'll learn how to track down undocumented features. Rather than provide a smorgasbord of undocumented features as I've done in previous books, this chapter shows how to find these hidden goodies yourself. You'll learn how to use Profiler to find undocumented features and commands, as well as how to search the text of system procedures for undocumented DBCC commands and trace flags. With the skills and data you acquire in this chapter, you should be able to dig up undocumented features and commands on your own.

Chapter 25: DTSDIAG

In this chapter, I'll introduce you to a utility implemented via a collection of DTS packages that can collect diagnostic data from SQL Server. Using this tool, you can concurrently collect Profiler traces, blocking script output, SQLDIAG reports, Perfmon logs, event logs, and a number of other useful diagnostics. This tool demonstrates several useful DTS techniques including how to automate a DTS package from Visual Basic, how to modularize a DTS application by breaking it up into separate packages, and how to use a DTS package as a workflow manager for other tasks.

Chapter Pairs

It's probably pretty self-evident, but I guess I should point out my intent to construct much of the book using "chapter pairs." A chapter pair is a pair of chapters where the second chapter builds directly on the information shared in the first one. You'll see these throughout the book. For example, rather than assume that the typical DBA has an intimate understanding of the Windows scheduler (and can, therefore, explain why SQL Server implements its own scheduler), I provide a chapter that explains in detail how the Windows scheduler works. The book is aimed at the database professional who may or may not have an in-depth understanding of Windows internals. I felt an obligation to explain some of these foundational concepts rather than flippantly assuming most of my readers already understood them well. I could have constantly referred to external books and other sources, but I felt that would be taking the easy way out, and I also felt I had something to add to the discussion of Windows application fundamentals that has not been said before.

I build on this foundational information throughout the rest of the book as I delve into the various parts of SQL Server. For example, in the User Mode Scheduler chapter, I leverage the discussion of the Windows scheduler from earlier in the book. The same is true of the Memory Fundamentals chapter and the SQL Server Memory Management chapter: The first chapter lays the groundwork for the second one. Ditto for the Networking chapter and the SQL Server as a Server chapter—one plays off the other. Each of the main chapters in the Foundations section sets up one or more chapters later in the book that cover specific SQL Server technologies or components. Because of this, you will likely want to read through the Foundations section before you dive into the rest of the book. If it doesn't make complete sense the first time through or its applicability isn't immediately apparent, don't worry—it will become clearer as you work through the remainder of the book.

If you already have a good understanding of Windows internals, COM, XML, and so on, you may be able to skip these foundational chapters. As I said in the Introduction, I'm well aware that such details may not be for everyone. If you have doubts about the value of some of this information to you or your work, my suggestion would be to start with the SQL Server–specific coverage (e.g., Chapter 9, SQL Server as a Server) and see whether you understand it reasonably well without first reading through the earlier material (e.g., Chapter 3, Processes and Threads). If so, good for you. If not, you have a thorough tutorial on many of the foundational concepts you'll need right here in this book. Either way you go about it, you should find all you need in this book to learn a good deal about SQL Server architecture and internals.

About the Code

With the sheer volume of code in this book and the emphasis on exploring SQL Server as a program, it might at first appear that you'd need to be a seasoned coder to really understand the book. That's not my intent. I wanted to take a fresh approach to the discussion of SQL Server's architecture and the way that its various components are constructed and fit together, so this book explores the product from the perspective of the professional developer. I think this is appropriate given that SQL Server is, after all, an application. It was obviously built by developers. There is no greater insight into the way an application works—no higher level of mastery—than to understand the application in the same the people that built it do. By exploring SQL Server as an application, we attempt to get inside the heads of the people who built it, to understand what they were thinking when they designed it. Of course, there are limits as to how far we can go—we didn't write the app and we don't have source code for it. But there is a great deal we can learn just by approaching SQL Server as we would any other complex Windows application. By using tools such as WinDbg, Perfmon, and others, we can look under the hood, so to speak, and gain a deep understanding of much of the architecture and internals of the product. In my opinion, there is no better way to master SQL Server or any other third-party application.

So, do you need to be a coder to master SQL Server or glean everything this book has to teach? No, but it certainly wouldn't hurt. If you don't consider yourself a coder, my suggestion would be not to fret. Read through the text and examples in this book, retrace my steps where you can, and work at your own pace. The fact that the book is an in-depth study of a particular program doesn't mean that it's only for programmers. It's my hope that many readers who don't consider themselves coders will discover their inner programmer and, in taking their coding skill to the next level, come to understand SQL Server in ways that would otherwise not be possible and as they never have before. And it's my hope that they will then be sufficiently equipped to continue the exploration of SQL Server on their own. Rather than just divulging a mother lode of technical data as is so often the case with even the best technical books, I wanted to teach readers *how* to investigate complex Windows applications such as SQL Server. The investigatory skills you pick up in this book should be applicable regardless of the product or program you're studying and should allow you to continue your exploration of SQL Server for years to come.

CHAPTER 2

Windows Fundamentals

You have two ears and one mouth. If you use them in those proportions, we'll get along just fine.

—Neil Coy

As I said in the Introduction, knowing how Windows works is foundational to understanding how a complex Windows application such as SQL Server works. Without a good understanding of how the operating system (OS) works, you have neither the tools nor the frame of reference to understand how SQL Server works. Humans store knowledge in neural networks built through associating new knowledge with existing knowledge. The knowledge and insight you gain from exploring SQL Server fits within the larger framework of how Windows works and how Windows applications in general are constructed. My purpose in this chapter is to acquaint you with some of Windows' fundamental elements and to lay the groundwork for the deeper discussions of these topics that follow in the chapters ahead.

The Win32 API

The Win32 API is the programming interface for 32-bit Windows. Windows applications make calls to this API in order to invoke OS services. The actual code behind this API is located in a collection of dynamic-link libraries (DLLs) such as Kernel32.DLL, User32.DLL, and GDI32.DLL and, of course, in the OS kernel itself, which resides primarily in a file named NTOSKRNL.EXE.

The programming interface slated for use with the original version of 32-bit Windows was not the Win32 API. It was the OS/2 Presentation Manager API. Midway through the development of what was to become the first version of Windows NT, Windows 3.0 was released, and adoption of Windows as a development platform exploded. Microsoft then decided that the 32-bit programming API should be compatible with the 16-bit API in order to make porting apps from Windows 3.x easier. This was the genesis of the Win32 API and is why it may seem a bit incongruous or uneven at times—it was designed to be as compatible as possible with the old 16-bit Windows API.

Given that SQL Server is a complex Windows application, it of course makes heavy use of the Win32 API. In the first section of this book, we will explore many of the Win32 API functions that SQL Server uses. You'll learn how they work and how to use them, and you'll gain some insight into how SQL Server makes use of them. You'll see the relationship between certain key SQL Server features and the Win32 API functions they rely upon.

You can download the Platform SDK, which contains the C header files and libraries, as well as the online documentation for the Win32 API, directly from the Microsoft Web site. The Platform SDK also ships with several of Microsoft's development tools and is included with the MSDN Library.

User Mode vs. Kernel Mode

In order to keep misbehaving application code from destabilizing the system, Windows uses two processor modes: user mode and kernel mode. User application code runs in user mode; OS code and device drivers run in kernel mode. Kernel mode has a higher hardware privilege level than user mode and provides access to all system memory and all CPU instructions. By running at a higher privilege than application software, Windows can keep a misbehaving application from directly destabilizing the system.

The Intel x86 family of processors actually supports four operating modes (also known as rings). These are numbered 0 through 3, and each is isolated from the others by the hardware—a crash in a lower-priority mode will not destabilize higher-priority modes. Because it was originally designed to support chips such as the Compaq Alpha and the Silicon Graphics MIPS that provide only two processor modes, Windows uses only two of these modes (rings 0 and 3, for kernel and user modes, respectively). Now that these chips are no longer supported, it would probably make sense for Windows to use at least one additional operating mode on the Intel x86 processor family. Doing so would allow device drivers, for example, to run at a lower privilege level than the OS and would prevent an errant driver from being able to bring down the entire system.

Processes and Threads

An instance of a running application is known as a process. Actually, that's a misnomer. Processes don't actually run—threads do. Every process has at least one thread (the main thread) but can have many. Each thread represents an independent execution mechanism. Any code that runs within an application runs via a thread.

Each process is allotted its own virtual memory address space. All threads within the process share this virtual memory space. Multiple threads that modify the same resource must synchronize access to the resource in order to prevent erratic behavior and possible access violations. A process that correctly serializes access to resources shared by multiple threads is said to be thread-safe.

Each thread in a process gets its own set of volatile registers. A volatile register is the software equivalent of a CPU register. In order to allow a thread to maintain a context that is independent of other threads, each thread gets its own set of volatile (software) registers that are used to save and restore hardware registers. These volatile registers are copied to/from the CPU registers every time the thread is scheduled/unscheduled to run by Windows. The process by which this happens is known as a context switch.

Processes can be initiated by many different types of applications. Console apps, graphical user interface (GUI) apps, Windows services, out-of-process COM servers, and so on are examples of EXEs that can be executed to instantiate a process. SQL Server can run as both a console app and a Windows service.

Virtual Memory vs. Physical Memory

Windows provides all processes a 4GB virtual memory sandbox in which to play. By "virtual" I mean that the memory isn't memory in the traditional sense. It is merely a range of addresses with no physical storage implicitly associated with it. As a process makes memory allocations, these addresses are used and physical storage is associated with them. However, this physical storage is not necessarily (and not usually) physical memory. It is usually disk drive space. Specifically, it's space in the system paging file(s). That's how multiple applications can run on a system with 128MB of memory, each with a virtual address space of 4GB—it's not real memory, but it seems like it to the application. Windows transparently handles copying data to and from the paging file so that the app can allocate more memory than physically exists in the machine and so that multiple apps can have equal access to the machine's physical RAM.

This 4GB address space is divided into two partitions: the user mode partition and the kernel mode partition. By default, each of these is sized at 2GB, though you can change this through BOOT.INI switches on the Windows NT family of the OS. (Windows NT, Windows 2000, Windows XP, and Windows Server 2003 are members of the Windows NT family; Windows 9x and Windows ME are not.)

Although each process receives its own virtual memory address space, OS code and device driver code share a single private address space. Each virtual memory page is associated with a particular processor mode. In order for the page to be accessed, the processor must be in the required mode. This means that user applications cannot access kernel mode virtual memory directly; the system must switch into kernel mode in order for kernel mode memory to be accessible.

We'll talk more about virtual memory and how Windows manages it in Chapter 4, Memory Fundamentals. For now, just understand that virtual memory does not necessarily correlate to physical memory. It is a service provided by Windows that allows applications (and Windows itself) to allocate and use more primary storage (memory) than physically exists in a machine without having to handle paging data to and from secondary storage (disk drives).

Subsystems

Windows ships with three environment subsystems: Win32, OS/2, and POSIX. Each of these provides a different environment or personality for the OS. Of these, Win32 is preeminent because it's not optional (it must always be running, regardless of the environmental subsystem chosen and regardless of whether anyone is logged in) and because it provides the most direct and most complete access to Windows itself. The other environment subsystems aren't used much and don't provide the same level of functionality as the Win32 subsystem. Applications that run on Windows are compiled and linked to run under a particular environment subsystem. Obviously, most of these, including SQL Server, are Win32 applications.

The Win32 environment subsystem can be broken down into the following major components.

- Csrss.exe, the environment subsystem process, supports creating processes and threads, console windows, portions of the 16-bit virtual DOS machine, and miscellaneous functions.
- Win32k.sys, the kernel mode device driver, includes two facilities: (1) the window manager, the facility responsible for collecting input from the keyboard and mouse, for managing screen output, and for passing messages to applications; and (2) the Graphics Device Interface (GDI), the facility responsible for output to graphics devices.
- The subsystem DLLs (which include Kernel32.DLL, User32.DLL, GDI32.DLL, and Advapi32.DLL) handle translating Win32 API functions into kernel mode service calls.

Windows applications interact with the OS kernel via the subsystem DLLs. These DLLs hide the actual native OS calls (which are undocumented) from the application. The purpose of these DLLs is to translate Win32 API calls into OS service calls. These calls may or may not involve sending a message to the environment subsystem process hosting the application.

Given my statement that user mode code cannot access kernel mode memory, you may be wondering how user mode code can invoke code and access data that is obviously in the kernel—after all, the operating system's core functionality is implemented in the kernel, hence the name. The way this works is that user mode applications make Win32 API calls to functions exported from subsystem DLLs. These DLLs then make calls to undocumented native API functions in NTDLL.DLL. The functions in NTDLL.DLL then invoke the platform-specific instructions to switch the processor chip into kernel mode and invoke the appropriate code in the OS kernel. This code may reside in the kernel executable, NTOSKRNL.EXE, or in the kernel mode device driver, Win32k.sys. (Purists may quibble that it's a little more complicated than that, but this gives you a basic picture of how a user mode app interacts with the Windows kernel.)

Dynamic-Link Libraries

A DLL is a binary file that serves as a shared library of routines that can be dynamically loaded and unloaded at runtime by applications that use the routines. Runtime libraries and class libraries for language products such as Visual C++ and Delphi can take the form of DLLs. The user mode portion of the Win32 API is ensconced in DLLs such as Kernel32.DLL and User32.DLL. One advantage of a DLL over a static library is that multiple applications can share a single DLL. Windows ensures that only one copy of a DLL's code is mapped into memory regardless of the number of applications that reference it.

DLLs make the functions they contain visible to the outside world by exporting them. A DLL's export table can be viewed using external tools such as the Depends tool that comes with Visual Studio or the dumpbin utility that comes with several Microsoft products. A DLL routine can be exported by name or ordinal or both. DLLs (and executables) also have import tables—tables listing the DLLs they depend on and the functions they statically import. I'll talk more about static importing in just a moment.

A process can load DLLs through one of two means: either implicitly when it starts or explicitly via a call to the LoadLibrary(Ex) API. The manner in which it loads a particular DLL is determined by the way in which its executable references the functions exported (made visible to the outside world) by the DLL. There are two ways these references can occur. When an executable is compiled and linked, it can statically import the functions exported by a DLL by importing the DLL's .LIB file. (.LIB files are not universally required by all compilers and linkers for static linking but are most prominent with C and C++ products—e.g., neither Visual Basic nor Delphi require or use .LIB files.) A static import causes the DLL to load automatically when the executable is started. If the DLL can't be located, the executable won't start. Static importing is usually the way Windows apps load DLLs. It requires less code and is managed mostly by the OS. All Windows apps statically import at least Kernel32.DLL, and most also import User32.DLL because these DLLs contain the lion's share of the Win32 API.

A DLL can also be loaded at runtime by an executable through a call to the LoadLibrary API. In this case, LoadLibrary is passed the name of the DLL to load and returns a module handle if it finds it (if it doesn't, it returns NULL). Then, this module handle is passed into GetProcAddress to get the address of a specific function exported by the DLL. This address can then be cast to the appropriate function type so that it can be called. This is how SQL Server calls extended procedures, for example, and is the way the SQL Server Net-Libraries are loaded. Anytime an application doesn't know at compile/link time whether a DLL it might want to load will be present on the system, it must use LoadLibrary to load it. For example, when an application loads replaceable database drivers via ODBC, ODBC loads the

DLLs that house them via LoadLibrary because there was no way for it to know which drivers would be present on a given system when it was compiled and linked.

So, when a DLL is loaded into a process's address space, it becomes code the process can call. Each DLL has a default load address within the 4GB process address space that is specified when it is linked. If nothing occupies the address range where the DLL was configured to load in the calling process, it will load at that address. If something else is already there, it will have to be "rebased," which involves reading the entire image and updating all fix-ups, debugging information, checksums, and time-stamp values to use a different base address. Because this amounts to updating pages contained in the DLL image, Windows must load each page that must be modified into virtual memory and make the changes there.

As I said earlier and as Chapter 4 details, the normal mode of operation for allocations within a process's address space is that those allocations are backed by the paging file (or physical memory). An exception is made in the case of binary code, though, because it is normally read-only and copying it to the paging file is wasteful. Instead, the EXE or DLL file itself "backs" (provides physical storage for) the range of virtual memory addresses within a process's address space set aside for the executable or DLL. So, when the process makes a call to a part of the executable or DLL that is not in physical memory, it will not go to the paging file to get that page of the EXE or DLL file. Instead, it will go to the appropriate binary file and load the page into physical memory directly from it. In that sense, EXE and DLL files become read-only extensions of the paging file.

Normally, only one copy of the pages that make up a DLL or EXE file is maintained in memory regardless of the number of processes using it. An exception to this is when a process makes a change to a global or static variable in the DLL or EXE. When this occurs, Windows makes a copy of the page that's local to the process, carries out the change, then alters the process to reference the new version of the page going forward. The mechanism by which this happens is known as copy-on-write memory.

The ability to use a DLL or EXE as the physical storage for the virtual memory address range it occupies relies on Windows' memory-mapped file facility, which can actually be used with any type of file, not just binaries. A memory-mapped file serves as the physical storage for the virtual memory it occupies. Rather than copying the file to the system paging file, Windows uses the file as though it were a paging file itself and automatically saves/ loads pages to/from this file as the virtual memory into which it has been mapped is referenced. Virtual memory is just that: virtual. It doesn't represent actual memory until physical storage is committed to it. Windows' memory-mapped file facility provides applications the ability to treat files as though they were memory, with Windows handling all the I/O behind the scenes. Windows itself uses this facility when it accesses EXEs and DLLs. This is all explained in great detail in Chapter 4.

Tools

In this section, I'll touch on a few of the tools we'll use throughout the book to explore SQL Server. These tools come from a variety of sources, and you certainly don't need all of them to work through the book. I mention them in various places in order to point out their usefulness and to give you some tips on how to leverage them to solve a particular problem or examine a particular piece of data. That said, you can work through most of the examples in the book with little more than the tools that come with Windows and Microsoft's freely downloadable WinDbg debugger.

TList

This tool comes on the Windows Support Tools CD. You can use it to list the running processes and to list the modules loaded within each process. A variety of other process-specific information can be returned as well.

Pviewer

Pviewer also comes with the Windows Support Tools. It allows you to view information about running processes and threads. You can also kill processes and change process priority classes. One really handy aspect of it is that you can use it to view processes on your local machine as well as those across a network on a remote machine.

Pview

This tool comes with the Platform SDK and is essentially the same tool as Pviewer. It offers the same functionality and displays the same type of information. Of course, the features it sports vary based on the release of the SDK and how recent the build you have is, but it is basically the same tool as Pviewer.

Perfmon

Windows' Performance Monitor is probably the single most valuable tool included with the product for looking under the hood to see what's happening within the OS. Perfmon (or Sysmon, as it's now known) provides the ability to monitor several key statistics about running processes and threads, memory and CPU utilization, disk use, and a bevy of other interesting objects and diagnostics.

You use Perfmon by adding counters to a data collection, then allowing the tool to sample them over time as the system runs. You can view these counters as lines on a chart, as literal values, or as bars on a histogram. You can save logs created by Perfmon as binary files, as delimited text files, and as SQL Server tables. Throughout the book, I'll mention Perfmon counters that are useful in exploring a particular technology or subsystem within Windows or SQL Server.

WinDbg

As I mentioned in the Introduction, we'll frequently use Microsoft's freely downloadable standalone debugger, WinDbg, to peer under the SQL Server hood. We won't actually be using WinDbg for the normal purpose debuggers are typically used for: debugging apps. Instead, WinDbg will serve as a type of "X-ray machine" for SQL Server, a tool that lets us see what's happening behind the scenes.

A version of WinDbg comes with Windows, and you can also download it from the Microsoft public Web site (as of this writing, you can find it at http://www.microsoft.com/ddk/debugging/default.asp). For working through the examples in this book, I suggest you get WinDbg from the Microsoft Web site so that you can be sure to have the latest version.

NOTE: Microsoft also includes a command line debugger, cdb.exe, in its Debugging Tools for Windows package that you may find preferable to WinDbg if you prefer command lines to GUIs. This debugger uses the same debugger "engine" as WinDbg, and the debugger commands presented in this book will work equally well with it.

Probably the single most important thing to remember when using WinDbg or any symbolic debugger is that, in order to successfully debug much of anything, you must have debugging symbols and the debugger's symbol path must be set so that it can find them. Debugging symbols are generated by your compiler/linker product. For Microsoft products, the standard symbol file format is the Program Database (PDB) format and is automatically produced for debug builds in Visual C++ and for any executable in VB whose Create Symbolic Debug Info project property is set. Typically, if you have debug symbols, you will find a PDB file corresponding to your EXE or DLL name in the same folder with the executable.

An exception to this is SQL Server. SQL Server's symbol files are located in the exe and dll subfolders under the main SQL Server Binn folder. (The symbols for sqlservr.exe, the main SQL Server executable, are in the exe folder; the symbols for the key DLLs it uses are in the dll folder.) These symbols are retail debug symbols—symbol files that have been stripped of many things essential to real-world debugging such as parameter types, local variables, and the like. These symbols aren't suitable for true debugging, but they're just right for our purposes. Retail symbols work fine for looking under the hood of an application and exploring a running process.

As I've mentioned, in order to successfully debug anything with WinDbg, you'll need to correctly set the symbol path. You can set the symbol path in WinDbg by pressing Ctrl+S or by choosing File | Symbol File Path from the menu system.

The retail symbols for much of Windows (and for many other products) are available over the Internet via Microsoft's symbols server. You don't have to download these—you simply point the debugger at the symbols server and it takes care of downloading (and caching) symbols files as it needs them. As of this writing, you can use http://msdl.microsoft.com/download/symbols in your symbol path to reference Microsoft's publicly available symbol server over the Internet. Microsoft has a great Web page explaining exactly how this works and how to use it at http://www.microsoft.com/ddk/debugging/symbols.asp. Read this page and set your symbol path accordingly in WinDbg. Currently, my WinDbg symbol path is set to SRV*c:\temp\symbols*http://msdl.microsoft.com/download/symbols.

When debugging a component or program to which you have source code, it's also important to set the WinDbg source path correctly. You can do this by pressing Ctrl+P or by selecting File | Source File Path in the WinDbg menu system. Setting the source path allows WinDbg to find the source code to your app while debugging so that you can step through it, set breakpoints, and so on.

NOTE: I should point out here that there's no guarantee that SQL Server will continue to ship symbol files of any kind. For now, they're included with the product, but they may not be at some point in the future. If that ever happens, hopefully Microsoft will make them available via its public symbols server as it has for some of its other products.

Recap

Windows is a sophisticated, robust operating system that is comprised of several subsystems. Programmed using the Win32 API, it provides a mechanism that allows user applications to (indirectly) make calls into the system kernel code.

Windows provides an architecture that protects the system from being destabilized by errant user applications. It provides a virtual memory facility to alleviate the need for apps to implement their own virtual memory managers. And it provides memory-mapped files and copy-on-write support for making advanced memory management easy and efficient.

Knowledge Measure

1. How much virtual memory does the user mode portion of a process have by default?
2. How many operating modes (rings) does the Intel x86 processor family support?
3. True or false: No code actually runs via a process itself—a thread is required to execute an application's code.
4. Explain the function of copy-on-write memory.
5. True or false: You must download symbolic debug information from Microsoft and copy it to a local symbols server in order to use WinDbg to debug a Microsoft product.
6. True or false: Windows uses all the operating modes supported by whatever processor chip it is running on.
7. Describe the relationship between the LoadLibrary and GetProcAddress Win32 API functions.
8. What is a context switch?
9. True or false: Windows provides a mechanism that an application can use to optionally load a DLL at runtime.
10. What's the single most important thing you must do in order to ensure a symbolic debugger is able to debug a process?

CHAPTER 3

Processes and Threads

It is necessary to the happiness of man that he be mentally faithful to himself. Infidelity does not consist in believing, or in disbelieving; it consists in professing to believe what he does not believe.

—Thomas Paine[1]

In this chapter, we'll explore processes and threads within Windows. We'll discuss how processes and threads differ and how they're similar, and we'll talk about the unique role each plays within the Windows operating system.

We'll also explore in detail how the Windows thread scheduler works and how threads are scheduled on and off of processors. We'll talk about thread synchronization and how multithreaded apps such as SQL Server use synchronization objects to serialize access to shared resources and ensure thread safety.

Processes

Key Process Terms and Concepts

✔ *Process*—the encapsulation of a running program in Windows. A process provides a context in which threads can carry out the work of an application.
✔ *Process address space*—the virtual memory address space for an application. This is limited to 4GB for 32-bit Windows applications. Addresses in Win32 applications are limited to 4GB because 4GB is the largest integer

---

1. Paine, Thomas. *The Age of Reason*, ed. Philip S. Foner. New York: Citadel Press, 1974, p. 50.

value a 32-bit pointer can store. Of these 4GB, by default 2GB are reserved for the kernel and 2GB are set aside for user mode access. On
some editions of the Windows NT family, the user mode address space
can be increased to 3GB (at the expense of kernel mode space) via the /
3GB BOOT.INI switch for applications that have been linked with a special flag that allows them to take advantage of this. All memory allocated
by an application comes from this space.

✔ *Main thread*—the first thread of an application. Windows automatically
allocates a main thread for every process it starts. This is also often referred to as the application's *primary thread*.

✔ *Entry-point function*—the function address at which a thread begins executing. For the main thread, this is the entry point of the application
(often a function named main() or something similar); for all other
threads, the entry-point function is specified when the thread is created
and is basically a simple callback routine.

Overview

A Win32 process is completely passive—it doesn't actually execute or do
anything. It is merely a container for threads. When you start or stop a process, you are actually starting and stopping its threads—the process itself
doesn't run. And, technically speaking, you don't terminate a process; you
terminate its threads. A process serves only to provide resources and context in which the threads that actually carry out the work of an application
can run.

Each process consists mainly of two components, a process kernel object and a virtual address space. The operating system uses the kernel object
to manage the process and to provide a means for applications to interact
with the process. The virtual address space contains the executable module's code and data, the code and data of the DLLs it loads, and dynamic
memory allocations such as thread stacks and heap allocations.

The fact that they provide the virtual address space for the application
means that processes require a lot more system resources than threads. The
creation of a process's virtual address space requires a significant amount of
system resources. The tracking and management of this space is handled by
the operating system's memory manager using virtual address descriptors
(VADs), and this requires resources that threads don't have to concern
themselves with.

I should mention here that the executable code (and data) that's contained within the process's virtual address space isn't actually loaded until needed. It is *mapped* within the virtual address space—which merely reserves certain address ranges for it within the space while the physical storage for the region remains the EXE or DLL file itself. It is loaded or unloaded as needed by the operating system in page-sized chunks (4K for Win32 on x86). Every executable or DLL file mapped into a process's address space is assigned a unique instance handle.

Beyond the kernel object and virtual address space, a process also encapsulates:

- A process-specific table of open handles to system resources such as files, events, mutexes, and semaphores
- An access token that defines the process's security context and identifies the user, privileges, and security groups associated with the process
- A unique identifier called a process ID or client ID
- At least one thread

Key Process APIs

Table 3.1 Key API Functions for Processes

Function	Description
CreateProcess	Creates a new process handle
ExitProcess	Exits the current process
OpenProcess	Opens an existing process
TerminateProcess	Terminates an existing process

Key Process Tools

As I mentioned in Chapter 2, there's a fair amount of overlap between the various system information tools and the data they return regarding system objects. Process-related tools are no exception to this. Table 3.2 summarizes the process-related information returned by several of these tools.

Table 3.2 Process-Related Tools and the Information They Display

	Process ID	Image Name	Priority Class	% CPU Time	Handle Count	% User Time	% Priv Time	Elapsed Time	Command Line
Perfmon	✔			✔	✔	✔	✔	✔	✔
Pstat	✔	✔							
Pviewer	✔	✔	✔	✔					
Qslice	✔	✔		✔		✔	✔		
TaskMgr	✔	✔	✔	✔	✔				
TList	✔	✔							✔

Key Perfmon Counters

Perfmon is an indispensable tool when working with processes. Table 3.3 lists some of the more important process-related Perfmon counters.

Table 3.3 Process-Related Perfmon Counters

Counter	Description
Process:% Privileged Time	The time the process has spent in kernel mode
Process:% User Time	The time the process has spent in user mode
Process:% Processor Time	The total processor time for the process; should be a sum of the first two counters and may exceed 100% on a multiprocessor machine
Process:Elapsed Time	The number of seconds that have passed since the process was created
Process:ID Process	The internal ID for the process
Process:Creating Process ID	The internal ID of the process that created this one
Process:Thread Count	The number of threads the process currently contains
Process:Handle Count	The number of handles in the process-specific handle table

Process Internals

Each thread runs within the context of the process that owns it. The process provides the resources and environment in which the thread executes its code. By virtue of Windows' process separation, a thread can't access the address space of other processes without a shared memory section or the use of the ReadProcessMemory or WriteProcessMemory functions.

Internally, a process is represented by an executive process (EPROCESS) block, which is stored in the system space along with its related data structures. Of these internal structures, only the process environment block (PEB) is stored within the process address space.

When a process object is first created (through a call to CreateProcess), Windows creates a process kernel object with an initial usage count of 1. Note that this object is not the process itself but a small data structure Windows uses to manage the process and track statistical information about it.

Once the kernel object is created, Windows creates the process's virtual address space and maps the code and data for the executable module (and any other required modules) into this space.

Note that CreateProcess can return TRUE before the process has been completely initialized, even before the operating system loader has located all the DLLs required by the executable. If a required module can't be located or fails to initialize, Windows terminates the new process. Because CreateProcess may have returned TRUE before this was known, the creating process is not aware of the problem and may attempt to erroneously use the process or thread handle returned by CreateProcess. One way to avoid this is to check the process status via the GetExitCodeProcess API function before attempting to use its process or main thread handle. GetExitCodeProcess will return FALSE if you pass it an invalid handle. Also, you can wrap calls to CloseHandle in exception blocks such that they trap the INVALID_HANDLE exception that's raised when CloseHandle is passed a bad handle.

Once a process is created, the system automatically creates its primary or main thread. Every process has at least one thread represented by an executive thread (ETHREAD) block in system memory.

After you've created a new process using CreateProcess, you should close the handle to its main thread in order to allow the corresponding thread object to be freed by the system when it is no longer needed. Closing this handle doesn't terminate the thread; it just releases the caller's reference to it. There is no advantage to keeping a handle to the spawned process's primary thread unless you intend to manipulate that thread directly through API calls. You can pass the handle of the process itself into a wait function if you want to wait on the process to finish executing before proceeding.

During the initialization of a new process, the instruction pointer for the process's primary thread is set to an undocumented and unexported function called BaseProcessStart. This is where all new processes begin executing in Win32.

Other Internal Structures

The PEB, EPROCESS block, and related structures aren't the only internal structures Windows uses to track processes. The Win32 subsystem process (CSRSS) maintains a parallel structure for each process that executes a Win32 program. Additionally, the kernel mode piece of the Win32 subsystem (Win32k.sys) maintains a per-process data structure that is created the first time a thread in the process calls a Win32 USER or GDI function that is implemented in kernel mode.

Process Termination

A process can be terminated by using one of the following four methods.

1. The primary thread's entry-point function returns. This is preferable because it ensures that:
   a. Any C++ objects created by the thread will have their destructors called and the runtime library (RTL) will be allowed to run its cleanup code.
   b. Windows will immediately release the memory used by the thread's stack.
   c. The process's exit code will be set to the return value of the thread's entry-point.
   d. Windows will decrement the corresponding process kernel object's usage count.
2. A thread in the process calls ExitProcess. You want to avoid this because it prevents C++ object destructors and RTL cleanup code from being called.
3. A thread in another process calls TerminateProcess. Avoid this because it does not notify the process's DLLs of the termination, nor are object destructors or RTL cleanup routines allowed to run. Note that TerminateProcess is asynchronous—the process isn't guaranteed to be terminated by the time the function returns. You can use WaitForSingleObject to suspend execution of the calling thread until the process becomes signaled (terminates).
4. All the threads in the process terminate on their own. This is fairly rare.

Once terminated, a process will leak absolutely nothing. Windows ensures that all resources allocated by the process are freed when it exits.

Speaking of process termination, here's what happens when a process terminates.

- All object handles opened by the process are closed.
- All threads in the process also terminate.
- The kernel process object becomes signaled.
- All the process's threads become signaled.
- GetExitCodeProcess will return the exit value of the process rather than STILL_ACTIVE.

SetErrorMode

Each process has a set of flags associated with it that tells the system how the process should respond to serious errors such as unhandled exceptions, media failures, and file open failures. You can set these flags via the SetErrorMode API call. Table 3.4 summarizes the options available to you.

SQL Server calls this function on startup, and, as a rule, you should never call it from code that runs within the SQL Server process (e.g., from

Table 3.4 SetErrorMode Parameters and Their Meanings

Value	Meaning
0	The system default—display all error dialog boxes.
SEM_FAILCRITICALERRORS	Don't display dialog boxes for critical errors; instead, send the error to the calling process.
SEM_NOALIGNMENTFAULTEXCEPT	Automatically fix any memory alignment problems (this applies only to RISC processors).
SEM_NOGPFAULTERRORBOX	Don't display the General Protection Fault dialog.
SEM_NOOPENFILEERRORBOX	Don't display a dialog box when file find error occurs; instead, send the error to the calling process.

an extended procedure or in-process COM object) as this could interfere with the server's ability to handle errors.

Exercises

In these exercises, we'll monitor various aspects of the SQL Server process. We'll check out its CPU usage, the threads it creates, and the modules it loads. You can use these same techniques to monitor other types of Win32 processes.

Exercise 3.1   Monitoring Process CPU Usage

In this exercise, we'll monitor a CPU spike in the SQL Server process. You'll learn how to monitor processor use via Task Manager. To complete the exercise, follow these steps.

1. Start SQL Server (*this should not be a production system*) it if isn't already started and connect to it with Query Analyzer. Ideally, you should be the only user on the system.
2. Start Task Manager (e.g., press Ctrl+Shift+Esc).
3. Click the Processes tab, then click the CPU column to sort the list so that processes with high CPU usage appear at the top of the list.
4. Minimize Task Manager, then switch back to Query Analyzer and run the following query:

```
declare @var int
set @var=1
while @var<100000 begin
  set @var=@var+1
end
```

5. Switch back to Task Manager while the query runs. In the Processes list, you should see that sqlservr.exe has moved near the top of the list.

The effect will be more dramatic on uniprocessor machines and, of course, on slower processors, but you should see some type of spike in the CPU use by the SQL Server process.

If you'd like to see a graphical depiction of this spike, run the query again and switch to the Performance tab in Task Manager. On a uniprocessor machine, you will see a chart like the one in Figure 3.1.

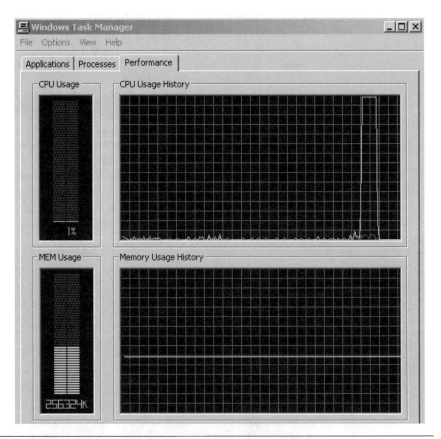

Figure 3.1 A spike in CPU use by SQL Server can spike the CPU use for the entire machine.

Exercise 3.2 Monitoring Thread Creation in SQL Server

Multithreaded applications usually take one of two approaches in deciding when to create new threads: Either all threads are created at application start-up, or they are created as needed while the application runs. SQL Server creates new worker threads as necessary up to the maximum number of worker threads specified with sp_configure (or in Enterprise Manager). To see how this works, follow these steps.

1. Stop and restart SQL Server. *This should not be a production server* and you should be its only user for the duration of this test.
2. Start Perfmon and click the Add Counters button.

3. In the Add Counters dialog, change the Performance Object to Process.
4. In the instances list, find sqlservr and click it. (This may have #1 or #2 or some other number appended to it if you have multiple instances of SQL Server running; make sure you know which instance you select.)
5. Select Thread Count from the counters list.
6. Click the Add button. You should now see a line chart in Perfmon indicating the current number of threads running within the SQL Server process. Make a note of how many threads are currently running (the Last field will tell you the exact count from the last sample interval). Figure 3.2 illustrates how to add the counter.
7. Open a command window, change to a folder into which you can copy some files and run some tests, and copy the files STRESS.CMD and STRESS.SQL from the CH03 folder on the CD accompanying this book. STRESS.CMD runs a specified T-SQL script or scripts using a specified number of connections (it calls osql.exe). You can use it to simulate multiple users connecting to your server and running a given query or queries. Run it without parameters to see usage help. STRESS.SQL simply dumps the pubs..authors table, then pauses for 15 seconds via the T-SQL WAITFOR DELAY. Start STRESS.CMD with this command line:

```
STRESS STRESS.SQL 15 N normal Y YourServerName\Instance
```

Replace YourServerName\Instance with your SQL Server machine name and instance.

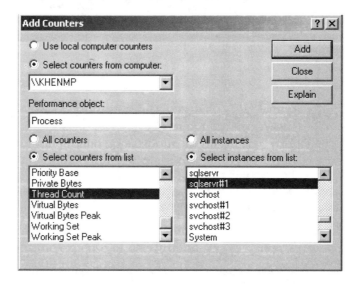

Figure 3.2 Adding the thread count to a Perfmon session

You should see 15 command windows open, each of them running STRESS.SQL.

8. Now switch back to Perfmon. You should see a noticeable increase in the number of threads within the SQL Server process. This is because your new connections have forced the server to create new worker threads to service them. Note that there's no strict ratio between worker threads and connections. SQL Server can often effectively service thousands of connections with only a few hundred worker threads.

9. About 15 seconds after you started STRESS.CMD, you should see the command windows it opened automatically close. However, you won't see SQL Server's worker thread count dip immediately. The server will not immediately destroy its newly created worker threads even though they're currently sitting idle because it may need them when the next wave of work comes rolling in. Caching idle worker threads allows SQL Server to provide stable performance in environments where the number of connections and queries being sent into the server varies significantly over time. At the same time, the server doesn't continue to use system resources that aren't needed—after 15 minutes, SQL Server will time out an idle worker thread and destroy it.

Note that a process's thread count can also be viewed by numerous other tools—you don't have to use Perfmon. One tool I'm particularly fond of is Pview (from the Platform SDK tools). Figure 3.3 illustrates viewing the thread count for SQL Server using Pview.

Exercise 3.3   Listing Modules and Processes within SQL Server

In this last exercise, you'll use a custom extended procedure, xp_modlist, to list the currently loaded modules and processes under SQL Server. You'll see all DLLs within the SQL Server process space, as well as any executables it has spawned. While Windows does not provide an official mechanism for establishing parent-child relationships between processes, there are undocumented functions that a routine can use to get this information. To run xp_modlist under SQL Server, follow these steps.

1. Start Query Analyzer and connect to a development or test SQL Server instance. *This should not be a production server*, and, ideally, you should be its only user.

2. Copy the file xp_sysinfo.dll from the CH03\xp_sysinfo\release subfolder on the CD accompanying this book to the binn folder under your SQL Server installation root.

3. Install xp_modlist by running this command from Query Analyzer:

```
sp_addextendedproc 'xp_modlist','xp_sysinfo.dll'
```

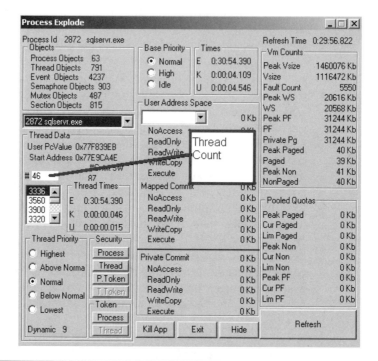

Figure 3.3 Viewing the thread count using Pview

4. Run the following command to instantiate a child process under SQL Server:

```
xp_cmdshell 'notepad'
```

Note: You will not see Notepad started unless you are running SQL Server as a console application. Don't worry about that—we're only starting it in order to have a subprocess that never completes.

5. Your xp_cmdshell call will appear to hang. Open a new Query Analyzer window and run the following command:

```
xp_modlist
```

You should see a list of processes that looks something like this:

```
ParentProcessID ProcessID Handle      ModuleName
--------------- --------- ----------  ----------------------------
264             3544      0x00400000  C:\PROGRA~1\MICROS~3\MSSQL$~2
264             3544      0x77F80000  C:\WINNT\System32\ntdll.dll
264             3544      0x77E80000  C:\WINNT\system32\KERNEL32.DLL
```

264	3544	0x77DB0000 C:\WINNT\system32\ADVAPI32.DLL
264	3544	0x77D30000 C:\WINNT\system32\RPCRT4.DLL
264	3544	0x77E10000 C:\WINNT\system32\USER32.DLL
264	3544	0x77F40000 C:\WINNT\system32\GDI32.dll
264	3544	0x41060000 C:\PROGRA~1\MICROS~3\MSSQL$~2
264	3544	0x41070000 C:\PROGRA~1\MICROS~3\MSSQL$~2
264	3544	0x42AE0000 C:\PROGRA~1\MICROS~3\MSSQL$~2
264	3544	0x41080000 C:\PROGRA~1\MICROS~3\MSSQL$~2
264	3544	0x25900000 C:\PROGRA~1\MICROS~3\MSSQL$~2
264	3544	0x410D0000 C:\PROGRA~1\MICROS~3\MSSQL$~2
264	3544	0x26A70000 C:\PROGRA~1\MICROS~3\MSSQL$~2
264	3544	0x26B10000 C:\PROGRA~1\MICROS~3\MSSQL$~2
264	3544	0x10000000 C:\PROGRA~1\MICROS~3\MSSQL$~2
264	3544	0x10010000 C:\WINNT\system32\PSAPI.DLL
3544	652	0x4AD00000 C:\WINNT\system32\cmd.exe
3544	652	0x77F80000 C:\WINNT\System32\ntdll.dll
3544	652	0x77E80000 C:\WINNT\system32\KERNEL32.dll
3544	652	0x77E10000 C:\WINNT\system32\USER32.dll
3544	652	0x77F40000 C:\WINNT\system32\GDI32.dll
652	3468	0x01000000 C:\WINNT\system32\notepad.exe
652	3468	0x77F80000 C:\WINNT\System32\ntdll.dll
652	3468	0x77E80000 C:\WINNT\system32\KERNEL32.dll
652	3468	0x77F40000 C:\WINNT\system32\GDI32.dll
652	3468	0x77E10000 C:\WINNT\system32\USER32.dll
652	3468	0x77DB0000 C:\WINNT\system32\ADVAPI32.dll
652	3468	0x76620000 C:\WINNT\system32\MPR.DLL

Note the three different ParentProcessId values. When you call xp_cmdshell, it calls the command interpreter, Cmd.exe, which in turn calls Notepad.exe, the command you passed into xp_cmdshell. By calling your process using cmd.exe, xp_cmdshell allows it to use command shell services such as piping and redirection.

6. If you are running SQL Server as a service, you may have to cycle your server machine in order to get rid of the Notepad instance you just started, depending on the user account you're logged in with and its permissions.

Process Recap

Although we tend to think of processes as objects that carry out the work of an application, a process is really just a context provider for threads. In Windows, threads carry out the work of the application; processes provide an environ-ment in which to do that work.

SQL Server is a process that can run as either a service or a console mode application. As with all other Windows processes, it consists of threads, a vir-tual address space, kernel objects, and so forth.

Process Knowledge Measure

1. What Windows API routine is used to construct a new process object?
2. What is the preferred method of shutting down a process?
3. Is it possible for an application to leak handles once it has been terminated?
4. What does GetExitCodeProcess return for a process that is still running?
5. In which of the two main sections of the process address space—the user mode section and the kernel section—is the process environ-ment block (PEB) stored?
6. Of the 4GB set aside for a 32-bit process's address space, how much is reserved for the kernel and how much is resolved for user mode space by default?
7. True or false: It's possible to create a new process that does not have a main thread, but this is not recommended since the app won't be able to do anything.
8. What is the largest size an application's user mode space can be set to under 32-bit Windows?
9. What file contains the kernel mode piece of the Win32 subsystem?
10. True or false: It is safe to call SetErrorMode from an extended stored procedure so long as you wrap the call in an exception han-dling block.
11. What is the signal status of a process that is terminated using Task Manager?
12. What BOOT.INI switch is used to configure Windows to provide ap-plications with a larger-than-normal user mode address space?
13. True or false: Because of the way that Windows protects processes from each other, it is impossible for one process to alter memory al-located within another process's address space.
14. True or false: CreateProcess can return TRUE even when the new process cannot be created because DLLs on which it depends can-not be located.

Threads

A thread is the facility by which program code is executed in Windows. It is the only Windows object capable of running code. A thread is always created within the context of a process and lives its entire life within that process.

A thread is the only means by which a process carries out work. Without threads, processes can't do anything.

Key Thread Terms and Concepts

✔ *Entry-point function*—the function address at which a thread begins executing. For the main thread, this is the entry point of the application (often a function named main() or something similar); for all other threads, the entry-point function is specified when the thread is created and is basically a simple callback routine.

✔ *Thread*—the Windows object by which application code is executed. Every thread runs within the context of an application or the operating system.

✔ *Context switch*—what happens when Windows saves off the contextual information for one thread and loads that of another so that the other thread can run. This consists of saving/loading volatile register values and other elements pertinent to the runtime environment of the thread.

✔ *Fiber*—a lightweight, thread-like user mode construct that runs within the context of a thread. Fiber mode imposes a number of restrictions on SQL Server that you may find unacceptable (e.g., you can't use SQLXML when running fiber mode). For this reason, fiber mode is generally not recommended, but it is sometimes useful for achieving greater scalability by reducing context switching.

✔ *SEH*—structured exception handling, specifically that provided by Windows. SEH constructs provide the mechanisms necessary to allow an application to logically divide the tasks it wants to carry out from the steps it must take if one of those tasks fails for some reason.

✔ *TLS*—thread local storage, a mechanism by which threads can store data that is unique to each thread. TLS values are accessed by index. You use the Win32 API function TlsAlloc to allocate a TLS index and the functions TlsSetValue and TlsGetValue to set and get values, respectively.

Key Thread APIs

Table 3.5 Key Thread-Related Win32 API Functions

Function	Description
CreateThread	Creates a new thread object
ExitThread	Exits the current thread
TerminateThread	Terminates another thread
GetExitCodeThread	Gets the return code of the thread's entry-point function

TIP: Note that you can pass a pseudohandle into a Win32 API function that requires a process or thread handle. This causes the function to perform its action on the calling process or thread.

Key Thread Tools

As I said in Chapter 2, there is considerable overlap between the various system diagnostic tools. Thread-related diagnostic tools are no exception. Table 3.6 summarizes many of the ways you can access basic thread information.

Table 3.6 Basic Thread Diagnostic Tools and the Information They Return

	Thread ID	Start Address	% CPU Time	Context Switches	Thread State	% User Time	% Priv Time	Reason for Last Wait State	Last Error
Perfmon	✔	✔	✔	✔	✔	✔	✔	✔	
Pstat	✔	✔		✔					
Pviewer	✔	✔		✔	✔	✔	✔	✔	
Qslice			✔			✔	✔		
TList	✔				✔			✔	✔

Key Perfmon Counters

As with processes, Perfmon is invaluable for monitoring thread usage in an application and across the system. Table 3.7 lists some of the more useful thread-related Perfmon counters.

Table 3.7 Useful Thread-Related Performance Counters

Counter	Description
Process:Priority Base	The base execution priority of the owning process
Thread:% Privileged Time	The percentage of time the thread has spent in kernel mode
Thread:% User Time	The percentage of time the thread has spent in user mode
Thread:% Processor Time	The percentage of time the thread has used the CPU; should be a sum of the % Privileged Time and % User Time counters
Thread:Context Switches/sec	The number of context switches per second
Thread:Elapsed Time	The elapsed time since the thread was started
Thread:Id Process	The internal ID of the owning process
Thread:Id Thread	The internal ID of the thread
Thread:Priority Base	The thread's priority base
Thread:Priority Current	The thread's current priority
Thread:Start Address	The thread's start address
Thread:Thread State	The current thread state, an integer from 0 to 7 (see Table 3.11 on page 64)
Thread:Thread Wait Reason	If the thread is waiting, the reason it is waiting

Thread Internals

A Win32 thread includes the following components:

- A set of volatile CPU registers that represent the state of the processor.
- A stack for executing in kernel mode.

- A stack for executing in user mode.
- A TLS area.
- A unique identifier known as a thread ID. (As with processes, this is also internally called a client ID—process and thread IDs never overlap because they are generated from the same namespace.)
- An optional security context. (By default, a thread inherits the security context of its parent process. Multithreaded apps will sometimes obtain a separate access token for individual threads in order to impersonate the security context of the clients they serve.)

The TLS area, registers, and thread stacks are collectively known as a thread's context. Data about them is stored in the thread's CONTEXT structure. CONTEXT is the only processor-dependent structure in the Win32 API. The structure itself is contained in the thread's kernel object.

Of the items stored in the CONTEXT structure, the thread's instruction pointer and stack pointer registers are probably the two most important. When a thread's kernel object is initialized, the stack pointer is set to the address of the location of the thread's entry-point function on the thread's stack. The instruction pointer is set to the undocumented Base-ThreadStart function.

All threads in a process share the process's virtual memory address space and handle table. By default, they also inherit the process's security access token, though they can obtain their own for impersonation if necessary, as mentioned above. And, as I mentioned in the Processes section, the system prevents threads from accessing the address space of other processes without a shared memory section or the use of the ReadProcessMemory or WriteProcessMemory API functions.

A thread is represented at the system level by an ETHREAD block. As with the process EPROCESS block, the ETHREAD block and related structures live in the system address space. The lone exception is the thread environment block (TEB), which lives in the user mode address space. The TEB stores context information for the image loader and various Win32 DLLs and is located in the process space because they need a structure that is writable from user mode.

As with processes, the Win32 subsystem (CSRSS) maintains a parallel structure for each thread created in a Win32 process. And for threads that have called a Win32 subsystem USER or GDI function, Win32k.sys, the kernel mode portion of the Win32 subsystem, maintains a parallel data structure (a W32THREAD struct) that the ETHREAD block references.

The Primary Thread

When CreateProcess creates a new process, the system handles automatically creating its first thread. This thread is usually referred to as the primary thread or main thread. For single-threaded applications, this is the only thread the process will contain. For multithreaded applications, the primary thread will usually either spawn or at least interact with the other threads in the process. These other threads are usually referred to as worker or background threads.

When a process finishes its work and is ready to shut down, it should signal any worker threads it has created that they need to return from their entry-point functions, then simply return from the entry point to its main thread. Returning from the primary thread's entry-point function ensures that:

- Any objects created by the thread will have their destructors called so that they can be destroyed properly.
- Windows will immediately release the memory used by the thread's stack.
- The process's exit code will be set to the entry-point function's return value.
- The system will decrement the usage count of the process kernel object for the thread's owning process.

Processes vs. Threads

Given that threads use fewer system resources than processes, it makes sense to try to solve your programming problems using threads rather than processes when possible. The overhead of managing the virtual address space is not insignificant; creating too many processes on a machine can run the system out of virtual memory and bring performance to a standstill.

That said, don't assume that every problem is better solved with multiple threads rather than multiple processes. Some designs are better implemented using separate processes. My advice is to educate yourself as to the trade-offs with each approach and weigh them against one another before deciding which way to go.

Beyond the obvious efficiencies with respect to system resources, multi-threading an application also allows its interface to be simplified. If certain tasks that you normally trigger by clicking menu options or buttons can be performed automatically in the background by separate threads, you may be able to eliminate those user interface elements altogether. Keep in mind, though, that in most apps, a single thread should handle all user interface updates. This is because, unlike other types of objects, the window handles to user interface components such as buttons and text boxes are actually owned by individual threads, not the parent process. Synchronizing multiple user interface threads such that the app displays and works correctly is usually more trouble than it's worth.

Multithreading also allows an application to scale. If your machine has multiple CPUs, you can truly run multiple tasks simultaneously by creating multiple threads, each of which might get its own CPU.

For all its benefits, keep in mind that multithreading is not the best way to solve every problem. Performing tasks over multiple threads introduces complexities into an app that would otherwise not be there—there are always trade-offs. Some developers believe the first thing you do with a complex task is break it up into multiple threads. This is a questionable design practice that will get you into trouble as an application builder if you follow it.

Creating and Destroying Threads

When CreateThread is called, the system creates a thread kernel object to manage the thread. This object's initial usage count is 2. The thread's kernel object will not be destroyed until the thread terminates *and* the handle returned by CreateThread is closed.

Creating a thread initializes its stack. This stack is allocated from the process's virtual address space since threads don't have an address space of their own. Once the stack is allocated, the system writes two values to the upper end of it (thread stacks always build from high memory addresses downward): the entry-point function address that was supplied to CreateThread and the value of the user-defined parameter that was passed in along with it.

The routine pointed to by the instruction pointer immediately after thread initialization depends on the type of thread being created. If the thread being initialized is the process's main thread, the instruction pointer will be set to the undocumented (and unexported) function BaseProcessStart. If the thread is one created by the application (a worker or background thread), the instruction pointer is set to the BaseThreadStart function (also undocumented and unexported).

NOTE: Usually, developers aren't concerned with the thread ID of a newly created thread—they only need the object handle in order to interact with the thread. Therefore, CreateThread allows you to pass NULL for its final parameter, lpThreadId, and this is a common practice among experienced NT developers. This works fine on the Windows NT family of operating systems (which includes Windows NT, Windows 2000, and all subsequent versions of Windows) but will cause an access violation on Windows 9x. If you want your code to run on Win9x, you must pass a value for this parameter whether you actually intend to do anything with it or not.

Thread Termination

You can terminate a thread using one of the following four methods.

1. Return from the thread's entry-point function. This is the cleanest and best way to shut down a thread. It ensures that C++ object destructors are called, RTL cleanup code runs, buffers are flushed to disk, and so on.
2. Have the thread commit suicide by calling ExitThread. This approach prevents C++ object destructors and RTL cleanup code from running, so you should avoid it.
3. Call TerminateThread from the same or another process. You shouldn't use TerminateThread to kill a thread for three reasons.
   a. The thread doesn't receive any notification that it is dying. Naturally, this can present problems with running cleanup code.
   b. Code wired up to the DLL_THREAD_DETACH notification doesn't run when you use TerminateThread. Again you may have cleanup issues because of this. Note also that TerminateThread is asynchronous. It can return before the thread is signaled (terminated). You can use a wait function to pause the execution of the calling thread until the thread is actually signaled.
   c. The memory in which the thread's stack is stored is not freed up until the process terminates. TerminateThread was implemented this way so that other threads that might still be running and accessing variables that were on the terminated thread's stack can continue to run unaffected.
4. Terminate the containing process. This has the same caveats as TerminateThread since it basically calls TerminateThread for every thread in the process.

When a thread terminates, the following happens.

- The thread kernel object is signaled.
- Windows frees all user object handles owned by the thread. As I said earlier, usually a process owns the objects created by its threads. However, there are two exceptions: windows and hooks. When a thread terminates, any window or hook handles it has open are freed.
- Windows changes the thread's exit code from STILL_ACTIVE to the return value of the entry-point function or the value passed to ExitThread or TerminateThread.
- Windows decrements the thread kernel object's usage count by 1.
- Windows considers the process terminated if the thread is the last active thread in the process.

NOTE: For obvious reasons, many of the thread-specific Win32 API functions are not available from Visual C++ if you link with the single-threaded runtime library. You'll get "unresolved external" errors for functions such as CreateThread and _beginthreadex if you attempt to call these functions while linking with the single-threaded RTL. The single-threaded version of the RTL is the default when you build a non-MFC application, but the multithreaded RTL is the default when you build an MFC app or use the extended stored procedure wizard to build a SQL Server extended procedure. If you're going to write code that is to run in a multithreaded environment you must link with the multithreaded version of the RTL because, in addition to multithreading-specific functions not even being present in the single-threaded RTL, several base RTL functions are not thread-safe in the single-threaded version of the library. Examples include errno, _strerror, tmpnam, strtok, and many, many others. And, in case you're wondering, there are separate single-threaded and multithreaded RTLs for C because the original RTL was created around 1970 before threads were available on operating systems.

_beginthreadex and _endthreadex

Even though CreateThread and ExitThread are the standard Win32 API functions for creating and ending threads, Visual C++ developers should consider using _beginthreadex and _endthreadex instead. There are three main reasons for this.

1. _beginthreadex allocates a structure (known as a tiddata block) that allows certain C/C++ RTL functions (such as those mentioned in the note above) to work correctly when accessed simultaneously by multiple threads.

2. _beginthreadex uses an entry-point function that wraps your thread entry-point function in an SEH frame. This frame handles many conditions and errors that would not be caught were you to create the thread directly with CreateThread.

3. When _endthreadex is used instead of ExitThread to terminate a thread, the thread's tiddata block is freed (it is leaked until process shutdown when ExitThread is used).

Given that CreateThread is the only way to create a new thread in Windows, _beginthreadex does ultimately call it. However, it makes a few changes en route that make your code more robust and protect it from thread-safety issues in the RTL. It pulls this off by substituting its own thread entry-point function for yours and storing the address of your function, along with the user-defined parameter you originally supplied, in the tiddata structure it allocates from the RTL heap for your thread. It then calls CreateThread and passes its thread entry-point function (_threadstartex) as the entry-point function and the address of the tiddata block as the user-defined parameter. This _threadstartex function sets up the SEH frame I mentioned earlier, does some other initialization work, then retrieves the address of your entry-point function from the tiddata block passed into it and calls it, passing it the user-defined parameter you originally passed to _beginthreadex. The end result is a far safer and more robust thread creation mechanism. SQL Server uses _beginthreadex and _beginthread to instantiate new threads.

The parameter lists differ slightly between CreateThread/_beginthreadex and ExitThread/_endthreadex, so you may have to do some casting to pass muster with the compiler, but these functions are very similar, so this shouldn't be too difficult.

Thread Functions

A thread function is the entry point for the thread. It's where execution begins when the thread starts. A few points about these types of functions appear below.

- Thread functions can be named anything.
- You don't have the ANSI/Unicode issues that you have with the primary thread and its main/wmain and WinMain/wWinMain entry points.
- A thread function must return a value.
- You should try to use function parameters and local variables as much as possible; using static and global variables makes your code inherently unthread-safe.

In order to ensure that system cleanup code runs properly, you want to write code such that it returns from your entry-point function rather than calling ExitThread/_endthreadex. Returning properly from your thread function ensures the following.

- The destructors of your C++ objects will be called so that the objects can be disposed of properly.
- Windows will release the memory used by the thread's stack immediately (rather than waiting until process shutdown).
- The thread's exit code (stored in the thread's kernel object) will be set to your thread function's return value.
- The usage count of the thread's kernel object will be decremented.

Threads and Exception Handling

Windows has built-in support for structured exception handling (SEH). This allows you to write code that separates the task at hand from what it is supposed to do if an error occurs.

SEH is different from language exceptions (implemented through key-words such as throw and catch) in that the operating system, rather than the RTL, provides the facilities that make it work. You can certainly use both types of exceptions in your code; in fact, in Visual C++, language exceptions are implemented under the covers using Windows' SEH facilities.

When an operating system exception occurs that is not handled by a thread, the system's default handler is triggered (unless the application has installed its own), a dialog box is displayed, and the process is shut down. (What actually happens when an unhandled exception occurs can be changed with SetErrorMode, as mentioned earlier.)

Of course, this has important implications for code you write that runs inside the SQL Server process. What happens when you call an xproc from T-SQL and the xproc causes an exception to be raised? The answer depends on whether the exception was raised within the context of the SQL Server worker thread or a thread created by the xproc.

If the exception was raised by the SQL Server worker thread running the xproc, the thread's default exception handler catches the exception and kills the connection responsible for causing it. If the exception was raised by a thread created by the xproc (and the thread has no exception handling code of its own), SQL Server will generate a symptom dump file, then write a message to the error log indicating that it is terminating, and exit. *This means that an unhandled exception in a thread created by an xproc could cause your server to crash*—not a pleasant scenario.

How do you protect against this? Always wrap the thread entry-point function for any threads you create in an xproc (or in an in-process COM object) with SEH code. Listing 3.1 provides an example.

Listing 3.1 A Thread Function with SEH Code in Place

```
DWORD WINAPI StartThrd(LPVOID lpParameter)
{
  __try
  {
  CHAR *pCh=NULL;
  //null pointer ref -- forces an exception
  *pCh='x';
  }
  __except(EXCEPTION_EXECUTE_HANDLER)
  {
    MessageBeep(0);
  }
  return 1;
}
```

In this example, we intentionally try to dereference a NULL pointer in order to force an exception. When the exception occurs, we simply execute the MessageBeep Win32 API function. Obviously, in a real application, you'd do something more substantial in your exception handling block, but you get the point.

GetLastError

Every thread stores the result of the last Win32 API call, commonly referred to as last error. Though there's no guarantee that a Win32 function will set the last error value on an error condition, it's very unusual for this not to be the case. You can retrieve this value using the GetLastError API function. In addition to setting last error on an error condition, some functions also set it when no error occurs—in other words, they reset it. You can set the value of last error via the SetLastError API function.

You should call GetLastError immediately after API function calls from which you wish to obtain error information because, as I've mentioned, some functions reset this value when they complete without an error. Once a last error value has been lost because a function has reset it, there's no way to retrieve it.

You can use bitwise operators to retrieve important information from last error values. For example, bit 29 indicates that the error is a user-defined error. No system error will have this bit set. If you're defining your own error codes, be sure to set this bit in order to ensure that it does not conflict with a system-defined error code.

The file winerror.h in the Platform SDK documents the exact format of Win32 error codes and includes #defines for the most common ones. You can also use NET HELPMSG nnnn from the command prompt to display a brief description of the most common Win32 error codes. For example, type this at a command prompt:

```
NET HELPMSG 5
```

You should see:

```
Access is denied.
```

This means that Win32 error code 5 indicates an access denied error condition.

The Win32 API FormatMessage allows you to translate an error code into its textual description. You can use this function to display a message when an error occurs or to return an error string to a caller. For example, you could use FormatMessage to translate a Win32 error encountered in an extended procedure into a string that you can return to SQL Server. SQL Server will then pass this message on to the client.

Fibers

Fibers are often thought of as lightweight threads. They were added to Windows to make porting UNIX server applications easier. UNIX doesn't implement threading in the same sense that Windows does. If we view them from the perspective of the Windows threading model, UNIX apps are single-threaded but can serve multiple clients. This basically means that UNIX developers have created their own threading library that they use to simulate the type of pure threading offered by Windows. This package does many of the same things Windows does when managing threads and thread context—it saves/restores certain CPU registers, maintains multiple stacks, and switches between these thread contexts in order to service client requests.

The chief difference between threads and fibers in Windows is that threads are kernel objects, while fibers are user objects. The operating system knows threads intimately and has highly tuned and tunable methods of scheduling them, synchronizing them, and managing them to maximize system performance and concurrency. Fibers, by contrast, are invisible to the operating system kernel. They are implemented in user mode code of which the kernel knows nothing.

SQL Server can be configured to use Windows' fiber APIs. This is something Microsoft generally recommends against, and you should do so only when instructed to by Microsoft or a Microsoft partner. There are numerous facilities in SQL Server that either do not work at all or that cannot work correctly when the system is in fiber mode. For example, the SQLXML facilities in SQL Server (e.g., sp_xml_preparedocument) are not available when the system is in fiber mode. This same is true of SQLMAIL—you can't use it while in fiber mode. Seemingly innocuous activities such as initializing COM from an xproc that in thread mode would have potentially affected just one SQL Server worker could conceivably affect many workers when the server is running in fiber mode since a single thread can own multiple fibers. A word to the wise is sufficient: Avoid fiber mode if you can.

That said, what would be a valid scenario in which it would be appropriate to consider enabling fiber mode on SQL Server? Again, you should do so only when instructed to by Microsoft, but a common scenario that fiber mode may be able to help address is the situation we see when there are far too many context switches between SQL Server's worker threads. Context switches are expensive; too many of them can bring system performance to a crawl. Furthermore, since threads are kernel objects, waiting on them (which SQL Server does most of the time) causes the thread to switch from user to kernel mode, which is, again, a costly (~1,000 CPU cycles) operation. Since fibers are user objects (implemented in Kernel32.DLL), it's possible to use fiber mode to improve SQL Server's performance in pathological situations where context switches are contending heavily with the real work of the server for CPU resources. In such scenarios, you may find that the many cons of using fiber mode are outweighed by its benefits to your specific situation.

Exercises

In these exercises, we'll investigate SQL Server's ability to handle exceptions and do some general research into how it manages threads. We'll begin in Exercise 3.4 by creating an extended procedure whose whole purpose is to raise different types of exceptions within the SQL Server process to see how it handles them. Working through this example will give you a greater understanding of the methods Win32 processes in general—and SQL Server in particular—typically use to deal with critical errors.

Exercise 3.5 takes you through attaching to SQL Server with a debugger so that we can look under the hood a bit and see how to inspect thread-relevant information for a running process. You'll use Microsoft's standard WinDbg debugger to attach to SQL Server, list some thread stacks, and do some other basic tasks having to do with threading.

Exercise 3.4   Exceptions in Extended Procedures

In this exercise, we'll explore what can happen when an extended procedure causes an exception within the SQL Server process. *This exercise will cause your SQL Server to stop, so be sure to run the exercise against a test or development server.* Ideally, you should be the only user on the server. Let's begin by setting up an xproc called xp_exception in the master database by following these steps.

1. Locate the file xp_exception.dll in the CH03 subfolder on the CD accompanying this book.
2. Copy it to the binn folder under your SQL Server.
3. Start Query Analyzer and add the xproc to the master database using sp_addextendedproc, like this:

```
exec sp_addextendedproc 'xp_exception','xp_exception.dll'
```

For curious readers, Listing 3.2 provides the main routine in xp_exception.

Listing 3.2 xp_exception's Main Module

```
RETCODE __declspec(dllexport) xp_exception(SRV_PROC *srvproc)
{

int iParams=srv_rpcparams(srvproc);
BYTE bType;
ULONG cbMaxLen;
ULONG cbActualLen;
BYTE bCrashType;
BOOL bNull;
DWORD dwThreadID;


if (0==iParams) bCrashType=0;
else srv_paraminfo(srvproc,1,&bType,&cbMaxLen,&cbActualLen,
    &bCrashType,&bNull);
```

```
switch (bCrashType)
{
case 0: {  //Crash the worker thread
    srv_sendmsg(srvproc,SRV_MSG_INFO,0,(DBTINYINT)0,(DBTINYINT)0,
        NULL,0,0,
    "Generating an access violation on the worker thread",
        SRV_NULLTERM);

    CHAR *pCh=NULL;
    //null pointer ref
    *pCh='x';
    break;
    }
case 1: {  //Crash a new thread with exception handling
    srv_sendmsg(srvproc,SRV_MSG_INFO,0,(DBTINYINT)0,(DBTINYINT)0,
        NULL,0,0,
    "Generating an access violation on a new thread with exception
        handling",SRV_NULLTERM);

    CreateThread(NULL,
    0,
    (LPTHREAD_START_ROUTINE)StartThrdHandled,
    NULL,
    0,
    (LPDWORD)&dwThreadID);
    break;
    }
case 2: {  //Throw a language exception
    srv_sendmsg(srvproc,SRV_MSG_INFO,0,(DBTINYINT)0,(DBTINYINT)0,
        NULL,0,0,
    "Generating a language exception on a new thread without
        exception handling",SRV_NULLTERM);

    CreateThread(NULL,
    0,
    (LPTHREAD_START_ROUTINE)StartThrdLanguageException,
    NULL,
    0,
    (LPDWORD)&dwThreadID);
    break;
    }
case 3: {  //Crash a new thread WITHOUT exception handling
    srv_sendmsg(srvproc,SRV_MSG_INFO,0,(DBTINYINT)0,(DBTINYINT)0,
        NULL,0,0,
```

```
"Generating an access violation on a new thread WITHOUT
    exception handling -- your server should crash",
    SRV_NULLTERM);

CreateThread(NULL,
0,
(LPTHREAD_START_ROUTINE)StartThrdUnhandled,
NULL,
0,
(LPDWORD)&dwThreadID);
break;
}
}
  return XP_NOERROR ;
}
```

As you can see, the xproc takes a single parameter—an integer—then fails in different ways based on the parameter passed. Table 3.8 lists the supported parameter values and what each one causes to happen.

Table 3.8 xp_exception Parameter Values and Their Meanings

Value	Action
0	Generates an exception on the calling SQL Server worker thread
1	Generates an exception on a new thread that includes an SEH wrapper
2	Generates a language exception
3	Generates an exception on a new thread that does not include an SEH wrapper

4. Now, let's run the xproc. Let's start by passing it a parameter value of 0:

```
exec xp_exception 0
```

You should see something like this in Query Analyzer:

```
ODBC: Msg 0, Level 20, State 1
Stored function 'xp_exception' in the library
'xp_exception.dll'
generated an access violation. SQL Server is terminating
```

```
process 51.
Generating an access violation on the worker thread
```

```
Connection Broken
```

The SEH block that SQL Server sets up for its worker threads caught the exception generated by the xproc and killed the corresponding connection.

5. Let's see what happens when we generate an exception on a new thread that has an SEH wrapper around its entry-point function:

```
exec xp_exception 1
```

All you should see in Query Analyzer is a message returned by the xproc—SQL Server is unaffected by the exception because of the SEH code:

```
Generating an access violation on a new thread with
exception handling
```

6. Now let's see what happens when we force a language exception to be generated on a new thread without an SEH wrapper:

```
exec xp_exception 2
```

Again, all you see in Query Analyzer is the message returned by the xproc itself—SQL Server is unaffected by the language exception:

```
Generating a language exception on a new thread without
exception handling
```

As I said earlier in the chapter, language exceptions and Win32 exceptions are two different things. A language exception won't bring down the server, but a Win32 exception can if not handled properly.

7. Now let's try an access violation on a new thread without an SEH wrapper around its entry-point function. (Warning: This will cause your server to stop.)

```
exec xp_exception 3
```

Here's what we see in Query Analyzer:

```
Generating an access violation on a new thread WITHOUT
exception handling -- your server should crash
```

If you then check your server status in SQL Server Service Manager, you should find that it has stopped. The unhandled exception generated by xp_exception caused the process to crash. This should reinforce how important it is, especially in multithreaded xprocs, to handle any exceptions your code might raise. Failing to do so can quickly cause a server crash.

Note that I don't recommend that you necessarily handle all exceptions in the main thread (the SQL Server worker thread from which it was called) of an xproc. If you want to have the calling connection killed in the event of a catastrophic failure in your xproc, you can simply allow SQL Server's default SEH handling to take care of this for you—there's no need to set up your own version of it.

That said, you should definitely handle all exceptions in any new threads you create in an xproc. Failing to do so will bring down your server when an exception occurs.

If you check the LOG folder under your SQL Server installation, you should find two new files: an exception log file and a stack dump file. Both are text files that you can view with Notepad. Feel free to open each of these and inspect them for additional data about the exception that was raised. The dump file in particular contains interesting details about DLLs loaded within the SQL Server process address space and the call stacks of the worker threads when the exception was raised.

Exercise 3.5   Displaying Thread Information Using a Debugger

In this next exercise, we'll attach to SQL Server using WinDbg and inspect some thread-related information exposed by the debugger. To take a peek under the SQL Server hood, follow these steps.

1. If your server is still stopped from the previous exercise, restart it. As before, this should be a test or development server, and, ideally, you should be the only user on it (since attaching to it with a debugger will also stop it momentarily).
2. Start WinDbg. As I mentioned in Chapter 2, be sure your symbol path is set correctly.
3. Press F6 to attach to SQL Server. Find the sqlservr.exe instance in the list of processes and select it. If you have more than one instance running there may be more than one sqlservr.exe in the list. If so, expand the tree node of each sqlservr.exe process to view its command line— you should be able to identify each instance from its command line. If you just restarted your SQL Server, the correct instance should be near the bottom of the list of processes.
4. Once you've attached, the Disassembly window should open automatically. Close it. If the Disassembly window reopens at any point during this exercise, close it—we won't be using it for the time being.
5. Find the command window and dump the thread stacks using this command:

```
~*kv
```

You should see the call stacks of every thread in the SQL Server process listed. You'll notice that most of the threads are in Win32's WaitForSingleObject API function. This is because they are waiting on a synchronization object of some type to be signaled; we'll talk more about WaitForSingleObject and synchronization objects later in the chapter.

6. Now run this command:

```
!teb
```

This will dump the TEB for the current thread. The current thread is indicated by the prompt to the left of the edit box in the command window. (Given that we haven't changed it, this should be the last worker thread in the SQL Server process space.) Your TEB will likely look something like this:

```
TEB at 7FF99000
       ExceptionList:       26caffdc
       Stack Base:          26cb0000
       Stack Limit:         26cae000
       SubSystemTib:        0
       FiberData:           1e00
       ArbitraryUser:       0
       Self:                7ff99000
       EnvironmentPtr:      0
       ClientId:            bcc.cf8
       Real ClientId:       bcc.cf8
       RpcHandle:           0
       Tls Storage:         f3b38
       PEB Address:         7ffdf000
       LastErrorValue:      0
       LastStatusValue:     0
       Count Owned Locks:0
       HardErrorsMode:      0
```

Note the inclusion of the LastErrorValue in the output. This is the value you would see were the thread to call the Win32 API GetLastError at this point.

7. You can also retrieve the last error value for the current thread via this command:

```
!gle
```

This dumps the last error value as well as the last status value for the thread:

```
LastErrorValue: (Win32) 0 (0) - The operation completed
successfully.
LastStatusValue: (NTSTATUS) 0 - STATUS_WAIT_0
```

8. Let's conclude by dumping SQL Server's process environment block (PEB):

```
!peb
```

This displays a wealth of information, including a list of all the modules currently loaded in the SQL Server process space, the command line specified for the process, its DLL path, and many other useful tidbits.

9. You can now exit the debugger. If you are running on a version of Windows prior to Windows XP, you will have to restart SQL Server because exiting the debugger leaves it stopped.

Thread Recap

A thread is the mechanism by which code gets executed in Windows. No application can execute a single instruction without doing so via a thread. Threads run within the context of their owning process and terminate when the process terminates. Although the relationship between fibers and threads is similar to that of threads and processes, it's usually better to rely on threads and avoid fiber mode if you can, both in the apps you build and in those you use, such as SQL Server. Windows was designed to use threads and has been optimized to work with them. There are numerous scenarios where the functionality of Win32 fibers falls well short of that offered by kernel-based threads.

Thread Knowledge Measure

1. What happens if an application starts a new worker thread that terminates due to an exception and the thread's entry-point function does not have an SEH wrapper?
2. What is the name of the only processor-dependent structure in the entire Win32 API, and why is it processor-dependent?
3. In what section of a process's address space—kernel space or user mode space—is the TEB stored?
4. True or false: You can use the TList utility to list the percentage of CPU utilization for a given process.

5. True or false: When a new process is created, the system will automatically create its first thread regardless of the parameters passed into CreateProcess.
6. What happens if you attempt to compile and link a Visual C++ program that calls the CreateThread Win32 API function but links with the single-threaded version of the runtime library?
7. What is the preferred method of terminating a thread?
8. True or false: When designing most types of complex applications, the first thing an application architect should do is divide the work the app must perform into threaded tasks and design threads to carry them out.
9. Name the main reason creating a process is slower and more resource intensive than creating a thread.
10. What WinDbg command do we use to list the PEB for a thread?
11. Describe the purpose of the ReadProcessMemory Win32 API function.
12. What Win32 API function is used to create a thread?
13. What WinDbg command can we use to list only the last error value and last status value for the current thread?
14. True or false: It's possible for thread and process IDs to overlap because they are generated from different namespaces.
15. What Win32 API function is used to allocate a TLS index?
16. What is the source of error code 0x80000004—Windows or a user application?
17. I have received a last error value of 6. What command line sequence can I use to display the textual description for this error code?
18. What does the Thread:% Privileged Time Perfmon counter indicate?
19. What WinDbg command do we use to list only the TEB for a thread?
20. True or false: The LastErrorValue field included in WinDbg's TEB output is the same information as that returned by the Win32 GetLastError API function.

Thread Scheduling

A preemptive, multitasking operating system must use some type of formal process to determine which threads should run and for how long. The algorithms Windows uses to determine when a thread gets scheduled aren't always well documented, but Microsoft has designed them to be as fair and as

generally applicable as possible. Below, I'll document how a few of these algorithms work; just understand that future versions of Windows may alter
them significantly.

Before we go any further, I should stop and point out that SQL Server
does not use the Windows scheduler and the scheduling APIs as you might
expect. That's because it handles most of its thread scheduling needs itself
via its UMS component. One noteworthy side effect of this is that, to the
operating system, only one SQL Server thread generally appears to be active at a time per processor. So, even though the server may have hundreds
of worker threads at any given time, only one of them for each processor on
the server appears to Windows to be actually doing anything.

I'll talk more about the reasons for this in Chapter 10, but just understand for the time being that SQL Server makes use of the Windows scheduler and scheduling APIs in different ways than you might expect. We'll
plumb the depth of those differences and the reasons behind them later.

Key Scheduling Terms and Concepts

- ✔ *Context switch*—what happens when Windows saves off the contextual
  information for one thread and loads that of another so that the other
  thread can run. This consists of saving/loading volatile register values
  and other elements pertinent to the runtime environment of the thread.
- ✔ *Quantum*—the time slice a thread is given to run by the Windows
  scheduler.
- ✔ *Preemption*—what happens when Windows stops one thread before its
  quantum has expired so that another thread can run.
- ✔ *Clock interval*—the frequency at which the CPU's clock interrupt fires.
- ✔ *Thread state*—the current execution status of a thread, represented by
  an integer value between 0 and 7.
- ✔ *Process priority*—the execution priority of a process ranging from Idle
  through Real-Time.
- ✔ *Thread priority*—the process-relative execution priority of a particular
  thread ranging from Idle through Time-Critical.
- ✔ *Processor affinity*—a bitmap indicating the processors on which a process or thread can run.
- ✔ *Ideal processor*—the processor considered the best host for a particular
  thread. Windows gives preference to this processor when scheduling the
  thread to run but will allow the thread to run on another processor if its
  ideal processor is busy.
- ✔ *Thread starvation*—what happens when a lower-priority thread is continuously preempted by higher-priority threads and not allowed to run.

Overview

Windows schedules work using a priority-driven, preemptive scheduling system. This means that the highest-priority thread that is ready to run (runnable) preempts lower-priority threads (within the limits of processor affinity, which we'll discuss more in a moment). When a lower-priority thread is preempted, it is interrupted (perhaps just momentarily) while a higher-priority thread is allowed to run. Thread starvation occurs when a thread is continually preempted and not allowed to run for an extended period of time.

Windows schedules work at thread granularity. Given that processes don't run but only provide an environment in which threads can run, this makes sense.

Windows creates the illusion that all threads run concurrently by partitioning the time each thread is allowed to run into time slices called quantums. It hands quantums to threads in a round-robin fashion.

There is no single routine within Windows that performs all task scheduling. Within the Windows kernel, there are numerous routines and modules involved in the scheduling of work. We refer to them collectively as the kernel's dispatcher or scheduler.

Key Thread Scheduling APIs

Table 3.9 Key Thread Scheduling APIs

Function	Description
Suspend/ResumeThread	Pauses/resumes a thread
Sleep/SleepEx	Suspends execution of the current thread for a specified amount of time
Get/SetPriorityClass	Gets/sets the base priority for the specified process
Get/SetThreadPriority	Gets/sets the process-relative priority for the specified thread
Get/SetProcessAffinityMask	Gets/sets the processors a process is allowed to run on
SetThreadAffinityMask	Sets the processors a thread is allowed to run on
Get/SetThreadPriorityBoost	Gets/sets the system's ability to temporarily boost the priority of a thread
SetThreadIdealProcessor	Sets the ideal processor on which a thread should run
Get/SetProcessPriorityBoost	Gets/sets the system's ability to temporarily boost the priority of a process
SwitchToThread	Allows a thread to give up the remainder of its quantum so that other threads can run

Key Thread Scheduling Tools

Perfmon is, again, a key diagnostic tool here. Pview and Pviewer are also very valuable for monitoring what's happening with specific processes. Given that much of the scheduling code actually resides in the kernel, there is only so much information that user mode tools can provide (Table 3.10).

Table 3.10 Scheduling-Related Tools and the Information They Provide

	Process Base Priority	Process Priority Class	Thread Base Priority	Thread Current Priority
TaskMgr		✔		
Perfmon	✔		✔	✔
Pstat	✔			✔
Pviewer	✔			✔

Thread Scheduling Internals

The scheduling of threads is handled by the Windows kernel and is transparent to applications. Unlike 16-bit Windows' cooperative multitasking architecture, every version of Windows since Windows NT 3.1 (the very first version of the Windows NT product family, currently represented by Windows 2000, Windows XP, and Windows Server 2003) has implemented a scheduling system that does not require an application to do anything special to allow other applications to run smoothly or to perform multiple tasks at once. One thread or process need not yield to another in order to keep the system humming along.

Quantums

As I've mentioned, a quantum refers to the length of time a thread is allowed to run before the system interrupts it. The quantum value isn't actually a time length—it's an integer value that represents what are commonly referred to as quantum units. Each time a thread is scheduled, it starts with a certain amount of quantum units. Each time the processor's clock interrupt fires, a given number of these units are deducted from this amount. When this count reaches 0, the thread is interrupted and another thread is allowed to run.

Of course, this assumes that no higher-priority threads are waiting for the thread's processor. If a higher-priority thread needs to run and has affinity with the processor on which a lower-priority thread is currently running, all bets are off—the higher-priority thread preempts the lower-priority thread and runs regardless of whether the latter has finished its quantum.

The frequency of the clock interval varies from platform to platform. Clock interrupt frequency is dictated by Windows' hardware abstraction layer (HAL), not the kernel. On most x86 uniprocessor systems, the clock interval is 10 milliseconds (ms); on most x86 multiprocessor systems, it's 15 ms.

The number of quantum units deducted for each clock interrupt is 3. On Windows 2000 Professional and Windows XP, the default quantum amount for a thread is 6. On Windows 2000 Server and Windows Server 2003, it's 36. Given a uniprocessor clock interval of 10 ms, this means that a thread quantum can span 2 clock interrupts (approximately 20 ms) on Windows XP, or 12 clock interrupts (120 ms) on Windows Server 2003. And on a multiprocessor system with a clock interval of 15 ms, a thread's quantum can last for a maximum of 30 ms on Windows XP, and 180 ms on Windows Server 2003.

As I've mentioned, a thread might not get to complete its quantum. The numbers above are maximums: if a higher-priority thread becomes schedulable for a given processor, it will preempt a running lower-priority thread.

You might be wondering why a quantum is expressed as a multiple of 3 per clock tick rather than the simpler 1:1 ratio. The reason for this is to allow for partial quantum decay when a thread comes out of a wait state. When a thread whose base priority is less than 14 executes a wait function (e.g., WaitForSingleObject), its quantum is reduced by 1. (Threads with a base priority of 14 or higher have their quantums reset after coming out of a wait state.) So, instead of possibly having its entire 6-unit quantum remaining when it comes out of its wait state, it will have, at most, 5 remaining quantum units. This addresses the situation where a thread continuously runs and goes to sleep between clock ticks. Were it not for the system enforcing quantum decay on the thread each time it came out of its wait state, it would have what amounted to an infinite quantum so long as it did not happen to be running when the clock interrupt fired.

Thread States

If you start Perfmon and display the explanation for the Thread State counter for the Thread object, you'll see that there are eight potential thread states (Table 3.11).

Table 3.11 Thread States and Their Values

Value	State
0	Initialized
1	Ready—waiting on a processor
2	Running—currently using a processor
3	Standby—about to use a processor
4	Terminated—has been stopped
5	Wait—waiting on a peripheral operation or a resource
6	Transition—waiting for resource in order to execute
7	Unknown

You will probably be surprised to learn that most threads spend most of their time waiting. In almost any given application, threads spend the majority of their time waiting for some event—keyboard input, a mouse click, I/O operations, and so on—to occur or complete. This is certainly the case with SQL Server, as we discovered earlier in the chapter when we dumped the SQL Server thread stacks using WinDbg.

Thread Priorities

Windows supports 32 priority levels, ranging from 0 to 31—31 being the highest. Threads begin life inheriting the base priority of their process. This priority can be set when the process is first created with CreateProcess and can be changed afterward by using SetPriorityClass or externally by using Task Manager or a similar tool. Table 3.12 summarizes the process priorities supported by Windows.

Once created, a thread's priority can be changed using SetThreadPriority. You never set an exact thread priority value but instead use one of the predefined constants provided by the Win32 API (e.g., THREAD_PRIORITY_NORMAL, THREAD_PRIORITY_ABOVE_NORMAL, and so on) to set the priority of a thread. The precise numeric values of these constants are subject to change (and have changed) between releases of Windows. Table 3.13 lists the currently supported thread priority levels.

As I've mentioned, higher-priority threads preempt lower-priority ones. This means that, all other things being equal, as long as a higher-priority thread is runnable, lower-priority threads will not get time on the proces-

Table 3.12 Process Priority Levels

Priority	Description
Idle	The threads in this process run only when the system is idle.
Below normal	On Windows 2000 and later, threads in a Below normal priority process run at a lower priority than Normal but at a higher one than Idle.
Normal	This process has no special scheduling needs.
Above normal	On Windows 2000 and later, process threads in the Above normal class run at a higher priority than Normal but at a lower one than High.
High	This class is used for time-critical tasks. Task Manager runs at this class so that it can kill processes that are CPU-intensive.
Real-Time	This class is used for time-critical tasks. Threads in a time-critical process must respond immediately to events. Note that tasks with this base priority compete with the operating system for processor time and can adversely affect overall system performance. You should not use this priority class unless absolutely necessary.

Table 3.13 Thread Priority Levels

Priority	Description
Idle	The thread runs at a priority level of 1 for Above normal, Below normal, High, Idle, and Normal priority processes, and a priority level of 16 for Real-Time priority processes.
Lowest	The thread runs at 2 points below the Normal priority for the base priority class.
Below normal	The thread runs at 1 point below the Normal priority for the base priority class.
Normal	The thread runs at Normal priority for the priority class.
Above normal	The thread runs at 1 point above the Normal priority for the base priority class.
Highest	The thread runs at 2 points above Normal priority for the base priority class.
Time-critical	The thread runs at a base priority level of 15 for Above normal, Below normal, High, Idle, and Normal priority processes, and a base priority level of 31 for Real-Time priority processes.

sor—they will starve indefinitely until the higher-priority thread either terminates or enters a wait state.

All priorities are not equally available to applications. Priorities 17–21 and 27–30 are not available to user mode applications (but they are available to device drivers). Also, only one thread in the system can run at priority 0: Windows' zero page thread. The zero page thread's job is to zero free pages in RAM when there are no other runnable threads. It runs only when the system is otherwise completely idle. The system always tries to keep the CPU busy and sits idle only when there is absolutely no work to do.

If the scheduler sees that a thread has completed its quantum and there are no other threads at its priority, it will reschedule the thread to run for another quantum. This is why it's so easy for lower-priority threads to become starved—the fact that a thread has just completed its quantum has no bearing on whether it will be allowed to run again.

That said, when the scheduler detects that a thread has been starved for about 3–4 seconds, it boosts the thread's priority in hopes of allowing it to run. It also doubles its quantum length. Once the thread runs, its priority is reset to its former level and its quantum is restored to its default length.

TIP: You can change the base priority of an interactive (nonservice) application by using Task Manager. Simply right-click the process in the Processes list and select Set Priority from the menu. You can also start a process using a nondefault priority using the Windows start command and one of the priority command line switches such as /abovenormal, /high, or /realtime.

Foreground Process Tweaking

Using Windows' Performance Options dialog (My Computer | Properties | Advanced in Windows 2000), you can opt to have Windows boost the performance of foreground applications. In this dialog, you have two application prioritization options: Applications and Background services. If you select Background services, no boost occurs. But if you select Applications, Windows will increase the quantum length of whatever process is currently in the foreground whenever the foreground application changes. This will generally make the application that currently has focus more responsive but will do so at the expense of background services such as SQL Server. On Windows 2000 Professional and Windows XP, the default is Applications. On Windows 2000 Server and Windows Server 2003, the default is Background services.

Real-Time Threads

A real-time thread is a thread whose priority is 16 or higher. Although you can create a process with a base priority of real-time, keep in mind that real-time threads can block system threads, which may cause Windows to behave erratically. Important system functions such as disk writes and memory allocations may be delayed by your real-time thread. The mode in which a thread is running (user mode versus kernel mode) has no bearing on preemption: A thread running in user mode can preempt a kernel mode thread and vice versa. This means, of course, that as long as a priority 31 thread remains schedulable on a given processor, no other thread—kernel mode or otherwise—can run on that processor.

An important difference between real-time threads and threads in other priority classes is that real-time thread quantums are reset when they're preempted. So, whereas a normal thread would retain whatever was remaining of its quantum when it was preempted and, once rescheduled, would run for the remainder of that quantum or until again preempted, a real-time thread gets a brand new quantum once it's rescheduled after preemption. This gives real-time threads yet another advantage over regular threads in terms of scheduling and means that, in general, high-priority threads should not be schedulable most of the time if you want even system throughput.

Note that "real-time" within the world of Windows does not mean real-time in the traditional sense of the term. Windows doesn't provide conventional real-time operating system features such as guaranteed interrupt latency or a way for a thread to obtain a guaranteed execution time. Even real-time threads can be preempted—by other higher-priority real-time threads.

Scheduling Queues

The first thing to understand about the scheduling queue is that it is really a series of queues, one for each scheduling priority. Each of the 32 thread priority levels has its own scheduling queue. When Windows begins looking for a thread to run, it simply starts with the highest-priority thread queue (31) and works downward through the other queues until it finds a ready thread.

In order to avoid having to physically walk all 32 thread queues every time it needs to find a ready thread, Windows maintains a 32-bit bitmap called the ready summary. Each bit in the bitmap indicates that one or more threads for the corresponding priority level are ready to run. This allows Windows to quickly detect which thread queues to search for ready threads without having to iterate through all of them.

Windows also maintains a bitmap that indicates which processors are idle. This allows it to quickly find an idle processor when it needs to schedule a thread to run.

Approximately every 20 ms, Windows examines all the thread kernel objects that have been created. Usually, most of these are not runnable because they are waiting on something else to occur (an event, I/O, and so on). Some, however, will be schedulable, so Windows will select one, load the CPU register values using the ones last saved to the thread's CONTEXT structure, and schedule it to run. This process is called a context switch.

Once scheduled, a thread executes code and manipulates data in the process's address space until it is either preempted or its quantum expires. When the system switches to another thread, it saves the CPU registers back to the currently running thread's CONTEXT structure, restores those saved with the thread about to be scheduled, and schedules the new thread. This process of switching between threads begins at system startup and continues until system shutdown. It is Windows' main loop, if you will.

Context Switching

As I mentioned earlier, a context switch involves swapping the values in the CPU registers with those in each thread's CONTEXT structure. Specifically, a context switch causes the following pieces of data to be saved/loaded:

- The process status register
- User and kernel stack pointers
- Other register contents
- The program counter
- A pointer to the address space in which the thread runs

Windows actually keeps track of how many times a thread gets scheduled, as you can see by inspecting the thread with Spy++ or by checking the Thread:Context Switches/sec Perfmon counter.

Threads and Processor Affinity

By default, a process's threads can execute on any of the processors in the host machine. If a process has multiple threads and the host machine has multiple processors, Windows will attempt to distribute the threads such that the processors are kept as busy as possible.

It's usually preferable to allow Windows to decide which processor a thread can run on. Windows always strives to keep the processors in the host machine as active as possible, and it goes to great lengths to ensure that the selection and scheduling process is fair.

There are situations when it's advantageous to limit the processors on which a thread may run. For example, you may have a high-priority task for which you want to dedicate a CPU. You can set the thread-processor affinity for the other threads in the process such that they will not be scheduled on a particular CPU. This leaves the CPU for use by your high-priority task (and by other processes), whose thread you can then affinitize to it. This technique of partitioning an application such that certain threads run only on certain processors is fairly common in high-end, high-performance software.

Sometimes you'll find that a combination of the two approaches is best—you affinitize some threads but let Windows decide what processors the others can run on. For example, in the scenario above, it would likely be better to leave the high-priority task's thread unaffinitized. All other things being equal, Windows will not attempt to schedule the thread on processors that are busy doing other things if there is an idle processor in the system. Furthermore, since Windows defaults to running a thread on the processor on which it last ran, once the thread is scheduled on the dedicated processor, it will likely stay there (because the other threads cannot be scheduled on that processor due to their affinity masks). In that particular scenario, the hybrid approach is probably more scalable overall because it allows for the possibility that you might add another concurrent high-priority task thread at some point. In that case, you'd likely leave the new thread unaffinitized as well. And even though you've set aside a single processor on which the two threads can run, by not affinitizing them, you allow for the possibility that another processor may become available and permit one of the high-priority threads to run without requiring it to wait on the other high-priority task to complete. In other words, even though you've set aside one processor to serve the needs of your high-priority task threads, you allow them to run on a different processor if the dedicated processor is busy. Since other threads cannot use that processor, the only time when this will occur is when the dedicated CPU is busy with one of the high-priority tasks and the other one needs to run. By not affinitizing them, you avoid wasting unused CPU resources in the machine and you keep from having to set up a dedicated processor for every high-priority task your application needs to carry out.

Of course, moving threads between processors is expensive because the likelihood that each processor's secondary cache will be optimally used is much lower than if a thread always runs on the same processor. So, there are certainly situations where it makes sense to set up strict affinities for the threads in a process rather than allowing Windows to decide what processor each thread runs on. There is no right answer for all applications. My advice is to allow Windows to manage processor-thread affinity unless there is simply no other way to get the performance and scalability you need. You can usually find a way via thread priorities and synchronization to get the performance you need without resorting to hard processor affinity. Once you get to the place in application tuning that you are down to considering setting aside dedicated CPUs for certain tasks, trial and error will probably be your best approach—you will have to experiment a little, and experience will be your guide.

Types of Affinity

Threads in a Windows process can have one of three basic types of processor affinity: last processor (or soft) affinity, ideal affinity, and hard affinity. Hard affinity is the type of affinity we were just discussing and is what typically comes to mind when we talk about processor affinity: A thread is assigned to a given set of processors and can run on no others. Once a thread has been affinitized to a particular processor or processors, Windows ensures that it runs only on those processors. Even though other processors may be sitting idle while the thread waits for its processor(s) to become available, the system will force the thread to wait. You can set the hard affinity for an individual thread by calling the SetThreadAffinityMask Win32 API function.

You can also set processor affinity in the header of an executable, but there's no linker switch for it. You can, however, edit the executable header with ImageCfg.exe to change a processor affinity for a process.

TIP: The Windows Task Manager allows you to set processor affinity for a process via the Set Affinity menu option. Find the process in the Processes list, right-click it, and select Set Affinity from the menu. Note that this option is available only on multiprocessor computers and only on the Windows NT family. (Windows 9x offers no special support for multiprocessor machines.)

As I've mentioned, from a performance standpoint, hard affinity is often not the most optimal approach. You might limit a thread to a particular process while other processors on the machine sit idle. In that scenario, ideal affinity may be a better solution. Setting a thread's ideal affinity tells the system which processor you'd prefer that the thread ran on but allows it to schedule the thread on other processors if the preferred processor is busy. You can set the ideal processor for a thread using the Win32 API call SetThreadIdealProcessor.

The third type of thread-processor affinity model supported by Windows is last processor affinity. By default, Windows employs this type of affinity—all other things being equal, Windows attempts to schedule a thread on the processor on which it last ran. This helps maximize the use of the secondary case on the processor (the hope is that some of the thread's data may still be in the cache when the thread gets a new quantum).

Windows knows which processor a thread last ran on because it tracks this information in the thread's kernel block. In fact, Windows maintains two CPU numbers for each thread—the last processor on which the thread ran and its ideal processor.

When a thread is ready to be scheduled, Windows will first check to see whether it has an ideal processor. If it does, Windows will attempt to schedule it on that processor. If that processor is busy or the thread does not have an ideal processor, Windows will attempt to schedule it on the currently executing processor—the CPU on which the scheduler itself is currently running. If that processor is not idle, the system will select the first idle processor it finds by scanning the idle processor mask from highest- to lowest-numbered CPU.

If there are no idle processors, Windows checks the priority of the thread against the priority of the thread currently executing on its ideal processor. If the thread has a higher priority than the one running on its ideal processor, it preempts the other thread and is scheduled on that processor.

If it has a lower priority than the thread running on its ideal processor (or doesn't have an ideal processor), Windows checks the processor on which it last ran. If it has a higher thread priority than the thread currently running on that processor, it preempts that thread and the system sets it up to run.

If the thread cannot preempt either the thread running on its ideal processor or the one running on its last processor, the system checks the other processors on the system to see whether it can preempt any of their running threads. The CPUs are checked beginning with the highest processor in the active affinity mask down to the lowest one. If a thread with a lower priority is found executing on one of these processors, the system will preempt it in favor of the ready thread.

If a thread has a hard processor affinity mask associated with it, this obviously limits the processors visible to the preceding search process. For example, even though a thread may have an ideal processor associated with it, if that processor is not in its processor affinity mask, the thread will never run on its ideal processor.

If no processors are idle and the thread cannot preempt any other running threads, the thread will be placed in the ready queue and reevaluated for scheduling on the next go-round. Note that Windows never moves threads to make room for affinitized threads. If Thread A has affinity to CPU 0 and CPU 0 is busy, but Thread B has affinity to both CPU 0 and CPU 1 (which is idle), the system will not move Thread B from CPU 0 to CPU 1 in order to allow Thread A to run. Thread A will simply have to wait its turn on CPU 0.

Thread Selection

When the scheduler needs to find a new thread to run on a CPU that is currently executing code (e.g., when the currently executing thread goes into a wait state, lowers its priority, changes it affinity, and so on), Windows uses a simple algorithm for picking which thread gets to run. On a single processor system, it picks the first ready thread in the list of ready queues, starting with the highest-priority ready queue and working downward. For a multiprocessor machine, it picks a thread that meets one of the following conditions:

- It executed last on the processor.
- It has the specified processor set as its ideal processor.
- It has a thread priority greater than or equal to 24.
- It has been ready to run longer than 2 quantums.

Suspending and Resuming Threads

Windows allows threads to be suspended and resumed using the Suspend-Thread and ResumeThread API calls, respectively. A suspended thread uses no CPU time and will not be scheduled until you resume it.

The system maintains a suspend count for each thread in its kernel object. The suspend count for a thread indicates how many times the thread has been suspended. As long as this is not 0, the thread will not be scheduled. When a thread's suspend count reaches 0, it is schedulable unless it is waiting for some other event (e.g., I/O to complete).

When an application first creates a thread, Windows sets its suspend count to 1 to prevent it from being scheduled while it is being initialized. Once the thread is initialized, the system checks to see whether the thread was created with the CREATE_SUSPENDED flag. If it was, the suspend count is left unchanged; otherwise it is reset to 0. When a thread is created in a suspended state, an application must call ResumeThread in order to allow it to run.

When ResumeThread is successful, it returns the thread's previous suspend count. If it's not successful, it returns 0xFFFFFFFF (-1). This is useful information to have given that you must resume as many times as you suspend in order for a thread to be schedulable. For example, you could use ResumeThread's return value as the control variable for a loop so that you could be sure a thread's suspend count was set to 0 when you wanted it to run.

It should be self-evident that a thread can suspend itself, but it can't resume itself. Once a thread is suspended, another thread will have to resume it in order for it to run.

You have to be careful about suspending running threads because you don't necessarily have a good idea of what a thread is up to when you suspend it. It's usually preferable to code your thread functions so that a thread enters a wait state (e.g., because it is waiting on a synchronization object) when you want to momentarily suspend it than to force it to pause by calling SuspendThread when you may not know exactly what it is doing. For example, if you suspend a thread with an open mutex or critical section, you may inadvertently block other threads from executing that are waiting for the object to be released.

Putting a Thread to Sleep

In addition to being able to suspend a thread indefinitely (until it is resumed by another thread), Windows allows you to suspend a thread for a specified period of time by putting it to sleep. You use either the Sleep or SleepEx functions to put a thread to sleep for a specified number of milliseconds.

As with Win32's wait functions, you can pass in the constant INFINITE to Sleep/SleepEx to cause a thread to sleep indefinitely, but I can't think of a practical application of this. If you're using Sleep, you won't be able to awaken the thread in order to make further use of it, so you would be better off destroying it in order to free up the system resources associated with it. If you're using SleepEx, an INFINITE delay can be terminated only by an I/O completion callback or an asynchronous procedure call (APC).

Note that you can pass a delay of 0 into Sleep/SleepEx to cause the thread to allow other threads of at least the same priority to run. On versions of Windows prior to Windows Server 2003, if you want lower-priority threads to be allowed to run, you'll have to put the thread to sleep for a longer duration (even sleeping for a single millisecond will allow lower-priority threads to run). Prior to Windows Server 2003, sleeping with a duration of 0 will cause the calling thread to be rescheduled immediately even if lower-priority threads are being starved.

An interesting alternative to using Sleep to yield to other runnable threads is the SwitchToThread function. SwitchToThread exists for the very purpose of allowing a thread to surrender the remainder of its time slice and allow other threads to run, regardless of whether they have a lower priority than the current thread.

Exercises

In these exercises, you'll experiment with SQL Server and thread/process priorities. You'll learn to start SQL Server as a real-time process and how to view process priority using Task Manager. You'll learn how SQL Server "sleeps" while it waits for T-SQL commands such as WAITFOR DELAY to complete. And you'll use an xproc to look under the hood a bit and display thread priorities, affinities masks, and other useful information for SQL Server's worker threads.

Exercise 3.6   Running SQL Server at Real-Time Process Priority

You're probably aware that you can configure SQL Server to run at the High process priority. You do this in Enterprise Manager via the Processor tab in the Properties dialog for your server.

When you change this setting and restart your server, Task Manager will show that it's running at High priority. Microsoft doesn't normally recommend that customers change this setting, but it's not uncommon to find those who have.

You can take this a step farther and actually run SQL Server as a real-time process. Again, this isn't recommended, but, from a technical standpoint, it is possible. As I mentioned earlier, running a process at Real-Time priority will cause its threads to contend with operating system threads for processor time, possibly slowing down or even blocking key operating systems such as disk I/O and memory allocations. So, I offer the following to you merely as an experiment. You should not run SQL Server at the Real-Time priority in production, nor should you conduct the following tests on anything but a test or development machine as the OS itself may become unresponsive.

To start SQL Server in Real-Time mode, follow these steps.

1. Stop your SQL Server via the SQL Server Service Manager. Again, this should be a test or development instance, and, ideally, you should be its only user.

2. Open a command prompt and switch to the folder that contains sqlservr.exe, the SQL Server executable. This should be the binn sub-folder under your SQL Server main installation folder.

3. Start sqlservr.exe in console mode with the following command:

```
start /realtime sqlservr.exe -c -sYourInstanceName
```

Replace YourInstanceName with the name of the instance you're starting. Omit the -s parameter altogether if you're starting a default instance.

4. You should see SQL Server start as a console application in a separate window. Switch to Task Manager and check the base process priority column. (If the Base Pri column isn't visible in Task Manager, select the View | Select Columns menu option and select it from the list of available columns.) The base process priority should now be Real-Time.

5. Let's do a quick test to see whether running at Real-Time priority helps CPU-intensive queries finish more quickly. Connect to your SQL Server instance using Query Analyzer and run the following query.

```
declare @var int
set @var=1
while @var<100000 begin
   set @var=@var+1
end
```

6. Note the amount of time it takes to run. Depending on your processor, this shouldn't be more than a few seconds.

7. Now stop your SQL Server (go to the console window and press Ctrl+C) and restart it using SQL Server Service Manager. This should put it back at its default process priority.

8. Now run the query again from Query Analyzer and check how much time it takes to run.

On my system, the execution times of the two runs are the same—running SQL Server at Real-Time priority didn't speed up my CPU-intensive query. Normally, I wouldn't expect running SQL Server at a higher priority to make much difference unless there were other things running on the machine at the same time and they had a high enough base priority that they would often preempt SQL Server.

My point is this: You shouldn't expect running SQL Server at a higher priority to automatically turbocharge your system all by itself. Setting a process's priority affects who wins when there's contention for processor resources; it does not automatically speed anything up in and of itself.

For this reason—and because SQL Server has not been certified to be safe to run at Real-Time priority—I recommend that you leave SQL Server at its default priority.

Exercise 3.7 Determining How SQL Server Sleeps

In this exercise, you'll learn what SQL Server does when you tell it to put a connection to sleep with the Transact-SQL WAITFOR DELAY command. Having just learned about the Win32 API Sleep and SleepEx functions, it might seem obvious that SQL Server calls one of these functions to put a thread to sleep when you execute WAITFOR DELAY in Transact-SQL. Understanding how the server actually handles this scenario and how it handles language events versus remote procedure call (RPC) events will give us some insight into how it works internally. Let's take a peek under the hood by following these steps.

1. Start an instance of SQL Server to which you can attach a debugger. *This should not be a production machine*, and, ideally, you should be its only user. You may find that starting the server as a console application is preferable to starting it as a service because doing so prevents SQL Server Agent from running because it depends on the service.
2. Start WinDbg and make sure that your symbol path is set correctly, as outlined in Chapter 2.
3. Attach to your SQL Server using the debugger (press F6). Find sqlservr.exe in WinDbg's list of running processes and double-click it. If you just started the SQL Server instance, sqlservr.exe should be near the bottom of the list.
4. When the Disassembly window opens, close it. We won't need it for this exercise. If it reopens at any time during the exercise, feel free to close it then as well.
5. Type g in the command prompt window and hit Enter. This will cause the SQL Server process to continue running.
6. Open a Query Analyzer connection to the server and run the following command:

```
WAITFOR DELAY '00:00:30'
```

This will cause the connection to pause for 30 seconds.
7. Return to the debugger now, and hit Ctrl+Break to stop the SQL Server process. Type the following command to see what each thread is doing:

```
~*kv
```

This will list off the call stack for each thread. We'll be able to tell what each thread is up to during our WAITFOR call by examining these stacks.
8. If you look closely at each call stack (and provided that you are the server's lone user), you should see that nearly all of the threads are performing identical work except one. Skip past the first few threads, as these are system threads that don't correspond to user connections. Scan down through the list of call stacks, and you should find

one thread with a list of function calls that differs markedly from the others. Its stack features a call to a function named language_exec. See if you can find it. Note that the topmost function on this call stack is not Sleep or SleepEx. If this is the thread servicing our WAITFOR DELAY command, it obviously isn't using the Sleep or SleepEx functions to do it. Under my instance of WinDbg, the stack that contains the call to language_exec (set in boldface type below) looks like this:

```
21  Id: 8f8.65c Suspend: 1 Teb: 7ffa6000 Unfrozen
ChildEBP RetAddr  Args to Child
2619f674 77e8780f 000002fc 00000001 00000000 ntdll!
NtWaitForSingleObject+0xb (FPO: [3,0,0])
2619f69c 4107149d 000002fc ffffffff 00000001 KERNEL32!
WaitForSingleObjectEx+0x71 (FPO: [Non-Fpo])
2619f6b8 4107173f 251c8bd8 251c86e0 00bc66d8 UMS!
UmsThreadScheduler::Switch+0x58
2619f6dc 410717ff 00bc66d8 251c8bd8 42dd36fc UMS!
UmsScheduler::IdleLoop+0x11f
2619f6f4 41071918 00007530 00000001 42dd36ec UMS!
UmsScheduler::Suspend+0x7e
2619f710 0040129c 00007530 00000000 00000000 UMS!
UmsEvent::Wait+0x95
2619f754 00637256 00007530 00a6997c 00000000
sqlservr!ExecutionContext::WaitForSignal+0x1b5
2619f7a8 004160db 42dc8060 42dd3240 42dc8060 sqlservr!
CStmtWait::XretExecute+0x128
2619f814 00415765 42dd3550 00000000 2619f8d4
sqlservr!CMsqlExecContext::ExecuteStmts+0x27e
2619f858 00415410 00000000 00000000 42dd3240 sqlservr!
CMsqlExecContext::Execute+0x1c7
2619f8a4 00459a54 00000000 4200e700 42dd4038 sqlservr!
CSQLSource::Execute+0x343
2619fa64 004175d8 42dd6090 0024004c 251c43c0
sqlservr!language_exec+0x3c8
2619fefc 410735d0 42dd6090 2619fe90 00000000 sqlservr!
process_commands+0xe0
2619ff68 4107382c 00bc6770 00bc6770 00bc66d8 UMS!
ProcessWorkRequests+0x264
2619ff80 7800c9eb 251c21b0 0024004c 00530053 UMS!
ThreadStartRoutine+0xbd
2619ffb4 77e887dd 251c43c0 0024004c 00530053 MSVCRT!
_beginthread+0xce
2619ffec 00000000 7800c994 251c43c0 00000000 KERNEL32!
BaseThreadStart+0x52 (FPO: [Non-Fpo])
```

The topmost function on this stack is a call to the NtWaitForSingle-Object function, the native API function that calls into the Windows kernel to actually carry out the wait requested by WaitForSingleObject. So, as I've said, if this thread is executing our WAITFOR DELAY call (we'll answer that question definitively in a moment), we can say with certainty that WAITFOR DELAY does not result in a call to the Win32 Sleep function. (If you think about it, this makes sense without even knowing anything about UMS—WAITFOR also supports waiting until an absolute date/time and supports being canceled, which Sleep obviously could not service.)

9. We might infer from language_exec's name that it's what gets executed when we submit a T-SQL language batch to the server. To verify that, let's set a breakpoint on it and see what happens when we run our command again. Type this command into the command window:

```
bp language_exec
```

You can type bl in the command window to verify that your breakpoint is set. You should see output like this from bl:

```
0 e 004597ef     0001 (0001)  0:*** sqlservr!language_exec
```

It's important that the second column of the output is set to e, indicating that the breakpoint is enabled.

10. Type g in the command prompt window and hit Enter. This will cause the SQL Server process to continue running.

11. Return to Query Analyzer and click the stop button to cancel your query, then run it again.

12. Return to WinDbg, and you should see the debugger stopped at your breakpoint. Your output should look something like this:

```
Breakpoint 0 hit
eax=00000000 ebx=0097fb00 ecx=0000003c edx=00000000
esi=42d9a090 edi=00000001
eip=004597ef esp=260afa68 ebp=260afefc iopl=0
nv up ei pl zr na po nc
cs=001b  ss=0023  ds=0023  es=0023  fs=0038  gs=0000
efl=00000246
sqlservr!language_exec:
004597ef b8ff619300         mov       eax,0x9361ff
```

This tells us that we hit the breakpoint we set earlier, but, beyond the inference we're drawing from its name, how do we *know* that language_exec is the function called when a T-SQL language event is received by the server? Let's test sending an RPC event to the server to see whether the language_exec breakpoint is tripped in that situation.

13. Type bd 0 in the command window and press Enter. This will disable the breakpoint we set up earlier. We need to disable this breakpoint for now so that we can create a procedure for use in our RPC event.

14. Type g in the command prompt window and hit Enter. This will cause the SQL Server process to continue running.

15. Return to Query Analyzer and stop your query if it is still running. Open a new Query Analyzer window and create a new procedure in the pubs database using this command:

```
USE pubs
GO
CREATE PROC waiter as WAITFOR DELAY '00:00:30'
```

Run this command batch to create your new procedure.

16. Now open a new Query Analyzer window and type the following into it:

```
{CALL waiter}
```

This syntax will submit a call to the waiter stored procedure as an RPC event. Do not run it yet.

17. Return to WinDbg and press Ctrl+Break to stop the SQL Server process.

18. Now reenable your breakpoint by typing this command in the command window and pressing Enter:

```
be 0
```

19. Type g in the command prompt window and hit Enter. This will cause the SQL Server process to continue running.

20. Return to Query Analyzer and run the waiter procedure via the RPC syntax you typed in earlier.

21. Switch back to WinDbg and see whether your breakpoint was hit. It should not have been. This gives us pretty conclusive evidence that language_exec is the internal function used for T-SQL language events in SQL Server. Feel free to try some other queries to see whether they trip the breakpoint you set up on language_exec. Unless you submit the query using the RPC syntax outlined above, each batch you submit to the server should trip the breakpoint at least once. Those with GOs embedded will trip it multiple times as these are submitted separately to the server by Query Analyzer.

22. You may be wondering what internal function is called due to an RPC event. Let's find out. Hit Ctrl+Break to stop the SQL Server process, then type ~*kv to list the call stacks of the process's threads.

23. As before, the call stacks of most of the nonsystem threads are virtually identical except for one that features a call to a routine named execute_rpc. Let's set a breakpoint on execute_rpc to see whether it gets tripped when we submit our RPC event. Type the following into the WinDbg command window:

```
bp execute_rpc
```

24. Type g in the command prompt window and hit Enter. This will cause the SQL Server process to continue running.

25. Return to Query Analyzer and stop your procedure call if it is still running, then run it again.

26. Return to WinDbg and you should see that your breakpoint has been hit. Your output should look something like this:

```
Breakpoint 1 hit
eax=00000000 ebx=0097fb00 ecx=00000018 edx=42dd30a8
esi=42dd6090 edi=00000003
eip=0043b7d2 esp=2619fa68 ebp=2619fefc iopl=0
nv up ei pl zr na po nc
cs=001b  ss=0023  ds=0023  es=0023  fs=0038  gs=0000
efl=00000246
sqlservr!execute_rpc:
0043b7d2 55                    push    ebp
```

So, we can reasonably conclude that language_exec is called when a language event comes into the server, and execute_rpc is called when an RPC event is received. Feel free to experiment with other language and RPC events to see how this works.

27. Type q to quit the Debugger. You will then need to restart your SQL Server instance with SQL Server Service Manager.

Exercise 3.8   Viewing Thread Priorities, Affinities, and Other Useful Information

In this last exercise, you'll run an extended procedure to iterate through SQL Server's currently active worker threads and list important information for each one. Follow these steps.

1. Copy the file xp_sysinfo.dll from the CH03\xp_sysinfo\release subfolder on the CD accompanying this book to the binn folder under your SQL Server installation path. (This DLL may already be installed from a previous exercise in this chapter.)

2. Install xp_threadlist by running this command in Query Analyzer:

```
sp_addextendedproc 'xp_threadlist','xp_sysinfo.dll'
```

3. Open the xp_threadlist.sql T-SQL script from CH03\xp_sysinfo subfolder in Query Analyzer. Do not run it yet.

4. Create a scratch folder on your hard drive and copy to it the files STRESS.CMD and STRESS.SQL from the CH03 subfolder on the CD.

5. Run STRESS.CMD with a command line like this one, substituting your server name for the one specified:

```
stress stress.sql 15 N normal Y YourServerName
```

6. You should see 15 windows open on your desktop, all of them using osql.exe to run a select against a table in pubs, then issuing a WAIT-FOR DELAY command.

7. While the queries run, switch back to Query Analyzer and run the script you loaded previously. You should see output like this:

ThreadID	ImpersonationLevel	HasAccessToken	TebBaseAddress	AffinityMask	BasePriority	SID
556	N/A	0	0x7FF9A000	3	9	S-1-
1784	N/A	0	0x7FFDC000	3	9	S-1-
2784	N/A	0	0x7FF98000	3	9	S-1-
2808	N/A	0	0x7FF9B000	3	9	S-1-
2908	N/A	0	0x7FF91000	3	9	S-1-
2912	N/A	0	0x7FF9C000	3	9	S-1-
2920	N/A	0	0x7FF95000	3	9	S-1-
3068	N/A	0	0x7FF96000	3	8	S-1-
3232	N/A	0	0x7FF90000	3	9	S-1-
3280	N/A	0	0x7FF8D000	3	9	S-1-
3292	N/A	0	0x7FF92000	3	9	S-1-
3372	N/A	0	0x7FF97000	3	9	S-1-
3380	N/A	0	0x7FF93000	3	9	S-1-
3404	N/A	0	0x7FFA1000	3	9	S-1-
3452	N/A	0	0x7FFDD000	3	9	S-1-
3640	N/A	0	0x7FFA4000	3	9	S-1-
3812	N/A	0	0x7FF94000	3	9	S-1-

8. On a multiprocessor box, you can experiment with SQL Server's processor affinity to cause different values to show up in the AffinityMask column. In the above example, each thread has an affinity to processors 1 and 2 in the box, resulting in a bitmask of 3.

You can also use linked server queries to set up impersonation for a particular worker thread. The threads in the example output above have all inherited SQL Server's security context and do not have access tokens of their own.

Note that you may see different values for the BasePriority column depending on when you run the xproc and what the system is doing. I've personally seen a fair amount of fluctuation across the worker threads.

Note also that the threads listed are the currently *active* worker threads; inactive or idle threads are not listed. If you want to see all the threads currently instantiated within the SQL Server process, use a tool like Perfmon or Pview.

9. The 15 windows should close on their own and your system should now be back to normal.

Thread Scheduling Recap

Windows implements a preemptive, priority-based scheduler for scheduling and running application code via threads. The system is designed to keep a single application from taking over the system and to provide for even performance across the system.

There are 32 priority levels at which a thread can run. Threads running at higher priorities preempt those running at lower priorities.

Each thread gets a schedule time slice called a quantum in which to run. The exact length of the quantum varies between versions of Windows and between multiprocessor and uniprocessor machines. A thread is not guaranteed a full quantum because it may be preempted by a higher-priority thread.

SQL Server does not use the Windows scheduler and scheduling APIs in the same way that most multithreaded applications do. This is because it handles most of its scheduling needs using its UMS facility.

Thread Scheduling Knowledge Measure

1. What is a quantum?
2. Name one thing that happens during a context switch.
3. What Win32 API sets the ideal processor for a thread?
4. True or false: One of the eight thread states (numbered 0 through 7) is Suspended, indicating that the thread has been suspended through a call to SuspendThread.
5. True or false: Task Manager cannot display the base priority for individual threads in a process.
6. What part of the Windows architecture determines clock interrupt frequency?
7. What is the highest process priority available on Windows?
8. True or false: No threads in the system run at a thread priority of 0.
9. Name the term for what happens when a lower-priority thread is continuously preempted by higher-priority threads and not allowed to run.
10. What does Windows do when it sees that a thread has not been allowed to run for 3–4 seconds? What happens after the thread gets to run?
11. True or false: Windows implements a cooperative multitasking system wherein processes must be careful to yield to one another in order to keep the system running smoothly.
12. What Win32 API is used to set the processor affinity for an individual thread?
13. What is the clock interval on most x86 uniprocessor machines?

14. For each clock interrupt, how many quantum units are deducted from a thread's quantum?

15. True or false: Windows automatically takes into account the fact that a thread has just completed its quantum when it decides which thread to schedule next and will automatically allow lower-priority threads to run before allowing the high-priority thread to run again.

16. Name the term that describes associating a thread or process with a given set of CPUs.

17. True or false: When a thread with a priority lower than 14 successfully waits on a kernel object using WaitForSingleObject, the system automatically deducts 1 unit from its quantum.

18. True or false: The function responsible for performing the lion's share of scheduling within the Windows kernel is named Schedule-Thread.

19. When you issue a Sleep(0) call, are lower-priority threads allowed to run?

20. True or false: Windows keeps a separate ready list for each thread priority and maintains a bitmap to make accessing that list faster.

21. What happens to the quantum of a thread with a priority of 14 or higher that has just successfully waited on a kernel object via Wait-ForSingleObject?

22. What internal function within SQL Server is responsible for processing language events? How about RPC events?

23. True or false: SQL Server does not use the Win32 Sleep or SleepEx API functions in order to service the Transact-SQL WAITFOR DE-LAY command.

24. True or false: Running SQL Server with a Real-Time process priority will speed up CPU-intensive queries on an otherwise idle system.

25. True or false: You can change the base priority for a process using the Windows Task Manager.

26. True or false: The Spy++ utility included with the Platform SDK and recent versions of Visual Studio can display the number of context switches for a given thread.

27. What is the default quantum length on Windows 2000 Professional and Windows XP?

28. Describe the functionality of the SwitchToThread API function.

29. At what numeric priority level is a thread considered a real-time thread?

30. True or false: If a thread's ideal CPU is not in its affinity mask, it can still be scheduled on that CPU because Windows will ignore the mask when the two conflict.

Thread Synchronization

When you get beyond the simplicity of single-threaded applications and begin to explore the world of multithreaded programming, one of the first things you discover is the need to synchronize the activities of the threads in your application. Allowing one thread to modify a global variable while another is using it to control flow logic is a recipe for erratic application behavior and possibly even an access violation. The fact that multiple threads can truly execute simultaneously on multiprocessor machines does not mean that you literally want all of them running all of the time. There are times when you need one thread to wait on others to finish what they're doing before proceeding. There are times when you need to synchronize them.

The single most important element of thread synchronization is atomic access—ensuring that a thread has access to a resource in a manner that guarantees that no other thread will access the same resource simultaneously. Windows provides a number of objects and API calls to facilitate atomic access. We'll discuss each of these and delve into each one separately.

Key Thread Synchronization Terms and Concepts

✔ *Synchronization*—ensuring that resources are accessed by threads in a manner that allows them to be used safely and their data to be trusted.
✔ *Deadlock*—what happens when two or more threads wait indefinitely on resources owned by each other.
✔ *Wait function*—one of the Win32 functions designed to put a thread to sleep until a resource becomes available or a timeout period expires.
✔ *Signaled*—the state of an object when it is available for use by a thread or when a Win32 wait function should not wait on it.
✔ *Unsignaled*—the state of an object when it is not available for use by a thread or when a Win32 wait function should wait on it.
✔ *Spinlock*—a user mode construct that continuously polls a resource to check its availability. Spinlocks often make use of the interlocked family of functions.
✔ *Interlocked function*—a member of the Win32 family of functions that provides simple, atomic updates of variables.
✔ *Kernel synchronization object*—one of several different types of kernel objects that can be used to synchronize access to a resource. Examples of kernel synchronization objects include mutexes, semaphores, and events, to name just a few.

✔ *Thread-safe code*—code that has been designed such that multiple threads accessing the same resources do so in a safe and predictable manner.

✔ *Atomic access*—ensuring that a thread retrieves, modifies, and returns a value or resource as a single operation without having to be concerned about another thread modifying the value simultaneously.

Key Thread Synchronization APIs

Table 3.14 Key Synchronization-Related API Functions

Function	Description
EnterCriticalSection	Denotes a section of code that only one thread can access at a time
LeaveCriticalSection	Leaves a section of code that was designed for single-threaded access
InterlockedExchange	Assigns one value to another in an atomic fashion
InterlockedExchangeAdd	Adds one value to another in an atomic fashion
CreateEvent	Creates a kernel event object
SetEvent/ResetEvent	Signals/unsignals an event object
CreateSemaphore	Creates a semaphore object
ReleaseSemaphore	Releases a reference to a semaphore
CreateWaitableTimer	Creates a waitable timer object
SetWaitableTimer	Configures a waitable timer
CreateMutex	Creates a mutex (mutually exclusive) object
ReleaseMutex	Releases an owned mutex
WaitForSingleObject	Waits for a kernel object to become signaled
WaitForMultipleObjects	Waits for multiple kernel objects to become signaled

Key Thread Synchronization Tools

Given that most synchronization objects are kernel mode objects, there's a limit to how much information a user mode tool can give us about thread synchronization. A kernel mode debugger is unfortunately the best option here. That said, the tools in Table 3.15 provide several useful pieces of synchronization-related data.

Table 3.15 Thread Synchronization Diagnostic Tools

	Handle Count	Context Switches	Thread Security Context	Kernel Object Count by Type	Thread Priority	Thread State	CPU Times
Perfmon	✔	✔		✔		✔	✔
Pview	✔	✔	✔	✔	✔	✔	✔
Spy++	✔	✔			✔	✔	✔

Synchronization Using User Mode Constructs

Windows provides two types of thread synchronization: user mode synchronization and kernel mode synchronization. User mode synchronization is implemented by functions in Kernel32.DLL and, as the name suggests, does not require the thread to switch into kernel mode. User mode synchronization is consequently faster than synchronizing threads using kernel objects. On the other hand, user mode objects cannot be used to synchronize threads in multiple processes and cannot be used with the Win32 wait functions, which allow a thread to wait on a resource without consuming any CPU resources and allow the waiter to timeout. Examples of user mode synchronization objects/constructs include spinlocks and critical sections.

Spinlocks

Simply put, a spinlock is a loop that iterates until a resource becomes available. Listing 3.3 shows a simple example in C++.

Listing 3.3 A Simple Spinlock Implementation

```
void CSpinLock::GetLock() {
  while (TRUE == InterlockedExchange(&g_bLocked, TRUE))
    SwitchToThread();

  // use the resource
```

```
// "unlock" the resource
InterlockedExchange(&g_bLocked, FALSE);


}
```

InterlockedExchange, which we'll talk about more in a moment, assigns the value of its second parameter to its first parameter in an atomic fashion and returns the original value of the first parameter. The spinlock code above simply loops while the original value of g_bLocked is TRUE—in other words, while the global resource in question is locked. It continuously assigns TRUE to g_bLocked until InterlockedExchange no longer returns TRUE. When InterlockedExchange returns FALSE—meaning that the resource was not locked when the function was called—the loop exits. Since InterlockedExchange has already set g_bLocked to TRUE, other threads calling the GetLock method will stop at the while loop until g_bLocked is set to FALSE by the thread that just acquired the spinlock.

As you can see, a spinlock isn't a separate type of user mode object; rather, it is implemented by using user mode objects and code—in this case, a global variable and one of the interlocked functions. Though it is often wrapped in a class of some type in object-oriented languages such as C++, as far as Windows is concerned, a spinlock is really more of a programming construct than a distinct type of synchronization object.

Spinlocks and CPU Use

Even though the above example tries to be as CPU efficient as possible by calling SwitchToThread in its spin loop, it's still using some amount of CPU time while it waits on the resource. This is, unfortunately, unavoidable without the assistance of a scheduling facility (such as the one provided by Windows) that can maintain lists of waiting threads and the resources they need independent of the threads themselves, basically putting them to sleep until the resources they need become available.

This is the main reason that kernel mode objects such as mutexes and semaphores have a distinct advantage over spinlocks in terms of CPU usage. Because Windows can act on behalf of a waiting thread and allow the thread to consume no resources while the resources it needs are unavailable, waiting on a kernel object is often more CPU efficient than using a spinlock to wait on a resource even though a thread must transition from user mode to kernel mode in order to wait on a kernel object.

Because they are not coordinated by the operating system, spinlocks like the one above must make a few assumptions.

1. Spinlocks assume that all threads run at the same thread priority level. (You might want to disable thread priority boosting for this very reason.)

2. Spinlocks assume that the lock variable and the data to which the lock provides access are maintained in different CPU cache lines. If they are on the same cache line, you'll see contention between the processor using the resource and any CPUs waiting on it. In other words, the continual assignment of the control variable by the other CPUs will contend with the code accessing the protected resource.

3. For this reason, spinlocks assume you are running on a multiprocessor machine. If the threads attempting to access the resource and the one that currently has it locked share a single processor, you will see significant contention as the waiting threads continually assign the control variable.

Generally speaking, you should avoid techniques and design elements that continuously poll for resource availability. Windows provides a rich set of tools for waiting on resources with minimal CPU usage. It makes sense to use what you get for free in the OS box.

Often you'll find that a hybrid approach is the best fit for a particular scenario—use spinlocks and critical sections to protect some types of resources; use kernel objects for others. Or, use a spinlock to wait a fixed number of iterations, then transition to a kernel object if it appears that the thread might have to wait for an extended period of time. This is, in fact, how critical sections themselves are implemented. A critical section starts off using a spinlock that iterates a specified number of times, then transitions to kernel mode where it waits on the resource in question.

The Interlocked Functions

Windows provides a family of API functions commonly referred to as the interlocked functions. You saw a basic example of their use above. These functions provide simple, lightweight thread synchronization that does not rely on kernel objects. Table 3.16 summarizes the interlocked functions.

You'll note that there's no interlocked function for reading a value. That's because none is necessary. If a thread attempts to read a value that is always modified using an interlocked function, it can depend on getting a good value. That is, it can assume that it will see either the value before it

Table 3.16 The Interlocked Family of Functions

Function	Operation
InterlockedIncrement	Allows a variable to be incremented and its value to be checked in a single atomic operation
InterlockedDecrement	Allows a variable to be decremented and its value to be checked in a single atomic operation
InterlockedExchangePointer	Atomically exchanges the value pointed to by the first parameter for the value passed in the second parameter
InterlockedExchangeAdd	Atomically adds the value passed in the second parameter to the first parameter
InterlockedCompareExchangePointer	Atomically compares two values and replaces the first value with a third value based on the outcome of the comparison

was changed or the value afterward—the system guarantees that it will be one or the other.

Critical Sections

A critical section is a user mode object you can use to synchronize threads and serialize access to shared resources. A critical section denotes a piece of code that you want executed by only one thread at a time. The process of using a critical section goes something like this.

1. Initialize the critical section with a call to InitializeCriticalSection. This frequently occurs at program startup and is often used to set up a critical section stored in a global variable.
2. On entrance to a routine that you want only one thread to execute at a time, call EnterCriticalSection, passing in the previously initialized critical section structure. Once you've done this, any other thread that attempts to enter this routine will be put to sleep until the critical section is exited.

3. On exit, call LeaveCriticalSection.
4. On program shutdown (or some other similar termination event that occurs after the critical section is no longer needed), call DeleteCriticalSection to free up the system resources used by the object.

Because you can't specify the amount of time to wait before giving up on a critical section, it's entirely possible for a thread to wait indefinitely for a resource. This happens, for example, when a critical section has been orphaned due to an exception. The waiting threads have no way of knowing that the thread that previously acquired the critical section never released it, so they wait indefinitely on a resource that will never be available.

One way to mitigate this all-or-nothing proposition is to use TryEnterCriticalSection rather than EnterCriticalSection. TryEnterCriticalSection will never allow a thread to be put into a wait state. It will either acquire the critical section or return FALSE immediately. The fact that it has this ability to return immediately is the reason that it has a return value while EnterCriticalSection does not.

When a thread calls EnterCriticalSection for a critical section object that is already owned by another thread, Windows puts the thread in a wait state. This means that it must transition from user mode to kernel mode, costing approximately 1,000 CPU cycles. This transition is usually cheaper than using a spinlock of some type to continuously poll a resource to see whether it is available.

You can integrate the concept of a spinlock with a critical section by using the InitializeCriticalSectionAndSpinCount function. This function allows you to specify a spin count for entrance into the critical section. If the critical section is not available, the function will spin for the specified number of iterations before going into a wait state. For short-duration waits, this may save you the expense of transitioning to kernel mode unnecessarily.

Note that it makes sense to specify a spin count only on a multiprocessor machine. The thread owning the critical section can't relinquish it if another thread is spinning, so InitializeCriticalSectionAndSpinCount ignores a nonzero spin count specification on uniprocessor machines and immediately enters a wait state if the critical section is not available.

You can set the spin count for a specific critical section using the Win32 API function SetCriticalSectionSpinCount. The optimal value will vary from situation to situation, but the fact that the critical section that's used to synchronize access to a process's heap has a spin count of 4000 can serve as a guide to you.

As a rule, use one critical section variable per shared resource. Don't try to conserve system resources by sharing critical sections across different resources. Critical sections don't consume that much memory in the first place, and attempting to share them unnecessarily can introduce complexities and deadlock potential into your code that don't need to be there.

Threads and Wait States

As I've mentioned, while your thread is waiting on a resource, the system acts as an agent on its behalf. The thread itself consumes no CPU resources while it waits. The system puts the thread in a wait state and automatically awakens it when the resource(s) it has been waiting for becomes available.

If you check the states of the threads across all processes on the system, you'll discover that most are in a wait state of some type most of the time. It is normal for most of the threads in a process to spend most of their time waiting on some event to occur (e.g., keyboard or mouse input). This is why it's particularly important for the operating system to provide mechanisms for waiting on resources that are as CPU efficient as possible.

Thread Deadlocks

A thread deadlock occurs when two threads each wait on resources the other has locked. If each is set up to wait indefinitely, the threads are for all intents and purposes dead and will never be scheduled again. Unlike SQL Server, Windows does not automatically detect deadlocks. Once threads are caught in a deadly embrace, the only resolution is to terminate them. Listing 3.4 presents some C++ code that illustrates a common deadlock scenario.

Listing 3.4 A Classic Deadlock Scenario

```
// deadlock.cpp
//

#include "stdafx.h"
#include "windows.h"

CRITICAL_SECTION g_CS1;
CRITICAL_SECTION g_CS2;

int g_HiTemps[100];
int g_LoTemps[100];

DWORD WINAPI ThreadFunc1(PVOID pvParam)
{
```

```
  EnterCriticalSection(&g_CS1);
  Sleep(5000);
  EnterCriticalSection(&g_CS2);

  for (int i=0; i<100; i++)
    g_HiTemps[i]=g_LoTemps[i];

  printf("Exiting ThreadFunc1\n");

  LeaveCriticalSection(&g_CS1);
  LeaveCriticalSection(&g_CS2);

  return(0);
}

DWORD WINAPI ThreadFunc2(PVOID pvParam)
{
  EnterCriticalSection(&g_CS2);
  EnterCriticalSection(&g_CS1);

  for (int i=0; i<100; i++)
    g_HiTemps[i]=g_LoTemps[i];

  printf("Exiting ThreadFunc2\n");

  LeaveCriticalSection(&g_CS2);
  LeaveCriticalSection(&g_CS1);

  return(0);
}


int main(int argc, char* argv[])
{
  DWORD dwThreadId;
  HANDLE hThreads[2];

  InitializeCriticalSection(&g_CS1);
  InitializeCriticalSection(&g_CS2);

  hThreads[0]=CreateThread(NULL,0,ThreadFunc1,NULL,0,&dwThreadId);
  hThreads[1]=CreateThread(NULL,0,ThreadFunc2,NULL,0,&dwThreadId);

  WaitForMultipleObjects(2,hThreads,TRUE,INFINITE);
```

```
    DeleteCriticalSection(&g_CS1);
    DeleteCriticalSection(&g_CS2);

    return 0;
}
```

The problem with this code is that the two worker threads access resources in different orders: ThreadFunc1 enters the critical sections in numerical order; ThreadFunc2 does not. I placed the call to Sleep after the first critical section is entered in order to allow the second thread function to start up and allocate the second critical section before Thread 1 can enter it. Once Sleep expires, Thread 1 then tries to enter the second critical section but is blocked by Thread 2. Thread 2, on the other hand, is waiting on critical section 1, which Thread 1 already owns. So, each thread waits indefinitely on resources the other has locked, constituting a classic deadlock scenario.

The moral of the story is this: Always request resources in a consistent order in multithreaded applications. This is a good design practice regardless of whether you are working with user mode or kernel objects.

Synchronization Using Kernel Objects

As I've mentioned, synchronizing threads via user mode objects is faster than synchronizing them using kernel mode objects, but there are trade-offs. User mode objects can't be used to synchronize multiple processes, nor can you use the Win32 wait functions to wait on them. Because you can't specify a timeout value when waiting on user mode objects such as critical sections, it's easier to block other threads and to get into deadlock situations. On the other hand, each transition to kernel mode costs you about a thousand x86 clock cycles (and this doesn't include the actual execution of the kernel mode code that implements the function you're calling), so there are definitely performance considerations when trying to decide whether to perform thread synchronization using kernel objects. As with many things, the key here is to use the right tool for the job.

Signaling

Kernel mode objects can typically be in one of two states: signaled or unsignaled. You can think of this as a flag that gets raised when the object is signaled and lowered when it isn't. Signaling an object allows you to notify other threads (in the current process or outside it) that you are ready for them to do something or that you have finished a task. For example, you might have a background thread signal an object when it has finished making a backup copy of the file being currently edited in your custom programmer's editor. Your background thread saves the file, then "raises a flag" (it signals an object) to let your foreground thread know that it's done.

Kernel mode objects such as events, mutexes, waitable timers, and semaphores exist to be used for thread synchronization and resource protection through signaling. In themselves, they do nothing. They exist solely to assist with resource protection and management—especially in multithreaded applications—by being signalable in different ways. Processes, threads, jobs, events, semaphores, mutexes, waitable timers, files, console input, and file change notifications can all be signaled or unsignaled.

Some kernel objects, such as event objects, can be reset to an unsignaled state after having been signaled, but some can't. For example, neither a process nor a thread object can be unsignaled once it has been signaled. This is because for either of these objects to be signaled, they have to terminate. You cannot resume a terminated process or thread.

Wait Functions

I've mentioned the Win32 wait functions in some of the examples we've looked at thus far, and now we'll delve into them a bit. The wait functions allow a thread to suspend itself until another object (or objects) becomes signaled. The most popular Win32 wait function is WaitForSingleObject. It takes two parameters: the handle of the object on which to wait, and the number of milliseconds to wait. You can pass in the INFINITE constant (0xFFFFFFFF, or -1) to wait indefinitely.

As the name suggests, WaitForMultipleObjects can wait for multiple objects (up to 64) to be signaled. Rather than passing in a single handle for its first parameter, you pass in an array containing the handles of the objects to wait for. WaitForMultipleObjects can wait for all objects to be signaled or just one of them. When a single object causes WaitForMultipleObjects to return, its return value indicates which object was signaled. This value will be somewhere between WAIT_OBJECT_0 and WAIT_OBJECT_0 + NumberOfHandles – 1. If you wish to call the function again with the same handle array, you'll need to first remove the signaled object or the function will return immediately without waiting.

If a wait function times out while waiting on an object, it will return WAIT_TIMEOUT. You can use this ability to implement a type of spinlock that waits for a short period of time, times out, carries out some work, then waits again on the desired resource. This keeps the thread from being completely unschedulable while it waits on a required resource and gives you a finer granularity of control over the blocking behavior of your threads.

There are several other wait functions (e.g., MsgWaitForSingleObject, MsgWaitForMultipleObjects, MsgWaitForMultipleObjectsEx, WaitForMultipleObjectsEx, WaitForSingleObjectEx, SignalObjectAndWait, and so on) that I won't go into here. You can consult the Windows Platform SDK reference for details about these functions. They are mostly variations of either WaitForSingleObject or WaitForMultipleObjects.

Events

Event objects are exactly what they sound like: objects that allow threads to signal to one another that something has occurred. They are commonly used to perform work in steps. One thread performs the first step or two of a task and then signals another thread via an event to carry out the remainder of the task.

Events come in two varieties: manual-reset events and auto-reset events. You call SetEvent to signal an event and ResetEvent to unsignal it. Auto-reset events are automatically unsignaled as soon as a single thread successfully waits on them; a manual-reset event must be reset through a call to ResetEvent. When multiple threads are waiting on an auto-reset event that gets signaled, only one of the threads gets scheduled. When multiple threads are waiting on a manual-reset event that gets signaled, all waiters become schedulable.

You call the CreateEvent API function to create a new event. Other threads can access the event by calling CreateEvent, DuplicateHandle, or OpenEvent.

Waitable Timers

Waitable timers are objects that signal themselves at a specified time or at regular intervals. You create a waitable timer with CreateWaitableTimer and configure it with SetWaitableTimer. You can pass in an absolute or relative time (pass a negative DueDate parameter to indicate a relative time in the future) or an interval at which the timer is supposed to signal. Once the interval or time passes, the timer signals and optionally queues an APC routine. If you created the timer as a manual-reset timer, it remains signaled until you call SetWaitableTimer again. If you created it as an auto-reset timer, it resets as soon as a thread successfully waits on it.

As the name suggests, you can cancel a waitable timer using the Cancel-WaitableTimer function. Once a manual-reset timer is signaled, there's no need to cancel it; you can simply close its handle.

As I mentioned, a waitable timer can optionally queue an APC routine. You won't likely use this facility much because you can always just wait on the timer to be signaled, then execute whatever code you want. In the event that you do decide to use an APC routine, keep in mind that it's pointless for a thread to wait on a timer's handle and wait on the timer alertably at the same time. Once the timer becomes signaled, the thread wakes (which takes it out of the alertable state), causing the APC routine not to be called.

If you've built many apps for Windows, you're probably familiar with Windows' user timer object. This is a different beast than a kernel mode waitable timer. The biggest difference between them is that user timers require a user interface harness in your app, making them relatively resource consumptive. Also, as with the other kernel mode objects we've been discussing, waitable timers can be shared by multiple threads and can be secured.

Windows' user timer object generates WM_TIMER messages that come back either to the thread that called SetTimer or to the thread that created the window. This means that only one thread is notified when the timer goes off. Conversely, a waitable timer can signal multiple threads at once, even across processes.

The decision of whether to use a waitable timer object or a user timer should come down to whether you're doing very much user interface manipulation in response to the timer. If so, a user timer is probably a better choice since you will have to wait on both the object and window messages that might occur if you use a waitable timer. If you end up using a waitable timer in a GUI app and need the thread that's waiting on the timer to respond to messages while it waits, you can use MsgWaitForMultipleObjects to wait on the object and messages simultaneously.

Semaphores

Typically, a kernel semaphore object is used to limit the number of threads that may access a resource at once. While a mutex, by definition, allows just one thread at a time to access a protected resource, a semaphore can be used to allow multiple threads to access a resource simultaneously and to set the maximum number of simultaneous accessors. You specify the maximum number of simultaneous accessors when you create the semaphore, and Windows ensures that this limit is enforced.

When you first create a semaphore object, you specify not only the maximum value for the semaphore but also its starting value. As long as its value remains greater than 0, the semaphore is signaled, and any thread that attempts to wait on it will return immediately, decrementing the semaphore as it returns. Say, for example, that you want a maximum of five threads (out of a pool of ten) to access a particular resource simultaneously. You would create the semaphore with a maximum value of 5, then as each thread needed access to the resource, it would call one of the wait functions to wait on the semaphore. The first five would return immediately from the wait function, and each successful wait would decrement the semaphore's value by 1. When the sixth thread began waiting on the semaphore, it would be blocked until one of the first five released the semaphore. If, say, Thread 5 then called ReleaseSemaphore, Thread 6 would return immediately from its wait state. All the while, the number of threads with simultaneous access to the resource would never exceed five.

Mutexes

Mutexes are among the most useful and widely used of the Windows kernel objects. They have many practical uses—from serializing access to critical resources to making code thread-safe—and they are often found in abundance in sophisticated multithreaded Windows apps.

Mutexes are very similar to critical sections except, of course, that they're kernel objects. This means that accessing them can be slower, but they are generally more functional than critical sections because they can be shared across processes and because you can use the wait functions to wait on them with a specified timeout.

Mutexes are unusual in that they are the only kernel object that supports the notion of thread ownership. Each mutex kernel object has a field that contains the thread ID of the owning thread. If the thread ID is 0, the mutex is not owned and is signaled. If the thread ID is other than 0, a thread owns the mutex, and the mutex is unsignaled.

Unlike all other kernel objects, a thread that owns a mutex can wait on it multiple times without releasing it and without waiting. Each time a thread successfully waits on a mutex, it becomes its owner (its thread ID is stored in the mutex's kernel object), and the object's recursion counter is incremented. This means that you must release the mutex (using ReleaseMutex) the same number of times that you waited on it in order for it to become signaled, thus allowing other threads to take ownership of it.

Windows also makes sure that a mutex isn't abandoned by a terminated thread, potentially blocking other threads infinitely. If a thread that owns a mutex terminates without releasing it, Windows automatically resets the mutex object's thread ID and recursion counter to 0 (which signals the object). If another thread is waiting on the mutex, the system gives it ownership of the mutex by setting the mutex's thread ID to reference the waiting thread and sets its recursion counter to 0. The wait function itself will return WAIT_ABANDONED so that the waiter can determine how it came to own the mutex.

As I've mentioned, suspending or terminating or a thread can cause a mutex to be held indefinitely or even abandoned. It's always better to let a thread's entry-point function return normally when possible.

I/O Completion Ports

An I/O completion port allows multiple threads conducting asynchronous I/O operations to be synchronized through a single object. You associate file handles with an I/O completion port through the Win32 API function CreateIOCompletionPort. When an asynchronous I/O operation that was started on a file associated with an I/O completion port finishes, an I/O completion packet is queued to the port.

A thread can wait on the port by calling the GetQueuedCompletionStatus function. If no I/O completion packet is ready, the thread will go into a wait state. When a packet is queued to the port, the function will return immediately.

Note that you can use I/O completion ports to synchronize operations besides those involving asynchronous I/O. Using the PostQueuedCompletionStatus API function in tandem with GetQueuedCompletionStatus, you can create a multithread signaling mechanism that is more scalable than the SetEvent/WaitForMultipleObjects approach. This is due to the fact that WaitForMultipleObjects is limited to waiting on a maximum of 64 worker threads. Using an I/O completion port, you can create a synchronization system that can wait on as many threads as the process can create. Here's an example of how you could implement a mechanism that could wait on more than 64 threads simultaneously.

1. The main thread of your process creates an I/O completion port that is not associated with a particular file or files by passing NULL for its FileHandle parameter.
2. The main thread creates as many threads as your process requires—let's say it starts with a pool of 100 worker threads.
3. Once all the threads are created, the main thread calls GetQueuedCompletionStatus to wait on the I/O completion port.
4. Whenever a worker thread has finished its work and wants to signal the main thread, it calls PostQueuedCompletionStatus to post an I/O

completion packet to the port. For example, it might do this before returning from its entry-point function or before going to sleep while it waits on, say, a global event associated with the main thread. In order to let the main thread know which thread completed its work, the worker thread could pass its thread ID into PostQueued-CompletionStatus.

5. The main thread returns from its call to GetQueuedCompletion-Status when it sees the packet.

6. Because the main thread knows how many threads it created, it calls GetQueuedCompletionStatus again, looping repeatedly until all the worker threads have indicated that they have completed their work.

Because a thread need not terminate to be signaled and because the main thread (or any thread) can wait on as many other threads as it wants, an I/O completion port provides a nicely scalable alternative to waiting on multiple threads using WaitForMultipleObjects or a similar API call.

Exercises

In this next exercise, you'll experiment with an application that is intentionally not thread-safe. You'll get to see firsthand what happens when an application does not synchronize access to shared resources. This should give you a greater appreciation for the lengths SQL Server must go to in order to ensure that its worker threads can access shared resources in a manner that is both safe and fast.

In the final exercise in this chapter, you'll learn to implement a spinlock based on a kernel mutex object. SQL Server uses spinlocks to guard access to shared resources within the server; understanding how they work will give you greater insight into how SQL Server works.

Exercise 3.9   What Happens When Threads Aren't Synchronized?

The following C++ application demonstrates three methods for accessing a shared resource (in this case, a global variable) from multiple resources. You can find it in the CH03\thread_sync subfolder on the CD accompanying this book. Load the application into the Visual C++ development environment and compile and run it in order to work through the exercise.

The app creates 50 threads that check the value of a global variable and, if it's less than 50, increment it. The end result of this should be a value of 50 in the global variable once all the threads have terminated, but that's not always the case. Let's looks at the code (Listing 3.5).

Listing 3.5 Thread Synchronization Options

```cpp
// thread_sync.cpp : Defines the entry point for the
// console application.
//

#include "stdafx.h"
#include "windows.h"

#define MAXTHREADS 50
//#define THREADSAFE
//#define CRITSEC
//#define MUTEX

long g_ifoo=0;
HANDLE g_hStartEvent;

#ifdef CRITSEC
CRITICAL_SECTION g_cs;
#endif

#ifdef MUTEX
HANDLE hMutex;
#endif

DWORD WINAPI StartThrd(LPVOID lpParameter)
{
  WaitForSingleObject(g_hStartEvent, INFINITE);
#ifdef CRITSEC
  EnterCriticalSection(&g_cs);
#endif
#ifdef MUTEX
  WaitForSingleObject(hMutex,INFINITE);
#endif
#ifdef THREADSAFE
  if (g_ifoo<50) InterlockedIncrement(&g_ifoo);
#else
  if (g_ifoo<50) g_ifoo++;
#endif
#ifdef CRITSEC
  LeaveCriticalSection(&g_cs);
```

```
#endif
#ifdef MUTEX
  ReleaseMutex(hMutex);
#endif
  return 0;
}

int main(int argc, char* argv[])
{
  DWORD dwThreadID;
  HANDLE hThreads[MAXTHREADS];
#ifdef CRITSEC
  InitializeCriticalSection(&g_cs);
#endif
#ifdef MUTEX
  hMutex=CreateMutex(NULL,FALSE,NULL);
#endif
  g_hStartEvent=CreateEvent(NULL,true,false,NULL);
  for (int i=0; i<MAXTHREADS; i++) {
    hThreads[i]=CreateThread(NULL,
      0,
      (LPTHREAD_START_ROUTINE)StartThrd,
      0,
      0,
      (LPDWORD)&dwThreadID);
  };
  SetEvent(g_hStartEvent);
  WaitForMultipleObjects(i,hThreads,true,INFINITE);

  printf("g_ifoo=%d\n",g_ifoo);
#ifdef CRITSEC
  DeleteCriticalSection(&g_cs);
#endif
#ifdef MUTEX
  CloseHandle(hMutex);
#endif
  return 0;
}
```

Three #define constants control how (and whether) the program synchronizes access to the global variable. By default, THREADSAFE, CRITSEC, and MUTEX are undefined, so access to the global variable is not synchronized. If you run the program on a multiprocessor machine enough times, you will eventually see a situation where g_ifoo does not end up with a value of 50. This is because access to the variable was not synchronized, and there was an overlap between the time one thread retrieved the value and another incremented it, as illustrated by the scenario outlined in Table 3.17.

Because of the overlap, two threads set g_ifoo to the same value, causing g_ifoo to end up with a value less than 50 because there are only 50 worker threads.

If you then uncomment the //#define THREADSAFE line and recompile, this overlap should be impossible. This is because the code then uses InterlockedIncrement to ensure atomicity of the increment operation. In the scenario shown in Table 3.17, this means that steps 3, 5, and 7 are performed as a single operation, as are steps 4, 6, and 8. Since Thread 10 completes its increment operation before Thread 11 is allowed to do so, Thread 11 sees 11, not 10, as the current value of g_ifoo when it performs its increment.

You can take this a step further by commenting out the #define for THREADSAFE and uncommenting CRITSEC. Access to the global variable is then synchronized with a critical section.

You can provide the ultimate in multithread synchronization by commenting out CRITSEC and uncommenting MUTEX. The code will then use a mutex kernel object to serialize access to the global variable.

Experiment with all four techniques and see what results you get. Generally speaking, when building applications, you should choose from among them in the order in which I've presented them here: If you don't need thread synchronization, don't code for it. If you do, try to use the interlocked functions. If they don't meet your needs, perhaps a critical section will do the job. If a critical section doesn't work for you (perhaps because you need to allow

Table 3.17 An Example of Unsynchronized Resource Access by Multiple Threads

Step	Action
1	Thread 10: Is g_ifoo < 50—Yes
2	Thread 11: Is g_ifoo < 50—Yes
3	Thread 10: Get g_ifoo's value—currently 10
4	Thread 11: Get g_ifoo's value—currently 10
5	Thread 10: Increment it (to 11)
6	Thread 11: Increment it (to 11)
7	Thread 10: Move the new value back to g_ifoo
8	Thread 11: Move the new value back to g_ifoo

for a timeout on the wait or you need to synchronize multiple processes), move up to a kernel object such as a mutex.

Exercise 3.10   Implementing a Kernel Mode Spinlock by Using a Mutex

Earlier in the chapter, I showed an example of the traditional implementation of a spinlock—a user mode construct that uses one of the interlocked functions to ensure atomic access to the lock variable. You can also set up spinlocks that are based on kernel mode objects. That may seem like a strange thing to do, but one very natural use of a kernel spinlock is to execute other code on a thread while you wait on a kernel object. You basically code the spinlock to time out on a fairly short interval, execute whatever code you're wanting to execute while you wait, then return to the wait loop. This keeps the thread semi-busy while it waits on a resource, which you may find preferable to simply having it go to sleep until the resource is available.

The example below demonstrates a kernel object–based spinlock. You can find it in the CH03\kernel_spinlock subfolder on the CD accompanying this book. Load it into the Visual C++ development environment, then compile and run it. Listing 3.6 shows the code.

Listing 3.6 A Kernel Object–Based Spinlock Implementation

```
// kernel_spinlock.cpp : Defines the entry point for the
// console application.
//

#include "stdafx.h"
#include "windows.h"

#define MAXTHREADS 2
#define SPINWAIT 1000

HANDLE g_hWorkEvent;

class CSpinLock {
public:
  static void GetLock(HANDLE hEvent);
};

void CSpinLock::GetLock(HANDLE hEvent) {
  int i=0;
  while (WAIT_TIMEOUT==WaitForSingleObject(hEvent, SPINWAIT)) {
```

```
     printf("Spinning count=%d for thread 0x%08x\n",++i,
        GetCurrentThreadId());
     //Put other code here to execute while we wait on the resource
   }
}

DWORD WINAPI StartThrd(LPVOID lpParameter)
{
   printf("Inside thread function for thread 0x%08x\n",
      GetCurrentThreadId());
   CSpinLock::GetLock(g_hWorkEvent);
   printf("Acquired spinlock for thread 0x%08x\n",
      GetCurrentThreadId());
   Sleep(5000);
   SetEvent(g_hWorkEvent);
   return 0;
}

int main(int argc, char* argv[])
{
   DWORD dwThreadID;
   HANDLE hThreads[MAXTHREADS];

   g_hWorkEvent=CreateEvent(NULL,false,true,NULL);

   for (int i=0; i<MAXTHREADS; i++) {
     hThreads[i]=CreateThread(NULL,
     0,
     (LPTHREAD_START_ROUTINE)StartThrd,
     0,
     0,
     (LPDWORD)&dwThreadID);
   };
   WaitForMultipleObjects(i,hThreads,true,INFINITE);

   return 0;
}
```

In this example, the spinlock is implemented in its own class and exposed via a static method. (The static method allows you to avoid having to create an instance of the CSpinLock class in order to use it.) You could pass any kernel object into the spinlock; in this example we use an event object.

The main function creates two threads that acquire the spinlock, sleep for five seconds, then release the spinlock by signaling the event. Since only one of the threads can acquire the spinlock at a time, the second thread to start waits on the first one to complete by spinning for as many one-second durations as it takes until the spinlock is released (i.e., the event is signaled).

Since the event is an auto-reset event, it immediately resets to unsignaled once a thread successfully waits on it. So, when GetLock successfully waits on the event object for the first thread, the event is immediately set back to unsignaled, and the second thread must wait for the first thread to signal it before proceeding. Given that the thread function sleeps for five seconds, this will be at least five seconds after the first thread acquires the spinlock.

Compile and run the code, experimenting with different sleep times for the thread function and different numbers of threads. You should see output like the following when you run the application:

```
Inside thread function for thread 0x00000d00
Acquired spinlock for thread 0x00000d00
Inside thread function for thread 0x00000f20
Spinning count=1 for thread 0x00000f20
Spinning count=2 for thread 0x00000f20
Spinning count=3 for thread 0x00000f20
Spinning count=4 for thread 0x00000f20
Spinning count=5 for thread 0x00000f20
Acquired spinlock for thread 0x00000f20
```

Thread Synchronization Recap

Windows provides a rich suite of thread synchronization functions. Thread synchronization comes in two basic varieties: user mode synchronization and kernel mode synchronization. User mode synchronization usually involves spinlocks, critical sections, and interlocked functions. Kernel mode synchronization involves kernel objects such as mutexes, semaphores, events, threads, processes, and waitable timers.

SQL Server makes use of both types of synchronization. Its UMS component spends a fair amount of time waiting on kernel mode synchronization objects, but it also implements a variety of spinlocks and does its best to avoid switching a thread into kernel mode unless absolutely necessary.

The key to successful thread synchronization is ensuring atomic access to resources. Modifying the same resource from multiple threads simultaneously is a recipe for disaster. Effective thread synchronization prevents this.

Thread Synchronization Knowledge Measure

1. True or false: The single most important element of thread synchronization is ensuring atomic access to resources.
2. Give two examples of user mode synchronization objects or constructs.
3. What happens when a thread successfully waits on an auto-reset event?
4. What happens when a thread successfully waits on a semaphore?
5. What happens when a thread successfully waits on a mutex?
6. What is the only kernel object that supports the concept of a thread owner?
7. If you want to protect a routine in a DLL shared by several processes from being executed by more than one process at a time, what type of synchronization object should you use?
8. If you are building a windows GUI and want to update the GUI at certain regular intervals, should you use a waitable timer object or a Windows user timer?
9. What API function is used to set the signal frequency for a waitable timer object?
10. True or false: A spinlock is a kernel mode object that spins (loops) until it acquires a lock on a resource.
11. Explain the function of the InterlockedExchange API function.
12. True or false: You cannot specify a timeout value when waiting on a critical section object.
13. What action does the system take when a thread that owns a mutex terminates?
14. What is the maximum number of objects that WaitForMultipleObjects can wait on simultaneously?
15. What type of message does a Windows user timer object produce?
16. True or false: Generally speaking, you should avoid techniques and design elements that continuously poll for resource availability.
17. True or false: Windows detects thread deadlocks, selects one of the participating threads as the deadlock victim, and terminates it.
18. What API routine does a thread use to acquire a critical section object?
19. What API routine does a thread use to release a critical section object?
20. Name a mechanism discussed in this chapter for waiting on more objects than the maximum supported by WaitForMultipleObjects.
21. True or false: A spinlock consumes no CPU resources while it waits.

22. True or false: A process object is the only type of kernel object that cannot be signaled.
23. True or false: The order in which you access kernel resources has no bearing on thread deadlocks because they are kernel resources.
24. True or false: Synchronizing threads using kernel mode objects is generally faster than synchronizing them via user objects.
25. When a semaphore's value reaches 0, is it signaled or unsignaled?

CHAPTER 4

Memory Fundamentals

You must lay aside all prejudice on both sides, and neither believe nor reject anything, because any other persons, or descriptions of persons, have rejected or believed it. Your own reason is the only oracle given you by heaven, and you are answerable, not for the rightness, but the uprightness of the decision.

—Thomas Jefferson[1]

Understanding an operating system's memory architecture is probably the single most important thing you can do to understand how the operating system itself works. Like all operating systems, Windows has its own methods of managing memory resources and providing memory-related services to applications. We'll delve into how Windows manages memory and how applications typically make use of Windows' memory management features in this chapter. We'll also talk about the different types of Windows memory: virtual memory, heaps, and shared memory.

Memory Basics

Memory access is so integral to application architecture and performance that a considerable portion of the Windows infrastructure is devoted to managing it and making it accessible to applications. Effective memory management is key to achieving application performance that is both acceptable and consistent. Despite the relatively low prices of today's RAM modules, memory is still a finite resource and is probably the single most important factor affecting application performance and overall system

---

1. Jefferson, Thomas. Letter to nephew, Peter Carr, from Paris. August 10, 1787; Reprinted in *Thomas Jefferson: Writings*, ed. Merrill D. Peterson. New York: Library of America, 1994, pp. 900–906.

throughput. In many instances, you'll get a better performance boost from adding RAM to a machine than you will by upgrading to a faster CPU.

Key Memory Terms and Concepts

✔ *Process address space*—the 4GB address space for an application. Addresses in Win32 applications are limited to 4GB because 4,294,967,296 (2^{32}) is the largest integer value a 32-bit pointer can store. Of these 4GB, 2GB are reserved by default for the kernel and 2GB are set aside for user mode access. On some editions of Windows, the user mode address space can be increased to 3GB (at the expense of kernel mode space) via the /3GB BOOT.INI switch for applications that are configured to take advantage of it. All memory allocated by an application comes from this space.

✔ *Virtual memory*—the facility by which a memory manager provides more memory than physically exists in a machine. The Windows virtual memory manager makes it appear to applications as though 4GB of memory exists in the machine, regardless of how much physical memory there actually is. Windows virtual memory is implemented primarily through the system paging file.

✔ *Page size*—the memory page size that a given processor architecture requires. On the x86, this is 4K. All Windows memory allocations must occur in multiples of the system page size.

✔ *Allocation granularity*—the boundary at which virtual memory reservations must be made under Windows. On all current versions of Windows, this is 64K, so user mode virtual memory reservations must be made at 64K boundaries within the process address space.

✔ *System paging file*—the file (or files) that Windows uses to provide physical storage for virtual memory. Windows uses the paging file to swap physical memory pages to and from disk in a manner that is transparent to the application. The total physical memory storage on a given machine is equal to the size of the physical memory plus the size of all the paging files combined.

✔ *Address translation*—the process of translating a virtual memory address into a physical one.

✔ *Page fault*—a condition raised by the memory management unit (MMU) of a processor that causes the Windows fault-handling code to load a page from the system paging file into physical memory if it can be located.

✔ *Thrashing*—a condition that occurs when the system is pressured for physical memory and continually swaps pages to and from the system paging file, often preventing applications from running in a timely fashion.

✔ *NULL pointer assignment partition*—the first 64K of the user mode address space; it's marked off limits in order to make NULL pointer references easier to detect.

✔ *Large-address-aware application*—an application whose executable has the IMAGE_FILE_LARGE_ADDRESS_AWARE flag set in its header. An application that is large address aware will receive a 3GB user mode address space when executed on an appropriate version of Windows that has been booted with the /3GB option.

✔ *AWE*—Address Windowing Extensions, the facility Windows provides for accessing physical memory above 4GB.

✔ *Application memory tuning*—the facility whereby a large-address-aware application can use up to 3GB of the process address space.

Key Memory APIs

Table 4.1 Key Memory-Related Win32 API Functions

Function	Description
GetSystemInfo	Gets system-level information about machine resources such as processors and memory
VirtualAlloc	Reserves, commits, and resets virtual memory
AllocateUserPhysicalPages	Allocates physical memory for use with Windows' AWE facility
MapUserPhysicalPages	Maps a portion of the AWE physical memory into a virtual memory buffer set aside by VirtualAlloc
ReadProcessMemory	Allows one process to read memory belonging to another
WriteProcessMemory	Allows one process to write memory belonging to another

Key Memory Tools

The best all around tool for monitoring Windows memory statistics and performance is Perfmon. Task Manager is also surprisingly helpful. Keep in mind that Task Manager's Mem Usage column lists each process's working set size, not its total virtual memory usage. Since this column includes shared pages, you can't total it to get the total physical memory used by all processes. Also, Task Manager's VM Size column actually lists a process's private bytes (its private committed pages), not its total virtual memory size.

Table 4.2 Key Memory-Monitoring Tools

	Reserved Virtual Memory	Paging File Size	Page Faults	Working Set Size	Paged Pool	Nonpaged Pool
Perfmon	✔	✔	✔	✔	✔	✔
Pstat	✔	✔	✔	✔	✔	✔
Pview	✔		✔	✔	✔	✔
pmon	✔		✔		✔	✔
TaskMgr	✔		✔	✔	✔	✔
TList	✔			✔		

Key Perfmon Counters

Table 4.3 Key Memory-Related Perfmon Counters

Counter	Description
Memory:Committed Bytes	The committed private address space (in both the paging file and physical memory)
Memory:Commit Limit	The amount of memory that can be committed without causing the system paging file to grow
Memory:% Committed Bytes In Use	Memory:Committed Bytes divided by Memory:Commit Limit
Process:Virtual Bytes	The total size of the process address space (shared and private pages)
Process:Private Bytes	The size of the nonshared committed address space
Process:Page File Bytes	Same as Process:Private Bytes
Process:Page File Peak	The peak value of the Process:Page File Bytes counter

Addresses

Because Windows is a 32-bit operating system, all user processes have a flat 4GB address space. This space is limited to 4GB because a 32-bit pointer can have one of 4,294,967,296 (2^{32}) values. This means that pointer values in Windows applications can range from 0x00000000 to 0xFFFFFFFF.

On 64-bit Windows, processes have a flat 16EB (exabyte) address space. A 64-bit pointer can have one of 18,446,744,073,709,551,616 (2^{64}) values, ranging from 0x0000000000000000 to 0xFFFFFFFFFFFFFFFF.

The fact that user processes are limited to 4GB of address space on 32-bit Windows doesn't mean that apps can't access more than 4GB of physical memory. As you're probably aware, it's not unusual for server machines to have more than 4GB of RAM installed. Windows' AWE facility allows applications to fully utilize the physical memory available in their host machines. We'll discuss AWE in more detail later in the chapter. For now, just keep in mind that it allows an application to access physical memory beyond 4GB. Windows 2000 Professional and Windows 2000 Server both support up to 4GB of physical memory. Windows 2000 Advanced Server supports up to 8GB, and Windows 2000 Data Center supports up to 64GB. Through AWE, an application can make use of as much physical memory as the operating system supports.

Keep in mind that the 4GB that a 32-bit process has to work with is *virtual* address space, not physical storage. By *virtual*, I mean that the address space is simply a range of memory addresses. Physical storage must be mapped to portions of this space before an application can make use of it without causing an access violation.

Basic Memory Management Services

In its bare essence, Windows memory management consists of implementing virtual memory and managing the interchange between virtual memory and physical memory. This involves a couple of fundamental tasks:

1. Mapping the virtual space for a process into physical memory
2. Paging memory to and from disk when process threads attempt to use more physical memory than is currently available

Beyond the virtual memory management services it provides, the memory manager also provides core services to Windows' environment subsystems. These include the following:

- Memory-mapped files
- Support for apps using sparsely populated address spaces
- Copy-on-write memory

Granularities

All processor chips define a fixed page size for working with memory. The page size on the x86 family of processors is 4K. Any allocation request an application makes is rounded up to the nearest page boundary. This means, for example, that a 5K allocation request will actually require 8K of memory.

Like most operating systems, 32-bit Windows has a fixed allocation granularity—a boundary on which all application memory reservations must occur. The boundary will always be a multiple of the system page size. In the case of 32-bit Windows, this boundary is 64K, so when an application requests a memory reservation, that reservation must begin on a 64K boundary in the process address space. Though many apps let Windows decide the precise location of the buffers they allocate, some make allocations at specific addresses. For those that do, they must pass a starting reservation address into Windows that aligns with a 64K boundary in the process address space. Windows will round down any starting reservation address that does not correctly align with the allocation granularity.

An app that's not mindful of the system's 64K allocation granularity can cause address space to be wasted. If an application reserves a virtual memory region less than 64K in size, the remainder of the 64K region is unusable by the application thanks to the system-enforced allocation granularity. Because an app cannot then specify a reservation that occupies the remainder of the region without having the system automatically round it down to the start of the 64K region, the unused address space is essentially wasted. So, it's possible to exhaust the address space for a process without actually reserving or allocating much memory. We'll talk more about memory reservation and commitment in the Virtual Memory section below.

You can retrieve both the system allocation granularity and the system page size via the Win32 GetSystemInfo API function. It's conceivable that both of these could vary in future versions of Windows, so it's wise not to hard-code references to them. See Exercise 4.4 later in the chapter for an example of how to use GetSystemInfo in a SQL Server extended procedure.

Process Memory Protection

Windows isolates processes from one another such that no user process can corrupt the address space of another process or of the OS itself. This makes Windows more robust and protects applications from one another. There are four fundamental aspects of this protection.

1. All processor chips supported by Windows provide some form of hardware-based memory protection.
2. System-wide data structures and memory areas used by kernel mode components are accessible only while in kernel mode—user mode code can't touch them.

3. Windows provides each process a private address space. Threads belonging to other processes are prohibited from accessing it.
4. Shared memory sections have standard Access Control Lists (ACLs) that are checked when processes access them.

These four aspects of the Windows memory management architecture make the operating system far more robust than it otherwise would be. They help prevent intentional and unintentional corruption of one process's address space by another, and they help make Windows itself resilient in the face of catastrophic application errors.

NOTE: As I've mentioned earlier, Windows *does* provide API functions such as ReadProcessMemory and WriteProcessMemory that allow one process to access another's address space. That said, using these functions requires specific access rights; you cannot accidentally read or modify memory belonging to another process. Typically (but not always), these functions are used by a debugger to access the memory of a process being debugged. Also note that, by default, when one process spawns another via a call to CreateProcess, the parent process has the access permissions required to access the child process's virtual memory. Again, this is typically used to facilitate debugging.

Partitions

At a high level, the 4GB process address space is organized as shown in Table 4.4.

Table 4.4 The Process Address Space and What It Contains

Address Range	Description
0x00000000–0x7FFFFFFF	Application and DLL code, global variables, thread stacks—user mode memory
0x80000000–0xBFFFFFFF	Kernel and executive, HAL, boot drivers
0xC0000000–0xC07FFFFF	Process page tables, hyperspace
0xC0800000–0xFFFFFFFF	System cache, paged pool, nonpaged pool

Unless the /3GB boot option has been enabled, the user mode portion of this space takes up the first 2GB, and the kernel occupies the remaining 2GB. If /3GB has been enabled, the user mode portion occupies the first 3GB (0x00000000–0xBFFFFFFF) and the kernel is squeezed into the remaining 1GB. See the subsection titled Application Memory Tuning on page 122 for more information on this option. For purposes of this discussion, we'll assume that /3GB is not enabled.

Within the user mode portion, there are several smaller partitions (Table 4.5). The following subsections briefly discuss these partitions.

NULL Pointer Assignment Partition

Have you ever wondered why NULL (address 0x00000000) can't be used by an application? After all, isn't it just another address within the process address space (the first address, in fact) just like any other address? No, it

Table 4.5 Partitions in the User Mode Portion of a Process's Address Space

Address Range	Size	Description
0x00000000–0x0000FFFF	64K	Off-limits region (prevents NULL pointer assignments).
0x00010000–0x7FFEFFFF	2GB–~192K	Private process address space.
0x7FFDE000–0x7FFDEFFF	4K	TEB for the process's main thread. TEBs for other threads reside at the previous page (0x7FFDD000) and working backward.
0x7FFDF000–0x7FFDFFFF	4K	The process's PEB.
0x7FFE0000–0x7FFE0FFF	4K	Shared user data page.
0x7FFE1000–0x7FFEFFFF	60K	Off-limits region (remainder of 64K containing shared user data page).
0x7FFF0000–0x7FFFFFFF	64K	Off-limits region (prevents buffers from straddling the user mode/kernel mode boundary).

isn't. And the reason it isn't is because, in the interest of helping programmers catch NULL pointer assignments, Windows has marked the first 64K of the process address space as off limits.

The NULL pointer assignment partition is a very simple yet surprisingly useful feature in the operating system that helps programs catch failed allocations. For example, consider the following C code.

```
char *pszLastName = (char *)malloc(LAST_NAME_SIZE);
strcpy(pszLastName,"Smith");
```

This code performs no error checking. If malloc is unable to allocate a buffer of the requested size, it returns NULL. Because Windows has marked the entirety of the first 64K of the process's address space as off limits (including address 0x00000000—NULL), any attempt to access a NULL pointer will result in an access violation. In the code above, if the call to malloc returns NULL, the call to strcpy will cause an access violation to be raised. This isn't because Windows checks every pointer reference to make sure that it doesn't equal NULL; it's because no address within the first 64K of the user mode space—0x00000000 or otherwise—may be used.

Does this mean that the operating system wastes 64K of the memory in your system? No, not at all. Remember: A process's address space is *virtual*—those sections marked off limits by the operating system are not backed by physical memory. For such a useful feature as the NULL pointer assignment partition, you give up only a 64K range of memory *addresses*—no physical memory is wasted.

Why is the NULL assignment partition 64K in size? Why not just make the NULL address, 0x00000000, off limits, or, at most, a single 4K page? Windows makes the entire 64K off limits for two reasons.

1. Reservations by user mode apps are required to be on allocation granularity (64K) boundaries. So, even if only the first 4K page was marked off limits, you still couldn't reserve memory in the remaining 60K of the first 64K of address space.
2. NULL pointer references are often buried in pointer arithmetic where a NULL memory address is not actually referenced, but one based on NULL plus an offset of some kind is. This means that your NULL pointer reference may actually end up causing your app to reference a memory location other than 0x00000000. Marking the entire 64K region off limits helps catch many of these situations.

This is best explained by way of example. Exercises 4.1 through 4.3 later in this chapter walk you through building a few test applications that demonstrate NULL pointer references and how Windows helps you detect them.

Process Private Address Space Partition

A process's private address space is where an application's executable and DLLs are loaded. All private memory allocations come from this region, and memory-mapped files are mapped here as well. It's the space within which an application operates.

Kernel Mode Partition

The kernel mode partition is where the code for file system support, thread management, memory management, networking support, and all device drivers resides. Everything residing in the kernel mode partition is shared among all processes.

You may be wondering whether the kernel really needs the top half of the process address space. Unfortunately, the answer is yes, it does. The kernel needs this space for OS code, device I/O cache buffers, process page tables, device driver code, and so forth. To be sure, the kernel could really make good use of much more space. It finally gets all the space it needs in 64-bit Windows.

One thing to keep in mind about kernel mode space: If you boot with the /3GB option (discussed below), the kernel space is reduced to just 1GB. This, in turn, limits the sizes of some of the data structures typically stored in the kernel mode space. For example, when /3GB is enabled, you may access only 16GB of total system memory because the size of the process page table is constricted by the limited kernel mode space.

PEB and TEB Regions

The PEB and TEB areas aren't regions that you'll make direct use of much, but it's instructive to know about them and what they are. As I mentioned in Chapter 3, each process has a process environment block (PEB) that's allocated in the user mode space. As Table 4.5 indicates, the precise address of a process's PEB is 0x7FFDF000. This means that you can dump this region of memory from under a debugger in order to view the PEB for a process. WinDbg has a special command for doing exactly this, !peb. The next time you attach to SQL Server with WinDbg, try the !peb command. You'll see that it returns a number of interesting pieces of data including the modules currently loaded within the process, the command line passed into the process, the address of the default heap, and many others.

As I said in Chapter 3, every thread has an associated thread environment block (TEB). The user mode address space contains a TEB for each thread owned by the process. As with the PEB, these blocks are stored in the user mode space in order to allow the system to access them without having to switch to kernel mode.

As shown in Table 4.5, the address of the TEB for a process's main thread is at 0x7FFDE000. You can list the contents of a TEB using the WinDbg !teb command. If you execute !teb without any parameters, you get the TEB for the current thread. If you pass an address into !teb, you'll get the TEB at that address if there is one.

TEBs for the worker threads in a multithreaded application are stored on the page at address 0x7FFDD000 and the pages immediately preceding it in memory (e.g., 0x7FFDC000, 0x7FFDB000, and so on).

Shared User Data Page

The memory page at 0x7FFE0000 is known as the shared user data page. It contains global items such as the clock tick count, the system time, the version number, and various other system-level data elements. It is read-only and is backed by a memory page that actually resides in the kernel address space. It exists in the user mode space in order to allow API routines to access key system data without having to switch to kernel mode.

Boundary Partitions

The last two regions of the user mode address space are off limits to applications. The first is the remainder of the 64K region containing the shared user data page. This 60K region is marked off limits by the operating system; any attempt to access it will result in an access violation. The fact that the remainder of the 64K region containing the shared user data page is marked off limits doesn't really affect user mode applications because that region would be inaccessible to them anyway given that user mode reservations must begin on an allocation granularity boundary.

The second region is the last 64K of the user mode address space. Windows marks it off limits in order to prevent an application from accessing a region of virtual memory that straddles the boundary between user mode and kernel mode. Because routines such as WriteProcessMemory are actually validated by kernel mode code, they can access address regions normally off limits to user mode code. By marking the last 64K of user mode space off limits, Windows protects against memory access that starts in the user mode space and extends into the kernel mode space.

The System Paging File

In order to implement virtual memory—that is, in order to allow applications to access more memory than physically exists in the machine—the Windows memory manager transparently copies pages to and from disk as necessary. The file it uses to store these pages is called the system paging file.

From an application standpoint, the system paging file increases the amount of memory available for use. It makes the system appear to have much more physical memory than it actually does. This is why a machine with, say, 1GB of physical memory can run many apps simultaneously, each having a 4GB process address space that is, perhaps, 50% backed by physical storage.

Conceptually, it's helpful to think of the physical storage behind virtual memory as the system paging file. Even though pages are constantly being copied in and out of physical RAM, the vast majority of the physical storage behind the virtual memory in the system is typically in the system paging file.

Although it is possible to run Windows without a paging file, this isn't usually recommended. In a typical configuration, the system paging file is considerably larger than the physical memory in the machine and provides apps with an efficient mechanism for accessing more memory than the machine actually has.

The paging file size is the most important variable affecting how much storage is available to an application. The amount of RAM has very little impact on the physical storage available to an app, but it does, of course, affect performance very significantly. When physical RAM is too low, the system will constantly copy data pages to and from the paging file (a condition known as thrashing), and, of course, performance will suffer commensurately.

Address Windowing Extensions

Windows' AWE facility exists to allow applications to access more than 4GB of physical memory. As I mentioned earlier, a 32-bit pointer is an integer that is limited to storing values of 0xFFFFFFFF or less—that is, to references within a 4GB memory address space. AWE allows an application to circumvent this limitation and access all the memory supported by the operating system.

At a conceptual level, AWE is nothing new—operating systems and applications have been using similar mechanisms to get around pointer limitations practically since the dawn of computers. For example, back in the DOS days, 32-bit extenders (e.g., Phar Lap, Plink, and others) were commonly used to allow 16-bit apps to access memory outside their normal address space. Special-purpose managers and APIs for extended and expanded memory were common; you may even remember products such as Quarterdeck's QEMM-386 product, which was commonly used for this sort of thing way back when.

Typically, mechanisms that allow a pointer to access memory at locations beyond its direct reach (i.e., at addresses too large to store in the pointer itself) pull off their magic by providing a window or region within the accessible address space that is used to transfer memory to and from the inaccessible region. This is how AWE works: You provide a region in the process address space—a window—to serve as a kind of staging area for transfers to and from memory above the 4GB mark.

In order to use AWE, an application follows these steps.

1. Allocate the physical memory to be accessed using the Win32 AllocateUserPhysicalPages API function. This function requires that the caller have the Lock Pages in Memory permission.
2. Create a region in the process address space to serve as a window for mapping views of this physical memory using the VirtualAlloc API function. We'll discuss VirtualAlloc further in just a moment.
3. Map a view of the physical memory into the virtual memory window using the MapUserPhysicalPages or MapUserPhysicalPagesScatter Win32 API functions.

While AWE exists on all editions of Windows 2000 and later and can be used even on systems with less than 2GB of physical RAM, it's most typically used on systems with 2GB or more of memory because it's the only way a 32-bit process can access memory beyond 3GB, as I mentioned earlier in the chapter. If you enable AWE support in SQL Server on a system with less than 3GB of physical memory, the system ignores the option and uses conventional virtual memory management instead.

One interesting characteristic of AWE memory is that it is never swapped to disk. You'll notice that the AWE-specific API routines refer to the memory they access as *physical* memory. This is exactly what AWE memory is: physical memory outside the control of the Windows virtual memory manager.

The virtual memory window used to buffer the physical memory provided by AWE requires read-write access. Hence, the only protection attribute that can be passed into VirtualAlloc when you set up this window is PAGE_READWRITE. Not surprisingly, this also means that you can't use VirtualProtect to protect pages within this region from modification or access.

Application Memory Tuning

The /3GB boot option is available on the Advanced Server and Data Center editions of Windows 2000 (and later). It allows a process's user mode address space to be expanded from 2GB to 3GB at the expense of the kernel mode address space (which is reduced from 2GB to 1GB). In Windows parlance, this facility is known as application memory tuning or 4GB tuning (4GT).

You enable application memory tuning by adding "/3GB" (without the quotes) to the appropriate line in the [operating systems] section of your BOOT.INI. It's common for people to configure their systems to be bootable with and without /3GB by setting up the entries in the [operating systems] section of BOOT.INI such that they can choose either option at startup.

WARNING: You can also boot Windows 2000 Professional, Windows 2000 Server, and Windows XP with the /3GB switch. However, this has the negative consequence of reducing kernel mode space to 1GB without increasing user mode space. In other words, you gain nothing for the kernel mode space you give up.

NOTE: Windows Server 2003 introduced a new boot option to set the user mode process space, /USERVA. You add /USERVA to your BOOT.INI just as you would /3GB. The advantage of /USERVA over /3GB is that it gives you a finer level of control over exactly how much address space to set aside for user mode use versus kernel mode use. For example, /USERVA=2560 configures 2.5GB for user mode space and leaves the remaining 1.5GB for the kernel. The caveats that apply to the /3GB switch apply here as well.

Large-Address-Aware Executables

Before support for /3GB was added to Windows, an application could never access a pointer with the high bit set. Only addresses that could be represented by the first 31 bits of a 32-bit pointer could be accessed by user mode applications. This left 1 bit unused, so some developers, being the clever coders they were and not wanting to waste so much as a bit in the process address space, made use of it for other purposes (e.g., to flag a pointer as referencing a particular type of application-specific allocation). This caused a conundrum when /3GB was introduced because these types of apps would not be able to easily distinguish a legitimate pointer that happened to reference memory above the 2GB boundary from a pointer that referenced memory below 2GB but had its high bit set for other reasons. Basically, booting a machine with /3GB would likely have broken such apps.

To deal with this, Microsoft added support for a new bit flag in the Characteristics field of the Win32 Portable Executable (PE) file format (the format that defines the layout of executable files—EXEs and DLLs—under Windows) that indicates whether an application is large address aware. When this flag (IMAGE_FILE_LARGE_ADDRESS_AWARE) is enabled, bit 32 in the Characteristics field in an executable file's header will be set. By having this flag set in its executable header, an application indicates to Windows that it can correctly handle pointers with the high bit set—that it doesn't do anything exotic with this bit. When this flag is set and the appropriate version of Windows has been booted with the /3GB option, the system will provide the process with a 3GB private user mode address space. You can check whether an executable has this flag enabled by using utilities such as DumpBin and ImageCfg that can dump the header of an executable file.

Visual C++ exposes IMAGE_FILE_LARGE_ADDRESS_AWARE via its /LARGEADDRESSAWARE linker switch. (You can also change this flag in an existing executable using ImageCfg.) SQL Server has this flag enabled, so if you boot with the /3GB switch on the appropriate version of Windows, the system will set the size of SQL Server's private process address space to 3GB.

NOTE: The IMAGE_FILE_LARGE_ADDRESS_AWARE flag is checked at process startup and is ignored for DLLs. DLLs must always behave appropriately when presented with a pointer whose high bit is set.

/3GB vs. AWE

The ability to increase the private process address space by 50% is certainly a handy and welcome enhancement to Windows' memory management facilities; however, Windows' AWE facility is far more flexible and scalable. As I said earlier, when you increase the private process address space by a gigabyte, that gigabyte comes from the kernel mode address space, which shrinks from 2GB to 1GB. Since the kernel mode code is already cramped for space even when it has the full 2GB to work with, shrinking this space means that certain internal kernel structures must also shrink. Chief among these is the table Windows uses to manage the physical memory in the machine. When you shrink the kernel mode partition to 1GB, you limit the size of this table such that it can manage a maximum of only 16GB of physical memory. For example, if you're running under Windows 2000 Data Center on a machine with 64GB of physical memory and you boot with the /3GB option, you'll be able to access only 25% of the machine's RAM—the remaining 48GB will not be usable by the operating system or applications.

AWE also allows you to access far more memory than /3GB does. Obviously, you get just one additional gigabyte of private process space via /3GB. This additional space is made available to apps that are large address aware automatically and transparently, but it is limited to just 1GB. AWE, by contrast, can make the entirety of the physical RAM that's available to the operating system available to an application provided it has been coded to make use of the AWE Win32 API functions. So, while AWE is more trouble to use and access, it's far more flexible and open ended.

Address Translation

Address translation refers to the process of translating a virtual address into a physical RAM address. This occurs each time a process attempts to access a block of data using its virtual address. Each time a process tries to access a data block by address, three things can happen.

1. The address will be valid and the page will already reside in physical memory.
2. The address will be valid and the page will be stored in the system paging file. In this case, the data will be paged into physical memory so that it can be accessed. This is known as a page fault. (You can track the page faults for a process via Perfmon's Process:Page Faults/ sec counter and via Task Manager's Page Faults column.)
3. The address will be invalid and the system will raise an access violation exception (user mode) or blue screen (kernel mode).

Virtual addresses aren't mapped directly to physical addresses. Instead, each virtual address is composed of three elements: the page directory index, the page table index, and the byte index. These elements establish the mapping between the virtual address and the physical RAM it references.

For each process, the Windows memory manager creates a page directory that it uses to map all the page tables for the process. Windows stores the physical address of this page directory in each process's KPROCESS block (the kernel process block stored within the EPROCESS block mentioned in Chapter 3) and maps it to address 0xC0300000 in the process address space.

The CPU keeps track of the address of a process's page directory table via a special register (CR3, or Control Register 3, on x86; the PDR, or Page Directory Register, on Alpha). Each time a context switch occurs wherein a thread from a different process is scheduled on the CPU, this register is loaded from the KPROCESS block so that the CPU's MMU can determine where the page directory table resides. Context switches among threads in the same process do not require the register to be reloaded because all threads in a process share the same address space.

This special register serves as a bootstrap for the system's memory management facilities. Without it, a process's page directory cannot be located. Without the page directory, the process address space itself cannot be accessed. The register provides the entry point for the CPU's memory management hardware to access an individual process's address space.

Each page directory consists of a series of page directory entries. The first 10 bits of a 32-bit virtual address store a page directory entry (PDE) index that tells Windows which page table to use to locate the physical memory associated with the address.

Each page table consists of series of page table entries. The second 10 bits of a 32-bit virtual address provide an index into this table and indicate which page table entry (PTE) contains the address of the page in physical memory to which the virtual address is mapped.

On x86 processors, the last 12 bits of a 32-bit virtual address contain the byte offset on the physical memory page to which the virtual address refers. The system page size determines the number of bits required to store the offset. Since the system page size on x86 processors is 4K, 12 bits are required to store a page offset ($4,096 = 2^{12}$).

When an address is translated, the following events occur.

1. The CPU's MMU locates the page directory for the process using the special register mentioned above.
2. The page directory index (from the first 10 bits of the virtual address) is used to locate the PDE that identifies the page table needed to map the virtual address to a physical one.
3. The page table index (from the second 10 bits of the virtual address) is used to locate the PTE that maps the physical location of the virtual memory page referenced by the address.
4. The PTE is used to locate the physical page. If the virtual page is mapped to a page that is already in physical memory, the PTE will

contain the page frame number (PFN) of the page in physical memory that contains the data in question. (Processors reference memory locations by PFN.) If the page is not in physical memory, the MMU raises a page fault, and the Windows page fault–handling code attempts to locate the page in the system paging file. If the page can be located, it is loaded into physical memory, and the PTE is updated to reflect its location. If it cannot be located and the translation is a user mode translation, an access violation occurs because the virtual address references an invalid physical address. If the page cannot be located and the translation is occurring in kernel mode, a bug check (also called a blue screen) occurs.

The four-step process required to resolve a virtual address to a physical one may seem inefficient at first glance. It may seem that it would be far simpler and more efficient to compose a virtual address of two basic components: (1) a PTE that stores the reference to the page in physical storage to which the virtual address maps and (2) a page offset that pinpoints the precise data location of the data block referenced by the address. However, the x86 and Alpha processors take the four-step approach they do in order to conserve memory. If we simplify this process into a basic one-step translation where each virtual address is composed of only two components as I've just described, we end up consuming far more memory to manage this table than we do in the four-step process, especially on systems where the majority of the address space is unallocated. We would need 1,048,576 PTEs to map a 4GB address space (4GB ÷ 4K page size = 1,048,576). With each PTE requiring a 32-bit pointer, we would need 4MB of physical memory to map the address space for each process (1,048,576 × 4 bytes = 4MB). Using the four-step process that x86 and Alpha processors employ, only the page directory must be fully defined—memory for the page directory can be allocated as necessary. Given that the address space for many processes is mostly unallocated, the physical memory this approach saves is significant.

That said, if this process occurred with every memory access, performance would likely be very poor, so the x86 and Alpha processors cache virtual-to-physical address translation pairs. The cache memory set aside for storing these address pairs is known as a Translation Buffer (TB) or Translation Look-aside Buffer (TLB). When the MMU is presented with a virtual address, it takes the virtual page number and compares it with the virtual page number of every entry in the cache. If it finds a match, it bypasses the four-step process and simply locates the PFN in physical memory from the cache entry. A downside of the Windows scheduler switching from one process to another is that cache entries associated with the process being taken off the scheduler must be cleared. The four-step process then fills the cache with entries from the new process.

Physical Address Extension

Intel processors starting with the Pentium Pro and later include support for a memory-mapping model called Physical Address Extension (PAE). PAE can provide access for up to 64GB of physical memory. In PAE mode, the MMU still implements page directories and page tables, but a new level exists above them: the page directory pointer table. Also, in PAE mode, PDEs and PTEs are 64 bits wide (rather than the standard 32 bits.) The system can address more memory than the standard translation because PDEs and PTEs are twice their standard width, not because of the page directory pointer table. The page directory pointer table is needed to manage these high-capacity tables and the indexes into them.

A special version of the Windows kernel is required to use PAE mode. This kernel ships with every version of Windows 2000 and later and resides in Ntkrnlpa.exe for uniprocessor machines and in Ntkrnlpamp for multiprocessor machines. You enable PAE use by adding the /PAE switch to your BOOT.INI file, just as you might add /3GB or /USERVA.

Exercises

Earlier in the chapter we discussed NULL pointer references and how Windows helps applications detect them (though it cannot completely prevent them). The next three exercises take you through some sample code that exhibits different types of NULL pointer references and shows how Windows handles each type.

Exercise 4.1 NULL Pointer References

1. Create a console app based on Listing 4.1 by loading and compiling the Visual Studio project in the CH04\memexamp00 subfolder on the CD accompanying this book. I'm assuming that you're working with Visual Studio C++ (VC++) version 6.0 or later in the steps that follow.

Listing 4.1 A NULL Pointer Reference

```
// memexamp00.cpp : NULL pointer reference example.
//

#include "stdafx.h"
#include "stdlib.h"
#include "string.h"

#define LAST_NAME_SIZE 2147483647

int main(int argc, char* argv[])
{
  char *pszLastName = (char *)malloc(LAST_NAME_SIZE);
  strcpy(pszLastName,"Smith");
  return 0;
}
```

2. Set a breakpoint on the strcpy line and run the app.
3. When the app stops at the strcpy, place your mouse over pszLastName in the VC++ editor window. A tool-tip hint should display indicating that pszLastName has a value of 0x00000000. Why is this? The pointer is NULL because we requested a larger memory allocation (2GB) than Windows could satisfy.

   Because the code does no error checking, strcpy will attempt to copy the string "Smith" into this invalid address.
4. Hit F10 to execute the strcpy line. You should now see an access violation. Windows has intercepted the attempted access of memory address 0x00000000 (NULL) and raised the error you see. Press Shift+F5 to stop debugging.

Exercise 4.2   An Obscured NULL Pointer Reference

Now let's modify the app to cause a NULL pointer reference that is not so obvious.

1. Change your code to look like Listing 4.2 (or load memexamp01 from the CD).

Listing 4.2 A Less Obvious NULL Pointer Reference

```
// memexamp01.cpp : NULL pointer reference example.
//
```

```
#include "stdafx.h"
#include "stdlib.h"
#include "string.h"

#define LAST_NAME_SIZE 2147483647
char szLastName[]="Smith";

int main(int argc, char* argv[])
{
  char *pszLastName = (char *)malloc(LAST_NAME_SIZE);
  *(pszLastName+strlen(szLastName)+1)='\0';
  strncpy(pszLastName,szLastName,strlen(szLastName));
  return 0;
}
```

2. In this code, we use strncpy rather than strcpy to fill the address referenced by pszLastName with data. strncpy is often preferred over strcpy
   because it helps prevent buffer overruns—you can control the number
   of characters copied. Because we've used strncpy, we have to take
   care of terminating the string referenced by pszLastName, so we begin
   by placing an ASCII 0 character at the end of the target buffer for
   szLastName. To compute the target address for the string terminator,
   we simply take the string length of szLastName, add it to the address
   contained in pszLastName, and add 1.
3. Unfortunately, this code also assumes that the malloc call won't fail.
   When malloc fails, it returns NULL into pszLastName. This address is
   then used when we compute where to put the string terminator. Since
   it's 0, we're effectively attempting to place an ASCII 0 at a memory address that's equivalent to the length of the string referenced by szLast-
   Name plus 1. So, rather than a plain NULL reference, we are referring
   to address 0x00000006—5 (the length of "Smith") + 1.
4. This is easy to see by looking at the disassembly for our app.

```
13:        char *pszLastName = (char *)malloc(LAST_NAME_SIZE);
00401028   push        7FFFFFFFh
0040102D   call        malloc (00401220)
00401032   add         esp,4
00401035   mov         dword ptr [ebp-4],eax
14:        *(pszLastName+strlen(szLastName)+1)='\0';
00401038   push        offset szLastName (00421a30)
0040103D   call        strlen (004011a0)
00401042   add         esp,4
00401045   mov         ecx,dword ptr [ebp-4]
00401048   mov         byte ptr [ecx+eax+1],0
```

   a. The call to malloc (Line 13) begins by pushing 0x7FFFFFFF onto the stack. This is the value of our LAST_NAME_SIZE constant: 2,147,483,647, or 2GB minus 1.

   b. Register eax contains the return value from malloc. Because we know the call will fail, we know that this value is NULL or 0x00000000. This value is moved into pszLastName immediately before our attempt to set up the string terminator.

   c. Line 14 computes the string length of szLastName, adds that value to the previous value stored in pszLastName plus 1, and attempts to treat this new value as an address (to dereference it) so that it can assign the string terminator. The actual dereference (and the cause of the ensuing access violation) appears in bold type in Listing 4.2.

  5. Because address 0x00000006 is within the first 64K of the process address space, an access violation is raised when we attempt to dereference it.

In the next exercise, we'll cause a NULL pointer reference by overwriting a pointer value. This is a common problem in applications, especially those that feature pointers prominently such as C and C++.

Exercise 4.3   A NULL Pointer Reference Due to a Memory Overwrite

Here's a fairly contrived example that demonstrates, once again, the usefulness of the NULL pointer access partition.

  1. Load the app shown in Listing 4.3 from the CD (CH04\memexamp02) and compile it.

Listing 4.3 A NULL Pointer Reference Caused by Pointer Corruption

```
// memexamp02.cpp : NULL pointer reference caused by pointer
// corruption.
//

#include "stdafx.h"
#include "stdlib.h"
#include "string.h"

#define MAX_FIRST_NAME_SIZE 10
#define MAX_LAST_NAME_SIZE 30
```

```
#pragma pack(1)

struct NAME
{
  char szFirstName[MAX_FIRST_NAME_SIZE];
  char *pszLastName;
} nmEmployee;

int main(int argc, char* argv[])
{
  int dwFirstNameLen=__min(strlen(argv[1]),MAX_FIRST_NAME_SIZE);
  int dwLastNameLen=__min(strlen(argv[2]),MAX_LAST_NAME_SIZE);

  nmEmployee.pszLastName=(char *)malloc(dwLastNameLen);

  strncpy(nmEmployee.szFirstName,argv[1],dwFirstNameLen);
  strncpy(nmEmployee.pszLastName,argv[2],dwLastNameLen);

  nmEmployee.szFirstName[dwFirstNameLen+2]='\0';
  nmEmployee.pszLastName[dwLastNameLen+2]='\0';

  strupr(nmEmployee.pszLastName);

  printf("First Name=%s Last
    Name=%s\n",nmEmployee.szFirstName,nmEmployee.pszLastName);
  return 0;
}
```

This code will work fine so long as the first argument passed into it is 8 characters or less. Thanks to the faulty pointer arithmetic used throughout the app, but especially when the name strings are terminated, a first name that's longer than 8 characters will cause the pszLastName pointer to be overwritten with an ASCII 0.

2. To see how this works, set the command line parameters (Alt+F7 | Debug | Program arguments) to "Wolfgangus Mozart" (without quotes).

3. Set a breakpoint at the line that assigns the string terminator for szFirstName:

   ```
   nmEmployee.szFirstName[dwFirstNameLen+2]='\0';
   ```

4. Now, run the app from inside the VC++ IDE. When the debugger stops at your breakpoint, add nmEmployee to your Watch window, then expand it so that you can see its members as you step through the code.

5. Press F10 to step over the breakpoint line. You should notice in the Watch window that not only was szFirstName changed by the line just executed but pszLastName was changed as well (both members should appear red in the Watch window). This is because the ASCII 0 assigned to the end of szFirstName was actually written 3 bytes past the end of the string. Because szFirstName is 10 characters wide and because arrays in C++ are always zero-based, the valid indexes for sz-FirstName are 0–9. However, dwFirstNameLen equals 10. Assigning ASCII 0 to szFirstName[dwFirstNameLen] would have also overwritten pszLastName but would have gotten only the first byte of the four-byte pointer. Adding 2 to this offset pushes us into the third byte of the ps-zLastName pointer. By zeroing this byte, we change the address to one that happens to be in the first 64K of the process address space.

6. Now attempt to step over the next line. Because the previous line corrupted the pszLastName pointer, you should see an access violation. The specific reason for the access violation is that you are referencing an address in the first 64K of memory, and Windows' NULL pointer access partition protection has caught that invalid reference.

I mentioned earlier in the chapter that you can retrieve the system's page size and allocation granularity through a call to the GetSystemInfo Win32 API function. In this next exercise, you'll build and run a SQL Server extended procedure that returns this same information.

Exercise 4.4   A GetSystemInfo Extended Stored Procedure

1. Copy the xp_sysinfo project from the CH04\xp_sysinfo subfolder on the book's CD onto your hard drive and load it into Visual C++. For curious readers, Listing 4.4 shows the complete source code of the xp_sysinfo extended procedure.

Listing 4.4 An Extended Procedure That Returns System Memory Information

```
RETCODE __declspec(dllexport) xp_sysinfo(SRV_PROC *srvproc)
{

    DBCHAR colname[MAXCOLNAME];
    DBCHAR szProcType[MAX_PATH];
    DBCHAR szMinAddress[MAXCOLNAME];
    DBCHAR szMaxAddress[MAXCOLNAME];
    DBCHAR szAffinityMask[MAXCOLNAME];
    SYSTEM_INFO si;
```

```
GetSystemInfo(&si);

//Set up the column names
wsprintf(colname, "PageSize");
srv_describe(srvproc, 1, colname, SRV_NULLTERM, SRVINT4,
    sizeof(DBINT), SRVINT4, sizeof(DBINT), &si.dwPageSize);

wsprintf(colname, "AllocationGranularity");
srv_describe(srvproc, 2, colname, SRV_NULLTERM, SRVINT4,
    sizeof(DBINT), SRVINT4, sizeof(DBINT),
    &si.dwAllocationGranularity);

wsprintf(colname, "NumberOfProcessors");
srv_describe(srvproc, 3, colname, SRV_NULLTERM, SRVINT4,
    sizeof(DBINT), SRVINT4, sizeof(DBINT),
    &si.dwNumberOfProcessors);

wsprintf(colname, "ProcessorType");
switch (si.wProcessorArchitecture)
{
  case PROCESSOR_ARCHITECTURE_INTEL :
  {
    strcpy(szProcType,"Intel ");
    switch (si.wProcessorLevel)
    {
    case 3 :
      {
        strcat(szProcType,"386");
        break;
      }
    case 4 :
      {
        strcat(szProcType,"486");
        break;
      }
    case 5 :
      {
        strcat(szProcType,"Pentium");
        break;
      }
    case 6 :
      {
        strcat(szProcType,"Pentium II or Pentium Pro or later");
        break;
      }
```

```
      case 7 :
        {
          strcat(szProcType,"Pentium III");
          break;
        }
      case 8 :
        {
          strcat(szProcType,"Pentium 4");
          break;
        }
      default :
        {
          strcat(szProcType,"Unknown");
          break;
        }

    }
    break;
}
case PROCESSOR_ARCHITECTURE_MIPS :
  {
  strcpy(szProcType,"MIPS ");
  switch (si.wProcessorLevel)
  {
  case 4:
    {
      strcat(szProcType,"R4000");
      break;
    }
  default:
    {
      strcat(szProcType,"Unknown");
      break;
    }
  }
  break;
  }
case PROCESSOR_ARCHITECTURE_ALPHA :
  {
  strcpy(szProcType,"Alpha ");
  switch (si.wProcessorLevel)
  {
  case 21064:
```

```
      {
        strcat(szProcType,"21064");
        break;
      }
    case 21066:
      {
        strcat(szProcType,"21066");
        break;
      }
    case 21164:
      {
        strcat(szProcType,"21164");
        break;
      }
    default:
      {
        strcat(szProcType,"Unknown");
        break;
      }
    }
    break;
    }
  case PROCESSOR_ARCHITECTURE_PPC :
    {
    strcpy(szProcType,"PPC ");
    switch (si.wProcessorLevel)
    {
    case 1:
      {
        strcpy(szProcType, "601");
        break;
      }
    case 3:
      {
        strcpy(szProcType, "603");
        break;
      }
    case 4:
      {
        strcpy(szProcType, "604");
        break;
      }
```

```
        case 6:
          {
            strcpy(szProcType, "603+");
            break;
          }
        case 9:
          {
            strcpy(szProcType, "604+");
            break;
          }
        case 20:
          {
            strcpy(szProcType, "620");
            break;
          }
        default:
          {
            strcat(szProcType,"Unknown");
            break;
          }
      }
      break;
      }
  default :
    {
    strcpy(szProcType,"Unknown ");
    break;
    }
}
srv_describe(srvproc, 4, colname, SRV_NULLTERM, SRVCHAR,
    strlen(szProcType), SRVCHAR, strlen(szProcType),
    &szProcType);

wsprintf(colname, "ProcessorAffinityMask");
wsprintf(szAffinityMask,"0x%08X",si.dwActiveProcessorMask);
srv_describe(srvproc, 5, colname, SRV_NULLTERM, SRVCHAR,
    strlen(szAffinityMask), SRVCHAR, strlen(szAffinityMask),
    &szAffinityMask);

wsprintf(colname, "MinimumAppAddress");
wsprintf(szMinAddress,"0x%08X",si.lpMinimumApplicationAddress);
srv_describe(srvproc, 6, colname, SRV_NULLTERM, SRVCHAR,
    strlen(szMinAddress), SRVCHAR, strlen(szMinAddress),
    &szMinAddress);
```

```
wsprintf(colname, "MaximumAppAddress");
wsprintf(szMaxAddress,"0x%08X",si.lpMaximumApplicationAddress);
srv_describe(srvproc, 7, colname, SRV_NULLTERM, SRVCHAR,
    strlen(szMaxAddress), SRVCHAR, strlen(szMaxAddress),
    &szMaxAddress);

wsprintf(colname, "UserModeAddressSpace");
DWORD dwUserModeSpace = ((DWORD)si.lpMaximumApplicationAddress -
    (DWORD)si.lpMinimumApplicationAddress);
srv_describe(srvproc, 8, colname, SRV_NULLTERM, SRVINT4,
    sizeof(DBINT), SRVINT4, sizeof(DBINT), &dwUserModeSpace);

srv_sendrow(srvproc);

// Now return the number of rows processed
srv_senddone(srvproc, SRV_DONE_MORE | SRV_DONE_COUNT,
    (DBUSMALLINT)0, 1);

    return XP_NOERROR;


}
```

2. Compile the project. This should produce a DLL named xp_sysinfo.dll in the Release subfolder under your root xp_sysinfo folder.
3. Copy xp_sysinfo.dll to the binn folder under your SQL Server installation's root folder. If you've worked through the exercises in previous chapters, you may be asked whether to replace the existing xp_sysinfo. Answer Yes to this prompt.
4. Add the xproc to the master database with this command:

   ```
   sp_addextendedproc 'xp_sysinfo','xp_sysinfo.dll'
   ```

5. Run xp_sysinfo from Query Analyzer. You should see output something like this (results abridged):

```
PageSize   AllocGranularity  Processors  ProcessorType      AffinityM
---------  ----------------  ----------  ----------------   ---------
4096       65536             2           Intel Pentium...   0x0000000
```

As you can see, the system page size is 4K and the allocation granularity is 64K. Note that these numbers may differ on other processors or in future versions of Windows.

Note also the UserModeSpace column. On this machine, the maximum user mode space is roughly 2GB. This tells us that the /3GB boot option was not successfully enabled. Since SQL Server is a large-address-aware application, it would reflect a user mode address space of roughly 3GB if it were running on an appropriate version of Windows and the system had been booted with /3GB.

Memory Basics Recap

Windows provides a rich set of facilities for making memory available to applications. Even though a machine may have a relatively small amount of physical RAM installed, Windows provides each process a 4GB virtual address space in which to run and transparently handles swapping physical memory to and from disk as necessary.

The x86 family of processors has a memory page size of 4K. This means that all memory allocations under Windows are actually carried out in multiples of 4K. For example, a 5K allocation request actually requires 8K of memory.

AWE and /3GB provide applications mechanisms for accessing memory beyond the standard 2GB user mode partition. The /3GB option actually limits the total amount of physical memory that Windows can manage, so it is generally not recommended. AWE is the more flexible of the two and can make all the physical memory that's visible to the operating system available to applications.

Memory Basics Knowledge Measure

1. What is the system page size on the x86 family of processors?
2. What is the allocation granularity size on 32-bit Windows?
3. True or false: A page fault causes an exception to be raised that will crash an application if the application does not trap it with structured exception-handling (SEH) code.
4. If you enable the /3GB option on Windows 2000 Professional, how much user mode address space will SQL Server be allotted when it starts up?
5. True or false: Address translation refers to the two-step process in which the two components of a virtual address, the page table index and the page offset, are used to translate a virtual address into a physical one.
6. True or false: Thrashing is the condition in which physical memory pages are continually swapped to and from the system paging file, often preventing applications from running in a timely fashion.

7. What address region is set aside by Windows to help applications detect NULL pointer assignments?

8. How large is the default user mode space in a 32-bit Windows process?

9. How much total physical memory can Windows 2000 Data Center manage?

10. True or false: Using the AWE functions causes the kernel mode space to be so compressed that only 16GB of total physical memory can be accessed by Windows.

11. What VC++ linker switch enables an executable to be large address aware?

12. Before support for the /3GB boot option was added to Windows, how many bits in a virtual address could a user mode application use to reference virtual memory directly?

13. True or false: The system paging file can actually consist of several physical files that may reside on different disk drives.

14. What does Task Manager's Mem Usage column indicate for a process?

15. When an address translation is attempted on an invalid user mode address, what happens?

16. What Windows API function covered in this chapter will return both the system page size and the system allocation granularity?

17. True or false: The PEB is not allocated at a specific address in a process's virtual address space, and its location will almost always vary between processes.

18. True or false: All processor chips supported by Windows have some form of built-in memory protection.

19. What's the typical difference between Perfmon's Process:Private Bytes and Process:Page File Bytes counters?

20. True or false: Because Windows is a 32-bit operating system, all user processes have a flat 4GB address space.

21. What is the WinDbg command for displaying a process's PEB?

22. What does Task Manager's VM Size column indicate for a process?

23. What Win32 API function covered in this chapter can you use to deduce whether a process has an oversized user mode address space?

24. True or false: Because the largest integer a 32-bit pointer can store is 2^{32}, the maximum memory that a user mode application may access is 4GB.

25. True or false: The majority of the physical storage used to implement virtual memory comes from the physical RAM installed in the machine.

26. What special-purpose register is used to store the location of the page directory on x86 processors?

27. True or false: If a process needs more than the standard 2GB of virtual memory space, AWE is generally preferred over the /3GB option.
28. What is a Translation Look-aside Buffer (TLB)?
29. True or false: The shared user data page is actually backed by a page in kernel mode memory.
30. True or false: Although an application can specify the size of a memory allocation it wants to make, it cannot specify the precise location for the allocation.

Virtual Memory

Windows offers three distinct types of memory to applications: virtual memory, heaps, and shared memory. Virtual memory is best used for managing large arrays or collections of objects or structures of varying sizes. It is the primary mechanism by which SQL Server allocates memory and is the focus of this section.

You allocate virtual memory using the VirtualAlloc and VirtualAllocEx API functions. VirtualAlloc allocates memory only in the calling process's address space; VirtualAllocEx can allocate memory in another process's address space. VirtualAlloc is by far the more commonly used of the two, and it's the one we'll use throughout this chapter.

Pages in virtual memory are always in one of three states: free, reserved, or committed. You use VirtualAlloc to reserve and/or commit virtual memory, and you use VirtualFree to decommit and/or release allocated memory. Released memory is not reserved or committed—it's free.

Key Virtual Memory Terms and Concepts

✔ *Page size*—the memory page size that a given processor architecture requires. On the x86, this is 4K. All Windows memory allocations must occur in multiples of the system page size.
✔ *Allocation granularity*—the boundary at which virtual memory reservations must be made under Windows. On all current versions of Windows, this is 64K, so user mode virtual memory reservations must be made at 64K boundaries within the process address space.
✔ *Reserved memory*—a region of virtual memory addresses that has been set aside for use by a process. A reserved region does not require physical storage. Memory reservations should always be made on allocation granularity boundaries. Reserved memory cannot be accessed until it is committed.

✔ *Committed memory*—a region of virtual memory that is backed by physical storage.

✔ *Copy-on-write*—a Windows facility in which an attempted modification of a page causes the page to be duplicated and the new page modified instead. This mechanism is used, for example, when multiple instances of an application are running and one of them makes a change to one of its data pages (e.g., by changing a global variable).

✔ *Guard page*—a page that has been flagged with the PAGE_GUARD page protection attribute. The first time a process attempts to access the guard page, Windows fails the operation and either raises a STATUS_GUARD_PAGE exception or returns a last error code of STATUS_GUARD_PAGE_VIOLATION. This also resets the page's guard status, so the next attempt to access it succeeds.

Key Virtual Memory APIs

Table 4.6 Key Virtual Memory–Related API Functions

Function	Description
VirtualAlloc	Reserves, commits, and resets virtual memory
VirtualFree	Decommits and releases virtual memory
VirtualProtect	Changes the page protection attributes for a range of virtual memory pages
VirtualLock/VirtualUnlock	Locks/unlocks virtual memory pages in physical memory
VirtualQuery(Ex)	Returns system-level information about a virtual memory region
SetWorkingSetSize	Sets the number of virtual memory pages a process may lock in physical memory
GetSystemInfo	Gets system-level information about machine resources such as processors and memory

Page Protection Attributes

When an application allocates virtual memory using VirtualAlloc, Windows permits the allocating process to specify protection attributes for the range of pages allocated. These attributes are passed on to the system's memory management hardware, which helps implement them. In Visual C++, these attributes are specified by combining the various PAGE_ constants. Table 4.7 lists each attribute constant and its purpose.

Table 4.7 Page Protection Attributes

Protection Attribute	Purpose
PAGE_GUARD	Accessing this page causes a STATUS_GUARD_PAGE exception to be raised (or a STATUS_GUARD_PAGE_VIOLATION error to be returned) and resets the guard page protection. Cannot be combined with PAGE_NOACCESS.
PAGE_EXECUTE	Prevents writing to the page.
PAGE_EXECUTE_READ	Prevents writing to the page.
PAGE_EXECUTE_READ_WRITE	Permits any attempted access.
PAGE_EXECUTE_WRITECOPY	Writing to the page causes the system to copy the page and give the process the new copy. Execution of the page is permitted.
PAGE_NOACCESS	Prevents any attempted access.
PAGE_NOCACHE	Prevents the page from being cached. Not recommended for general use. Used mostly by device drivers.
PAGE_READONLY	Prevents writing to the page.
PAGE_READWRITE	Permits any attempted access.
PAGE_WRITECOMBINE	Causes multiple writes to a single device to be combined into a single operation in order to improve performance. Used mostly by device drivers.
PAGE_WRITECOPY	Writing to the page causes the system to copy the page and give the process the new copy. Execution of the page is not permitted.

NOTE: Execute-only access is not supported by the x86 family of processors. As far as the x86 family is concerned, if a page is readable, it is also executable. This means, for example, that the PAGE_EXECUTE and PAGE_READONLY protection attributes are functionally equivalent when Windows is running on an x86 processor.

It's not uncommon for memory allocation routines to make use of the PAGE_GUARD protection attribute to detect buffer overruns. The way this works is that, for every allocation it makes, the routine will allocate a page with the PAGE_GUARD attribute set (a guard page) just after the newly allocated region. If a memory access then attempts to write past the end of the allocated region, a STATUS_GUARD_PAGE exception is raised and the access fails.

When a process is started, Windows protects the executable's code pages with the PAGE_EXECUTE_READ attribute. This allows multiple copies of the same executable to share the same physical storage. For example, if you run multiple instances of Explorer, only one copy of explorer.exe is physically mapped into memory.

Copy-On-Write

Knowing that multiple instances of an application share the same physical storage for the executable's code pages, you may be wondering about its data pages. If all instances of an executable are mapped to the same physical storage, how can one instance change, say, a global variable without affecting the others? The answer lies in understanding the PAGE_WRITECOPY page protection attribute. When a process starts, Windows protects its data pages with the PAGE_WRITECOPY attribute. When a process modifies one of its data pages, it gets a private copy of that page. This functionality is known as copy-on-write and conserves physical storage while still allowing instances of an executable to make changes to global data without affecting other instances.

The Windows NT family of operating systems (Windows NT, Windows 2000, Windows XP, and Windows Server 2003) has always supported copy-on-write functionality. Most flavors of UNIX also support some type of copy-on-write functionality. However, some operating systems (such as Windows 9x and OpenVMS) do not. In operating systems that do not offer copy-on-write functionality, the standard practice is to make a private copy of all of an executable's data pages when a process first starts. Obviously, the approach taken in the Windows NT family is much more efficient.

In the Windows NT family, the system always allocates space in the system paging file to accommodate an executable's data pages. However, the storage set aside for each data page is not actually used until the page is written to. This conserves physical storage while still guaranteeing that an application will be able to write to its data pages when it needs to.

WARNING: Don't pass the PAGE_WRITECOPY or PAGE_EXECUTE_WRITECOPY attributes when calling VirtualAlloc to reserve or commit memory. If you do, the allocation will fail with an ERROR_INVALID_PARAMETER error. These page protection attributes are reserved for system use only.

Reserving Memory

Windows allows a process to reserve memory address space without actually consuming any committed pages or affecting the process's page file quota (which is not necessarily page file space but rather limits the number of committed pages a process can consume). A virtual memory reservation simply sets aside a contiguous block of process address space; it does not actually make any new memory available to the application for use. The application must commit the memory in order to use it.

Most developers aren't accustomed to being able to set the exact address where a region of memory will be reserved. Generally, memory allocation facilities such as malloc and the C++ **new** operator do not permit an application to specify *where* memory will be allocated—they only allow the application to control the *size* of the allocation. Windows, however, gives the developer control over both aspects of an allocation, which can have important implications for how an application is coded, as you'll see in just a moment.

As far as Windows is concerned, reserving memory is relatively inexpensive because all that happens when memory is reserved is that the relatively small virtual address descriptors (VADs) for the process are updated. The operation is normally speedy because no physical memory is actually being committed and the process page quota isn't impacted.

Windows' two-step approach to allocating virtual memory is used by the operating system itself. One prime example is the way in which the stack space for a thread is allocated. When it creates a thread, Windows reserves a region of virtual memory to store the thread's stack. This region is 1MB by default; you can override it for an individual thread by specifying a different stack size in the call to CreateThread, or for all threads via the /STACK linker flag (for Visual C++; most other compilers support a similar option) or by using tools such as ImageCfg that can edit an executable file's header.

Even though it has reserved the full stack space for the thread, Windows waits to commit pages within that region until they're needed. It begins by committing just one page in the reserved region and flags the page just beyond it as a guard page. When the system attempts to expand a thread's stack into the guard page, Windows traps the STATUS_GUARD_PAGE exception that results and expands the stack by committing the guard page (the page's guard status was already reset by the attempted access). It then flags the next page following the newly committed page as a guard page, and the thread is allowed to continue to execute. This process continues until the end of the region originally reserved for the thread's stack is reached. In this way, we're able to ensure that the address area used by the thread stack is contiguous, but we don't use physical storage until we absolutely have to.

As I've mentioned, the allocation granularity on 32-bit Windows is 64K. You should always reserve memory in allocation granularity–sized chunks because the unreserved address space that's left when you reserve only part of a 64K region is inaccessible to user mode allocation requests. Given that the starting address of each reservation request you make is rounded down to the nearest allocation boundary, there's no way for an application to force Windows to reserve the orphaned address space. Over time, this can lead to the process running out of address space even if there's plenty of physical storage available, which can cause catastrophic problems for an application. For example, getting down to less than 1MB of contiguous address space will prevent most applications from creating new threads since the default thread stack size is 1MB. (For SQL Server, the default thread stack size has been reduced to .5MB, but it is still quite possible to exhaust the virtual memory address space to the point that new worker threads cannot be created.)

Even though Windows requires user mode allocation requests to begin on an allocation granularity boundary, kernel mode allocations are not thus restricted. It's common and normal for system allocations such as the region that stores a process's PEB and TEBs to begin on a non-64K boundary.

Committing Memory

You must commit virtual memory before you can use it. Attempting to access memory that has only been reserved will cause an access violation. Committing a region of virtual memory is as simple as calling VirtualAlloc with the MEM_COMMIT flag. You can commit at the same time you reserve, or you can use a separate call to VirtualAlloc. If you want to reserve and commit simultaneously, you use a bitwise OR operator to combine the MEM_RESERVE and MEM_COMMIT flags, like this:

```
pBuf=(Buf *)VirtualAlloc(NULL, 65536, MEM_RESERVE|MEM_COMMIT,
    PAGE_READWRITE);
```

If you commit the pages in a reserved region in a separate operation, you're not required to commit all of them at once. You can select individual pages within the region to commit. This allows you to easily set up sparsely populated data structures that combine the benefits of contiguous address blocks with the efficiency of allocating physical storage only when needed. SQL Server's buffer pool is a good example of this type of sparse data structure. It is reserved in its entirety at process startup, and individual pages are committed within it as needed.

The size of any commit request you issue will be rounded up to the nearest page boundary. For example, if you attempt to commit a 10K region, your request will be rounded up to 12K. Here's an example of a virtual memory commit request.

```
//Begin by reserving a 64K buffer
pBuf=(Buf *)VirtualAlloc(NULL, 65536, MEM_RESERVE,
    PAGE_READWRITE);



...



//Commit the second page of the previously reserved buffer
VirtualAlloc((void *)(pBuf+4096), 4096, MEM_COMMIT,
    PAGE_READWRITE);
```

Initializing and Modifying Pages

If a committed page is private and has never been accessed, it is created the first time it's accessed as a zero-initialized page (also known as a demand zero page). This means that each virtual memory page starts out filled with zeros.

Windows automatically writes a private committed page that has been modified to disk as demands on system memory resources require. Windows writes committed pages to disk through the normal modified page writing process, which moves pages from the system working set to the modified list and then to disk. You can cause mapped file pages to be written immediately to disk by calling the Win32 FlushViewOfFile API function. Of course,

Windows will automatically reload a page from disk into physical memory as necessary.

If you've modified a page but want Windows to treat it as though it was not modified so that it will not be paged to disk when system memory demands dictate, you can call VirtualAlloc with the MEM_RESET flag. This tells Windows that you don't want the data on the page preserved if the system determines that it needs the physical memory the page occupies to satisfy other memory requests. If you reset the contents of a page currently in the system paging file, the page will be discarded. If the page is in physical memory, it will be marked as not modified so that the system can simply overwrite it if it needs that particular memory page. The next time the page is accessed, it will be filled with zeros, as it was when it was first accessed. Properly structured, your code can use the knowledge that a page is zeroed when reset to detect when it needs to reload the data for the page.

Resetting unneeded pages can improve application performance because it alleviates the need to write modified pages to the system paging file unnecessarily. Of course, you could also just decommit the page or pages, which would have the same effect. By resetting rather than decommitting you avoid the overhead associated with committing a new page. The page remains committed but is zero-filled on your next access.

Note that VirtualAlloc rounds the base address and allocation size differently when you pass the MEM_RESET flag. Normally, it rounds the base address down to the nearest page or allocation granularity boundary and rounds the allocation size up to the nearest integral number of pages. However, when you pass MEM_RESET into VirtualAlloc, it rounds the base address up to the nearest page boundary and rounds the allocation size down to the nearest page boundary. This is done in order to keep you from resetting a page by accident. If you want to reset a page, it must be completely encompassed within the region you supply to VirtualAlloc—pages not wholly contained within the region will not be reset.

Freeing Memory

Committed pages are either private (not shareable) or mapped to shared memory. Once a page has been committed, an application is free to access it. It can call VirtualProtect to change the protection attributes on the page, VirtualLock to lock the page in physical memory, and VirtualFree to release the page.

You can call VirtualFree to release the storage that's been committed for an address block without releasing its reservation. This is called decommitting. When you decommit, you can specify how much of the committed region to free up. You can also free up the address range associated with an allocation. This is called releasing. When you release a block of virtual memory addresses, you may not specify how much of the region to release—either the entire region is released or none of it is. Here are some examples.

```
//Begin by reserving a 64K buffer
pBuf=(Buf *)VirtualAlloc(NULL, 65536, MEM_RESERVE,
    PAGE_READWRITE);
```

...

```
//Commit the second page of the previously reserved buffer
VirtualAlloc((void *)(pBuf+4096), 4096, MEM_COMMIT,
    PAGE_READWRITE);
```

...

```
//Decommit the page just committed
VirtualFree((void *)(pBuf+4096), 4096, MEM_DECOMMIT);
```

...

```
//Release the entirety of the previous reservation
VirtualFree((void *)(pBuf),0,MEM_RELEASE);
```

When you decommit a region of memory, you can do so without having to be concerned about which pages within the region are actually committed versus only reserved. Decommitting an uncommitted page does not raise an error.

Locking Pages in Memory

By default, a process is limited to locking a maximum of 30 pages in memory. If an app wants to lock more pages than this in physical memory, it must first call the SetWorkingSetSize API in order to increase the size of the process's working set. This is the API that SQL Server calls when you enable the set working set size advanced configuration option. An app calls VirtualUnlock to unlock a page that has been locked in physical memory.

Note that pages locked into physical memory using VirtualLock can still be paged to disk in some circumstances. If all the threads in a process are in a wait state, Windows is free to prune such pages from the system working set, which would ultimately result in their being written to disk if they have been modified.

In this next exercise, you'll explore what transpires when an application re-serves virtual memory. You'll learn about the way in which VirtualAlloc rounds allocation requests to page boundaries, and you'll see how the system alloca-tion granularity affects virtual memory reservations.

Exercise 4.5   Exploring the Process of Reserving Virtual Memory

1. Copy the vm_reserve project from the CH04\vm_reserve subfolder on the book's CD to your local hard drive and load it into the VC++ devel-opment environment. Alternatively, you can copy the executable from the Release subfolder and run it separately if you aren't interested in building it from VC++.

2. Let's begin by looking at the source code for vm_reserve (Listing 4.5).

Listing 4.5 A Simple App That Reserves a Region of Memory

```
int main(int argc, char* argv[])
{

   void *pv=VirtualAlloc(
      (void *)0x7FF01000,
      4096,
      MEM_RESERVE,
      PAGE_READWRITE);

   if (pv)  {
      MEMORY_BASIC_INFORMATION mbi;
      DWORD dwLen=sizeof(MEMORY_BASIC_INFORMATION);

   VirtualQueryEx(GetCurrentProcess(),pv,&mbi,dwLen);
      printf("%d bytes reserved at 0x%08X.\n",
         mbi.RegionSize,pv);
   }
   else printf("Error reserving mem %d.\n",
      GetLastError());

   return 0;
}
```

3. This app begins by calling VirtualAlloc to reserve a 4K buffer at a particular memory address. The notion of reserving or committing memory at a specific address is foreign to most new Windows developers but is something Win32 has always supported. If the address requested is not on a page boundary (4K on x86) or is not on an allocation granularity boundary (64K on 32-bit Windows), the system will round the address as necessary to make sure it is properly aligned.

4. The app next calls VirtualQueryEx to retrieve the size of the newly reserved region, which it then displays. We use VirtualQueryEx rather than VirtualQuery because there are situations where VirtualQuery can return inaccurate information on systems with huge amounts of memory.

5. Run the app and compare its output to the original VirtualAlloc request. Two elements in the output should stand out. Your output should look something like the following:

```
8192 bytes reserved at 0x7FF00000.
```

6. First, notice that we reserved 8192 bytes rather than 4096. Why is that? It's because the starting address and allocation size we specified caused the reservation to span two pages in the virtual memory address space. As I mentioned earlier, if you specify a starting address for a reservation, it is always rounded down to the nearest allocation granularity boundary. If the size of the reservation causes it to span a page, the reservation is rounded up to the next page boundary. Hence, in this case, we end up reserving two pages instead of one.

7. Second, notice the starting address of the reservation. It differs from the one we specified. As I've mentioned, the Windows memory manager will round down a specified starting address so that it properly aligns with the system page size and allocation granularity. Since this is a reservation, the starting address is rounded down to the nearest allocation granularity. If this were instead a commit request, it would be rounded down to the nearest page boundary.

8. Last, take note of the region size returned by VirtualQueryEx. Even though the system allocation granularity is 64K, we reserve only 8K. This means that the remaining virtual memory addresses between the end of the reservation and the next allocation granularity boundary (the 56K of address space between 0x7FF02000 and 0x7FF0FFFF) are wasted. They're not accessible because any attempted reservation within this area will be rounded down to start at 0x7FF00000. As a rule, you should never reserve less than 64K of virtual memory space. Doing so wastes address space without really providing any upside. It doesn't conserve memory because you're not actually allocating memory when you reserve it—you're merely flagging a range of addresses as in use by the application. You can always commit individual pages

within a reserved range, so it's not as though reserving 64K means you have to also commit 64K worth of physical storage. And keep in mind that if you run a process out of address space (regardless of the amount of available physical storage), your app will likely go down in flames—any new reservation request for your process (including system-initiated reservations, such as one to reserve a new thread stack) will fail.

In this next exercise, you'll walk through the process of reserving a region of memory, then committing and releasing individual pages within that region. After each step, we'll print out the status of each page in the region to verify that what we think is happening actually is.

Exercise 4.6   Reserving, Committing, and Releasing Virtual Memory

1. Copy the vm_release sample project from the CH04\vm_release subfolder on the book's CD to your hard drive, and load it into the VC++ development environment. Then compile and run it. Alternatively, you can copy the executable from the Release subfolder and run it outside Visual Studio if you are not interested in compiling it first.

2. The app begins by allocating a 64K region of address space. It then commits the second page in this space. It then decommits this page and finishes up by releasing the entire 64K region.

3. At each step, we call a routine named DumpRegionMemoryStatus that iterates through the pages in a region and lists the status—reserved, committed, or free—of each one. Listing 4.6 shows the source code for vm_release.

Listing 4.6 A Sample App That Takes Virtual Memory through Its Paces

```
// vm_release.cpp : Reserve, commit, decommit, and release
// sample app.
//

#include "stdafx.h"
#include "conio.h"
#include "windows.h"

void DumpRegionMemoryStatus(char *szMsg, char * pV, DWORD
    dwRegionSize)
{
```

```
  //Display title message
  printf("\n%s\n",szMsg);

  //Get system page size
  SYSTEM_INFO si;
  GetSystemInfo(&si);

  MEMORY_BASIC_INFORMATION mbi;
  DWORD dwLen=sizeof(mbi);

  char * pCur=pV;
  while ((DWORD)pCur < ((DWORD)pV + dwRegionSize)) {
    VirtualQueryEx(GetCurrentProcess(),pCur,&mbi,dwLen);

    printf("Page at 0x%08x is %s\n",pCur,
      MEM_COMMIT==mbi.State?"Committed":
      MEM_RESERVE==mbi.State?"Reserved":"Free");
    pCur+=si.dwPageSize;
  }
}

#define REGIONSIZE 65536

int main(int argc, char* argv[])
{

  char *pv=(char *)VirtualAlloc((void *)0x7FF00000,
                                REGIONSIZE,
                                MEM_RESERVE,
                                PAGE_READWRITE);

  if (pv)  {
    DumpRegionMemoryStatus("Memory status after reserving the
        region",pv,REGIONSIZE);

    VirtualAlloc((void *)(pv+4096),4096,
        MEM_COMMIT,PAGE_READWRITE);
    DumpRegionMemoryStatus("Memory status after committing a
        page",pv,REGIONSIZE);

    VirtualFree((void *)(pv+4096),4096,MEM_DECOMMIT);
    DumpRegionMemoryStatus("Memory status after decommitting a
        page",pv,REGIONSIZE);
```

```
      VirtualFree((void *)pv,0,MEM_RELEASE);
      DumpRegionMemoryStatus("Memory status after releasing the
          region",pv,REGIONSIZE);
  }
  else printf("Error reserving mem %d.\n",GetLastError());

  return 0;
}
```

4. Run the app and study the output. Your output should look something like this:

```
Memory status after reserving the region
Page at 0x7ff00000 is Reserved
Page at 0x7ff01000 is Reserved
Page at 0x7ff02000 is Reserved
Page at 0x7ff03000 is Reserved
Page at 0x7ff04000 is Reserved
Page at 0x7ff05000 is Reserved
Page at 0x7ff06000 is Reserved
Page at 0x7ff07000 is Reserved
Page at 0x7ff08000 is Reserved
Page at 0x7ff09000 is Reserved
Page at 0x7ff0a000 is Reserved
Page at 0x7ff0b000 is Reserved
Page at 0x7ff0c000 is Reserved
Page at 0x7ff0d000 is Reserved
Page at 0x7ff0e000 is Reserved
Page at 0x7ff0f000 is Reserved

Memory status after committing a page
Page at 0x7ff00000 is Reserved
Page at 0x7ff01000 is Committed
Page at 0x7ff02000 is Reserved
Page at 0x7ff03000 is Reserved
Page at 0x7ff04000 is Reserved
Page at 0x7ff05000 is Reserved
Page at 0x7ff06000 is Reserved
Page at 0x7ff07000 is Reserved
Page at 0x7ff08000 is Reserved
Page at 0x7ff09000 is Reserved
```

```
Page at 0x7ff0a000 is Reserved
Page at 0x7ff0b000 is Reserved
Page at 0x7ff0c000 is Reserved
Page at 0x7ff0d000 is Reserved
Page at 0x7ff0e000 is Reserved
Page at 0x7ff0f000 is Reserved

Memory status after decommitting a page
Page at 0x7ff00000 is Reserved
Page at 0x7ff01000 is Reserved
Page at 0x7ff02000 is Reserved
Page at 0x7ff03000 is Reserved
Page at 0x7ff04000 is Reserved
Page at 0x7ff05000 is Reserved
Page at 0x7ff06000 is Reserved
Page at 0x7ff07000 is Reserved
Page at 0x7ff08000 is Reserved
Page at 0x7ff09000 is Reserved
Page at 0x7ff0a000 is Reserved
Page at 0x7ff0b000 is Reserved
Page at 0x7ff0c000 is Reserved
Page at 0x7ff0d000 is Reserved
Page at 0x7ff0e000 is Reserved
Page at 0x7ff0f000 is Reserved

Memory status after releasing the region
Page at 0x7ff00000 is Free
Page at 0x7ff01000 is Free
Page at 0x7ff02000 is Free
Page at 0x7ff03000 is Free
Page at 0x7ff04000 is Free
Page at 0x7ff05000 is Free
Page at 0x7ff06000 is Free
Page at 0x7ff07000 is Free
Page at 0x7ff08000 is Free
Page at 0x7ff09000 is Free
Page at 0x7ff0a000 is Free
Page at 0x7ff0b000 is Free
Page at 0x7ff0c000 is Free
Page at 0x7ff0d000 is Free
Page at 0x7ff0e000 is Free
Page at 0x7ff0f000 is Free
```

As you can see, committing an individual page within a reserved region is fairly trivial. Decommitting is equally simple, as is releasing the entire region.

In this next exercise, you'll learn how the PAGE_GUARD page protection attribute works. You'll allocate a memory buffer that's initially guarded, then turn off the guard attribute for one of its pages by attempting to lock it in memory.

Exercise 4.7   Guarding Memory with the PAGE_GUARD Attribute

1. Let's start with the source code to vm_guard, the sample app we'll use to investigate how PAGE_GUARD works. Take a quick look at the code in Listing 4.7 and see whether you can understand how it works on first glance. I'll go through it step-by-step in just a moment.

Listing 4.7 A PAGE_GUARD Sample App

```
// vm_guard.cpp : Example that demonstrates how PAGE_GUARD works.
//

#include "stdafx.h"
#include "conio.h"
#include "windows.h"

#define REGIONSIZE 65536

int main(int argc, char* argv[])
{

  char *pv=(char *)VirtualAlloc(NULL,
                    REGIONSIZE,
                    MEM_RESERVE | MEM_COMMIT,
                    PAGE_READWRITE | PAGE_GUARD);

  if (pv)  {

    //Attempt to lock a page — will fail because of PAGE_GUARD
      bool bLocked=VirtualLock((void *)pv,4096);
      if (!bLocked) {
        printf("First VirtualLock failed for 0x%08X, Last error =
            0x%08X\n", pv, GetLastError());
      } else printf("First VirtualLock succeeded for 0x%08X\n",
                pv);
```

```
      //Retry page lock — will succeed since PAGE_GUARD was reset
      bLocked=VirtualLock((void *)pv,4096);
      if (!bLocked) {
        printf("Second VirtualLock failed for 0x%08X, Last error
        = 0x%08X\n", pv, GetLastError());
      } else printf("Second VirtualLock succeeded for 0x%08X\n",
                    pv);

      VirtualFree((void *)pv,0,MEM_RELEASE);
  }
  else printf("Error reserving/committing memory.  Last error=
            %d.\n",GetLastError());

  return 0;
}
```

2. Load this code from the CH04\vm_guard subfolder on the CD and compile and run it. Your output should look like this:

```
First VirtualLock failed for 0x00440000, Last error = 0x80000001
Second VirtualLock succeeded for 0x00440000
```

3. This code begins by allocating a virtual memory block that it protects
   with the PAGE_GUARD attribute. The entirety of the block is off limits to
   access because of PAGE_GUARD.
4. It then attempts to lock the first page of the block into physical memory
   using VirtualLock. (I've hard-coded the page size for simplicity's sake;
   you should always use GetSystemInfo to retrieve the system page size
   at runtime in your own code.)
5. This first VirtualLock call has two results: it fails, and it resets the
   PAGE_GUARD attribute for the first page in the region.
6. You'll note that the GetLastError output from the failed call is
   0x80000001, which is equivalent to the
   STATUS_GUARD_PAGE_VIOLATION return code I mentioned earlier in
   the chapter.
7. Because it resets the PAGE_GUARD status for the first page of the region, the second attempt to lock this page succeeds. This is how
   PAGE_GUARD works: You get a one-shot failure mechanism that can
   help you detect invalid page accesses.

NOTE: Note that VirtualQuery(Ex) always reports the page protection attributes of a page as it was *originally* allocated—neither changes made with VirtualProtect nor those made as a result of the PAGE_GUARD attribute being reset are reflected in the output from VirtualQuery(Ex). I was surprised when I initially discovered this, but it *is* consistent with the Platform SDK documentation.

Another interesting use of VirtualQuery is in inspecting SQL Server's memory. Because you can create and run extended procedures, you have the ability to load a DLL within the SQL Server process space and run the code it contains as though it were part of SQL Server itself. You can use this ability to inspect various internal structures within the server, including the server's own memory allocations. In this next exercise, we'll build an extended procedure that details SQL Server's virtual memory allocations.

Exercise 4.8   Inspecting SQL Server Memory Allocations with VirtualQuery

Let's begin with the source code to the xproc. Based on what you've learned thus far about virtual memory, take a quick look through the code in Listing 4.8 and see if you can figure out how it works. I'll go through it step-by-step in just a moment.

Listing 4.8 The Source Code for xp_vmquery

```
#include <stdafx.h>

#define XP_NOERROR          0
#define XP_ERROR            1
#define MAXADDRLEN          12
#define MAXSIZELEN          12
#define MAXPROTLEN          128
#define MAXSTATELEN         20
#define MAXTYPELEN          20


#ifdef __cplusplus
extern "C" {
#endif

RETCODE __declspec(dllexport) xp_vmquery(SRV_PROC *srvproc);
```

```
#ifdef __cplusplus
}
#endif

RETCODE __declspec(dllexport) xp_vmquery(SRV_PROC *srvproc)
{

  bool bByPage=false;
  DWORD dwParams=srv_rpcparams(srvproc);

  if (1==dwParams) {

    BYTE bType;
    ULONG cbMaxLen;
    ULONG cbActualLen;
    char szByPage[2];
    BOOL fNull;

    srv_paraminfo(srvproc, 1, &bType, &cbMaxLen, &cbActualLen,
        (BYTE *)&szByPage, &fNull);

    //Enable Page mode if "P" passed in
    bByPage=(!stricmp("P",szByPage));
  }

  //Set up the column names
  char szColName[129];

    wsprintf(szColName, "Address");
    srv_describe(srvproc, 1, szColName, SRV_NULLTERM, SRVCHAR,
        MAXADDRLEN, SRVCHAR, 0, NULL);

    wsprintf(szColName, "Size");
    srv_describe(srvproc, 2, szColName, SRV_NULLTERM, SRVCHAR,
        MAXSIZELEN, SRVCHAR, 0, NULL);

    wsprintf(szColName, "Protection");
    srv_describe(srvproc, 3, szColName, SRV_NULLTERM, SRVCHAR,
        MAXPROTLEN, SRVCHAR, 0, NULL);

    wsprintf(szColName, "State");
    srv_describe(srvproc, 4, szColName, SRV_NULLTERM, SRVCHAR,
        MAXSTATELEN, SRVCHAR, 0, NULL);
```

```
    wsprintf(szColName, "Type");
    srv_describe(srvproc, 5, szColName, SRV_NULLTERM, SRVCHAR,
        MAXTYPELEN, SRVCHAR, 0, NULL);

//Get user mode address info
SYSTEM_INFO si;
GetSystemInfo(&si);
char * pszStart=(char *)si.lpMinimumApplicationAddress;

char szProt[256];
char szState[256];
char szType[256];
char szBase[12];
char szSize[12];

//Set the column data bindings
srv_setcoldata(srvproc, 1, szBase);
srv_setcoldata(srvproc, 2, szSize);
srv_setcoldata(srvproc, 3, szProt);
srv_setcoldata(srvproc, 4, szState);
srv_setcoldata(srvproc, 5, szType);

MEMORY_BASIC_INFORMATION mbi;
int i=0;
while ((pszStart) &&
    (pszStart<si.lpMaximumApplicationAddress)) {

  //Get info for the current memory block
  VirtualQuery(pszStart,&mbi,sizeof(mbi));

  //Set up the Address column
  wsprintf(szBase,"0x%lp",mbi.BaseAddress);

  //Set up the Size column
  wsprintf(szSize,"%010d",mbi.RegionSize);

  //Set up the Protection column
  szProt[0]='\0';
  if (mbi.Protect & PAGE_READONLY) strcat(szProt,"READONLY ");
  if (mbi.Protect & PAGE_READWRITE) strcat(szProt,"READWRITE ");
  if (mbi.Protect & PAGE_WRITECOPY) strcat(szProt,"WRITECOPY ");
  if (mbi.Protect & PAGE_EXECUTE) strcat(szProt,"EXECUTE ");
  if (mbi.Protect & PAGE_EXECUTE_READ)
    strcat(szProt,"EXECUTE_READ ");
```

```
if (mbi.Protect & PAGE_EXECUTE_READWRITE)
  strcat(szProt,"EXECUTE_READWRITE ");
if (mbi.Protect & PAGE_EXECUTE_WRITECOPY)
  strcat(szProt,"EXECUTE_WRITECOPY ");
if (mbi.Protect & PAGE_GUARD) strcat(szProt,"GUARD ");
if (mbi.Protect & PAGE_NOACCESS) strcat(szProt,"NOACCESS ");
if (mbi.Protect & PAGE_NOCACHE) strcat(szProt,"NOCACHE ");

//Get rid of trailing space
if (szProt[0]) szProt[strlen(szProt)-1]='\0';
else strcpy(szProt,"UNKNOWN");

//Set up the State column
szState[0]='\0';
if (mbi.State & MEM_FREE) strcat(szState, "Free ");
else {
  if (mbi.State & MEM_RESERVE) strcat(szState, "Reserved ");
  if (mbi.State & MEM_COMMIT) strcat(szState, "Commit ");
}

//Get rid of trailing space
if (szState[0]) szState[strlen(szState)-1]='\0';

//Set up the Type column
szType[0]='\0';
if (mbi.Type & MEM_IMAGE) strcat(szType,"Image ");
else if (mbi.Type & MEM_MAPPED) strcat(szType,"Mapped ");
else if (mbi.Type & MEM_PRIVATE) strcat(szType,"Private ");

if (szType[0]) szType[strlen(szType)-1]='\0';
else strcpy(szType,"Unknown");

//Set current column lengths
srv_setcollen(srvproc, 1, strlen(szBase));
srv_setcollen(srvproc, 2, strlen(szSize));
srv_setcollen(srvproc, 3, strlen(szProt));
srv_setcollen(srvproc, 4, strlen(szState));
srv_setcollen(srvproc, 5, strlen(szType));

//Send the row to the client
  srv_sendrow(srvproc);
i++;

//Move to the next page or region
```

```
    if (bByPage) pszStart+=si.dwPageSize;
    else pszStart+=mbi.RegionSize;
  }


    return XP_NOERROR ;
}
```

1. Copy the binary for this xproc from CH04\xp_vmquery on the CD to the binn folder under your SQL Server installation.
2. Install it into the master database by running this command in Query Analyzer:

```
sp_addextendedproc 'xp_vmquery','xp_vmquery.dll'
```

3. Run it from Query Analyzer like this:

```
xp_vmquery
```

4. You should see output like this:

Address	Size	Protection	State	Type
0x00010000	0000004096	READWRITE	Committed	Private
0x00011000	0000061440	NOACCESS	Free	Unknown
0x00020000	0000004096	READWRITE	Committed	Private
0x00021000	0000061440	NOACCESS	Free	Unknown
0x00030000	0000454656	UNKNOWN	Reserved	Private
0x0009F000	0000004096	READWRITE GUARD	Committed	Private
0x000A0000	0000065536	READWRITE	Committed	Private
0x000B0000	0000282624	READWRITE	Committed	Private
0x000F5000	0000061440	UNKNOWN	Reserved	Private
0x00104000	0000004096	READWRITE	Committed	Private
0x00105000	0000700416	UNKNOWN	Reserved	Private
0x001B0000	0000004096	READWRITE	Committed	Mapped
0x001B1000	0000061440	UNKNOWN	Reserved	Mapped
0x001C0000	0000090112	READONLY	Committed	Mapped
0x001D6000	0000040960	NOACCESS	Free	Unknown
0x001E0000	0000192512	READONLY	Committed	Mapped
0x0020F000	0000004096	NOACCESS	Free	Unknown

5. As with the vm_release example, this extended procedure uses Virtual-Query to walk through the SQL Server process space and report on each region of allocated memory. Using this procedure, you can quickly

tally up how much reserved versus committed memory is allocated within the process and how much virtual memory remains unused (free). You can tell which pages are private pages (normal allocations), image pages (those belonging to EXEs and DLLs), and mapped pages (pages from memory-mapped files).

6. Use OSQL to run xp_vmquery with its 'P' option (page mode) in order to view the allocation information for every page in the SQL Server process (as opposed to each region, as in step 4). I suggest you run this via OSQL in order to avoid running out of virtual memory in Query Analyzer as xp_vmquery will return hundreds of thousands of rows when executed in page mode.

Virtual Memory Recap

Windows' virtual memory management is among its more powerful facilities. By providing a vast process address space that can be committed to physical storage in piecemeal fashion, the operating system provides applications with the simplicity of contiguous addressing combined with the efficiency and paucity of sparse resource consumption.

Every page in virtual memory is in one of three states: reserved, committed, or free. An application can allocate specific pages in memory or can allow Windows to choose the precise location of the pages allocated to fulfill an allocation request.

An application can reserve and commit memory as separate operations or simultaneously, and it can commit individual reserved pages. Pages within a reservation can and frequently do have different protection attributes. These protection attributes can be assigned during the reservation or commit operation or by calling VirtualProtect after the fact.

VirtualFree can be used to decommit committed pages as well as to release reserved pages. VirtualLock can be used to lock pages in physical memory; VirtualUnlock can be used to unlock them.

The physical storage behind virtual memory is often the system paging file, though, of course, some pages will be backed by physical memory. Virtual memory can also be backed by a file on disk. Windows uses this ability to share an application's executable code between multiple instances of it. The physical storage behind the virtual memory set aside in each process to store the application's code and data is the EXE or DLL file itself. When an application attempts to change one of its data pages, Windows' copy-on-write facility makes a copy of the page and instructs the modifying process to use it instead of the original. This way, multiple instances share as many pages as possible of the underlying executable's code and data as long as possible.

Virtual Memory Knowledge Measure

1. True or false: Even if I reserve only a 32K virtual memory address range, Windows still reserves a 64K range because of the system allocation granularity.

2. What page protection attribute does Windows use to mark the end of the committed range of a thread stack?

3. True or false: Even though a page has been locked in physical memory via a call to VirtualLock, it can still be paged to disk if memory demands dictate.

4. What happens when a process attempts to modify a page that has been flagged with the PAGE_WRITECOPY protection attribute?

5. True or false: SQL Server makes the majority of its memory allocations via the system heap.

6. What is SQL Server's default thread stack size?

7. Is it possible to reserve and commit memory in a single call to VirtualAlloc, or must an application make separate calls to reserve and commit memory?

8. True or false: All virtual memory requests—regardless of whether they are user mode or kernel mode requests—are subject to the system allocation granularity.

9. What type of application most typically uses the PAGE_WRITECOMBINE page protection attribute?

10. True or false: An application can use the PAGE_EXECUTE_WRITECOPY protection attribute to implement Windows' write copy functionality for committed pages in the user mode address space.

11. What Win32 API function is used to release a reserved region of virtual memory addresses?

12. True or false: The PAGE_EXECUTE and PAGE_READONLY attributes are functionally equivalent on x86 processors.

13. True or false: An application can specify the size of a virtual memory allocation but not the exact location—the Windows memory manager decides the precise memory location of an allocation.

14. What flag can you pass into VirtualAlloc to tell it to reset a region of committed memory in order to prevent that memory from being swapped to disk if memory demands dictate?

15. True or false: You call the VirtualReserve function to reserve a region of virtual memory addresses that you do not yet wish to commit.

16. True or false: The VirtualRelease function can release a region of reserved virtual memory without first decommitting it.

17. What VC++ linker switch can an application developer use to adjust the default stack size?

18. True or false: You can cause mapped file pages to be written immediately to disk by calling the Win32 FlushViewOfFile API function.

19. True or false: Attempting to access a page with the PAGE_GUARD protection attribute causes a STATUS_GUARD_PAGE exception to be raised and resets the guard page protection.

20. True or false: Virtual memory that has been decommitted is still reserved until you release it.

21. What Windows API function does SQL Server call when the set working set size option has been enabled?

22. Is it possible to alter the amount of virtual memory reserved for a new thread's stack via the call to CreateThread?

23. By default, how many virtual memory pages can a process lock in physical memory?

24. True or false: The VirtualDecommit API function can be used to decommit previously committed virtual memory pages that span allocation granularity boundaries.

25. True or false: When committing a region of reserved memory, Windows will round the commit request to the nearest allocation granularity boundary.

Heaps

A heap is a memory region consisting of one or more pages of reserved space that can be suballocated into smaller pieces by the heap manager. Heaps are most useful for allocating large numbers of similarly sized, relatively small objects and structures. You should not use heaps for blocks of 1MB or more; use VirtualAlloc and company for large allocations such as this.

On the plus side, heaps allow you to ignore the system's allocation granularity and page size boundaries. On the negative side, heaps are a bit slower to access and don't provide the same level of control that the virtual memory APIs do. For example, you can't reserve a heap region without also committing it—VirtualAlloc is the only Win32 allocation function that separates these two functions.

The exact algorithms used by the heap manager to commit and decommit physical storage for heaps are undocumented and have changed between releases of Windows. If you need precise information about and/or control over the process the heap manager uses to manage the physical storage behind heaps, don't use heaps in the first place—use virtual memory instead.

Key Heap Terms and Concepts

✔ *Default heap*—the built-in heap that Windows provides every process by default. The default process heap has a base size of 1MB, but this can be changed via a linker switch.

✔ *Private (or custom) heap*—a heap created by a process for its own private use that is separate from the default process heap.

✔ *Heap serialization*—the facility whereby the Windows heap manager ensures that multiple threads do not corrupt a heap through simultaneous access.

Key Heap APIs

Table 4.8 Key Heap-Related API Functions

Function	Description
HeapCreate	Creates a private heap
HeapAlloc	Allocates memory from a heap
HeapFree	Frees a block of memory allocated from a heap
HeapDestroy	Destroys (releases) a private heap
GetProcessHeap	Returns a handle to a process's default heap

The Default Heap

Windows provides every process with a default heap. Applications use the default heap to service allocation facilities such as malloc and the C++ **new** operator. Several Win32 API functions also make use of the default heap, including the old 16-bit LocalAlloc and GlobalAlloc functions.

A process's heap is 1MB in size by default but can be changed via the /HEAP linker switch (in Visual C++; most other compilers provide a similar option) or with utilities that can edit an executable's file header. This small size is why heaps aren't ideal for large allocations. You should leave those to virtual memory.

By default, Windows serializes access to the process heap. This means that only one thread at a time can access the default heap. This prevents multithreaded heap synchronization errors and protects the heap from corruption. Note that you can disable this synchronization for individual allocations from the heap, but this is not generally recommended.

You cannot destroy the default process heap with a call to HeapDestroy. If you pass the handle of the default heap into HeapDestroy, the system ignores the call. If you want to limit the physical size of the default heap, use the /HEAP linker option.

Allocating Heap Memory

You use the HeapAlloc and HeapFree routines to allocate and deallocate memory from a heap. Both of these functions require a handle to the heap from which you want to allocate or deallocate memory. This handle can be one returned either from a call to HeapCreate or from the GetProcessHeap function (if you want to work with memory from the default heap).

In order to allocate memory from a heap, HeapAlloc must perform the following steps.

1. Scan the linked list of allocated and freed blocks for the first free block that is large enough to satisfy the request.
2. Allocate the block by marking the free block as allocated.
3. Add the new block to the linked list managed by the heap manager.

HeapAlloc supports three flags: HEAP_ZERO_MEMORY, HEAP_GENERATE_EXCEPTIONS, and HEAP_NO_SERIALIZE. You can combine these by using a bitwise OR operator to pass them into HeapAlloc's second parameter.

As its name suggests, the HEAP_ZERO_MEMORY flag causes each block of allocated memory to be zero-filled just as virtual memory pages are zero-filled on their first access. This can be handy for tracking down uninitialized buffer errors.

HEAP_GENERATE_EXCEPTIONS causes HeapAlloc to throw exceptions when an error occurs rather than return NULL. When this happens, one of two exceptions will be raised: STATUS_NO_MEMORY (indicating an out-of-memory condition) or STATUS_ACCESS_VIOLATION, indicating heap corruption or improper function parameters.

HEAP_NO_SERIALIZE disables any thread synchronization that would normally occur when accessing the heap. As I mentioned, the default system heap is always created with serialization enabled by default. You can also create custom heaps with serialization enabled. You can disable this serialization for a specific allocation by passing HEAP_NO_SERIALIZE into HeapAlloc.

HeapRealloc allows a block to be resized. If you are suballocating your block, be careful with this because increasing the size of a block can cause it to be moved within the heap. If a block moves, any pointers that reference it would obviously need to be changed as well. You can keep the block from moving by passing in the HEAP_REALLOC_IN_PLACE_ONLY flag. This causes the reallocation to fail if the block needs to grow in size and would need to be moved in order to do so.

Custom Heaps

An application can create a custom heap by calling the HeapCreate function. There are several good reasons for creating your own custom heap, including the following.

- Component isolation—by placing components in their own heap, you prevent errant modifications to one component from corrupting other components.
- Efficient memory management—by allocating your own heap, you can size it so that it stores a given number of evenly sized objects as efficiently as possible.
- Proximity allocations—by allocating things close to each other, you lower the possibility that the system will thrash when iterating through a list of memory objects.
- Avoidance of the overhead of thread synchronization—if you know that you do not need thread synchronization (e.g., your app is single threaded), you can do away with the overhead of synchronizing heap access by creating your own heap.
- Fast and easy deallocation—regardless of the number of individual allocations you've made from a custom heap using HeapAlloc, you can free all of them at once by destroying the heap through a call to HeapDestroy.

When you create a custom heap, you can specify the HEAP_NO_SERIALIZE or HEAP_GENERATE_EXCEPTIONS flags or a combination of the two. As I mentioned earlier, HEAP_NO_SERIALIZE disables serialized access to the heap. Thread serialization is enabled by default. I'll cover this more below, but, generally speaking, you should not use this option unless you're absolutely sure you do not need thread synchronization when accessing your heap.

Also, as with HeapAlloc, passing the HEAP_GENERATE_EXCEPTIONS flag into HeapCreate causes the system to throw an exception when an attempt to allocate (or reallocate) a heap memory block fails. Normally, a failed allocation results in the return of a NULL pointer. You can use this flag to tell the heap manager to throw an exception instead.

The second parameter to HeapCreate specifies the number of bytes initially committed to the heap. HeapCreate rounds this up to a multiple of the CPU's page size as necessary.

The third parameter to HeapCreate specifies the heap's maximum size. Specify 0 if you want to create a heap with no fixed size limit.

You can use HeapDestroy to destroy a custom heap. If you fail to destroy a custom heap, it remains in memory until the process terminates.

Heap Serialization

When you create a custom heap, the HEAP_NO_SERIALIZE flag controls whether access to the heap is automatically serialized. When an app has more than one thread accessing a heap whose synchronization has been disabled, multiple threads can simultaneously grab the same memory block, and you have a veritable time bomb waiting to go off at the most inopportune moment. The fact that you've got such a serious bug may not be immediately evident. For example, you may not see a problem until your app is executed on a multiprocessor machine or on a machine with a much faster processor than your development machine. Thread synchronization errors are notoriously difficult to track down because they are almost always timing related. The very act of stepping through your code under a debugger can make them seem to go away.

Potential multithreaded heap synchronization problems include those listed below.

- The heap's linked list of blocks becomes corrupted.
- Multiple threads end up sharing the same memory block.
- One thread might free a block that other threads are still using. These threads then overwrite unallocated memory, which, in turn, corrupts the heap.

Generally speaking, you really shouldn't use HEAP_NO_SERIALIZE unless you're absolutely sure that you don't need heap serialization. Specifically, you shouldn't use it unless one of the following conditions is true.

- Your process is single threaded.
- Your process has multiple threads, but only one of them accesses the heap.
- Your process is multithreaded and multiple threads access the heap, but your app handles serializing their heap access itself.

Exercises

You can override the C++ new and delete operators in order to allocate objects from custom heaps. When a C++ compiler encounters a call to new, it checks to see whether the class has overloaded the new operator. If it has, the compiler generates a call to that function rather than generating code that allocates the object on the default heap. You can use operator overloading to cause new to use any memory allocation facility you choose. The code in the exercise below overloads new and delete to allocate objects on a custom heap.

Exercise 4.9   Overloading New and Delete to Allocate Memory from a Custom Heap

1. Load the code shown in Listing 4.9 from the CH04\heapnew subfolder on the book's CD or type it into the VC++ environment, then compile and run it.

Listing 4.9 Overloading New and Delete to Use a Custom Allocation Facility

```
// heapnew.cpp : Overload new and delete to use a custom heap
//

#include "stdafx.h"
#include "windows.h"


class CMemObj {
public:
  static HANDLE s_hPrivateHeap;
  static DWORD s_dwBlocks;
  void* operator new (size_t size);
  void  operator delete(void *p);
};
```

```
HANDLE CMemObj::s_hPrivateHeap=NULL;
DWORD CMemObj::s_dwBlocks=0;

void* CMemObj::operator new (size_t size) {

  //Create the private heap if it does not exist
  if (NULL==s_hPrivateHeap) {
    s_hPrivateHeap=HeapCreate(HEAP_NO_SERIALIZE,0,0);
    if (NULL==s_hPrivateHeap) return NULL;
  }

  //Allocate the memory
  void* p=HeapAlloc(s_hPrivateHeap,0,size);

  //Increment the block count
  if (p) s_dwBlocks++;
  return p;
}

void CMemObj::operator delete(void *p) {

  //Deallocate the memory
  if (HeapFree(s_hPrivateHeap,0,p)) {

    //Decrement the block count
    s_dwBlocks--;

    //If all blocks have been freed, release the heap
    if (0==s_dwBlocks)
      if (HeapDestroy(s_hPrivateHeap))
        s_hPrivateHeap=NULL;
  }
}

int main(int argc, char* argv[])
{

  //Allocate an object on the private heap
  CMemObj *pMO = new CMemObj();
  printf("Custom heap after first new: %d block(s),
      handle=0x%08x\n",CMemObj::s_dwBlocks,
      CMemObj::s_hPrivateHeap);

  //Allocate a second object on the private heap
```

```
CMemObj *pMO2 = new CMemObj();
printf("Custom heap after second new: %d block(s),
    handle=0x%08x\n",CMemObj::s_dwBlocks,
    CMemObj::s_hPrivateHeap);

//Delete the second object from the heap
delete pMO2;
printf("Custom heap after first delete: %d block(s),
    handle=0x%08x\n",CMemObj::s_dwBlocks,
    CMemObj::s_hPrivateHeap);

//Delete the first object from the heap (this causes the heap
//to be released)
delete pMO;
printf("Custom heap after second delete: %d block(s),
    handle=0x%08x\n",CMemObj::s_dwBlocks,
    CMemObj::s_hPrivateHeap);

return 1;
}
```

2. Run this application and observe its output. Your output should look something like this:

```
Custom heap after first new: 1 block(s), handle=0x00440000
Custom heap after second new: 2 block(s), handle=0x00440000
Custom heap after first delete: 1 block(s), handle=0x00440000
Custom heap after second delete: 0 block(s), handle=0x00000000
```

3. In this code, we automatically allocate and deallocate the private heap as needed. CMemObj uses a static member, s_hPrivateHeap, to store the pointer to our private heap. It's initialized to NULL at program startup. If a call is made to CMemObj's new operator, we check s_hPrivateHeap to see whether it's NULL. If so, we create a new heap using HeapCreate and assign it to s_hPrivateHeap. We then allocate a memory block from s_hPrivateHeap to satisfy the allocation request. If we're successful, we increment another static member, s_dwBlocks, that we use to keep track of the number of blocks allocated in the heap.

4. When CMemObj's delete operator is called, we begin by deallocating the block in question using HeapFree. If successful, we decrement s_dwBlocks to indicate that the heap has one less block allocated within it. If s_dwBlocks reaches 0, we release the heap itself by calling

HeapDestroy. This keeps us from wasting the memory resources required to maintain the heap if it isn't being used. Because we assign NULL to s_hPrivateHeap when we destroy it, we allow for the possibility that another code line might call CMemObj's new operator after we've destroyed the private heap. If that happens, the private heap is simply recreated.

5. You may be wondering why the code uses static members for the private heap handle and the block counter. The reason for this is that we want all instances of CMemObj to share the same private heap. If these members were not declared as static, each CMemObj would get its own private heap—not only wasteful but also illogical. The whole point of the design is to allocate CMemObj instances from a common private heap. Because all the objects will be the same size and are relatively small, this is an efficient and logical use of a heap.

6. You may also be wondering why the code uses a separate member variable to track the number of allocations from the private heap. After all, couldn't we get this same information from the HeapWalk API function without requiring a separate member variable? Yes, we certainly could; however, this would be terribly inefficient. For every allocation or deallocation, we'd have to walk the entirety of the heap and count up the blocks that make it up, being careful to skip those allocations that are for maintenance of the heap itself (the heap's overhead). In an app that made a large number of allocations, this would negatively affect performance and would likely have a detrimental impact on CPU use.

In this next exercise, you'll use an extended procedure to allocate custom heaps within SQL Server. You'll store some data in these heaps, then return it via a query. Because you will be attaching with a debugger, you should work through this exercise only on a test or development machine, and, ideally, you should be its only user.

Exercise 4.10   Allocating Heaps within SQL Server

1. Begin by copying xp_array.dll from the CH04\xp_array\release subfolder on the CD accompanying this book into the binn subfolder under your SQL Server main installation folder.
2. Register the extended procedures contained in xp_array with SQL Server by opening and running xp_array.sql from the CH04\xp_array subfolder on the CD.
3. Attach to SQL Server with WinDbg. When the WinDbg command prompt displays, type !heap to display a list of the heaps currently allocated by the process. You will likely see quite a few entries in this list, perhaps as many as 20 or 30. Take note of the exact number, then type g and hit Enter to allow SQL Server to continue running.

4. Now load arrays.sql from the CD's CH04\xp_array subfolder into Query Analyzer and run it. This will install a number of user-defined functions that make calling the xprocs you've just installed very easy.

5. Next, load leapheap.sql from CH04\xp_array and run it. leapheap.sql will create a heap-based array using the xprocs you installed earlier and will then load into it a couple of columns from the Northwind..Orders table.

6. Return to the debugger and press Ctrl+Break to stop execution, then type !heap at the command prompt to again list the heaps that have been allocated within the SQL Server process. This list should match the one you saw earlier because, by default, the xp_array code makes its allocations from the default process heap—it doesn't create a private heap.

7. Type g and hit Enter to allow SQL Server to continue running.

8. Return to Query Analyzer and edit leapheap.sql, changing

```
SET @hdl=fn_createarray(1000, 0)
```

to

```
SET @hdl=fn_createarray(1000, 1)
```

   This will cause the xp_array code to allocate its own heap when fn_createarray is first called. Note: You should never use this option when calling the xp_array code from multiple connections. Always use the default system heap when there is a possibility that multiple worker threads may call into xp_array simultaneously.

9. Use the mouse to select the entirety of the script text in Query Analyzer up to (but not including) the call to fn_destroyarray, then press F5 to run it. By not including the call to fn_destroyarray in the call to the server, we'll leave the array and its heap in memory for now. Congratulations, you've just created your own private heap within the SQL Server process space!

10. Return to the debugger, press Ctrl+Break, and run !heap again in the command window. You should see that a new heap has shown up in the list.

11. Next, run !heap 0 to list segment information for each heap. A heap can consist of up to 64 separate segments. Each time Windows needs to grow a heap, it will allocate a new segment for it. The last heap in the list—the one you just created—should have just one segment.

12. To verify that this is our heap, let's search for some of its data. The segment information for your new heap should list its starting and ending addresses. It should look something like this:

```
23:    10010000
     Segment at 10010000 to 10020000 (00008000 bytes committed)
```

The numbers set in bold are the segment's starting and ending addresses.

13. Use the starting and ending addresses to search for the entry in the array corresponding to Northwind CustomerId "TOMSP", like this:

```
s -a 10010000 10020000 'TOMSP'
```

The WinDbg s command searches a region of memory for a data value. Its -a parameter tells it to search for an ANSI string. The two memory addresses indicate the beginning and ending of the search range, and, of course, the character string in single quotes specifies the value we want to search for. Once you run this, you should see displayed the memory address at which this value resides in your heap. Though this isn't conclusive, it's a pretty good indication that this is the heap our xprocs used. Type g and press Enter to allow SQL Server to continue to run.

14. Return to Query Analyzer and load leakheaps.sql from the CH04\xp_ array subfolder on the CD and run it. This will cause 128 new heaps to be created within the SQL Server process.

15. Return to WinDbg and press Ctrl+Break to stop the SQL Server process. Run !heap again at the command prompt. You should see your new heaps in the heap list.

There is no functional limit to the number of heaps you can allocate within a process. I can't think of a practical reason to allocate as many as we've allocated in this exercise, but be aware that it is technically possible. When you need to dig into what heaps have been allocated within a process and what they contain, WinDbg's !heap is a good way to start.

16. Type q and press Enter to stop debugging SQL Server, then exit the debugger.

17. Restart SQL Server as necessary.

Heap Recap

A heap is a block of memory that's made up of one or more pages of reserved space that is suballocated by the heap manager. A heap is most useful for allocating similarly sized, relatively small objects and structures. A heap should not be used to allocate blocks of 1MB or more in size; virtual memory functions such as VirtualAlloc should be used instead.

An application can create custom heaps as necessary. One key decision in creating a custom heap is whether to have the heap manager serialize access to the heap. If an app has multiple threads and these threads make their own allocations from the heap, access to it must be serialized in order to prevent the heap from becoming corrupted. If an app is single-threaded or provides its own thread synchronization mechanisms, it may be able to safely disable heap serialization on custom heaps.

Heap Knowledge Measure

1. What Win32 API function allocates a block from a heap?
2. True or false: Before destroying a heap with HeapDestroy, a process should use HeapFree to free any allocations it has made from it.
3. Are allocations from a heap subject to the limitations imposed by the system page size and the system allocation granularity?
4. True or false: An application can improve its performance by omitting the HEAP_NO_SERIALIZE flag when it creates a private heap.
5. True or false: When an application allocates memory from a heap, it can reserve memory without committing it by specifying the correct parameters to HeapAlloc.
6. What is the default size of the default process heap?
7. True or false: Because pointers may already reference a block of heap memory allocated via HeapAlloc, the heap manager will not move a heap block once it has been allocated.
8. What maximum size should you specify to HeapCreate if you want to create a heap that automatically grows as allocations are made from it?
9. What Win32 API function returns a handle to the default process heap?
10. True or false: Several Win32 API functions make use of the default process heap.
11. What flag should you pass into HeapAlloc if you want it to zero-fill a newly allocated page?
12. True or false: If you fail to destroy a custom heap, it remains in memory until the process terminates.
13. Is it possible to disable heap serialization for individual allocations from a serialized heap?
14. True or false: Attempting to destroy the default process heap will cause an access violation.
15. What types of allocations are best suited for heaps?
16. True or false: By default, Windows does not serialize access to the default process heap, but you can create a private heap and enable serialization if your app requires it.
17. When the HEAP_GENERATE_EXCEPTIONS flag is passed into HeapAlloc, how does it change the behavior of the heap manager?

18. Can the Perfmon tool monitor the system paging file size?

19. True or false: STATUS_NO_MEMORY is an exception that the heap manager may raise in certain circumstances.

Shared Memory

In this section, we'll discuss Windows' shared memory facilities. Shared memory is memory that is visible to multiple processes or that is present in the virtual address space of multiple processes. It's the tool of choice when you need to rapidly exchange data between multiple processes. Because data is exchanged via shared virtual memory pages, each process that accesses it must already know how to interpret it and how to work with it. Unlike data that comes in over a TCP/IP socket or, say, through a Windows message, data accessed via shared memory consists of committed pages within a process's address space. The process must know something about what these pages should contain in order to make use of their data.

Key Shared Memory Terms and Concepts

✔ *Shared memory*—memory that is visible to multiple processes or that is present in the virtual address space of multiple processes.

✔ *Memory-mapped file*—a file on disk that has been mapped into virtual memory such that it serves as the physical storage for the virtual memory.

✔ *Section object*—the kernel object responsible for implementing shared memory and memory-mapped files.

Key Shared Memory APIs

Table 4.9 Key Shared Memory–Related API Functions

Function	Description
CreateFileMapping	Creates a file-mapping object (a section object) for use with shared memory or a memory-mapped file.
MapViewOfFile	Maps a view of a file into memory such that the file serves as the physical storage for the memory. The file can be a file on disk or the system paging file.
FlushViewOfFile	Writes the modified pages in a mapped file view to disk.

SQL Server and Shared Memory

Shared memory is used in a number of places within SQL Server. A prime example of this is the shared memory Net-Library. When a client application resides on the same machine as SQL Server, it can connect to the server using the shared memory Net-Library, for example, by specifying the server name as **.** (a period) or **(local)** or by prefixing the server\instance name with **lpc:**. This means that, rather than communicating using a protocol such as TCP/IP or Named Pipes and the full network stack, the client and server use a simple shared memory buffer to exchange data. Because both processes are running on the same machine, this is not only sensible but also far more efficient than using the network stack.

You may be wondering how access to this shared memory area is coordinated—that is, how can we keep the server from reading client-side data before it's ready and vice versa? This is handled using a named event object. Think back to our discussion of event objects in Chapter 3. In order to synchronize access to the memory area used by the shared memory Net-Library, the client and server signal an event object to tell the other party when it can safely access the buffer. So, the server enters a wait state by calling WaitForSingleObject on this event object, and the client signals the event when it's ready for the server to access the buffer. The client then calls WaitForSingleObject and waits on the event object itself. When the server finishes its work in the buffer, it signals the event, and the client takes over again. This process continues as long as the client remains connected to the server.

Section Objects

The fundamental kernel object used to implement shared memory is known as a section object. In Win32 API parlance, a section object is known as a file-mapping object. File mapping amounts to associating the contents of a file with a range of virtual memory addresses by having the file serve as the physical storage for the range. The file can be a file on disk or the system paging file. Regardless of the physical storage behind a file mapping, the shared memory it provides can be accessed by multiple processes.

Because it can be opened by one process or by multiple processes, a section object doesn't necessarily equate to shared memory. Though it is used to implement shared memory, a section object can also be used by just one process to map a file into virtual memory.

You can connect a section object to an open disk file to create a mapped file or to committed virtual memory in order to set up shared memory. A section object that is committed to virtual memory is considered "paging file backed" because its pages can be written to the system paging file as necessary. Keep in mind that because Windows can run without a paging file, these pages might instead be backed by physical memory.

Identically to a private committed page, a shared committed page is always zero-filled the first time a process accesses it. A shared page is zero-filled only once, regardless of how many processes access it.

Memory-Mapped Files

Windows provides a set of API functions that support mapping a file to a region of virtual addresses. An application can use these functions to conveniently perform file I/O by making a file appear in the virtual address space as memory. To manipulate the file, the application simply reads and writes the virtual memory associated with it.

To set up a memory-mapped file, an application follows these steps.

1. Call CreateFile to create a process-local handle for the file on disk.
2. Call CreateFileMapping to create a file-mapping object for the file.
3. Call MapViewOfFile to map the file into the process's address space. The pointer returned by MapViewOfFile is the starting address of the memory region that's mapped to the file.

If the application doesn't want to map a file on disk in order to perform I/O on it but is interested only in setting up a shared memory region, the app follows just two required steps.

1. Call CreateFileMapping to create a file-mapping object. Pass INVALID_HANDLE_VALUE as the file handle. This will cause the shared memory region to be backed by the system paging file. When the system paging file backs a shared memory region, you must tell CreateFileMapping how large to make the area. (When mapping a disk file, omitting the file size parameters causes CreateFileMapping to create a mapping object based on the physical size of the file.)
2. Call MapViewOfFile to retrieve a pointer to the shared memory region.

Image File Mappings

At process startup, Windows opens the application's executable file and determines the size of its code and data. Windows then reserves a region of the process address space large enough to cover the executable's code and data and sets the physical storage for these addresses as the executable file itself. As mentioned in the Virtual Memory section, executable pages are marked with the PAGE_EXECUTE attribute; data pages are marked with the PAGE_WRITECOPY attribute. All instances of a given executable share the same physical storage: the executable file itself. When a process makes a change to one of its data pages (e.g., it assigns a value to a global variable), Windows makes a copy of the data page and tells the process to use the new page instead of the old one. This copy-on-write functionality keeps address space usage to a minimum while still allowing applications to change their data pages whenever they need to.

An executable image (an EXE or DLL file) that serves as the physical storage for a region of virtual addresses is a type of memory-mapped file. Just as an application can connect a region of addresses with a file on disk, Windows uses its own file-mapping facility to make executable images easy to load and process.

Note that some types of media require Windows to copy the entirety of an executable image into virtual memory rather than allowing it to reside on disk. An image that's loaded from a floppy disk will be copied in its entirety into virtual memory. This is done so that setup programs loaded from floppy can continue to run even after the floppy has been swapped for another during the setup process. Loading an image from other types of removable media such as a CD-ROM or network drive does not cause Windows to copy the image into virtual memory unless it was linked with the /SWA-PRUN:CD or /SWAPRUN:NET switches.

Exercises

In the next exercise, we'll use shared memory to share data between multiple processes, and we'll use a synchronization object to make access to this data thread-safe. You'll create a single application, then spawn multiple instances of it to see how processes can share data between them by using shared memory.

Exercise 4.11   Using Shared Memory to Share Data between Processes

1. Copy the sharedmem_client example app from the CH04\sharedmem_client subfolder on the CD to your hard drive, and load it into the VC++ development environment (MSDEV). Compile and link the application so that sharedmem_client.exe is written to the Release subfolder.

Alternatively, you can just copy the executable from the CD if you aren't interested in compiling it first.

2. Start Explorer and change to the Release subfolder containing sharedmem_client.exe. Double-click the executable to start it.

3. Type Y a few times to allow the app to continue its modification loop. You'll see that it retrieves an integer from shared memory, then increments and assigns it back to shared memory.

4. After a few iterations of this, leave sharedmem_client.exe running and return to Explorer. Double-click sharedmem_client.exe a second time in Explorer to start a second instance of it. You'll notice that it appears to hang.

5. Return to the first instance of the app and type Y to allow it to continue. It will now appear to hang.

6. Return to the second instance and you'll see that it finally began to run. What's happening here is that the app uses a named event object to synchronize access to the shared memory area. This means that only one instance of the app can modify it at a time. When one app has control of the shared memory area, the other must wait for it to complete before continuing. You'll notice that each execution of the modification loop, regardless of which process it is, increments the integer by 1.

7. You can start as many instances of sharedmem_client.exe as you want. The effect will be the same: Only one of them at a time will be allowed to read or write the shared memory.

8. Type N in each of the sharedmem_client.exe instances you've started to shut them down.

For curious readers, Listing 4.10 shows the code for sharedmem_client.exe.

Listing 4.10 A Shared Memory Client App That Synchronizes by Using an Event Object

```
// sharedmem_client.cpp : Uses shared memory to share data between
// processes and synchronizes access to the data using a named
// event object
//

#include "stdafx.h"
#include "windows.h"
#include "conio.h"

#define SHARED_MEM_NAME "GGSharedMem"
#define EVENT_NAME "GGSharedMemEvent"
```

```
int main(int argc, char* argv[])
{
  //Create the event to synchronize access to the shared mem
  HANDLE hEvent=CreateEvent(NULL,false,true,EVENT_NAME);

  if (INVALID_HANDLE_VALUE==hEvent) return 0;

  LPVOID lpSharedMemory;
  DWORD dwValue;

  HANDLE hMapFile;

  //Create a file mapping based on the system paging file
  hMapFile = CreateFileMapping(INVALID_HANDLE_VALUE,
                               NULL,
                               PAGE_READWRITE,
                               0,
                               0x1000,
                               SHARED_MEM_NAME);

  if (NULL == hMapFile)
  {
    printf("Could not create file mapping object.
       Last error=%s\n",GetLastError());
    return 1;
  }


  //Get a pointer to the shared memory
  lpSharedMemory = MapViewOfFile
     (hMapFile, FILE_MAP_ALL_ACCESS, 0, 0, 0);

  if (NULL == lpSharedMemory)
  {
    printf("Could not map view of file.
       Last error=%s\n",GetLastError());
    return 1;
  }


  __try
  {
    char ch='N';
```

```
      do {
        //Wait on the object to be signaled
        //Since it's an auto-reset event, this also resets it
        WaitForSingleObject(hEvent,INFINITE);

        //Read a value from the shared memory area
        dwValue = *((LPDWORD) lpSharedMemory);
        printf("\n\ndwValue READ = %d for process 0x%08x\n",
                dwValue,GetCurrentProcessId());

        //Increment the private copy of the data
        dwValue++;

        //Assign the private value back to the shared memory
        *((LPDWORD) lpSharedMemory) = dwValue;
        printf("dwValue WRITE = %d for process 0x%08x\n",
                dwValue,GetCurrentProcessId());

        printf("Continue? ");
        ch=getche();

        //Signal the event (another client can now access)
        SetEvent(hEvent);


      } while ('Y'==toupper(ch));
    }

    //Make sure cleanup code runs
    finally
    {
      //Undo the file mapping view
      if (!UnmapViewOfFile(lpSharedMemory))
      {
        printf("Could not unmap view of file.
            Last error=%d\n",GetLastError());
      }

      //Close the handle for synchronization event
      CloseHandle(hEvent);
    }

    return 0;
}
```

9. In this code, we begin by creating a named event object. Whenever a process attempts to create a named object that already exists, it receives a process-local handle to the existing object. This means that all instances of sharedmem_client.exe will use the same event object to synchronize access to the shared memory area.

10. We next create a named file-mapping object that's backed by the system paging file. As with the event object, every process that attempts to create this named object will get a handle to the same kernel object if it already exists. This means that multiple instances of this executable will refer to the same file-mapping object and will thus use the same shared memory area.

11. Once we've created the file-mapping object, we set up the shared memory itself through the call to MapViewOfFile. The pointer returned by this function is the start of the shared memory area.

12. We then call WaitForSingleObject to wait on the event. Since the event was created in a signaled state (see the third parameter to CreateEvent), WaitForSingleObject will return immediately when it is called by the first instance of sharedmem_client.exe. Because the event was created as an auto-reset event (see CreateEvent's second parameter), the event will immediately return to a nonsignaled state as soon as WaitForSingleObject successfully waits on it. This keeps multiple instances of the process from gaining access to the shared memory region simultaneously. Each instance must wait until the first one to successfully wait on the event signals it.

13. We next retrieve the value from shared memory by simply dereferencing and casting the first DWORD in the buffer. We then increment the private copy of the integer and assign it back to the shared memory buffer.

14. We finish up by asking the user whether we should continue in the update loop. If the user types Y, we attempt to go through another round of incrementing and printing the first DWORD in the shared memory area. Once the user responds, we immediately signal the event, regardless of the response. If another instance of the app is waiting on the event, it will be allowed to run before we can cycle back through the loop. We will then wait until it finishes with the shared memory area and signals the event. This continues perpetually until all client instances have been terminated.

NOTE: I wouldn't normally recommend that you code apps so that they hang on to a kernel object while they wait on user input because this could block other apps needing access to the object indefinitely. I've coded this example to do so in order to make the progression of events easier to follow.

In this last exercise, we'll create a shared memory object that will be accessed by a couple of processes, then we'll view this object using WinObj, a tool from the Platform SDK.

Exercise 4.12   Using WinObj to View Named Shared Memory Objects

The app we'll be using to create a shared memory object we can inspect with WinObj is called SuperRecorder. It is an app I originally wrote about ten years ago and have enhanced a few times since then. To understand how and why it uses shared memory, let me give you some of its history and discuss how it evolved over time.

Some of you old-timers may remember the Windows 3.x Recorder accessory. Recorder allowed you to record mouse and keyboard events as a macro and play back that macro in any app with a keystroke combination. The ability to record both keyboard and mouse events was unusual at the time, and, being the keyboard-centric guy that I am, I used the tool very heavily and had numerous macros defined on my Win 3.x systems.

Sometime around 1992, it occurred to me that having Recorder's functionality in a component of some type that I could drop into an app and instantly provide programmable keyboard/mouse macros facilities would be quite powerful. I looked around at the various resources then available and didn't find anything in existence like this for Windows, so I decided to build it myself.

I had built several programmer's editors in the 1980s that included macro functionality of varying levels of sophistication (e.g., Cheetah, TurboEdit, TEdit, and so on), so I had a pretty good idea of what I wanted to do and how I would handle the mechanics of storing lists of input events. The question was how to do it within the Windows environment.

I began researching this and found that recording and playing back Windows messages, as I'd originally thought I might do, would not work reliably. Posting a WM_KEYDOWN for VK_SHIFT followed by VK_A didn't necessarily result in a capital A being typed into the current app. This was before tools like VB's SendKeys function existed (and that's a keyboard-only mechanism anyway), so I was left to find another way.

I finally discovered how Recorder itself had pulled off its magic—it was using a combination of global system hooks (to trap keyboard and mouse events) and the journal record/playback API functions. The global system hooks allowed it to capture keyboard and mouse events in a manner similar to an interrupt service routine in DOS that some of my programmer's editors had used. The journaling API functions allowed Recorder to reliably record and play back both mouse and keyboard events. I decided to take this same approach in my component. I began by building a DLL (system hooks require a DLL to host their callback function), then wrapped the functions exposed by the DLL in a component.

I called this library/component combo WinMacro and sold it for a few years over CompuServe and other venues before the World Wide Web really took off. It allowed a Windows developer to drop a component into an app and instantly have all the functionality of the Recorder accessory programmatically available in the app. The app could start or stop recording, record mouse as well as keyboard events, and play them back based on a mouse/keyboard event or through an API call. I used the facility in several of my own apps (e.g., the DB-Library and ODBC versions of my Sequin SQL Editor for Windows app) and even gave a talk at a developer conference on how I'd built the library and how it worked internally. Life was good.

Then came 32-bit Windows. On testing the WinMacro demo app I'd built, SuperRecorder, on the first version of Windows NT (Windows NT 3.1), I discovered that, while macros recorded in a process would play back in that process, other processes were completely unaware of them. One of the niftier features of WinMacro was that you could record a macro in, say, Notepad, then go to Word and play it back. This allowed you to create global, system-wide macros that had the same hotkeys and played back the same regardless of the app. The same functionality had been available in the original Recorder accessory. However, try as I might, I could not get it to work in my initial tests on the pubescent Windows NT.

I looked into this a bit and discovered why WinMacro macros recorded in one process would not play back in another. Win32's process isolation was preventing the linked list of macros I'd recorded in one process from being visible to other processes. I had designed the original WinMacro to depend on the inherent process memory sharing in Windows 3.x, which was, by design, no longer there in 32-bit Windows.

(I also discovered that the Recorder accessory had vanished in 32-bit Windows—it was nowhere to be found. I have always suspected that this was because it worked the same way SuperRecorder did and would have required a rewrite in order to run on 32-bit Windows.)

Clearly, the design I'd used for 16-bit Windows wasn't going to work on Win32, so, in about 1994, I set out to rewrite WinMacro for Win32. I called the new version WinMac32.

For WinMac32, the fundamental problem I had to solve was how to make linked lists that may have been allocated in one process visible to other processes. I soon discovered Win32's shared memory facilities and designed WinMac32 to use shared memory to store its linked list of macros and keyboard/mouse events. This, coupled with system hooks and DLL injection, allowed me to provide the same functionality to Win32 apps that I'd originally provided Win 3.x apps. WinMac32 has shipped on the CD with a couple of my other books, and the full source to it (along with the old Win 3.x source) is included on the CD accompanying this book. The library's SendKeys and AppActivate routines, which do not actually use the engine itself, have been shipped with Borland's Delphi product since version 4.0.

For purposes of this exercise, we'll start the WinMac32 demo app, Super-Recorder, and record a macro, then we'll go to Notepad and play that macro back. While the two apps are running, we'll check for the named WinMac32 shared memory object using WinObj.

1. Begin by starting SuperRecorder. It's in the CH04\WinMac32 subfolder on the CD accompanying this book and is named srecorder.exe. You can use SuperRecorder's Options menu to configure it before you start recording.

2. Tab to the Scratch Area, then press Ctrl+Alt+Shift+F11 to start recording.

3. Type anything you want in the scratch area. Feel free to use the mouse to select some of the text you type, then cut, copy, and paste it.

4. When you're done, press Ctrl+Alt+Shift+F11 a second time to stop recording. You'll be prompted for a keyboard/mouse combo to associate with the macro. Hit the backquote key (`, the unshifted character on the tilde key on most keyboards) to assign the macro to the backquote key. Name the macro Shared Memory Test and click OK.

5. Now, start Notepad and press the backquote key. You should see your keyboard and mouse events played back.

6. Start WinObj (from the Platform SDK) and click the node in the tree labeled BaseNamedObjects.

7. Scroll the list of named objects to the right until you find an object named WinMac32SharedData. Double-click this object to display its properties. You'll see that, among other things, WinObj knows that it's a section (shared memory) object. This is the shared memory object that WinMac32 uses to store its shared data structures and is the means by which memory allocations made by one process (macro recordings) can be accessed by another.

8. While we're at it, you can use the TList utility to check out the DLL injection technique that WinMac32 uses to insert itself into processes as you type or use the mouse. Given that it has to set system hooks (using the SetWindowsHookEx API) to grab both the keyboard and mouse events before a process sees them, WinMac32 will actually cause itself to be loaded into every process in which you type or use the mouse. While SuperRecorder and Notepad are still running, run TList from the command prompt to list the process IDs for all processes.

9. Take the IDs returned for SuperRecorder and Notepad and pass each of them into TList separately to list the modules loaded into each process. You'll notice that WinMac32 is loaded into the SuperRecorder process space. This is no big surprise given that SuperRecorder is a demo app for the library. But you'll also notice that WinMac32 is loaded into Notepad's process space. Now, we know that Notepad didn't explicitly load WinMac32 or reference it via an implicit import, so

how did WinMac32 get loaded into the process? Through DLL injection. Because the hooks that WinMac32 sets are system-wide and because the callback code to service those hooks lives in WinMac32.DLL itself, Windows loads the DLL into every process where the hook code will need to execute—that is, into every process where you type or use the mouse. In fact, if you use TList to check the module list for the WinObj tool you were just running, you'll find WinMac32.DLL loaded there as well because you've typed or used the mouse in it since SuperRecorder was started.

10. If you now close the SuperRecorder application, you'll see that not only does this behavior stop (you won't see WinMac32.DLL injected into any new processes) but WinMac32.DLL is also unloaded from all existing processes. I coded it this way so that you could easily turn off the macro facility by closing the recorder app. Although, technically, you can record in any app and play back in any other, I coded the demo app so that closing it turns off the macro engine and unloads it across the system. If I hadn't done this, you'd have had to close every process in which WinMac32.DLL had been injected in order to unload it completely from memory. DLL injection has its pros and cons. One of the cons is that it can spread like a plague throughout a system, and I didn't believe that users would want to have to forcibly eradicate it from all running processes in order to disable it.

WinMac32 makes use of several Win32 API functions that you may want to explore further. It sets four system-wide hooks using SetWindowsHookEx (a keyboard hook, a mouse hook, a journal record hook, and a journal playback hook). It installs a message handler for interprocess communication (with CreateWindow) and a shared memory area backed by the system paging file using the CreateMappedFile and MapViewOfFile API functions.

The journaling API functions are how we trap keyboard and mouse events in a process and play them back reliably. They necessarily interact at a very low level with the Windows input subsystems, and I've seen them cause blue screens on systems with faulty keyboard or mouse drivers.

Other than the occasional recompile, I haven't upgraded WinMac32 in years, and I noticed that it became somewhat unstable with the advent of Service Pack 3 for Windows NT 4. I haven't taken the time to investigate what changed in this service pack and may not do so anytime soon given that I no longer sell WinMac32. One of the advantages of giving away software free of charge is that you can decide how much time you have to spend supporting it. I haven't really had time to support any of my freeware in years, and I doubt that will change anytime in the near future.

Because WinMac32 is freeware, I don't recommend you use it in production. Study the code and learn about Windows and the Windows API functions, but don't rely too heavily on the tool itself.

If you want to compile WinMac32 yourself, you'll need Delphi 2.0 or later. To compile WinMacro (the Windows 3.x version), you'll need Delphi 1.0. For the embedded assembly language, you'll need an assembler compatible with TASM 1.5 or later (MASM will probably do). For more recent versions of Delphi, you can just use the embedded assembler—no need for separate assembly.

Note that you can also view section objects using WinDbg's !handle command. To do so, follow these steps.

1. Execute !handle at the WinDbg command prompt to get a list of all the process-local handles in the process's handle table. Running !handle without parameters causes it to list every handle (and its object type) in the process's handle table.

2. Find the handles in the list identified as section objects. Run !handle again, this time specifying the handle number of each section object handle you want to view. You can also pass an option mask to !handle that tells it what information you'd like listed for the handle. For example, say that you're wanting to list information for handle number a3c, a section object. You could do something like this:

```
!handle a3c 4
```

In this example, a3c is the handle number, and 4 is the option mask. Passing 4 to !handle tells it to list the name of the object if there is one.

Shared Memory Recap

Windows provides a rich set of facilities for allocating and working with shared memory. Shared memory and memory-mapped files are used throughout the operating system itself; using them is as easy as using any other type of memory. Sharing data between processes or mapping a file into virtual memory is relatively painless and quite powerful.

Shared Memory Knowledge Measure

1. In Win32 API parlance, what is a section object?
2. True or false: The system paging file can be used as the physical storage for shared memory.
3. Does Windows zero-fill shared memory pages on first access in the same way that it zero-fills private committed pages?
4. When a client connects to SQL Server using shared memory, what type of kernel object do SQL Server and the client use to coordinate access to the shared memory area?

5. What Win32 API function is used to write the modified pages in a mapped file immediately to disk?

6. What value must an application pass to CreateFileMapping to instruct it to use the system paging file to back the shared memory it is setting up?

7. True or false: When Windows loads an executable into virtual memory from a hard drive, it uses the system paging file to provide the physical storage for the executable's code and data.

8. What Windows API function actually provides the pointer to a shared memory area?

9. True or false: Though shared memory is slower than exchanging data using the network stack, it is still the tool of choice when you want to exchange data reliably.

10. True or false: Although it is used to implement shared memory, a section object does not necessarily equate to shared memory because it can also be used by a single process to map a file into virtual memory.

11. True or false: In order to initialize a shared memory area for use, an application must first call the Win32 API function AllocateUserPhysicalPages, then call MapUserPhysicalPages to map a view of the shared memory into the virtual address space.

12. What kernel object is responsible for implementing shared memory and memory-mapped files?

13. What WinDbg command can you use to display information about a kernel object that corresponds to a shared memory region?

14. Assume that I'm connecting to a SQL Server named khen\ss2k_sp4 via an instance of Query Analyzer that's running on the same machine as the server. What four-character prefix can I use with my server name to force Query Analyzer to attempt to connect using the shared memory Net-Library?

CHAPTER 5

I/O Fundamentals

Free thought is the repudiation of all coercion of authority or tradition in philosophy, theology, and ideology. It is the commitment to the theory that the power of cultural institutions can be morally exercised only when that power is limited by guaranteed and protected civil liberties possessed equally by all citizens.

—Richard Bozarth[1]

I have always believed that the best way to learn about a technology is to use it to build things. Every computer technology I've ever learned—from hardware to operating systems to programming languages to applications and tools—I've learned by getting my hands dirty. There is no substitute for practical experience; there's no better way to get your mind around how something works than to see it for yourself.

I still remember the first time I experienced the wonderment that comes from experimenting with computing technology and seeing it come to life before your very eyes. It was a Saturday afternoon, and I had sat down at a computer terminal with the goal of learning my first programming language. After about five minutes of reading through syntax diagrams and some exceedingly dull prose in the language manual, I decided just to build an application myself and see what would happen. It would be my very first program.

Most people build something along the lines of a "Hello World" app their first time out with a new language. Not me. For me, the power of the computer was in its ability to do repetitive tasks extremely fast, not in its ability to produce output. Humans can produce output—carbon dioxide, cave drawings, the *Mona Lisa*, this book—and they don't need computers to do it. For me, the most intriguing aspect of the computer was its ability to carry out logic-based tasks faster and more precisely than I or any other human could ever hope to. For me, the most useful innovation in computing was the concept of the *logical loop*—it was to computing what the invention

---

1. Bozarth, Richard. "Free Thought." *Truth Seeker,* 119(1):15, 1987.

of the wheel had been to mankind. I could see all sorts of seemingly complex problems suddenly becoming readily solvable because of the computer's ability to precisely repeat a given task over and over until a logical condition became true or some type of resolution was reached.

So, my first program was an app that accepted as input an integer and produced the factors of the number as output. The eureka feeling I experienced when I hit the submit key and watched the output of my app appear magically on the CRT is almost beyond description, and it is still vivid in my mind to this day. This has been my standard approach to learning new technologies for over two decades now, and I never grow tired of the profound satisfaction that comes from seeing my handiwork take flight with the press of a key or the click of a mouse.

In this chapter, we'll investigate Windows' I/O facilities using this hands-on approach. We'll talk about conceptual definitions and how things work architecturally, then we'll dive in and write some code. Before we're done, you'll have a good grasp of how Windows I/O facilities work and how applications such as SQL Server can make use of them.

I/O Basics

We'll begin our exploration of Windows I/O with the basics. We'll talk about key I/O terms and concepts, then delve into how Windows I/O works from an architectural standpoint.

Key I/O Terms and Concepts

✔ *File system*—the overall structure in which files are named, stored, and organized in an operating system. File systems consist of drives, files, directories, and the metadata needed to locate and access them. A file system is not only the logical representation of the machine's secondary storage but also the part of the operating system responsible for translating application file operation requests into low-level, sector-oriented calls into the device drivers that control the disk drives.

A file system's format defines the way in which file data is stored and directly affects the file system's features. For example, a format that doesn't allow files to be larger than 2GB obviously limits the file sizes the file system can support.

The Windows NT family supports several file systems (e.g., FAT16, FAT32, NTFS, and so on), but NTFS is its native file system. NTFS provides more features and performs more efficiently than any other file system Windows supports. Cluster indexes are 64 bits wide in NTFS, so it can theoretically address up to 16EB (16 exabytes—16 billion GB) of disk space. However, since Windows limits NTFS volume sizes so that they remain addressable with 32-bit cluster indexes, the largest an NTFS volume can be is 128TB (using 64K clusters).

✔ *File object*—the kernel object used to access files and devices under Windows. Like other types of kernel objects, file objects are system resources that multiple processes can share, that can be named, that support synchronization (i.e., the notion of being signaled or unsignaled), and that can be protected by object-based security.

✔ *Synchronous I/O*—causes a thread to pause until a pending I/O operation completes.

✔ *Asynchronous I/O*—allows a thread that initiates an I/O operation to continue executing without waiting on the operation to complete. The thread can check the status of its pending I/O operation through a variety of means which we'll discuss shortly.

Key I/O APIs

Table 5.1 Key I/O-Related API Functions

Function	Description
CreateFile	Creates or opens a file; can also be used to create or open other types of objects
ReadFile	Reads a buffer from a file into memory
WriteFile	Writes a buffer from memory to disk
CloseHandle	Closes the handle associated with a kernel object (e.g., a file)

Key I/O Tools

Table 5.2 Key I/O Monitoring Tools

	Reads	Bytes Read	Writes	Bytes Written	% Disk Read Time	% Disk Write Time	Average Disk Queue Length	Disk Reads/ sec	Disk Writes/ sec
Perfmon	✔	✔	✔	✔	✔	✔	✔	✔	✔
pmon	✔	✔	✔	✔					
TaskMgr	✔	✔	✔	✔					

Key Perfmon Counters

Perfmon is the undisputed king of I/O-related information under Windows. There are too many counters to go into here—just understand that you can retrieve a veritable treasure trove of I/O-related information from Perfmon. Table 5.3 lists a few of the more useful I/O-related performance counters.

Table 5.3 Key I/O-Related Perfmon Counters

Counter	Description
Physical Disk:Disk reads/sec	The rate of read operations on a disk
Physical Disk:Disk writes/sec	The rate of write operations on a disk
Physical Disk:% Disk Read Time	The percentage of elapsed time spent servicing read requests
Physical Disk:% Disk Write Time	The percentage of elapsed time spent servicing write requests
Physical Disk:Avg. Disk Queue Length	The average number of read and write requests queued to the disk during a sample interval
Cache:Lazy Write Flushes/sec	The rate at which the lazywriter thread is flushing data to disk
Cache:Lazy Write Pages/sec	The rate at which the lazywriter thread is writing pages to disk

Overview

In Windows, you perform most I/O operations via kernel file objects. File objects are unusual in that they are not strictly memory constructs. They are memory objects that provide access to the actual resource, which is on disk. Unlike events, semaphores, and other types of kernel objects, file objects do not manage resources that reside only in memory—they provide a means of interacting with resources that reside primarily outside of memory.

If you've done any Windows programming, you may have noticed that the SDK documentation recommends that you use CreateFile rather than OpenFile when opening a file. (OpenFile has been deprecated and is for backward compatibility with 16-bit apps only.) Why is this? Does it not seem a little counterintuitive to have to create something when you only want to open it? What if the file already exists? Would this overwrite it? No, it wouldn't—not if you call it properly. Here's why: You use CreateFile rather than OpenFile to open a file because you are creating a kernel object, not because you are (necessarily) creating a file on disk. What you're creating is a kernel object that will allow you to read from or write to the file using other Win32 API functions. CreateFile creates a kernel file object and returns a process-local handle to it. Whether it attempts to create a physical file on disk depends entirely on the parameters you pass into it. It can open an existing file, or it can create a new one—it all depends on how you call it.

Because it's not the actual resource it manages but only an in-memory representation of it, a file object contains only data that is specific to a particular object handle. The file itself contains the shareable data. When a thread opens a file handle, Windows creates a new file object with its own set of handle-based attributes. So, even though multiple file objects may reference the same file, each one contains data that is specific to its handle (e.g., the current offset in the file where the next I/O operation will occur).

Each file object is process-unique unless a process duplicates a file handle in another process via a call to the DuplicateHandle API function. In other words, even though, as with other kernel objects, file objects can obviously have names, two processes that open a file object with the same name will get two different objects. This differs from other types of kernel objects and is the result of the resource itself residing on disk rather than in memory.

Even though a file handle is process-local, the file itself isn't; therefore, threads must synchronize their access to it, just as they must for any other shared resource. We wouldn't want one thread writing to a file while another is trying to read it, for example. A thread that intends to write to a file should either open the file with exclusive write access or use the LockFile Win32 API function to block other threads from accessing it while the writes are occurring.

Synchronous I/O

Most application I/O operations are synchronous. This means that the calling thread waits on the operation to complete before proceeding. Windows' synchronous I/O facility mirrors the I/O facilities found in other operating systems and programming environments, and it's semantically familiar to most developers.

Applications perform synchronous I/O by calling the basic Win32 I/O functions and waiting on them to complete. If a file isn't explicitly opened for asynchronous I/O, threads will wait on I/O operations against it to complete before proceeding. Let's look at some code.

Exercise

The app below dumps the end of a text file to the console. There are various versions of tail utilities out there; this is just a simple one to demonstrate synchronous file I/O using the Win32 I/O functions. You can specify both the file to dump and an optional offset from the end of the file at which to begin listing file contents. If you don't specify an offset, the utility will either dump the last 1K of the file or its last one-fourth, whichever is smaller.

Exercise 5.1   A Simple Utility That Demonstrates Synchronous I/O

1. Load and compile the app shown in Listing 5.1 from the CH05\tail subfolder on the book's CD.

Listing 5.1 A Simple Tail Utility

```
// tail.cpp : A utility to dump the end of a file to the console
//

#include "stdafx.h"
#include "windows.h"
#include "stdlib.h"

int main(int argc, char* argv[])
{
  if (argc<2) {
    printf("Usage is:  tail filename [number of bytes]\n");
    return 1;
  }
  HANDLE hFile=CreateFile(argv[1],
                          GENERIC_READ,
                          FILE_SHARE_READ,
                          NULL,
                          OPEN_EXISTING,
                          FILE_ATTRIBUTE_NORMAL,
                          NULL);

  if (INVALID_HANDLE_VALUE==hFile) {
    printf("Unable to open file %s.  Last error=%d\n",
           argv[1],GetLastError());
    return 1;
  }

  DWORD dwFileOfs=1024;
```

```
if (argc>=3)
  dwFileOfs=atoi(argv[2]);

DWORD dwFileSizeHigh;
DWORD dwFileSizeLow;
dwFileSizeLow=GetFileSize(hFile,&dwFileSizeHigh);

if ((-1==dwFileSizeLow) &&
    (NO_ERROR!=(dwError=GetLastError()))) {
  printf("Unable to get the size of file %s.  Last error=%d\n",
         argv[1],GetLastError());
  return 1;
}

DWORDLONG dwlFileSize=(dwFileSizeHigh * MAXDWORD) +
                       dwFileSizeLow;

DWORDLONG dwlOfs = dwlFileSize / 4;
  if (dwlOfs<dwFileOfs)
    dwFileOfs = dwlOfs;

DWORD dwNewPos=SetFilePointer(hFile,dwFileOfs * -1,0,FILE_END);

char *pszTail = (char *)HeapAlloc(GetProcessHeap(),
                        HEAP_ZERO_MEMORY,
                        dwFileOfs+1);
DWORD dwBytesRead;
ReadFile(hFile,pszTail,dwFileOfs,&dwBytesRead,NULL);
printf("%s\n",pszTail);

HeapFree(GetProcessHeap(),0,pszTail);

CloseHandle(hFile);

return 0;
}
```

2. Run the app either from the VC++ development environment or from the command prompt and pass in the name of a text file for which you want to list the final 1K.

3. As you can see, this app takes a file name as an input and lists the last *n* bytes of it. This is handy for large files where you're only interested in the end of the file and don't want to have to list or search the entire file to reach the end.

4. The app begins by calling CreateFile. The CreateFile call stipulates that the file must exist (OPEN_EXISTING) or the function will fail. By not passing the FILE_FLAG_OVERLAPPED flag into CreateFile, the app is indicating that it wants to perform I/O against the file in a synchronous manner.

5. Once the file is open, we compute the offset at which to begin listing file contents. This defaults to the last 1K of the file but can also be specified on the command line to the utility.

6. We next call SetFilePointer, the Win32 API responsible for adjusting the current file offset. SetFilePointer moves the file pointer to a relative position based on the beginning of the file, the current file position, or the end of the file. Because we pass in FILE_END, we're specifying that we want to move relative to the end of the file. In order to move the file pointer backward, you must specify a negative file offset, so we multiply the previously computed file offset by –1 as we pass it into SetFilePointer. Given that we opened the file in synchronous I/O mode, the process's main thread will block while the file pointer is moved.

   SetFilePointer can fail, but since we have computed the offset in a manner that should be foolproof, I've omitted error-checking code for simplicity's sake.

7. We next allocate a buffer from the process heap to hold the section of the file that we'll read and display. We allocate the buffer using the HEAP_ZERO_MEMORY switch. Given that we are going to overwrite all but the last character in the buffer when we read the file, it would actually have been more efficient to have set only the final character in our buffer to 0, but I am lazy, so I'll let the heap manager zero the entire buffer for me. Notice that we set the size of this buffer to be one character larger than the size of the region we'll read from the end of the file. We do this in order to ensure that the buffer will end with an ASCII 0 so that we can safely write the buffer to the console using printf.

8. We next call the Win32 ReadFile API function in order to read the end of the file into memory. ReadFile can also fail and can return fewer bytes than were requested. However, for simplicity's sake, I've omitted any error-handling code and assumed that we'll get a valid buffer back from ReadFile.

9. Because the file is opened for synchronous I/O, we pass NULL into ReadFile for the OVERLAPPED structure parameter. For asynchronous I/O, we'd pass a pointer to a valid structure. Given that we're doing synchronous I/O, ReadFile will block until the read operation completes.

10. We finish up by writing the buffer we've just read to the console, then we free the buffer and close the file handle. You call the Win32 API function CloseHandle to close a file when you're done processing it.

So, that's synchronous I/O in a nutshell. It's very similar to the I/O mechanisms you'll find in other operating systems and programming environments: You open a file, you read or write to it, then you close it—not terribly complicated.

I/O Basics Recap

Windows provides a rich set of I/O-related facilities. We've touched on a few of them here; we'll explore the rest in the remainder of the chapter.

Most I/O in Windows occurs via a file handle. You use CreateFile rather than OpenFile to open an existing file because you're creating a kernel file object. Whether the system creates a new disk file for you or opens an existing one depends on the parameters you pass into the CreateFile call.

A kernel file object is different from other kernel objects in that it does not actually contain the resource it manages. The resource resides on disk— it's the file itself. If multiple threads need to make changes to the same file simultaneously, you'll obviously have to synchronize their access to it, just as you would any other shared resource.

Synchronous I/O is probably the most common type of I/O used by applications. A synchronous I/O operation blocks the calling thread until it completes. This type of I/O is common in applications and operating systems and is the most basic type of file I/O supported by Windows.

Windows provides a standard set of API functions that make performing synchronous I/O as easy as possible in a Windows app. You open a file for synchronous I/O just as you do for any other type of I/O: by calling CreateFile. You read the file with ReadFile and write to it using WriteFile. When you're finished, you close your file handle by calling the CloseHandle API function.

I/O Basics Knowledge Measure

1. When opening an existing file, which Win32 API should you call, OpenFile or CreateFile?
2. True or false: Regardless of whether you're initiating a synchronous or asynchronous I/O operation, you must pass a pointer to a valid OVERLAPPED structure into ReadFile and WriteFile.
3. True or false: When you're finished with a file you've opened, you should always close it via the CloseFile Win32 API function.
4. Which Windows API function can you call to move the current file pointer?
5. If you instruct Windows to open an existing file but the file does not actually exist, what handle value is returned to your application?
6. True or false: By not passing the FILE_FLAG_OVERLAPPED flag when it opens a file, an app indicates to Windows that it wants to perform I/O against the file in a synchronous manner.
7. What is the largest NTFS volume size supported by Windows?

8. True or false: A thread can call the LockFile API function to lock part of a file and prevent other threads from accessing it while it writes to the file.

9. Can the SetFilePointer Win32 API function fail?

10. In contrast to other types of kernel objects, where does the actual resource managed by a file object reside?

Asynchronous and Nonbuffered I/O

In this section, we'll continue the discussion of Windows' I/O facilities and delve into asynchronous and nonbuffered I/O. If you haven't yet read the first part of this chapter, you should probably take a quick read through it before continuing.

Key Asynchronous and Nonbuffered I/O Terms and Concepts

✔ *Sector*—a hardware-addressable block on a storage medium such as a hard disk. The sector size for hard disks on x86 computers is almost always 512 bytes. This means that if Windows wants to write to byte 11 or 27, it must write to the first sector of the disk; if it wants to write to byte 1961, it must write to the fourth sector of the disk. You can retrieve the sector size for a disk via the GetDiskFreeSpace Win32 API function.

✔ *Cluster*—an addressable block of sectors that many file systems use. A cluster is the smallest unit of storage for a file. A cluster is usually larger than a sector and is always a multiple of the sector size. Clusters are used by file systems to manage disk space more efficiently than would be possible with individual sectors. By encompassing multiple sectors, a cluster helps divide a disk into more manageable pieces. The downsides are that large cluster sizes may waste disk space or result in fragmentation since file sizes aren't usually exact multiples of the cluster size. You can retrieve the cluster size of a disk via the GetDiskFreeSpace Win32 API function.

✔ *Asynchronous I/O*—allows a thread that initiates an I/O operation to continue executing without waiting on the operation to complete. The thread can check the status of its pending I/O operation through a variety of means, which we'll discuss shortly.

✔ *Overlapped I/O*—a synonym for asynchronous I/O.

✔ *Nonbuffered I/O*—allows Windows to open a file without intermediate buffering or caching. When combined with asynchronous I/O, nonbuffered I/O gives the best overall asynchronous performance because operations are not slowed down by the synchronous operations of the memory manager. That said, some operations will actually be slower because data cannot be loaded from the cache. SQL Server uses nonbuffered I/O to eliminate the latency between logical disk writes and the data being physically written to disk.

✔ *APC*—asynchronous procedure call, a special type of callback function that executes in an asynchronous fashion in the context of a given thread. Each thread has its own APC queue. There are two types of APCs—kernel mode APCs and user mode APCs. When a kernel mode APC is queued to a thread, the APC will execute the next time the thread is scheduled. When a user mode APC is queued to a thread, the APC will execute the next time the thread enters an alertable state. A thread enters an alertable state when it calls a wait function that supports alerting. Examples of alertable wait functions include WaitForSingleObjectEx, WaitForMultipleObjectsEx, and SleepEx.

The ReadFileEx and WriteFileEx asynchronous I/O routines will cause a user mode APC to be queued when an asynchronous operation completes. An application can also queue its own APC via the Win32 QueueUserAPC function

Key Asynchronous and Nonbuffered I/O APIs

Table 5.4 Key Asynchronous I/O–Related API Functions

Function	Description
ReadFileEx	Reads a buffer asynchronously from a file into memory
WriteFileEx	Writes a buffer asynchronously from memory to disk
GetOverlappedResult	Retrieves the result of an overlapped (asynchronous) I/O operation, optionally waiting on the operation to complete
HasOverlappedIoCompleted	Returns a Boolean indicating whether an asynchronous operation has completed
GetDiskFreeSpace	Returns system information for a drive including its sector and cluster sizes
WaitForSingleObjectEx	Waits for an object to be signaled in an optionally alertable state

Overview

As I mentioned earlier, Windows' asynchronous I/O facility allows an application to initiate an I/O operation and continue running while the operation completes. Naturally, this can improve the performance of an application because it allows the application to do multiple things at once. In the same way that multithreading can improve overall application throughput, asynchronous I/O can help an app accomplish more work more quickly because it allows the application to perform other tasks while the I/O operation proceeds.

For the most part, you use the same basic Win32 file I/O API functions to carry out asynchronous I/O that you use to perform synchronous I/O; you just pass different parameters. (Although ReadFileEx and WriteFileEx are used exclusively for asynchronous I/O operations, ReadFile and WriteFile can be used for either type.) In order to set up a file for asynchronous I/O processing, you must pass the FILE_FLAG_OVERLAPPED switch into CreateFile. When you then call ReadFile/ReadFileEx or WriteFile/WriteFileEx, you pass a pointer to an OVERLAPPED structure that specifies the starting position for the operation (and is also used by Windows for managing the asynchronous operation).

You can check the status of a pending asynchronous operation via the HasOverlappedIoCompleted and GetOverlappedResult Win32 API functions. If you want to wait on an asynchronous operation to complete before proceeding, you have several options.

- You can call one of the Win32 wait functions (e.g., WaitForSingleObject) and pass in either the optional event you associated with the OVERLAPPED structure or the handle of the file object itself. If specified, this event should be a manual-reset event, not an auto-reset event. Windows will signal the event associated with the OVERLAPPED structure once an asynchronous operation that was initiated with ReadFile or WriteFile (but not ReadFileEx or WriteFileEx) has completed. It will also signal the file on which the operation has completed, however, if you have several concurrent asynchronous operations on the file in progress, you won't be able to tell from this alone which one of them has completed, so you have to be careful if you decide to wait on the file object itself.
- You can tell GetOverlappedResult to wait until the operation completes before returning by specifying TRUE for its bWait parameter. If you want to use GetOverlappedResult to wait on an asynchronous operation to complete and multiple asynchronous operations are oc-

curring simultaneously on the specified file, you must create an event object and assign it to the hEvent member of the OVERLAPPED structure passed into ReadFile/WriteFile and GetOverlappedResult. If you don't associate an event object with the OVERLAPPED structure and you specify a value of TRUE for GetOverlappedResult's bWait parameter, the function will wait on the specified file object to be signaled. As I mentioned in the previous bullet point, this isn't reliable when multiple asynchronous operations are occurring concurrently, so you must provide an event via the OVERLAPPED structure instead. When the OVERLAPPED structure contains a reference to an event object, GetOverlappedResult waits on it, rather than the file, to be signaled. Since each asynchronous operation must have its own OVERLAPPED structure, this is a reliable way to determine the status of a pending I/O request. See the fstring sample application later in the chapter for an example of this technique.

■ You can wait on some other object using an alertable wait function and allow the APC function passed into ReadFileEx or WriteFileEx to cause the wait function to return when an asynchronous operation completes. See the unicode_convert sample application later in this chapter for an example of this technique.

■ You can use an I/O completion port to manage the process of waiting on asynchronous I/O. See the I/O Completion Ports section later in the chapter for details.

You will likely need to synchronize access to files opened for asynchronous writes. If multiple asynchronous write operations are taking place concurrently, you will naturally need to ensure that the file does not become corrupted due to thread synchronization issues. You can use GetOverlappedResult and the Win32 wait functions to help ensure that only one asynchronous write operation transpires at a time.

Regardless of whether you specify synchronous or asynchronous I/O processing from an application standpoint, most I/O requests are carried out internally by Windows using asynchronous I/O. That is, once Windows' I/O subsystem has initiated an I/O request on a device, the device driver usually returns immediately. Whether or not the I/O subsystem then returns immediately to your application depends on whether you created the file object with the FILE_FLAG_OVERLAPPED switch, whether you've passed a valid OVERLAPPED structure pointer into the API function responsible for carrying out the operation, and various other factors.

I should stop here and point out something that may not be immediately obvious. You can create a file object with the FILE_FLAG_OVERLAPPED switch and pass a valid OVERLAPPED structure pointer into ReadFile or WriteFile and still not initiate an asynchronous I/O operation. With ReadFile and WriteFile, Windows makes the final decision as to whether the operation is carried out synchronously or asynchronously. Although you may call these routines with the expectation that an operation will be carried out asynchronously, you have to code for the possibility that it might not be. ReadFile will return TRUE when it carries out an operation synchronously. It will return false and GetLastError will return ERROR_IO_PENDING when it has queued an operation to be carried out asynchronously. Examples of when a ReadFile/WriteFile operation that was initiated as an asynchronous operation runs synchronously include the following.

- The file being processed is compressed with NTFS compression. This is yet another good reason not to compress files that SQL Server makes use of, especially data and log files.
- The requested operation is increasing the size of the file (e.g., a WriteFile operation to the end of a file that causes the file to grow in size).
- The operation can be completed immediately because it is working with cached data. Many I/O drivers are coded such that if an operation can be completed immediately against a data cache (this can be a read or a write of the data in the cache), it occurs synchronously.
- The operation is against a buffered (cached) file, but the cache manager and memory manager are saturated. This is more likely if an application makes a large number of I/O requests for data that is not in the cache. By making use of nonbuffered I/O on its data and log files, SQL Server avoids this issue altogether. We'll talk more about nonbuffered I/O later in the chapter.

The best way to ensure that an I/O operation is carried out asynchronously is to use ReadFileEx and WriteFileEx rather than ReadFile and WriteFile. ReadFileEx and WriteFileEx always run asynchronously, regardless of other activity on the system. In fact, unlike ReadFile and WriteFile, ReadFileEx and WriteFileEx don't even accept a counter to return the number of bytes processed as a parameter because they are not designed to be used by themselves to process file I/O—you retrieve the bytes processed from the APC function they cause to be queued when an I/O operation completes.

Exercise

Let's take a look at some code. In this sample application, we'll explore a utility that converts the text in a UNICODE file to a different code page (e.g., ANSI). The tool works similarly to Notepad's Save As command in that it allows you to write a UNICODE text file in a different file format.

Exercise 5.2   A Utility That Converts a UNICODE Text File by Using Asynchronous I/O

1. Load the sample application shown in Listing 5.2 from the CH05\unicode_convert subfolder on the book's CD into the Visual Studio development environment (MSDEV).

Listing 5.2 A UNICODE File Converter

```
// unicode_convert.cpp : Converts a UNICODE file to a different
// code page
//

#include "stdafx.h"
#include "windows.h"
#include "stdlib.h"

#define INPUT_BUFFER_SIZE 0x1000

//Allow for a 4x size increase during conversion
#define OUTPUT_BUFFER_SIZE (INPUT_BUFFER_SIZE * 4)

DWORD dwBytesWritten=0;
DWORD dwTotalBytesWritten=0;

VOID CALLBACK WriteCompleted(
   DWORD dwErrorCode,                    // completion code
   DWORD dwNumberOfBytesTransferred,  // number of bytes transferred
   LPOVERLAPPED lpOverlapped             // I/O information buffer
)
{
   printf("Async operation completed.  Transferred %d bytes.
      Error code=%d.\n",dwNumberOfBytesTransfered,dwErrorCode);
   dwBytesWritten=dwNumberOfBytesTransfered;
   dwTotalBytesWritten+=dwBytesWritten;
}
```

```
int main(int argc, char* argv[])
{
  if (argc<3) {
    printf("Usage is:  unicode_convert inputfilename
        outputfilename [codepage]\n");
    return 1;
  }

  DWORD dwCodePage=CP_ACP;
  if (4==argc)
    dwCodePage=atoi(argv[3]);


  HANDLE hInputFile=CreateFile(argv[1],
                              GENERIC_READ,
                              FILE_SHARE_READ,
                              NULL,
                              OPEN_EXISTING,
                              FILE_ATTRIBUTE_NORMAL,
                              NULL);

  if (INVALID_HANDLE_VALUE==hInputFile) {
    printf("Unable to open file %s.  Last error=%d\n",argv[1],
        GetLastError());
    return 1;
  }

  HANDLE hOutputFile=CreateFile(argv[2],
                              GENERIC_WRITE,
                              0,
                              NULL,
                              CREATE_ALWAYS,
                              FILE_ATTRIBUTE_NORMAL |
                              FILE_FLAG_OVERLAPPED,
                              NULL);

  if (INVALID_HANDLE_VALUE==hOutputFile) {
    printf("Unable to open file %s.  Last error=%d\n",argv[2],
        GetLastError());
    return 1;
  }


  wchar_t *pwszBuffer = (wchar_t *)HeapAlloc(GetProcessHeap(),
```

```
HEAP_ZERO_MEMORY,

INPUT_BUFFER_SIZE * sizeof(wchar_t));
char *pszBuffer = (char *)HeapAlloc(GetProcessHeap(),
HEAP_ZERO_MEMORY,
OUTPUT_BUFFER_SIZE);

OVERLAPPED olIO;

ZeroMemory(&olIO,sizeof(olIO));

DWORD dwBytesRead;
DWORD dwTotalBytesRead=0;

while ((ReadFile(hInputFile,
                         pwszBuffer,
                         INPUT_BUFFER_SIZE * sizeof(wchar_t),
                         &dwBytesRead,NULL))
                         && (dwBytesRead)) {

  if (dwTotalBytesRead) {

WaitForSingleObjectEx(GetCurrentProcess(),INFINITE,true);
    if ((MAXDWORD - olIO.Offset) < dwBytesWritten) {
      olIO.OffsetHigh++;
      olIO.Offset=(MAXDWORD - olIO.Offset);
    }
    else olIO.Offset+=dwBytesWritten;
  }

  DWORD dwBytesConverted=
    WideCharToMultiByte(dwCodePage,
                         0,
                         pwszBuffer,
                         dwBytesRead / sizeof(wchar_t),
                         pszBuffer,
                         OUTPUT_BUFFER_SIZE,
                         NULL,
                         NULL);

  if (!dwBytesConverted) {
    printf("Error converting file %s near offset %d.  Last
        error=%d\n",argv[1],dwTotalBytesRead,GetLastError());
    return 1;
  }
```

```
WriteFileEx(hOutputFile,
                pszBuffer,
                dwBytesConverted,
                &olIO,&WriteCompleted);

    dwTotalBytesRead+=dwBytesRead;

}

WaitForSingleObjectEx(GetCurrentProcess(),INFINITE,true);

printf("Converted %s to %s using code page %s.  Read %d bytes,
    Wrote %d bytes\n", argv[1], argv[2], argv[3],
    dwTotalBytesRead, dwTotalBytesWritten);

HeapFree(GetProcessHeap(),0,pwszBuffer);
HeapFree(GetProcessHeap(),0,pszBuffer);

CloseHandle(hInputFile);
CloseHandle(hOutputFile);

return 0;
}
```

2. Run the utility from MSDEV, passing in the name of a UNICODE file as the first parameter and the target name for the output file to create as the second parameter. (Press Alt+F7 in Visual Studio 6.0 and select the Debug tab to set the command line parameters.) If you don't have a UNICODE file handy, there's one on the CD named "UNICODE.TXT."

3. You can specify an optional code page number as the utility's third parameter. (See Table 5.5 for a list of common code pages and their corresponding integer values.) If you don't specify a third parameter, the ANSI code page is used by default.

4. The unicode_convert app begins by opening both files. It opens the input file in synchronous mode. Since we are converting the contents of the input file, there isn't a lot we can do until each I/O request against it has completed. There's therefore no reason to attempt to read it asynchronously.

5. We do, however, open the output file in asynchronous mode. The thinking is this: By not waiting on a write to the output file to complete before reading the next buffer from the input file, we allow the application to read the input and write the output simultaneously. As each new

Table 5.5 Popular Code Pages and Their Win32 API Constant Values

Code Page	Win32 API Function Integer Value
ANSI	0
OEM	1
MAC	2
The current thread's code page	3
Symbol	42
UTF-7	65000
UTF-8	65001

buffer is read from the input file, we are writing the previous buffer to the output file.

6. Whenever a Windows application wishes to process input or output asynchronously, it must not only open the file with the FILE_FLAG_OVERLAPPED switch but also pass in a pointer to an OVER-LAPPED structure to the ReadFile/ReadFileEx or WriteFile/WriteFileEx call that it uses to transfer data between the file on disk and memory. Before passing in the pointer to an OVERLAPPED structure, the app must initialize the structure with the offset at which to begin reading or writing. That's why we pass our structure into ZeroMemory before we enter the processing loop. It is also the reason that we increment the file offset stored in the OVERLAPPED structure after each write. The Offset and OffsetHigh fields of the OVERLAPPED structure tell the system at what file offset an asynchronous operation is to begin. Since we're writing the file asynchronously, failing to do this would cause us to write each converted text buffer to the same offset in the file—the zero offset—not a pretty sight.

7. The actual work of converting the input text from one code page to another is done by the Win32 WideCharToMultiByte function. We loop through the input file, convert each buffer we read using WideCharTo-MultiByte, then call WriteFileEx to write each converted buffer to the output file.

   We use WriteFileEx rather than WriteFile to ensure that the operation is processed asynchronously. You'll recall that I mentioned earlier that WriteFile will run synchronously when you are increasing the size of its target file. Since we're creating a new file here, that's exactly what we're doing. By calling WriteFileEx rather than WriteFile, we force the operation to be processed asynchronously in spite of this.

8. We pass a pointer to our OVERLAPPED structure as well as the address of an APC function into WriteFileEx. Windows signals that the requested asynchronous operation has completed by calling the specified APC function. In this case, this is our global WriteCompleted function.

9. In order to ensure that we've written each converted text buffer to disk before altering it through another call to WideCharToMultiByte, we use WaitForSingleObjectEx to pause execution of the calling thread until the previously initiated asynchronous write operation has completed. When we call WaitForSingleObjectEx, we pass in the handle to the current process. This object is actually not used by WriteFileEx and will not be signaled by the asynchronous operation (in fact, it won't be signaled until the process exits). We use it here as a kind of placeholder object so that we can be notified when the write operation began by Write-FileEx completes. In order for the APC routine we passed into Write-FileEx to be called, we have to enter an *alertable* state. We do that by calling one of the Win32 wait functions that support being alerted while they wait and passing TRUE for its bAlertable parameter. So, while WaitForSingleObjectEx waits indefinitely on our process object, the asynchronous write operation we initiated via the WriteFileEx call will complete and cause the wait function to return because we have specified that it is alertable.

You may be wondering why we don't just wait on the file object itself using WaitForSingleObjectEx rather than intentionally waiting on an object that will never be signaled as long as the process is running. The reason we do this is that an alertable wait on an object for which an asynchronous I/O operation is under way will not allow the specified APC function to run once the operation completes. Windows will signal the object and cause the wait function to return immediately without executing the APC. If you initiate an alertable wait on a different object, however, Windows will interrupt it with an alert when the asynchronous operation completes and will cause the APC function to execute within the context of the thread that initiated the operation.

Another way to cause thread execution to pause until the write operation completes is to call the GetOverlappedResult Win32 API function and set its bWait parameter to TRUE. This would cause the calling thread to wait until the pending asynchronous I/O on the specified file (and referenced by the supplied OVERLAPPED structure) had completed.

10. In addition to using it to tally the total number of bytes read, we use the dwTotalBytesRead counter as a flag to allow us to determine whether we're in the first iteration of the loop. The counter will be 0 the first time through the loop because we have not yet reached its increment instruction at the bottom of the loop. The reason we don't want to wait

on the write operation the first time through the loop is that we've not yet initiated it. If we call WaitForSingleObjectEx and begin waiting to be alerted before the asynchronous operation has even been started, we'll effectively hang the calling thread.

The reason we pause the calling thread until the previously initiated asynchronous operation has completed is twofold: (1) we don't want to alter the buffer WriteFileEx is writing to disk by initiating another call to the WideCharToMultiByte function before it completes, and (2) we don't want to initiate another asynchronous write operation before the one pending has completed. This is what I was referring to when I said that an app must provide for thread synchronization when performing asynchronous writes. In this case, we keep things pretty basic and simply prevent multiple asynchronous writes from occurring simultaneously. In a more complex app, you would likely have several overlapped I/O operations occurring at once, and you might use one of the multiobject wait functions (e.g., WaitForMultipleObjectsEx) to wait on all of them at once (or use a more complex I/O mechanism such as an I/O completion port).

11. We loop until we've processed the entire input file. Once ReadFile either returns FALSE or we see 0 bytes read from the input file, we exit the loop. Note the final call to WaitForSingleObjectEx. This is necessary to ensure that the last file write request has completed before we print our conversion tallies and close the files. Again, we block on this call until the asynchronous operation has completed.

12. It would probably be instructive to step through the app under the Visual C++ debugger. Begin by stepping through the main processing loop and the APC function. Pay special attention to the dwBytesRead and dwBytesWritten counters—they're the best indicators of how far along ReadFile and WriteFileEx are at any given point in time.

So, that's how asynchronous I/O works in Windows. You create the file object using the FILE_FLAG_OVERLAPPED flag, then pass a pointer to an OVERLAPPED structure into ReadFile/ReadFileEx or WriteFile/WriteFileEx to initiate the asynchronous operation. You then use either GetOverlappedResult or one of the Win32 wait functions to synchronize access to the file and check the progress of the asynchronous operation.

Nonbuffered I/O

As I mentioned earlier, nonbuffered I/O allows an application to bypass the Windows cache manager and read and write a file directly with no intermediate buffer or cache. This can provide better performance, especially when performing asynchronous I/O, because it prevents the synchronous operation of the cache manager from becoming an I/O bottleneck. Some operations may be slower, however, when using nonbuffered I/O because they cannot benefit from being able to read data from the cache.

One thing worth mentioning about nonbuffered I/O is that it alleviates the problem I mentioned earlier in which Windows may decide to carry out an asynchronous I/O request synchronously because of memory manager or cache manager saturation. By bypassing the system cache, you avoid that possibility altogether.

SQL Server uses nonbuffered I/O extensively. By circumventing the system cache (and performing its own internal cache management), SQL Server has greater control over whether operations are carried out asynchronously or synchronously and can ensure better data integrity because it does not have to be concerned with disk writes appearing to be complete but not actually being written to the physical media until the cache manager decides to write them.

To open a file without buffering, pass the FILE_FLAG_NO_BUFFERING flag into CreateFile. Certain requirements must be met in order for a thread to open a file with FILE_FLAG_NO_BUFFERING.

1. Access to the file must begin at byte offsets that are evenly divisible by the disk's sector size.
2. File reads and writes must be for numbers of bytes that are evenly divisible by the disk's sector size. Assuming a default sector size of 512 bytes, an application can read and write buffers of 1,024 and 8,192 bytes, but not 1,025 or 10,000 bytes.
3. The buffers used for reads and writes must be aligned on memory addresses that are evenly divisible by the disk's sector size. This means that 0x7FF01000 is a valid buffer start address, but 0x7FF01001 is not.

A good way to ensure that the last requirement is met is to allocate the memory used for nonbuffered I/O using VirtualAlloc. As I mentioned in Chapter 4, VirtualAlloc allocates memory on system page size boundaries. Since the system page size and a disk's sector size are both expressed as powers of 2, allocating a buffer with VirtualAlloc ensures that it will be aligned on sector size boundaries.

The next exercise is the first of several in this book that will take you through the process of building a sample application that searches a text file for a specified string. Each sample app uses a different type of Windows file I/O or uses it in a different way than the others. By exploring each type of

I/O using a common metaphor, you should be able to compare and contrast the types of I/O facilities that Windows offers user mode applications and ascertain the strengths and weaknesses of each one compared with the others. We'll start with simple apps, then gradually increase their complexity as we go—the hope being that you'll add an understanding of the unique characteristics of each new sample app to what you learned about the previous ones.

Exercise

Exercise 5.3 takes you through an application that makes use of nonbuffered I/O. It opens each file that matches a given file mask in both nonbuffered and overlapped (asynchronous) mode and searches it for a string. It uses multiple worker threads to search through the file in parallel, keeps a tally of the number of matches it finds, and prints out each line containing a match.

Exercise 5.3   A String Search Utility That Uses Nonbuffered Asynchronous I/O

1. Load the fstring sample app from the CH05\fstring subfolder on the book's CD into the Visual C++ development environment. Compile and run it, specifying a text file and search string to search for as parameters. If you don't have a file handy that you'd like to search, the CD includes a file named INPUT.TXT. It contains a few instances of the string "ABCDEF" that you can search for.
2. Find the CreateFile call for the input file in fstring.cpp. You'll find that it passes both the FILE_FLAG_NO_BUFFERING and FILE_FLAG_OVERLAPPED switches. This causes the file to be processed without using the system cache and in asynchronous mode when possible.
3. The fstring app consists of two main source code modules: fstring.cpp and bufsrch.cpp. fstring.cpp contains the program's entry point function and the parts of the code that invoke a search against each file matching the specified file mask. bufsrch.cpp implements the code necessary to search a given buffer for a specified string, count the number of matches, and output matches to the console. This is best explored by going through the code itself. Let's start with fstring.cpp (Listing 5.3).

Listing 5.3 fstring.cpp, the Main Source Code Module for the fstring Utility

```cpp
// fstring.cpp : Multithreaded file search that uses
// nonbuffered I/O

#include "stdafx.h"
#include "windows.h"
#include "stdlib.h"
#include "process.h"
#include "bufsrch.h"

#define IO_STREAMS_PER_PROCESSOR 6

//Entry point routine for the worker threads
unsigned __stdcall StartSearch(LPVOID lpParameter)
{

  //Cast the parameter supplied to _beginthreadex
  //as a CBufSearch * and call its Search method

  return ((CBufSearch*)lpParameter)->Search();

}

//Search a specified file for a given search string
//using nonbuffered, asynchronous I/O
DWORD SearchFile(DWORD dwClusterSize,
                 DWORD dwNumStreams,
                 LPCRITICAL_SECTION pcsOutput,
                 char *szPath,
                 char *szFileName,
                 char *szSearchStr)
{
  char szFullPathName[MAX_PATH+1];
  DWORD dwNumThreads;
  HANDLE hPrivHeap;
  HANDLE *hThreads;
  HANDLE *hEvents;

  strcpy(szFullPathName,szPath);
  strcat(szFullPathName,szFileName);

  //Open the file for both nonbuffered and
  //overlapped (asynchronous) I/O
```

```
HANDLE hFile=CreateFile(szFullPathName,
                        GENERIC_READ,FILE_SHARE_READ,
                        NULL,
                        OPEN_EXISTING,
                        FILE_ATTRIBUTE_NORMAL
                        | FILE_FLAG_OVERLAPPED
                        | FILE_FLAG_NO_BUFFERING
                        ,NULL);

if (INVALID_HANDLE_VALUE==hFile) {
  printf("Error opening file.  Last error=%d\n",
         GetLastError());
  return 1;
}

DWORD dwFileSizeHigh;

DWORD dwFileSizeLow=GetFileSize(hFile,&dwFileSizeHigh);

DWORD dwlFileSize=(dwFileSizeHigh*MAXDWORD)+dwFileSizeLow;

DWORD dwNumClusts=dwlFileSize / dwClusterSize;
if (dwNumClusts<1) dwNumClusts=1;

//If file is less than 4GB and we have more requested
//streams (IO threads) than clusters, set the # of
//threads = to the # of clusters
if ((dwlFileSize<0xFFFFFFFF) && (dwNumStreams>dwNumClusts))
  dwNumThreads=dwNumClusts;
else
  dwNumThreads=dwNumStreams;

//Create a private heap so that we can free all
//allocations at once
hPrivHeap=HeapCreate(0,0,0);


//Create the thread and synchronization event arrays
hThreads=(HANDLE *)HeapAlloc(hPrivHeap,
                             HEAP_ZERO_MEMORY,
                             dwNumThreads*sizeof(HANDLE));
if (NULL==hThreads) {
  printf("Error allocating worker thread array.  Aborting.\n");
  return 1;
}
```

```
hEvents=(HANDLE *)HeapAlloc(hPrivHeap,
                            HEAP_ZERO_MEMORY,
                            dwNumThreads*sizeof(HANDLE));
if (NULL==hEvents) {
  printf("Error allocating event array.  Aborting.\n");
  return 1;
}

//Create the worker threads and the
//CBufSearch instance for each thread
CBufSearch *pbFirst=NULL;
unsigned uThreadId;

for (DWORD i=0; i<dwNumThreads; i++) {

  hEvents[i]=CreateEvent(NULL,false,false,NULL);

  pbFirst=new CBufSearch(pbFirst,
                         pcsOutput,
                         szFileName,
                         hFile,
                         dwClusterSize,
                         szSearchStr,
                         hEvents[i]);

  hThreads[i]= (HANDLE)_beginthreadex(NULL,
                                      0,
                                      &StartSearch,
                                      pbFirst,
                                      0,
                                      &uThreadId);

  if (!hThreads[i]) {
    printf("Error creating thread.  Aborting.\n");
    return -1;
  }
}

//Wait for all threads to signal that they've started
WaitForMultipleObjects(dwNumThreads,hEvents,true,INFINITE);

//Main loop -- loop through the file, reading it in
//dwClusterSize chunks and starting dwNumThreads, searching it
//concurrently
```

```
DWORDLONG dwlFilePos=0;
do {
  for (CBufSearch *pbCurrent=pbFirst;
    NULL!=pbCurrent;
    pbCurrent=pbCurrent->m_pbNext) {

      pbCurrent->m_OverlappedIO.Offset=
          (DWORD)(dwlFilePos / MAXDWORD);
      pbCurrent->m_OverlappedIO.Offset=
          (DWORD)(dwlFilePos % MAXDWORD);

      //Zero-fill the read buffer so that we don't
      //get search hits at the end of a partially
      //filled buffer (from previous contents)
      ZeroMemory(pbCurrent->m_szBuf,dwClusterSize+1);

      //Read a buffer full of data from the file
      //using asynchronous I/O if possible
      if (!ReadFile(hFile,pbCurrent->m_szBuf,
                            dwClusterSize,
                            &pbCurrent->m_dwBytesRead,
                            &pbCurrent->m_OverlappedIO)) {

        DWORD dwLastErr=GetLastError();
        if (ERROR_IO_PENDING!=dwLastErr)    {

          //Terminate the thread's main loop
          //on any error except ERROR_IO_PENDING
          //including EOF
          pbCurrent->m_bTerminated=true;

          //Abort if the error isn't an EOF
          if (ERROR_HANDLE_EOF!=dwLastErr) {
            printf("Error reading file.  Last
                    error=%d",dwLastErr);
            throw -1;
          }
        }
        else {
          //We have an asynchronous operation
          pbCurrent->m_bOverlapped=true;
        }
      }
```

```
      else {
        //ReadFile returned true; the operation
        //is synchronous
        pbCurrent->m_bOverlapped=false;
      }

      //Signal the worker thread to begin searching
      SetEvent(pbCurrent->m_hMainEvent);

      dwlFilePos+=dwClusterSize;
    }

    //Wait on all the worker threads to finish searching their
    //buffers.  Each one will signal the event we provided it
    //when it's ready for another buffer.
    WaitForMultipleObjects(dwNumThreads,hEvents,true,INFINITE);

  } while (dwlFilePos<dwlFileSize);

  //Get total tally and destroy search objects
  DWORD dwFindCount=0;
  CBufSearch *pbNext;
  for (; NULL!=pbFirst; pbFirst=pbNext) {
    pbFirst->m_bTerminated=true;
    dwFindCount+=pbFirst->m_dwFindCount;
    pbNext=pbFirst->m_pbNext;
    delete pbFirst;
  }

  //Close the thread and event handles
  for (i=0; i<dwNumThreads; i++) {
    CloseHandle(hThreads[i]);
    CloseHandle(hEvents[i]);
  }

  CloseHandle(hFile);

  //Free all of our previous heap allocations
  //by destroying the private heap we created
  HeapDestroy(hPrivHeap);

  //Return the find count for the specified file
  return dwFindCount;
}
```

```
//Search the files matching a given mask for a
//specified string
bool SearchFiles(char *szFileMask, char *szSearchStr)
{

  char szPath[MAX_PATH+1];

  //Extract the file path from the specified mask
  char *p=strrchr(szFileMask,'\\');
  if (p) {
    strncpy(szPath,szFileMask,(p-szFileMask)+1);
    szPath[(p-szFileMask)+1]='\0';
  }
  else
    //If no path was specified, use the current
    //folder
    GetCurrentDirectory(MAX_PATH,szPath);

  //Add a trailing backslash as necessary
  if ('\\'!=szPath[strlen(szPath)-1])
    strcat(szPath,"\\");

  printf("Searching for %s in %s\n\n",szSearchStr,szFileMask);

  //Loop through all the files matching the mask
  //and search each one for the string
  WIN32_FIND_DATA fdFiles;
  HANDLE hFind=FindFirstFile(szFileMask,&fdFiles);

  if (INVALID_HANDLE_VALUE == hFind) {
    printf("No files match the specified mask\n");
    return false;
  }

  //Get the number of processors
  //for the current system.
  //This will be used to compute
  //the number of I/O streams
  //to use to search each file
  SYSTEM_INFO si;
  GetSystemInfo(&si);

  //Get the cluster size from the drive
  //This will always be a multiple of the
```

```
    //sector size, so it is a good choice for
    //use with nonbuffered I/O
    DWORD dwSectorsPerCluster;
    DWORD dwBytesPerSector;
    DWORD dwNumberOfFreeClusters;
    DWORD dwTotalNumberOfClusters;
    GetDiskFreeSpace(NULL,&dwSectorsPerCluster,&dwBytesPerSector,
                &dwNumberOfFreeClusters,&dwTotalNumberOfClusters);

    DWORD dwClusterSize=(dwSectorsPerCluster * dwBytesPerSector);

    CRITICAL_SECTION csOutput;
    InitializeCriticalSection(&csOutput);

    DWORD dwFindCount=0;
    do {
      dwFindCount+=SearchFile(dwClusterSize,
        si.dwNumberOfProcessors*IO_STREAMS_PER_PROCESSOR,
        &csOutput,
        szPath,fdFiles.cFileName,
        szSearchStr);
    } while (FindNextFile(hFind,&fdFiles));

    FindClose(hFind);

    DeleteCriticalSection(&csOutput);

    printf("\nTotal hits for %s in %s:\t%d\n",szSearchStr,
        szFileMask,dwFindCount);
    return true;
}

int main(int argc, char* argv[])
{
  if (argc<3) {
    printf("Usage is: fstring filemask searchstring\n");
    return 1;
  }

  try
  {
    return (!SearchFiles(argv[1], argv[2]));
  }
```

```
  catch (...)
  {
    printf("Error reading file\n");
    return 1;
  }
}
```

4. Let's start with the main function. It takes the parameters passed into it and calls the global SearchFiles function. SearchFiles accepts a file mask and a search string, then locates each file matching the mask using the FindFirstFile and FindNextFile Win32 API functions.

5. SearchFiles creates a critical section which will be used to synchronize access to the console, which it then passes into the routine responsible for searching each file, SearchFile. I'll explain why we use a critical section in a moment.

6. SearchFiles also computes the cluster size for the current drive by calling the GetDiskFreeSpace function. We need to compute the cluster size on the drive because we intend to process files using nonbuffered I/O and Windows requires that I/O requests against nonbuffered files be aligned on disk sector boundaries. Since a disk's cluster size is always a multiple of its sector size, setting our read buffer to match the cluster size is a reasonable way to meet Windows' requirements.

7. SearchFiles retrieves the number of processors installed on the system and uses it to specify a requested number of I/O streams when it calls SearchFile. The number of I/O streams specifies the number of threads to use to search a file. We use a multiple of the processors on the system because each thread will spend a certain amount of time waiting on I/O and we want to keep the CPU(s) as busy as possible.

8. SearchFiles then calls the global SearchFile function to search each file for the string.

9. SearchFile begins by opening the specified file using CreateFile and passing in the FILE_FLAG_NO_BUFFERING and FILE_FLAG_OVERLAPPED switches. It then computes the size of the file and makes certain that it does not have more I/O streams than clusters in the file since we are reading the input file in cluster-sized chunks.

10. SearchFile next creates a private heap that it will use to store the two arrays of handles that it will need, the worker thread handle array and the event synchronization array. It then uses this private heap to allocate these two arrays. Because these are both allocated from a private heap, SearchFile can easily free them by simply destroying the heap prior to exiting. You may recall that I mentioned this technique in Chapter 4.

11. SearchFile next enters a loop wherein it allocates a CBufSearch object for each I/O stream and creates a worker thread for each CBufSearch instance. The entry point for each worker thread is the global function StartSearch, which casts the user parameter that was passed into _beginthreadex as a CBufSearch pointer and uses it to call the CBuf-Search::Search method. We'll talk more about CBufSearch in just a moment.

12. Once the search objects and worker threads have been created, SearchFile waits on the worker threads to signal it (via the event synchronization array) that they're ready to begin processing data.

13. Once the worker threads signal that they're ready, SearchFile enters a loop wherein it iterates through the CBufSearch objects and reads a cluster from the file asynchronously for each one. Once it has read a cluster for each CBufSearch object, it signals the object to begin processing the buffer. After a search has been queued for each of the CBufSearch objects, SearchFile waits on them all to finish before queuing more requests. This process continues until the entire file has been searched.

14. SearchFile checks the return value of ReadFile so that it can provide for the possibility that Windows might decide to process the read synchronously even though we've opened the file with the FILE_FLAG_OVERLAPPED switch and passed in a valid OVERLAPPED structure. As I mentioned earlier, there are situations in which Windows will process an asynchronous I/O request synchronously, and you have to code for that possibility. Here, we set a member in the CBufSearch object (m_bOverlapped) to indicate whether an asynchronous I/O operation was successfully initiated. CBufSearch needs to know whether the read was initiated asynchronously so that it can determine whether to call GetOverlappedResult to wait on the pending operation before attempting to search the read buffer.

15. To see how this works, set a breakpoint in SearchFile on each line that assigns m_bOverlapped, then run fstring under the Visual C++ debugger. If you pass in INPUT.TXT as the file mask, you should see that it reads this file asynchronously. Now, stop the debugger, open Explorer, bring up the file properties for INPUT.TXT and flag it as a compressed file, then rerun your test. You should see that the file is now read synchronously. As I mentioned earlier, one sure way to defeat Windows' ability to read or write a file asynchronously is to compress it with NTFS file compression.

16. Once the file is completely read and searched, SearchFile closes the input file, frees up the resources it allocated, and returns a match count tally to SearchFiles.

17. The real work of searching each file is done by the CBufSearch class. Let's have a closer look at it (Listing 5.4).

Listing 5.4 bufsrch.cpp, the Source Code Module for the CBufSearch Class

```cpp
//bufsrch.cpp -- a utility class that we use to search
//a buffer for a string

#include "bufsrch.h"

//Ctor
CBufSearch::CBufSearch(CBufSearch *pbNext, LPCRITICAL_SECTION
pcsOutput, char *szFileName, HANDLE hFile, DWORD dwClusterSize,
char *szSearchStr, HANDLE hSearchEvent)
{
  //Initialize the OVERLAPPED structure
  ZeroMemory(&m_OverlappedIO, sizeof(m_OverlappedIO));
  m_OverlappedIO.hEvent=CreateEvent(NULL,true,false,NULL);

  //Cache constructor parameters for later use
  m_pbNext=pbNext;
  m_szFileName=szFileName;
  m_hFile=hFile;
  m_pcsOutput=pcsOutput;
  m_szSearchStr=szSearchStr;
  m_dwClusterSize=dwClusterSize;
  m_hSearchEvent=hSearchEvent;

  //Create the event the main thread
  //will signal when it's ready for
  //a worker thread to begin processing a buffer
  m_hMainEvent=CreateEvent(NULL,false,false,NULL);

  //Allocate the read buffer.
  //Use VirtualAlloc so that we can ensure that
  //the buffer is aligned on a page size
  //boundary.  This will also ensure that it's
  //aligned on a sector size boundary since both
  //are expressed as a power of 2.  In order to
  //perform nonbuffered I/O, the read or write
  //buffer must be aligned on an even multiple of
  //the disk's sector size.
  //Allocate one more byte than the cluster size
  //(which will result in an additional page of
  //virtual memory being committed and reserved)
  //so that we don't have to worry about strstr
  //running off the end of our buffer looking
```

```
   //for a null terminator.
   m_szBuf=(char *)VirtualAlloc(NULL,m_dwClusterSize+1,
                                MEM_RESERVE | MEM_COMMIT,
                                PAGE_READWRITE);

   //Initialize the remaining member variables
   m_bTerminated=false;
   m_bOverlapped=true;
   m_dwFindCount=0;


}

//Dtor
CBufSearch::~CBufSearch()
{
   //Close the event handles we created
   //in the constructor
   CloseHandle(m_OverlappedIO.hEvent);
   CloseHandle(m_hMainEvent);

   //Decommit and release the memory for
   //the read buffer
   VirtualFree(m_szBuf,0,MEM_RELEASE);
}

//From an offset in a buffer, find the start of the line
char *CBufSearch::FindLineStart(char *szStartPos)
{
   char *szStart;
   for (szStart=szStartPos; ((szStart>m_szBuf) &&
       (cLINE_DELIM!=*(szStart-1)))); szStart--);
   return szStart;
}

//From an offset in a buffer, find the end of the line
// -- assumes null-termination
char *CBufSearch::FindLineEnd(char *szStartPos)
{
   return strchr(szStartPos,cLINE_DELIM);
}

//Search the read buffer for
//every line containing a previously
```

```
//specified search string
bool CBufSearch::Search()
{
  char *szBol;
  char *szEol;
  char *szStringPos;
  DWORD dwNumChars;
  char *szStartPos;
  bool bRes=false;
  char szFmt[32];
  DWORDLONG dwlFilePos;

  //Signal to the main thread that we're
  //ready for processing
  SetEvent(m_hSearchEvent);

  //Main thread sets m_bTerminated
  //to false at EOF or in the case
  //of an error reading the file
  while (!m_bTerminated) {

    //Wait for the main thread to signal
    //that it's OK to process the read buffer
    WaitForSingleObject(m_hMainEvent,INFINITE);

    //If the terminate member was set while
    //we were asleep, exit the loop
    if (m_bTerminated) break;

    //We start the search at the beginning
    //of the read buffer
    szStartPos=m_szBuf;

    //The current file position (which we'll need
    //later to indicate where we found the string)
    //can be extracted from the OVERLAPPED structure
    //used by the read operation.
    dwlFilePos=(m_OverlappedIO.OffsetHigh*MAXDWORD)
    +m_OverlappedIO.Offset;

    //If we have an overlapped (asynchronous)
    //operation, use GetOverlappedResult to
    //wait on it to complete
    if (m_bOverlapped) {
```

```
      if ((!GetOverlappedResult(m_hFile,&m_OverlappedIO,
          &m_dwBytesRead,true)) ||
        (!m_dwBytesRead)) {
        printf("Error getting pending IO.  Last error=
            %d\n",GetLastError());
        break;
      }
    }

    __try
    {
      //Loop while our search start marker is not NULL,
      //is within our read buffer,
      //and strstr continues to find the search string
      while ((szStartPos) &&
            (szStartPos<(m_szBuf+m_dwBytesRead)-1) &&
            (NULL!=(szStringPos=
            strstr(szStartPos,m_szSearchStr)))) {

        //If we get in here, we have a search hit
        m_dwFindCount++;

        //Compute the line start and end so that we
        //can write it to the console
        szBol=FindLineStart(szStringPos);
        szEol=FindLineEnd(szStringPos);

        //Compute the number of characters to output
        //We'll use this later to build a printf
        //format string
        if (szEol) {
          dwNumChars=szEol-szBol;
          if (szEol<(m_szBuf+m_dwBytesRead)-1)
              szStartPos=szEol+1;
          else szStartPos=NULL;
        }
        else {
          dwNumChars=MAXLINE_LEN;
          szStartPos=NULL;
        }

        EnterCriticalSection(m_pcsOutput);

#if(_DEBUG)
        printf("Thread %08d: Offset: %010I64d %s ",
        GetCurrentThreadId(),dwlFilePos+
        (szStringPos-m_szBuf),m_szFileName);
```

```
      #else
          printf("Offset: %010I64d %s ",dwlFilePos+
              (szStringPos-m_szBuf),m_szFileName);
      #endif
          //Build format string that limits output to
          //current line
          strcpy(szFmt,"%.");
          sprintf(szFmt+2,"%ds\n",dwNumChars);

          //Output current line
          printf(szFmt,szBol);

          LeaveCriticalSection(m_pcsOutput);

          bRes=true;


        }
      }
      __except(EXCEPTION_EXECUTE_HANDLER)
      {
        //Eat the exception -- should never get here
        //given that the read buffer is guaranteed to
        //be null-terminated.
  #if(_DEBUG)

        //Assumes we got an access violation from going
        //past the end of the read buffer -- could actually
        //be some other type of error
        printf("Thread %08d reached end of buffer\n",
        GetCurrentThreadId());
  #endif
      }

      //Signal to the main thread that we're done
      //with this buffer
      SetEvent(m_hSearchEvent);
    }

    //If we exit the loop abnormally, be sure
    //to signal our event to prevent an infinite
    //wait by the main thread
    SetEvent(m_hSearchEvent);
    return bRes;
}
```

18. The CBufSearch constructor begins by zeroing the class's OVER-LAPPED structure and creating an event to associate with it. As I mentioned earlier in the chapter, an event object is required if you intend to use GetOverlappedResult to wait on an asynchronous operation to complete and have multiple asynchronous operations running concurrently for a given file. Although, technically speaking, creating the event is optional, GetOverlappedResult will not work reliably without it if multiple asynchronous operations are executing concurrently against the specified file. The telltale sign that this is an issue is when GetOverlappedResult returns FALSE but GetLastError returns 0.

19. The CBufSearch constructor next creates an event that the main thread will use to signal a worker thread that it can process the read buffer. Synchronization between the main thread and the worker threads is accomplished by using two event objects for each worker thread. The first event—the one created by CBufSearch's constructor—is used to signal the worker thread that it's safe to process the read buffer. The second—the one created by the main thread—is used to signal the main thread that the worker thread is done processing its buffer and is ready for another.

20. The CBufSearch constructor next allocates the memory for the read buffer. It uses VirtualAlloc to do this so that we can guarantee that the buffer will be aligned on a sector size boundary in memory, a requirement of Windows' nonbuffered I/O facility. As I mentioned earlier, because VirtualAlloc always allocates memory on page boundaries, and because the system page size and the sector size of a disk are always expressed as powers of 2, we can be certain that any buffer allocated with VirtualAlloc will be properly aligned for use with nonbuffered I/O.

21. Note the fact that we size the VirtualAlloc allocation to 1 byte greater than the cluster size. This is so that we can be sure that the search buffer will be null-terminated. We always zero-fill the read buffer between reads, so the buffer will always end with a 0, even after a read has completed, because the read buffer is larger than the read size specified in the ReadFile call. We need to ensure that the buffer is always null-terminated because we use C/C++ RTL functions such as strstr and strchr to search the buffer for matching strings and characters. There are no memstr or strnstr functions in the RTL, so we rely on null-termination to mark the end of the search buffer. Another way to handle this situation is to allocate a guard or no access page beyond the read buffer and simply trap the exception that will be generated when strstr attempts to traverse memory beyond our read buffer. You'll see a variation on this technique employed in the Memory-Mapped File I/O section later in the chapter.

22. The actual work of searching each read buffer is carried out by the CBufSearch::Search method. Once a worker thread is started, it calls this method and never exits it until the end of the input file is reached.

23. CBufSearch::Search begins by signaling the main thread that it has started up and is ready for a buffer to search. Just after creating the worker threads, the main thread passes the event array into WaitFor-MultipleObjects in order to wait on all the worker threads to start up and enter CBufSearch::Search before it begins to read the input file. Once each of them signals that it's ready, the main thread begins processing the file.

24. CBufSearch::Search next enters a loop controlled by the m_bTerminated member. It will stay in this loop until a catastrophic error occurs that forces it to exit or the main thread sets the member to FALSE because the end of the input file has been reached.

25. Next, Search checks to see whether we have a pending asynchronous I/O operation by inspecting the m_bOverlapped member. If an asynchronous I/O is pending, Search calls GetOverlappedResult to wait on it to complete. This causes GetOverlappedResult to wait on the event we associated with the OVERLAPPED structure to be signaled. Once it is, execution continues.

26. After acquiring a valid read buffer, Search loops through it, scanning for each occurrence of the search string. When it finds a match, it outputs the line on which the match occurs and moves to the next line to continue searching. This means that each line in the input file will register at most one match, regardless of how many times the search string occurs on the line.

27. When it finds a match and prepares to output a line to the console, Search enters the critical section originally created in the SearchFiles routine in order to prevent other worker threads from writing to the console simultaneously. This is necessary because we use two printfs to write the output to the console: one to indicate the file name and the offset at which we found the string, another to output the matching line itself. If not for the critical section, another thread could send output to the console in between the two printfs, making the output difficult to interpret. We use two printfs so that we can avoid copying the matching line into a second buffer before writing it to the console. Instead, we compute the start and end of the line in the read buffer itself, then use a printf format string to print the string starting at the matching line's beginning and continuing for the number of characters between the beginning of the line and the end of the line. This allows us to avoid first copying the matching line to a secondary buffer because we output directly from the read buffer itself. As you'll see in the sample apps later in the chapter, there's a simple modification we could make to the code here that would alleviate the need for the two separate printf calls and the use of the critical section. I took the approach I did in this app to demonstrate the conventional use of a critical section—to prevent multiple threads from executing a block of code simultaneously.

28. Once Search has processed its read buffer, it signals the main thread that it's ready for another buffer and waits on the main thread to signal it that a new read buffer is ready for processing. If the end of the input file is reached while Search waits on the main thread, CBufSearch's m_bTerminated member will be set to TRUE when Search exits Wait-ForSingleObject and will cause it to immediately exit its main loop. This, in turn, will cause the thread to exit. As I mentioned in Chapter 3, it's always preferable to allow a thread to shut down normally rather than forcing it to terminate by calling TerminateThread or ExitThread.

So, that's the fstring sample app from start to finish. As you can see, non-buffered and asynchronous I/O can be combined to carry out some very useful tasks in an efficient manner.

You may have noticed that fstring can't detect search string matches that straddle buffer boundaries. Assuming we have a cluster size of, say, 4K, a string match that straddles the 4K boundary will not be detected by fstring. This is a limitation of page-oriented searching algorithms, which we will address in the Memory-Mapped File I/O section later in the chapter. As designed, fstring is only intended to demonstrate how asynchronous, non-buffered I/O can be used by a multithreaded program to scan a file in parallel—it's not intended to be a general-purpose text search tool. There are, however, plenty of uses for page-oriented search tools. As long as your data is organized such that it does not span buffer boundaries (as it might be in a database program, for example), a page-oriented search algorithm can be used to search it.

Another point worth making about fstring is that, because it is multithreaded, the string matches it reports may not be listed in order. There's no guarantee that matches found early in a file will be listed before those found later. Multiple threads are being used to scan the input file(s) simultaneously, so the exact timing of when a particular match is found and written to the console is not predictable and will likely vary from run to run of the application. You could resolve this by writing the matches to memory and sorting them before writing them to the console, but this might require huge amounts of virtual memory and slow down the app considerably. You could change the search algorithm so that you don't search individual files in parallel but instead align the worker threads along file boundaries so that each file is searched by its own thread. This would resolve the issue, but it might not fully utilize your system resources (especially if you have a multiprocessor machine) if you were searching only a single file. If you were searching only one file, regardless of how large the file was, you'd have to wait while a single thread scanned through it in a synchronous fashion. A better solution is to use the SORT filter. Windows provides several filters you can make use of to filter or process the output from console applications and OS commands. You can use SORT to order fstring's output such that all the match lines for each file are written to the console in offset order. Here's the syntax:

```
fstring INPUT.TXT ABCDEF | SORT
```

I intentionally formatted the output lines so that they could be reordered using SORT. That's why the offset is zero-padded and the text on each match line has a uniform length up to the point where the file name starts.

Asynchronous and Nonbuffered I/O Recap

Asynchronous I/O allows a thread to continue to run while an I/O operation completes. In order to initiate an asynchronous operation, you must create the file object with the appropriate bit flags and must pass a valid OVER-LAPPED structure into the Win32 function you use to read or write the file. Even though you may instruct Windows to initiate an I/O operation asynchronously, it may decide to process it synchronously in certain circumstances.

A thread can call GetOverlappedResult to wait on a pending asynchronous I/O request. It can also wait on the event associated with the OVER-LAPPED structure or on the file object itself. Moreover, Win32 functions such as ReadFileEx and WriteFileEx can queue an APC function to notify a thread that an asynchronous operation has completed. An I/O completion port is yet another mechanism that can be used to notify a thread that an asynchronous operation has finished.

Nonbuffered I/O allows a thread to circumvent the system cache as it performs I/O operations on a file. It has a set of requirements that a thread must meet to make use of it. In order for a file to be processed with nonbuffered I/O, the file object must be created with the FILE_FLAG_NO_BUF-FERING switch. Access to the file must begin on even multiples of the disk's sector size. File reads and writes must be for a number of bytes that is also an even multiple of the disk's sector size. Finally, the buffer used in a nonbuffered read or write operation must be aligned on a memory address that is an even multiple of the disk's sector size. One sure way to guarantee this is to use VirtualAlloc to allocate the buffer. Since VirtualAlloc always allocates memory on system page size boundaries, and since disk sector sizes and the system page size are always expressed as a power of 2, a buffer allocated using VirtualAlloc will always be aligned on a sector size boundary.

Using nonbuffered I/O helps ensure the best performance when using asynchronous I/O. It is also a good way to help direct Windows to process an asynchronous I/O operation asynchronously since it bypasses the system cache, a potential cause of synchronous processing of asynchronous operations.

SQL Server uses nonbuffered and asynchronous I/O extensively. All writes to SQL Server data or log files are nonbuffered and asynchronous.

Asynchronous and Nonbuffered I/O Knowledge Measure

1. Is it true that a sector can actually be larger than a cluster on a hard disk?
2. What sector size is by far the most prevalent on x86 computers?
3. True or false: Passing in the FILE_FLAG_OVERLAPPED and FILE_FLAG_NO_BUFFERING switches to CreateFile will guarantee that Windows will not process I/O requests against the file synchronously.
4. What memory allocation function can you use to ensure that the read or write buffer for a nonbuffered I/O operation is aligned on a disk sector boundary?
5. What Win32 API function returns the sector and cluster size of a disk?
6. True or false: Passing the FILE_FLAG_NO_BUFFERING switch into CreateFile instructs Windows to circumvent the system cache when processing I/O requests for the specified file.
7. What type of callback routine do the ReadFileEx and WriteFileEx routines cause to be queued when an asynchronous I/O operation completes?
8. True or false: One of the circumstances in which Windows will process an asynchronous I/O request synchronously is when the file being read or written is on a network drive.
9. In what situation is the event handle that can be optionally associated with an OVERLAPPED structure required in order for GetOverlappedResult to function properly?
10. If an application is executing a loop that reads through a file using ReadFileEx, is it necessary to adjust the OVERLAPPED structure that is passed into ReadFileEx between calls to the function?
11. True or false: You can retrieve the number of bytes processed by an asynchronous I/O operation initiated by WriteFileEx by passing in a DWORD by reference for WriteFileEx's dwBytesTransferred parameter.

12. What Win32 API can be used to queue an APC?
13. What must a thread do in order to allow an APC to run?
14. What two types of APCs does Windows support?
15. What is the typical use of a critical section?
16. Assuming an event object has been associated with the OVER-LAPPED structure you're using for asynchronous I/O, when an operation initiated with ReadFileEx completes, will the event be signaled?
17. Explain the use of the Offset and OffsetHigh members of the OVERLAPPED structure in relation to asynchronous I/O.
18. True or false: An application can call the Win32 HasOverlappedIo-Completed function to determine whether a pending asynchronous I/O operation has completed.
19. Explain why you should not initiate an alertable wait against a file object that has a pending asynchronous I/O operation initiated by WriteFileEx.
20. True or false: SQL Server avoids using nonbuffered I/O because it leverages the Windows' lazywriter facility in order to achieve maximum I/O performance.
21. Can you specify parameters to GetOverlappedResult such that it waits on a pending asynchronous operation to complete before returning?
22. When ReadFile successfully initiates an asynchronous I/O operation, what value does GetLastError return?
23. True or false: Compressing a file with NTFS compression will prevent it from being processed asynchronously by ReadFile and WriteFile.
24. What's another term for overlapped I/O?
25. True or false: One of the requirements for initiating a nonbuffered I/O operation against a file is that access to the file must begin at byte offsets that are evenly divisible by the disk's sector size.

Scatter-Gather I/O

In this section, we'll explore Windows' scatter-gather I/O facility and build a sample app that makes use of it. If you haven't yet read the first part of this chapter, you should probably do so before continuing.

Key Scatter-Gather I/O Terms and Concepts

✔ *Sector*—a hardware-addressable block on a storage medium such as a hard disk. The sector size for hard disks on x86 computers is almost always 512 bytes. This means that if Windows wants to write to byte 11 or 27, it must write to the first sector of the disk; if it wants to write to byte 1961, it must write to the fourth sector of the disk. You can retrieve the sector size for a disk via the GetDiskFreeSpace Win32 API function.

✔ *Cluster*—an addressable block of sectors that many file systems use. A cluster is the smallest unit of storage for a file. A cluster is usually larger than a sector and is always a multiple of the sector size. Clusters are used by file systems to manage disk space more efficiently than would be possible with individual sectors. By encompassing multiple sectors, a cluster helps divide a disk into more manageable pieces. The downsides are that large cluster sizes may waste disk space or result in fragmentation since file sizes aren't usually exact multiples of the cluster size. You can retrieve the cluster size of a disk via the GetDiskFreeSpace Win32 API function.

✔ *Asynchronous I/O*—allows a thread that initiates an I/O operation to continue executing without waiting on the operation to complete. The thread can check the status of its pending I/O operation through a variety of means, which we'll discuss shortly.

✔ *Nonbuffered I/O*—allows Windows to open a file without intermediate buffering or caching. When combined with asynchronous I/O, nonbuffered I/O gives the best overall asynchronous performance because operations are not slowed down by the synchronous operations of the memory manager. That said, some operations will actually be slower because data cannot be loaded from the cache. SQL Server uses nonbuffered I/O to eliminate the latency between logical disk writes and the data being physically written to disk.

✔ *Scatter-gather I/O*—allows an app to issue a single read or write operation to move data between multiple virtual memory buffers and a contiguous file region. Before support for scatter-gather I/O was introduced into Windows, a read or write operation against a file always targeted a contiguous memory buffer. Scatter-gather I/O allows this memory buffer to consist of multiple smaller pieces that are not necessarily contiguous.

Key Scatter-Gather I/O APIs

Table 5.6 Key Scatter-Gather I/O–Related API Functions

Function	Description
ReadFileScatter	Reads a buffer asynchronously from a file into an array of memory buffers
WriteFileScatter	Writes a buffer asynchronously from an array of memory buffers to disk

Overview

First introduced via a service pack for Windows NT 4.0, Windows supports a special type of file I/O known as scatter-gather. You make use of scatter-gather I/O in an application by calling the ReadFileScatter and WriteFile-Scatter functions. Scatter-gather I/O works like this: You supply an array of buffers to either "scatter" data from a file into memory or "gather" data from memory and write it to a contiguous region of a file. The buffers into which data is scattered or from which it is gathered need not be contiguous. The source or destination file region is always contiguous. The purpose of scatter-gather I/O is to allow data to be transferred between a contiguous region of a file and a series of buffers that may be scattered throughout memory without requiring the use of an intermediate, contiguous buffer.

In order to use scatter-gather I/O, an application must meet the following requirements.

- The file must be opened with the FILE_FLAG_NO_BUFFERING and FILE_FLAG_OVERLAPPED switches.
- The scatter-gather buffers must be aligned on sector-size boundaries.
- The requested number of bytes to transfer must be an even multiple of the target disk's sector size.

As you may have noticed, these requirements are a combination of the requirements for nonbuffered I/O and asynchronous I/O. This is because scatter-gather I/O requires nonbuffered I/O and is asynchronous by default. As with regular asynchronous I/O requests, the system can decide to process scatter-gather I/O synchronously in certain circumstances (e.g., if the target file has been compressed with NTFS compression).

The scatter-gather I/O facility was originally added to Windows specifically for use by SQL Server. SQL Server makes heavy use of it as it reads and writes data and log files. Doing so allows it to quickly fill pages in the buffer pool with data from disk when reading from a database's data or log files and allows it to quickly flush multiple pages in the buffer pool to disk when writing data.

Scatter-gather I/O is best understood by seeing it in action. Let's look at some code.

Exercise

In this exercise, we'll walk through a sample app that's a variation on the fstring sample presented earlier. You'll recall that fstring accepts a file mask and a search string as parameters, then lists each line containing the search string in each of the files matching the mask. In that app, we used regular asynchronous I/O to process the file in cluster-sized chunks. In this one, we'll use scatter-gather I/O to grab several clusters worth of data at once, then search each one with a separate thread.

Exercise 5.4   A File Search Utility That Uses Scatter-Gather I/O

1. Load the fstring_scatter sample from the CH05\fstring_scatter subfolder on the CD into the Visual Studio development environment and compile it.
2. The source code to fstring_scatter is distributed mostly across two files: fstring_scatter.cpp and bufsrch.cpp. You'll notice that bufsrch.cpp is virtually identical to the one used by fstring.
3. Conceptually, fstring_search is very similar to fstring. We iterate through the files matching a given mask and search each one for a specified string. For each file, we read through it asynchronously and pass each read buffer to a worker thread to carry out the search. The difference between the two apps is in how the asynchronous I/O is carried out. In the case of fstring, we read the buffer for each worker thread separately. With fstring_scatter, we read them all at once via a single call to ReadFileScattered. Let's look at the source code (Listing 5.5).

Listing 5.5 The Source Code for the bufsrch.cpp Utility

```cpp
// bufsrch.cpp -- a utility class that we
// use to search a buffer for a string

#include "bufsrch.h"

//Ctor
CBufSearch::CBufSearch(CBufSearch *pbNext, char *szFileName,
HANDLE hFile, DWORD dwClusterSize, int iIndex, char *szBuf,
char *szSearchStr, HANDLE hSearchEvent, OVERLAPPED *pOverlappedIO)
{
  //Cache constructor parameters for later use
  m_pbNext=pbNext;
  m_szFileName=szFileName;
  m_hFile=hFile;
  m_szSearchStr=szSearchStr;
  m_dwClusterSize=dwClusterSize;
  m_hSearchEvent=hSearchEvent;
  m_pOverlappedIO=pOverlappedIO;
  m_iIndex=iIndex;

  //Create the event the main thread
  //will signal when it's ready for
  //a worker thread to begin processing a buffer
  m_hMainEvent=CreateEvent(NULL,false,false,NULL);

  m_szBuf=szBuf;

  //Initialize the remaining member variables
  m_bTerminated=false;
  m_bOverlapped=true;
  m_dwFindCount=0;


}

//Dtor
CBufSearch::~CBufSearch()
{
  //Close the event handles we created
  //in the constructor
  CloseHandle(m_hMainEvent);
```

```
}

//From an offset in a buffer, find the start of the line
char *CBufSearch::FindLineStart(char *szStartPos)
{
  char *szStart;
  for (szStart=szStartPos;
    ((szStart>m_szBuf) && (cLINE_DELIM!=*(szStart-1)));
      szStart--);
  return szStart;
}

//From an offset in a buffer, find the end of the line
// -- assumes null-termination
char *CBufSearch::FindLineEnd(char *szStartPos)
{
  return strchr(szStartPos,cLINE_DELIM);
}

//Search the read buffer for
//every line containing a previously
//specified search string
bool CBufSearch::Search()
{
  char *szBol;
  char *szEol;
  char *szStringPos;
  DWORD dwNumChars;
  char *szStartPos;
  bool bRes=false;
  char szFmt[32];
  char szOffsetOutput[255];

  DWORDLONG dwlFilePos;

  //Signal to the main thread that we're
  //ready for processing
  SetEvent(m_hSearchEvent);

  //Main thread sets m_bTerminated
  //to false at EOF or in the case
  //of an error reading the file
  while (!m_bTerminated) {
```

```
//Wait for the main thread to signal
//that it's OK to process the read buffer
WaitForSingleObject(m_hMainEvent,INFINITE);

//If the terminate member was set while
//we were asleep, exit the loop
if (m_bTerminated) break;

//We start the search at the beginning
//of the read buffer
szStartPos=m_szBuf;

//The current file position (which we'll need
//later to indicate where we found the string)
//can be extracted from the OVERLAPPED structure
//used by the read operation.
dwlFilePos=
      (m_pOverlappedIO->OffsetHigh*MAXDWORD)+
       m_pOverlappedIO->Offset+(m_iIndex*m_dwClusterSize);

//If we have an overlapped (asynchronous)
//operation, use GetOverlappedResult to
//wait on it to complete
if (m_bOverlapped) {
  if ((!GetOverlappedResult(m_hFile,m_pOverlappedIO,
    &m_dwBytesRead, true)) ||
    (!m_dwBytesRead)) {
    printf("Error getting pending IO.  Last error=%d\n",
      GetLastError());
      break;
    }
}

__try
{
  //Loop while our search start marker is not NULL
  //and is within our read buffer
  //and strstr continues to find the search string
  //in our read buffer
  while ((szStartPos) &&
         (szStartPos<(m_szBuf+m_dwBytesRead)-1) &&
         (NULL!=(szStringPos=
             strstr(szStartPos,m_szSearchStr)))) {
```

```
        //If we get in here, we have a search hit
        m_dwFindCount++;

        //Compute the line start and end so that we
        //can write it to the console
        szBol=FindLineStart(szStringPos);
        szEol=FindLineEnd(szStringPos);

        //Compute the number of characters to output
        //We'll use this later to build a printf
        //format string
        if (szEol) {
          dwNumChars=szEol-szBol;
          if (szEol<(m_szBuf+m_dwBytesRead)-1)
              szStartPos=szEol+1;
          else szStartPos=NULL;
        }
        else {
          dwNumChars=MAXLINE_LEN;
          szStartPos=NULL;
        }


#if(_DEBUG)
    sprintf(szOffsetOutput,
    "Thread %08d: Offset: %010I64d %s ",
    GetCurrentThreadId(),dwlFilePos+
    (szStringPos-m_szBuf),m_szFileName);
#else
    sprintf(szOffsetOutput,
    "Offset: %010I64d %s ",dwlFilePos+
    (szStringPos-m_szBuf),m_szFileName);
#endif
//Build format string that limits output to current line
    strcpy(szFmt,"%s %.");
    sprintf(szFmt+5,"%ds\n",dwNumChars);

    //Output current line
    printf(szFmt,szOffsetOutput,szBol);

    bRes=true;


  }
}
```

```
      __except(EXCEPTION_EXECUTE_HANDLER)
      {
        //Eat the exception -- should never get here
        //given that the read buffer is guaranteed to
        //be null-terminated.
#if(_DEBUG)

        //Assumes we got an access violation from going
        //past the end of the read buffer -- could actually
        //be some other type of error
        printf("Thread %08d reached end of buffer\n",
            GetCurrentThreadId());
#endif
      }

      //Signal to the main thread that we're done
      //with this buffer
      SetEvent(m_hSearchEvent);
    }

    //If we exit the loop abnormally, be sure
    //to signal our event to prevent an infinite
    //wait by the main thread
    SetEvent(m_hSearchEvent);

    return bRes;
}
```

4. As you'll see if you compare the version of bufsrch.cpp presented here with the one in Example 5.3, CBufSearch is largely the same between the two samples. The main difference between the two is the way in which this version uses the buffer index passed into it to help compute the file offset for a match string.

5. As mentioned above, fstring_scatter is very similar to fstring in many ways. As you might expect, one important way in which they differ is that fstring_scatter calls ReadFileScatter to load a contiguous region from each input file into a noncontiguous set of memory buffers. Examine in Listing 5.6 the code for the SearchFile function that calls ReadFileScatter. You'll notice that it's called outside the loop that iterates through the CBufSearch objects. That's because, unlike fstring, we can do all the I/O for all the worker threads with a single asynchronous call.

Listing 5.6 The Source Code for the fstring_scatter Utility

```cpp
// fstring_scatter.cpp : A multithreaded file
// search utility that uses scatter-gather I/O
//

#include "stdafx.h"
#include "windows.h"
#include "stdlib.h"
#include "process.h"
#include "bufsrch.h"

#define IO_STREAMS_PER_PROCESSOR 6

//Entry point routine for the worker threads
unsigned __stdcall StartSearch(LPVOID lpParameter)
{

  //Cast the parameter supplied to _beginthreadex
  //as a CBufSearch * and call its Search method

  return ((CBufSearch*)lpParameter)->Search();

}

//Search a specified file for a given search string
//using scatter-gather I/O
DWORD SearchFile(DWORD dwClusterSize,
                 DWORD dwNumStreams,
                 char *szPath,
                 char *szFileName,
                 char *szSearchStr)
{
  char szFullPathName[MAX_PATH+1];
  DWORD dwNumThreads;
  HANDLE hPrivHeap;
  HANDLE *hThreads;
  HANDLE *hEvents;
  FILE_SEGMENT_ELEMENT *pSegments;

  strcpy(szFullPathName,szPath);
  strcat(szFullPathName,szFileName);

  //Open the file for both nonbuffered and
  //overlapped (asynchronous) I/O
```

```
HANDLE hFile=CreateFile(szFullPathName,
                        GENERIC_READ,FILE_SHARE_READ,
                        NULL,
                        OPEN_EXISTING,
                        FILE_ATTRIBUTE_NORMAL
                        | FILE_FLAG_OVERLAPPED
                        | FILE_FLAG_NO_BUFFERING
                        ,NULL);

if (INVALID_HANDLE_VALUE==hFile) {
  printf("Error opening file.  Last error=%d\n",
        GetLastError());
  return 1;
}

DWORD dwFileSizeHigh;

DWORD dwFileSizeLow=GetFileSize(hFile,&dwFileSizeHigh);

DWORD dwlFileSize=
    (dwFileSizeHigh*MAXDWORD)+dwFileSizeLow;

DWORD dwNumClusts=dwlFileSize / dwClusterSize;
if (dwNumClusts<1) dwNumClusts=1;

//If file is less than 4GB and we have more requested
//streams (IO threads) than clusters, set the # of
//threads = to the # of clusters
if ((dwlFileSize<0xFFFFFFFF) &&
  (dwNumStreams>dwNumClusts))
  dwNumThreads=dwNumClusts;
else
  dwNumThreads=dwNumStreams;

//Create a private heap so that we can free all
//allocations at once
hPrivHeap=HeapCreate(0,0,0);

//Create the thread and synchronization event arrays
hThreads=(HANDLE *)HeapAlloc(hPrivHeap,
                            HEAP_ZERO_MEMORY,
                            dwNumThreads*sizeof(HANDLE));
```

```
if (NULL==hThreads) {
  printf("Error allocating worker thread array.  Aborting.\n");
  return -1;
}

hEvents=(HANDLE *)HeapAlloc(hPrivHeap,
                                HEAP_ZERO_MEMORY,
                                dwNumThreads*sizeof(HANDLE));
if (NULL==hEvents) {
  printf("Error allocating event array.  Aborting.\n");
  return -1;
}

//Create the array of file segment
//element pointers to be used with
//ReadFileScatter
//This is sized at one more than the
//# of threads because the last
//element must be NULL
pSegments=(FILE_SEGMENT_ELEMENT *)HeapAlloc(hPrivHeap,
                                                HEAP_ZERO_MEMORY,
                                                (dwNumThreads+1)*
                                    sizeof(FILE_SEGMENT_ELEMENT));
if (NULL==pSegments) {
  printf("Error allocating segment array.  Aborting.\n");
  return -1;
}

//Set up the OVERLAPPED structure
//that ReadFileScatter requires
//and that all the worker threads
//will use
OVERLAPPED OverlappedIO;
ZeroMemory(&OverlappedIO,sizeof(OverlappedIO));
OverlappedIO.hEvent=CreateEvent(NULL,true,false,NULL);

//Create the worker threads and the
//CBufSearch instance for each thread
CBufSearch *pbFirst=NULL;
unsigned uThreadId;

//Loop backward so that the CBufSearch linked list
//entries will have the correct ordinal index value
//which they use to compute their offset in the file
for (int i=dwNumThreads-1; i>=0; i--) {

  hEvents[i]=CreateEvent(NULL,false,false,NULL);
```

```
//Allocate the read buffer.
//Use VirtualAlloc so that we can ensure that
//the buffer is aligned on a page size
//boundary.  This will also ensure that it's
//aligned on a sector size boundary since both
//are expressed as a power of 2.  In order to
//perform scatter-gather I/O, the read or write
//buffer must be aligned on an even multiple of
//the disk's sector size.

//Allocate one more byte than the cluster size
//(which will result in an additional page of
//virtual memory being committed and reserved)
//so that we don't have to worry about strstr
//running off the end of our buffer looking
//for a null terminator.
pSegments[i].Buffer=
   (PVOID64)VirtualAlloc(NULL,dwClusterSize+1,
                         MEM_RESERVE | MEM_COMMIT,
                         PAGE_READWRITE);

pbFirst=new CBufSearch(pbFirst,
                       szFileName,
                       hFile,
                       dwClusterSize,
                       i,
                       (char *)pSegments[i].Buffer,
                       szSearchStr,
                       hEvents[i],
                       &OverlappedIO);

hThreads[i]=
(HANDLE)_beginthreadex(NULL,
                       0,
                       &StartSearch,
                       pbFirst,
                       0,
                       &uThreadId);

if (!hThreads[i]) {
  printf("Error creating thread.  Aborting.\n");
  return -1;
}
}
```

```
//Wait for all threads to signal that they've started
WaitForMultipleObjects(dwNumThreads,hEvents,true,INFINITE);


bool bTerminated=false;
bool bOverlapped;

//Main loop -- loop through the file, reading it in
//chunks of dwClusterSize * dwNumThreads size.  Each
//time we fill a set of scatter buffers, signal the
//worker threads to search them
DWORDLONG dwlFilePos=0;
do {

  bOverlapped=true;

  OverlappedIO.Offset=
      (DWORD)(dwlFilePos / MAXDWORD);
  OverlappedIO.Offset=
      (DWORD)(dwlFilePos % MAXDWORD);

  //Zero-fill the read buffers so that we don't
  //get search hits at the end of a partially
  //filled buffer (from previous contents)
  for (DWORD j=0; j<dwNumThreads; j++)
    ZeroMemory(pSegments[j].Buffer,dwClusterSize+1);

  //Fill the scatter buffers using
  //asynchronous I/O if possible
  if (!ReadFileScatter(hFile,pSegments,
                       dwClusterSize*dwNumThreads,
                       NULL,
                       &OverlappedIO)) {

    DWORD dwLastErr=GetLastError();
    if (ERROR_IO_PENDING!=dwLastErr)    {

      //Terminate the thread's main loop
      //on any error except ERROR_IO_PENDING
      //including EOF
      bTerminated=true;

      //Abort if the error isn't an EOF
      if (ERROR_HANDLE_EOF!=dwLastErr) {
```

```
      printf("Error reading file.  Last error=%d",
            dwLastErr);
      return -1;
    }
  }
  else {
    //We have an asynchronous operation
    Overlapped=true;
  }
}
else {
  //ReadFile returned true; the operation
  //is synchronous
  bOverlapped=false;
}

for (CBufSearch *pbCurrent=pbFirst;
  NULL!=pbCurrent;
  pbCurrent=pbCurrent->m_pbNext) {

  pbCurrent->m_bTerminated=bTerminated;
  pbCurrent->m_bOverlapped=bOverlapped;

  //Signal the worker thread to begin searching
  SetEvent(pbCurrent->m_hMainEvent);
}

//Wait on all the worker threads to finish searching their
//buffers.  Each one will signal the event we provided it
//when it's ready for another buffer.
WaitForMultipleObjects(dwNumThreads,hEvents,true,INFINITE);

dwlFilePos+=dwClusterSize*dwNumThreads;

} while (dwlFilePos<dwlFileSize);

//Get total tally and destroy search objects
DWORD dwFindCount=0;
CBufSearch *pbNext;
for (; NULL!=pbFirst; pbFirst=pbNext) {
  pbFirst->m_bTerminated=true;
  dwFindCount+=pbFirst->m_dwFindCount;
  pbNext=pbFirst->m_pbNext;
  delete pbFirst;
}
```

```
//Close the file, thread, and event handles
for (i=0; i<dwNumThreads; i++) {
  CloseHandle(hThreads[i]);
  CloseHandle(hEvents[i]);
}

CloseHandle(hFile);
CloseHandle(OverlappedIO.hEvent);

//Free the scatter buffers
for (DWORD j=0; j<dwNumThreads; j++)
  VirtualFree(pSegments[j].Buffer,0,MEM_RELEASE);

//Free all of our previous heap allocations
//by destroying the private heap we created
HeapDestroy(hPrivHeap);

//Return the find count for the specified file
return dwFindCount;
}

//Search the files matching a given mask for a
//specified string
bool SearchFiles(char *szFileMask, char *szSearchStr)
{

char szPath[MAX_PATH+1];

//Extract the file path from the specified mask
char *p=strrchr(szFileMask,'\\');
if (p) {
  strncpy(szPath,szFileMask,(p-szFileMask)+1);
  szPath[(p-szFileMask)+1]='\0';
}
else
  //If no path was specified, use the current
  //folder
  GetCurrentDirectory(MAX_PATH,szPath);

//Add a trailing backslash as necessary
if ('\\'!=szPath[strlen(szPath)-1])
  strcat(szPath,"\\");

printf("Searching for %s in %s\n\n",szSearchStr,szFileMask);
```

```
//Loop through all the files matching the mask
//and search each one for the string
WIN32_FIND_DATA fdFiles;
HANDLE hFind=FindFirstFile(szFileMask,&fdFiles);

if (INVALID_HANDLE_VALUE == hFind) {
  printf("No files match the specified mask\n");
  return false;
}

//Get the number of processors
//for the current system.
//This will be used to compute
//the number of I/O streams
//to use to search each file
SYSTEM_INFO si;
GetSystemInfo(&si);

//Get the cluster size from the drive
//This will always be a multiple of the
//sector size, so it is a good choice for
//use with scatter-gather I/O
DWORD dwSectorsPerCluster;
DWORD dwBytesPerSector;
DWORD dwNumberOfFreeClusters;
DWORD dwTotalNumberOfClusters;
GetDiskFreeSpace(NULL,&dwSectorsPerCluster,
                &dwBytesPerSector,
                &dwNumberOfFreeClusters,
                &dwTotalNumberOfClusters);

DWORD dwClusterSize=(dwSectorsPerCluster * dwBytesPerSector);

DWORD dwFindCount=0;
do {
  dwFindCount+=SearchFile(dwClusterSize,
                          si.dwNumberOfProcessors*
                          IO_STREAMS_PER_PROCESSOR,
                          szPath,
                          fdFiles.cFileName,
                          szSearchStr);
} while (FindNextFile(hFind,&fdFiles));

FindClose(hFind);
```

```
    printf("\nTotal hits for %s in %s:\t%d\n",
          szSearchStr,szFileMask,
          dwFindCount);
    return true;
}

int main(int argc, char* argv[])
{
  if (argc<3) {
    printf("Usage is: fstring_scatter filemask searchstring\n");
    return 1;
  }

  try
  {
    return (!SearchFiles(argv[1], argv[2]));
  }
  catch (...)
  {
    printf("Error reading file\n");
    return 1;
  }
}
```

6. Note that, as with the other asynchronous I/O examples in this book, we have to code for the possibility that Windows may decide to process our I/O operation synchronously. If that happens, we set each CBuf-Search's m_bOverlapped member to FALSE so that it will not attempt to wait on the operation to complete using GetOverlappedResult.

7. We assign each CBufSearch instance an ordinal index number so that it can use this index to compute the file offset it is processing. It needs this offset so that it can accurately list the location in the input file for each match it finds. In the fstring sample app, we retrieved the starting offset from the OVERLAPPED structure that was specific to each CBuf-Search object. In this sample, we use a single OVERLAPPED structure for all CBufSearch objects because only one asynchronous operation is occurring at any given time given that ReadFileScatter can fill multiple read buffers with a single call. Because the OVERLAPPED structure now reflects the starting position of the entire scatter-gather operation and not an individual asynchronous operation, we need another method of computing the exact file offset for each match we find. That's what we use CBufSearch's m_iIndex member for. It is set by the class constructor using the index value that was passed in during ob-

ject creation. This member reflects the object's ordinal position in the CBufSearch linked list. We iterate backward through the loop that creates the linked list of CBufSearch objects because we always add new objects to the head of the list. Since this results in the last object added becoming the head of the list, the index numbers would be reversed if we iterated through the loop in a forward direction. It's important that we keep the ordinal index values and the linked list properly sequenced because ReadFileScatter places data into the read buffers in sequential order. That is, the first buffer gets the first chunk read from the file, the second buffer gets the second one, and so forth, until all the buffers have been filled.

8. Note that the pSegments array is sized one element larger than the number of worker threads. This is a requirement of the scatter-gather functions: The last element in the buffer array must be a NULL pointer. Given that we zero-fill the array when we allocate it and never touch the array's last element thereafter, this will always be the case.

9. A pointer to each CBufSearch object's read buffer is passed in when the object is first created. This is the same buffer that ReadFileScatter will fill directly with data—because ReadFileScatter can scatter file data it reads into multiple buffers, there's no need to fill the buffers one by one or to use an intermediate contiguous buffer.

10. Once ReadFileScatter returns, SearchFile signals each of the worker threads to begin processing their output buffers. If the operation was initiated asynchronously, each CBufSearch object will call GetOverlappedResult to wait on the operation to complete. Because they all share the same OVERLAPPED structure that was initialized and passed in from SearchFile, they all effectively wait on the same event object that was originally associated with the OVERLAPPED structure. This is one reason why it's important that the event be a manual-reset event. If it were created as an auto-reset event, only one waiter thread would be awakened when the event was signaled because it would immediately be reset to nonsignaled as a side effect of the successful wait.

So, that's scatter-gather I/O in a nutshell. Study the app further, stepping through it under the Visual C++ debugger. Pay special attention to whether the I/O operation is carried out synchronously or asynchronously and how the app handles each situation.

Scatter-Gather I/O Recap

Using scatter-gather I/O allows a thread to fill multiple noncontiguous buffers with data from a contiguous region of a file and to write the contents of multiple noncontiguous memory buffers to a contiguous file region. Before the advent of scatter-gather, an app that wanted to write several noncontiguous buffers to disk had to either write them separately or copy them to an intermediate contiguous buffer before writing them. Neither alternative is very efficient, so scatter-gather I/O support was added at the operating system level to allow programs like SQL Server to perform this type of I/O more efficiently.

The requirements for performing scatter-gather I/O are a combination of those for asynchronous and nonbuffered I/O. This is because scatter-gather I/O is nonbuffered and executes asynchronously by default.

SQL Server makes extensive use of scatter-gather I/O when it reads and writes the database and log files associated with databases. Because the buffers it needs to load data into or write it out of may be stored at noncontiguous locations in the buffer pool, scatter-gather I/O allows SQL Server to read and write buffer pool data in a high-performance manner.

Scatter-Gather I/O Knowledge Measure

1. True or false: The buffers allocated for use with scatter-gather I/O must be contiguous in memory.
2. Can a thread call GetOverlappedResult to wait on a scatter-gather I/O operation?
3. True or false: When a scatter operation fills a set of memory buffers with data from a file, it fills them in reverse order (the last buffer in the array gets the first chunk of the disk file, the second-to-last gets the second chunk, and so forth).
4. What Win32 API function can a thread call to return a disk's sector size?
5. True or false: In order for a file to be used in scatter-gather I/O operations, its file object must be created with the FILE_FLAG_SCATTER_GATHER switch set.
6. What Win32 API function is used to gather buffers from memory and write them to a contiguous file region?
7. True or false: Unlike other types of asynchronous I/O, a scatter-gather I/O operation will never be processed synchronously by Windows.
8. Does an application that is looping through a file with ReadFileScatter need to adjust the members of the OVERLAPPED structure it passes into the function between reads? Why or why not?
9. Can a thread use scatter-gather I/O to write to noncontiguous regions of a file if the file has been opened for random access?
10. True or false: By default, Windows bypasses the system cache when performing scatter-gather I/O operations.

I/O Completion Ports

In this section, we'll talk about Windows' I/O completion port facility and build a sample app that uses it to control concurrency and assist with thread synchronization. If you haven't yet read through the first part of this chapter, please do so before proceeding. Many of the concepts we discuss here build on those covered earlier in the chapter.

Key I/O Completion Port Terms and Concepts

✔ *I/O completion port*—a mechanism that allows threads to wait on asynchronous I/O and/or coordinate access to resources in a highly efficient manner. When an I/O completion port is associated with a file and an asynchronous I/O operation that has been initiated for the file completes, an I/O completion packet is queued to the port. Threads can wait on these packets and respond accordingly rather than waiting directly on the asynchronous operations themselves. Moreover, the I/O completion port can control the concurrency (the number of threads allowed to process completion packets at once) and can activate waiting threads if an active thread becomes blocked. An I/O completion port can also be created without being associated with a file. In that scenario, an app can call the PostQueuedCompletionStatus API function to post its own special-purpose I/O completion packets to the port, which other threads can dequeue and respond to.

Key I/O Completion Port APIs

Table 5.7 Key I/O Completion Port–Related API Functions

Function	Description
CreateIoCompletionPort	Creates an I/O completion port, optionally associating with a file
GetQueuedCompletionStatus	Checks for a queued I/O completion packet and dequeues it if one is available; also associates the calling thread with the port
PostQueuedCompletionStatus	Posts an application-defined, special-purpose completion packet to an I/O completion port

Overview

One of the challenges facing server application designers is deciding how parallel to make the application—how many threads to create to process client requests. A server app with too few threads will likely starve clients; clients will wait in line until one of the server's limited number of worker threads gets around to responding to it. Although a server application could set up a single thread such that it could respond to multiple clients, this approach requires a good deal of complexity and may not take advantage of multiple processors.

Going to the other extreme, a server app with too many threads will likely spend a significant amount of time context switching. Having too many threads usually leads to a thread thrashing condition wherein a large number of threads wake up, carry out some work on the processor, block while waiting on I/O or a synchronization object, and then block again while waiting on a new request. The threads are continually scheduled on and off the system's processor(s) even though they may not be doing that much actual work.

An efficient server application strikes a balance between limiting context switching and providing for parallelism. A high-performance software scheduler will keep a thread running as long as there are pending work requests rather than swapping it off the processor for another thread that will then carry out the same work. This type of design requires decoupling worker threads from work requests. Ideally, you would have just one active thread per processor at any given time, and you would attempt to avoid having the thread become blocked so long as there was work to be carried out. As you'll see in Chapter 10, this is exactly how SQL Server's User Mode Scheduler works.

In order for a server to avoid context switching while providing maximum parallelism, it needs a way to activate another thread when a thread that's processing a client request becomes blocked (e.g., while waiting on I/O or another resource). That's where I/O completion ports come in. Because Windows' I/O completion mechanism can actively control the concurrency of an application, you can use an I/O completion port to minimize context switches while still keeping the CPU(s) in a machine as busy as possible should a running thread become blocked.

You create an I/O completion port by calling the Win32 CreateIoCompletionPort API function. Typically, an I/O completion port is associated with a file when it's created. When an asynchronous I/O operation completes on the file, Windows queues a completion packet to the port. The application can then dequeue the packet and respond accordingly.

Note that an I/O completion port can also be created such that it is not associated with a particular file. In this scenario, an application usually calls the Win32 API function PostQueuedCompletionStatus to queue its own special-purpose completion packets to the port. As I mentioned in Chapter 3, an application can use this mechanism to synchronize resource access by multiple threads.

The CreateIoCompletionPort Win32 API function allows the caller to specify a concurrency value when creating the port. This value controls the number of threads that may concurrently process I/O completion packets from the port. If you specify 0 for this parameter, Windows defaults to allowing as many threads as there are processors on the system. As a rule, Microsoft recommends that you set the concurrency value roughly equal to the number of processors on the system and code your app such that a worker thread will avoid being blocked as long as there are pending work requests. It's easy to experiment with different concurrency values to get the most out of your system.

A thread dequeues an I/O completion packet by calling the GetQueuedCompletionStatus Win32 API function. This also has the effect of associating the thread with the completion port. A thread can be associated with just one I/O completion port at a time. Regardless of the number of worker threads that associate themselves with a completion port, the system will attempt to keep the number of running threads equal to or less than the concurrency value passed into CreateIoCompletionPort.

GetQueuedCompletionStatus returns a couple of output parameters that the calling thread can use. The most important of these is the pointer to the OVERLAPPED structure that was used to initiate the asynchronous I/O request. You can use this to ascertain which I/O has just completed if you have multiple overlapped I/O operations running at once. You can't assume anything from the order in which the I/O completion packets are retrieved from the port; the asynchronous I/O operations that queued them may have taken different amounts of time to run. Since each asynchronous I/O operation should have its own OVERLAPPED structure, you should be able to design your software such that you can use the OVERLAPPED pointer returned by GetQueuedCompletionStatus to locate the buffer the asynchronous operation has just filled or written to disk.

The second useful output parameter returned by GetQueuedCompletionStatus is the bytes transferred counter. You can use it to determine how many bytes were read or written by the associated asynchronous operation.

Windows keeps track of which threads are associated with a completion port and whether they are running. If a thread that is actively processing completion packets becomes blocked, Windows will attempt to activate another thread that is waiting on the port. This means, of course, that it's possible for the number of worker threads actively processing completion packets to momentarily exceed the specified concurrency value. Consider what happens when an active thread becomes blocked, another thread is activated, and the first thread awakens while the second one is still running. In that scenario, the number of active threads would temporarily exceed the concurrency value specified for the port. No other threads waiting on the port would be allowed to run until the number of active threads dipped below the concurrency value originally specified for the port.

Windows awakens threads that block on a completion port in LIFO order (the last thread to wait is the first one awakened). When a thread is awakened to dequeue an I/O completion packet from the port, it gets the oldest packet in the queue.

The scalability benefits provided by an I/O completion port are probably best understood by way of example. Let's say you have a server application that has twelve worker threads, and let's say that twelve client requests come into it. Without using an I/O completion port or fashioning a similar mechanism yourself, you might allow all twelve threads to run at once. While this would provide maximum parallelism to the app's clients, if the system has less than twelve processors, you'll likely see a relatively high degree of context switching. In other words, the CPU(s) in your machine won't spend all their time processing work requests; they'll spend some of it—perhaps a relatively high percentage—switching between threads because you do not have enough processors to truly run them concurrently. Windows must fake the apparent concurrency by continually swapping threads on to and off of the system processor(s).

But suppose you used an I/O completion port to manage the concurrency within your app, and suppose the system had just two processors. If you created the I/O completion port with its default concurrency setting, it would allow just two worker threads to run concurrently. And rather than being continually swapped on and off the processors, these two worker threads would remain active on their respective processors (so long as they did not become blocked) until all twelve work requests had been processed. Provided the work requests were of similar length, each thread would likely process about six of them. Thus, you'd have a net gain in performance because your CPUs would have spent nearly all their time processing client requests instead of wasting processor power switching between worker threads.

You might be wondering: Why not just limit the total number of worker threads to match the number of CPUs in the machine? Wouldn't that address the context switch issue? The problem with this approach is that threads can be and often are blocked at different times while they run. If your target machine has just two processors and you therefore create only two worker threads, what happens when both of them block while waiting on I/O or a synchronization object? Your processors might sit idle while the threads slept. If, on the other hand, you create more worker threads than CPUs but use an I/O completion port to manage your app's concurrency, when an active thread goes into a wait state, Windows will allow another thread to run, thereby more fully utilizing the system's processor power.

Exercises

As with all the other types of Windows I/O we've discussed in this book, we'll explore I/O completion ports by working through an exercise. The sample app presented in the following exercise, fstring_io_comp, is a variation on the fstring sample we've been working with throughout the chapter. It's similar to several of the other I/O sample apps in that it searches the files matching a specified mask for a given string. It differs from the others in that it uses an I/O completion port to manage concurrency and also to assist with thread synchronization.

Exercise 5.5 A Multithreaded, Multifile Search Utility That Uses an I/O Completion Port

1. Load the fstring_io_comp sample from the CH05\fstring_io_comp subfolder on the CD into the Visual Studio development environment.
2. There are two primary classes used by fstring_io_comp: CBufSearch and CIoBuf. You probably remember CBufSearch from the other asynchronous I/O sample apps earlier in this chapter. It is largely unchanged in this app. CIoBuf, on the other hand, is a new class. We'll talk more about it in just a moment.
3. From a 30,000-feet view, fstring_io_comp works like this.
   a. The main thread opens a file to search and associates it with an I/O completion port.
   b. The main thread enters a loop wherein it dequeues a read buffer from the linked list of CIoBuf objects (by changing the buffer's state from BUF_STATE_INACTIVE to BUF_STATE_READING) and passes it into ReadFile to be used to read the file asynchronously.
   c. Each time an asynchronous operation completes, an I/O completion packet is queued to the completion port.

  d. CIoBuf::CheckForIoPacketAndSetState (which is called from a worker thread) dequeues this completion packet by calling the Win32 GetQueuedCompletionStatus API function and uses the OVERLAPPED pointer it provides to locate the matching CIoBuf object originally associated with the asynchronous operation. When the function locates the matching buffer, its sets the buffer's state to BUF_STATE_READY.

  e. CBufSearch::Search continuously polls the work request queue for a buffer whose state has been set to BUF_STATE_READY. When it finds one, it changes its state to BUF_STATE_SEARCHING, scans it for the search string, and writes the matching lines to the console. Once it finishes with a buffer, it enqueues it by setting its state back to BUF_STATE_INACTIVE.

  f. This continues until each input file has been completely read and searched.

4. The fstring_io_comp app consists of three main source code modules: fstring_io_comp.cpp, bufsrch.cpp, and iobuf.cpp. The first of these, fstring_io_comp.cpp (Listing 5.7), is similar to the main source modules of the other fstring sample apps in this book. Let's start with it.

Listing 5.7 fstring_io_comp.cpp, the Main Source Code Module for fstring_io_comp

```
// fstring_io_comp.cpp : Multithreaded file
// search that uses an I/O completion port
//

#define _WIN32_WINNT 0x500

#include "stdafx.h"
#include "windows.h"
#include "stdlib.h"
#include "process.h"
#include "bufsrch.h"
#include "iobuf.h"

#define IO_STREAMS_PER_PROCESSOR 2

//Entry point routine for the worker threads
unsigned __stdcall StartSearch(LPVOID lpParameter)
{

  //Cast the parameter supplied to _beginthreadex
  //as a CBufSearch * and call its Search method
```

```
    return ((CBufSearch*)lpParameter)->Search();

}

void __stdcall DisplayOutput(DWORD dwParam)
{
  char *pszMsg=(char *)dwParam;
  printf(pszMsg);
}



//Search a specified file for a given search string
//using nonbuffered, asynchronous I/O
DWORD SearchFile(DWORD dwClusterSize,
                 DWORD dwNumStreams,
                 char *szPath,
                 char *szFileName,
                 char *szSearchStr,
                 HANDLE hMainThread)
{
  char szFullPathName[MAX_PATH+1];
  DWORD dwNumThreads;
  HANDLE hPrivHeap;
  HANDLE *hThreads;

  strcpy(szFullPathName,szPath);
  strcat(szFullPathName,szFileName);

  //Open the file for both nonbuffered and
  //overlapped (asynchronous) I/O
  HANDLE hFile=CreateFile(szFullPathName,
                     GENERIC_READ,FILE_SHARE_READ,
                     NULL,
                     OPEN_EXISTING,
                     FILE_ATTRIBUTE_NORMAL
                     | FILE_FLAG_OVERLAPPED
                     | FILE_FLAG_NO_BUFFERING
                     ,NULL);

  if (INVALID_HANDLE_VALUE==hFile) {
    printf("Error opening file.  Last error=%d\n",
      GetLastError());
    return -1;
  }
```

```
    DWORD dwFileSizeHigh;

    DWORD dwFileSizeLow=GetFileSize(hFile,&dwFileSizeHigh);

    DWORD dwlFileSize=(dwFileSizeHigh*MAXDWORD)+
        dwFileSizeLow;

    DWORD dwNumClusts=dwlFileSize / dwClusterSize;
    if (dwNumClusts<1) dwNumClusts=1;

    //If file is less than 4GB and we have more requested
    //streams (IO threads) than clusters, set the # of
    //threads = to the # of clusters
    if ((dwlFileSize<0xFFFFFFFF) && (dwNumStreams>dwNumClusts))
      dwNumThreads=dwNumClusts;
    else
      dwNumThreads=dwNumStreams;


#if(_DEBUG)
    printf("Using %d threads\n\n",dwNumThreads);
#endif

    //Create a private heap so that we can free all
    //allocations at once
    hPrivHeap=HeapCreate(0,0,0);


    //Create the thread array
    hThreads=(HANDLE *)HeapAlloc(hPrivHeap,
                                 HEAP_ZERO_MEMORY,
                                 dwNumThreads*sizeof(HANDLE));
    if (NULL==hThreads) {
      printf("Error allocating worker thread array.  Aborting.\n");
      return -1;
    }

    //Create the I/O completion port
    HANDLE hPort=CreateIoCompletionPort(hFile,NULL,0,0);
    if (INVALID_HANDLE_VALUE==hPort) {
      printf(
        "Error creating IO completion port.  Last error=%d\n",
        GetLastError());
      return -1;
    }
```

```
//Create the worker threads and the
//CBufSearch and CIoBuf objects
CBufSearch *pbFirst=NULL;
CIoBuf *pIoFirst=NULL;
unsigned uThreadId;


for (DWORD i=0; i<dwNumThreads; i++) {

  pIoFirst=new CIoBuf(pIoFirst,hPort,dwClusterSize+1);

  pbFirst=new CBufSearch(pbFirst,
                         szFileName,
                         szSearchStr,
                         &DisplayOutput,
                         hMainThread);

  hThreads[i]=
  (HANDLE)_beginthreadex(NULL,
                         0,
                         &StartSearch,
                         pbFirst,
                         CREATE_SUSPENDED,
                         &uThreadId);

  if (!hThreads[i]) {
    printf("Error creating thread.  Aborting.\n");
    return -1;
  }
}


//Set the CBufSearch objects'
//pointer to the head of the
//CIoBuf list
pbFirst->s_pIoFirst=pIoFirst;

//Set the CIoBuf objects'
//pointer to the head of the
//CIoBuf list
pIoFirst->s_pIoFirst=pIoFirst;

//Set statics so that multiple
//file searches work
```

```
pIoFirst->s_bTerminated=false;
pIoFirst->s_bOverlapped=true;

//Once the static members are set,
//start the worker threads
for (i=0; i<dwNumThreads; i++)
  ResumeThread(hThreads[i]);

//Main loop -- loop through the file, reading it in
//dwClusterSize chunks
DWORDLONG dwlFilePos=0;
do {
  for (CBufSearch *pbCurrent=pbFirst;
    NULL!=pbCurrent;
    pbCurrent=pbCurrent->m_pbNext) {

    CIoBuf *pIoBuf=
        pIoFirst->SpinToFindBuf(BUF_STATE_INACTIVE,
                                BUF_STATE_READING);

    //Set the starting offset for the next read
    pIoBuf->m_OverlappedIO.OffsetHigh=
      (DWORD)(dwlFilePos / MAXDWORD);
    pIoBuf->m_OverlappedIO.Offset=
      (DWORD)(dwlFilePos % MAXDWORD);

    //Zero-fill the read buffer so that we don't
    //get search hits at the end of a partially
    //filled buffer (from previous contents)
    ZeroMemory(pIoBuf->m_szBuf,dwClusterSize+1);

    //Read a buffer full of data from the file
    //using asynchronous I/O if possible
    if (!ReadFile(hFile,pIoBuf->m_szBuf,
                        dwClusterSize,
                        &pIoBuf->m_dwBytesRead,
                        &pIoBuf->m_OverlappedIO)) {

      DWORD dwLastErr=GetLastError();
      if (ERROR_IO_PENDING!=dwLastErr)   {

        //Terminate the thread's main loop
        //on any error except ERROR_IO_PENDING
```

```
            //including EOF
            InterlockedExchange(
                  (LPLONG)&pIoBuf->s_bTerminated,
                  (long)true);

            //Abort if the error isn't an EOF
            if (ERROR_HANDLE_EOF!=dwLastErr) {
              printf(
              "Error reading file.  Last error=%d",
              dwLastErr);
                return -1;
            }
            break;
          }
          else {
            //We have an asynchronous operation
            InterlockedExchange(
                  (LPLONG)&pIoBuf->s_bOverlapped,
                  (long)true);
          }
        }
        else {
          //ReadFile returned true; the operation
          //is synchronous
          InterlockedExchange(
                  (LPLONG)&pIoBuf->s_bOverlapped,
                  (long)false);
          pIoBuf->SetState(BUF_STATE_READY);

        }

        dwlFilePos+=dwClusterSize;
      }

  } while ((dwlFilePos<dwlFileSize) &&
      (!pIoFirst->s_bTerminated));


  //Signal that we're done reading the file
  InterlockedExchange(
          (LPLONG)&pIoFirst->s_bTerminated,
          (long)true);
```

```
//Wait on all the worker threads to finish
WaitForMultipleObjects(dwNumThreads,hThreads,
                       true,
                       INFINITE);

//Dequeue any output that was queued
//via APC calls
while (WAIT_IO_COMPLETION==SleepEx(0,true));


//Get total tally and destroy search objects
DWORD dwFindCount=0;
CBufSearch *pbNext;
for (; NULL!=pbFirst; pbFirst=pbNext) {
  dwFindCount+=pbFirst->m_dwFindCount;
  pbNext=pbFirst->m_pbNext;
  delete pbFirst;
}

//Delete the buf objects
CIoBuf *pIoNext;
for (; NULL!=pIoFirst; pIoFirst=pIoNext) {
  pIoNext=pIoFirst->m_pIoBufNext;
  delete pIoFirst;
}

//Close the I/O completion port
CloseHandle(hPort);

//Close the thread handles
for (i=0; i<dwNumThreads; i++) {
  CloseHandle(hThreads[i]);
}

CloseHandle(hFile);

//Free all of our previous heap allocations
//by destroying the private heap we created
HeapDestroy(hPrivHeap);

//Return the find count for the specified file
return dwFindCount;
}
```

```
//Search the files matching a given mask for a
//specified string
bool SearchFiles(char *szFileMask, char *szSearchStr)
{

  char szPath[MAX_PATH+1];

  //Extract the file path from the specified mask
  char *p=strrchr(szFileMask,'\\');
  if (p) {
    strncpy(szPath,szFileMask,(p-szFileMask)+1);
    szPath[(p-szFileMask)+1]='\0';
  }
  else
    //If no path was specified, use the current
    //folder
    GetCurrentDirectory(MAX_PATH,szPath);

  //Add a trailing backslash as necessary
  if ('\\'!=szPath[strlen(szPath)-1])
    strcat(szPath,"\\");

  printf("Searching for %s in %s\n\n",szSearchStr,
    szFileMask);

  HANDLE hMainThread=
        OpenThread(THREAD_ALL_ACCESS,
        0,
        GetCurrentThreadId());

  //Loop through all the files matching the mask
  //and search each one for the string
  WIN32_FIND_DATA fdFiles;
  HANDLE hFind=FindFirstFile(szFileMask,&fdFiles);

  if (INVALID_HANDLE_VALUE == hFind) {
    printf("No files match the specified mask\n");
    return false;
  }

  //Get the number of processors
  //for the current system.
  //This will be used to compute
```

```
        //the number of I/O streams
        //to use to search each file
        SYSTEM_INFO si;
        GetSystemInfo(&si);

        //Get the cluster size from the drive
        //This will always be a multiple of the
        //sector size, so it is a good choice for
        //use with nonbuffered I/O
        DWORD dwSectorsPerCluster;
        DWORD dwBytesPerSector;
        DWORD dwNumberOfFreeClusters;
        DWORD dwTotalNumberOfClusters;
        GetDiskFreeSpace(NULL,&dwSectorsPerCluster,
                                &dwBytesPerSector,
                                &dwNumberOfFreeClusters,
                                &dwTotalNumberOfClusters);

        DWORD dwClusterSize=(dwSectorsPerCluster * dwBytesPerSector);

        DWORD dwFindCount=0;
        do {
          dwFindCount+=
                SearchFile(  dwClusterSize,
                             si.dwNumberOfProcessors*
                             IO_STREAMS_PER_PROCESSOR,
                             szPath,
                             fdFiles.cFileName,
                             szSearchStr,
                             hMainThread);

        } while (FindNextFile(hFind,&fdFiles));

        FindClose(hFind);

        printf("\nTotal hits for %s in %s:\t%d\n",
          szSearchStr,szFileMask,dwFindCount);

        CloseHandle(hMainThread);

        return true;
    }

int main(int argc, char* argv[])
```

```
{
  if (argc<3) {
    printf(
            "Usage is: fstring_io_comp filemask searchstring\n");
    return 1;
  }

  try
  {
    return (!SearchFiles(argv[1], argv[2]));
  }
  catch (...)
  {
    printf("Error reading file.  Last error=%d\n",
      GetLastError());
    return 1;
  }
}
```

5. The plumbing necessary to iterate through the files matching the specified mask and call the SearchFile routine is identical to that found in the other fstring samples, so I won't go through it here. Let's begin our examination with the CreateFile call in the SearchFile function.

6. Notice that we open the file for both overlapped (asynchronous) and nonbuffered I/O. Because we are going to associate our I/O completion port with this file, we want to ensure, as much as we possibly can, that we'll be able to successfully initiate asynchronous I/O operations. An I/O completion port that's associated with a file isn't much good if you're doing synchronous I/O. Enabling both of these switches when we open the file gives us the best chance of getting asynchronous I/O.

7. Next, note the call to CreateIoCompletionPort. We pass in the file handle in order to associate it with the port. We pass in a concurrency value of 0 so that the system will set the concurrency for the port to match the number of processors in the system.

8. We next create the worker threads and the CBufSearch and CIoBuf objects. Prior to calling SearchFile, the SearchFiles function retrieved the number of processors in the system via the GetSystemInfo Win32 API function and multiplied it by the IO_STREAMS_PER_PROCESSOR constant, which is currently set to 2. It then passed this value into Search-File via the dwNumStreams parameter. This parameter specifies the number of worker threads SearchFile creates to search each file. This means that if there are four processors on the system, SearchFile will create eight worker threads to search it. We do this in order to keep the

CPUs as busy as possible because we assume that each worker thread will spend a certain amount of time waiting on I/O. Regardless of the number of worker threads we create, the I/O completion port we're using will still determine the number of active threads.

9. The CBufSearch class has the same purpose it has had in every sample app in which it has appeared in this book: It scans a buffer of text for a specified string and sends the matching lines to the console. CIoBuf is new in this exercise. Because we need to decouple work requests from worker threads when leveraging I/O completion ports (as I mentioned earlier), the I/O-related elements that, in the other fstring samples, have been encapsulated by CBufSearch have been moved to their own class, CIoBuf. CIoBuf represents an item in a work request queue— each CIoBuf instance represents a buffer that needs to be searched. We'll talk more about CBufSearch and CIoBuf in just a moment.

10. We create each thread in a suspended state so that we can set some static class members before the worker threads start running. The worker threads rely on these members being set correctly, so we hold off on starting the threads until we've set them.

11. We next enter the main processing loop wherein we read the input file and queue asynchronous I/O operations and work requests. The asynchronous I/O operations are queued via the ReadFile calls. The work requests are queued when a worker thread detects that Windows has sent a completion packet to the I/O completion port when each asynchronous operation completes.

12. Each I/O operation we carry out is encapsulated in a CIoBuf object. The buffer that will receive the file data as it's read, as well as a state field and the OVERLAPPED structure required by asynchronous operations, are all members of the CIoBuf class.

13. CIoBuf's state field can have one of four values. Table 5.8 lists each one and what it indicates.

Table 5.8 CIoBuf States and Their Meanings

State	Meaning
BUF_STATE_INACTIVE	The buffer is unused and can be used in an asynchronous read operation.
BUF_STATE_READING	The buffer is being used by a read operation.
BUF_STATE_READY	The buffer has been filled by a read operation and is ready to be searched.
BUF_STATE_SEARCHING	The buffer is being searched.

14. We begin the read loop by locating a buffer whose state is set to BUF_STATE_INACTIVE. An inactive buffer is one that isn't being used for anything. By virtue of the SpinToFindBuf call, we find and acquire this buffer in one step by changing its state to BUF_STATE_READING. BUF_STATE_READING indicates that we're reading data into the buffer.

15. As with the other asynchronous I/O sample apps, we allow for the possibility that Windows will decide to process an I/O request synchronously. If the ReadFile call returns TRUE, we know we have a synchronous call and that the read has already completed, so we immediately change the buffer state to BUF_STATE_READY. This means that it's ready to be searched.

16. In the case of a synchronous read, we also set a static member of the CIoBuf class so that we don't later attempt to wait on the I/O completion port. By using a static member, we're assuming that if we get one synchronous read, they will likely all be synchronous for a given file.

17. If ReadFile initiated an asynchronous call, we have to wait until the operation completes before we can change the buffer state. A method of the CIoBuf class takes care of that, as we'll see shortly.

18. If you've worked through the other asynchronous I/O sample apps in this chapter, you've probably noticed that the event objects that we've typically used to synchronize our worker threads are conspicuously absent in this app. For example, instead of waiting on an array of event objects to be signaled once we finish reading the file, we wait on the threads themselves to be signaled (terminated). We don't need the event objects in this app because we're handling thread synchronization using the I/O completion port and a couple of the interlocked functions. (Recall that we discussed the interlocked family of functions in Chapter 3.)

19. Once the threads finish running, we clean up our resources and return a match count to SearchFiles.

20. Let's next look at CBufSearch (Listing 5.8). It doesn't differ much from the CBufSearch classes in the other examples in this chapter.

Listing 5.8 bufsrch.cpp, the Source Code Module for the CBufSearch Class

```
//bufsrch.cpp -- a utility class that
//we use to search a buffer for a string

#include "bufsrch.h"

CIoBuf *CBufSearch::s_pIoFirst=NULL;

//Ctor
```

```
CBufSearch::CBufSearch(CBufSearch *pbNext,
                          char *szFileName,
                          char *szSearchStr,
                          PAPCFUNC pOutputCallback,
                          HANDLE hMainThread)
{

  //Cache constructor parameters for later use
  m_pbNext=pbNext;
  m_szFileName=szFileName;
  m_szSearchStr=szSearchStr;
  m_pOutputCallback=pOutputCallback;
  m_hMainThread=hMainThread;

  //Initialize the remaining member variables
  m_dwFindCount=0;

  //Create the private heap that we'll use for output
  m_hOutputHeap=HeapCreate(HEAP_NO_SERIALIZE,0x1000,0);


}



CBufSearch::~CBufSearch()
{
  //Destroy the private output heap
  HeapDestroy(m_hOutputHeap);
}

//From an offset in a buffer, find the start of the line
char *CBufSearch::FindLineStart(char *szStartPos)
{
  char *szStart;
  for (szStart=szStartPos;
    ((szStart>m_pIoCurrent->m_szBuf) &&
     (cLINE_DELIM!=*(szStart-1))); szStart--);
  return szStart;
}

//From an offset in a buffer, find the end of the line
// -- assumes null-termination
char *CBufSearch::FindLineEnd(char *szStartPos)
{
```

```
      return strchr(szStartPos,cLINE_DELIM);
}

//Search the read buffer for
//every line containing a previously
//specified search string
bool CBufSearch::Search()
{
  char *szBol;
  char *szEol;
  char *szStringPos;
  DWORD dwNumChars;
  char *szStartPos;
  bool bRes=false;
  char szFmt[32];
  char szOffsetOutput[255];
  DWORDLONG dwlFilePos;
  char szMsg[1024];

  while (1) {

    __try
    {

      //Spin until we find a buffer to search
      if ((NULL==(m_pIoCurrent=
        s_pIoFirst->SpinToFindBuf(BUF_STATE_READY,
                              BUF_STATE_SEARCHING))) &&
                          (s_pIoFirst->s_bTerminated))
        break;

      //We start the search at the beginning
      //of the read buffer
      szStartPos=m_pIoCurrent->m_szBuf;

      //Get the starting file offset from
      //the buf object for display later
      dwlFilePos=m_pIoCurrent->FilePos();


      //Loop while the search start marker is not NULL
      //and is within the read buffer
      //and strstr continues to find the search string
      //in the read buffer
```

```
      while ((szStartPos) &&
            (szStartPos<(m_pIoCurrent->m_szBuf+
                    m_pIoCurrent->m_dwBytesRead)-1) &&
            (NULL!=(szStringPos=
                strstr(szStartPos,m_szSearchStr)))) {

        //If we get in here, we have a search hit
        m_dwFindCount++;

        //Compute the line start and end so that we
        //can write it to the console
        szBol=FindLineStart(szStringPos);
        szEol=FindLineEnd(szStringPos);

        //Compute the number of characters to output
        //We'll use this later to build a printf
        //format string
        if (szEol) {
          dwNumChars=szEol-szBol;
          if (szEol<(m_pIoCurrent->m_szBuf+
            m_pIoCurrent->m_dwBytesRead)-1)
            szStartPos=szEol+1;
          else szStartPos=NULL;
        }
        else {
          dwNumChars=MAXLINE_LEN;
          szStartPos=NULL;
        }

#if(_DEBUG)
      sprintf(szOffsetOutput,
              "Thread %08d: Offset: %010I64d %s ",
              GetCurrentThreadId(),
              dwlFilePos+
                (szStringPos-m_pIoCurrent->m_szBuf),
              m_szFileName);
#else
      sprintf(szOffsetOutput,
              "Offset: %010I64d %s ",
              dwlFilePos+
                (szStringPos-m_pIoCurrent->m_szBuf),
              m_szFileName);
#endif
      //Build format string that limits output to current line
```

```
          strcpy(szFmt,"%s %.");
          sprintf(szFmt+5,"%ds\n",dwNumChars);


          //Output current line
          sprintf(szMsg,szFmt,
                  szOffsetOutput,
                  szBol);

          char *pszMsg=(char *)HeapAlloc(m_hOutputHeap,
                                         0,
                                         strlen(szMsg)+1);

          strcpy(pszMsg,szMsg);
          if (!QueueUserAPC(m_pOutputCallback,
                            m_hMainThread,
                            (DWORD)pszMsg))
            printf("Error queuing output\n");

          bRes=true;

        }
      }
      __except(EXCEPTION_EXECUTE_HANDLER)
      {
        //Eat the exception -- should never get here
        //given that the read buffer is guaranteed to
        //be null-terminated.
#if(_DEBUG)

        //Assumes we got an access violation from going
        //past the end of the read buffer -- could actually
        //be some other type of error
        printf("Thread %08d reached end of buffer\n",
          GetCurrentThreadId());
#endif
      }

    m_pIoCurrent->SetState(BUF_STATE_INACTIVE);

  }

  return bRes;
}
```

21. The most important thing to note about this code is the call to SpinToFindBuf at the top of the Search method. This is the means by which the Search method acquires the read buffer that it will search for matching strings.

22. Another noteworthy feature of CBufSearch is its use of APCs for delivering output to the console. In an attempt to keep our worker threads from being blocked while they wait on console I/O, we queue each match line to the main thread via an APC. We allocate each match line output string on a private heap (each instance of CBufSearch has its own heap), then we pass a pointer to this string in the call to QueueUserAPC. After the main thread finishes reading the file and waiting on the worker threads to complete, it repeatedly calls SleepEx until all the queued APCs are executed. Each queued APC simply writes to the console the output string we allocated earlier. This funnels all screen output through the main thread and allows the worker threads to process work requests without waiting on console I/O. Naturally, this requires all match strings to be stored in memory temporarily, so this technique wouldn't be ideal if we had a huge number of matches. In that situation, you might set up a separate thread to handle console output and construct a message loop such that worker threads could post messages to the output thread when they wanted to send text to the console. Another option would be to use an I/O completion port to queue each thread's output just as we're using one to manage the input queue. You'll see that technique employed in the next exercise.

   Once it dequeues all queued APCs, the main thread destroys its list of CBufSearch objects, which has the effect of also freeing their private heaps (which contain the output strings). This helps ensure that we don't leak memory between files.

23. After a buffer has been fully scanned, Search enqueues it by setting its state back to BUF_STATE_INACTIVE. This allows the main thread to use it the next time it needs to acquire a buffer for use with ReadFile.

24. Once Search finds the buffer list empty and the app has signaled that it has read the entirety of the input file (by setting CIoBuf::s_bTerminated to TRUE), it exits its loop, causing the thread to exit normally.

25. Let's now examine the CIoBuf class (Listing 5.9). As I said earlier, each CIoBuf object encapsulates an I/O operation. The linked list of CIoBuf objects serves as a type of work request queue. As long as there are buffers in the queue that need to be processed, CBufSearch's Search method will continue to search them.

Listing 5.9 iobuf.cpp, the Source Code Module for the CIoBuf Class

```cpp
//iobuf.cpp -- implements a simple
//buffer manager for asynchronous
//file reads

#include "iobuf.h"

bool CIoBuf::s_bOverlapped=true;
bool CIoBuf::s_bTerminated=false;
CIoBuf *CIoBuf::s_pIoFirst=NULL;

//Ctor
CIoBuf::CIoBuf(CIoBuf * pIoBufNext,
                       HANDLE hPort,
                       DWORD dwBufSize)
{
  m_dwState=BUF_STATE_INACTIVE;

  m_dwBufSize=dwBufSize;
  m_szBuf=(char *)VirtualAlloc(NULL,
                                m_dwBufSize,
                                MEM_RESERVE
                                | MEM_COMMIT,
                                PAGE_READWRITE);
  m_pIoBufNext=pIoBufNext;
  m_hPort=hPort;

  ZeroMemory(&m_OverlappedIO,
                sizeof(m_OverlappedIO));
  m_OverlappedIO.hEvent=
    CreateEvent(NULL,true,false,NULL);
}

//Dtor
CIoBuf::~CIoBuf()
{
  VirtualFree(m_szBuf,0,MEM_RELEASE);
  CloseHandle(m_OverlappedIO.hEvent);
}
```

```
//Spin until we locate a buffer
//with a state of dwOldState,
//atomically set it to dwNewState,
//and return it to the caller
CIoBuf *CIoBuf::SpinToFindBuf(DWORD dwOldState,
                                    DWORD dwNewState)
{
  bool bWasTerminated;
  do {
    //Check for and process new I/O completion packets
    CheckForIoPacketAndSetState(BUF_STATE_READY);

    //Save off termination status before
    //entering the search loop
    bWasTerminated=s_bTerminated;

    //Iterate through the buf list
    //If we find one with the desired state,
    //set it to the new state and return it
    for (CIoBuf *pIoCurrent=this;
        NULL!=pIoCurrent;
        pIoCurrent=pIoCurrent->m_pIoBufNext) {
      if (dwOldState==
        (DWORD)InterlockedCompareExchange(
              (volatile long *)&pIoCurrent->m_dwState,
              dwNewState,
              dwOldState))
        return pIoCurrent;
    }

    //If termination was signaled
    //before we began the loop
    //and we didn't find any
    //matching buffers, exit
  } while (!bWasTerminated);
  return NULL;
}

//Atomically set the buffer state
void CIoBuf::SetState(DWORD dwNewState)
{
  InterlockedExchange((long *)&m_dwState,dwNewState);
}
```

```
//Return the buffer state
DWORD CIoBuf::GetState()
{
  return m_dwState;
}


//Calc the current file position
//using the OVERLAPPED member
DWORDLONG CIoBuf::FilePos()
{
  return (m_OverlappedIO.OffsetHigh*MAXDWORD)+
    m_OverlappedIO.Offset;
}

//Check for pending I/O completion packets
//If we get one, match its OVERLAPPED structure
//pointer with one in the buffer list and set
//the matching buffer's bytesread and state members
//appropriately
void CIoBuf::CheckForIoPacketAndSetState(DWORD dwNewState)
{
  if (!s_pIoFirst->s_bOverlapped) return;
  DWORD dwKey;
  DWORD dwBytesRead;
  LPOVERLAPPED pOverlappedIO;
  if (GetQueuedCompletionStatus(m_hPort,
                                &dwBytesRead,
                                &dwKey,
                                &pOverlappedIO,
                                1))
  {
    for (CIoBuf *pIoCurr=s_pIoFirst;
      NULL!=pIoCurr;
      pIoCurr=pIoCurr->m_pIoBufNext) {
        if (&pIoCurr->m_OverlappedIO==pOverlappedIO) {
          InterlockedExchange(
                  (long *)&pIoCurr->m_dwBytesRead,
                  dwBytesRead);
          pIoCurr->SetState(dwNewState);
          return;
        }
      }
```

```
        //Should never get here
        assert(false);
    }



}
```

26. I should begin the detailed discussion of CloBuf by discussing why it exists in the first place. Because we are using an I/O completion port to control the concurrency of the app and also to help synchronize our worker threads, we needed to design the app such that a given worker thread could continue to run and process as many pending work requests as possible before going into a wait state or being switched out for another thread. After all, that's the whole point of using the I/O completion port in the first place: to keep context switches to a minimum while still providing a reasonable level of parallelism. This obviously meant that we couldn't use the same model we'd used in the other fstring samples where the work requests (the read buffers) were effectively embedded in the CBufSearch class, the class that also encapsulated the worker threads themselves. That design would not have allowed all worker threads to access all work requests—there was an implicit 1:1 relationship between worker threads and work requests. Processing a new work request meant scheduling the containing worker thread and allowing it to search its own buffer. To make full use of the I/O completion port, we needed a means of placing each read buffer and its attendant information in a global queue that all worker threads could access and dequeue as necessary. In the other fstring examples, CBufSearch contains the read buffer and the OVERLAPPED structure used by Windows' ReadFile API function. In this app, those members have been moved to CloBuf, and a new member has been added that indicates the state of a given buffer. The linked list of CloBuf objects serves as a work request queue from which each worker thread retrieves buffers that have been read from the file and are ready to be searched. Because the buffer information is no longer stored along with each worker thread's entry-point class, all the worker threads can see all the read buffers and can dequeue them, one at a time, in order to search them.

Another approach to moving the OVERLAPPED structure we need for asynchronous I/O would have been to derive the CloBuf class from it. This would have allowed us to pass a pointer to a CloBuf instance into the functions that need a pointer to an OVERLAPPED structure (e.g., ReadFile) and would have alleviated the need for the search code in the CheckForIoPacketAndSetState method (discussed below). You'll see this technique employed in the next exercise.

27. To enqueue or dequeue a buffer, a thread simply changes its state member. Setting a buffer's state to BUF_STATE_INACTIVE or BUF_STATE_READY enqueues it. Setting it to BUF_STATE_READING or BUF_STATE_SEARCHING dequeues it. That's the purpose of the call to SpinToFindBuf: It scans the buffer list for a buffer whose state matches the requested state (dwOldState) and changes it to the specified state (dwNewState). This has the effect of either enqueuing or dequeuing the buffer, depending on the new state and the potential consumer. SpinToFindBuf changes the buffer state in an atomic fashion in order to avoid collisions with other threads. Worker threads use SpinToFindBuf to acquire buffers to search; the main thread uses it to acquire buffers for use with ReadFile.

28. SpinToFindBuf spins (loops) until it finds a buffer with the requested state. In the case of CBufSearch::Search, the requested state will always be BUF_STATE_READY. When it finds a matching buffer, SpinToFindBuf uses InterlockedCompareExchange to change the buffer's state to dwNewState so that other threads will not acquire the same buffer. It then returns the address of the corresponding CIoBuf object to the caller.

29. Note the call to CheckForIoPacketAndSetState on entry to SpinToFindBuf. This is the method that actually calls GetQueuedCompletionStatus. It checks for a pending I/O completion packet, and, if it finds one, uses the OVERLAPPED pointer returned by GetQueuedCompletionStatus to locate the CIoBuf object that corresponds to the original asynchronous I/O operation. It then sets this object's state field to BUF_STATE_READY, which indicates that the asynchronous read operation that was using its buffer has now completed. It also sets the object's bytes read field so that CBufSeach::Search will know how much of the buffer to search (in case the end of the file was encountered while filling it).

30. At the start of its spin loop, SpinToFindBuf detects whether the main thread has signaled that it has finished reading the input file. It then searches the buffer list for a buffer with the desired state, and if it doesn't find one and termination was signaled before it entered the search loop, it exits. This prevents termination in the middle of the loop before all buffers have been searched while still allowing the object to detect that the file has been completely read and all pending work requests should be in the buffer list. It is conceivable that an asynchronous I/O operation could take so long to complete that the buffer queue will be empty after s_bTerminated has been set to TRUE, causing the polling worker thread to exit prematurely; however, the I/O sizes we are working with here are so small that this is a very remote possibility, and I have not coded this sample app to account for it.

In this next exercise, we'll explore a variation on fstring_io_comp that uses an I/O completion port to queue the output for each worker thread. This is another way of helping ensure that, once a CBufSearch thread begins actively processing I/O completion packets, it does not block on I/O or become otherwise unschedulable any more than absolutely necessary.

Exercise 5.6   A File Search Utility That Uses an I/O Completion Port for Both Input and Output

1. Load the fstring_io_comp_out sample from the CH05\fstring_io_comp_ out subfolder on the book's CD into the Visual Studio development environment.
2. Most of the code in fstring_io_comp_out is identical to that of the previous exercise; bufsrch.cpp is the only module with substantive changes. Let's have a look at it (Listing 5.10).

Listing 5.10 A Version of CBufSearch That Uses an I/O Completion Port to Queue Output

```
//bufsrch.cpp -- a utility class that
//we use to search a buffer for a string

#include "bufsrch.h"

CIoBuf *CBufSearch::s_pIoFirst=NULL;

//Ctor
CBufSearch::CBufSearch(CBufSearch *pbNext,
                               char *szFileName,
                               char *szSearchStr)
{

  //Cache constructor parameters for later use
  m_pbNext=pbNext;
  m_szFileName=szFileName;
  m_szSearchStr=szSearchStr;

  //Initialize the remaining member variables
  m_dwFindCount=0;
```

```
//Create the private heap that we'll use for output
m_hOutputHeap=HeapCreate(HEAP_NO_SERIALIZE,0x1000,0);

//Create the I/O completion port that we'll use for
//queuing output
m_hOutputIoCompletionPort=
  CreateIoCompletionPort(INVALID_HANDLE_VALUE,NULL,0,0);

}


CBufSearch::~CBufSearch()
{

  //Dequeue the I/O completion packets
  //from the output queue and print
  //the output
  DWORD dwLineCount=0;
  DWORD dwBytesWritten;
  DWORD dwKey;
  OUTPUT_OVERLAPPED *pOutputOverlapped;
  while (dwLineCount<m_dwFindCount)  {
    GetQueuedCompletionStatus(m_hOutputIoCompletionPort,
                              &dwBytesWritten,
                              &dwKey,
                              (OVERLAPPED **)
                                &pOutputOverlapped,INFINITE);
    printf(pOutputOverlapped->pszMsg);
    dwLineCount++;
  }

  //Destroy the private output heap
  HeapDestroy(m_hOutputHeap);

  //Close the output I/O completion port
  CloseHandle(m_hOutputIoCompletionPort);
}

//From an offset in a buffer, find the start of the line
char *CBufSearch::FindLineStart(char *szStartPos)
{
  char *szStart;
  for (szStart=szStartPos;
```

```
    ((szStart>m_pIoCurrent->m_szBuf) &&
      (cLINE_DELIM!=*(szStart-1)))); szStart--);
  return szStart;
}


//From an offset in a buffer, find the end of the line
// -- assumes null-termination
char *CBufSearch::FindLineEnd(char *szStartPos)
{
  return strchr(szStartPos,cLINE_DELIM);
}


//Search the read buffer for
//every line containing a previously
//specified search string
bool CBufSearch::Search()
{
  char *szBol;
  char *szEol;
  char *szStringPos;
  DWORD dwNumChars;
  char *szStartPos;
  bool bRes=false;
  char szFmt[32];
  char szOffsetOutput[255];
  DWORDLONG dwlFilePos;
  char szMsg[1024];

  while (1) {

    __try
    {

      //Spin until we find a buffer to search
      if ((NULL==(m_pIoCurrent=
        s_pIoFirst->SpinToFindBuf(BUF_STATE_READY,
            BUF_STATE_SEARCHING))) &&
            (s_pIoFirst->s_bTerminated))
        break;

      //We start the search at the beginning
      //of the read buffer
      szStartPos=m_pIoCurrent->m_szBuf;
```

```
        //Get the starting file offset from
        //the buf object for display later
        dwlFilePos=m_pIoCurrent->FilePos();


        //Loop while the search start marker is not NULL
        //and is within the read buffer
        //and strstr continues to find the search string
        //in the read buffer
        while ((szStartPos) &&
               (szStartPos<(m_pIoCurrent->m_szBuf+
                        m_pIoCurrent->m_dwBytesRead)-1) &&
               (NULL!=(szStringPos=
                    strstr(szStartPos,m_szSearchStr)))) {

          //If we get in here, we have a search hit
          m_dwFindCount++;

          //Compute the line start and end so that we
          //can write it to the console
          szBol=FindLineStart(szStringPos);
          szEol=FindLineEnd(szStringPos);

          //Compute the number of characters to output
          //We'll use this later to build a printf
          //format string
          if (szEol) {
            dwNumChars=szEol-szBol;
            if (szEol<(m_pIoCurrent->m_szBuf+
                  m_pIoCurrent->m_dwBytesRead)-1)
                  szStartPos=szEol+1;
            else szStartPos=NULL;
          }
          else {
            dwNumChars=MAXLINE_LEN;
            szStartPos=NULL;
          }

#if(_DEBUG)
sprintf(szOffsetOutput,"Thread %08d: Offset: %010I64d %s ",
            GetCurrentThreadId(),
            dwlFilePos+(szStringPos-m_pIoCurrent->m_szBuf),
            m_szFileName);
#else
```

```
        sprintf(szOffsetOutput,"Offset: %010I64d %s ",
                dwlFilePos+(szStringPos-m_pIoCurrent->m_szBuf),
                m_szFileName);
#endif
  //Build format string that limits output to current line
    strcpy(szFmt,"%s %.");
    sprintf(szFmt+5,"%ds\n",dwNumChars);


    //Build the output line
    sprintf(szMsg,szFmt,
                 szOffsetOutput,
                 szBol);


  //Allocate a structure to serve as an output packet
    OUTPUT_OVERLAPPED *pOutputOverlapped=
    (OUTPUT_OVERLAPPED *)
         HeapAlloc(m_hOutputHeap,
         0,
         sizeof(OUTPUT_OVERLAPPED));

    //Allocate memory for the message string within
    //the output packet structure
    pOutputOverlapped->pszMsg=
       (char *)HeapAlloc(m_hOutputHeap,
                         0,
                         strlen(szMsg)+1);

    //Copy the output message to the output packet
    strcpy(pOutputOverlapped->pszMsg,szMsg);

    //Queue the output packet

    PostQueuedCompletionStatus(
                 m_hOutputIoCompletionPort,
                 0,
                 0,(OVERLAPPED *)pOutputOverlapped);

    bRes=true;

  }
}
__except(EXCEPTION_EXECUTE_HANDLER)
```

```
      {
        //Eat the exception -- should never get here
        //given that the read buffer is guaranteed to
        //be null-terminated.
#if(_DEBUG)

        //Assumes we got an access violation from going
        //past the end of the read buffer -- could actually
        //be some other type of error
        printf("Thread %08d reached end of buffer\n",
          GetCurrentThreadId());
#endif
      }

    m_pIoCurrent->SetState(BUF_STATE_INACTIVE);

  }

  return bRes;
}
```

3. Let's begin with the CBufSearch constructor. Notice that it now creates an I/O completion port for the exclusive use of a CBufSearch object and that this completion port is not associated with a file. Also notice that we no longer receive a handle to the main thread or a callback address. These are no longer needed since we won't be queuing output to the main thread using an APC as we did in fstring_io_comp.

4. Take a look at the section of CBufSearch::Search that builds the output line once a match has been found. Here we allocate an OUTPUT_OVERLAPPED structure and copy the output line to it. OUTPUT_OVERLAPPED is derived from OVERLAPPED and is defined like this in bufsrch.h:

```
struct OUTPUT_OVERLAPPED : OVERLAPPED
{
  char *pszMsg;
};
```

This means that it includes all the members of the OVERLAPPED structure, and, in addition, includes a single string pointer. Because we've derived it from OVERLAPPED, we can pass it into functions that require a pointer to an OVERLAPPED structure, such as PostQueued-CompletionStatus and GetQueuedCompletionStatus. When these routines internally cast the pointer they receive to an OVERLAPPED structure pointer and dereference it, they'll still be able to access the fields they expect to find in the locations where they expect to find them. Here, we use the technique to allow us to send some additional data along with the OVERLAPPED structure so that we can later retrieve it.

OUTPUT_OVERLAPPED encapsulates an output packet. It allows us to queue CBufSearch output while a worker thread is searching and defer our console I/O until later.

5. Once we've allocated the OUTPUT_OVERLAPPED structure and copied the output line to it, we post it to our output completion port using PostQueuedCompletionStatus. You may recall that PostQueuedCompletionStatus can be used by an application to post its own special-purpose I/O completion packets. That's exactly what we're doing here. We're posting output to the completion port that we will later retrieve using GetQueuedCompletionStatus.

6. Let's finish up by having a look at the destructor, ~CBufSearch. It's responsible for writing all the output from the output queue to the console and ultimately freeing up the resources allocated by the object, including the private heap containing its output. It begins by entering a loop in which it repeatedly calls GetQueuedCompletionStatus to dequeue I/O completion packets. Each time it dequeues a packet, it takes the OVERLAPPED structure pointer it receives from the call, casts it as an OUTPUT_OVERLAPPED structure, and writes the output line it contains to the console. Because there should be one line of output for every string match, it continues this until the number of retrieved I/O completion packets equals the number of string matches.

You may be wondering why we don't open a handle to the console using the FILE_FLAG_OVERLAPPED switch and simply write to it asynchronously from CBufSearch::Search. The reason we don't is that all console output is synchronized. An application cannot write to the console asynchronously. Although you can certainly open a new file handle for console output (using the special string CONOUT$ as the file name), any writes to it will be processed synchronously. In fact, an attempt to write to the console with WriteFileEx will fail, and GetLastError will report that the file handle is invalid. (The file handle isn't actually invalid, but it is invalid for use with asynchronous I/O.) In order to make multithreaded apps easier to write, Windows synchronizes all console I/O, so writing our output (directly) to the console asynchronously is not an option. That's why we've explored using an APC function and an I/O completion port to keep worker threads from waiting on I/O while they're searching.

You've now worked through two real-world applications that use I/O completion ports to control concurrency, assist with thread synchronization, and serve as queuing mechanisms. There are a fair number of these types of problems for which an I/O completion port can provide a ready solution. SQL Server makes use of I/O completion ports as well, so it's important to understand how they work and how they can be used.

I/O Completion Port Recap

An I/O completion port provides an efficient mechanism for allowing multiple threads to wait on asynchronous I/O and can be used as a general-purpose signaling mechanism independent of files and file I/O. The real power of I/O completion ports is that they can help manage the concurrency in an app, actively assisting the app with keeping the CPUs as busy as possible running application code rather than context switching.

I/O Completion Port Knowledge Measure

1. By default, how does an I/O completion port decide how many threads should be allowed to actively process I/O completion packets?
2. True or false: A characteristic of a high-performance server application is that it attempts to minimize context switches among worker threads as much as possible while still maintaining a sufficient degree of parallelism.
3. In what state must a thread be in order for a user mode APC to execute?
4. What happens if you specify a timeout value of 0 when you call GetQueuedCompletionStatus and there's no pending I/O completion packet?
5. What is the maximum number of completion ports with which a thread can be associated at one time?
6. True or false: Packets are dequeued from an I/O completion port in FIFO (first in, first out) order.
7. What API function is used to create an I/O completion port?
8. Is it possible to create an I/O completion port that is not associated with a file?
9. True or false: In order to wait on a completion packet to be queued to an I/O completion port, a thread calls one of the Win32 wait functions and passes it the handle of the I/O completion port.

10. What does the OVERLAPPED structure pointer that's returned by GetQueuedCompletionStatus refer to?

11. How can an application determine the number of bytes transferred by an asynchronous I/O operation that was initiated via a ReadFile call against a file associated with an I/O completion port?

12. True or false: SQL Server's User Mode Scheduler attempts to maximize processor utilization by avoiding context switches as much as possible.

13. Describe the purpose of the InterlockedExchange Win32 API function.

14. True or false: When working with I/O completion ports, it is generally preferable to decouple work requests from worker threads in such a manner that any thread can process any work request.

15. What common condition often exists in applications where too many worker threads are allowed to run concurrently?

16. What Win32 API can be used to post a special-purpose I/O completion packet to an I/O completion port?

17. True or false: If possible, threads that are actively processing I/O completion packets should avoid operations that cause them to be blocked.

18. Can SleepEx be used to dequeue an APC in the same way that WaitForSingleObjectEx can?

19. True or false: Once the concurrency value for an I/O completion port has been set, the system ensures that the number of threads actively processing I/O completion packets never exceeds the value specified.

20. What Win32 API function can a thread call to explicitly queue an APC to a thread?

21. True or false: Calling GetQueuedCompletionStatus has the effect of associating a thread with an I/O completion port.

22. What does the InterlockedCompareExchange Win32 API function do?

23. Is it possible for an asynchronous I/O request on a file that's associated with an I/O completion port to be processed synchronously by Windows?

24. Describe a potential fallacy of the software design approach that sets a hard limit for the number of worker threads in an app equal to the number of processors in the system.

25. What type of object does ReadFileEx cause to be queued when an asynchronous operation it has initiated completes?

Memory-Mapped File I/O

This section concludes our discussion of Windows' I/O facilities. We'll finish up by discussing how to process files using memory-mapped file I/O. We'll construct a couple of sample apps that build on what we've done earlier in the chapter and use memory-mapped file I/O to scan a text file for a string. This section will leverage the things we've covered earlier in the chapter and in the rest of the book. If you haven't yet read the first part of the chapter, please work through it before continuing. You will probably also want to read Chapter 4 if you haven't already done so.

Key Memory-Mapped File I/O Terms and Concepts

✔ *Shared memory*—memory that is visible to multiple processes or that is present in the virtual address space of multiple processes.
✔ *Memory-mapped file*—a file on disk that has been mapped into virtual memory such that it serves as the physical storage for the virtual memory.
✔ *Section object*—the kernel object responsible for implementing shared memory and memory-mapped files.

Key Memory-Mapped File I/O APIs

Table 5.9 Key Win32 APIs for Working with Memory-Mapped Files

Function	Description
CreateFileMapping	Creates a file-mapping object (a section object) for use with shared memory or a memory-mapped file.
MapViewOfFile	Maps a view of a file into memory such that the file serves as the physical storage for the memory. The file can be a file on disk or the system paging file.
FlushViewOfFile	Writes the modified pages in a mapped file view to disk.

Overview

As I mentioned in Chapter 4, Windows' memory-mapped file I/O facility allows I/O to be performed on a file as though it were memory. Rather than backing a range of virtual memory addresses with the physical storage in the system page file, the file itself is the physical storage behind the virtual memory used by a memory-mapped file.

Threads that access the file simply access memory as though it were one large, contiguous array. As the memory is accessed, the Windows memory manager handles paging the file in and out of physical memory behind the scenes. If a thread makes changes to this memory, the memory manager writes the changes to the file as part of the normal paging process.

Windows' mapped file I/O facility is produced jointly by the I/O system and the memory manager. It's an important part of the I/O subsystem and is used throughout the OS. The system cache manager, for example, uses mapped file I/O to map files into virtual memory and provide better response time for I/O-bound applications. While most caching systems allocate a fixed amount of memory for caching files, Windows' use of mapped file I/O for this purpose means that the amount of physical memory set aside for caching files can vary based on what else is going on in the system. If a lot of physical memory is being consumed, the buffer shrinks to accommodate this consumption. If physical memory is relatively unused, the cache can be quite large and can provide excellent performance even with very large files.

Another way in which Windows makes use of its own mapped file I/O facility is with image file activation. When an executable or DLL is brought into a process's address space, it is loaded as a mapped file. As Windows needs to access a particular code or data page within the binary, it's automatically loaded into physical memory via the normal paging process. In this case, the range of virtual memory addresses occupied by the binary is backed by the executable or DLL file itself rather than the system paging file.

To map a file into virtual memory, an application follows these steps.

1. Open the file through a call to CreateFile.
2. Create a file-mapping object (a section object, in kernel parlance) through a call to CreateFileMapping.
3. Pass the handle to the file-mapping object into MapViewOfFile. MapViewOfFile is responsible for actually mapping the file into virtual memory and returns a pointer to the starting virtual address where the mapping begins.

Once a file has been mapped into virtual memory, it can be accessed as though it had actually been copied from disk into memory. The advantage of mapping the file into memory versus actually copying it from disk is that because the file is never copied from its original location into the system paging file, the "load" is extremely fast and doesn't waste physical storage that might be used for other purposes.

Note that because a mapped file resides in the virtual memory address space, it's subject to the same limitations as any other virtual memory allocation. If there's insufficient contiguous address space to create the specified mapping, it will fail, just as virtual memory reservation that's too large might. Also, given that the entire user mode address space is at most 3GB, you can't map a file entirely into memory that's larger than 3GB. You might be able to map a smaller segment of it, but you won't be able to access the entire file as one large sequential memory buffer.

Exercises

Let's examine memory-mapped file I/O up close by building an app that uses it. The following exercise presents an app that uses mapped file I/O to search a text file.

Exercise 5.7 Using Memory-Mapped File I/O to Perform a File Search

This exercise takes you through a sample app that uses memory-mapped file I/O to search the files matching a given mask for a specified string. It is a variation on the sample app presented earlier in this chapter that used nonbuffered, asynchronous I/O to perform a similar search.

1. Load the fndstr sample app from the CH05\fndstr subfolder on the book's CD into Visual Studio and compile it.
2. Run the app under the VC++ debugger, passing it a text file to search and a string to locate. If you don't have a text file handy, the CD includes a file named INPUT.TXT that you can use for testing. It contains several instances of the string "ABCDEF."
3. If you step through the code, you'll notice that the actual process of searching a given file is carried out by a single call to the strstr C/C++ RTL function. Because the entirety of the file appears to be loaded into a contiguous memory buffer, we can easily search it using strstr. There's no need to process the file in buffer-sized chunks, nor do we need to be concerned with search string matches that happen to span a buffer boundary. Unlike some of the other I/O sample apps, fndstr will locate every occurrence of the search string within a file, regardless of where it physically resides.

4. Note that, because we're mapping the file into virtual memory, we are subject to the limitations of the virtual memory address space. To begin with, if the system is unable to find a contiguous region of virtual memory addresses that's large enough to map the entire file, the code below will fail. This could occur if the user mode address space is fragmented by other allocations or file mappings. Moreover, if the file is larger than the user mode space (either 2GB or 3GB on 32-bit Windows), the mapping will also fail. So, this technique isn't suitable for processing extremely large files or for processing even moderate-sized files in situations where virtual memory may be heavily fragmented.

5. As with most of the other sample applications in this book, the best way to understand how they work is to walk through the code itself. Listing 5.11 shows fndstr.cpp, the main source code file for the fndstr sample app.

Listing 5.11 fndstr.cpp, the Main Source Code Module for the fndstr Utility

```
// fndstr.cpp : A file search utility that uses
// memory-mapped file I/O to read each file
//

#include "stdafx.h"
#include "windows.h"
#include "stdlib.h"

#define MAXLINE_LEN 0x1000
const char cLINE_DELIM='\n';

//From an offset in a buffer, find the start of the line
char *FindLineStart(char *szStartPos, char *szFileStart)
{
  char *szStart;
  for (szStart=szStartPos;
    ((szStart>szFileStart) && (cLINE_DELIM!=*(szStart-1)));
      szStart--)
;
  return szStart;
}

//From an offset in a buffer, find the end of the line
// -- assumes null-termination
char *FindLineEnd(char *szStartPos)
{
```

```
          return strchr(szStartPos,cLINE_DELIM);
}

//Search a buffer for a specified string
DWORD Search(char *szStart, char *szEnd, char *szSearchStr,
     char *szFileName)
{
  DWORD dwFindCount=0;

  char *szBol;
  char *szEol;
  char *szStringPos;
  DWORD dwNumChars;
  char *szStartPos=szStart;
  char szFmt[32];
  __try
  {
    while ((szStartPos) &&
           (szStartPos<szEnd) &&
           (NULL!=(szStringPos=strstr(szStartPos,szSearchStr)))) {

      dwFindCount++;

      szBol=FindLineStart(szStringPos, szStart);
      szEol=FindLineEnd(szStringPos);

      if (szEol) {
        dwNumChars=szEol-szBol;
        if (szEol<szEnd) szStartPos=szEol+1;
        else szStartPos=NULL;
      }
      else {
        dwNumChars=MAXLINE_LEN;
        szStartPos=NULL;
      }

      printf("%s Offset: %010d ",szFileName,
             szStringPos-szStart);

      //Build format string that limits output
      //to current line

      strcpy(szFmt,"%.");
      sprintf(szFmt+2,"%ds\n",dwNumChars);
```

```
      //Output current line
      printf(szFmt,szBol);


    }
  }
  __except(EXCEPTION_EXECUTE_HANDLER)
  {
    //Eat the exception
#if(_DEBUG)
    printf("Scanned past end of buffer\n");
#endif
  }

  if (!dwFindCount)
    printf("Not found\n");
  return dwFindCount;
}

//Scan a single file for the search string
DWORD SearchFile(char *szPath, char *szFileName,
    char *szSearchStr)
{
  char *szFileData;
  char szFullPathName[MAX_PATH+1];
  DWORD dwFindCount;

  strcpy(szFullPathName,szPath);
  strcat(szFullPathName,szFileName);

  //Open the file
  HANDLE hFile=CreateFile(szFullPathName,
                          GENERIC_READ,
                          FILE_SHARE_READ,
                          NULL,
                          OPEN_EXISTING,
                          FILE_ATTRIBUTE_NORMAL,
                          NULL);

  //Create a file-mapping object for the file
  HANDLE hMappingObject=
    CreateFileMapping(hFile,
                      NULL,
                      PAGE_READONLY,
                      0,
                      0,
                      NULL);
```

```
  //Retrieve a pointer to the file data
  //by mapping it into virtual memory
  szFileData=
    (char *)MapViewOfFile(hMappingObject,
                          FILE_MAP_READ,
                          0,
                          0,
                          0);

  //Get the size of the mapped area
  //using VirtualQueryEx
  //so that we'll know the boundaries
  //of our search area
  MEMORY_BASIC_INFORMATION mbi;
  VirtualQueryEx(GetCurrentProcess(),
                 szFileData,
                 &mbi,
                 sizeof(mbi));

  //Search the file
  dwFindCount=Search(szFileData,
                     szFileData+mbi.RegionSize,
                     szSearchStr,
                     szFileName);

  //Unmap the file
  UnmapViewOfFile(szFileData);

  //Close the mapping object and file handles
  CloseHandle(hMappingObject);
  CloseHandle(hFile);

  return dwFindCount;
}

//Search the files matching a given mask
//for a specified string
bool SearchFiles(char *szFileMask, char *szSearchStr)
{

  char szPath[MAX_PATH+1];
  char *p=strrchr(szFileMask,'\\');
  if (p) {
    strncpy(szPath,szFileMask,(p-szFileMask)+1);
    szPath[(p-szFileMask)+1]='\0';
```

```
  }
  else
    GetCurrentDirectory(MAX_PATH,szPath);

  if ('\\'!=szPath[strlen(szPath)-1])
    strcat(szPath,"\\");

  printf("Searching for %s in %s\n\n",szSearchStr,szFileMask);

  WIN32_FIND_DATA fdFiles;
  HANDLE hFind=FindFirstFile(szFileMask,&fdFiles);

  if (INVALID_HANDLE_VALUE == hFind) {
    printf("No files match the specified mask\n");
    return false;
  }

  DWORD dwFindCount=0;
  do {
    dwFindCount+=
          SearchFile(szPath,fdFiles.cFileName,szSearchStr);
  } while (FindNextFile(hFind,&fdFiles));

  FindClose(hFind);

  printf("\nTotal hits for %s in %s:\t%d\n",szSearchStr,
          szFileMask,dwFindCount);
  return true;
}

int main(int argc, char* argv[])
{
  if (argc<3) {
    printf("Usage is: fndstr filemask searchstring\n");
    return 1;
  }

  return (!SearchFiles(argv[1], argv[2]));
}
```

6. The basic plumbing for iterating through the files matching a particular mask and calling a search function is the same in this and the other file search sample apps in this book, so I won't put you through the tedium of walking back through it. If you want specifics on how the SearchFiles routine works, see the Asynchronous and Nonbuffered I/O

section earlier in the chapter where we originally introduced the Search-Files function and examined the routine in detail. For the adventurous, it wouldn't be a lot of work to take the search algorithms in the I/O samples in this book (implemented via the SearchFile function in each sample app) and encapsulate them such that they implemented the Strategy design pattern (as outlined in the book *Design Patterns* by Erich Gamma and company[2]) and were interchangeable. Time and topical constraints do not permit me to do so here, but it would be an interesting exercise for the curious.

7. Let's begin by examining the global Search function. It's fairly simple in construction. It receives a starting pointer and an ending pointer and finds every occurrence of the search string between them. The mechanics of actually locating each string occurrence are handled by the strstr C/C++ RTL function. Once we find a match, we output the line on which it occurs, reposition the search start just beyond the end of the line, and continue looking. Once we've searched the whole buffer, we return a find count to the caller.

8. Note the exception-handling code we use to trap situations where strstr may scan past the end of our buffer in search of a null-terminator. Because we can't pad the file as it appears in virtual memory without physically changing it, it's possible that we'll read past the end of the buffer if the file happens to end on an exact system page boundary. So, assuming a system page size of 4K, if a file is exactly 4K in size and does not happen to end with a null-terminator, strstr will scan past the end of it while looking for the end of the string. Given that we can't commit an extra page past the end of the mapped region, this possibility is, unfortunately, unavoidable with the memory-mapped file technique. If the end of the file does *not* fall on a page boundary, we can rest assured that the remainder of its final page will be zero-filled on its first access, so strstr will find its null-terminator regardless of the file contents. However, if that's not the case and strstr attempts to access uncommitted address space, an access violation will be raised. When that happens, our structured exception-handling code will discard the exception and allow the program to continue searching other files. If compiled as a debug build, fndstr will note that the end of the buffer was likely passed by printing a message to the console. The fndstr app ignores the exception based on the assumption that an access violation due to strstr going past the end of the mapped file memory is the only type of exception we should see in our main search loop. Although other types of obscure exceptions could be raised, this is a fairly safe assumption.

2. Gamma, Erich, Richard Helm, Ralph Johnson, and John Vlissides. *Design Patterns: Elements of Reusable Object-Oriented Software.* Reading, MA: Addison-Wesley, 1995.

9. Now let's have a look at the SearchFile routine itself. It begins by opening the file and creating a file-mapping object for it, a requirement of memory-mapped file I/O. It next calls the MapViewOfFile Win32 function to map the file into a contiguous range of virtual memory addresses and return a pointer to the start of this range. We use the pointer returned by MapViewOfFile as the access point into the file. Our search routines will use it as their starting address.

10. SearchFile next calls VirtualQueryEx to retrieve the size of the region set aside for the file mapping. This should be the file size rounded up to the next page boundary. We use this to compute the end of the search buffer. Since the system zero-fills a committed virtual memory page the first time it's accessed, we can be sure that search routines based on strstr will not find false matches past the end of the file due to data remnants that may have been left in memory from previous operations.

So, that's the fndstr sample app from beginning to end. Thanks to memory-mapped file I/O, the app itself is fairly simple and doesn't have to be concerned much with searching multiple buffers and the idiosyncrasies of searching for a string that may straddle a buffer boundary.

Given that the nonbuffered, asynchronous sample app fstring (introduced earlier in the chapter) was multithreaded, you may be wondering why we don't scan the mapped file in parallel. After all, searching the file is simply a matter of scanning memory, and we can do that for the most part without having to be concerned about synchronizing simultaneous access by multiple threads because we are reading, not writing, the memory.

In the next sample app, we'll explore that very possibility. Because we will be logically dividing the file into multiple pieces in order to scan it with multiple threads, we will again face the possibility that a match string could straddle a buffer boundary. However, because the entirety of the file has been mapped into memory and appears as one contiguous buffer of address space, we can solve the problem in a novel way without giving up the ability to scan the file with multiple threads.

Exercise 5.8 A Multithreaded File Scanner That Uses Mapped File I/O

1. Load the findstring sample app from the CH05\findstring subfolder on the CD into Visual Studio and compile it.

2. Findstring consists of two main source code modules: findstring.cpp and rngsrch.cpp. Findstring.cpp implements the plumbing necessary to iterate through the files matching a specified mask and call a search routine to scan each one for a given string. Its main function, SearchFiles, is similar enough to the other samples in this chapter that I won't

go back through it here. If you'd like specifics on SearchFiles, consult the discussion of the fstring sample app earlier in the chapter where I discuss it in detail.

3. The SearchFile function is responsible for searching each file. It opens each one with CreateFile, creates a file-mapping object for it, then maps it into memory using MapViewOfFile. As with the previous exercise, we use the pointer returned by MapViewOfFile as the starting point for the search operation.

4. One of the parameters passed into SearchFile is the number of processors on the system. The SearchFiles routine computes this at program startup and passes it into SearchFile. SearchFile then creates a worker thread for each processor on the system. If you have a two-processor system, you'll see two worker threads created. If you have a four-processor system, you'll see four worker threads created. Because the search is done entirely in virtual memory, there's little benefit in creating more threads than processors.

5. Note the way in which SearchFile checks the number of pages in the file and lowers the number of threads it will use if the file has fewer pages than there are processors on the system. This way we can be sure that each thread gets at least one memory page to search.

6. SearchFile next creates a linked list of CRangeSearch objects and a suspended worker thread to correspond to each instance. When it creates a worker thread, SearchFile passes a pointer to a CRangeSearch object as the user-defined void pointer parameter to _beginthreadex. The thread entry-point function, StartSearch, then casts this parameter back to a CRangeSearch pointer and calls its Search method. Once Search has been called, it never exits until the thread is ready to shut down. We'll discuss CRangeSearch (implemented in rngsrch.cpp) in detail in just a moment.

7. Each CRangeSearch object is passed a starting and ending offset to search. So, by virtue of the fact that the file is mapped into a range of contiguous virtual memory addresses, we only need to compute offset pairs in order to scan it with multiple threads. If you have two worker threads, each thread will scan approximately half of the file.

8. Once all the worker threads have been created, SearchFile starts them running by calling ResumeThread. We initially create the worker threads in a suspended state so that each CRangeSearch object can recompute the end of its search range before the actual search process begins. As I mentioned earlier, because we are dividing the virtual memory region into which the file has been mapped into multiple logical pieces so that we can scan them in parallel, we again face the situation where a search match may span a buffer boundary. To handle this, as we create each CRangeSearch object, we adjust its ending scan offset such that it coincides with the last complete text line in the

region. In other words, if the last character in the buffer is not an end-of-line marker, we move the end of the buffer backward until we find the last end-of-line marker in the buffer. This prevents a search match from spanning a buffer boundary. It also necessitates that the next CRange-Search object start its search just after this final end-of-line marker in the buffer, so CRangeSearch's RecalcEnd method returns the new starting offset, and this is passed into the next CRangeSearch object's constructor so that it can set its starting position accordingly.

9. Once all the threads are started, we call WaitForMultipleObjects to wait on them to complete. Once they complete, we tally up the results, release the resources we've allocated, and return a find count to SearchFiles.

10. This procedure is best understood by looking at the code itself. Listing 5.12 shows findstring.cpp.

Listing 5.12 findstring.cpp, the Main Source Code Module for the findstring Utility

```cpp
// findstring.cpp : Multithreaded file search
// using memory-mapped file I/O
//

#include "stdafx.h"
#include "windows.h"
#include "stdlib.h"
#include "process.h"
#include "rngsrch.h"

//Thread entry-point function
unsigned __stdcall StartSearch(LPVOID lpParameter)
{
  return ((CRangeSearch*)lpParameter)->Search();
}

//Search a file for a specified string
DWORD SearchFile(DWORD dwPageSize,
                 DWORD dwNumProcessors,
                 char *szPath,
                 char *szFileName,
                 char *szSearchStr)
{
  char *szFileData;
  char szFullPathName[MAX_PATH+1];
```

```
strcpy(szFullPathName,szPath);
strcat(szFullPathName,szFileName);

//Open the file
HANDLE hFile=
  CreateFile(szFullPathName,
             GENERIC_READ,
             FILE_SHARE_READ,
             NULL,
             OPEN_EXISTING,
             FILE_ATTRIBUTE_NORMAL,
             NULL);

//Create the file-mapping object
HANDLE hMappingObject=
  CreateFileMapping(hFile,
                    NULL,
                    PAGE_READONLY,
                    0,
                    0,
                    NULL);

//Map the file into memory and return
//a pointer to the start of the memory
szFileData=
  (char *)MapViewOfFile(hMappingObject,
                        FILE_MAP_READ,
                        0,
                        0,
                        0);

//Get the size of the mapped region
MEMORY_BASIC_INFORMATION mbi;
VirtualQueryEx(GetCurrentProcess(),
                        szFileData,
                        &mbi,
                        sizeof(mbi));

//Make sure we don't have more threads
//than pages
DWORD dwNumThreads;
DWORD dwNumPages=(mbi.RegionSize / dwPageSize);
```

```
if (dwNumProcessors>dwNumPages)
  dwNumThreads=dwNumPages;
else
  dwNumThreads=dwNumProcessors;

//Compute the number of pages
//each thread will scan
DWORD dwPagesPerThread=dwNumPages / dwNumThreads;

//Allocate the thread handle array
HANDLE *hThreads=
          (HANDLE *)HeapAlloc(GetProcessHeap(),
                              0,
                              dwNumThreads*sizeof(HANDLE));
if (NULL==hThreads) {
  printf("Error allocating worker thread array.  Aborting.\n");
  return 1;
}

CRangeSearch *prsFirst=NULL;
char *szNextStartOfs=szFileData;
char *szEndOfs=szFileData;
unsigned uThreadId;

//Allocate the CRangeSearch objects
//and create the worker threads
for (DWORD i=0; i<dwNumThreads; i++) {

  if (i<dwNumThreads-1) {
    szEndOfs+=(dwPagesPerThread*dwPageSize)-1;
  }
  else szEndOfs=szFileData+mbi.RegionSize-1;

  prsFirst = new CRangeSearch(prsFirst,
                              szFileName,
                              szFileData,
                              szNextStartOfs,
                              szEndOfs,
                              szSearchStr);

  if (i<dwNumThreads-1)
    szNextStartOfs=prsFirst->RecalcEnd()+1;

  hThreads[i]=
```

```
           (HANDLE)_beginthreadex(NULL,
                                  0,
                                  &StartSearch,
                                  prsFirst,
                                  CREATE_SUSPENDED,
                                  &uThreadId);

    }

    //Once all CRangeSearch objects have
    //been created, start the threads up
    for (i=0; i<dwNumThreads; i++)
      ResumeThread(hThreads[i]);

    //Wait for the threads to finish searching the file
    WaitForMultipleObjects(dwNumThreads,hThreads,true,INFINITE);

    //Get total tally and destroy search objects
    DWORD dwFindCount=0;
    CRangeSearch *prsNext;
    for (; NULL!=prsFirst; prsFirst=prsNext) {
      dwFindCount+=prsFirst->m_dwFindCount;
      prsNext=prsFirst->m_prsNext;
      delete prsFirst;
    }

    //Free the thread handles
    for (i=0; i<dwNumThreads; i++)
      CloseHandle(hThreads[i]);

    //Free the thread handle array
    HeapFree(GetProcessHeap(),0,hThreads);

    //Unmap the file and close
    //the mapping object and file handles
    UnmapViewOfFile(szFileData);
    CloseHandle(hMappingObject);
    CloseHandle(hFile);

    return dwFindCount;
}

bool SearchFiles(char *szFileMask, char *szSearchStr)
{
```

```
char szPath[MAX_PATH+1];
char *p=strrchr(szFileMask,'\\');
if (p) {
  strncpy(szPath,szFileMask,(p-szFileMask)+1);
  szPath[(p-szFileMask)+1]='\0';
}
else
  GetCurrentDirectory(MAX_PATH,szPath);

if ('\\'!=szPath[strlen(szPath)-1])
  strcat(szPath,"\\");

printf("Searching for %s in %s\n\n",szSearchStr,szFileMask);

WIN32_FIND_DATA fdFiles;
HANDLE hFind=FindFirstFile(szFileMask,&fdFiles);

if (INVALID_HANDLE_VALUE == hFind) {
  printf("No files match the specified mask\n");
  return false;
}

SYSTEM_INFO si;
GetSystemInfo(&si);

DWORD dwFindCount=0;
do {
  dwFindCount+=
    SearchFile(si.dwPageSize,
               si.dwNumberOfProcessors,
               szPath,
               fdFiles.cFileName,
               szSearchStr);

} while (FindNextFile(hFind,&fdFiles));

FindClose(hFind);

printf("\nTotal hits for %s in %s:\t%d\n",szSearchStr,
       szFileMask,dwFindCount);
return true;
}

int main(int argc, char* argv[])
```

```
{
  if (argc<3) {
    printf("Usage is: findstring filemask searchstring\n");
    return 1;
  }

  return (!SearchFiles(argv[1], argv[2]));
}
```

11. The work of actually searching each logical piece of the file is done by the CRangeSearch class. It's implemented in rngsrch.cpp. Listing 5.13 provides that code.

Listing 5.13 rngsrch.cpp, the Source Code Module for the CRangeSearch Class

```
// rngsrch.cpp -- utility class for
// searching a range of virtual memory
// for a given string

#include "rngsrch.h"

//Ctor
CRangeSearch::CRangeSearch(CRangeSearch *prsNext,
char *szFileName, char *szFileData, char *szStart, char *szEnd,
char* szSearchStr)
{
  //Cache ctor params for later use
  m_prsNext=prsNext;
  m_szFileName=szFileName;
  m_szFileData=szFileData;
  m_szStart=szStart;
  m_szEnd=szEnd;
  m_szSearchStr=szSearchStr;

  m_dwFindCount=0;
}

//Recompute the end of a
//search buffer so that a line
//does not straddle two buffers
char *CRangeSearch::RecalcEnd()
{
```

```
  m_szEnd=FindLineStart(m_szEnd);
  if (m_szEnd) m_szEnd--;
  return m_szEnd;
}


//From an offset in a buffer, find the start of the line
char *CRangeSearch::FindLineStart(char *szStartPos)
{
  char *szStart;
  for (szStart=szStartPos;
    ((szStart>m_szStart) && (cLINE_DELIM!=*(szStart-1)));
      szStart--);
  return szStart;
}
//From an offset in a buffer, find the end of the line
// -- assumes null-termination
char *CRangeSearch::FindLineEnd(char *szStartPos)
{
  return strchr(szStartPos,cLINE_DELIM);
}


//Continuously search a given buffer
//for a specified string
bool CRangeSearch::Search()
{
  char *szBol;
  char *szEol;
  char *szStringPos;
  DWORD dwNumChars;
  char *szStartPos=m_szStart;
  bool bRes=false;
  char szFmt[32];
  char szOffsetMsg[255];

    __try
    {
      while ((szStartPos) &&
          (szStartPos<m_szEnd) &&
          (NULL!=(szStringPos=strstr(szStartPos,m_szSearchStr)))) {

        m_dwFindCount++;

        szBol=FindLineStart(szStringPos);
        szEol=FindLineEnd(szStringPos);
```

```
      if (szEol) {
        dwNumChars=szEol-szBol;
        if (szEol<m_szEnd) szStartPos=szEol+1;
        else szStartPos=NULL;
      }
      else {
        dwNumChars=MAXLINE_LEN;
        szStartPos=NULL;
      }

#if(_DEBUG)
sprintf(szOffsetMsg,"Thread %08d: Offset: %010d %s ",
        GetCurrentThreadId(),
        szStringPos-m_szFileData,m_szFileName);
#else
sprintf(szOffsetMsg,"Offset: %010d %s ",
        szStringPos-m_szFileData,m_szFileName);
#endif

  //Build format string that limits output to current line
    strcpy(szFmt,"%s %.");
    sprintf(szFmt+5,"%ds\n",dwNumChars);

    //Output current line
    printf(szFmt,szOffsetMsg,szBol);

    bRes=true;


  }
}
__except(EXCEPTION_EXECUTE_HANDLER)
{
  //Eat the exception
#if(_DEBUG)
  printf("Thread %08d reached end of buffer\n",
        GetCurrentThreadId());
#endif
}

if (!bRes)
  printf("Not found\n");
return bRes;
}
```

12. The key method in the CRangeSearch class is its Search method. As I mentioned earlier, once a worker thread enters this method, it never exits until the thread has finished scanning the range of memory for which it's responsible.

13. The Search method uses a simple loop based on calls to the strstr C/C++ RTL function to find the matches in its buffer. For each match, it outputs the line containing the match, then repeats the scan beginning with the end of the current line. When it runs out of matches, the thread is done and exits normally.

14. As with the previous sample app, the possibility remains that strstr could scan past the end of the virtual address range into which the file has been mapped while looking for a null-terminator. This is much more likely if the file happens to end on an exact page boundary. If strstr runs past the end of the mapped region, an access violation may be raised, so we trap and eat any exceptions raised by the search loop. Again, we're doing this based on the assumption that an access violation caused by strstr running off the end of the mapped file area is the only likely cause of an exception from this routine even though there remains the possibility that some other obscure condition could raise an exception within the loop. The code isn't intended to demonstrate exhaustive or even robust exception handling; the idea is to keep it as simple as possible while remaining functional enough that you get a sense of some of the practical uses of memory-mapped file I/O.

You should now have an understanding of some of the things you can do with mapped file I/O and multithreading. SQL Server uses memory-mapped files in several places itself, so understanding the basics of how mapped file I/O can be put to work by an application will give you some insight into how SQL Server makes use of it.

Memory-Mapped File I/O Recap

In addition to using Windows' shared memory facilities to share data between processes, you can use it to map files into virtual memory for easy access. A memory-mapped file becomes the physical storage for the range of virtual addresses into which it has been mapped, so the file need not be copied from disk into the system paging file. Reading the file is as simple as reading memory. Writing it is as simple as changing memory. Because the file appears to be loaded into a single, contiguous buffer, you have options for processing it that would otherwise not be available or that would be much more difficult. An example of this type of functionality is demonstrated in the RecalcEnd method in the findstring sample.

Memory-Mapped File I/O Knowledge Measure

1. Which Win32 API function is responsible for mapping a file into memory and returning a pointer to its starting address?
2. True or false: Windows will relocate DLLs and other images that have been mapped into a process's address space to make room for a file you are attempting to map into memory.
3. What's the simplest way for an application to change the contents of a file that's been mapped into memory?
4. True or false: In order for a file to be mapped into memory, its file object must have been created with the FILE_FLAG_MAPPED switch.
5. What Win32 API function is used to create a file-mapping object?
6. True or false: Because a memory-mapped file is subject to the same limitations as virtual memory itself, you cannot map an entire file into virtual memory whose size exceeds 3GB on 32-bit Windows.
7. True or false: Windows' mapped file I/O facility is produced jointly by the I/O system and the memory manager.
8. When a file is mapped into virtual memory, at what point does Windows copy it to the system paging file?
9. What Win32 API can a thread call to flush the modified pages in a memory-mapped file immediately to disk?
10. What kernel object is responsible for implementing shared memory?
11. What Win32 API function did we use in this chapter to get the exact size of the memory region into which a file is mapped?
12. True or false: Although a file that has been mapped into virtual memory serves as the physical storage for the memory, it takes longer to map a file into memory than to allocate a memory buffer and copy the file from disk because the Windows memory manager almost always processes I/O synchronously.
13. What Win32 API function do we call to undo a file mapping?
14. True or false: The address range set aside for a memory-mapped file comes from the default system heap.
15. True or false: One way in which Windows makes use of its own mapped file I/O facility is with image file activation.

CHAPTER 6

Networking Fundamentals

It is impossible to calculate the moral mischief, if I may so express it, that mental lying has produced in society. When a man has so far corrupted and prostituted the chastity of his mind as to subscribe his professional belief to things he does not believe, he has prepared himself for the commission of every other crime.

—Thomas Paine[1]

The purpose of network software is to take a client request for a resource, execute the request on the remote machine containing the requested resource, and return the results to the client. Before networking functionality was built into operating systems, this was a nontrivial proposition. All sorts of ill-fitting and interim-type solutions were used to provide basic connectivity between machines and to make it as seamless as possible (e.g., TSRs, topology-dependent utilities, and so on). With the advent of OS-integrated network support, interconnectivity is not only trivial and commonplace, it is expected. Today, we've moved beyond basic connectivity to things like WiFi and Gigabit Ethernet. Intermachine networking has become as humdrum as running water and electricity.

Overview

Key Networking Terms and Concepts

- ✔ *Named pipe*—a connection-oriented networking protocol, based on Server Message Blocks and NetBIOS.
- ✔ *Socket*—the end point of an interprocess communication across a network transport. In Windows, you establish and interact with socket connections using the Winsock API.

---

1. Paine, Thomas. *The Age of Reason*, ed. Philip S. Foner. New York: Citadel Press, 1974, p. 50.

311

✔ *RPC*—Remote Procedure Call, a networking API that presents a call-level interface (CLI) in place of the traditional I/O model of network programming.

✔ *Connection-oriented Winsock application*—an application that makes use of a stream or reliable connection to communicate using the Winsock API.

✔ *Connectionless Winsock application*—an application that makes use of a datagram or unreliable connection to communicate using the Winsock API.

✔ *Name resolution*—the process of translating a machine name into a network address.

✔ *Network stack*—the collection of interrelated software used to allow applications to communicate with one another over a network.

Key Networking APIs

Table 6.1 Key Network-Related Win32 APIs

Function	Description
CreateNamedPipe	Creates a named pipe
ConnectNamedPipe	Waits on a client to connect to a named pipe
WSAStartup	Initializes the Winsock API library
WSASocket	Creates a new socket (Microsoft-specific)
socket	Creates a new socket (BSD Sockets–compatible)
listen	Instructs a socket to begin listening for client connections
accept	Waits on a Winsock client to connect
connect	Connects to a Winsock server
send	Sends data over a Winsock socket
recv	Receives data from a Winsock socket
ReadFile	Reads data from a resource represented by a file handle, including sockets and named pipes
WriteFile	Writes data to a resource represented by a file handle, including sockets and named pipes

Traditionally, networking software is structured around an I/O paradigm—a client typically interacts with networking resources using standard operating system API calls. In Windows, a network operation is automatically initiated when an application requests access to a remote resource. The system detects that the request is for a remote resource and forwards it to a redirector. The redirector acts as a type of remote file system. It passes the operation to the remote machine where the resource is located, which then routes the request to the appropriate operating system component to fulfill it. Once the request is fulfilled, the remote system returns the results across the network to the redirector, which then returns them to the client. All the while, the client does not even need to be aware that the network operation took place because the request was intercepted, redirected, and fulfilled transparently.

Successful networking requires that a machine be able to figure out how to get to a machine containing a remote resource and what communications protocols that machine can use. The process of translating a machine name into a network address is known as name resolution. The process of negotiating a compatible set of communications protocols is known as negotiation.

Once name resolution and protocol negotiation have been successfully completed, a network request must be altered for transmission across the network by dividing it into packets that the physical medium can transport. When the request reaches the destination, it must be reassembled from its packets, checked for completeness, decoded, and passed on to the appropriate OS component for fulfillment. Once the OS component fulfills the request, the process must be reversed in order to send the results back to the client.

The OSI Reference Model

Networking software can be classified into four basic categories: services, APIs, protocols, and network adapter device drivers. Each type is layered on top of the next to form what's commonly referred to as the network stack. The components in Windows that implement the network stack correspond loosely to the Open Systems Interconnection (OSI) reference model, first introduced in 1974 by the International Organization for Standardization (ISO). You can download the OSI reference model from the ISO Web site at http://www.iso.org. Table 6.2 details the seven layers of the model.

Keep in mind that this is more of a conceptual model than something that vendors implement exactly. It's often used to discuss networking in the

Table 6.2 The OSI Reference Model

Layer Number	Layer	Description
7	Application	Responsible for transferring information between two machines in a network conversation. It handles such things as machine identification, security validation, and starting the data exchange.
6	Presentation	Responsible for the formatting of data, including the type of line-break character(s) used, data compression, data encoding, etc.
5	Session	Responsible for managing the connection itself, including coordination of who is sending and who is receiving at any given time.
4	Transport	Responsible for dividing messages into packets on the client and assigning them sequence numbers and for reassembling packets on the server that have been received from the client. It's also responsible for abstracting the hardware layer in such a way as to protect the Session layer from changes to it.
3	Network	Responsible for packet headers and routing, internetworking, and congestion control. It is the topmost layer that is aware of the network topology—the physical configuration of the network (the machines on the network, bandwidth limitations, etc.).
2	Data-link	Responsible for transmitting low-level data frames, checking to make sure they were received, and retransmitting frames lost due to unreliable lines.
1	Physical	Responsible for sending data to the physical network transmission medium (the network cable, wireless device, etc.).

abstract, with implementation details left to vendors. The important thing is to glean its key tenets and understand how Windows implements them.

Each layer in the model exists to provide services to the higher layers and to provide an abstract interface to the services provided by lower layers. It's helpful to think of each layer built on top of the Physical layer as another level of indirection removed from the actual process of transmitting bits over the network cabling. As we travel up the stack, we get further and further away from the physical transmission of data until we get to the Application layer, which is completely unaware of how data is physically moved between machines.

Consider how the layers on one machine communicate with those on another in a network conversation. Conceptually, each layer on the first machine talks to the same layer on the other machine, and both layers use the same protocol. For example, a Windows Socket application on one machine will behave as though it is communicating directly with a Windows Socket application on the other machine. Physically, however, data must travel down each machine's network stack to the physical medium, then across the medium to the other machine and back up the other machine's network stack. So, although the Transport layers on each machine involved in a network conversation may logically appear to be talking to one another, in actuality, they are communicating with their own Network, Data-link, and Physical layers, and it is the Physical layers of the two machines that actually communicate directly with one another over the network cabling.

By convention, the seven layers of the model are further divided into two broader tiers. The bottom four layers are commonly referred to as the transport, and the top three are referred to as clients of the transport or users of the transport. The OSI Transport layer is where we start to get into the physical logistics of getting from one machine to another, so dividing the seven layers along these lines is useful from a conceptual standpoint.

Windows Networking Components

As with other operating systems, Windows doesn't implement the OSI reference model precisely. It has some layers that the OSI model doesn't have, and a few of its layers span more than one OSI layer. Table 6.3 lays out the OSI-to-Windows network component mapping.

Windows supports multiple network APIs in order to be compatible with industry standards and to provide support for legacy applications. For example, Windows' Sockets implementation closely resembles that of Berkeley

Table 6.3 Windows Network Components and Their OSI Reference Model Mappings

Layer Number	Windows Networking Component	OSI Layer	Comments
7	Network application	Application	
6	Network API DLL	Presentation	Allows applications to communicate across a network in a manner that's independent of transport protocol.
5		Session	
5	Network API driver	Session	Kernel mode drivers responsible for the kernel mode portion of a network API's implementation.
	Transport Driver Interface		Specifies a common API for kernel mode device drivers.
4	Protocol driver (TCP/IP, IPX, etc.)	Transport	
3		Network	
	NDIS protocol drivers		Kernel mode drivers that process I/O requests from TDI clients.
2	NDIS library and miniport	Data-link	The NDIS library encapsulates the kernel mode environment for adapter drivers. NDIS miniport drivers are kernel mode drivers that interface a TDI transport with a specific network adapter.
	Hardware abstraction layer		
1	Ethernet, IrDa, etc.	Physical	

Software Distribution (BSD) Sockets, the standard for Internet communication on UNIX since the 1980s, in order to make porting UNIX applications to Windows simpler.

As with any technology decision, which network API you should use in a particular application comes down to how well the API meets your application's needs. What a network API can offer an application can vary a great deal in terms of the network protocols it can use, what types of communication it supports (reliable versus unreliable, bidirectional versus unidirectional, and so on), and its portability to other versions of Windows or other operating systems that you might want it to either run on or be easily portable to. There's no single networking API that is better than every other networking API in every situation.

Windows' key networking APIs include the following:

- Common Internet File System
- Named Pipes
- Windows Sockets
- Remote Procedure Call
- NetBIOS

Of these, we'll discuss RPC, Named Pipes, and Windows Sockets because SQL Server offers network libraries for each of them (the multiprotocol Net-Library uses Windows' RPC facility). Common Internet File System is the mechanism by which files are shared on a Windows network. NetBIOS is mostly a legacy API that predates the emergence of TCP/IP and Sockets as the prevalent internetworking technology for computers.

Named Pipes

Windows' named pipes technology was originally developed for OS/2 LAN Manager and ported to the first release of Windows NT. You can still see a few vestiges of LAN Manager in Windows networking today (e.g., the LM-HOSTS file—"LM" stands for LAN Manager), and named pipes is a technology that has stood the test of time.

Named pipes allows applications to set up reliable, bidirectional communications across a network. It leverages Windows' security facilities, which allows a server to control which clients can access a pipe and what they can do with it.

The named pipe facility is tightly integrated with Windows. Most of the Named Pipes API functions are implemented in Kernel32.dll, the Win32 client-side DLL. ImpersonateNamedPipeClient is actually implemented in AdvApi32.dll, but the other Named Pipes functions are implemented in Kernel32. Working with named pipes to access network resources is as similar as possible to working with other types of Windows resources such as files and synchronization objects.

Named pipe names conform to Windows' Universal Naming Convention (UNC) standard (a protocol-independent method of identifying network resources) and have the form \\Server\Pipe\PipeName. The Server portion of the name can be a DNS name, an IP address, or a NetBIOS name. If you are creating a pipe, this portion of the name must refer to the current machine given that you can't create pipes on other machines. Windows supports the use of a period (.) as shorthand for the current machine, so you can use \\.\ instead of actually naming the machine when referring to a local pipe. The Pipe portion must actually be the word "Pipe." The PipeName portion can be anything you choose and can include subdirectories.

To start a conversation over named pipes, a machine creates a pipe using the CreateNamedPipe Win32 API call. The machine that does this is known as the named pipe server. Once it creates a pipe, it can begin accepting client connections by calling ConnectNamedPipe. ConnectNamedPipe can be executed synchronously or asynchronously.

A client connects to a named pipe server via a CreateFile call that specifies the pipe name as the file name. It sends and receives data on the pipe by calling the Win32 WriteFile and ReadFile API functions that we discussed earlier in the book. There's no difference to the client between working with a file versus working with a pipe. In fact, a program can be made to work with a named pipe—that is, to become a named pipe client—without the app itself even being aware of it, as you'll see in just a moment when we get to the exercises.

CreateNamedPipe allows the application to specify the mode in which to open the pipe (in-bound, out-bound, or full-duplex), the pipe mode (byte or message), the default sizes for I/O buffers, the security attributes to apply to the pipe, and a host of other parameters. Named pipes' support of a message mode is noteworthy. Most network APIs support byte mode exclusively. This means that receiving a single message might require multiple calls to the receive function in order to build up the complete message. You can use named pipes' message mode to eliminate this—each send will require exactly one receive.

Another noteworthy characteristic of named pipes is that a server can impersonate the security credentials of a client. It does this by calling the ImpersonateNamedPipeClient function. SQL Server uses this facility when making linked server connections and accessing other types of resources where it wants a named pipe client's credentials to be used to authenticate access.

Named pipes uses the Windows' redirector file system driver to communicate across the network. This means that it relies indirectly on the Common Internet File System protocol and also means that it can be layered on top of any protocol that CIFS supports, including IPX, TCP/IP, and NetBEUI. A system that has at least one of these protocols installed can support named pipe applications.

Exercise

In the following exercise, we'll take the fstring example originally introduced in Chapter 5 and adapt it to accept a named pipe as either input or output or both. You'll recall that fstring accepted a file mask as input and wrote its output to the console. Here we'll take the fstring_io_comp_out sample from Chapter 5 and retrofit it to work with named pipes. It will still work with file masks and the console as before but will also be able to accept input or output from a named pipe.

Exercise 6.1   A Find String Utility That Uses Named Pipes

1. Load the fstring_pipe sample project from the CH06\fstring_pipe sub-folder on the book's CD into the Visual Studio development environment.
2. Only the main source code module, fstring_pipe.cpp, differs significantly from the fstring_io_comp_out example, so we'll go through only that module in this exercise. Listing 6.1 shows the code.

Listing 6.1 fstring_pipe.cpp, the Main Source Code Module for the fstring_pipe Utility

```
// fstring_pipe.cpp : Multithreaded file
// search that can open pipes for input and
// output
//

#include "stdafx.h"
#include "windows.h"
#include "stdlib.h"
#include "process.h"
#include "bufsrch.h"
#include "iobuf.h"

#define IO_STREAMS_PER_PROCESSOR 2
```

```
//Entry-point routine for the worker threads
unsigned __stdcall StartSearch(LPVOID lpParameter)
{

  //Cast the parameter supplied to _beginthreadex
  //as a CBufSearch * and call its Search method

  return ((CBufSearch*)lpParameter)->Search();

}


//Search a specified file for a given search string
//using nonbuffered, asynchronous I/O
DWORD SearchFile(DWORD dwClusterSize,
                 DWORD dwNumStreams,
                 char *szPath,
                 char *szFileName,
                 HANDLE hOutputFile,
                 char *szSearchStr,
                 HANDLE hInputFile=INVALID_HANDLE_VALUE
                 )
{
  char szFullPathName[MAX_PATH+1];
  DWORD dwNumThreads;
  HANDLE hPrivHeap;
  HANDLE *hThreads;
  bool bPipe;

  char szMsg[1024];
  DWORD dwOutput;

  strcpy(szFullPathName,szPath);
  strcat(szFullPathName,szFileName);

  DWORD dwFileSizeHigh;
  DWORD dwFileSizeLow;
  DWORD dwlFileSize;

  bPipe=(INVALID_HANDLE_VALUE!=hInputFile);

  if (!bPipe) {
```

```
    //Open the file for both nonbuffered and
    //overlapped (asynchronous) I/O
    hInputFile=CreateFile(szFullPathName,
                          GENERIC_READ,FILE_SHARE_READ,
                          NULL,
                          OPEN_EXISTING,
                          FILE_ATTRIBUTE_NORMAL
                          | FILE_FLAG_OVERLAPPED
                          | FILE_FLAG_NO_BUFFERING
                          ,NULL);

  if (INVALID_HANDLE_VALUE==hInputFile) {
    printf("Error opening file.  Last error=%d\n",
      GetLastError());
    return -1;
  }

}

sprintf(szMsg,"Searching for %s in %s\n\n",szSearchStr,
        szFileName);

WriteFile(hOutputFile,szMsg,strlen(szMsg),&dwOutput,NULL);

DWORD dwRetries=0;

do {

  dwFileSizeLow=GetFileSize(hInputFile,&dwFileSizeHigh);

  dwlFileSize=(dwFileSizeHigh*MAXDWORD)+
        dwFileSizeLow;

} while ((bPipe) &&
            (0==dwlFileSize) &&
            (++dwRetries<12) &&
            (printf("Waiting on data from pipe client\n")) &&
            (!SleepEx(5000,false))
            );

if (0==dwlFileSize) return -1;

DWORD dwNumClusts=dwlFileSize / dwClusterSize;
```

```
    if (dwNumClusts<1) dwNumClusts=1;

    //If file is less than 4GB and we have more requested
    //streams (IO threads) than clusters, set the # of
    //threads = to the # of clusters
    if ((dwlFileSize<0xFFFFFFFF) && (dwNumStreams>dwNumClusts))
      dwNumThreads=dwNumClusts;
    else
      dwNumThreads=dwNumStreams;

#if(_DEBUG)
    sprintf(szMsg,"Using %d threads\n\n",dwNumThreads);
    WriteFile(hOutputFile,szMsg,strlen(szMsg),&dwOutput,NULL);
#endif

    //Create a private heap so that we can free all
    //allocations at once
    hPrivHeap=HeapCreate(0,0,0);


    //Create the thread array
    hThreads=(HANDLE *)HeapAlloc(hPrivHeap,
                                  HEAP_ZERO_MEMORY,
                                  dwNumThreads*sizeof(HANDLE));
    if (NULL==hThreads) {
      printf("Error allocating worker thread array.  Aborting.\n");
      return -1;
    }

    //Create the I/O completion port
    HANDLE hPort=CreateIoCompletionPort(hInputFile,NULL,0,0);
    if (INVALID_HANDLE_VALUE==hPort) {
      printf("Error creating IO completion port.  Last error=%d\n",
        GetLastError());
      return -1;
    }

    //Create the worker threads and the
    //CBufSearch and CIoBuf objects
    CBufSearch *pbFirst=NULL;
    CIoBuf *pIoFirst=NULL;
    unsigned uThreadId;
```

```
for (DWORD i=0; i<dwNumThreads; i++) {

  pIoFirst=new CIoBuf(pIoFirst,hPort,dwClusterSize+1);

  pbFirst=new CBufSearch(pbFirst,
                         szFileName,
                         szSearchStr,
                         hOutputFile);

  hThreads[i]=
  (HANDLE)_beginthreadex(NULL,
                         0,
                         &StartSearch,
                         pbFirst,
                         CREATE_SUSPENDED,
                         &uThreadId);

  if (!hThreads[i]) {
    printf("Error creating thread.  Aborting.\n");
    return -1;
  }
}


//Set the CBufSearch objects'
//pointer to the head of the
//CIoBuf list
pbFirst->s_pIoFirst=pIoFirst;

//Set the CIoBuf objects'
//pointer to the head of the
//CIoBuf list
pIoFirst->s_pIoFirst=pIoFirst;

//Set statics so that multiple
//file searches work
pIoFirst->s_bTerminated=false;
pIoFirst->s_bOverlapped=true;

//Once CBufSearch's static member is set,
//start the worker threads
for (i=0; i<dwNumThreads; i++)
  ResumeThread(hThreads[i]);
```

```
//Main loop -- loop through the file, reading it in
//dwClusterSize chunks
DWORDLONG dwlFilePos=0;
bool bEof=false;
do {
  for (CBufSearch *pbCurrent=pbFirst;
    NULL!=pbCurrent;
    pbCurrent=pbCurrent->m_pbNext) {

    CIoBuf *pIoBuf=
      pIoFirst->SpinToFindBuf(BUF_STATE_INACTIVE,
                              BUF_STATE_READING);

    //Set the starting offset for the next read
    pIoBuf->m_OverlappedIO.OffsetHigh=
      (DWORD)(dwlFilePos / MAXDWORD);
    pIoBuf->m_OverlappedIO.Offset=
      (DWORD)(dwlFilePos % MAXDWORD);

    //Zero-fill the read buffer so that we don't
    //get search hits at the end of a partially
    //filled buffer (from previous contents)
    ZeroMemory(pIoBuf->m_szBuf,dwClusterSize+1);

    //Read a buffer full of data from the file
    //using asynchronous I/O if possible
    if (!ReadFile(hInputFile,pIoBuf->m_szBuf,
                  dwClusterSize,
                  &pIoBuf->m_dwBytesRead,
                  &pIoBuf->m_OverlappedIO)) {

      DWORD dwLastErr=GetLastError();
      if (ERROR_IO_PENDING!=dwLastErr)   {

        //Terminate the thread's main loop
        //on any error except ERROR_IO_PENDING
        //including EOF
        InterlockedExchange(
            (LPLONG)&pIoBuf->s_bTerminated,
            (long)true);

        //Abort if the error isn't an EOF
        if ((ERROR_HANDLE_EOF!=dwLastErr) &&
            (ERROR_BROKEN_PIPE!=dwLastErr)) {
```

```
        printf(
          "Error reading file.  Last error=%d\n",
          dwLastErr);
            return -1;
      }
      else
          bEof=true;
      break;
    }
    else {
      //We have an asynchronous operation
      InterlockedExchange(
          (LPLONG)&pIoBuf->s_bOverlapped,
          (long)true);
    }
  }
  else {
    //ReadFile returned true; the operation
    //is synchronous
    InterlockedExchange(
        (LPLONG)&pIoBuf->s_bOverlapped,
        (long)false);
    pIoBuf->SetState(BUF_STATE_READY);

  }

  dwlFilePos+=dwClusterSize;
}

} while ((((!pIoFirst->s_bOverlapped) && (!bEof)) ||
  ((pIoFirst->s_bOverlapped) &&
  (dwlFilePos<dwlFileSize) &&
  (!pIoFirst->s_bTerminated)));


//Signal that we're done reading the file
InterlockedExchange((LPLONG)&pIoFirst->s_bTerminated,
      (long)true);

//Wait on all the worker threads to finish
WaitForMultipleObjects(dwNumThreads,hThreads,
                          true,
                          INFINITE);
```

```
    //Get total tally and destroy search objects
    DWORD dwFindCount=0;
    CBufSearch *pbNext;
    for (; NULL!=pbFirst; pbFirst=pbNext) {
      dwFindCount+=pbFirst->m_dwFindCount;
      pbNext=pbFirst->m_pbNext;
      delete pbFirst;
    }

    //Delete the buf objects
    CIoBuf *pIoNext;
    for (; NULL!=pIoFirst; pIoFirst=pIoNext) {
      pIoNext=pIoFirst->m_pIoBufNext;
      delete pIoFirst;
    }

    //Close the I/O completion port
    CloseHandle(hPort);

    //Close the thread handles
    for (i=0; i<dwNumThreads; i++) {
      CloseHandle(hThreads[i]);
    }

    if (!bPipe)
      CloseHandle(hInputFile);


    //Free all of our previous heap allocations
    //by destroying the private heap we created
    HeapDestroy(hPrivHeap);

    sprintf(szMsg,"\nTotal hits for %s in %s:\t%d\n",
          szSearchStr,szFileName,dwFindCount);

    WriteFile(hOutputFile,szMsg,strlen(szMsg),&dwOutput,NULL);

    //Return the find count for the specified file
    return dwFindCount;
}

HANDLE OpenOutputFile(char *szOutput)
{
  HANDLE hOutputFile;
```

```
    if (strcmp(szOutput,"CONOUT$")) {
      do {
        hOutputFile=
          CreateFile(szOutput,
                     GENERIC_WRITE,
                     FILE_SHARE_READ,
                     NULL,
                     CREATE_ALWAYS,
                     FILE_ATTRIBUTE_NORMAL,
                     NULL);

        if (INVALID_HANDLE_VALUE==hOutputFile) {
          printf(
            "Waiting on output file/pipe.  Last error=%d\n",
            GetLastError());
        }
      } while ((INVALID_HANDLE_VALUE==hOutputFile) &&
                  (!SleepEx(5000,false)));

    }
    else
      hOutputFile=
        GetStdHandle(STD_OUTPUT_HANDLE);

  return hOutputFile;
}

//Search the files matching a given mask for a
//specified string
bool SearchFiles(char *szFileMask, char *szSearchStr,
    char *szOutput, DWORD dwPeriod=0)
{

  char szPath[MAX_PATH+1];
  char szMsg[1024];
  DWORD dwOutput;
  HANDLE hOutputFile;

  //Extract the file path from the specified mask
  char *p=strrchr(szFileMask,'\\');
  if (p) {
    strncpy(szPath,szFileMask,(p-szFileMask)+1);
    szPath[(p-szFileMask)+1]='\0';
  }
```

```
  else
    //If no path was specified, use the current
    //folder
    GetCurrentDirectory(MAX_PATH,szPath);

  //Add a trailing backslash as necessary
  if ('\\'!=szPath[strlen(szPath)-1])
    strcat(szPath,"\\");

  printf("Searching for %s in %s\n\n",szSearchStr,
    szFileMask);

  //Get the number of processors
  //for the current system.
  //This will be used to compute
  //the number of I/O streams
  //to use to search each file
  SYSTEM_INFO si;
  GetSystemInfo(&si);

  //Get the cluster size from the drive.
  //This will always be a multiple of the
  //sector size, so it is a good choice for
  //use with nonbuffered I/O
  DWORD dwSectorsPerCluster;
  DWORD dwBytesPerSector;
  DWORD dwNumberOfFreeClusters;
  DWORD dwTotalNumberOfClusters;
  GetDiskFreeSpace(NULL,&dwSectorsPerCluster,
                        &dwBytesPerSector,
                        &dwNumberOfFreeClusters,
                        &dwTotalNumberOfClusters);

  DWORD dwClusterSize=(dwSectorsPerCluster * dwBytesPerSector);

  DWORD dwFindCount=0;

  HANDLE hInputPipe=INVALID_HANDLE_VALUE;

  strupr(szFileMask);

  char *pipestr=strstr(szFileMask,"\\PIPE\\");
  if (pipestr) {
```

```
while (1) {

  hOutputFile=OpenOutputFile(szOutput);

  printf("Opening pipe %s\n",szFileMask);

  hInputPipe=CreateNamedPipe(szFileMask,
                              PIPE_ACCESS_INBOUND
                              ,PIPE_TYPE_BYTE,
                              PIPE_UNLIMITED_INSTANCES,
                              si.dwPageSize,
                              si.dwPageSize,
                              INFINITE,
                              NULL);

  if (INVALID_HANDLE_VALUE==hInputPipe) {
  sprintf(szMsg,
    "Error creating named pipe.  Last error=%d\n",
    GetLastError());

    WriteFile(hOutputFile,
        szMsg,
        strlen(szMsg),
        &dwOutput,
        NULL);
        return false;
  }

  printf(
  "Waiting on client to connect to pipe %s\n",
      szFileMask);
  ConnectNamedPipe(hInputPipe
      ,NULL
      );

  dwFindCount+=SearchFile(dwClusterSize,
                      si.dwNumberOfProcessors*
                      IO_STREAMS_PER_PROCESSOR,
                      szFileMask,
                      "",
                      hOutputFile,
                      szSearchStr,
                      hInputPipe
                      );
```

```
    DisconnectNamedPipe(hInputPipe);

    CloseHandle(hInputPipe);

    if (GetStdHandle(STD_OUTPUT_HANDLE)!=hOutputFile)
      CloseHandle(hOutputFile);

  };
}
else {

  do {

    DWORD dwpFindCount=0;  //Count for period

    //Loop through all the files matching the mask
    //and search each one for the string
    WIN32_FIND_DATA fdFiles;
      HANDLE hFind=FindFirstFile(szFileMask,&fdFiles);
    if (INVALID_HANDLE_VALUE == hFind) {
      printf("No files match the specified mask\n");
      return false;
    }

    do {
      hOutputFile=OpenOutputFile(szOutput);
      dwpFindCount+=SearchFile(dwClusterSize,
                        si.dwNumberOfProcessors*
                        IO_STREAMS_PER_PROCESSOR,
                        szPath,
                        fdFiles.cFileName,
                        hOutputFile,
                        szSearchStr,
                        hInputPipe
                        );

      dwFindCount+=dwpFindCount;

      if (GetStdHandle(STD_OUTPUT_HANDLE)!=
                  hOutputFile)
        CloseHandle(hOutputFile);

    } while (FindNextFile(hFind,&fdFiles));
```

```
        FindClose(hFind);

        if (dwPeriod)
          printf(
            "\nTotal hits for %s in %s:\t%d for this
                polling period\n",
            szSearchStr,
            szFileMask,
            dwpFindCount);

        printf("\nTotal hits for %s in %s:\t%d\n",
          szSearchStr,szFileMask,dwFindCount);

      } while ((dwPeriod) && (!SleepEx(dwPeriod,false)));
    }

    return true;
  }

int main(int argc, char* argv[])
{
  if (argc<3) {
    printf("Usage is: fstring_pipe filemask|pipe searchstring
        outputfilename|pipe polling_interval_secs \n");
    return 1;
  }

  try
  {

    //Get the optional output path
    //default to the console
    char szOutpath[MAX_PATH+1];
    if (argc>=4)
      strncpy(szOutpath,argv[3],MAX_PATH);
    else
      strcpy(szOutpath,"CONOUT$");

    //Get the optional poll interval
    DWORD dwPeriod=0;
    if (argc>=5)
      dwPeriod=atol(argv[4])*1000;

    return (!SearchFiles(argv[1], argv[2],
              szOutpath,dwPeriod));
  }
```

```
catch (...)
{
  printf("Error reading file.  Last error=%d\n",
    GetLastError());
  return 1;
}
}
```

3. Let's start with the CreateNamedPipe function in the SearchFiles routine. It looks like this:

```
hInputPipe=CreateNamedPipe(szFileMask,
                           PIPE_ACCESS_INBOUND
                           ,PIPE_TYPE_BYTE,
                           PIPE_UNLIMITED_INSTANCES,
                           si.dwPageSize,
                           si.dwPageSize,
                           INFINITE,
                           NULL);
```

We create the pipe as an inbound pipe (that is, it will receive data from clients but not send it). We set up a byte (rather than a message) pipe and specify that an unlimited number of instances of this pipe can be created. We set the default send and receive buffer sizes to match the system page size, and we set the pipe's default wait time to INFINITE so that any client that calls WaitNamedPipe will wait indefinitely until the pipe is available.

4. We get into the code path that calls CreateNamedPipe by virtue of finding the string "\pipe\" in the file mask specified on the command line. If we detect that a pipe name has been specified as input, we skip trying to iterate through files matching the mask and go straight to creating the pipe and waiting on a client to connect to it.

5. The next code to take a look at is the call to ConnectNamedPipe. It's just below the call to CreateNamedPipe and looks like this:

```
ConnectNamedPipe(hInputPipe
    ,NULL
    );
```

We received hInputPipe back from our call to CreateNamedPipe. We pass in NULL for the OVERLAPPED structure pointer because this parameter is optional if the FILE_FLAG_OVERLAPPED switch was not specified when the pipe was created. When a pipe is created using the

FILE_FLAG_OVERLAPPED switch, ConnectNamedPipe's OVERLAPPED pointer parameter cannot be NULL.

6. ConnectNamedPipe doesn't return until a client connects. Once it does, the SearchFile routine is called and the search processes as though it were reading a file.

7. Note the new parameter for SearchFile, hInputFile. This allows us to open the file SearchFile will scan and send it into the routine rather than allowing SearchFile to open the file itself. If we pass in a valid file handle, SearchFile doesn't attempt to open or close it—it merely carries out the search and returns. Other than that, SearchFile works as it did in all the other fstring samples: It processes the data returned by the pipe as though it were reading a file. It attempts to read the pipe asynchronously, but if it can't, it falls back to synchronous processing.

8. As I said, fstring_pipe also supports having its output written directly to a pipe. Technically, you could simply use command line redirection in the command shell to send the console output from fstring_pipe or any other command line utility to a specified pipe. However, I wanted to show you how to do this using Win32 API calls, so I've coded fstring_pipe to take a new optional command line parameter specifying the output destination. If you omit this parameter (or specify the CONOUT$ console output file name), the output will be written to the console as it has been in the other fstring examples. If you specify a file name, it will be overwritten with fstring_pipe's output. And if you specify a pipe, fstring_pipe will write its output to the pipe instead of to the console or to a file. This means, of course, that one instance of fstring_pipe could serve as the named pipe client for another instance. To do that, you'd start two instances with command lines something like the following:

```
REM This is the server
start fstring \\.\pipe\fstring ABCDEF

  REM This is the client
fstring INPUT*.TXT ABCDEF \\.\pipe\fstring
```

This also means that you could daisy-chain several instances of fstring_pipe together to run text through a series of filters before outputting it to the console. If you want to give your network administrator a fun-filled day, set up 20 or 30 of these running simultaneously to pass a multigigabyte text file between them and scan it for string matches.

So, that's fstring_pipe. It opens a new pipe with CreateNamedPipe and reads and writes named pipes using the Win32 basic file I/O routines, ReadFile and WriteFile.

Windows Sockets

Windows Sockets, or Winsock as it's commonly known, is Windows' implementation of BSD Sockets. As I mentioned earlier, BSD Sockets is an API that became the standard for Internet connectivity on UNIX systems in the 1980s. By providing API-level compatibility with Sockets, Windows makes porting UNIX network apps relatively easy. In addition to supporting functionality already present in BSD Sockets, Winsock also includes some Microsoft-specific enhancements. We'll talk about a few of these in just a moment.

Like BSD Sockets, Winsock supports both reliable (connection-oriented) communication and unreliable (connectionless) communication. These are known as stream and datagram connections, respectively. Winsock also supports scatter-gather and asynchronous I/O, protocol extensibility (so that it can be used with protocols other than the Microsoft-required protocols), integrated namespaces (allowing a server to publish its name in a directory service and a client to find it there), quality of service (QoS) conventions (when a network on which Winsock is running supports QoS, applications can negotiate bandwidth and latency requirements via QoS conventions and receive preferential treatment from the network), and multipoint messages (allowing a message to be transmitted to multiple receivers simultaneously).

Winsock is implemented in Ws2_32.dll. An easy way to tell that an application is using the Winsock API is to check whether Ws2_32.dll is mapped into its process space. (You could also check the executable's import table, but this might not include Ws2_32.dll if it is being loaded via LoadLibrary or by another DLL.) For example, you can verify that a SQL Server installation that is listening over TCP/IP uses the Winsock library by running the TList utility against the SQL Server process. If the server is listening for a TCP/IP socket connection, you should see Ws2_32.dll in the list of loaded modules.

Once a Windows-specific initialization function, WSAStartup, is called, a Winsock application can call BSD Sockets–compliant API functions to create and interact with sockets. There are also often Windows-specific API functions that perform the same basic function as their BSD counterparts but offer additional options or enhanced functionality (these are usually prefixed with *WSA*). For example, the first step a socket server application usually performs is to create a socket and begin listening on it so that clients can connect. The socket represents a communications end point in a socket conversation. An app can create a socket by calling the socket function or by calling WSASocket. Regardless of which way it created the socket, the app then listens for client connections on the socket by calling the listen function. The socket and listen functions are both ports of BSD Socket functions. WSASocket, on the other hand, is a Microsoft-specific extension.

Before it can be used to listen for client connections, a socket must be bound to an address on the host machine. Keep in mind that Winsock is an API, not a network protocol. It must make use of a network protocol in order to communicate with other machines on the network. As an API, it can bind to any protocol over which Windows supports layering it, including TCP/IP, NetBEUI, and IPX.

Binding is the glue that holds the network stack together. There are different types of binding within the typical network stack. APIs are usually bound to protocols in some way, while protocols are bound to network interface cards. Usually, when we're talking about network binding, we're talking about the latter, but we'll also discuss it in terms of binding APIs such as Winsock to specific network protocols.

Connection-Oriented Winsock Applications

Once it has been bound to an address, a connection-oriented (stream) Winsock app begins listening for client connections by calling the listen function. In the listen call, the app indicates how many concurrent connections it will allow. It then calls accept to block until a client connects. The accept function returns a new socket object to the calling app. This socket represents the server's end of the conversation. By sending and receiving data over this socket (e.g., using functions such as send and recv), the server can transmit data to and from the client.

Note that a server can also call the Microsoft-specific WSAAccept, which supports conditional acceptance of a client connection request, as well as AcceptEx, which provides some performance enhancements over accept, as we'll discuss below. Regardless of the method of accepting a connection, once a connection has been made, the server can then begin interacting with the client by using the returned socket in function calls such as send and recv.

A connection-oriented client establishes a connection to the server by calling the Socket connect function and specifying a network address. Once it has connected, the client can begin transmitting and receiving data by calling the send and recv functions.

Exercise

Let's take a look at a simple socket app to see how all this works. The following exercise presents a basic socket server app and a basic client app that you can work through to better understand how applications make use of Windows Sockets to communicate across a network.

Exercise 6.2 A Basic Socket Server and Client

1. Load the socket_server Visual C++ workspace from the CH06\socket_server subfolder on the CD into the Visual Studio development environment and run it.
2. As you can see from the display, it begins by binding the socket and listening for a client connection. Let's have a closer look at the code (Listing 6.2).

Listing 6.2 A Simple Socket Server

```
// socket_serv.cpp : A basic Winsock server app
//

#include "windows.h"
#include "stdafx.h"
#include "winsock2.h"

#define BUFF_SIZE 0x1000

int main(int argc, char* argv[])
{

  DWORD dwError;
  WORD wVersionRequested;
  WSADATA wsaData;

  char szBuf[BUFF_SIZE+1];

  //Initialize WSA and make sure
  //we have the right version
  wVersionRequested=MAKEWORD(2,0);

  dwError=WSAStartup(wVersionRequested,&wsaData);
  if (dwError!= 0 ) {
```

```
      printf("Error starting Winsock: %d\n",dwError);
      return 1;
}

if (LOBYTE(wsaData.wVersion) != 2 ||
   HIBYTE(wsaData.wVersion) != 0 ) {
   WSACleanup( );
   printf("Cannot locate Winsock 2.0 or later\n");
   return 1;
}

//Get a socket for the server
SOCKET hServerSocket=
   WSASocket(AF_INET,
             SOCK_STREAM,
             0,
             NULL,
             0,
             0);
SOCKET hClientSocket;


sockaddr_in  soServerAddress;
ZeroMemory(&soServerAddress,sizeof(soServerAddress));

soServerAddress.sin_family=AF_INET;
soServerAddress.sin_addr.s_addr=htonl(INADDR_ANY);
soServerAddress.sin_port=htons(1234);

printf("Binding socket.\n");

//Bind to the specified address/port
bind(hServerSocket,
   (sockaddr *)&soServerAddress,
   sizeof(soServerAddress));

printf("Listening...\n");

//Allow only one connection at a time
listen(hServerSocket, 1);

sockaddr_in  soClientAddress;
int iAddrSize=sizeof(soClientAddress);
ZeroMemory(&soClientAddress, sizeof(soClientAddress));
```

```
//Wait on a client connection
hClientSocket = accept(hServerSocket,
                       (sockaddr*)(&soClientAddress),
                       &iAddrSize);

printf("Client connected\n");


HANDLE hStdOut=GetStdHandle(STD_OUTPUT_HANDLE);

//Poll for strings and
//write them to the console
dwError=0;
do {
  int iBytesRead=recv(hClientSocket,szBuf,BUFF_SIZE,0);
  if (SOCKET_ERROR!=iBytesRead) {
    if (iBytesRead) {

      //Make sure buff is null-terminated
      szBuf[iBytesRead]='\0';

      //Display bytes read count in red
      CONSOLE_SCREEN_BUFFER_INFO cbi;
      GetConsoleScreenBufferInfo(hStdOut,&cbi);
      WORD wAttribs=cbi.wAttributes;
      SetConsoleTextAttribute(hStdOut,
          FOREGROUND_RED|
          FOREGROUND_INTENSITY);
      printf(
        "Received %d bytes.  Contents=\n",iBytesRead);

      //Restore normal attributes for actual text
      SetConsoleTextAttribute(hStdOut,wAttribs);
      printf("%s\n",szBuf);
    }
  }
  else {
    dwError=WSAGetLastError();
    printf(
      "Error receiving data from socket.  Last error=%d\n",
      dwError);
  }
} while (!dwError);
```

```
//Close the sockets
closesocket(hClientSocket);
closesocket(hServerSocket);

//Uninitialize WSA
WSACleanup();
return 0;
}
```

3. We begin by calling the required WSAStartup initialization function and checking to make sure we have a recent version of Winsock installed. There's nothing about this code that depends on Winsock 2.0 being installed, but it's still a good idea to check to be sure that you aren't working with an ancient version of the library. Windows 2000 ships with Winsock 2.2, and the most recent version of Winsock is available for download from the Microsoft Web site for all supported Windows platforms.

4. After we check the Winsock version, we create a socket. In this case, we call the WSASocket function and pass it the AF_INET family, indicating that we intend to bind to the TCP/IP protocol.

5. Let's next have a look at the assignments to the soServerAddress structure. This is where we set up the address to which we'll be binding. We begin by setting the address family to AF_INET, indicating that we are specifying a TCP/IP address. We then specify INADDR_ANY as the actual address. This means that we'll bind to any available IP address on the machine. If the machine is multihomed (that is, if TCP/IP is bound to multiple network cards in the machine), this could be one of several addresses. INADDR_ANY maps to an integer value of 0 in Winsock2.h, but this might change someday, so you should always use INADDR_ANY rather than 0 in your programs. Note the use of the htonl function. htonl converts an unsigned long (in this case, containing an IP address) from host byte order to TCP/IP networking byte order, which is big-endian.

6. We finish assigning soServerAddress by specifying the port we'll use, which is 1234. Again, we have to switch the byte order, so we call htons, which converts an unsigned short to TCP/IP network byte order.

7. Once the address to which we want to bind is set up, we call the bind function to actually bind to it. Once the bind has completed, we call listen in order to listen for clients to connect. The listen function doesn't block but gets the socket ready to receive a client connection. Note that we pass 1 for the second parameter to the listen function. This indicates that we will allow just one client at a time to connect to the socket.

8. Once we've begun listening, we call accept to wait on a connection. The accept function takes two output parameters into which it will put information about the address of a client that connects. It also returns a new socket that we will then use to transfer data to and from the client.

9. We finish up by entering a loop in which we call the recv function to read data from the client. The recv function returns a count of the bytes read from the client. As long as this count is nonzero, we continue to read strings from the client and write them to the console.

So, that's the server app. Now let's have a look at the client app.

1. While the server app is still running, start another instance of the Visual C++ development environment and load the socket_client project into it from the CH06\socket_client subfolder on the CD.

2. Let's have a look at the code (Listing 6.3) before we run it. You'll notice that much of it is very similar to the socket_server app.

Listing 6.3 A Simple Socket Client

```cpp
// socket_client.cpp : A basic Winsock client app
//

#include "windows.h"
#include "stdafx.h"
#include "winsock2.h"
#include "stdlib.h"

#define BUFF_SIZE 0x1000

// Client, just simple connect to server, and send a message
int main(int argc, char* argv[]) {


  if (argc<2) {
    printf(
      "Usage: socket_client hostname:port [L] (for looping) \n");
      return -1;
  }

  WORD wVersionRequested;
  WSADATA wsaData;
  int iErr;
```

```
wVersionRequested = MAKEWORD(2,0);

iErr = WSAStartup(wVersionRequested,&wsaData);
if (iErr != 0) {
  return -1;
}

if (LOBYTE(wsaData.wVersion) != 2 ||
  HIBYTE(wsaData.wVersion) != 0 ) {
    WSACleanup( );
    return -1;
}

char szHostName[MAX_PATH+1];
char *p=strchr(argv[1],':');
if (!p) {
  printf("Invalid or missing port specification\n");
  return -1;
}
strncpy(szHostName,argv[1],p-argv[1]);
szHostName[p-argv[1]]='\0';

p++;
int iPort=atoi(p);

HOSTENT *heServer=gethostbyname(szHostName);

if (!heServer) {
  printf("Unknown host %s\n",szHostName);
  return -1;
}

bool bLoop=((argc>2) && (!stricmp(argv[2],"L")));

SOCKET soServer=WSASocket(AF_INET,
                          SOCK_STREAM,
                          0,
                          NULL,
                          0,
                          0
                          ) ;

char szBuffer[BUFF_SIZE];
sockaddr_in saServerAddress;
```

```
ZeroMemory(&saServerAddress, sizeof(saServerAddress));

saServerAddress.sin_family = AF_INET;

memcpy(&(saServerAddress.sin_addr),
  heServer->h_addr_list[0],
  heServer->h_length);

saServerAddress.sin_port = htons(iPort);

printf("Connecting to the server ...\n");
if (connect(soServer,
              (sockaddr *)&saServerAddress,
              sizeof(saServerAddress))) {
  printf("Connection failed %d\n",WSAGetLastError());
}

DWORD dwLastErr=0;

do {
  sprintf(szBuffer,
    "Greetings from process %d\n",GetCurrentProcessId());
  printf ("Sending message ...\n");
    if (SOCKET_ERROR==
      send(soServer, (char*)(&szBuffer), BUFF_SIZE, 0))
    {
      dwLastErr=WSAGetLastError();
      printf("Send error. %d\n", dwLastErr);
    }
    else Sleep(5000);
} while ((bLoop) && (!dwLastErr));
closesocket(soServer);
WSACleanup();
return 0;
}
```

3. Once again, we begin by checking the Winsock version and creating a socket. We then break the hostname:port parameter that was passed into the app into its component pieces since the host name and target port are separate elements in the sockaddr_in structure we'll pass into the connect function. After we've done this, we take the host name and resolve its IP address through a call to gethostbyname. The gethostbyname function returns the network address of the specified host.

(You cannot pass an IP address into gethostbyname, by the way; you must pass an actual network name.) Since this address is already in the proper byte order, we simply call memcpy to move it into the sockaddr_in structure that we'll use to connect to the server.

4. Once we've assigned the target port, we then call the connect method to connect to the server. If connect completes successfully, it returns 0. It also returns two output parameters which provide address information for the server we've just connected to.

5. After we connect, we enter a loop in which we begin sending a string to the server every 5 seconds until an error occurs. When an error occurs (e.g., the server closes the socket or fails to respond), we fall through the loop and exit the program.

6. Let's try running the app now. Check the command line parameters in the Visual Studio IDE and be sure they're set to the following:

```
localhost:1234 L
```

The host name localhost should resolve to 127.0.0.1, the loop back address. Every TCP/IP address in the 127.n.n.n range loops back to the current machine. The number on the right side of the colon specifies the destination port. We specify 1234 here since that's what we specified in the server app. The L parameter tells the client app to loop continuously, sending the same message over and over. Once you've verified the parameters, run the client app.

7. Now switch back to the running server app. You should see output like the following in the server app console window:

```
Received 4096 bytes.  Contents=
Greetings from process 3512
```

8. These messages will continue to show up in the server until you stop the client. You can stop both the client and the server by pressing Ctrl+C in their respective console windows. Go ahead and stop them both now.

So, that's what a basic Winsock client and server look like. SQL Server's Net-Library code calls some of these very same API functions to transfer data between the client and server when you connect using the Super Socket Net-Library.

Connectionless Winsock Applications

Once it has bound to a network address, a connectionless server and a connectionless client behave similarly: Each sends and receives messages over the appropriate socket simply by specifying the remote address with each message. There is no accept or connect call—each party in the conversation simply includes the destination address in every datagram transmission using functions like sendto and recvfrom.

Sockets and the Win32 API

Because a socket is really just a file handle in disguise, Windows apps can use basic I/O functions such as WriteFile and ReadFile to send and receive data over sockets. Basically, you just pass the socket into the desired Win32 I/O function, casting it as a handle in the process.

Exercise

The best way to understand how socket handles can be interchanged with file handles is to explore some code that demonstrates how it works. The following exercise presents a socket server app that uses ReadFile in place of recv to read data from a socket client.

Exercise 6.3   A Winsock Server App That Uses Win32 I/O Functions to Interact with a Client

1. Close the socket_server workspace if it is still loaded and load the socket_server_rf project from the CH06\socket_server_rf subfolder on the CD.
2. The only part of the code that differs significantly from the socket_server app is the loop that receives data from the client. Let's have a look at it (Listing 6.4).

Listing 6.4 A Variation on socket_server That Uses Win32 I/O Functions

```
dwError=0;
do {
  DWORD dwBytesRead;
  if (!ReadFile((HANDLE)hClientSocket,
          szBuf,
          BUFF_SIZE,
          &dwBytesRead,
          NULL)) {
    dwError=GetLastError();
```

```
    if (ERROR_HANDLE_EOF==dwError)
      break;
    printf("Error reading socket %d\n",dwError);
  }
  else {
    if (dwBytesRead) {

      //Make sure buff is null-terminated
      szBuf[dwBytesRead]='\0';

      //Display bytes read count in red
      CONSOLE_SCREEN_BUFFER_INFO cbi;
      GetConsoleScreenBufferInfo(hStdOut,&cbi);
      WORD wAttribs=cbi.wAttributes;
      SetConsoleTextAttribute(hStdOut,
          FOREGROUND_RED|
          FOREGROUND_INTENSITY);
      printf(
          "Received %d bytes.  Contents=\n",
          dwBytesRead);

      //Restore normal attributes for actual text
      SetConsoleTextAttribute(hStdOut,wAttribs);
      printf("%s\n",szBuf);
    }
    else break;
  }
} while (!dwError);
```

3. Note the call to Win32's ReadFile function. We call it synchronously (note the NULL OVERLAPPED structure pointer), so it functions in a manner that's very similar to the recv function in the socket_server app we looked at above. Instead of relying on the return value of the function to provide the number of bytes received, we pass a DWORD into ReadFile, just as we would were we issuing a synchronous read against a file or named pipe.

4. We used a cast so that we could pass the socket into ReadFile. Even though both a socket and a handle are actually pointers, we still couldn't successfully pass a socket into a Win32 I/O function such as ReadFile if sockets weren't integrated into the Windows I/O system. Because of this integration, we can treat sockets in a more generic fashion and use them in many places where we might use a file. This

sample shows a simple example of this functionality; we'll look at a more complex one in just a moment.

5. Go ahead and run the app now. While it's running, restart the socket_client app. You'll see that the client app is able to transmit data over the socket to the new app just as it did to the original socket_server app. Once you've let both apps run for a few seconds, go ahead and stop both of them and close the Visual Studio instances into which they're loaded.

So, that's socket_server_rf. It uses a Win32 I/O function, ReadFile, to read a TCP/IP socket as though it were a file.

Winsock Extensions

Note that Winsock supports asynchronous as well as synchronous operations. Winsock supports connecting, reading, writing, and performing other operations using a socket asynchronously. Similarly to other asynchronous I/O operations, once an asynchronous socket operation completes, an application can receive a notification via a Windows message, a callback function, or an I/O completion packet.

Beyond functions that mirror those in BSD Sockets, Winsock also supports two that are completely absent from the BSD Sockets API. TransmitFile is used for sending a complete file to a client. Because it is integrated with the system file cache, the file can be sent directly from the cache without first being copied to a secondary buffer (this is known as a zero-copy file transfer because the file doesn't have to be copied to another buffer to be transmitted). Also, TransmitFile allows the caller to add data before or after the file in the transmission stream (e.g., to prepend a header), again helping to prevent having to first copy a file to a secondary buffer before transmitting it to a client.

In addition to performing the work of the standard accept function, AcceptEx returns the client's address and its first message, thereby saving the calling application the trouble of having to make multiple calls to get the same information. This can make a noticeable difference in performance, particularly when a client connects, sends a single message, and disconnects. Using AcceptEx rather than accept or WSAAccept in this situation can cut in half the API calls the server must make.

Sockets vs. Pipes

In this final section on Winsock, I'll present a sample app that allows you to compare and contrast working with named pipes and working with sockets in an application. There's not that much difference between them, and each API has its strengths and weaknesses.

Exercise

The following exercise takes the familiar fstring sample app we've worked with throughout the book and retrofits it to accept as input or output a socket, a named pipe, or a file. In the case of output, the file, of course, can be the system console (whose special system name is CONOUT$). By working through this exercise and comparing the code involved with setting up a pipe versus what's required to set up a socket, you'll begin to get a feel for how the two compare and in what situations you might choose one over the other.

Exercise 6.4   An fstring Variant That Works with Both Sockets and Pipes

1. Load the fstring_pipe_socket workspace from the CH06\fstring_pipe_socket subfolder on the CD into the Visual Studio development environment.
2. This is a variant of the fstring_pipe sample presented earlier in the chapter that, in addition to supporting I/O over named pipes, also supports the use of Windows Sockets. Only two routines, SearchFiles and OpenOutputFile, have significant changes from the earlier example, so we'll focus on them in this exercise. Let's begin with SearchFiles (Listing 6.5).

Listing 6.5 fstring_pipe_socket's SearchFiles Routine

```
//Search the files matching a given mask for a
//specified string
bool SearchFiles(char *szFileMask,
                 char *szSearchStr,
                 char *szOutput,
                 DWORD dwPeriod=0)
{

  char szPath[MAX_PATH+1];
  char szMsg[1024];
  DWORD dwOutput;
  HANDLE hOutputFile;
```

```
//Extract the file path from the specified mask
char *p=strrchr(szFileMask,'\\');
if (p) {
  strncpy(szPath,szFileMask,(p-szFileMask)+1);
  szPath[(p-szFileMask)+1]='\0';
}
else
  //If no path was specified, use the current
  //folder
  GetCurrentDirectory(MAX_PATH,szPath);

//Add a trailing backslash as necessary
if ('\\'!=szPath[strlen(szPath)-1])
  strcat(szPath,"\\");

printf("Searching for %s in %s\n\n",szSearchStr,
  szFileMask);

//Get the number of processors
//for the current system.
//This will be used to compute
//the number of I/O streams
//to use to search each file
SYSTEM_INFO si;
GetSystemInfo(&si);

//Get the cluster size from the drive.
//This will always be a multiple of the
//sector size, so it is a good choice for
//use with nonbuffered I/O
DWORD dwSectorsPerCluster;
DWORD dwBytesPerSector;
DWORD dwNumberOfFreeClusters;
DWORD dwTotalNumberOfClusters;
GetDiskFreeSpace(NULL,&dwSectorsPerCluster,
                      &dwBytesPerSector,
                      &dwNumberOfFreeClusters,
                      &dwTotalNumberOfClusters);

DWORD dwClusterSize=(dwSectorsPerCluster * dwBytesPerSector);

DWORD dwFindCount=0;

HANDLE hInputPipe=INVALID_HANDLE_VALUE;
```

```
DWORD dwInputType=INPUT_TYPE_FILE;

strupr(szFileMask);

char *pszPipe=strstr(szFileMask,"\\PIPE\\");
char *pszPort=PortString(szFileMask);
if (pszPipe) dwInputType=INPUT_TYPE_PIPE;
else {
  if (pszPort)
    dwInputType=INPUT_TYPE_SOCKET;
  }
switch (dwInputType) {
case INPUT_TYPE_PIPE :
  {
    while (1) {

        hOutputFile=OpenOutputFile(szOutput);

        printf("Opening pipe %s\n",szFileMask);

        hInputPipe=CreateNamedPipe(szFileMask,
                        PIPE_ACCESS_INBOUND
                        ,PIPE_TYPE_BYTE,
                        PIPE_UNLIMITED_INSTANCES,
                        si.dwPageSize,
                        si.dwPageSize,
                        INFINITE,
                        NULL);

        if (INVALID_HANDLE_VALUE==hInputPipe) {
        sprintf(szMsg,
            "Error creating named pipe.  Last error=%d\n",
            GetLastError());
          WriteFile(hOutputFile,
                    szMsg,
                    strlen(szMsg),
                    &dwOutput,
                    NULL);
          return false;
        }

        printf(
            "Waiting on client to connect to pipe %s\n",
                szFileMask);
```

```
        ConnectNamedPipe(hInputPipe
            ,NULL
            );

        dwFindCount+=SearchFile(dwClusterSize,
                    si.dwNumberOfProcessors*
                    IO_STREAMS_PER_PROCESSOR,
                    szFileMask,
                    "",
                    hOutputFile,
                    szSearchStr,
                    hInputPipe);

        DisconnectNamedPipe(hInputPipe);
        CloseHandle(hInputPipe);
        CloseOutputFile(szOutput,hOutputFile);
      };
      break;
  }
case INPUT_TYPE_SOCKET :
  {
    while (1) {
      if (!InitializeWSA()) {
        return false;
      }

      hOutputFile=OpenOutputFile(szOutput);

      printf("Opening socket for %s\n",szFileMask);
      //Get a socket for the server
      SOCKET hServerSocket=
        WSASocket(AF_INET,
                  SOCK_STREAM,
                  0,
                  NULL,
                  0,
                  0);
      SOCKET hClientSocket;


      sockaddr_in  soServerAddress;
      ZeroMemory(&soServerAddress,
        sizeof(soServerAddress));
```

```
u_short usPort=atoi(pszPort);
soServerAddress.sin_family=AF_INET;

soServerAddress.sin_addr.s_addr=
     htonl(INADDR_ANY);

soServerAddress.sin_port=htons(usPort);

//Bind to the specified address/port
bind(hServerSocket,
    (sockaddr *)&soServerAddress,
    sizeof(soServerAddress));

//Allow only one connection at a time
listen(hServerSocket, 1);

sockaddr_in  soClientAddress;
int iAddrSize=sizeof(soClientAddress);
ZeroMemory(&soClientAddress,
     sizeof(soClientAddress));

//Wait on a client connection
printf(
    "Waiting on client to connect to socket on
    %s\n",
    szFileMask);
hClientSocket = accept(hServerSocket,
    (sockaddr*)(&soClientAddress),
    &iAddrSize);

dwFindCount+=SearchFile(dwClusterSize,
                  si.dwNumberOfProcessors*
                    IO_STREAMS_PER_PROCESSOR,
                  szFileMask,
                  "",
                  hOutputFile,
                  szSearchStr,
                  (HANDLE)hClientSocket);

//Close the sockets
closesocket(hClientSocket);
closesocket(hServerSocket);

CloseOutputFile(szOutput, hOutputFile);
```

```
          //Uninitialize WSA
          WSACleanup();
       }
       break;

    }
    case INPUT_TYPE_FILE:
      {
        do {

          DWORD dwpFindCount=0;   //Count for period

          //Loop through all the files matching the mask
          //and search each one for the string
          WIN32_FIND_DATA fdFiles;
          HANDLE hFind=
                FindFirstFile(szFileMask,&fdFiles);

          if (INVALID_HANDLE_VALUE == hFind) {
            printf("No files match the specified mask\n");
            return false;
          }

          do {
            hOutputFile=OpenOutputFile(szOutput);
            dwpFindCount+=SearchFile(dwClusterSize,
                  si.dwNumberOfProcessors*
                  IO_STREAMS_PER_PROCESSOR,
                  szPath,
                  fdFiles.cFileName,
                  hOutputFile,
                  szSearchStr,
                  hInputPipe);

            dwFindCount+=dwpFindCount;

            CloseOutputFile(szOutput,hOutputFile);

          } while ((FindNextFile(hFind,&fdFiles)));

          FindClose(hFind);
```

```
        if (dwPeriod)
          printf(
            "\nTotal hits for %s in %s:\t%d for this
                polling period\n",
            szSearchStr,
            szFileMask,
            dwpFindCount);

        printf("\nTotal hits for %s in %s:\t%d\n",
          szSearchStr,szFileMask,dwFindCount);

    } while ((dwPeriod) &&
        (!SleepEx(dwPeriod,false)));
    break;
  }
}

return true;
}
```

3. The salient point to be gleaned here can be found in exploring the switch (dwInputType) statement. After determining what type of input we have—a pipe, a socket, or a file mask—we drop into this switch statement and execute different code for each input type. For a file mask, we iterate through the files matching the mask and call Search-File for each one. For a named pipe input, we create a pipe, wait on a client to connect, then pass the pipe into SearchFile, which then reads it as though it were an input file. For a socket, we verify the Winsock version, open a socket, call listen to begin listening for connections, then call accept to block until we get one. Once we have a connection, we pass the resulting socket handle into SearchFile, which, again, reads it as though it were an input file. The key concept to get here is that we are able to treat pipes and sockets virtually identically for two reasons: (1) they offer a similar API metaphor and (2) they're both integrated with the Windows I/O model and, hence, can be used interchangeably in Win32 I/O calls.

4. Now let's have a look at the OpenOutputFile function. It handles the prospect of three types of potential output: a pipe, a socket, or a file (or the console). Listing 6.6 shows the code.

Listing 6.6 fstring_pipe_socket's OpenOutputFile Routine

```
HANDLE OpenOutputFile(char *szOutput)
{
  HANDLE hOutputFile;
  if (stricmp(szOutput,"CONOUT$")) {

    //Socket
    char *pszPort=PortString(szOutput);
    if (pszPort) {
        if (!InitializeWSA()) {
        return INVALID_HANDLE_VALUE;
        }

        char szHostName[MAX_PATH+1];
        strncpy(szHostName,szOutput,pszPort-szOutput-1);
        szHostName[pszPort-szOutput-1]='\0';

      HOSTENT *heServer=gethostbyname(szHostName);

        if (!heServer) {
          printf("Unknown host %s\n",szHostName);
          return INVALID_HANDLE_VALUE;
        }
        hOutputFile=(HANDLE)WSASocket(AF_INET,
                                      SOCK_STREAM,
                                      0,
                                      NULL,
                                      0,
                                      0) ;


        sockaddr_in saOutput;
        ZeroMemory((char *)&saOutput, sizeof(saOutput));

        u_short usPort=atoi(pszPort);

        saOutput.sin_family = AF_INET;
        memcpy(&(saOutput.sin_addr),
          heServer->h_addr_list[0],
          heServer->h_length);
        saOutput.sin_port = htons(usPort);

        do {
```

```
              } while ((connect((SOCKET)hOutputFile,
                                (sockaddr *) &saOutput,
                                sizeof(saOutput))) &&
                 (printf(
                   "Waiting on output socket.  Last error=%d\n",
                   WSAGetLastError())) &&
                 (!SleepEx(5000,false)));

        }
        else {
          //File or pipe
          do {
            hOutputFile=
              CreateFile(szOutput,
                         GENERIC_WRITE,
                         FILE_SHARE_READ,
                         NULL,
                         CREATE_ALWAYS,
                         FILE_ATTRIBUTE_NORMAL,
                         NULL);

          } while ((INVALID_HANDLE_VALUE==hOutputFile) &&
               (printf(
                 "Waiting on output file/pipe.  Last error=%d\n",
                 GetLastError())) &&
               (!SleepEx(5000,false)));
        }

      }
      else
        hOutputFile=
          GetStdHandle(STD_OUTPUT_HANDLE);

      return hOutputFile;
    }
```

5. Because we are setting an output rather than an input file here, Open-OutputFile establishes itself as a client application if either a pipe or socket is specified. If a file is specified, it simply opens the file or returns a pointer to the console if CONOUT$ is the specified file name. In the case of a socket or pipe, we make the necessary calls to connect the server and return the socket or pipe handle for use as the output device for the rest of the app. SearchFile will use this handle to write its output. If it's connected to a named pipe or socket server, it will function as a simple client of that server, using plain WriteFile calls to send data.

6. Set the app's parameters to localhost:1234 ABCDEF and run it. This will cause the app to open a socket on port 1234 on the current machine and wait on a client connection.

7. Next, open a command prompt and start a second instance of fstring_pipe_socket with these parameters: INPUT*.TXT ABCDEF localhost:1234. This instance will route its output to the first instance. You should see a separate connection made to the server app for each file the client app finds that matches INPUT*.TXT. You'll see more string matches than you might expect because fstring's header and footer titles also include the string being searched for. Because this is routed to the first instance of fstring_pipe_socket as input, it will cause string match hits just as the contents of the INPUT*.TXT files will.

8. Experiment with different combinations of pipe and socket inputs and outputs. Also, try using redirection as input to an fstring_pipe_socket instance you've started as a pipe server, like this:

```
TYPE INPUT3.TXT >\\.\pipe\fstring
```

This should demonstrate that you don't need an actual client app to send input to a pipe server—simple redirection will do just fine.

9. Also try starting up the socket_client app and sending text from it to fstring_pipe_socket. Unless you modify socket_client app, you'll want to change fstring_pipe_socket's search string to match something in the "greetings" string that socket_client sends.

This concludes our discussion of Winsock. Now let's move on to Windows' RPC facility.

Remote Procedure Call

In the early 1980s, the Open Software Foundation (now known as The Open Group) developed the RPC network programming standard as part of the Distributed Computing Environment (DCE) distributed computing standard. Microsoft's implementation of RPC is compatible with this original specification.

RPC makes use of other network APIs (e.g., Named Pipes, Message Queuing, or Winsock) in order to provide a programming model that hides most of the details of communicating over a network from the developer. Given that RPC actually rides on top of other APIs, it can use any network transport that those APIs support—it's compatible with any transport on the system.

An RPC app is composed of a series of procedures; some are local, some reside on other machines. To the app, they're all local. Procedures that actually reside on other machines have stub procedures on the local machine that match their calling conventions and parameter lists exactly. The application developer simply calls these routines, not necessarily cognizant of where they physically reside. For basic apps, these stub routines are typically linked statically into the application. For more complex apps, they often reside in separate DLLs. With Distributed COM (DCOM), which uses RPC as its means of executing code on other machines, the stub routines are usually in separate DLLs.

Marshaling

When a stub routine is called, the parameters passed into it must be marshaled for transport across the network to the actual routine. You can think of marshaling as a traffic cop or escort that takes care of the work necessary to route data between different execution contexts. In the case of marshaling between machines, you're obviously routing data from one process to another, so one thing that marshaling must take care of is dereferencing any pointers that are passed into the stub routine, encapsulating the data they reference, and sending it over to the other machine. It has to do this because a pointer in one process isn't going to be useful to another process, particularly if the data it references isn't even there. I like to think of marshaling as the process of taking the data represented by the parameters passed into a routine by the hand and making sure it gets to its destination in a usable form.

When a stub is called, it invokes RPC runtime routines that carry out the work of communicating with the destination computer, negotiating a compatible set of protocols, and sending the request to the other machine. When the destination machine gets the request, it unmarshals the parameters (by placing the encapsulated data back into memory allocations that can then be referenced by the original pointers and fixing up those pointers so that they reference the correct locations) and calls the original procedure with the correct parameter values. All the while, the whole process is transparent to the client-side application code—it simply called a procedure. Once the call completes on the remote system, the whole process is reversed in order to return the results to the caller.

Asynchronous RPC

Windows supports asynchronous RPC as well as synchronous RPC. When an asynchronous RPC is made, the calling app continues to execute. When the call completes, Windows' RPC facility signals an event that was originally associated with the call. The caller can detect this through the traditional means of checking the signal state of a kernel object such as calling WaitForSingleObject.

The RPC Runtime

The RPC runtime resides in Rpcrt4.dll. You can use TList to verify that this DLL is loaded into the SQL Server process space. This DLL is always loaded, regardless of whether SQL Server is configured to listen on the multiprotocol Net-Library, which uses the RPC API. This is because SQL Server's executable directly imports this DLL by name. (You can check this out yourself by using the Depends or DumpBin tools that ship with Visual Studio.)

Recap

SQL Server supports a variety of network transports and protocols. It's important to have a basic understanding of how these technologies work and how applications typically make use of them. Understanding how to use them in your own applications will help you better understand how they are employed by SQL Server.

From an architectural point of view, SQL Server is just another application on the network. When it communicates over the network with a client, it does so using network APIs just as any other application would. When a client connects to SQL Server over the network, it does so via the network stack, just as it would were it communicating with some other type of server.

Knowledge Measure

1. True or false: The Winsock listen API function causes the caller to block until a client connects.
2. What Win32 API function does a named pipe server call to wait on a client connection?

3. Can a socket handle be used with basic Win32 I/O functions such as ReadFile?

4. True or false: Winsock runs exclusively over the TCP/IP protocol.

5. Describe the process of marshaling RPC parameters and why it is needed.

6. What is the top layer of the OSI reference model?

7. True or false: Each layer in the OSI model exists to provide services to the higher layers and to provide an abstract interface to the services provided by lower layers.

8. True or false: Windows' networking model matches the OSI model precisely.

9. What is the difference between byte mode and message mode on a named pipe?

10. What must the second portion of a named pipe's name consist of?

11. What's the shorthand representation for referencing the current machine in a named pipe's name?

12. True or false: Although Windows' named pipes facility can make use of other OS facilities such as network transports, it cannot make use of Windows' security facilities because it is a port of code from OS/2 LAN Manager.

13. True or false: The purpose of network software is to take a client request for a resource, execute the request on the remote machine containing the requested resource, and return the results to the client.

14. True or false: A network redirector acts as a type of remote file system.

15. What does the term *name resolution* refer to?

16. True or false: Windows' named pipes facility runs exclusively over the NetBEUI protocol.

17. What is the special file name assigned by Windows to the console output device?

18. Name two functions mentioned in this chapter for use with connectionless Winsock clients and servers.

19. What byte order must be used to pass in IP addresses and port numbers to Winsock?

20. What are the bottom four layers of the OSI reference model commonly referred to as?

21. What underlying mechanism does DCOM use to run code across a network?

22. In what system DLL is most of the Named Pipes API implemented?

23. On what legacy API from UNIX is Windows' Winsock API based?

24. How many layers exist in the OSI reference model?

25. True or false: One advantage of the Named Pipes API over Winsock is that Named Pipes can be used with asynchronous I/O, whereas Winsock supports only synchronous I/O.

26. Name the three network protocols over which Windows supports layering Winsock.

27. What is the bottom layer of the OSI reference model?

28. What DLL contains the implementation of the Winsock API?

29. What flag must an application supply when creating a named pipe in order for the pipe to participate in asynchronous operations?

30. What DLL contains the runtime for Windows' RPC facility?

CHAPTER 7

COM

Having the right don't make it right.

—Kenneth E. Routen

Given COM's ubiquity both inside and outside of SQL Server, no section on application fundamentals would be complete without some discussion of it. I don't have the time or space to give COM the treatment I'd like to in this book, so I suggest you consult books such as Dale Rogerson's *Inside COM* (Redmond, WA: Microsoft Press, 1997) and Don Box's *Essential COM* (Reading, MA: Addison-Wesley, 1998) to get the details of how COM works and how applications can make use of it. In this chapter, I will update the coverage of COM from my previous books and cover COM from a high-level standpoint. We'll also talk about how SQL Server exposes some of its functionality via COM and how it makes use of external COM components. See Chapter 15 on ODSOLE for more information on accessing COM objects from Transact-SQL.

Overview

If you've built many Windows applications, you probably have at least a passing familiarity with COM, OLE, and ActiveX. OLE originally stood for Object Linking and Embedding and represented the first generation of cross-application object access and manipulation in Windows. The idea was to have a document-centric view of the world where an object from one application could happily reside in and interact with another. OLE 1.0 used Dynamic Data Exchange (DDE) to facilitate communication between objects. DDE is a message-based interprocess communication mechanism based on the Windows' messaging architecture. DDE has a number of shortcomings (it's slow, inflexible, difficult to program, and so on), so the second version of OLE was moved off of it.

The second iteration of OLE was rewritten to depend entirely on COM. And even though COM is more efficient and faster than DDE, OLE is still a bit of a bear to deal with. Why? Because it was the first-ever implementation of COM. We've learned a lot since then. That said, regardless of its implementation, OLE provides functionality that's very powerful and very rich. It may be big, slow, and hard to code to, but that's not COM's fault—that has to do with how OLE itself was built.

ActiveX is also built on COM. The original and still primary focus of ActiveX is on Internet-enabled components. ActiveX is a set of technologies whose primary mission is to enable interactive content (hence the "Active" designation) on Web pages. Formerly known as OLE controls or OCX controls, ActiveX controls are components you can insert into a Web page or Windows application to make use of packaged functionality provided by a third party.

COM is the foundation on which OLE and ActiveX controls are built. Through COM, an object can expose its functionality to other components and applications. In addition to defining an object's life cycle and how the object exposes itself to the outside world, COM also defines how this exposure works across processes and networks.

COM is Microsoft's answer to the fundamental questions: How do I expose the classes in my code to other applications in a language-neutral fashion? How do I provide an object-oriented way for users of my DLL to use it? How can people make use of my work without needing source code or header files?

Before COM

There was a time not so long ago in software development when it was quite normal to distribute full source code and/or header files with third-party libraries. In order to make use of these libraries, people simply compiled them (or included their header files) into applications. The end result was a single executable that might contain code from many different vendors. Since it was common for many developers to use the same third-party library, a version of the library might exist in the executables deployed with numerous products. Executables tended to be relatively large and there was little or no code sharing between them. Updating one of these third-party libraries required recompilation and/or relinking since the library was incorporated directly into the executable at compile time.

That all changed with the introduction of DLLs. Almost overnight, it became quite common for third-party vendors to ship only header files and binaries. Instead of being able to deploy a single executable, the developer would end up distributing a sometimes sizeable collection of DLLs with his or her application. At runtime, it was up to the application to load—either implicitly or explicitly—the DLLs provided by the third-party vendor. As applications became more complex, it was not uncommon to see executables that required dozens of DLLs with complex interdependencies between them.

NOTE: This is, in fact, how Windows itself works—Windows is an executable with a large collection of dynamically linked libraries. Windows apps make calls to the functions exposed by these DLLs.

This approach worked reasonably well, but it had several drawbacks. One of the main ones was that the interfaces to these DLLs weren't object-oriented and therefore were difficult to extend and susceptible to being broken by even minor changes to an exposed function. If a vendor added a new parameter to a function in its third-party library, the change might well break the code of everyone currently using that library. The approach most vendors took to address this was simply to create a new version of the function (often with an "Ex" suffix or something similar) that included the new parameter. The end result was call-level interfaces that became unmanageable very quickly. It was common for third-party libraries (and even Windows itself) to include multiple versions of the same function call in an attempt to be compatible with every version of the library that had ever existed. The situation quickly grew out of control, exacerbated by the fact that there was no easy, direct method for users of these libraries to know which of the many versions of a given function should be used. Coding to these interfaces became a trial-and-error exercise that involved lots of scouring of API manuals and guesswork.

Another big problem with this approach was the proliferation of multiple copies of the same DLL across a user's computer. Hard drive space was once much more expensive than it is now, so having multiple copies of a library in different places on an end user's system was something vendors sought to avoid. Unfortunately, their solution to the problem wasn't really very well thought out. Their answer was to put the DLLs their apps needed in the Windows system directory. This addressed the problem of having multiple copies of the same DLL, but it introduced a whole host of other issues.

Chief among these was the inherent problems with conflicting versions of the same DLL. If Vendor A and Vendor B depended on different versions of a DLL produced by Vendor C, there was a strong likelihood that one of their products would be broken by the other's version of the DLL. If the interface to the DLL changed even slightly between versions, it was quite likely that at least one of the apps would misbehave (if it worked at all) when presented with a version of the DLL it wasn't expecting.

Another problem with centralizing DLLs was the trouble that arose from centralized yet unmanaged configuration information. In the days before the Windows registry, it was common to have a separate configuration file (usually with a .INI extension) for every application (and even multiple configuration files for some applications). These configuration files might include paths to DLLs that the application made use of, further complicating the task of unraveling DLL versioning problems. Because these configuration files were not managed by Windows itself, there was nothing to stop an application from completely wiping out a needed configuration file, putting entries into it that might break other applications, or completely ignoring it. These .INI files were simply text files that an application could use or not use as it saw fit.

The progression used by Windows to locate DLLs was logical and well documented; however, the fact that an application might use Windows' LoadLibrary function and grab a DLL from anywhere it pleased on a user's hard drive might not mean anything in terms of knowing what code an application actually depended on. The app might pick up a load path from a configuration file that no one else even knew about, or it might just search the hard drive and load what it thought was the best version of the library. It was common for applications to have subtle interdependencies that made the applications themselves rather brittle. We had come full circle from the days of bloated executables and little or no code sharing—now everyone depended on everyone else, with the installation of one app frequently breaking another.

The Dawn of COM

Microsoft's answer to these problems was COM. Simply put, COM provides an interface to third-party code libraries that is

- Object-oriented
- Centralized

- Versioned
- Language-neutral

Since COM uses the system registry, the days of unmanaged or improperly used configuration information are gone. When an application instantiates a COM object (usually through a call to CreateObject), Windows checks the system registry to find the object's location on disk and loads it. There's no guesswork, and multiple copies of the same object aren't allowed—each COM object lives in exactly one place on the system.

NOTE: Microsoft has recently introduced the concept of COM redirection and side-by-side deployment. This allows multiple versions of the same COM object to reside happily on the same system. This functionality has all the hallmarks of an afterthought and applies only in limited circumstances. (You can't, for example, use COM redirection to load different copies of an object into different Web applications on an IIS implementation—though the Web pages may seem like different apps to users, there's actually just one application—IIS—in the scenario, and COM still limits a given app to just one copy of a particular object version.) The vast majority of COM applications still abide by the standard COM versioning constraints.

This isn't to say that you can't have multiple versions of an object on a system. COM handles this through multiple interfaces: Each new version of an object has its own interface and might as well be a completely separate object as far as its users are concerned. There may or may not be code sharing between the versions of the object. As an application developer, you try not to worry about this—you just code to the interface.

Lest I omit a very fundamental detail, an interface is similar to a class without a body or implementation. It's a programming construct that defines a functionality contract—a contract between the provider of the functionality and its users. By implementing an interface, the author of the object ensures that clients of the object can depend on a fixed set of functionality being present in the object. Regardless of what the object actually is, the client can code to the interface without being concerned about the details. If the author of the object ever needs to enhance his or her code in a way that might break client applications that depend on it, the author can simply define a new interface and leave the old one intact.

COM has its limitations (most of which are addressed in the .NET Framework), but it is ubiquitous and fairly standardized. The world has embraced COM, so SQL Server includes a mechanism for working with COM objects from Transact-SQL.

Basic Architecture

The fundamental elements of COM are the following:

- Interfaces (especially IUnknown)
- Reference counting
- The QueryInterface method
- Marshaling
- Aggregation

Let's talk about each of these separately.

Interfaces

From an object-oriented programming standpoint, and also from the perspective of COM, an interface is a mechanism for exposing functionality, as I mentioned earlier. Typically, an object uses an interface to make its capabilities available to the outside world. When an object uses an interface, the object is said to *implement* that interface. Users of the object can interact with the interface without knowing what the object actually is, and a single object can implement multiple interfaces.

Generally speaking, to implement an interface, the methods exposed by the interface are linked to an object's methods. The interface itself requires no memory and really just specifies the functionality that an object implementing it must have.

Each COM interface is based on IUnknown, the fundamental COM interface. IUnknown allows navigation to the other interfaces exposed by the object.

Each interface has an interface ID (IID), a GUID that identifies it uniquely. This makes it easy to support interface versioning. A new version of a COM interface is actually a separate interface with its own IID. The IIDs for the standard ActiveX, OLE, and COM interfaces are predefined.

Reference Counting

Unlike .NET and the Java Runtime, COM does not perform automatic garbage collection. Disposing of objects that are no longer needed is left to the developer. You use an object's reference count to determine whether the object can be destroyed.

The IUnknown methods AddRef and Release manage the reference count of interfaces on a COM object. When a client receives a pointer to a

COM interface (a descendent of IUnknown), AddRef must be called on the interface. When the client has finished using the interface, it must call Release.

In its most primitive form, each AddRef call increments a counter variable inside its object and each Release call decrements it. When this count reaches zero, the interface no longer has any clients and can be destroyed.

You can also implement reference counting such that each reference to an object (as opposed to an interface implemented by the object) is counted. In this scenario, calls to AddRef and Release are delegated to a central reference count implementation. Release frees the whole object when its reference count reaches zero.

The QueryInterface Method

The fundamental COM mechanism used to access an object's functionality is the QueryInterface method of the IUnknown interface. Since every COM interface is derived from IUnknown, every COM interface has an implementation of QueryInterface.

QueryInterface queries an object using the IID of the interface the caller wants a pointer to. If the object implements the specified interface, QueryInterface retrieves a pointer to it and also calls AddRef. If the object does not implement the interface, QueryInterface returns the E_NOINTERFACE error code.

Marshaling

I like to think of marshaling as a kind of traffic cop or escort for data from one process to another (marshaling sometimes occurs between threads within a process as well). Marshaling enables the COM interfaces exposed by an object in one process to be accessed by another process. If a structure contains a pointer to a piece of data within a process's address space, that pointer is meaningless to other processes. Marshaling it involves copying the reference and the data into a format that can be sent to the other process. Once the other process receives the marshaled data, the marshaling is reversed (or unmarshaled). The data is copied somewhere within the new process's address space and a reference to it is again established.

Through marshaling, COM either provides code or uses code provided by the implementer of the interface to pack a method's parameters into a format that can be shipped across processes or across the network to other machines and to unpack those parameters during the call. When the call returns, the process is reversed.

Marshaling is usually unnecessary when an interface is being used in the same process as the object that provides it. However, marshaling can still be required between threads.

Aggregation

For those situations when an object's implementer wants to make use of the services offered by another (e.g., third-party) object and wants this second object to function as a natural part of the first one, COM supports the concepts of aggregation and containment.

By aggregation, I mean that the containing object creates the contained object as part of its construction process and exposes the interfaces of the contained object within its own interface. Some objects can be aggregated, some can't. An object must follow a specific set of rules to participate in aggregation.

COM at Work

Practically speaking, COM objects are used through two basic means: early binding and late binding. When an application makes object references that are resolvable at compile-time, the object is early bound. To early bind an object in Visual Basic, you add a reference to the library containing the object to your project, then Dim specific instances of it. To early bind an object in tools like Visual C++ and Delphi, you import the object's type library and work with the interfaces it provides. In either case, you code directly to the interfaces exposed by the object as though they were interfaces you created yourself. The object itself may live on a completely separate machine and be accessed via Distributed COM (DCOM) or be marshaled by a transaction manager such as Microsoft Transaction Server or Component Services. Generally speaking, you don't care—you just code to the interface.

When references to an object aren't known until runtime, the object is late bound. In Visual Basic, you instantiate a late-bound object via a call to CreateObject and store the object instance in a variant. In Visual C++, you obtain a pointer to the object's IDispatch interface (all automation objects implement IDispatch), then call GetIDsOfNames and Invoke to call the object's methods and get and set its properties.

Since the compiler didn't know what object you were referencing at compile-time, you may encounter bad method calls or nonexistent properties at runtime. That's the trade-off with late binding: It's more flexible in that you can decide at runtime what objects to create and can even instantiate objects that didn't exist on the development system, but it's more error prone—it's easy to make mistakes when you late bind objects because your development environment can't provide the same level of assistance it can when it knows the objects you're dealing with.

Accessing COM objects via late binding is also slower than doing so via early binding, sometimes dramatically so. ProgIDs must be translated into IIDs, and the dispatch IDs of exposed methods and properties must be looked up at runtime in order to be callable. This takes time, and the difference in execution speed is often quite noticeable.

Once you have an instance of an object, you call methods and access properties on it like any other object. COM supports the notion of events (though they're a bit more trouble to use than they should be), so you can subscribe and respond to events on COM objects as well.

Threading Models

COM objects support two primary threading models: single-threaded apartment (STA, also known as "apartment-threaded") and multithreaded apartment (MTA, also known as "free-threaded"). Don't let the "apartment" concept confuse you or scare you away. The term helps define a conceptual framework that describes the relationships among threads, objects, and processes. It establishes an analogy wherein a process is the equivalent of a building, and the logical container in which COM threads and objects exist within a process is an apartment—that is, a set of rooms within the building. Thus an apartment is simply a logical container within a process. As the analogy suggests, an apartment might contain multiple threads and/or objects, depending on its type, and a single process might have many individual apartments.

Each object and each thread can belong to only one apartment. Only the threads within an apartment can access the objects in that apartment directly; all other threads go through COM proxies of some sort. A thread establishes residence in an apartment (and optionally specifies the threading model it wants to use) through a call to a COM initialization function such as CoInitialize, CoInitializeEx, or OleInitialize.

In the STA model, an apartment has a single thread and can contain multiple objects. In the MTA model, an apartment can have multiple threads and multiple objects. A process can have multiple STAs but only one MTA. This one MTA can coexist with multiple STAs in the same process.

As I've mentioned, an out-of-process COM server (i.e., an executable) specifies its threading model via a COM initialization function call. CoInitializeEx is the only one of the three main COM initializers that permits the threading model to be specified; CoInitialize and OleInitialize both force the STA model. A call to either CoInitialize or OleInitialize ultimately results in a call to CoInitializeEx with STA hard-coded as the threading model.

The threading model for an in-process COM server (a DLL) is not specified via a call to CoInitializeEx. Instead, it's specified via a registry key, like this:

```
HKEY_LOCAL_MACHINE\SOFTWARE\Classes\CLSID\InprocServer32\
ThreadingModel
```

The value of this key can be Apartment, Free, or Both. If the key is not found, STA is assumed.

As I've said, only the threads residing in the apartment in which a COM object was created can directly access the object. Other threads access the object through proxy objects. Given that only one thread resides in a given STA apartment, COM takes responsibility for synchronizing object access by other threads. It accomplishes this via Windows' messaging facilities. It creates a hidden window for each apartment and sets up proxies to post messages to the apartment owning an object in order to invoke it. The serialization of access to the object is managed through Windows' normal message queuing facilities. Methods on the object are called in response to messages posted to the apartment's hidden window. As messages are pulled out of the message queue (via PeekMessage and GetMessage) and dispatched (via DispatchMessage), the window procedure for the thread, which is implemented by COM, invokes the appropriate methods on the object. The process is reversed when the method call completes and results need to be returned to the calling thread. Messages are posted to the hidden window for the calling thread's apartment to provide the result(s) and indicate function completion. These messages are picked up by the calling thread, and it, in turn, returns through the proxy object method call, thus completing the method call on the object in the other apartment.

When a component is configured for the STA model, the objects it exposes are created on the Win32 thread that created it. Other threads can't access these object instances.

When a component is configured for the MTA model, COM automatically starts a host MTA and instantiates the objects in it. When a component's threading model has been configured as both STA and MTA compatible, the object is created in the calling STA.

The Main STA

The first thread to initialize COM using the STA threading model becomes the main STA. This STA is required to remain alive until all COM work is completed within a process because some in-process servers are always created in the context of the main STA.

OLE requires a single thread to be set up to respond to STA-related messages. This is the first caller of OleInitialize, so the first thread in a process to call OleInitialize becomes the main STA for the process.

COM and SQL Server

COM is evident in several places within SQL Server. To begin with, if you access SQL Server via ADO or OLE DB, you're doing so using COM—both ADO and OLE DB consist of collections of COM objects and interfaces. If you use Enterprise Manager, you're also using COM. As Chapter 15 demonstrates, Enterprise Manager is built on a collection of COM objects known as SQL-DMO. When you execute a linked server query, you're doing so via COM—OLE DB providers, as I've said, are COM components. When you call certain Transact-SQL commands, you're working with COM. For example, the BULK INSERT command is based on a COM object that loaded and accessed within the server.

When you use DTS or the ActiveX replication objects, you are again making use of COM. ActiveX scripts in SQL Server Agent as well as those in DTS packages use the ActiveX script COM interfaces for defining scripting languages and executing user code.

When you interact with SQLXML using the SQLXMLOLEDB provider or using the sp_xml_preparedocument procedure, you're interacting with COM. As the name suggests, SQLXMLOLEDB is an OLE DB provider. The sp_xml_preparedocument procedure (and its counterpart, sp_xml_removedocument) makes use of MSXML, Microsoft's XML parser, which is exposed to applications such as SQL Server via COM interfaces.

And, of course, when you instantiate COM objects from T-SQL using the sp_OA stored procedures, you're working with COM. As Chapter 15 details, the sp_OA functionality is based on COM's IDispatch interface and interacts with it in the same way that simple automation tools such as VBScript do.

Various other facilities within SQL Server also either use COM or expose their functionality via COM. COM is pervasive throughout SQL Server, just as it is throughout many complex Windows applications.

Recap

COM offers a language-independent mechanism for exposing the functionality in a DLL or executable to the outside world. It is based on interfaces and the concept of binding—an application that makes use of COM is said to be either early bound or late bound to the COM interfaces it uses.

SQL Server both exposes its own functionality via COM and makes use of functionality exposed by external COM components. Some examples of SQL Server functionality exposed via COM include its use of OLE DB and its own native OLE DB provider, SQLOLEDB, and SQL-DMO, the COM objects on which Enterprise Manager is based; and SQLXMLOLEDB, the OLE DB provider that exposes the client-side SQLXML functionality. Examples of external COM interfaces used by SQL Server include MSXML, the ActiveX scripting interfaces, and OLE DB providers accessed via linked server queries.

Knowledge Measure

1. What interface does an application interact with when accessing a COM object via late binding?
2. What three methods must all COM interfaces implement?
3. What interface do all COM interfaces ultimately descend from?
4. Describe what happens when data is marshaled from one process to another.
5. What COM library is used by SQL Server's sp_xml_prepare-document stored procedure?
6. True or false: Access to COM is limited to Microsoft programming language tools such as Visual Basic and Visual C++. Because COM is a proprietary Microsoft technology, you cannot create or access COM objects from third-party languages.
7. What mechanism is used with COM objects to keep track of how many references are currently pending for a given object?
8. Describe the purpose of QueryInterface.
9. Name the technology that allows a COM object on another machine to be instantiated remotely.
10. True or false: When accessing an object via late binding using its ProgID, the ProgID must be translated into an interface ID before the interfaces it implements can be accessed.

CHAPTER 8

XML

The most formidable weapon against errors of every kind is reason. I have never used any other, and I trust I never shall.

—Thomas Paine[1]

I've included a chapter on introductory XML in this book for four reasons. First, I wanted to update the coverage of XML from my last book, *The Guru's Guide to SQL Server Stored Procedures, XML, and HTML* (Boston, MA: Addison-Wesley, 2002), and felt this was a good time to do that. The language has evolved since I first wrote that book, and I've wanted to update what I said about XML for some time.

Second, I believe that the pervasiveness and ubiquity of XML justifies its acceptance as a core technology. It is strongly supported and relied upon by SQL Server's SQLXML technologies in the same way that COM, shared memory, and Windows sockets are used and leveraged in other parts of the product. The next release of SQL Server promises to provide even more XML support and features. XML has come into its own in the last few years, and I think it's high time we acknowledged that and added it to the list of foundational technologies that one must know something about in order to master modern, complex applications such as SQL Server. The day is soon approaching when you won't be able to claim to be a practicing technologist without at least a rudimentary knowledge of XML.

Third, since XML support is now a core component of SQL Server, I think it deserves to be covered in books that cover SQL Server. Given that I cover topics such as virtual memory management and thread synchronization in this book because I believe they are foundational to the architecture and design of SQL Server and because I believe understanding them helps us know SQL Server better, I feel compelled to cover XML as well—it is

---

1. Paine, Thomas. *The Age of Reason*, ed. Philip S. Foner. New York: Citadel Press, 1974, p. 49.

also a key foundational element in the SQL Server architecture. Understanding XML helps us better understand how SQL Server uses it and provides insight into how the product is designed. Important parts of SQL Server are based on XML, and that will only become truer as time goes by. Inasmuch as Windows sockets and shared memory deserve to be covered in a book focused on the architectural design of SQL Server, so does XML.

Fourth, many SQL Server practitioners are new to XML. I believe that teaching XML in a book that is principally about SQL Server gives those who haven't worked much with it a chance to gain valuable knowledge and deepen their skills. Knowing XML will make you a better SQL Server practitioner. By understanding a core tenet of the SQL Server architecture, you will understand the product and its technologies more viscerally. Understanding how XML works is fundamental to understanding not only the design and implementation of SQL Server's XML support but also the current and future course of the product.

Unfortunately, there isn't time or space to discuss XML as completely as I'd like to. Whole books (many of them, in fact) have been written on the subject of XML and the XML family of technologies. I'll try to hit the high points of what you need to know about XML to be able to use SQL Server's XML-related features. That said, you should probably supplement the coverage here with research of your own. (See the Resources section later in this chapter for some recommendations.)

Overview

Thanks to the World Wide Web, HTML has taken over the world. And yet, despite its popularity, HTML has always had a number of serious limitations. You don't have to build Web applications for very long before you run into some of them. HTML works reasonably well for formatting informal documents but not so well for more complex tasks. It was never intended to describe the structure of data, but business needs have caused it to be used to do just that. The fact that HTML is being used to do things it was never intended to do has highlighted many of its shortcomings. This has created the need for a more powerful markup language, one that's data-centric rather than display-centric, one that doesn't just know how to format data but can also give the data contextual meaning.

XML is the answer to many of the problems with HTML and with building extensible applications in general. XML is easy for anyone who understands HTML to learn but is overwhelmingly more powerful. XML is more than just a markup language—it's a *metalanguage*—a language that can be used to define new languages. With XML, you can create a language that's tailored to your particular application or business domain and use it to exchange data with your vendors, your trading partners, your customers, and anyone else that can speak XML.

Rather than replacing HTML, XML complements it. Beyond merely providing a means of formatting data, XML gives it context. Once data has contextual meaning, displaying it is the easy part. But displaying it is just one of the many things you can do with the data once it has context. By correctly separating the presentation of the data from its storage and management, we open up an almost infinite number of opportunities for using the data and exchanging it with other parties.

In this chapter, we'll explore the history of markup languages and how XML came into existence. We'll look at how data is presented in HTML and compare that with how XML improves on it. We'll touch on the basics of XML notation and how XML can be displayed through translation to HTML via XML style sheets. We'll talk about document validation using both Document Type Definitions (DTDs) and XML schemas, and we'll discuss some of the nuances of each. We'll finish up by touching on the Document Object Model (DOM) and how it's used to manipulate XML documents as objects.

Simplicity Comes at a Price

HTML's purpose is to format documents. It specifies display elements—titles, headings, fonts, captions, and so on. It's very presentation oriented. It's pretty good at laying out data. It's not good at describing that data or making it generally accessible.

Web site designers have worked around HTML's many shortcomings in some astonishingly novel ways. Still, HTML has serious flaws that make it ill suited for building complex, open information systems. Here are a few of them.

- HTML isn't extensible. Each browser supports a fixed set of tags, and you may not add your own.
- HTML is format-centric. Although it displays data reasonably well, HTML gives data no context. If the format of the data a program is accessing via HTML changes, the program will likely break.
- Once generated, HTML is static and not easily refreshable. Dynamic HTML (DHTML) and other technologies help alleviate this,

- but HTML, in its most basic essence, was never intended to serve up live data.
- HTML provides only a single view of data; because it is display-centric, changing the view of the data is more difficult than it should be. Again, technologies like DHTML help to some extent, but the bottom line is that we need a markup language that *knows* about its data.
- HTML has little or no semantic structure. There's no facility for representing data by *meaning* rather than by layout. As I've said, HTML's forte is displaying data, and sometimes it's not even terribly good at that.

If you've been around for awhile, you may be familiar with Standard Generalized Markup Language (SGML) and may be thinking that it would address many of HTML's shortcomings. Though SGML doesn't have the weaknesses that HTML does, its vast flexibility makes it extremely complex. Document Style Semantics and Specification Language (DSSSL), the language used to format SGML, is powerful and flexible, but this power comes at a price—it's extremely difficult to use. What we need is a language that's similar to HTML in terms of ease of use but features the flexibility of SGML.

A Brief History of XML

With the explosion of the Web and the massive amount of HTML development that consequently resulted, people began running into HTML's many shortcomings very quickly. At the same time, SGML proponents, who'd been working in relative obscurity for many years, began looking for a way to use SGML itself on the Web, instead of just one application of it (HTML). They realized that SGML itself was too complex for the task—most people couldn't or wouldn't use it—so they needed an alternative. Again, they were looking for something that blended the best aspects of HTML and SGML.

In mid-1996, Jon Bosak of Sun Microsystems approached the World Wide Web Consortium (W3C) about forming a committee on using SGML on the Web. The effort was given the green light by the W3C's Dan Connolly and, though organized, led, and underwritten by Sun, the actual work was shared among Bosak and people from outside Sun, including Tim Bray, C. M. Sperberg-McQueen, and Jean Paoli of Microsoft. By November

1996, the committee had the beginnings of a simplified form of SGML that was no more difficult to learn and use than HTML but that retained many of the best features of SGML. This was the birth of XML as we know it.

XML vs. HTML: An Example

You can create your own tags in XML. This is such a powerful, vital part of XML that it bears further discussion. If you're used to working in HTML, this concept is probably very foreign to you since HTML does not allow you to define your own tags. Though various browser vendors have extended HTML with their own custom tags, you still can't create your own—you have to use the tags provided to you by your browser.

So how do you define a new tag in XML? The simplest answer is: you don't have to. You just use it. You can control what tags are valid in an XML document by using DTD documents and XML schemas (we'll talk about each of these later), but, the bottom line is this: You simply use a tag to define it in XML. There is no typedef or similar construct.

To compare and contrast how HTML and XML represent data, let's look at the same data represented using each language. Listing 8.1 shows some sample HTML that displays a recipe.

Listing 8.1 A Basic HTML Document

```
<!-- The original html recipe -->
<HTML>
<HEAD>
<TITLE>Henderson's Hotter-than-Hell Habañero Sauce</TITLE>
</HEAD>
<BODY>
<H3>Henderson's Hotter-than-Hell Habañero Sauce</H3>
Homegrown from stuff in my garden
   (you don't want to know exactly what).
<H4>Ingredients</H4>
<TABLE BORDER="1">
<TR BGCOLOR="#308030"><TH>Qty</TH><TH>Units</TH><TH>Item</TH></TR>
<TR><TD>6</TD><TD>each</TD><TD>Habañero peppers</TD></TR>
<TR><TD>12</TD><TD>each</TD><TD>Cowhorn peppers</TD></TR>
<TR><TD>12</TD><TD>each</TD><TD>Jalapeño peppers</TD></TR>
<TR><TD></TD><TD>dash</TD><TD>Tequila (optional)</TD></TR>
</TABLE>
```

```
<P>
<H4>Instructions</H4>
<OL>
<LI>Chop up peppers, removing their stems,
   then grind to a liquid.</LI>
<!-- and so forth -->
</BODY>
</HTML>
```

If you read through the HTML in Listing 8.1, you'll no doubt notice that the recipe ingredients are stored in an HTML table. Figure 8.1 shows how it looks in a browser.

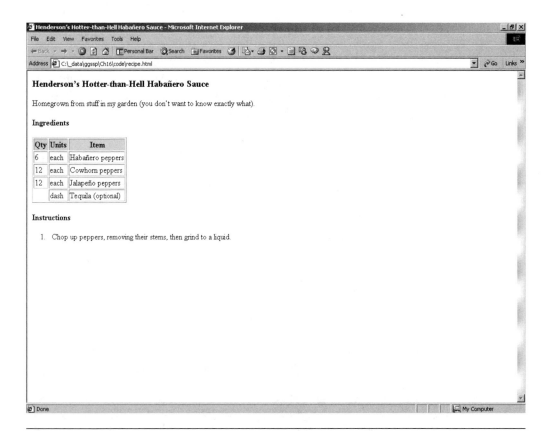

Figure 8.1 A simple HTML page containing some data

There are several positive aspects of how HTML represents this data.

- It's readable—if you look hard enough, you can tell what data the HTML contains.
- It can be displayed by any browser, even nongraphical ones.
- A cascading style sheet could be used to further control the formatting.

However, there's a really big negative aspect that outweighs the others insofar as data markup goes—there's nothing in the code to indicate the *meaning* of any of its elements. The data contained in the document has no context. A program could scan the document and pick out the items in the table, but it wouldn't know what they were. And while you could hard-code assumptions about the data (column 1 is Qty, column 2 is Units, and so on), if the format of the page were changed, your app would break.

The problem is further exacerbated by attempting to extract the data and store it in a database. Because the semantic information about the data was stripped out when it was translated into HTML, we have to resupply this information in order to store it meaningfully in a database. In other words, we have to translate the data back out of HTML because HTML is not a suitable storage medium for semantic information.

Now let's take a look at the same data represented as XML. You'll notice that the markup has nothing to do with displaying the data—it is all about describing content. Listing 8.2 shows the code.

Listing 8.2 The Recipe Data Stored as XML

```
<?xml version="1.0" ?>
<Recipe>
  <Name>Henderson&apos;s Hotter-than-Hell Habanero Sauce</Name>
  <Description> Homegrown from stuff in my garden
    (you don&apos;t want to know exactly what).</Description>
  <Ingredients>
    <Ingredient>
      <Qty unit="each">6</Qty>
      <Item>Habanero peppers</Item>
    </Ingredient>
    <Ingredient>
      <Qty unit="each">12</Qty>
      <Item>Cowhorn peppers</Item>
    </Ingredient>
```

```
  <Ingredient>
    <Qty unit="each">12</Qty>
    <Item>Jalapeno peppers</Item>
  </Ingredient>
  <Ingredient>
    <Qty unit="dash" />
    <Item optional="1">Tequila</Item>
  </Ingredient>
</Ingredients>
<Instructions>
  <Step> Chop up peppers, removing their stems, then grind to a
liquid.</Step>
  <!-- and so forth... -->
</Instructions>
</Recipe>
```

See the difference? The tags in Listing 8.2 relate to recipes, not format-ting. The file remains readable, so it retains the simplicity of the HTML for-mat, but the data now has context. A program that parses this file will know exactly what a Jalapeño is—it's an Item in an Ingredient in a Recipe.

And, regarding ease of use, I think you'll find that XML is actually more human readable than HTML. XML accomplishes the goal of being at least as simple to use as HTML, yet it is orders of magnitude more powerful. It explains the information in a recipe in terms of recipes, *not* in terms of how to display recipes. We leave the display formatting for later and for tools better suited to it.

Notational Nuances

It's important to get some of the nomenclature straight before we get too far into our discussion of XML. Let's reexamine part of our XML document.

```
<Item optional="1">Tequila</Item>
```

In this code, note the following.

1. Item is the tag name. As in HTML, tags mark the start of an element in XML. Elements are a key piece of the XML puzzle. XML docu-ments consist mostly of elements and attributes.
2. optional is an attribute name. An attribute is a field that further de-scribes an element. We could have called it something else—the

name we've come up with is entirely of our own choosing. Notice that the other elements in Listing 8.2 do not have this attribute.

3. "1" is the value of the optional attribute and the portion from optional through "1" comprises the attribute.

4. </Item> is the end tag of the Item element.

5. The portion from Item through /Item is the Item element.

XML tags do not always contain text. They can be empty or contain just attributes. For example, look at this excerpt:

```
<Qty unit="dash" />
```

Here, Qty is the element name, and unit is its only attribute. The forward slash at the end of the text indicates that the element itself is empty and therefore does not require a closing tag. It's shorthand for this:

```
<Qty unit="dash"></Qty>
```

Empty tags may or may not have attributes.

In addition to these basic structure rules, XML documents require stricter formatting than HTML. XML documents must be well formed in order for an XML parser to be able to process them. In mathematics, equations have particular forms they must follow in order to be logical; the ones that don't aren't well formed and aren't terribly useful for anything. XML has a similar requirement. In order for a parser to be able to parse an XML document, the document must meet certain rules. The most important of these are the following.

- Every document must have a root element that envelops the rest of the document. It need not be named root. In our earlier example, Recipe is the root element.
- All tags must have closing tags, either in the form of an end tag or via the empty tag symbol described above. HTML often doesn't enforce this rule—browsers typically try to guess where a closing tag should go if it's missing.
- All tags must be properly nested. If Qty is contained within Ingredient, you must close Qty before you close Ingredient. This is, again, not something that's rigorously enforced by HTML, but an XML parser will not parse tags that are improperly nested.
- Unlike element text, attribute values must always be enclosed in single or double quotes.

- The characters <, >, and " cannot be represented literally; you must use character entities instead. A character entity is a string that begins with an ampersand (&), ends with a semicolon (;), and takes the place of a special symbol in order to avoid confusing the parser. Since <, >, and " all have special meaning in XML, you must represent them using the special character entities <, >, and ", respectively. There are two other predefined special character entities you may use when necessary: & and '. The & entity takes the place of an ampersand. Since ampersands typically denote character entities in an XML document, using them in your data can confuse the parser. Similarly, ' represents a single quote—an apostrophe. Since attribute values can be enclosed in single quotes, a stray apostrophe can confuse the parser.
- Unlike HTML, if you wish to use character entities other than the predefined five we just talked about, you must first declare them in a DTD. We'll discuss DTDs shortly.
- Element and attribute names may not begin with the letters "XML" in any casing. XML reserves these for its own use.
- XML is case-sensitive. This means that an element named Customer is a different element than one named customer.

Well-Formed vs. Valid

There's a difference between a well-formed XML document and a valid one. A valid XML document is a well-formed document that has had additional validation criteria applied to it. Being well formed is only the beginning. Beyond being parsable, an XML document will typically have certain data relationships and requirements that make it sensible. A document that breaks these rules, while well formed, is not valid. For example, consider the XML fragment shown below.

```
<Car Name="Mustang" Make="Ford" Model="1966" LicensePlate="OU812">
  <Engine Type="Cleveland">341</Engine>
  <Engine Type="Winchester">302</Engine>
</Car>
```

Is it well formed? Yes. Is it valid? Perhaps not. Most cars don't have two engines. Consider the following modified excerpt from our earlier example document.

```
<Ingredient>
  <Qty unit="each">12</Qty>
  <Qty unit="each">10</Qty>
  <Item>Jalapeno peppers</Item>
</Ingredient>
```

Does it make sense for an ingredient to include two Qty specifications? No, probably not. While the document is well formed, it's most likely invalid.

How do you establish the validity rules for a document? Through DTDs and XML schemas. We'll discuss each of these in the sections that follow.

Document Type Definitions

There are two types of XML parsers: validating and nonvalidating. A non-validating parser checks an XML document to be sure that it's well formed and returns it to you as a tree of objects. A validating parser, on the other hand, ensures the document is well formed, *then* checks it against its DTD or schema to determine whether the document is valid. In this section, we'll discuss the first of these validation methods, the DTD.

A DTD is a somewhat antiquated though still widely used method of validating documents. DTDs have a peculiar and rather limited syntax, but they are still found in lots of XML implementations. Over time, it's likely that XML schemas will become the tool of choice for setting up data validation. That said, there's still plenty of DTD code out there (and there are a few things that DTDs can do that XML schemas can't), so DTDs are still worth knowing about.

A DTD can formalize and codify the tags used in a particular type of document. Since XML itself allows you to use virtually any tags you want so long as the document itself is well formed, a facility is needed to bring structure to documents, to ensure that they make sense. DTDs were the first attempt at doing this. And since DTDs define what tags can and cannot be used in a document, as well as certain characteristics of those tags, DTDs are also used to define new XML dialects, formalized subsets of XML tags and validation rules. Originally, DTDs put the X in XML—they were the means by which new applications of XML were designed.

Let's have a look at a DTD for our earlier recipe example. Listing 8.3 shows how it might look.

Listing 8.3 A DTD for the Recipe Data

```
<!-- Recipe.DTD, an example DTD for recipe.xml -->
<!ELEMENT Recipe (Name, Description?, Ingredients?,
   Instructions?, Step?)>
<!ELEMENT Name (#PCDATA)>
<!ELEMENT Description (#PCDATA)>
<!ELEMENT Ingredients (Ingredient)*>
<!ELEMENT Ingredient (Qty, Item)>
<!ELEMENT Qty (#PCDATA)>
<!ATTLIST Qty unit CDATA #REQUIRED>
<!ELEMENT Item (#PCDATA)>
<!ATTLIST Item optional CDATA "0">
<!ELEMENT Instructions (Step)+>
<!ELEMENT Step (#PCDATA)>
```

This DTD defines several characteristics of the document that are worth discussing. First, note the topmost noncomment line in the file (bolded). It indicates the elements that can be represented by a document that uses this DTD. A question mark after an element indicates that it's optional.

Second, notice the #PCDATA flags. They indicate that the element or attribute can contain character data and nothing else.

Third, take note of the #REQUIRED flag. This indicates that the unit attribute of the Qty element is required. Documents that use this DTD may not omit that attribute.

Fourth, note the default value supplied for the Item element's optional attribute. Rather than being required, this attribute can be omitted, as its name suggests. Moreover, for elements that omit the attribute, it defaults to "0."

From the listing, you can see that DTD syntax is not an XML dialect, nor is it terribly intuitive. That's why people are increasingly using schemas instead. We'll discuss XML schemas shortly.

You link a DTD and a document together by using a document type declaration element at the top of the document (immediately after the <?xml...> line). The document type declaration can contain either an inline copy of the DTD or a reference to its file name using a Uniform Resource Identifier (URI). The one for recipe.xml looks like this:

```
<!DOCTYPE Recipe SYSTEM "recipe.dtd">
```

Here's the document again with the DTD line included (Listing 8.4).

Listing 8.4 The recipe.xml Document with the DTD Reference Included

```
<?xml version="1.0" ?>
<!DOCTYPE Recipe SYSTEM "recipe.dtd">
<Recipe>
  <Name>Henderson&apos;s Hotter-than-Hell Habanero Sauce</Name>
  <Description> Homegrown from stuff in my garden
    (you don&apos;t want to know exactly what).</Description>
  <Ingredients>
    <Ingredient>
      <Qty unit="each">6</Qty>
      <Item>Habanero peppers</Item>
    </Ingredient>
    <Ingredient>
      <Qty unit="each">12</Qty>
      <Item>Cowhorn peppers</Item>
    </Ingredient>
    <Ingredient>
      <Qty unit="each">12</Qty>
      <Item>Jalapeno peppers</Item>
    </Ingredient>
    <Ingredient>
      <Qty unit="dash" />
      <Item optional="1">Tequila</Item>
    </Ingredient>
  </Ingredients>
  <Instructions>
    <Step> Chop up peppers, removing their stems, then grind to a
      liquid.</Step>
    <!-- and so forth... -->
  </Instructions>
</Recipe>
```

Validating the data against the DTD can be done through a number of means. If you're using Internet Explorer 5.0 or later, you can use Microsoft's built-in DTD validator simply by loading an XML document into the browser, right-clicking it, and selecting Validate. A number of GUI and command line tools exist to do the same thing. Several of them are listed on the W3C site, http://www.w3c.org.

XML Schemas

I mentioned earlier that DTDs were somewhat old-fashioned. The reason for this is that there's a newer, better technology for validating XML documents. It's called XML Schema. Unlike DTDs, you build XML Schema documents using XML. They consist of elements and attributes just like the XML documents they validate. They have a number of other advantages over DTDs, including the following.

- DTDs cannot control what kind of information a given element or attribute can contain. Merely being able to specify that an element stores text is not precise enough for most business needs. We might want to specify what format the text should have or whether the text is a date or a number. XML Schema has extensive support for data domain control.
- DTDs feature only 10 stock data types. XML Schema features over 44 base data types, plus you can create your own.
- All declarations in a DTD are global. This means that you can't define multiple elements with the same name, even if they exist in completely different contexts.
- Because DTD syntax is not XML, it requires special handling. It cannot be processed by an XML parser. This adds complexity to documents with associated DTDs and potentially slows down their processing.

A complete discussion on XML Schema is outside the scope of this book, but we should still touch on a few of the high points. Listing 8.5 presents a validation schema for the recipe.xml document we built earlier.

Listing 8.5 An XML Schema for the Recipe Document

```
<?xml version="1.0" ?>
<xsd:schema xmlns:xsd="http://www.w3.org/2000/10/XMLSchema"
    elementFormDefault="qualified">
  <xsd:element name="Recipe">
    <xsd:complexType>
      <xsd:sequence>
        <xsd:element name="Name" type="xsd:string"/>
        <xsd:element name="Description" type="xsd:string"/>
        <xsd:element name="Ingredients">
          <xsd:complexType>
```

```
<xsd:sequence>
  <xsd:element name="Ingredient"
      maxOccurs="unbounded">
    <xsd:complexType>
      <xsd:sequence>
        <xsd:element name="Qty">
          <xsd:complexType>
            <xsd:simpleContent>
              <xsd:restriction base="xsd:byte">
                <xsd:attribute name="unit"
                    use="required">
                  <xsd:simpleType>
                    <xsd:restriction
                        base="xsd:NMTOKEN">
                      <xsd:enumeration value="dash"/>
                      <xsd:enumeration value="each"/>
                      <xsd:enumeration value="dozen"/>
                      <xsd:enumeration value="cups"/>
                      <xsd:enumeration value="teasp"/>
                      <xsd:enumeration value="tbls"/>
                    </xsd:restriction>
                  </xsd:simpleType>
                </xsd:attribute>
              </xsd:restriction>
            </xsd:simpleContent>
          </xsd:complexType>
        </xsd:element>
        <xsd:element name="Item">
          <xsd:complexType>
            <xsd:simpleContent>
              <xsd:restriction base="xsd:string">
                <xsd:attribute name="optional"
                    type="xsd:boolean"/>
              </xsd:restriction>
            </xsd:simpleContent>
          </xsd:complexType>
        </xsd:element>
      </xsd:sequence>
    </xsd:complexType>
  </xsd:element>
</xsd:sequence>
</xsd:complexType>
</xsd:element>
<xsd:element name="Instructions">
```

```
        <xsd:complexType>
          <xsd:sequence>
            <xsd:element name="Step" type="xsd:string"/>
          </xsd:sequence>
        </xsd:complexType>
      </xsd:element>
    </xsd:sequence>
  </xsd:complexType>
</xsd:element>
</xsd:schema>
```

Look a little daunting? It's a bit longer than the DTD we looked at earlier, isn't it? However, it's not as bad as it might seem. Most of the document consists of opening and closing tags—the schema itself is not that complex.

The first thing you should notice is that each of the elements and attributes in the XML document is assigned a data type. When the document is validated with this schema, each piece of data in the document is checked to see whether it's valid for its assigned data type. If it isn't, the document fails the validation test.

Next, take a look at the maxOccurs element. Via a schema, you can specify a number of ancillary properties for elements including how many (or how few) times an element can appear in a document. The default for both minOccurs and maxOccurs is 1. You can make an element optional by setting its minOccurs attribute to 0.

Next, notice the xsd:enumeration elements under the unit attribute. In an XML schema, you can specify a list of valid values for an element or attribute. If an element or attribute attempts to store a value not in the list, the document fails validation.

Finally, notice the new data type for the Item element's optional attribute. I've changed it from an integer to a Boolean value, one of the stock data types supported by XML Schema. I point this out because I want you to realize the very rich data type set that XML Schema offers. Also understand that you can create new types by extending the existing ones. Furthermore, you can create complex types—elements that contain other elements and attributes. In the schema listed above, the Qty data type is a complex data type, as are the Ingredients and Instructions types. Any schema element that contains other elements or attributes is, by definition, a complex data type.

You might be wondering how you associate a schema with an XML document. You do so by adding a couple of attributes to the document's root element. For example, the root element in our recipe.xml document now looks like this:

```
Recipe xmlns:xsi="http://www.w3.org/2000/10/XMLSchema-instance"
xsi:noNamespaceSchemaLocation="D:\Ch08\code\recipe.xsd">
```

The first attribute makes the elements in the xsi (the XML Schema Instance) namespace available to the document. A namespace is a collection of names identified by a URI reference. You can define your own, or you can do as we've done here and refer to a namespace defined on the W3C Web site. As in many programming disciplines, an XML namespace provides name scoping to an application so that names from different sources do not collide with one another. Unlike traditional namespaces, the names within an XML namespace do not have to be unique. Without getting into why that is, for now just understand that a namespace gives scope to the names you use in XML. In this particular case, it provides access to the names in the xsi namespace, which is where XML Schema Instance elements reside. By referring to the namespace in this way, we can use XML Schema Instance elements in the document by prefixing them with xsi:.

The second attribute describes the location of the XML Schema document. This is the document listed above. It contains the schema information for our document.

Once these attributes are in place, XML Schema–aware tools will validate the document using the schema identified by the attribute.

Converting XML to HTML Using a Style Sheet

In the same way that cascading style sheets are commonly used to transform HTML documents, Extensible Stylesheet Language Transformations (XSLT) transforms XML documents. It can transform XML documents from one document format to another, into other XML dialects, or into completely different file formats such as PostScript, RTF, and TeX.

The best part about XSLT is that it's XML. An XSLT document is a regular XML document. "How can that be?" you may ask. "Wouldn't you have issues with circular references?" No—XSLT is just another XML dialect. Modern XML parsers are intelligent enough to know how to use the instructions encoded in an XSLT document (which are just ordinary XML tags and attributes and the like) to transform or provide structure to another document.

An XSLT style sheet is an XML document that's made up of a series of rules, called *templates*, that are applied to another XML document to produce a third document. These templates are written in XML using specific tags with defined meanings. Each time a template matches something in the source XML document, a new structure is produced in the output. This is often HTML, as the example we're about to examine demonstrates, but it does not have to be.

Listing 8.6 shows an XSLT style sheet that transforms our recipe.xml document into HTML that closely resembles the HTML we built by hand earlier in the chapter (Listing 8.1).

Listing 8.6 An XSLT Style Sheet That Transforms Our XML Document into HTML

```
<?xml version='1.0'?>
<xsl:stylesheet version="1.0"
xmlns:xsl="http://www.w3.org/1999/XSL/Transform">
<xsl:template match="/">
  <html>
  <HEAD>
  <TITLE>Henderson&apos;s Hotter-than-Hell Habanero Sauce</TITLE>
  </HEAD>
  <body>
    <H3>Henderson&apos;s Hotter-than-Hell Habanero Sauce</H3>
      Homegrown from stuff in my garden
      (you don&apos;t want to know exactly what).
      <H4>Ingredients</H4>
      <table border="2">
      <tr BGCOLOR="#00FF00">
        <TH>Qty</TH>
        <TH>Units</TH>
        <TH>Item</TH>
      </tr>
      <xsl:for-each select="Recipe/Ingredients/Ingredient">
      <tr>
        <td><xsl:value-of select="Qty"/></td>
        <td><xsl:value-of select="Qty/@unit"/></td>
        <td><xsl:value-of select="Item"/></td>
      </tr>
      </xsl:for-each>
    </table>
<P/>
      <H4>Instructions</H4>
      <OL>
```

```
        <xsl:for-each select="Recipe/Instructions">
          <LI><xsl:value-of select="Step"/></LI>
        </xsl:for-each>
        </OL>
      </body>
      </html>
  </xsl:template>
  </xsl:stylesheet>
```

This style sheet does several interesting things. First, note the xsl:template match="/" element. As I've said, XSLT transformations occur by applying templates to specific parts of the XML document. The match attribute of this element specifies, via what's known as XML Path (XPath) syntax, what part of the document the template should apply to. In this case, it's the root element. So, the style sheet is saying, "Locate the root element of the document, and when you find it, insert the following text into the output document." What follows are several lines of standard HTML that set up the header of the Web page.

Note the xsl: prefix on the template element. It refers to the xsl namespace. The xsl namespace is where the template element and the other xsl:-prefixed names are defined. Adding the namespace reference makes the xsl: prefix available to the document so that it can reference those names. The URI reference is at the top of the style sheet. It has the following form:

```
<xsl:stylesheet version="1.0"
xmlns:xsl="http://www.w3.org/1999/XSL/Transform">
```

Next, notice the HTML table header information that's generated by the style sheet. It contains three sets of HTML <TH> tags that set up the column headers for the table. This section of the code matches that of the original HTML document we created earlier.

The most interesting part of the document is the looping it does. This is where the real power of XSLT lies. Notice the first xsl:for-each loop (bolded). An XSLT for-each loop does exactly what it sounds like: It iterates through a collection of nodes at the same level in a document. The base node from which it works is identified by its select attribute. In this case, that's the Recipe/Ingredients/Ingredient node. As with the earlier match attribute, this is an XPath to the node we want to access. What this means is that we're going to loop through the ingredients for the recipe. For each one we find, we'll generate a new row in the table.

Note the way in which the nodes within each Ingredient element are referenced. We use the xsl:value-of element to insert the value of each field in each ingredient as we come to it. To access the unit attribute of the Qty element, we use the XPath attribute syntax, /@*name*, where *name* is the attribute we want to access.

Note the paragraph tag <P/> that follows the looping code. Traditional HTML would permit this tag to be specified without a matching closing tag, but not XML. And this brings up an important point: When you provide HTML code for a style sheet to generate, it must be well formed. That is, it must comply with the rules that dictate whether an XML document is well formed. Remember: A style sheet is an XML document in every sense of the word. It must be well formed or it cannot be parsed.

The code finishes up with another for-each loop. This one lists the Step elements in each Instructions element. Note the use of the HTML Ordered List (<OL>) and List Item (<LI>) tags. These work just like they do in standard HTML—they produce a numbered list.

You have several options for using this style sheet to transform the recipe.xml document. You could use Microsoft's standalone XSLT transformer, you could use a third-party XSLT transformer, or you could use the one that's built into your browser, if your browser supports direct XSLT transformations. See the Tools subsection below for more information, but, in my case, I'm using Internet Explorer's built-in XSLT transformer. This requires the addition of an <?xml-stylesheet> element to the XML document itself, just beneath the <?xml version> tag. Here's the complete element:

```
<?xml-stylesheet type="text/xsl" href="recipe3.xsl"?>
```

As you can see, the element contains an href attribute that references the style sheet using a URI. Now, every time I view the XML document in Internet Explorer, the style sheet will automatically be applied in order to transform it. Listing 8.7 shows the HTML code that's generated by using the style sheet.

Listing 8.7 The HTML Code Generated by the Transformation

```
<html>
<HEAD>
<TITLE>Henderson's Hotter-than-Hell Habanero Sauce</TITLE>
</HEAD>
<body>
<H3>Henderson's Hotter-than-Hell Habanero Sauce</H3>
```

```
   Homegrown from stuff in my garden
   (you don't want to know exactly what).
<H4>Ingredients</H4>
<table border="2">
<tr BGCOLOR="#00FF00">
<TH>Qty</TH>
<TH>Units</TH>
<TH>Item</TH>
</tr>
<tr>
<td>6</td>
<td>each</td>
<td>Habanero peppers</td>
</tr>
<tr>
<td>12</td>
<td>each</td>
<td>Cowhorn peppers</td>
</tr>
<tr>
<td>12</td>
<td>each</td>
<td>Jalapeno peppers</td>
</tr>
<tr>
<td></td>
<td>dash</td>
<td>Tequila</td>
</tr>
</table>
<P />
<H4>Instructions</H4>
<OL>
<LI>Chop up peppers, removing their stems, then grind to a liq-
uid.</LI>
</OL>
</body>
</html>
```

Figure 8.2 shows how Listing 8.7 looks when viewed from a browser.
While it's nifty to be able to translate the XML document into well-formed HTML that matches our original example, what does that really buy

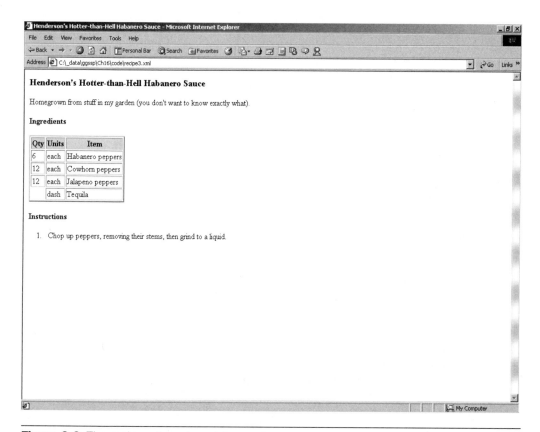

Figure 8.2 The recipe when viewed from a browser

us? Wouldn't it have been easier just to create the document using HTML in the first place?

Perhaps it would have been easier to create this one document in HTML without using XML and a style sheet. However, by separating the storage of the data from its presentation, we can radically alter its formatting without affecting the data. That's not true of HTML. To understand this, look over the style sheet shown in Listing 8.8.

Listing 8.8 A Completely Different Transformation for the Same XML Document

```
<?xml version='1.0'?>
<xsl:stylesheet version="1.0"
xmlns:xsl="http://www.w3.org/1999/XSL/Transform">
```

```
<xsl:template match="/">
  <html>
  <HEAD>
  <TITLE>Henderson&apos;s Hotter-than-Hell Habanero Sauce</TITLE>
  </HEAD>
  <body>
    <H3>Henderson&apos;s Hotter-than-Hell Habanero Sauce</H3>
      Homegrown from stuff in my garden
      (you don&apos;t want to know exactly what).
      <H4>Ingredients</H4>
      <UL>
        <xsl:for-each select="Recipe/Ingredients/Ingredient">
        <LI>
        <xsl:value-of select="Qty"/>&#9;<xsl:value-of
            select="Qty/@unit"/> of <xsl:value-of select="Item"/>
        </LI>
        </xsl:for-each>
      </UL>
      <P/>
      <H4>Instructions</H4>
      <table border="2">
      <tr BGCOLOR="#00FF00">
        <TH>#</TH>
        <TH>Step</TH>
      </tr>
      <xsl:for-each select="Recipe/Instructions">
      <tr>
        <td><xsl:value-of select="position()"/></td>
        <td><xsl:value-of select="Step"/></td>
      </tr>
      </xsl:for-each>
      </table>
  </body>
  </html>
</xsl:template>
</xsl:stylesheet>
```

We can use this style sheet to transform the XML document into a completely different HTML layout than the first one (you can specify a new style sheet for a document by changing the document's <?xml-stylesheet> element or by overriding it in your XSLT transformation tool). Figure 8.3 shows how the new Web page looks in a browser.

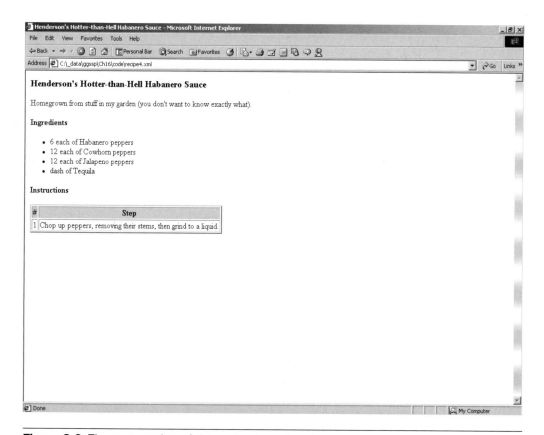

Figure 8.3 The new version of the recipe page in a browser

As you can see, the page formatting is completely different. The ingredients table is gone, replaced by a bulleted list. Conversely, the Instructions steps have been moved from an ordered list into a table. The formatting has changed completely, but the data is the same. The XML document didn't change at all.

Since the data now has context, we can access it directly. There's no need to hard-code table column or table row references to the HTML and translate the data out of HTML into a usable data format—the data is already in such a format. And, regardless of how we decide to transform or format the data, that will always be true. Because it's stored in XML, the data can be manipulated in virtually any way we see fit.

The xsl:for-each element in our style sheets gave us a glimpse of some of XSLT's power. Like most languages, much of its utility can be found in its ability to perform a task repetitively. XSLT defines a number of constructs that are similarly powerful, among them:

- xsl:if
- xsl:choose
- xsl:sort
- xsl:attribute
- Embedded scripting—IBM's LotusXSL package provides most of the functionality of XSLT, including the ability to call embedded ECMAScript, the European standard JavaScript, from XSLT templates.

You can check the XSLT specification itself for the full list, but suffice it to say—XSLT brings to bear some of the real power and extensibility of XML. It's an example of what I like to refer to as the "programmable data" aspect of XML. Via XSLT, we have the ability not only to specify how data is formatted but also to programmatically change it *from within the data itself*. That's powerful stuff indeed.

Because we've been carrying out formatting-related tasks with XSLT and XML, it might appear that XML is just a content management technology. That's not the case—it's far more than that. Certainly, from the perspective of Web masters, the XML family of technologies offers huge advancements over HTML. However, XML is about more than just formatting data or managing content. It is about *data* and giving that data sufficient context to be useful in a wide variety of situations. There's a whole world of applications outside the realm of browsers and Web pages. To add the power of XML to those types of applications, we use the DOM.

The Document Object Model

Thus far, we've explored XML from the standpoint of generalizing document formats. But XML's real power comes into play when it is used to structure information.

All XML documents consist of nested sets of elements. Every document is wrapped in a root element, which in turn houses other elements. The structure is a natural tree—a tree of elements—objects that represent the content of the document. The DOM goes beyond the simple text stream approach and provides a language-neutral means of working with an XML document as a tree of objects.

This object-oriented access to XML documents opens the door to a whole host of other uses for XML. It makes it trivial to incorporate XML as an interprocess or interapplication data interchange mechanism because all you deal with are objects in your programming language of choice. It's doesn't matter whether that language is Visual Basic, Java, or C#; you can read, manipulate, and generally process XML documents by calling methods on objects and accessing their properties.

Think of all the possibilities this brings with it. For example, imagine a database system where the entire database was represented as an XML document. Need a schema of the database? No problem—extract the XML schema from the DOM, run it through an XSLT transformation, and you've got yourself a browsable database schema that's always current. Want to write a unified tool that can administer objects on SQL Server, Oracle, DB2, and all the other big players in the DBMS space without having to code to each of the administrative APIs separately? Have them expose their database schemas as DOM trees, and you should be able to build a single tool that works with all of them.

Already, vendors are putting DOM and XML to use in scenarios like the ones I've just described. SQL Server has certainly done its fair share of this, as we'll discuss later in the book.

Processing XML with MSXML

MSXML supports two basic APIs for processing XML: DOM and SAX (the Simple API for XML). Let's start with DOM.

MSXML and DOM

As I've mentioned, the DOM method involves parsing an XML document and loading it into a tree structure in memory. An XML document parsed via DOM is known as a DOM document (or just DOM, for short). Listing 8.9 presents a simple VB application that demonstrates parsing an XML document via DOM and querying it for a particular node set. (You can find the source code for this app in the CH08\domltest subfolder on the CD accompanying this book.)

Listing 8.9 A VB App That Processes an XML Document via DOM

```
Private Sub Command1_Click()

  Dim bstrDoc As String

  bstrDoc = "<Songs> " & _
  "<Song title='One More Day' artist='Diamond Rio' />" & _
  "<Song title='Hard Habit to Break' artist='Chicago' />" & _
  "<Song title='Forever' artist='Kenny Loggins' />" & _
  "<Song title='Boys of Summer' artist='Don Henley' />" & _
  "<Song title='Cherish' artist='Kool and the Gang' />" & _
  "<Song title='Dance' artist='Lee Ann Womack' />" & _
  "<Song title='I Will Always Love You' artist= _
       'Whitney Houston' />" & _
"</Songs>"

  Dim xmlDoc As New DOMDocument30

  If Len(Text1.Text) = 0 Then
    Text1.Text = bstrDoc
  End If

  If Not xmlDoc.loadXML(Text1.Text) Then
    MsgBox "Error loading document"
  Else
    Dim oNodes As IXMLDOMNodeList
    Dim oNode As IXMLDOMNode

    If Len(Text2.Text) = 0 Then
      Text2.Text = "//Song/@title"
    End If
    Set oNodes = xmlDoc.selectNodes(Text2.Text)

    For Each oNode In oNodes
      If Not (oNode Is Nothing) Then
        sName = oNode.nodeName
        sData = oNode.xml
        MsgBox "Node <" + sName + ">:" _
           + vbNewLine + vbTab + sData + vbNewLine
      End If
    Next

    Set xmlDoc = Nothing
  End If
End Sub
```

We begin by instantiating a DOMDocument object. The DOMDocument object is the key to everything else we do with DOM using MSXML. We next call DOMDocument.loadXML to parse the XML document and load it into the DOM tree. Once the document is loaded into memory, we can query it via XPath queries or manipulate it further by making DOMDocument method calls. In this example, we call the selectNodes method to query the document via XPath. DOMDocument's selectNodes method returns a node list object, which we can then loop through using For Each. For each node in the node set, we display the node name followed by its contents. Parsing an XML document via DOM turns the document into a memory object that we can then work with just as we would any other object. We're able to access and manipulate the document as though it were an object because that's exactly what it is.

MSXML and SAX

Like DOM, SAX is a W3C standard. Rather than providing an application access to XML data by materializing the document entirely in memory, SAX is an event-driven API. An application processes an XML document via SAX by responding to SAX events. As the SAX processor reads through the document, it raises an event each time it encounters a new node or section of the document. It then triggers the appropriate application event handler code and passes the relevant data about the event to the application. The application can then decide what to do in response—it could store the event data in some type of tree structure, as is the case with DOM processing; it could ignore the event; it could search the event data for a particular node or value; or it could take some other action. Once the application handles the raised event, the SAX processor continues processing the document. At no point does it store the entire document in memory as DOM does. It's really just a parsing mechanism to which an application can attach its own functionality. This is, in fact, the case with MSXML's DOM loader—SAX is its underlying parsing mechanism. MSXML's DOM loader sets up SAX event handlers that store the data passed to them via SAX in a DOM tree.

Given that SAX doesn't persist document data in memory, it's inherently far less memory consumptive than DOM. SAX is also much more trouble to use. By persisting documents in memory, DOM makes working with XML documents as easy as working with any other kind of object.

Listing 8.10 shows some VB code that demonstrates how to use SAX. It consists of three main modules: the main form, a content handler class, and an error handler class. (You can find the full source code for this application in the SAX subfolder under the CH08 folder on the CD accompanying this book.)

Listing 8.10 A VB App That Processes an XML Document via SAX

```
' Main form
Option Explicit

Private Sub Command1_Click()

    'Create the SAX reader object
    Dim reader As New SAXXMLReader

    'Set up the event handlers
    Dim CHandler As New ContentHandler
    Set reader.ContentHandler = CHandler

    Dim EHandler As New ErrorHandler
    Set reader.ErrorHandler = EHandler

    Text1.text = ""
    On Error GoTo ErrorTrap

    reader.parseURL (App.Path & "\" & Text2.text)
    Exit Sub

ErrorTrap:
    Text1.text = Text1.text & "Error: " & Err.Number & " : "
        & Err.Description

End Sub

' Content handler
Option Explicit

Implements IVBSAXContentHandler

Private Sub IVBSAXContentHandler_startElement(strNamespaceURI
    As String, strLocalName As String, strQName As String, ByVal
    attributes As MSXML2.IVBSAXAttributes)

    Form1.Text1.text = Form1.Text1.text & "__ELEMENT START__" &
        vbCrLf & "<" & strLocalName
```

```
        Dim i As Integer
        For i = 0 To (attributes.length - 1)
            Form1.Text1.text = Form1.Text1.text & " " &
                attributes.getLocalName(i) & "=""" &
                attributes.getValue(i) & """"
        Next

        Form1.Text1.text = Form1.Text1.text & ">" & vbCrLf

End Sub

Private Sub IVBSAXContentHandler_endElement(strNamespaceURI
    As String, strLocalName As String, strQName As String)

        Form1.Text1.text = Form1.Text1.text & "__ELEMENT END__" &
            vbCrLf & "</" & strLocalName & ">" & vbCrLf

End Sub

Private Sub IVBSAXContentHandler_characters(text As String)
        text = Replace(text, vbLf, vbCrLf)
        Form1.Text1.text = Form1.Text1.text & "__CHARACTERS__" &
            vbCrLf & text & vbCrLf
End Sub

Private Property Set IVBSAXContentHandler_documentLocator
    (ByVal RHS As MSXML2.IVBSAXLocator)
        Form1.Text1.text = Form1.Text1.text & "__DOCUMENT_LOCATOR__" &
            vbCrLf
End Property

Private Sub IVBSAXContentHandler_endDocument()
        Form1.Text1.text = Form1.Text1.text & "__DOCUMENT END__" &
            vbCrLf
End Sub

Private Sub IVBSAXContentHandler_endPrefixMapping(strPrefix
    As String)
        Form1.Text1.text = Form1.Text1.text & "__PREFIX MAPPING__" &
            vbCrLf & strPrefix & vbCrLf
End Sub

Private Sub IVBSAXContentHandler_ignorableWhitespace(strChars
    As String)
```

```
        Form1.Text1.text = Form1.Text1.text & "__IGNORABLE
            WHITESPACE__" & vbCrLf & strChars & vbCrLf
End Sub


Private Sub IVBSAXContentHandler_processingInstruction(target
    As String, data As String)
        Form1.Text1.text = Form1.Text1.text & "__PROCESSING
            INSTRUCTION__" & vbCrLf & "<?" & target & " " &
            data & ">" & vbCrLf
End Sub


Private Sub IVBSAXContentHandler_skippedEntity(strName As String)
        Form1.Text1.text = Form1.Text1.text & "__SKIPPED ENTITY__" &
            vbCrLf & strName & vbCrLf
End Sub


Private Sub IVBSAXContentHandler_startDocument()
        Form1.Text1.text = Form1.Text1.text & "__DOCUMENT START__" &
            vbCrLf
End Sub


Private Sub IVBSAXContentHandler_startPrefixMapping(strPrefix
    As String, strURI As String)
        Form1.Text1.text = Form1.Text1.text & "__START PREFIX
        MAPPING__" & strPrefix & " " & strURI & " " & vbCrLf
End Sub

' Error handler
Option Explicit

Implements IVBSAXErrorHandler


Private Sub IVBSAXErrorHandler_fatalError
    (ByVal lctr As IVBSAXLocator, msg As String, ByVal
    errCode As Long)
        Form1.Text1.text = Form1.Text1.text & "Fatal error: " &
        msg & " Code: " & errCode
End Sub


Private Sub IVBSAXErrorHandler_error(ByVal lctr As IVBSAXLocator,
    msg As String, ByVal errCode As Long)
        Form1.Text1.text = Form1.Text1.text & "Error: " & msg &
            " Code: " & errCode
```

```
End Sub

Private Sub IVBSAXErrorHandler_ignorableWarning
    (ByVal oLocator As MSXML2.IVBSAXLocator,
    strErrorMessage As String, ByVal nErrorCode As Long)

End Sub
```

As I said earlier, an application makes use of the SAX engine by invoking the SAX parser and responding to the events it raises. To use MSXML's SAX engine in a VB application, you implement SAX interfaces such as IVBSAX-ContentHandler, IVBSAXErrorHandler, IVBSAXDeclHandler, IVBSAXDT-DHandler, and IVBSAXLexicalHandler. Implementing these interfaces amounts to setting up event handlers to respond to the events they define. In this example code, I've implemented IVBSAXContentHandler and IVBSAX-ErrorHandler via the ContentHandler and ErrorHandler classes.

We begin by instantiating a SAXXMLReader object. This object will process an XML document we pass it and raise events as appropriate as it reads through the document. The code in the ContentHandler and ErrorHandler classes will respond to these events and write descriptive text to the main form.

Resources

Further Reading

- I've found Liz Castro's book *XML for the World Wide Web: Visual QuickStart Guide* (Berkeley, CA: Peachpit Press, 2000) to be a concise yet thorough treatment of the subject. Liz writes good books, and I've found this one particularly useful.
- *XML in a Nutshell, 2nd Edition* (Sebastopol, CA: O'Reilly, 2001) by W. Scott Means and Elliotte Rusty Harold also offers a concise treatment of the subject material and even gets into some of the more esoteric areas of the language.
- Steve Holzner's *Inside XML* (Indianapolis, IN: New Riders, 2000) is also a good read. It's comprehensive and covers many key XML subjects in great detail.

- Erik T. Ray's *Learning XML* (Sebastopol, CA: O'Reilly, 2001) is another good introductory text. It contains a nice introduction to the many XML parsers out there and delves into a few topics (e.g., XML Schema) omitted by some of the other books.
- *XSLT Programmer's Reference* (Indianapolis, IN: Wrox, 2001) by Michael Kay will tell you everything you need to know about XSLT. Michael is also the author of SAXON, one of the best XSLT processors out there.
- The W3C's Web site (http://www.w3c.org) is as valuable a source on XML, HTML, and all things Web-related as you'll find. The specifications documents can be a little dry at times, but they're worth reading if you can get through them. The site also has a number of links to XML-related tutorials, free tools, and other resources.
- Most of the major software vendors have a large XML portal of some type available from their sites. I've found the Microsoft and Sun sites to be the most informative.

Tools

- You should begin by getting yourself a good XML/XSLT/XSD editor. I like XML Spy (http://www.xmlspy.com), but there are several good ones out there. Don't let anyone tell you that GUIs are for wimps. Using Notepad to spend hours doing what a GUI tool will do for you in seconds simply makes no sense. You end up wasting lots of time trudging around in clunky tools that could have been spent mastering the technology.
- You'll also want an XML Schema/DTD validator. I use the one that's freely downloadable from the Microsoft Web site, but there are several out there.
- Depending on your other tools, you may need a separate XSLT transform tool. I use Microsoft's XSLT tools, as well as James Clark's XT tool. Again, there are several freebies out there.
- If you run on Windows, get the latest version of the MSXML parser—it's the best one on the market.
- Michael Kay's SAXON tool is worth having even if you have other XSLT processors. It's a nice piece of software written by a master of the technology.
- The MSXML SDK is also worth having if you're on Windows. It contains some good sample code and documentation that will come in handy if you build applications using the MSXML APIs.

Recap

XML is programmable, hierarchical data. It is designed to be similar to HTML in terms of ease of use and similar to SGML in terms of power, extensibility, and expressiveness.

You can translate XML documents into other formats by using XSLT. Often the target format is HTML, but it does not have to be. Translating between divergent document formats is also quite common.

DTDs and XML schemas help ensure that an XML document is not only well formed but also valid. A document can be well formed and still have invalid data in it. It's up to a validating XML parser to check the document against its DTD or XML schema to ensure that it contains valid data.

DOM is a popular API for processing XML documents as objects. Put succinctly, DOM loads an XML document into a tree object, which you may then manipulate by getting and setting the object's properties and by calling its methods.

SAX is also an increasingly popular XML processing API. Unlike DOM, it does not load an entire XML document into memory. Instead, it reads through the document, raising events as it goes. It's up to the calling application to respond to those events.

XML is not just one technology—it's a whole family of technologies, and those technologies continue to evolve and continue to be adopted by more people around the world with each passing day. It's crucial to learn as much as you can about XML now so that you can make the best use of SQL Server's XML-related features—both those it has today and those coming in the future. Here's a bold prediction for you: The day will come when XML will be at least as important to SQL Server application development as Transact-SQL is today. It's definitely time to dive in.

Knowledge Measure

1. True or false: You can add your own tags to HTML, but you cannot add custom attributes.
2. What's the name of the MSXML SAX reader object?
3. Does XML support the notion of empty elements?
4. What's the maximum number of root nodes an XML document can have?
5. True or false: You use an XML schema to translate an XML document from one format into another.

6. In the code fragment <foo "bar"/>, what type of document node is "bar"?
7. True or false: It's possible for a document to be valid but not well formed.
8. What classic data structure does an XML document that's been loaded into memory via DOM most closely resemble?
9. True or false: Like HTML, XML is not case-sensitive.
10. Explain the function of xsl:for-each.
11. True or false: DOM document processing tends to be more memory consumptive than SAX document processing.
12. Is an XML element that contains attributes but no other elements or data considered empty?
13. Is the code fragment <Customer lastname=Brown/> a valid XML element?
14. True or false: XML parsers are typically more tolerant of tag nesting mismatches than HTML parsers.
15. Describe the functional difference, if there is one, between this XML:

```
<foo></foo>
```

and this XML:

```
<foo/>
```

PART II

Subsystems, Components, and Technologies

CHAPTER 9

SQL Server as a Server

> *We want to stand upon our own feet and look fair and square at the world—its good facts, its bad facts, its beauties, and its ugliness; see the world as it is and be not afraid of it. Conquer the world by intelligence and not merely by being slavishly subdued by the terror that comes from it.*
>
> —Bertrand Russell[1]

In this chapter, we'll talk about SQL Server as a Windows server application. Earlier in the book, we discussed the Win32 networking and I/O API functions that Windows servers call to carry out their work. We talked about the process and threading APIs, thread scheduling and synchronization, memory management, and COM. Here we'll talk about how some of these are used by SQL Server itself and where it fits in the general taxonomy of Windows server applications.

NOTE: In this chapter I assume that you've already read Chapters 5 and 6, I/O Fundamentals and Networking, respectively. If you haven't yet read through those chapters, you will probably want to before proceeding.

SQL Server and Networking

You'll recall that in the Networking chapter I said that SQL Server uses standard networking API calls to accept and process connections. You're probably already aware that SQL Server calls into its network library code

---

1. Russell, Bertrand. "What We Must Do." *Little Blue Book No. 1372.* Girard, KS: Haldeman-Julius Company, 1929, p. 20.

(which resides in separate DLLs) to accept and process user connections. What you may not be aware of is that these DLLs, in turn, call standard Windows networking API functions to carry out their work.

When listening for connections over TCP/IP, the Windows socket APIs that we discussed in the Networking chapter are used heavily. The SQL Server Net-Library code calls accept and WSAAccept to accept new connections and the various other socket and Win32 I/O API functions to process client requests and return data. As we saw in the Networking chapter, socket handles returned by Windows' implementation of the socket API can be used with standard Win32 file I/O functions such as ReadFile and WriteFile.

When listening for connections over named pipes, the Net-Library code uses the standard Win32 file I/O API functions to process new connection requests and process and return results from client requests. As you learned in the Networking chapter, Windows applications interact with named (and anonymous) pipes using the same Win32 I/O functions that are used when interacting with disk files.

SQL Server supports client connectivity using the multiprotocol Net-Library via the Win32 RPC API functions. Win32 applications communicate with one another over the RPC API via stub (or proxy) functions that the client calls. These stub functions, in turn, make RPC API calls to marshal each function call and its parameter data to the destination server. On the destination server, the call is unmarshaled and the actual server-side function to which the proxy function corresponded is called. In this way, the RPC API provides a call-level interface to network communications, rather than the packet-, byte-, or message-oriented interfaces normally presented by Windows networking API libraries. When a SQL Server client connects over the multiprotocol Net-Library to SQL Server, it essentially makes procedure calls into the server-side version of the library that are marshaled and sent across the network to the target SQL Server. The server-side Net-Library then processes these calls and feeds the client requests into the normal network I/O processing code line used by the other Net-Libraries.

SQL Server uses an I/O completion port to allow connection I/O to be processed asynchronously. As I mentioned in the I/O Fundamentals chapter, an I/O completion port that's associated with a file (or socket) object receives a new completion packet each time an asynchronous I/O operation that was initiated for the associated object completes. This design allows SQL Server to support a high number of concurrent client connections with a minimum number of dedicated network-related worker threads.

Each Net-Library receives a separate worker thread that it uses to listen for connections and process network-related I/O. If your server is listening on TCP/IP sockets and named pipes, each associated Net-Library uses its own worker thread.

You can see how SQL Server's Net-Library code makes use of the API functions we discussed in Chapters 5 and 6 by using WinDbg. Work through Exercise 9.1 to get a good feel for the types and frequency of the networking API calls that SQL Server makes.

Exercise 9.1 Inspecting SQL Server's Use of Windows Networking API Functions

1. Stop your development or test SQL Server instance if it is running. For this exercise, you should be the server's only user.
2. Start WinDbg and be sure your symbol paths are set correctly as described in Chapter 2.
3. From the WinDbg File menu, select Open Executable and locate your SQL Server executable (sqlservr.exe). Set the command line parameters to:

   ```
   -c -sYourInstanceName
   ```

   where YourInstanceName is the name of your SQL Server instance. If you are using the default instance, omit the -s parameter altogether.
4. Click the OK button to start SQL Server under WinDbg. Once you see the WinDbg command prompt, add the following breakpoints:

   ```
   bp WS2_32!WSAAccept
   bp WS2_32!accept
   bp WS2_32!listen
   ```

5. Now, type g in the WinDbg command window and press Enter to allow SQL Server to start up.
6. Start Query Analyzer and attempt to connect to your server. You should see some of your breakpoints tripped immediately. Add the following additional breakpoints:

   ```
   bp kernel32!GetQueuedCompletionStatus
   bp kernel32!ReadFile
   ```

7. Type g and press Enter again to allow SQL Server to run. Your new connection should succeed in Query Analyzer. Now open a new connection. Again, you should see some of your breakpoints tripped, including some of the new ones you just set. Type g and press Enter to bump through these. You should see that some of them are hit repeatedly as your new connection is processed and the default ODBC connection options are processed by the server.

8. At this point, you're done. Press Shift+F5 to stop debugging, then close WinDbg. You will need to restart your server to continue working with it as it should be stopped after your debugging session completes.

If you work through the preceding exercise, you'll see that the networking API functions we explored in Chapter 6 and many of the I/O functions we investigated in Chapter 5 are used very heavily by SQL Server's Net-Library code. Understanding how these work and what they're typically used for will give you good insight into how SQL Server itself works.

The SQL Server Executable

SQL Server's executable is named sqlservr.exe and resides in the binn folder under your main SQL Server installation. The folder is named binn because earlier releases of SQL Server shipped 16-bit client-side executables and libraries and these were stored in a folder named bin. The binn folder was reserved for 32-bit executables and libraries (the extra "n" signified "NT"). SQL Server no longer ships any 16-bit binaries, but the folder name for 32-bit binaries has remained unchanged.

The sqlservr.exe executable is a multithreaded console mode Win32 application. It can run as a console application or as a service and can write its output to the console, the error log, and to the Windows event log.

sqlservr.exe is linked with the LARGEADDRESSAWARE linker switch. This means that it can take advantage of user mode address space above 2GB. As I mentioned in Chapter 4, when a member of the Windows NT Server family (e.g., Windows 2000 Server, Windows Server 2003, and so on) is booted with the /3GB switch (or /USERVA switch on Windows Server 2003), Windows increases the user mode portion of a process's virtual address space at the expense of the kernel mode portion. SQL Server is linked and coded such that it can take advantage of this and use more than 2GB of user mode virtual memory address space when the operating system makes it available.

SQL Server's DLLs

SQL Server's main executable, sqlservr.exe, statically imports nine different DLLs. Table 9.1 lists these and indicates the main purpose of each one.

Table 9.1 SQL Server's Statically Linked DLLs

DLL Name	Purpose
Kernel32.dll	Win32 kernel function library
AdvApi32.dll	Win32 security function library
User32.dll	Win32 windowing and application library
Rpcrt4.dll	Win32 RPC runtime library
Opends60.dll	**SQL Server Open Data Services library**
Ums.dll	**SQL Server User Mode Scheduler library**
Msvcrt.dll	Multithreaded Visual C++ runtime library
Sqlsort.dll	**SQL Server collation and string comparison library**
Msvcirt.dll	Old Iostream Visual C++ library

Each of these must be present on the host system in order for SQL Server to start. Furthermore, any DLLs they require (Gdi32.dll, Ntdll.dll, and so on) must also be present in order for the server to successfully start. SQL Server also loads numerous DLLs dynamically on startup depending on the options selected (e.g., which Net-Libraries the server is configured to listen on) or when they're needed based on client requests and other activities on the server (e.g., OPENXML queries, linked server queries, BULK INSERT operations, and so on).

The three DLLs set in bold type in Table 9.1 ship with SQL Server and are, generally speaking, a matched set. Typically (but not always), these are updated together when a new service pack or hotfix is released for the product. Each of them includes a Windows version resource, so you can easily check their version strings by right-clicking them in Windows Explorer, selecting Properties, and selecting the Version tab in the Properties dialog.

SQL Server I/O

When running on a member of the Windows NT family, SQL Server performs as much file I/O as possible asynchronously. You'll recall from Chapter 5 that the standard Win32 API functions can be executed asynchronously when the file object they're working with has been opened with the FILE_FLAG_OVERLAPPED switch and a pointer to a valid OVERLAPPED structure is passed in to the functions that require it. For example, if you call CreateFile and pass in FILE_FLAG_OVERLAPPED, then call ReadFileEx with the returned file handle and a pointer to a valid OVERLAPPED structure, Windows will attempt to process your request asynchronously. SQL Server takes advantage of this Windows' facility to avoid blocking on I/O whenever possible.

There are situations, of course, that prevent SQL Server from processing I/O asynchronously. One obvious one is running it on a member of the Win9x family. Because Win9x doesn't support asynchronous file I/O, all SQL Server file I/O on Win9x is performed synchronously. SQL Server's UMS component is responsible for handling the scheduling of I/O requests and has special code to detect Win9x and perform I/O synchronously. See Chapter 10 for more information on UMS and its processing of asynchronous I/O.

Another example of a situation in which SQL Server can't use asynchronous I/O is when the MDF and LDF files that make up a database have been compressed using NTFS file compression. As I mentioned in Chapter 5, Windows prohibits the use of asynchronous file I/O against compressed files and will either turn any asynchronous request against such files into synchronous operations for those APIs that support synchronous I/O (e.g., ReadFile) or return an error for those that don't (e.g., ReadFileEx). This is one reason that Microsoft doesn't support the compression of database files.

SQL Server makes use of scatter-gather I/O in order to quickly load a contiguous disk file region into a set of buffers that may or may not be contiguous in memory. As we saw in Chapter 5, the ReadFileScatter and WriteFileGather Win32 API functions take a pointer to an array of I/O buffers, then either load data from disk into them or write data from them to disk. By supporting noncontiguous source and destination memory buffers, these API functions allow SQL Server to avoid having to use a contiguous intermediary buffer that matches the size of the disk file region being read or written to and copying it to or from a series of noncontiguous memory buffers. First introduced in a service pack for Windows NT 4.0, scatter-gather I/O allows SQL Server to achieve better scalability and greater performance than would otherwise be possible. It allows the BPool and MemToLeave memory managers to do what they do best—manage large numbers of noncontiguous buffers without having to be concerned with locating any of them in particular proximity to the others based on I/O requirements—while still allowing the storage engine to process I/O as quickly as possible. See Chapter 5 for more information on scatter-gather I/O.

SQL Server Components

I will end this chapter by talking in broad terms about the various SQL Server components involved in processing the typical client request. Several of these are discussed in more detail in other chapters; we'll just hit the high points here. A typical client request is one that queries the server for data that resides in a database. Understanding how these components interoperate and the workflow between them will give you some good insight into how the server works internally.

As I've mentioned, client requests come into the server via SQL Server's Net-Libraries. These requests are then scheduled for processing via UMS. The language processing and execution (LPE) component within the server then takes each request and passes it to the query processor (QP) for optimization. LPE and QP are members of the relational engine. Once a client query is optimized and an execution plan is produced for it, LPE executes it via calls from the relational engine to the storage engine (SE). The storage engine carries out the physical I/O, table and index traversal, data retrieval, and so on necessary to carry out the request from the relational engine. The communication between the LPE and SE components occurs via COM using calls to OLE DB interfaces. See Chapter 7 for more information on interfaces and COM in general.

So, the key components and technologies involved in the processing of a typical client request include the Net-Libraries, UMS, LPE, QP, SE, and OLE DB. All of these are touched every time a client submits a query against a SQL Server database for processing. All along the way, SQL Server's various memory managers are accessed each time a component within the server requires a memory allocation. See Chapter 12 for more information on the sequence of events that occurs when a query is processed. See Chapter 11 for more information on how SQL Server manages memory.

Recap

SQL Server is a complex Windows app. There's nothing magical about it that makes it different from other Windows apps; it simply makes heavy use of the Win32 API functions, C/C++ runtime library functions, COM interfaces, and so on that any Windows app can use. It presents a sophisticated, multithreaded Windows application that clients can connect to and to which they can submit requests for data from databases, requests related to the storage of that data, and other administrative commands in the form of Transact-SQL. As a request is processed, its results—if any—are sent back to the requesting client via the same mechanisms that delivered the request in the first place.

Knowledge Measure

1. What component within SQL Server is responsible for scheduling I/O operations?
2. When the multiprotocol Net-Library is used to connect to SQL Server, what underlying Windows API is used?
3. What Windows kernel object has a completion packet queued to it when an asynchronous I/O operation completes on a file or socket to which it has been linked?
4. SQL Server's LPE and QP components are members of which larger component within the server?
5. True or false: Scatter-gather I/O supports writing a set of contiguous memory buffers to a series of noncontiguous disk file regions using a single API call.
6. What is the purpose of the Sqlsort.dll file that ships with SQL Server?
7. True or false: Because SQL Server is linked with the LARGEAD-DRESSAWARE linker switch, it can take advantage of a 3GB user mode virtual memory address space if the operating system provides it.
8. What technology is used to communicate between the relational engine and the storage engine within the server?
9. True or false: Although SQL Server statically links several DLLs, it also explicitly loads several of them either at startup or as it runs, depending on the way it's configured and the commands executed by users.
10. In addition to /3GB, what other switch can be used with Windows Server 2003 to increase the size of the user mode virtual address space available to applications that are large address aware such as SQL Server?

CHAPTER 10

User Mode Scheduler

To those searching for the truth—not the truth of dogma and darkness but the truth brought by reason, search, examination, and inquiry, discipline is required. For faith, as well intentioned as it may be, must be built on facts, not fiction—faith in fiction is a damnable false hope.

—Thomas Edison[1]

Up through version 6.5, SQL Server used Windows' scheduling facilities to schedule worker threads, switch between threads, and generally handle the work of multitasking. This worked reasonably well and allowed SQL Server to leverage Windows' hard-learned lessons regarding scalability and efficient processor use.

Between versions 6.5 and 7.0, however, it became evident that SQL Server was beginning to hit a "scalability ceiling." Its ability to handle thousands of concurrent users and efficiently scale on systems with more than four processors was hampered by the fact that the Windows scheduler treated SQL Server like any other application. Contrary to what some people believed at the time, SQL Server 6.5 made use of no hidden APIs to reach the scalability levels it achieved. It used the basic thread and thread synchronization primitives we discussed earlier in this book, and Windows scheduled SQL Server worker threads on and off the processor(s) just as it did any other process. Clearly, this one-size-fits-all approach was not the most optimal solution for a high-performance app like SQL Server, so the SQL Server development team began looking at ways to optimize the scheduling process.

---

1. Edison, Thomas. As quoted in *The Book Your Church Does Not Want You to Read,* ed. Tim C. Leedom. San Diego, CA: The Truth Seeker Company, 1993, p. 4.

UMS Design Goals

Several goals were established at the outset of this research. The scheduling facility needed to:

- Support fibers, a feature new in Windows NT 4.0, and abstract working with them so that the core engine would not need separate code lines for thread mode and fiber mode
- Avoid causing a thread to switch into kernel mode whenever possible
- Avoid context switches as much as possible
- Support asynchronous I/O and abstract working with it so that the core engine would not need a separate code line for versions of Windows that do not support asynchronous file I/O (e.g., Windows 9x and Windows ME)

Ultimately, it was decided that SQL Server 7.0 should handle its own scheduling. From that decision, the User Mode Scheduler (UMS) component was born.

UMS acts as a thin layer between the server and the operating system. It resides in a file named UMS.DLL and is designed to provide a programming model that's very similar to the Win32 thread scheduling and asynchronous I/O model. Programmers familiar with one would instantly be at home in the other.

Its primary function is to keep as much of the SQL Server scheduling process as possible in user mode. This means that UMS necessarily tries to avoid context switching because that involves the kernel. As I mentioned in Chapter 3, context switches can be expensive and can limit scalability. In pathological situations, a process can spend more time switching thread contexts than actually working.

User Mode vs. Kernel Mode Scheduling

You may be wondering what the advantage of moving the scheduling management inside the SQL Server process is. Wouldn't SQL Server just end up duplicating functionality already provided by Windows? With all the smart people Microsoft must have working on Windows and its scheduler, how likely is it that the SQL Server team could come up with something that much more scalable?

I'll address this in detail below, but the short answer is that SQL Server knows its own scheduling needs better than Windows or any other code base outside the product could hope to. UMS doesn't duplicate the complete functionality of the Windows scheduler, anyway—it implements only the basic features related to task scheduling, timers, and asynchronous I/O and, in fact, relies on Windows' own thread scheduling and synchronization primitives. Several Windows scheduling concepts (e.g., thread priority) have no direct counterparts in UMS.

Preemptive vs. Cooperative Tasking

An important difference—in fact, probably the most important difference— between Windows' scheduler and SQL Server's UMS is that Windows' scheduler is a preemptive scheduler, while UMS implements a cooperative model. What does this mean? It means that Windows prevents a single thread from monopolizing a processor. As we discussed in Chapter 3, each thread gets a specified time slice in which to run, after which Windows automatically schedules it off the processor and allows another thread to run if one is ready to do so. UMS, by contrast, relies on threads to voluntarily yield. If a SQL Server worker thread does not voluntarily yield, it will likely prevent other threads from running.

You may be wondering why UMS would take this approach. If you're an old-timer like me, you might recall that Windows 3.x worked exactly the same way—it made use of a cooperative scheduler, and it wasn't difficult for a misbehaving app to take over the system. This was, in fact, why Windows NT was designed from the ground up to make use of a preemptive scheduler. As long as a single app could bring down the system, you could never have anything even approaching a robust operating system.

UMS takes the approach it does in order to keep from involving the Windows kernel any more than absolutely necessary. In a system where worker threads can be counted on to yield when they should, a cooperative scheduler can actually be more efficient than a preemptive one because the scheduling process can be tailored to the specific needs of the application. As I said earlier, UMS knows SQL Server's scheduling needs better than the operating system can be expected to.

How UMS Takes Over Scheduling

If UMS is to handle SQL Server's scheduling needs rather than allowing Windows to do so, UMS must somehow prevent the OS from doing what it does with every other process: schedule threads on and off the system's processor(s) as it sees fit. How do you do that in a preemptive OS? UMS pulls this off through some clever tricks with Windows event objects. Each thread under UMS has an associated event object. For purposes of scheduling, Windows ignores threads it does not consider viable—threads that cannot run because they are in an infinite wait state. Knowing this, UMS puts threads to sleep that it does not want to be scheduled by having them call WaitForSingleObject on their corresponding event object and passing INFINITE for the timeout value. As you'll recall from Chapter 3, when a thread calls WaitForSingleObject to wait on an object and passes INFINITE for the timeout value, the only way to awaken the thread is for the object to be signaled. When UMS wants a given thread to run, it signals the thread's corresponding event object. This allows the thread to come out of its wait state and permits Windows to schedule it to run on a processor.

In order to prevent Windows from scheduling multiple threads on the same processor and thereby incurring the overhead and expense of context switches, UMS attempts to keep just one thread viable—that is, not in an infinite wait state—per processor. There are exceptions to this (e.g., full-text queries, security validations, xproc invocations, linked server queries, and so on), but the system is designed to allow just one thread per processor to run at a time.

The UMS Scheduler

The UMS mechanism for managing the scheduling process and for ensuring that only one thread per processor is active at any given time is called a scheduler. When SQL Server starts, one UMS scheduler is created for each processor in the machine. These schedulers are not affinitized to specific processors by default, but Windows' scheduling algorithms work out such that, over time, with each UMS scheduler allowing just one thread to run, that thread should end up on its own processor.

The worker pool for the server—regardless of whether it consists of threads or fibers—is distributed evenly across the UMS schedulers. This means that if you have max worker threads set to the default of 255 and you have a four-processor machine, SQL Server creates four UMS schedulers, and each can host a maximum of approximately 64 workers.

Because workers are divided evenly among the UMS schedulers on the server, the more UMS schedulers you have, the fewer ill-behaved connections it takes to cause concurrency issues and other problems on the server.

For example, with an eight-processor machine, each UMS scheduler can host approximately 32 workers. If a spid associated with a particular scheduler holds locks on resources such that it causes a blocking chain that's 32 processes deep (certainly not unheard of) and these spids happen to also be associated with the same scheduler, the scheduler can become unresponsive and unable to process new work requests. The processing of new work requests on the scheduler would effectively stop until the blocking issue was resolved.

The UMS Scheduler Lists

Each UMS scheduler maintains five lists that support the work of scheduling threads: a worker list, a runnable list, a waiter list, an I/O list, and a timer list. Each of these plays a different role, and nodes are frequently moved between lists.

The Worker List

The worker list is the list of available UMS workers. A UMS worker is an abstraction of the thread/fiber concept and allows either to be used without the rest of the code being aware of which is actually being used under the covers. As I said, one of the design goals of UMS was to provide support for fibers in such a way as not to require the core engine code to be concerned with whether the system was using fibers or threads. A UMS worker encapsulates a thread or fiber that will carry out tasks within the server and abstracts it such that the server does not have to be concerned (for the most part) with whether it is in thread mode or fiber mode. Throughout this chapter, I'll refer to UMS workers instead of threads or fibers.

If your SQL Server is in thread mode (the default), a UMS worker encapsulates a Windows thread object. If your server is in fiber mode, a UMS worker encapsulates a Windows fiber, the handling of which is actually implemented outside of the Windows kernel, as I mentioned in Chapter 3.

The Connection Process

When a client connects to SQL Server, it is assigned to a specific UMS scheduler. The selection heuristics are very basic: Whichever scheduler has the fewest number of associated connections gets the new connection. Once a connection is associated with a scheduler, it never leaves that scheduler.

Regardless of whether its associated scheduler is busy and there are inactive schedulers on the system, UMS will not move a spid between schedulers. This means that it's possible to design scenarios where SQL Server's support for symmetric multiprocessing is effectively thwarted because an application opens multiple persistent connections that do not perform a similar amount of work.

Say, for example, that you have a two-processor machine, and a SQL Server client application opens four persistent connections into the server, with two of those connections performing 90% of the work of the application. If those two connections end up on the same scheduler, you may see one CPU consistently pegged while the other remains relatively idle. The solution in this situation is to balance the load evenly across the connections and not to keep persistent connections when the workload is unbalanced. Disconnecting and reconnecting is the only way to move a spid from one scheduler to another. (This movement isn't guaranteed—a spid that disconnects and reconnects may end up on the same scheduler depending on the number of users on the other schedulers.)

Once a spid is assigned to a scheduler, what happens next depends on the status of the worker list and whether SQL Server's max worker threads configuration value has been reached. If a worker is available in the worker list, it picks up the connection request and processes it. If no worker is available and the max worker threads threshold has not been reached, a new worker is created, and it processes the request. If no workers are available and max worker threads has been reached, the connection request is placed on the waiter list and will be processed in FIFO order as workers become available.

Client connections are treated within UMS as logical (rather than physical) users. It is normal and desirable for there to be a high ratio of logical users to UMS workers. As I've mentioned before, this is what allows a SQL Server with a max worker threads setting of 255 to service hundreds or even thousands of users.

Work Requests

UMS processes work requests atomically. This means that a worker processes an entire work request—a T-SQL batch execution, for example—before it is considered idle. It also means that there's no concept of context switching during the execution of a work request within UMS. While executing a given T-SQL batch, for example, a worker will not be switched away to process a different batch. The only time a worker will begin processing another work request is when it has completed its current work request. It may yield and execute, for example, I/O completion routines originally queued by another worker, but it is not considered idle until it has processed its complete work request, and it will not process another work request until it is finished with the current work request. Once that happens, the worker either activates another worker and returns itself to the worker list or enters an idle loop code line if there are no other runnable workers and no remaining work requests, as we'll discuss in just a moment.

This atomicity is the reason it's possible to drive up the worker thread count within SQL Server by simply executing a number of simultaneous WAITFOR queries as we did using the STRESS.CMD tool in Chapter 3. While each WAITFOR query runs, the worker that is servicing it is considered busy by SQL Server, so any new requests that come into the server require a different worker. If enough of these types of queries are initiated, max worker threads can be quickly reached, and, once that happens, no new connections will be accepted until a worker is freed up.

When the server is in thread mode and a worker has been idle for 15 minutes, SQL Server destroys it, provided doing so will not reduce the number of workers below a predefined threshold. This frees the virtual memory associated with an idle worker's thread stack (.5MB) and allows that virtual memory space to be used elsewhere in the server.

The Runnable List

The runnable list is the list of UMS workers ready to execute an existing work request. Each worker on this list remains in an infinite wait state until its event object is signaled. Being on the runnable list does not imply that the worker is schedulable by Windows. It will be scheduled by Windows as soon as its event object is signaled according to the algorithms within UMS.

Given that UMS implements a cooperative scheduler, you may be wondering who is actually responsible for signaling the event of a worker on the runnable list so that it can run. The answer is that it can be any UMS worker. There are calls throughout the SQL Server code base to yield control to UMS so that a given operation does not monopolize its host scheduler. UMS provides multiple types of yield functions that workers can call. As I've mentioned, in a cooperative tasking environment, threads must voluntarily yield to one another in order for the system to run smoothly. SQL Server is designed so that it yields as often as necessary and in the appropriate places to keep the system humming along.

When a UMS worker yields—either because it has finished the task at hand (e.g., processing a T-SQL batch or executing an RPC) or because it has executed code with an explicit call to one of the UMS yield functions—it is responsible for checking the scheduler's runnable list for a ready worker and signaling that worker's event so that it can run. The yield routine itself makes this check. So, in the process of calling one of the UMS yield functions, a worker actually performs UMS's work for it—there's no thread set aside within the scheduler for managing it. If there were, that thread would have to be scheduled by Windows each time something needed to happen in the scheduler. We'd likely be no better off than we were with Windows handling all of the scheduling. In fact, we might even be worse off due to contention for the scheduler thread and because of the additional overhead of the UMS code. By allowing any worker to handle the maintenance of the scheduler, we allow the thread already running on the processor to continue running as long as there is work for it to do—a fundamental design requirement for a scheduling mechanism intended to minimize context switches. As I said in Chapter 5 in the discussion of the I/O completion port–based scheduler that we built, a scheduler intended to minimize context switching must decouple the work queue from the workers that carry it out. In an ideal situation, any thread can process any work request. This allows a thread that is already scheduled by the operating system to remain scheduled and continue running as long as there is work for it to do. It eliminates the wastefulness of scheduling another thread to do work the thread that's already running could do.

The Waiter List

The waiter list maintains a list of workers waiting on a resource. When a UMS worker requests a resource owned by another worker, it puts itself on the waiter list for the resource and for its scheduler and enters an infinite wait state for its associated event object. When the worker that owns the resource is ready to release it, it is responsible for scanning the list of workers waiting on the resource and moving them to the runnable list as appropriate. And when it hits a yield point, it is responsible for setting the event of the first worker on the runnable list so that the worker can run. This means that when a worker frees up a resource, it may well undertake the entirety of the task of moving those workers that were waiting on the resource from the waiter list to the runnable list and signaling one of them to run.

The I/O List

The I/O list maintains a list of outstanding asynchronous I/O requests. These requests are encapsulated in UMS I/O request objects. When SQL

Server initiates a UMS I/O request, UMS goes down one of two code paths, depending on which version of Windows it's running on. If running on Windows 9x or Windows ME, it initiates a synchronous I/O operation (Windows 9x and ME do not support asynchronous file I/O). If running on the Windows NT family, it initiates an asynchronous I/O operation.

You'll recall from our discussion of Windows I/O earlier in the book that when a thread wants to perform an I/O operation asynchronously, it supplies an OVERLAPPED structure to the ReadFile/ReadFileEx or WriteFile/WriteFileEx function calls. Initially, Windows sets the Internal member of this structure to STATUS_PENDING to indicate that the operation is in progress. As long as the operation continues, the Win32 API HasOverlapped-IoCompleted will return false. (HasOverlappedIoCompleted is actually a macro that simply checks OVERLAPPED.Internal to see whether it is still set to STATUS_PENDING.)

In order to initiate an asynchronous I/O request via UMS, SQL Server instantiates a UMS I/O request object and passes it into a method that's semantically similar to ReadFile/ReadFileScatter or WriteFile/WriteFileGather, depending on whether it's doing a read or a write and depending on whether it's doing scatter-gather I/O. A UMS I/O request is a structure that encapsulates an asynchronous I/O request and contains, as one of its members, an OVERLAPPED structure. The UMS asynchronous I/O method called by the server passes this OVERLAPPED structure into the appropriate Win32 asynchronous I/O function (e.g., ReadFile) for use with the asynchronous operation. The UMS I/O request structure is then put on the I/O list for the host scheduler.

Once an IO request is added to the IO list, it is the job of any worker that yields to check this list to see whether asynchronous I/O operations have completed. To do this, it simply walks the I/O list and calls HasOverlappedI-oCompleted for each one, passing the I/O request's OVERLAPPED member into the macro. When it finds a request that has completed, it removes it from the I/O list, then calls its I/O completion routine. This I/O completion routine was specified when the UMS I/O request was originally created.

You'll recall from our discussion of asynchronous I/O that when an asynchronous operation completes, Windows can optionally queue an I/O completion APC to the original calling thread. As I said earlier, one of the design goals of UMS was to provide much of the same scheduling and asynchronous I/O functionality found in the OS kernel without requiring a switch into kernel mode. UMS's support for I/O completion routines is another example of this design philosophy. A big difference between the way Windows executes I/O completion routines and the way UMS does is that, in UMS, the I/O completion routine executes within the context of whatever worker is attempting to yield (and, therefore, checking the I/O list for completed I/O operations) rather than always in the context of the thread that originally initiated the asynchronous operation. The benefit of this is that a context switch is not required to execute the I/O completion routine. The worker that is already running and about to yield takes care of calling it before it goes to sleep. Because of this, no interaction with the Windows kernel is necessary.

If running on Windows 9x or ME, the I/O completion routine is called immediately after the Win32 I/O API call. Since the operation is handled synchronously by the operating system, there is no reason to go on the I/O list and have perhaps another worker actually run the I/O completion routine. Given that we know the I/O has completed when we return from the Win32 API call, we can go ahead and call the I/O completion routine before returning from the UMS I/O method call. This means that, on Windows 9x/ME, the I/O completion routine is always called within the context of the worker that initiated the asynchronous I/O operation in the first place.

The Timer List

The timer list maintains a list of UMS timer requests. A timer request encapsulates a timed work request. For example, if a worker needs to wait on a resource for a specific amount of time before timing out, it is added to the timer list. When a worker yields, it checks for expired timers on the timer list after checking for completed I/O requests. If it finds an expired timer request, it removes it from the timer list and moves its associated worker to the runnable list. If the runnable list is empty when it does this—that is, if no other workers are ready to run—it also signals the worker's associated event so that it can be scheduled by Windows to run.

The Idle Loop

If, after checking for completed I/O requests and expired timers, a worker finds that the runnable list is empty, it enters a type of idle loop. It scans the timer list for the next timer expiration, then enters a WaitForSingleObject call on an event object that's associated with the scheduler itself using a time-out value equal to the next timer expiration. You'll recall from our discussion of asynchronous I/O that the Win32 OVERLAPPED structure contains an event member that can store a reference to a Windows event object. When a UMS scheduler is created, an event object is created and associated with the scheduler itself. When an asynchronous I/O request is initiated by the scheduler, this event is stored in the hEvent member of the I/O request object's OVERLAPPED structure. This causes the completion of the asynchronous I/O to signal the scheduler's event object. By waiting on this event with a timeout set to the next timer expiration, a worker is waiting for either an I/O request to complete or a timer to expire, whichever comes first. Since it's doing this via a call to WaitForSingleObject, there's no polling involved and it doesn't use any CPU resources until one of these two things occurs.

Going Preemptive

Certain operations within SQL Server require that a worker "go preemptive"—that is, that it be taken off of the scheduler. An example is a call to an extended procedure. As I've said, because UMS is a cooperative multitasking environment, it relies on workers to yield at regular points within the code in order to keep the server running smoothly. Obviously, it has no idea of whether an xproc can or will yield at any sort of regular interval, and, in fact, there's no documented ODS API function that an xproc could call to do so. So, the scheduler assumes that an xproc requires its own thread on which to run. Therefore, prior to a worker executing an xproc, it removes the next runnable worker from the runnable list and sets its event so that the scheduler will continue to have a worker to process work requests. Meanwhile, the original worker executes the xproc and is basically ignored by the scheduler until it returns. Once the xproc returns, the worker continues processing its work request (e.g., the remainder of the T-SQL batch in which the xproc was called), then returns itself to the worker list once it becomes idle, as I mentioned earlier.

The salient point here is that because certain operations within the server require their own workers, it's possible for there to momentarily be multiple threads active for a single scheduler (and, by extension, for a single CPU within the machine since these logical schedulers will often find themselves on their own CPUs). This means that Windows will schedule these threads preemptively as it usually does, and you will likely see context switches between them. It also means that since executing an xproc effectively commandeers a UMS worker, executing a high number of xprocs can have a very negative effect on scalability and concurrency. Each xproc executed reduces UMS's ability to service a high number of logical users with a relatively low number of workers.

Besides xprocs, there are several other activities that can cause a worker to need to go preemptive. Examples include sp_OA calls, linked server queries, distributed queries, server-to-server RPCs, T-SQL debugging, and a handful of others. Obviously, you want to avoid these when you can if scalability and efficient resource use is a primary concern.

Fiber Mode

When the server is in fiber mode, things work a little differently. As I mentioned in Chapter 3, a fiber is a user mode concept—the kernel knows nothing of it. Since a thread is actually Windows' only code execution mechanism, code that is run via a fiber still has to be executed by a thread at some point. The way this is handled is that Windows' fiber management APIs associate a group of threads with a single thread object. When one of the fibers runs a piece of code, the code is actually executed via its host thread. Afterward, user code is responsible for switching to another fiber so that it can run—a concept not unlike the cooperative tasking offered by UMS.

Given that when SQL Server is in fiber mode, multiple workers could be sharing a single Windows thread, the process that's followed when taking a worker thread preemptive won't work when we need to switch to preemptive mode with a worker fiber. Because the execution mechanism within Windows is still a thread, the thread that hosted the fiber would have to be taken off of the scheduler, and this would, in turn, take all the other fiber workers hosted by the same thread off of the scheduler as well—not a desirable situation.

Instead, what happens here is that a hidden thread-based scheduler is created to service xprocs and other external calls that cause a worker to need to switch to preemptive mode. (The scheduler is hidden in the sense that it does not show up in the DBCC SQLPERF(umsstats) output.) When a worker fiber then needs to switch to preemptive mode to run one of these components, the work request is moved to this hidden scheduler and processed. Once it completes, the fiber is moved back to the original scheduler and processing continues as normal.

The upshot of this is that executing things like xprocs and linked server queries can be extremely inefficient in fiber mode. In fact, there are a number of components within the server that aren't even supported in fiber mode (sp_xml_preparedocument and ODSOLE, for example). If you need to run lots of xprocs, linked server queries, distributed transactions, and the like, fiber mode may not be your best option.

Hidden Schedulers

The server creates hidden schedulers for other uses as well. Other processes within the server require the same type of latch, resource management, and scheduling services that UMS provides for work request scheduling, so the server creates hidden schedulers that allow those processes to make use of this functionality without having to implement it themselves. An example of such a facility is SQL Server's backup/restore facility. Given that many backup devices do not support asynchronous I/O and the fact that doing a large amount of synchronous I/O on a regular UMS scheduler would negatively impact the concurrency of the entire scheduler because it would allow a single blocking synchronous I/O call to monopolize the worker (not unlike calling external code does), SQL Server puts backup/restore operations on their own scheduler. This allows them to contend with one another for processor time and permits Windows to preemptively schedule them with the other schedulers.

DBCC SQLPERF(umsstats)

I mentioned DBCC SQLPERF(umsstats) earlier, and you may already be aware of it given that, although it's undocumented, it's mentioned in the public Microsoft Knowledge Base. DBCC SQLPERF(umsstats) allows you to return a result set listing statistics for the visible UMS schedulers on the system. It can list the total number of users and workers for the scheduler, the number of workers on the runnable list, the number of idle workers, the number of outstanding work requests, and so on. It's very handy when you suspect you're experiencing some type of issue with a scheduler and need to know what's going on behind the scenes. For example, you should be able to quickly tell from this output whether a scheduler has reached its maximum number of workers and whether they're currently busy. Table 10.1 details the result set returned by DBCC SQLPERF(umsstats).

The output of DBCC SQLPERF(umsstats) is best understood by way of example. Say, for the sake of discussion, that SQL Server is running on a single-processor system. It will have just one visible UMS scheduler, so that scheduler's maximum number of workers will be equal to the max worker threads sp_configure setting. If you see from the DBCC SQLPERF(umsstats) output that the number of workers associated with the scheduler has already reached max worker threads and stays there, and you see that the

Table 10.1 DBCC SQLPERF(umsstats) Fields

Statistic	Meaning
Scheduler ID	The scheduler's zero-based ID number
num users	The number of user connections associated with the scheduler
num runnable	The number of workers on the runnable list
num workers	The total number of workers associated with the scheduler
idle workers	The number of idle workers
work queued	The number of items waiting to be processed in the work queue
cntxt switches	The number of switches between workers for the scheduler
cntxt switches(idle)	The number of times the idle loop was switched into
Scheduler Switches	The number of switches between schedulers (not used)
Total Work	The total number of work items processed by all schedulers

work queued column is consistently nonzero, you may reasonably infer that the scheduler is very busy and might have difficulty processing work in a timely fashion.

Recap

In order to increase scalability and support Windows fibers, SQL Server has managed its own scheduling since version 7.0 via UMS. UMS serves as a thin layer between the server and the operating system that provides much of the same functionality offered by the Win32 thread and scheduling primitives, but it does so without requiring as many transitions into kernel mode or as many context switches.

A key difference between UMS and Windows' scheduler is that UMS is a cooperative scheduler. It relies on workers to voluntarily yield often enough to keep the system running smoothly. By putting control of when a thread is scheduled under the direction of the server, a much greater responsibility is placed on SQL Server developers to write code that runs efficiently and yields often enough and in the appropriate places. However, this also provides a much finer granularity of control and allows the server to scale better than it could ever hope to using Windows' one-size-fits-all scheduling approach because SQL Server knows its own scheduling needs best.

Knowledge Measure

1. What mechanism within UMS encapsulates the scheduling facility for a single logical processor?
2. What list within UMS tracks the workers that are ready to run?
3. What kernel object does UMS use to put workers to sleep that it does not want to run at a particular point in time?
4. True or false: UMS provides a special thread for each processor that handles scheduling workers to run, processing expired timers, and so on.
5. True or false: By default, each UMS instance is affinitized to a particular processor when SQL Server is running on a multiprocessor machine.
6. What list within UMS is responsible for tracking outstanding I/O requests?
7. What part of UMS ultimately owns the event object that gets signaled when an asynchronous I/O request completes?
8. Describe what happens within UMS when SQL Server is in fiber mode and an xproc is executed.
9. Assuming the server is in thread mode, name a facility within the server that makes use of a hidden instance of the UMS scheduling facility.
10. True or false: All UMS I/O under Windows 9x is processed synchronously by SQL Server.
11. When a worker yields, whose responsibility is it to check the timer list to see whether any timers have expired?
12. Describe what it means for a UMS worker to "go preemptive."

13. True or false: An original UMS design goal was to provide support for using Windows fibers within SQL Server.

14. True or false: A key difference between UMS scheduling and Windows scheduling is that Windows provides a cooperative scheduling facility, while UMS provides a preemptive scheduling facility.

15. What list is used within UMS to track idle workers?

16. Explain what is meant by the statement that a thread in an infinite wait state is not considered "viable" by the Windows scheduler.

17. In what version of Windows did fiber support first appear?

18. When a worker is on the list UMS uses to track workers that are ready to run, what must occur in order for the worker to actually be schedulable by Windows?

19. True or false: A linked server query will cause a UMS worker to have to switch into preemptive mode.

20. True or false: Because SQL Server's max worker threads setting specifies the maximum number of workers for each instance of the UMS scheduling facility, a machine with two processors can have a total maximum of 510 worker threads by default.

CHAPTER 11

SQL Server Memory Management

Accustom a people to believe that priests, or any other class of men, can forgive sins, and you will have sins in abundance.

—Thomas Paine[1]

In this chapter, we'll explore SQL Server's memory management architecture. The way that an application manages critical resources such as memory tells us a lot about how it is designed. It tells us what priority the application designers placed on efficient resource utilization and on maximizing the performance of the application. As you will see in the discussion that follows, efficient memory management and maximum system performance were both of paramount importance to the designers of SQL Server. A considerable portion of the complex code within the product is dedicated to managing memory efficiently and effectively. There are always trade-offs with memory management. Too little memory usage makes your app efficient but slow. Too much memory usage may make your app fast, but it may not play well with others and it may become a resource hog in general. As you'll see, SQL Server attempts to strike a balance between getting the most out of the resources available to it and running well alongside other applications on the system.

---

1. Paine, Thomas. "Worship and Church Bells." In *The Complete Writings of Thomas Paine, Vol. II,* ed. Philip S. Foner. New York: Citadel Press, 1945, p. 726.

Memory Regions

SQL Server organizes the memory it allocates into two distinct regions: the BPool (buffer pool) and MemToLeave (memory to leave) regions. If you make use of AWE memory, there's actually a third region: the physical memory above 3GB made available by Windows' AWE support. (Refer to Chapter 4 for details on AWE.)

The BPool is the preeminent region of the three. It is SQL Server's primary allocation pool. MemToLeave consists of the virtual memory space within the user mode address space that is not used by the BPool. The AWE memory above 3GB functions as an extension of the BPool and provides additional space for caching data and index pages.

Sizing

When the server starts, it begins by computing the upper limit of the BPool. This upper limit is the maximum size to which the server will allow the BPool to grow. On a non-AWE system, this size will be set equal to the amount of physical memory in the machine or to the size of the user mode address space minus the size of the MemToLeave region, whichever is less. (If the sp_configure max server memory setting has been changed from the default and is less than or equal to the amount of physical memory in the machine, it will override this computation.) So, if the system has 1GB of physical memory installed, the BPool will be sized to 1GB, provided max server memory has not been adjusted.

On an AWE system, the BPool upper limit will be set to either the size of the total physical memory in the machine or to the max server memory setting, whichever is less. When AWE is used, the BPool isn't constrained by the size of the user mode address space or the size of the MemToLeave region.

By default, the MemToLeave region is sized at 384MB. Of this, 128MB is reserved for worker thread stacks (max worker threads = 255 × .5MB for each thread stack), and 256MB is reserved for allocations outside of the BPool. Examples of the types of memory allocations that come from MemToLeave include OLE DB provider allocations, in-process COM object allocations, and *any memory allocation by the server code itself that is larger than 8KB*. This last item is important because it means that large procedure or execution plans can be allocated from the MemToLeave region.

Although all allocations for a contiguous memory block larger than 8KB come from the MemToLeave region, the reverse is not always true. Because the server will attempt to use the uncommitted portion of a reserved block for other allocation requests, it's possible that allocations smaller than 8KB could end up coming from the MemToLeave region, depending on the version and service pack of SQL Server you're using. In order to make an allocation request, a memory consumer within the server first allocates a memory allocation object, which it then uses to request the allocation (this object implements the COM IMalloc interface, as we'll discuss later in the chapter). If multiple requests are made via a given allocation object, it's possible that some of them will be fulfilled using MemToLeave memory, even if they request less than 8KB. For example, if a consumer within the server requests 10KB of contiguous storage, the allocation object will allocate this from the MemToLeave region. If necessary, it will first reserve a region sized to match the system's allocation granularity (64KB on 32-bit Windows), then commit two 8KB pages to satisfy the request. If the memory consumer then uses the same allocation object to request, say, 4KB of additional space, the system will see the unallocated 6KB of space at the end of the two-page region it just allocated and will fulfill the new request from this space. Thus, it's possible for an allocation that's less than 8KB in size to be satisfied outside of the BPool.

Because OLE DB providers, COM objects, and other external consumers that may reside within the SQL Server process will know nothing of SQL Server's BPool or its memory management facilities, it's essential that the server leave some amount of virtual memory free within the user mode space. That's why MemToLeave exists—it is basically unused memory within the SQL Server process space. If an in-process COM object or other external consumer calls VirtualAlloc or HeapAlloc itself, it will require virtual memory address space in order to satisfy the allocation request. If the BPool were to take up all of this user mode address space itself, allocation requests of this type would always fail.

The size of the MemToLeave region can be adjusted using the -g command line parameter. The total memory required for the worker thread stacks cannot be changed without changing the max worker threads sp_configure value or modifying the default thread stack size by hacking the SQL Server executable, which you should definitely not do. However, you can increase or decrease the 256MB set aside for allocations outside of the BPool by passing a different value for the -g parameter. This parameter can be handy in situations where you have a lot of linked server queries, in-process COM objects, or other memory consumers contending for space in the MemToLeave region. By making it larger, you give them a bigger sandbox in which to play. Conversely, shrinking it can provide more virtual memory space for the BPool and may improve performance in some situations.

Even though the BPool can be sized based on the amount of physical memory in the machine, it is still based entirely in virtual memory, by default. The exception to this is when you make use of AWE memory. In that situation, part of the BPool is in virtual memory (but backed by pages locked in physical memory), and the rest is in physical memory above 3GB. AWE is the only way for a user mode process to access more than 3GB of memory. Since the maximum size of the user mode virtual address space is 3GB (even with /3GB or /USERVA enabled), AWE is the only means by which a process can access memory above the 3GB boundary. It just so happens that AWE memory is physical rather than virtual memory and must be mapped into the user mode space in order to be accessed.

The BPool

The vast majority of SQL Server's memory allocations come from the BPool. The BPool consists of up to 32 separate memory regions organized into 8KB pages. You'll recall from Chapter 4 our discussion of VirtualAlloc and the way it can be used to reserve contiguous blocks of memory. After the server has computed the maximum size of the BPool, it reserves the MemToLeave region in an attempt to ensure that this region will be a contiguous address range. If possible, it will reserve this using a single call to VirtualAlloc. If that's not possible (highly unlikely), the server will make multiple calls to VirtualAlloc to reserve the MemToLeave region. The server then attempts to reserve the BPool region from the user mode address space. (Put aside how AWE affects this for now; we'll return to it in just a moment.) With DLLs, memory-mapped files, and other allocations already in the user mode space, it's very unlikely that the entire BPool will be able to be reserved with a single call to VirtualAlloc. Instead, the BPool will likely have to consist of several fragments spread across the user mode space. The server will call VirtualAlloc repeatedly, each time with a smaller reservation request size until it succeeds. It will do this up to 32 times in order to reserve as much of the BPool's maximum size as possible. Once this completes, the server releases the MemToLeave region so that it will be available to external consumers. Because it was reserved before the BPool reservations were made and then released afterward, the MemToLeave region normally starts out as a single, contiguous block of free virtual address space.

When AWE is involved, the algorithm is slightly different. The repetitive calls to VirtualAlloc for the user mode portion of the BPool still occur. However, Windows does not support reserving and committing AWE memory using separate operations. As we discussed in Chapter 4, when using AWE, either the memory is allocated or it isn't. AllocateUserPhysicalPages does not support the concept of reserving, but not allocating, physical memory—memory is reserved and committed in one fell swoop. Once it is, it must be mapped into a window in the user mode space so that a 32-bit pointer can access it.

So, in this scenario, all of the memory set aside for the BPool is locked into physical memory. This applies to both the user mode portion as well as the AWE portion. Because physical memory is being locked, this can cause serious performance problems for other applications running on the same machine, including other instances of SQL Server. You typically set up a SQL Server this way when it is the only significant app running on a machine.

When AWE support is enabled in SQL Server, the user account under which the server is running must have the lock pages in memory privilege. SQL Server's setup program will automatically grant this privilege to the startup account you choose for the server. If you start the server from the command line or change the startup account, you have to take care of this yourself.

Hashing

In order to make locating particular pages faster, SQL Server hashes pages within the BPool. This basically amounts to creating a hash table over the pages in the BPool such that, given the database ID, file number, and page number of a data page, the server can quickly determine whether the BPool contains the data page and where it is located if it does.

When the server needs to access a particular data page, it hashes the page's database ID, file number, and page number such that the page maps to a particular bucket within the hash table. That bucket consists of a linked list of pointers to BPool pages. It is checked to see whether the page in question is on the list. If it is, it can be quickly accessed in memory. If it is not, it must first be loaded from disk.

Primitive Allocations

Before any pages can be allocated from the BPool, SQL Server must allocate the support structures required to manage it. The first of these that we'll talk about is a global variable to hold a reference to an instance of the class that defines the BPool. Because this variable has global scope, you can see it yourself using WinDbg and the public symbols that ship with SQL Server. Exercise 11.1 takes you through locating both the global variable and its host data type.

Exercise 11.1   Using WinDbg to Find the Buffer Pool

1. Attach to your nonproduction SQL Server with WinDbg.
2. Make sure your symbol path is set correctly as described in Chapter 2.
3. Our next step will be based on two assumptions.
   a. Due to its very nature and ubiquity within the server, the reference to the BPool is likely stored in a global variable or similar construct.
   b. It is likely named BPool, BufferPool, or some variation thereof.
4. At the WinDbg command prompt, type:

```
.reload -f sqlservr.exe
x sqlservr!*
```

   This will list all of the public symbols included in sqlservr.pdb, the program database (symbol) file for SQL Server.
5. Scroll to the top of the command window and click above the start of the output from the x command. Press Ctrl+F, type BPool, and press Enter.
6. You should find the first occurrence of a reference to the BPool class. This is actually a reference to one of its methods. We can deduce from this that SQL Server has a class named BPool. It's a fair guess that this is the data type of the object that stores the SQL Server buffer pool, but we'll establish that with a good degree of certainty in just a moment.
7. Now let's look for the global variable that we suspect stores the reference to the buffer pool. Scroll to the top of the output and repeat your search, this time specifying "bPool" for the search string (no quotes). Be sure to specify a case-sensitive search in the dialog. Because C++ is a case-sensitive language, it's common for developers to name an instance of a variable after its type using different case. We'll start by checking for that.
8. If your search was case-sensitive, it should not have found any symbols named "bPool," so we need to keep looking. Another common tactic is to spell out a type name but abbreviate the names of instances of it or vice versa. Since we already know the type name is BPool, let's look for it spelled out as BufferPool. Repeat your search, this time specifying BufferPool as the search criteria.
9. You should find a symbol named sqlserver!BufferPool. Notice that this isn't prefixed by a class name and a pair of colons (::) as the BPool ref-

erence you found earlier was. This means that it's a global of some type. Based on the name alone, we can deduce that it's probably not a global function. Thus, it's likely a global variable and probably the one that stores the reference to the SQL Server buffer pool.

10. At this point, you could dump the contents of the BufferPool variable to the console using the dd command or something similar. The value of the variable itself isn't terribly useful to us at this point; I just wanted you to see that it was indeed a global. All of SQL Server's BPool functionality is wrapped up in the BPool class and in BufferPool, the single, global instance of it.

11. Scroll back to the top of the command window and repeat your search, this time using "DropCleanBuffers" as your search string. You should find an entry for BPool::DropCleanBuffers in the symbol list.

12. Readers of my previous books will recall the discussions of the DBCC DROPCLEANBUFFERS command. This command was once undocumented but is handy for releasing the clean buffers from the BPool in order to test a query with a cold cache without cycling SQL Server. Given that the BPool class has a member named DropCleanBuffers, might this be what the DBCC command calls? Let's set a breakpoint and find out.

13. At the WinDbg command prompt, type:

```
bp sqlserver!BPool::DropCleanBuffers
g
```

14. Now, switch over to Query Analyzer, connect to your server, and run DBCC DROPCLEANBUFFERS in the editor. Switch back to WinDbg. You should see that execution has stopped at your breakpoint. This tells us definitively that DBCC DROPCLEANBUFFERS is implemented via a method off of the BPool class named DropCleanBuffers. It also reinforces our assertion that the BPool class we see in the debugger is the actual data type of SQL Server's global buffer pool instance.

15. Type q in the WinDbg command window and press Enter to stop debugging. You'll need to restart your SQL Server.

Page Arrays

I mentioned earlier that SQL Server makes up to 32 separate memory reservations to reserve the BPool. The BPool tracks these allocations in two parallel arrays—one array stores a list of pointers to the start of each region, the other stores a count of the 8K pages reserved in the region. Both arrays are private members of the BPool class.

BUF Array

SQL Server uses a special BUF structure to manage each page in the BPool. Before reserving the BPool, SQL Server calls VirtualAlloc to allocate an array of BUF structures from the MemToLeave region equal in size to the number of pages it will reserve for the BPool (including physical AWE pages). Each page in the BPool will have a corresponding BUF structure, as will each page of AWE memory allocated by the server, regardless of whether it has been mapped into virtual memory. Since each BUF structure is 64 bytes in size, this array isn't usually very large unless the server is using a significant amount of AWE memory.

Each page's BUF structure functions as a type of header for it. It stores information such as a pointer to the actual page in the BPool, the reference count for the page, the page's latch, and status bits that indicate whether the page is dirty, has I/O pending, is pinned in memory, and so on.

When the lazywriter traverses the pool looking for pages to free, this array of BUF structures is what it actually sweeps. We'll discuss the lazywriter further in just a moment.

Commit Bitmap

On startup, SQL Server allocates a bitmap from the default process heap that it uses to track committed pages in the BPool. The original reservations tracked by the page arrays are just that—reservations. As we discussed in Chapter 4, it's possible to reserve virtual memory address space without committing any physical storage to it. As each page in the BPool is committed, its corresponding bit in the commit bitmap is set.

AWE

Although the BPool keeps track of which pages in AWE memory it makes use of, it cannot access them directly due to the way that Windows' AWE facility works. It accesses them by mapping physical pages in and out of the user mode address space, as I mentioned in Chapter 4.

Note that if your server has less than 3GB of physical RAM and you enable AWE use via the sp_configure awe enabled option, SQL Server will ignore it. You must have 3GB or more of physical memory in order to use Windows' AWE facility with SQL Server, as we discussed earlier in the book.

The Lazywriter

The purpose of the lazywriter is twofold: (1) to keep a specified number of BPool buffers free so they can be allocated for use by the server and (2) to monitor and adjust the committed memory usage by the BPool so that enough physical memory remains free on the system to prevent Windows from paging (provided dynamic memory management is enabled so that the lazywriter can adjust the size of the BPool as necessary). SQL Server estimates the number of BPool buffers to keep free based on the system load and the number of stalls occurring (the number of times a memory consumer within the server has to wait on a free buffer page).

The amount of physical memory the lazywriter attempts to keep free usually varies between 4MB and 10MB. It is partially based on the computed page life expectancy for the pool (the number of seconds a page will stay in the buffer pool without being referenced). You can track the Buffer Manager:Page life expectancy Perfmon counter to see what this value is for a particular instance of SQL Server. As the page life expectancy increases (i.e., as the instance of SQL Server is less memory-pressured and, therefore, pages stay in the cache longer even when not being referenced), the amount of physical memory reserved for the OS climbs nearer to 10MB. As the page life expectancy decreases, the physical memory set aside for the OS continues to fall until it reaches approximately 4MB.

Keeping a minimum amount of physical memory available for use by the OS helps ensure that it doesn't page unnecessarily and helps keep it and the other processes on the SQL Server machine running smoothly. If the system begins to be pressured for physical memory—even if that pressure is not coming from SQL Server—the BPool will adjust its committed BPool memory downward so that more physical memory is available.

Computing Physical Memory

The manner in which the BPool determines the amount of available physical memory varies based on the OS. On Windows 2000, the Win32 API function GlobalMemoryStatusEx is called. If you're running SQL Server on Windows 2000, you can see this for yourself by attaching to SQL Server with WinDbg and setting a breakpoint in kernel32!GlobalMemoryStatusEx. If you list the call stack once your breakpoint is tripped, you'll see that GlobalMemoryStatusEx is being called by either BPool::AvailablePagingFile or BPool::AvailablePhysicalMemory. Obviously, the latter one is the call the

BPool is using to ensure that physical memory stays at or above the required threshold.

On Windows NT 4.0 and Windows 9x/ME, the Win32 API function GlobalMemoryStatus is called. This function is used rather than GlobalMemoryStatusEx because GlobalMemoryStatusEx is not supported on Windows NT 4.0 or Windows 9x/ME.

On Windows XP and Windows Server 2003, the BPool uses the CreateMemoryResourceNotification and QueryMemoryResourceNotification API functions to instruct Windows to notify the BPool when physical memory runs low. These APIs are not available on earlier versions of Windows, so their use is exclusive to Windows XP and Windows Server 2003.

Flushing and Freeing Pages

As I mentioned earlier, the BUF array contains an element for each page in the BPool. Each BUF structure functions as a kind of BPool page header and contains a reference count for its corresponding page. Each time a page is referenced, this reference count is incremented. Some more expensive pages—such as those that contain execution plans—begin with a higher reference count than other kinds of pages. This helps keep them in memory longer and helps the server avoid incurring the cost of recreating them or reloading them from disk unnecessarily.

Periodically, this BUF array is scanned. The reference count in each BUF structure is divided by four and the remainder is discarded. When the reference count for a page reaches zero, the page is checked to see whether it's dirty; if so, a write is scheduled via UMS to flush the dirty page to disk. (If a page's reference count reaches zero and the page is *not* dirty, it is simply freed—i.e., moved to the free list—without writing anything to disk.) Because SQL Server uses a write-ahead log, this flush to disk of the dirty page will be blocked while the transaction log is written to. Once a dirty page has been successfully written to disk, it is unhashed (removed from the hash table) and added to the free list. A dirty page is not usually decommitted in this scenario—it is merely moved on to a list of free buffers so that it can be reused. Avoiding unnecessary decommit/commit operations speeds up SQL Server's memory operations significantly and is a key design tenet of an effective memory cache.

The size of the free list is calculated internally by SQL Server based on the size of the BPool. The fact that SQL Server uses separate physical structures for a page and its header allows a page to be flushed to disk and to "move" from list to list without anything on the page actually changing.

When a dirty page is flushed to disk and freed, for example, information in the page's header (its BUF structure) changes, but the page itself does not have to be modified. Once flushed, its contents are considered disposable and can be overwritten when the page is reused. When a page needs to move from one list to another (e.g., when it's freed), the much smaller 64-byte BUF structure is moved from list to list rather than the 8KB page. The reason the size of the structure matters here has to do with the use of the processor's local cache. The smaller the structure, the more instances of it can be stored in the chip's onboard cache, and the more efficient the process of moving nodes between lists is. Leveraging the local cache on the CPU is another key tenet of an effective memory cache.

On the Windows NT family, this process of aging pages, flushing them to disk, and moving them to the free list is usually done by individual UMS workers. The dedicated lazywriter thread usually finds that it has very little to do. On Windows 9x and ME, though, the lazywriter thread plays a much bigger role. Because Windows 9x and ME do not support asynchronous file I/O, UMS is forced to perform all file I/O synchronously (see Chapter 10). This limits the ability of a UMS worker to perform lazywriter work; therefore, the dedicated lazywriter thread is much more active on Windows 9x/ME than it is on the Windows NT family.

The lazywriter checks the free buffer count and the available physical memory once per second or when signaled. You can see this for yourself by attaching to SQL Server with WinDbg and setting a breakpoint in the BPool::AvailablePhysicalMemory method that we discovered earlier, as shown below. (Note that due to page width limitations this code appears printed on two lines, but you must type it all together as one line.)

```
bp sqlservr!BPool::AvailablePhysicalMemory
".echo checking availphys; g"
```

Once you restart WinDbg, you'll see the message following .echo displayed once a second until you stop the debugger.

I should point out here that, until the BPool upper limit size is reached, the lazywriter doesn't free up buffers by flushing them to disk and putting them on the free list. Instead, it merely commits more reserved pages in the BPool each time the free list falls below the built-in threshold and changes the corresponding bits in the commit bitmap accordingly.

The lazywriter checks 16 BUF structures at a time. It keeps track of where it left off with each iteration and picks back up there on the next run (a second later or when signaled, as I've said). When the lazywriter reaches the end of the BUF array, it wraps back around to the start in a manner similar to a clock—it sweeps continuously through the BUF array not unlike the way the hands on a clock sweep indefinitely.

Checkpoint

The checkpoint process also scans the BPool and flushes dirty pages to disk. It does not, however, move pages to the free list. Freeing pages is the job of the UMS workers and the dedicated lazywriter thread. Checkpoint's job is to shorten the amount of time required to recover the system by keeping the number of dirty pages to a minimum. It's common for a checkpoint not to find many pages to flush to disk because dirty pages have already been flushed by the lazywriter thread or individual UMS workers.

Partitions

In order to provide for better scalability, SQL Server partitions the BPool free list by CPU. As we discussed in Chapter 10, a given UMS user is assigned to a particular scheduler when it first connects and remains with that scheduler until it disconnects. Each UMS scheduler is typically associated with a particular CPU. When a UMS user needs a free page, the partition associated with its CPU is checked first, followed by the other partitions if necessary. By partitioning the BPool free list by CPU, we make better use of the processor's local cache and improve the scalability of the server.

The Memory Managers

Rather than embed all of the complexities of memory management into the BPool itself, SQL Server spreads it across five major memory manager classes. This allows different memory consumers to allocate and manage memory independently of one another while still using a shared, managed memory pool.

Understand that a handful of allocations bypass these managers altogether. The transaction log implements its own caching mechanism, as does the backup/restore facility. There are other examples as well. Rather than go through a memory manager, these allocations come straight from the OS via calls to VirtualAlloc.

The five managers are the Connection, Query Plan, Optimizer, Utility, and General memory managers. Each is responsible for a different class of memory management within the server. Let's discuss each of these separately.

Connection

This memory manager is responsible for connection-related memory allocations. Each connection has a process status structure (PSS) and SRVPROC structure allocated for it, as well as one network send buffer and two network receive buffers. The Connection memory manager manages these types of allocations.

Query Plan

SQL Server uses the Query Plan memory manager mainly for allocations related to compiled plans and execution plans produced by the query optimizer (you can see these in the syscacheobjects system table). This memory manager also handles allocations related to cursors, RPC parameters, index creation, and certain DBCC commands that deal with indexes on computed columns.

   Note that the Query Plan memory manager is the only memory manager that the lazywriter can cause to free up memory. A page whose BUF header has a status bit indicating that the page is related to a query plan can be aged out of the cache by the lazywriter when its reference count reaches zero.

Optimizer

SQL Server uses the Optimizer memory manager to allocate and manage metadata and tree structures related to query optimization. The server limits this manager to 80% of the server's total memory.

Utility

SQL Server has a special memory manager for use by utility functions. As the name suggests, it uses the Utility memory manager for various utility-related allocations, including buffers used by the server-side trace facility, log manager initialization, cluster- and log shipping–related functions, bitmap comparisons, hash table searches, and so on.

General

This memory manager is for allocations that don't fit any of the above categories. Allocations for several different types of internal storage engine structures, including locks, are made using the General memory manager.

OS Memory Allocations

As a rule, the five major memory managers attempt to allocate memory from the BPool unless the request is larger than 8KB. For allocations larger than 8KB of contiguous memory, the request is usually passed on to the memory manager responsible for allocating memory from the MemToLeave region. This memory manager is commonly known as the OS or Reserved memory manager. It is not a separate manager class in the same sense as the five major ones we just discussed; instead, it provides functionality that all of them can make use of for large allocations.

When it processes an allocation request, the OS memory manager calls VirtualAlloc to reserve a sufficiently large region of the MemToLeave pool. This reservation will be rounded up to the system's allocation granularity (64KB on 32-bit Windows), as we discussed in Chapter 4. Within this reservation, the memory manager will commit a sufficient number of pages to satisfy the request. If additional allocation requests are received before the region is released, they may also be fulfilled by committing pages in this region. Once all pages have been decommitted, the memory manager calls VirtualFree to release the region.

The Low Memory Manager

SQL Server provides a special emergency condition memory manager that is used in rare circumstances when the normal memory managers have failed and the server must have some memory in order to continue without severe consequences (e.g., corruption) during such things as logging or recovery. The normal managers do not automatically use this memory manager when allocations they attempt fail; it is used only by certain very critical code paths within the server.

When SQL Server starts, this memory manager commits a 64KB region of virtual memory. Only one consumer can use this memory at a time. Each new consumer must wait until the others have released the memory before the new consumer can use it.

When this memory manager is used, it writes a warning message to the SQL Server error log:

```
Warning: Due to low virtual memory, special reserved memory used
%d times since startup. Increase virtual memory on server.
```

Due to its very nature, you'll normally see other errors or warnings accompanying this message when it occurs.

IMalloc

Internally, SQL Server uses a custom implementation of the COM IMalloc interface to handle individual memory allocations. As I mentioned earlier in the chapter, when a consumer needs to make a memory request, it first allocates a memory allocation object. It then uses this allocation object to make the request. Multiple requests can be made via a single allocation object. This allocation object implements the standard COM IMalloc interface.

IMalloc includes all the features you'd expect to find in a standard memory allocator: allocation, deallocation, resizing, functions to determine allocation block sizes, and so on. COM provides a standard implementation of this interface that uses the Win32 heap facilities to carry out allocation requests. Since SQL Server performs its own memory management, it doesn't use the standard COM implementation—it uses an internal implementation that allocates requests from the BPool or MemToLeave regions as appropriate.

Pulling It All Together

Thus far, we've explored the individual components of SQL Server's memory architecture in some detail. In this section, we'll pull these elements together so you can better understand how SQL Server manages memory overall and why it behaves the way it does in certain circumstances.

When you start SQL Server, the BPool's upper limit is computed based on the physical memory in the machine, the max server memory sp_configure value, and the size of the MemToLeave region. Once this size is computed, the MemToLeave region is set aside (reserved) so that it will not be fragmented by the BPool reservations that are to follow. The BPool region is then set aside, using as many as 32 separate reservations in order to allocate around the DLLs and other allocations that may already be taking up virtual address space within the SQL Server process by the time the BPool is reserved.

Once the BPool is reserved, the MemToLeave region is released. SQL Server does not hold on to the MemToLeave region because this region is intended for "external" (i.e., outside the core SQL Server code) consumption. It is used for internal SQL Server allocations that exceed 8KB of contiguous space and for allocations made by external consumers such as OLE DB providers, in-process COM objects, and the like. As I've said, SQL Server reserves the entire MemToLeave region at startup, then releases it after the BPool reservations are made in order to keep it from being fragmented by BPool reservations.

So, once the server has started, the BPool has been reserved, but not committed, and the MemToLeave region is essentially free space within the virtual memory address space of the process. If you view the Virtual Bytes Perfmon counter for the SQL Server process just after SQL Server has started, you'll see that it reflects the BPool reservation. I've seen people become alarmed because this number is often so high—after all, it usually reflects either the total physical memory in the machine or the maximum user mode address space minus the size of the MemToLeave region. This is nothing to worry about, however, because it is only reserved, not committed, space. As I said in Chapter 4, reserved space is just address space—it does not have physical storage behind it until it is committed.

Over time, the amount of memory committed to the BPool will increase until it reaches the upper limit computed when the server was originally started. You can track this via the SQL Server:Buffer Manager\Target Pages Perfmon counter. As different parts of the server need memory, the BPool commits the 8KB pages it originally reserved until this committed size reaches the computed target. Since this is virtual space as opposed to physical space, and since the majority of virtual memory is backed by the system paging file, not by physical RAM, this does not necessarily equate to more physical memory usage. You can track the BPool's use of committed virtual memory via the SQL Server:Buffer Manager\Total Pages Perfmon counter. You can track the server's overall use of committed virtual memory via the Private Bytes counter for the SQL Server process.

Because most of SQL Server's virtual memory usage comes from the BPool, these two counters will, generally speaking, increase or level off in tandem. If the Total Pages counter levels off but the Private Bytes counter continues to climb, this usually indicates continued allocations from the MemToLeave region. These allocations could be completely normal—for example, they could be allocations related to thread stacks as additional worker threads are created within the server—or they could indicate a leak by an external consumer such as an in-process COM object or an xproc. If the process runs out of virtual memory address space because the MemToLeave region is exhausted due to a leak or overconsumption (or if the maximum free block within the MemToLeave region falls below the default thread stack size of .5MB), the server will be unable to create new worker threads, even if the sp_configure max worker threads value has not been reached. In this situation, if the server needs to create a new worker thread in order to carry out a work request—for example, to process a new connection request—this work request will be delayed until the server can create the thread or another worker becomes available for it to use. This can prevent a user from connecting to the server because the connection may time out before a sufficient amount of MemToLeave space is freed or another worker becomes available to process the connection request.

A memory consumer within the server initiates a memory allocation by first creating a memory object to manage the request. This memory object is an implementation of the standard COM IMalloc interface. When the object allocates the request, it calls on the appropriate memory manager within the server to fulfill the request from either the BPool or the MemToLeave region. For requests of 8KB or less, the request is usually filled using memory from the BPool. For requests of more than 8KB of contiguous space, the request is usually filled using memory from the MemToLeave region. Because a single memory object may be used to carry out multiple allocations, it's actually possible for an allocation of less than 8KB to be allocated from the MemToLeave region, as I mentioned earlier.

Consumers of memory within the SQL Server process space are usually internal consumers, that is, consumers or objects within the SQL Server code itself that need memory to carry out a task, but they do not have to be. They can also be external consumers, as I've said. External consumers include OLE DB providers, xprocs, in-process COM objects, and so on. Usually, these external consumers use normal Win32 memory API functions to allocate and manage memory and, therefore, allocate space from the MemToLeave space since it is the only region within the SQL Server process that appears to be available. However, xprocs are a special exception. When an xproc calls the ODS srv_alloc API function, it is treated just like any other consumer within the server. Generally speaking, srv_alloc requests for 8KB of memory or less are allocated from the BPool. Larger allocations come from the MemToLeave space.

As the server runs, the lazywriter checks to make sure that a given amount of physical memory remains available on the server so that Windows and other apps on the server continue to run smoothly. This amount can vary between 4MB and 10MB (it trends closer to 10MB on Windows Server 2003) and is based on the system load and the page life expectancy for the BPool. If the physical memory on the server begins to dip below this threshold, the server decommits BPool pages in order to shrink its physical storage usage (assuming that dynamic memory configuration is enabled).

The lazywriter also ensures that a given number of pages remain free at any given point in time so that, as new allocation requests come in, they will not have to wait for memory to be allocated. By "free" I mean that the page is committed but not used. Unused committed BPool pages are tracked via a free list. As pages are used from this list, the lazywriter commits more pages from the BPool reservation until the entire reservation has been committed. You will see the Process:Private Bytes Perfmon counter increase gradually (and usually linearly) due to this activity.

There is a separate free list for each CPU on the system. When a free page is needed to satisfy an allocation request, the free list associated with the UMS worker requesting the allocation is checked first, followed by the lists for the other CPUs on the system. This is done to improve scalability by making better use of the local cache for each processor on a multiprocessor system. You can monitor a specific BPool partition via the SQL Server:Buffer Partition Perfmon object. You can monitor the free list for all partitions via the SQL Server:Buffer Manager\Free Pages Perfmon counter.

So, throughout the time that it runs, SQL Server's lazywriter process (whether run from the lazywriter thread or via a UMS worker) monitors the memory status of the system to be sure that a reasonable amount of physical memory remains available to the rest of the system and that a healthy number of free pages remains available for use by new memory allocation requests.

Of necessity, some of this changes when AWE memory is used by the server. Because Windows' AWE facility does not support the concept of reserving but not committing memory (i.e., dynamic memory commitment/decommitment), SQL Server doesn't support dynamic memory management when using AWE memory. The BPool begins by acquiring and locking physical memory on the machine. The amount of memory it locks varies based on whether max server memory has been set. If it has, the BPool attempts to lock the amount specified by max server memory. If it has not, the BPool locks all of the physical memory on the machine except for approximately 128MB, which it leaves available for other processes. The BPool then uses the physical memory above 3GB (the AWE memory) as a kind of paging file for data and index pages. It maps physical pages from this region into the virtual memory address space as necessary so they can be referenced via 32-bit pointers.

Recap

So there you have it: SQL Server memory management in a nutshell. Understanding how an application allocates and manages memory is essential to understanding how the application itself works. Memory is such an important resource and its efficient use is such an integral element of sound application design that understanding how memory is managed by an application gives you great insight into the overall design of the application.

Knowledge Measure

1. The BPool is the pool from which most memory allocations are made within SQL Server. What region is set aside for external consumers such as OLE DB providers that run in-process with the server?
2. Which of SQL Server's five memory managers manages memory related to connections?
3. How often does the lazywriter process run?
4. What Perfmon counter reflects the total amount of committed virtual memory within a process?
5. Describe, in general terms, the two main functions of the lazywriter process.
6. True or false: On all releases of SQL Server 2000 and later, allocations of 8KB or less always come from the BPool.
7. True or false: Allocations made by an xproc via the ODS srv_alloc API function are always allocated from the MemToLeave region, regardless of size.
8. What standard COM interface is used within SQL Server to manage individual memory allocations?
9. Which of the five memory managers is the only one the lazywriter can cause to free allocated pages?
10. On a system with 512MB of physical memory and a SQL Server startup parameter of -g768, what will be the maximum size to which the BPool can grow?
11. What Win32 API function is used by the lazywriter process on Windows 2000 to check the available physical memory in the machine?
12. True or false: Because UMS workers are often allowed to perform the work of the lazywriter process, the dedicated lazywriter often finds little to do when it runs on an instance of SQL Server installed on the Windows NT family of the Windows operating system.
13. Why is the virtual memory address space for the MemToLeave region reserved at system startup?
14. On a four-way SMP system, how many BPool free list partitions will SQL Server create?
15. What command line parameter can you pass into SQL Server to adjust the size of the MemToLeave region?
16. What operating system privilege must the SQL Server startup account have in order to make use of AWE memory?
17. True or false: When you configure SQL Server to use AWE memory on a system with less than 3GB of physical memory, the server will refuse to start and log an error in the system error log.

18. What mechanism does SQL Server use to track committed pages in the BPool?

19. What mechanism does SQL Server use to locate a data page in the BPool using its database ID, file number, and page number?

20. How many total reservations can be made at system startup to reserve the BPool?

21. On a SQL Server with 2GB of physical memory, a startup parameter of -g512, and a max server memory setting of 384, what will be the maximum size to which the BPool can grow?

22. By default, how much of the MemToLeave pool is set aside for thread stacks?

23. True or false: Because memory allocations by in-process COM objects that are 8K or less come from the BPool, they are automatically freed when the object is destroyed.

24. True or false: When AWE memory is being used by SQL Server, the physical memory behind the BPool is locked and will not be available to other processes.

25. True or false: By default, the lazywriter process tries to keep at least 384MB available for the MemToLeave region within the SQL Server process.

CHAPTER 12

Query Processor

*I believe in the equality of man; and I believe that religious duties con-
sist in doing justice, loving mercy and endeavoring to make our fellow
creatures happy.*

—Thomas Paine[1]

Query processing and performance is so important to optimal SQL Server usage that I've included a chapter on it in each of my SQL Server books. In this
book, I'll update the coverage from my last book, *The Guru's Guide to SQL
Server Stored Procedures, XML, and HTML*, and continue the discussion of
query optimization internals begun in that book. While providing a boatload
of individual performance tips would certainly have some short-term benefits,
it occurs to me that understanding the reasoning behind the how-to is actually
more important and will benefit you more in the long run. As I said in the Introduction, understanding the design behind a technology is more important
than merely learning how to use it. Your ability to tune Transact-SQL queries
is a product of your knowledge and understanding of SQL Server itself—how
it works, what it does when it processes a query, what resources it needs to
formulate an efficient plan, and so on. So, in this chapter, I'll balance the coverage of practical user information with a discussion of some of the internals
of SQL Server query processing. I'll talk about the various query stages and
what happens at each one. As you come to better understand how SQL
Server query processing works, you'll develop your own methods of speeding
up T-SQL code, and you'll use techniques that are sensible and safe because
you'll have a good understanding of how SQL Server was designed to work.

---

1. Paine, Thomas. *The Age of Reason*, ed. Philip S. Foner. New York: Citadel Press, 1974,
p. 50.

Key Terms and Concepts

✔ *Predicate*—an expression that evaluates to true, false, or unknown.

✔ *Cardinality*—strictly speaking, refers to the number of unique values in a table. Because SQL Server allows tables to have duplicate rows and indexes to have duplicate key values, cardinality often more generally refers to the number of rows in a table or the number of rows returned by a query plan operator when discussed from a SQL Server perspective. Cardinality can also refer to the number of unique values in an index.

✔ *Density*—refers to the uniqueness of values within a data set. An index's density is computed by dividing the number of rows that would correspond to a given key value by the number of rows in the table.

✔ *Selectivity*—a measure of the number of rows that will be returned by a particular predicate. It is represented as a percentage of the rows in the table.

Parsing

In order for a Transact-SQL query to be optimized by the SQL Server query optimizer, it must first be parsed into a tree of relational operators. These are the logical operators necessary to carry out the work the query has requested. For example, a simple query that joins the Northwind Customers and Orders tables might be parsed into a relational operator tree that includes an Inner Join logical operator between the two inputs.

SQL Server attempts to avoid redundantly parsing and optimizing queries by hashing the text of each newly submitted query and caching it in memory, along with the original query text and a link to the execution context and the execution plan that the original query resulted in. It checks the hashed query text of each newly submitted query against those already in memory. In order to allow for the possibility of hash collisions, if it finds a match, it then compares the original text of the new query with the one in memory to see whether they match exactly. If they do, the new query doesn't need to be reparsed and reoptimized—the original execution context and/or execution plan can be reused.

The process within SQL Server that handles parsing queries submitted via language events and RPCs into relational operator trees is known as language processing and execution (LPE). LPE is responsible for handing a parsed relational operator tree to the optimizer, then taking the optimized execution plan produced by the optimizer's conversion stage and executing it. LPE is not a single component or code line within the server but actually spans many modules and involves multiple facilities within the server.

Optimization Stages

Figure 12.1 outlines the query optimization process. Once the optimizer receives a relational operator tree into which the initial parsed query has been placed, it begins optimizing it—searching for a means of carrying out the

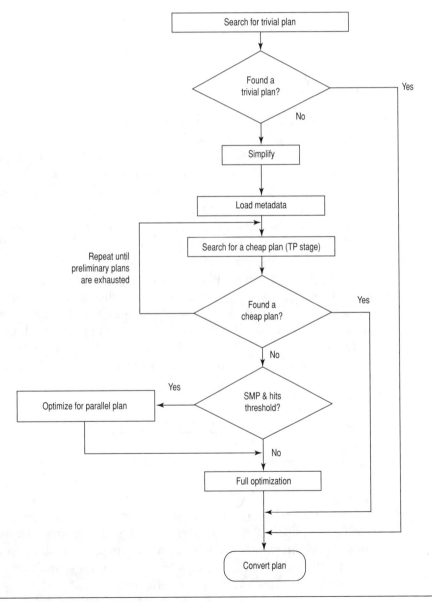

Figure 12.1 The query optimization process

work it requires with the least amount of cost and changing it as necessary to accomplish that. Generally speaking, each successive phase or stage of the optimization process allows more sophisticated (and often more expensive) options to be considered for transforming the initial relational operator tree presented by the parser into an optimized execution plan. If a suitably inexpensive plan is found during this process, it can be returned without requiring further optimization or evaluation of potential transformations. There are four distinct stages in the optimization process: trivial plan optimization, simplification, full optimization, and conversion. I'll describe each of these separately.

Trivial Plan Optimization

With certain queries, the most efficient execution plan is evident based on the query itself and doesn't require any cost estimation or comparisons between plans. For example, if a query uses an equality predicate to filter a query on a column with a unique index, there's no need to estimate the costs of various plans and compare them; a seek using the unique index is obviously the best choice. The optimizer also has trivial optimizations for certain types of covered queries, joins between tables with constraint relationships, DML statements, and a few others. (Note, however, that a query that contains a subquery is *not* eligible for a trivial plan.) When the optimizer detects that a trivial plan is the cheapest plan it can hope to obtain, it sends the plan on to the conversion stage so that it can be returned for execution. You can detect when a trivial plan has been chosen by enabling the 8759 trace flag. When this flag is enabled, the optimizer will write the first portion of a query for which a trivial plan is created to the error log.

Here's an example of a query that results in a trivial plan selection.

```
DECLARE @ordno int
SET @ordno=10248
SELECT * FROM Orders WHERE OrderId=@ordno
```

Because the only predicate used is an equality comparison predicate and there's a unique index on the Orders.OrderNo column, the optimizer will select a trivial plan that features an index seek to service this query. Note that the fact we're using a variable here to filter the query doesn't impair the optimizer's ability to select a trivial plan. Regardless of the value the variable ends up with at runtime, a simple equality operator is being used to compare the variable with a uniquely indexed column, and the optimizer intrinsically knows that a trivial plan is the best option.

The trivial optimization and full optimization stages are the only two optimization stages from which a plan can be generated and the optimization process can end. If a query cannot be optimized via a trivial optimization, it is passed to the simplification stage and then on to the full optimization stage.

Simplification

During the simplification stage, certain heuristics are applied that allow for easier and more effective optimization later. As the name suggests, the purpose of this stage is to simplify the query expression and facilitate better index and statistics usage during the full optimization process. Operators can be relocated in the tree, changed out for other operators, and generally simplified to make the ensuing full optimization process simpler, quicker, and more effective. For example, subqueries used in a predicate can be flattened into semi-joins and inner joins, filters that apply to just one table in a multitable query can be moved above the join in the tree, star schema relationships can be detected, certain operators can be replaced by more efficient equivalents, and so on. Here's an example of a query containing a subquery that is flattened into a semi-join by the optimizer during the simplification stage:

```
SELECT a.au_id
FROM authors a
WHERE au_id IN (SELECT au_id FROM titleauthor ta WHERE
    ta.au_id=a.au_id)
```

If you view the graphical showplan for this query in Query Analyzer, you'll see that the optimizer produces a plan featuring a Nested Loops/Left Semi Join operator. Although expressed as a subquery in the T-SQL code, the query is really asking for the rows in the authors table that have matches in the titleauthor table. Thus, rather than run the subquery for each row in the authors table, the optimizer is smart enough to normalize the query into a simple semi-join between the two tables.

Full Optimization

If the optimizer is unable to find a suitable trivial plan, the plan is simplified, then passed on to the full optimization stage. The full optimization stage attempts to project the cost of various alternate ways of returning the data the query requests and selects the one that is the least expensive. It does not go through this process indefinitely—a timeout governs how long the optimizer thrashes through the various ways of processing a query before it chooses one. If the optimizer hasn't found the most efficient execution plan by the time the timeout expires, it chooses the least expensive plan it has found up to that point and passes it on to the conversion stage so that it can be returned for execution.

The full optimization stage is composed of four smaller stages—steps, if you will—that the optimizer goes through when fully optimizing a query: the transaction processing, quick plan, parallel optimization, and full optimization steps. Understand that the optimizer may not actually go through all of these. If it finds a suitably cheap plan (one that is less expensive than a predetermined cost threshold), the optimizer will send the plan to the conversion stage so that it can be returned for execution without going through the remainder of the steps. Each step except for the parallel optimization step can produce an execution plan and send it on to the conversion stage. Also, if the machine on which SQL Server is running is not a multiprocessor machine, there's no need to execute the parallel optimization step. I'll discuss each of these steps in detail below.

Transaction Processing

During the transaction processing step, the optimizer applies a subset of the potential transformations available to it during full optimization. The purpose of this step is to find most of the transaction processing–oriented query plans that were not found during the trivial plan stage as quickly as possible. For the most part, only transformations involving a join with an indexed lookup are allowed during this step. When an operator does not support an indexed lookup, a transformation involving a hash may be permitted.

The transaction processing step doesn't permit more sophisticated transformations; those are saved for the full optimization step. Transformations involving join reordering, reformatting (dynamic index creation), and so on are not permitted or evaluated for costing during the transaction processing step. As I've said, the idea is to quickly check a wider range of plans than was checked during the trivial plan stage. If a plan is discovered whose estimated cost is less than approximately two-tenths of a second, that plan is selected and no further optimization occurs.

Quick Plan

The quick plan step permits all transformation rules supported by the optimizer. It allows transformations involving join reordering (of the bottom four tables of the relational operator tree) and will select the first plan it finds with an estimated cost of less than approximately one second.

Parallel Optimization

During the parallel optimization step, if the least expensive plan found up to that point exceeds the cost threshold for parallelism sp_configure setting (and SQL Server is running on a multiprocessor computer), the optimizer evaluates operators and transformations that could exploit the multiprocessing capabilities of the machine. These operators will be more fully explored during the full optimization step.

Full Optimization

If all other attempts at finding a suitably inexpensive execution plan fail, the full optimization step of the full optimization stage is entered. During this step, the optimizer recursively walks the relational operator tree as it exists after having passed through the other optimization stages and steps. This tree consists of relational AND/OR nodes and operators. The OR nodes represent a set of mutually exclusive operators (e.g., nested loop vs. hash join vs. merge join) for a particular plan step. The optimizer compares these with one another and selects the least expensive. AND nodes represent operators in which each child node needs to be optimized. The optimizer walks these child nodes and evaluates them separately. The cost of an OR node is equal to the child node with the lowest cost. The cost of an AND node is equal to the sum of the cost of the child nodes, plus some operator cost.

The recursive algorithm followed during this step is basically the same as that followed during earlier stages, it's just that a larger set of the potential transformations are considered. For example, given that the full optimization step comes after the parallel optimization step, parallel operators can be evaluated for cost during this step. Different types of joins can be compared with one another, and reformatting (on-the-fly index creation) and other advanced optimization strategies can be evaluated for cost and compared with one another.

Conversion

Regardless of the stage that actually produces the execution plan, the plan must first go through a conversion in order to be passed to the LPE process to be carried out. This is handled by the conversion stage of the optimization process. Each optimized query plan is processed by this stage before being returned for execution.

Optimization Limits

The optimizer uses multiple techniques to ensure that the process of comparing the cost of operators and plans does not continue indefinitely or even exorbitantly long. At some point during the optimization process, the optimizer can begin to reach a point of diminishing returns. After all, if the time required by the evaluation process far exceeds the execution time of even the most expensive plans, the optimization process may not be able to save that much processing time overall. In a pathological situation, it may be even more expensive than not optimizing at all. The optimizer is designed to avoid situations like this and, to the extent possible, ensure that there is a genuine performance benefit associated with its cost.

A couple of the optimizer's evaluation-limit techniques bear mentioning. The first is the concept of a cost goal. Each successive stage in the optimization process defines a cost goal for plans to be considered. Plans that exceed this cost are not considered further, allowing the optimizer to quickly narrow its search to the better candidate plans. During the trivial plan stage, this cost goal is infinite, which means that no plans will be discarded out-of-hand. For the stages that follow, the optimizer reduces this to 90% of the cheapest plan up to that point.

The optimizer also implements the notion of a timeout value. This timeout value is based on a set number of transformations the optimizer believes it can perform before it needs to time out. Throughout the optimization process, the optimizer checks to see whether it has exceeded this number of transformations and times out if so. Because the number of transformations used to compute the timeout is based on an assumption that the optimizer can perform a given number of transformations per second, this timeout has only a rough correlation to actual elapsed time. It is a semi-linear function that starts at around 10% of the initial cost estimate and increases more or less linearly until it levels off at approximately 60 seconds of elapsed time. Note that this timeout is only as accurate as the transformation time estimates made. There is no strictly enforced concept of a time-based timeout value. Because the number of transformations that the optimizer can apply per second can vary widely, the exact amount of time that may elapse before a query times out may change from query to query.

You can use trace flag 8675 to determine when the optimizer times out while generating a query plan. This flag will also tell you when the optimizer reaches the memory limit to which SQL Server restricts it (about 80% of the BPool). You can also often infer that an optimization timeout has occurred via the compile time returned by SET STATISTICS TIME ON. If this is around 60 seconds, you may indeed be seeing an optimization time-out, particularly in situations where you know that the optimizer has inexplicably failed to choose the best plan for a given query.

Parameter Sniffing

Prior to compiling an execution plan for a stored procedure, SQL Server attempts to "sniff" (i.e., discern) the values of the parameters being passed into it and use those values when compiling the plan. When these values are being used to filter a query (i.e., as part of a WHERE or HAVING predicate), this allows the optimizer to produce a more precise execution plan tailored to the values being passed into the stored procedure (using the statistics histograms for the columns they're used to filter) rather than based solely on the average density of the relevant table columns. Generally speaking, this is a good thing and results in improved performance over older versions of SQL Server.

You can get into trouble, however, when an atypical parameter value is passed in when a plan is first compiled for a procedure. The plan that's cached in memory may be suboptimal for the majority of the values that will be supplied for the parameter. When more typical values are supplied, they may reuse the old plan and may take longer to execute than they would have if the plan had been tailored to them instead.

You have a few options in this situation. You can mark the procedure for automatic recompilation using the WITH RECOMPILE option. This will cause the procedure's plan to be rebuilt each time it's executed. If the compilation time is negligible, this can be an easy solution for dealing with parameter values that vary a great deal in terms of their distribution across a table column.

You can also execute a procedure using the WITH RECOMPILE option—again causing the plan to be rebuilt. Similarly, you can use the sp_recompile procedure to cause a procedure's plan to be rebuilt the next time it's executed.

You can also "disable" parameter sniffing by filtering your query using local variables to which you've copied the parameter values. Using local variables instead of procedure parameters to filter a query is generally a bad idea because it inhibits the use of an index's statistics histogram in computing selectivity, but there are exceptions to the rule. When the optimizer can't use the statistics histogram to compute the number of rows that may be returned by a particular filter criterion, it uses magic numbers—hard-coded estimates of the percentage of rows that will be returned based on the comparison operator used. In some rare cases, these estimates may be more accurate than using the histogram itself. One such case is when the value used to scan the histogram is atypical and results in a skewed estimate of the number of rows that will normally match the supplied parameter.

You can sometimes also reorganize a query that's affected by errant parameter sniffing such that it runs in a distinct execution context that receives its own execution plan. This leverages the fact that when a procedure executes a T-SQL block dynamically or calls another procedure, each gets its own execution plan. Methods of using this technique to deal with parameter sniffing idiosyncrasies include using sp_executesql, EXEC(), and breaking a procedure into multiple procedures. With the sp_executesql and multiple procedure approach, you can still benefit from plan reuse. With EXEC(), you are not likely to—it's likely that your plan will have to be recompiled with each execution. Depending on what you're doing and how long compilation takes, this may or may not be desirable.

You can also explicitly clear the procedure cache with DBCC FREE-PROCCACHE. This will cause all compiled plans to be tossed from memory and force them to be recompiled the next time each procedure is executed. This is a fairly drastic measure but can apply in some circumstances. For example, you might use it before and after running a nightly job that executes a number of procedures with atypical parameter values that usually run during the day with more typical parameters. This would help make sure that you don't reuse the plans from earlier in the day and that the plans created for your nightly job run aren't reused the next day.

Another situation in which you can run into trouble with parameter sniffing is when an execution plan in the cache reflects typical parameter values that you pass, but you need to pass an atypical parameter into a procedure and you need it to execute as quickly as possible. In this case, the problem isn't that you have a suboptimal plan in the cache—for the majority of your queries, the plan *is* optimal. The problem is that these two queries shouldn't be sharing an execution plan. Say, for example, that you have a stored procedure to which you pass a country code so that it can return national sales figures. Most of the time, you pass in "US" because your business is based in the United States and most of your sales are in that country. Due to the fact that U.S.-based sales records make up most of your sales table, the optimizer generates an execution plan that uses a table scan. A table scan is more efficient in this situation than an index seek because most of the rows are being returned anyway. Sometimes, however, you pass in a different country code—a code for a country for which there may be only a few sales. You expect this query to return relatively quickly based on the handful of rows it will eventually yield, but it doesn't. It also results in a table scan because it reuses the plan originally compiled when you passed in "US." One potential solution would be to reorganize the procedure into multiple procedures—one for U.S.-based sales and one for all other countries. Given that your sales to countries outside the United States are relatively few and fairly evenly distributed, you will likely see an index seek (provided that an appropriate index exists) when querying for sales from these countries. Conversely, your queries for U.S.-based sales will continue to use table scans because that is the most efficient way to service them. Especially if a plan takes awhile to compile (and, hence, is not an ideal candidate for automatic recompilation with each execution), using multiple procedures in this manner may be a viable solution for you.

Auto-Parameterization

In order to increase the likelihood of plan reuse, SQL Server attempts to automatically parameterize ad hoc queries. By "auto-parameterize," I mean that the server can replace a constant value in an ad hoc query with a parameter marker so that the plan can be reused with different values for the constant. Consider the following query, for example:

```
SELECT * FROM Orders WHERE OrderId=10248
```

In this query, the value 10248 is a constant. If the server were unable to auto-parameterize the query, a value other than 10248 would result in a separate execution plan being generated. Instead, the server is intelligent enough to replace 10248 with a parameter marker and supply 10248 as the value of the parameter for a given execution context. Other executions of the same query with different parameters will each have their own execution contexts but will use the same execution plan.

Rather than relying on the server to correctly guess the parameters for a given query, you can specify them directly via sp_executesql or by using parameter markers in your query text. When you do this, there's no ambiguity, and you have more control over the data types used for each parameter. SQL Server infers each auto-parameter's data type based on the constant passed in, but it can occasionally guess wrong, causing a data type mismatch between the parameter and the column to which it is being compared. Given that this can possibly inhibit index usage, it's important to be aware of it. For example, in the query above, SQL Server guesses that the order ID parameter should be a smallint based on the value of 10248, which fits comfortably within the range of SQL Server's two-byte smallint data type. However, the OrderId column in the Orders table is actually a four-byte int, so the execution plan must include a CONVERT operator in order to reconcile the difference between the two.

The textual or graphical showplan for an auto-parameterized query will indicate that it has been parameterized. When an ad hoc query has been auto-parameterized, you'll see parameter placeholders such as @1 in place of at least some of the constant values in your query text, and you'll see that these placeholders have been used to filter your query.

The syscacheobjects table is also a good place to check for auto-parameterization. When SQL Server has auto-parameterized an ad hoc query, the automatically generated parameter placeholders and data types will be included at the start of the sql column in the query's rows in syscacheobjects. The query text listed in the sql column will also use these placeholders to filter the data it returns, like so:

```
(@1 smallint)SELECT * FROM [Orders] WHERE [OrderId]=@1
```

You can also turn on trace flag 8759 to detect when a query has been auto-parameterized. When trace flag 8759 is enabled, the first part of an auto-parameterized query is written to the SQL Server error log, as shown below.

```
SAFE auto-paramd query: (@1 smallint) SELECT * FROM [Orders] WHERE
    [OrderId]=@1
```

Indexing

There are few more beneficial things you can do to speed up query performance than to construct usable, efficient indexes. The name of the game with large data banks is I/O—you want to avoid as much of it as you can. Caching helps. Processing power helps. Fast hard drives help. But nothing affects query performance as fundamentally or as profoundly as indexing.

Without a useful index, SQL Server has little choice but to scan the entire table or tables to find the data you need. If you're joining two or more tables, SQL Server may have to scan some of them multiple times to find all the data needed to satisfy the query. Indexes can dramatically speed up the process of finding data as well as the process of joining tables together.

Storage

The sysindexes system table stores system-level information about SQL Server indexes. Every index has a row in sysindexes and is identified by its indid column, a 1-based integer indicating the order in which it was created—the clustered index is always indid 1. If a table has no clustered index, sysindexes will contain a row for the table itself with an indid value of 0.

The Index Allocation Map

SQL Server tracks the extents that belong to a table or index using Index Allocation Map (IAM) pages. A heap or index will have at least one IAM for each file on which it has allocated extents. An IAM is a bitmap that maps extents to objects; each bit indicates whether the corresponding extent belongs to the object that owns the IAM. Each IAM bitmap covers a range of 512,000 pages. The first IAM page for an index is stored in sysindexes' First-IAM column. IAM pages are allocated randomly in a database file and linked together in a chain. Even though the IAM permits SQL Server to efficiently prefetch a table's extents, individual rows must still be examined—the IAM just serves as an access method to the pages themselves.

Index Types

SQL Server supports two types of indexes: clustered and nonclustered. Both types have a number of features in common. Both consist of pages stored in B-(balanced) trees. The node levels of each type contain pointers to pages at the next level, while the leaf level contains the key values.

B-Trees

As I've said, SQL Server indexes are stored physically as B-trees. B-trees support the notion of searching through data by using a binary search-type algorithm. B-tree indexes store keys with similar values close together, with the tree itself being continually rebalanced in order to ensure that a given value can be reached with a minimum of page traversal. Because B-trees are balanced, the cost of finding a row is fairly constant, regardless of which row it is.

The first node in a B-tree index is the root node. A pointer to each index's root node is stored in sysindexes' root column. When searching for data using an index, SQL Server begins at the root node, then traverses any intermediate levels that might exist, finally either finding or not finding the data in the bottom-level leaf nodes of the index. The number of intermediate levels will vary based on the size of the table, the size of the index key, and the number of columns in the key. Obviously the more data there is or the larger each key is, the more pages you need.

Index pages above the leaf level are known as node pages. Each row in a node page contains a key or keys and a pointer to a page at the next level whose first key row matches it. This is the general structure of a B-tree. SQL Server navigates these linkages until it locates the data it's searching for or reaches the end of the linkage in a leaf-level node. The leaf level of a B-tree contains key values, and, in the case of nonclustered indexes, bookmarks to the underlying clustered index or heap. These key values are stored sequentially and can be sorted in either ascending or descending order on SQL Server 2000 and later.

Unlike nonclustered indexes, the leaf node of a clustered index actually stores the data itself. There is no bookmark, nor is there a need for one. When a clustered index is present, the data itself lives in the leaf level of the index.

The data pages in a table are stored in a page chain, a doubly-linked list of pages. When a clustered index is present, the order of the rows on each page and the order of the pages within the chain are determined by the index key. Given that the clustered index key causes the data to be sorted, it's important to choose it wisely. The key should be selected with several considerations in mind, including the following.

- The key should be as small as possible since it will serve as the bookmark in every nonclustered index.
- The key should be chosen such that it aligns well with common ORDER BY and GROUP BY queries.
- It should match reasonably well with common range queries (queries where a range of rows is requested based on the values in a column or columns).
- It should be a set of columns that is not updated extremely frequently because updating a table's clustered index key can require relocating a row and updating the bookmark in every nonclustered index on the table.

Beginning with SQL Server 7.0, all clustered indexes have unique keys. If a clustered index is created that is not unique (e.g., via CREATE INDEX without the UNIQUE keyword), SQL Server forces the index to be unique by appending a 4-byte value called a uniqueifier to key values as necessary to differentiate identical key values from one another.

Leaf-level pages in a nonclustered index contain index keys and book-marks to the underlying clustered index or heap. A bookmark can take one of two forms. When a clustered index exists on the table, the bookmark is the clustered index's key. If the clustered index and the nonclustered index share a common key column, it's stored just once. When a clustered index isn't present, the bookmark consists of a row identifier (RID) made up of the file number, the page number, and the slot number of the row referenced by the nonclustered key value.

The fact that a heap (a table without a clustered index) forces nonclustered indexes to reference it using physical location information is a good enough reason alone to create a clustered index on every table you build. Without it, changes to the table that cause page splits will have a ripple effect on the table's nonclustered indexes since the physical location of the rows they reference will change, perhaps quite often. This was, in fact, one of the major disadvantages of SQL Server indexing prior to version 7.0—nonclustered indexes always stored physical row locator information rather than the clustered key value and were thus susceptible to physical row location changes in the underlying table.

Nonclustered indexes are best at singleton selects—queries that return a single row. Once the nonclustered B-tree is navigated, the actual data can be accessed with just one page I/O, that is, the read of the page from the underlying table.

Covering Indexes

A nonclustered index is said to "cover" a query when it contains all the columns requested by the query. This allows it to skip the bookmark lookup step and simply return the data the query seeks from its own B-tree. When a clustered index is present, a query can be covered using a combination of nonclustered and clustered key columns since the clustered key is the nonclustered index's bookmark. That is, if the nonclustered index is built on the LastName and FirstName columns and the clustered index key is built on CustomerID, a query that requests the CustomerID and LastName columns can be covered by the nonclustered index. A covering nonclustered index is the next best thing to having multiple clustered indexes on the same table.

Performance Issues

Generally speaking, keep your index keys as narrow as possible. Wider keys cause more I/O and permit fewer key rows to fit on each B-tree page. This results in the index requiring a larger number of pages than it otherwise would and causes it to take up more disk space. In practice, you'll likely tailor your indexing strategy to meet specific business requirements. For example, if you have a query that takes an extremely long time to return because it needs an index with key columns none of your current indexes have, you may indeed want to widen an existing index or create a new one.

Naturally, there's a trade-off with adding additional indexes or index columns—namely, DML performance. Since the indexes on a table have to be maintained and updated as you add or change data, each new index you add brings with it a certain amount of overhead. The more indexes you add, the slower updates, inserts, and deletes against the underlying tables become, so it's important to keep your indexes as compact and narrow as possible while still meeting the business needs your system was designed to address.

Index Intersection

Prior to version 7.0, the SQL Server query optimizer would use just one index per table to resolve a query. SQL Server 7.0 and later can use multiple indexes per table and can intersect their sets of bookmarks before incurring the expense of retrieving data from the underlying table. This has some implications on index design and key selection, as I'll discuss in a moment.

Index Fragmentation

You can control the amount of fragmentation in an index through its fillfactor setting and through regular defrag operations. An index's fillfactor affects performance in several ways. First, creating an index with a relatively low fillfactor helps avoid page splits during inserts. Obviously, with pages only partially full, the potential for needing to split one of them in order to insert new rows is lower than it would be with completely full pages. Second, a high fillfactor can help compact pages so that less I/O is required to service a query. This is a common technique with data warehouses. Retrieving pages that are only partially full wastes I/O bandwidth.

An index's fillfactor setting affects only the leaf-level pages in the index. SQL Server normally reserves enough empty space on intermediate index pages to store at least one row of the index's maximum size. If you want your fillfactor specification applied to intermediate as well as leaf-level pages, supply the PAD_INDEX option of the CREATE INDEX statement. PAD_INDEX instructs SQL Server to apply the fillfactor to the intermediate-level pages of the index. If your fillfactor setting is so high that there isn't room on the intermediate pages for even a single row (e.g., a fillfactor of 100%), SQL Server will override the percentage so that at least one row fits. If your fillfactor setting is so low that the intermediate pages cannot store at least two rows, SQL Server will override the fillfactor percentage on the intermediate pages so that at least two rows fit on each page.

Understand that an index's fillfactor setting isn't maintained over time. It's applied when the index is first created but is not enforced afterward. DBCC SHOWCONTIG is the tool of choice for determining how full the pages in a table and/or index really are. The key indicators you want to examine are Logical Scan Fragmentation and Avg. Page Density. DBCC SHOWCONTIG shows three types of fragmentation: extent scan fragmentation, logical scan fragmentation, and scan density. Use DBCC INDEXDEFRAG to fix logical scan fragmentation; rebuild indexes to defrag the table and/or index completely.

Listing 12.1 shows some sample DBCC SHOWCONTIG output from the Northwind Customers table.

Listing 12.1 Sample DBCC SHOWCONTIG Output

```
DBCC SHOWCONTIG (Customers)

(Results)

DBCC SHOWCONTIG scanning 'Customers' table...
Table: 'Customers' (2073058421); index ID: 1, database ID: 6
TABLE level scan performed.
- Pages Scanned...............................: 5
- Extents Scanned.............................: 3
- Extent Switches.............................: 4
- Avg. Pages per Extent.......................: 1.7
- Scan Density [Best Count:Actual Count].......: 20.00% [1:5]
- Logical Scan Fragmentation .............: 40.00%
- Extent Scan Fragmentation ...................: 66.67%
- Avg. Bytes Free per Page....................: 3095.2
- Avg. Page Density (full)................: 61.76%
```

As you can see, the Customer table is a bit fragmented. Logical Scan Fragmentation is sitting at 40% and Avg. Page Density is at 61.76% (see lines set in bold). In other words, the pages in the table are, on average, approximately 40% empty. Let's defrag the table's clustered index and see if things improve any. Listing 12.2 shows the resulting output.

Listing 12.2 Output from the Customers Table After Defragmentation

```
DBCC INDEXDEFRAG(Northwind,Customers,1)
```

(Results)

Pages Scanned	Pages Moved	Pages Removed
1	0	1

```
    DBCC SHOWCONTIG (Customers)
```

(Results)

```
DBCC SHOWCONTIG scanning 'Customers' table...
Table: 'Customers' (2073058421); index ID: 1, database ID: 6
TABLE level scan performed.
- Pages Scanned...............................: 4
- Extents Scanned.............................: 3
- Extent Switches.............................: 2
- Avg. Pages per Extent.......................: 1.3
- Scan Density [Best Count:Actual Count].......: 33.33% [1:3]
- Logical Scan Fragmentation .............: 25.00%
- Extent Scan Fragmentation ..................: 66.67%
- Avg. Bytes Free per Page....................: 1845.0
- Avg. Page Density (full)................: 77.21%
```

As you can see, DBCC INDEXDEFRAG helped considerably. Logical Scan Fragmentation has dropped to 25% and Avg. Page Density is now at a little over 77%, an improvement of approximately 15%.

By default, DBCC SHOWCONTIG reports leaf-level information only. To scan the other levels of the table/index, specify the ALL_LEVELS option (Listing 12.3).

Listing 12.3 Using DBCC SHOWCONTIG to Show Fragmentation at All Levels

```
DBCC SHOWCONTIG (Customers) WITH TABLERESULTS, ALL_LEVELS
```

(Results abridged)

ObjectName	IndexName	AveragePageDensity	ScanDensity	LogicalFragmenta
Customers	PK_Customers	77.205337524414063	33.333333333333329	25.0
Customers	PK_Customers	0.95132195949554443	0.0	0.0

Table 12.1 lists the key data elements reported by DBCC SHOWCON-TIG and what they mean.

I use the Logical Scan Fragmentation and Avg. Page Density fields to determine overall table/index fragmentation. You should see them change in tandem as fragmentation increases or decreases over time.

Defragmenting

As you just saw, DBCC INDEXDEFRAG is a handy way to defragment an index. It's an online operation, so the index is still usable while it works. That said, it reorganizes the index only at the leaf level, performing a kind of bubble sort on the leaf-level pages. To fully defrag an index, you must rebuild it. You have several ways to do this. First, you could simply drop and recreate the index by using DROP/CREATE INDEX. The drawback to this, though, is that you have to take the index offline while you rebuild it, and you aren't allowed to drop indexes that support constraints. You could use DBCC DBREINDEX or the DROP_EXISTING clause of CREATE INDEX, but, again, the index is unavailable until it's rebuilt. The one upside is that the index can be created in parallel if you're running on the Enterprise Edition of SQL Server. Since SQL Server's parallel index creation scales almost linearly on multiple processors, the length of time that an index is offline while being recreated can be significantly less on an SMP system than on a single-processor system that is otherwise identical in terms of hardware resources.

Table 12.1 Key DBCC SHOWCONTIG Fields

SHOWCONTIG Field	Meaning
Avg. Bytes Free per Page	Average number of bytes free on each page
Pages Scanned	Number of pages accessed
Extents Scanned	Number of extents accessed
Out of order pages (not displayed, but used to compute Logical Scan Fragmentation)	Number of times a page had a lower page number than the previous page in the scan
Extent Switches	Number of times a page in the scan was on a different extent than the previous page in the scan

Generally speaking, DBCC INDEXDEFRAG is the best tool for the job unless you find widespread fragmentation in the non-leaf levels of the index and you feel this fragmentation is unacceptably affecting query performance. As I mentioned, you can check the fragmentation of the other levels of an index by passing the ALL_LEVELS option to DBCC SHOWCONTIG.

In addition to defragmenting the leaf-level pages, DBCC INDEXDE-FRAG also features a compaction phase wherein it compacts the index's pages using the original fillfactor as its target. It attempts to leave enough space for at least one row on each page when it finishes. If it can't obtain a lock on a particular page during compaction, it skips the page. It removes any pages that end up completely empty as a result of the compaction.

Indexes on Views and Computed Columns

Creating an index on a view or a computed column persists data that would otherwise exist only in a logical sense. Normally, the data returned by a view exists only in the tables the view queries. When you query the view, your query is combined with the one comprising the view and the data is retrieved from the underlying objects. The same is true for computed columns. Normally, the data returned by a computed column does not actually exist independently of the columns or expressions it references. Every time you request it from its host table, the expression that comprises it is reevaluated and its data is generated on-the-fly.

When you begin building indexes on a view, you must start with a unique clustered index. This is where the real data persistence happens. Just as with tables, a clustered index created on a view actually stores the data itself in its leaf-level nodes. Once the clustered index exists, you're free to create nonclustered indexes on the view as well.

This differs from computed columns in tables. With computed columns, you're not required to first create a clustered index in order to build nonclustered indexes. Since the column will serve merely as an index key value, a nonclustered index works just fine.

Prerequisites

SQL Server requires that seven SET options have specific values in order to create an index on a view or a computed column. Table 12.2 lists the settings and their required values. As you can see from the table, all settings except NUMERIC_ROUNDABORT must be set to ON.

Only deterministic expressions can be used with indexed views and indexes on computed columns. A deterministic expression is one that, when

Table 12.2 Required Settings for an Indexed View or Computed Column

Setting	Required Value
ARITHABORT	ON
CONCAT_NULL_YIELDS_NULL	ON
QUOTED_IDENTIFIER	ON
ANSI_NULLS	ON
ANSI_PADDING	ON
ANSI_WARNINGS	ON
NUMERIC_ROUNDABORT	OFF

supplied a given input, always returns the same output. The expression SUB-STRING('He who loves money more than truth will end up poor',23,7) is a deterministic expression; GETDATE isn't.

You can check to see whether a view or column is indexable using Transact-SQL's OBJECTPROPERTY and COLUMNPROPERTY functions (Listing 12.4).

Listing 12.4 Checking Whether a View or Column Is Indexable

```
USE Northwind
SELECT OBJECTPROPERTY (OBJECT_ID('Invoices'), 'IsIndexable')
SELECT COLUMNPROPERTY (OBJECT_ID('syscomments'), 'text' , 'IsIndexable')
SELECT COLUMNPROPERTY (OBJECT_ID('syscomments'), 'text' , 'IsDeterministic')
```

(Results)

```
-----------
0
```

```
-----------
0
```

```
-----------
0
```

One final prerequisite for views is that a view is only indexable if it was created with the SCHEMABINDING option. Creating a view with SCHEMABINDING causes SQL Server to prevent the objects it references from being dropped unless the view is first dropped or changed so that the SCHEMABINDING option is removed. Also, ALTER TABLE statements on tables referenced by the view will fail if they affect the view definition.

In the example above, the Invoices view is not indexable because it was not created with SCHEMABINDING. Here's a version of it that was, along with a subsequent check of IsIndexable (Listing 12.5).

Listing 12.5 The Indexable Invoices2 View

```
CREATE VIEW Invoices2
WITH SCHEMABINDING
AS
SELECT Orders.ShipName, Orders.ShipAddress, Orders.ShipCity,
  Orders.ShipRegion, Orders.ShipPostalCode, Orders.ShipCountry,
  Orders.CustomerID, Customers.CompanyName AS CustomerName,
  Customers.Address, Customers.City, Customers.Region,
  Customers.PostalCode, Customers.Country, Orders.OrderID,
  Orders.OrderDate, Orders.RequiredDate, Orders.ShippedDate,
  Shippers.CompanyName As ShipperName, "Order Details".ProductID,
  Products.ProductName, "Order Details".UnitPrice,
  "Order Details".Quantity, "Order Details".Discount,
  Orders.Freight
  FROM dbo.Shippers INNER JOIN
    (dbo.Products INNER JOIN
      (
        (dbo.Employees INNER JOIN
          (dbo.Customers INNER JOIN dbo.Orders
            ON Customers.CustomerID = Orders.CustomerID)
          ON Employees.EmployeeID = Orders.EmployeeID)
        INNER JOIN dbo.[Order Details]
          ON Orders.OrderID = "Order Details".OrderID)
      ON Products.ProductID = "Order Details".ProductID)
    ON Shippers.ShipperID = Orders.ShipVia
GO
SELECT OBJECTPROPERTY (OBJECT_ID('Invoices2'), 'IsIndexable')

(Results)

-----------
1
```

Note that all the object references now use two-part names (they don't in the original Invoices view). Creating a view with SCHEMABINDING requires all object references to use two-part names.

Once a view has been indexed, the optimizer can make use of the index when the view is queried. In fact, on the Enterprise Edition of SQL Server, the optimizer will even use the index to service a query on the view's underlying tables if it thinks that would yield the least cost in terms of execution time.

Normally, indexed views are not used at all by the optimizer unless you're running on Enterprise Edition. For example, consider the following index and query (Listing 12.6).

Listing 12.6 An Indexed View Query

```
CREATE UNIQUE CLUSTERED INDEX inv ON invoices2 (orderid, productid)
GO
SELECT * FROM invoices2 WHERE orderid=10844 AND productid=22
```

(Results abridged)

ShipName	ShipAddress	ShipCity	ShipRegion	ShipPostalCode
Piccolo und mehr	Geislweg 14	Salzburg	NULL	5020

Listing 12.7 shows an excerpt from the query plan.

Listing 12.7 The Query Plan for Listing 12.6

```
StmtText
-----------------------------------------------------------------------------
SELECT * FROM [invoices2] WHERE [orderid]=@1 AND [productid]=@2
  |--Nested Loops(Inner Join)
       |--Nested Loops(Inner Join)
       |    |--Nested Loops(Inner Join, OUTER REFERENCES:([Orders].[ShipVia]))
       |    |    |--Nested Loops(Inner Join, OUTER REFERENCES:([Orders].[Employ
       |    |    |    |--Nested Loops(Inner Join, OUTER REFERENCES:([Orders].[C
       |    |    |    |    |--Clustered Index Seek(OBJECT:([Northwind].[dbo].[O
       |    |    |    |    |--Clustered Index Seek(OBJECT:([Northwind].[dbo].[C
       |    |    |    |--Clustered Index Seek(OBJECT:([Northwind].[dbo].[Employ
       |    |    |--Clustered Index Seek(OBJECT:([Northwind].[dbo].[Shippers].[
       |    |--Clustered Index Seek(OBJECT:([Northwind].[dbo].[Order Details].[
       |--Clustered Index Seek(OBJECT:([Northwind].[dbo].[Products].[PK_Product
```

Though the plan text is clipped on the right, you can tell that the view index obviously isn't being used even though it contains both of the columns the query filters on. On versions of SQL Server other than Enterprise Edition, this is completely expected. Out of the box, only the Enterprise Edition of SQL Server will consider view indexes when formulating an execution plan. There is, however, a workaround. You can use the NOEXPAND query hint on non-EE versions of SQL Server to force the consideration of a view's index. Here's the query again, this time with the NOEXPAND keyword and the resultant query plan (Listing 12.8).

Listing 12.8 Using NOEXPAND to Force the Use of a View's Index

```
SELECT * FROM invoices2 WITH (NOEXPAND) WHERE orderid=10844 AND productid=22
```

(Results)

```
StmtText
--------------------------------------------------------------------------
SELECT * FROM invoices2 (NOEXPAND) WHERE orderid=10844 AND productid=22
  |--Clustered Index Seek(OBJECT:([Northwind].[dbo].[Invoices2].[inv]), SEEK:([
```

Notice that the index is now used. Using the NOEXPAND keyword forces the optimizer to use a view's index, even if doing so yields a suboptimal plan. You should regard NOEXPAND with the same skepticism that you do other query hints. It's best to let the optimizer do its job and override it only when you have no other choice.

Locking and Indexes

One telltale sign that a table lacks a clustered index is when you notice that it has RID locks taken out on it. SQL Server will never take out RID locks on a table with a clustered index; it will always take out key locks instead.

Generally speaking, you should let SQL Server control locking of all types, including locking with indexes. Normally, it makes good decisions and will do the best job of managing its own resources.

You can use the sp_indexoption system procedure to manually control what types of locks are allowed on an indexed table. You can use it to disable row and/or page locks, but I don't recommend that you normally do this. As with query hints, it's generally best to let the server decide what type of lock should be taken out on a resource.

Note that sp_indexoption applies only to indexes, so you can't control the locking with the pages in a heap. That said, when a table has a clustered index, it *is* affected by the settings specified via sp_indexoption.

Statistics

You've probably heard the term "statistics" bandied about in discussions of SQL Server query performance. Statistics are metadata that SQL Server maintains about index keys and, optionally, nonindexed column values. SQL Server uses statistics to determine whether using an index could speed up a query. In conjunction with indexes, statistics are the single most important source of data for helping the optimizer develop optimum execution plans. When statistics are missing or out-of-date, the optimizer's ability to formulate the best execution plan for a query is seriously impaired.

Let's cover a few basic statistics-related terms before we discuss statistics in more depth.

Cardinality

The cardinality of data refers to how many unique values exist in the data. In strict relational database theory, duplicate rows (tuples) are not permitted within a relation (a table), so cardinality would refer to the total number of tuples. That said, SQL Server *does* permit duplicate rows to exist in a table, so for our purposes, the term "cardinality" refers to the number of *unique* values within a data set.

Density

Density refers to the uniqueness of values within a data set. An index's density is computed by dividing the number of rows that would correspond to a given key value by the number of rows in the table. For a unique index, this amounts to dividing 1 by the table's total row count. Density values range from 0 through 1; lower densities are better.

Selectivity

Selectivity is a measure of the number of rows that will be returned by a particular query criterion. It expresses a relationship between your query criteria and the key values in an index. It is computed by dividing the number of keys being requested by the number of rows they access. Query criteria (usually specified in a WHERE clause) that are highly selective are the most useful to the optimizer because they allow it to predict with certainty how much I/O is required to satisfy a query.

Performance Issues

Indexes with high densities will likely be ignored by the optimizer. The most useful indexes to the optimizer have density values of 0.10 or lower. Let's take the example of a table called VoterRegistration with 10,000 rows, no clustered index, and a nonclustered index on its PartyAffiliation column. If there are three political parties registered in the voting precinct and they each have about the same representation across the voter base, PartyAffiliation will likely contain only three unique values. This means that a given key value in the index could identify as many as 3,333 rows in the table, perhaps more. This gives the index a density of 0.33 (3,333 ÷ 10,000) and virtually ensures that the optimizer will not use the index when formulating an execution plan for queries that require columns not covered by the index.

To better understand this, let's compare the cost of using the index versus not using it to satisfy a simply query. If we wanted to list all the voters in the precinct affiliated with the Democratic Party, we'd be talking about hitting approximately a third of the table, or 3,333 rows. If we use the PartyAffiliation index to access those rows, we're faced with 3,333 separate logical page reads from the underlying table. In other words, as we found each key value in the index, we'd have to look up its bookmark in the underlying table in order to get the columns not contained in the index, and each time we did this, we'd incur the overhead of a logical (and possibly physical) page I/O. All told, we might incur as much as 26MB of page I/O overhead to lookup these bookmark values (3,333 keys × 8K/page). Now consider the cost of simply scanning the table sequentially. If an average of 50 rows fit on each data page and we have to read the entire table to find all of the ones affiliated with the Democratic Party, we're still looking at only about 200 logical page I/Os (10,000 rows ÷ 50 rows/page = 200 pages). That's a big difference and is the chief reason you'll see high-density nonclustered indexes ignored in favor of table/clustered index scans.

At what point does a nonclustered index become sufficiently selective to be useful to the optimizer? In our example, 200 is the magic number—specifically, the optimizer would have to believe that retrieving data via the index would require fewer than 200 page I/Os in order for it to consider the index a more efficient access path than simply scanning the entire table. The original 3,333 estimate could be lowered by adding columns to the index (and also to the query) that make it more selective. There is a point of diminishing returns here, though. As you add columns to the index in an attempt to make it more selective, you increase the amount of overhead that comes with traversing the index's B-tree. By making the index larger, you also make it more expensive to navigate. At some point, it becomes cheaper just to scan the data itself than to incur the overhead of navigating the B-tree.

Storage

SQL Server stores statistics for an index key or a column in the statblob column of sysindexes. statblob is an image data type that stores a histogram containing a sampling of the values in the index key or column. For composite indexes, only the first column is sampled, but density values are maintained for the other columns.

During the index selection phase of query optimization, the optimizer decides whether an index matches up with the columns in filter criteria, determines index selectivity as it relates to that criteria, and estimates the cost of accessing the data the query seeks.

If an index has only one column, its statistics consist of one histogram and one density value. If an index has multiple columns, a single histogram is maintained, as well as density values for each prefix (left-to-right) combination of key columns. The optimizer uses this combination of an index's histogram and densities—its statistics—to determine how useful the index is in resolving a particular query.

The fact that a histogram is stored only for the first column of a composite index is one of the reasons you should position the most selective columns in a multicolumn index first—the histogram will be more useful to the optimizer. Moreover, this is also the reason that splitting up composite indexes into multiple single-column indexes is sometimes advisable. Since the server can intersect and join multiple indexes on a single table, you retain the benefits of having the columns indexed, and you get the added benefit of having a histogram for each column (column statistics can help out here, as well). This isn't a blanket statement—don't run out and drop all your composite indexes—just keep in mind that breaking down composite indexes is sometimes a viable performance tuning option.

Column Statistics

Besides index statistics, SQL Server can also create statistics on nonindexed columns. (This happens automatically when you query a nonindexed column while AUTO_CREATE_STATISTICS is enabled for the database.) Being able to determine the likelihood that a given value might occur in a column gives the optimizer valuable information in determining how best to service a query. It allows the optimizer to estimate the number of rows that will qualify from a given table involved in a join, allowing it to more accurately select join order. Also, the optimizer can use column statistics to provide histogram-type information for the other columns in a multicolumn index. Basically, the more information you can give the optimizer about your data, the better.

Listing Statistics

SQL Server uses statistics to track the distribution of key values across a table. The histogram that's stored as part of an index's statistics contains a sampling of up to 200 values for the index's first key column. Besides the histogram, the statblob column also contains:

- The number of rows the histogram and densities are based on
- The average length of the index key
- The date and time of the last statistics generation
- Density values for other prefix combinations of key columns

The range of key values between each of the 200 histogram sample values is called a step. Each sample value denotes the end of a step, and each step stores three values:

1. EQ_ROWS—the number of rows with a key value matching the sample value
2. RANGE_ROWS—the number of other values inside the range
3. RANGE_DENSITY—a density computation for the range itself

DBCC SHOW_STATISTICS lists the EQ_ROWS and RANGE_ROWS values verbatim and uses RANGE_DENSITY to compute the DISTINCT_RANGE_ROWS and AVG_RANGE_ROWS for the step. It computes DISTINCT_RANGE_ROWS (the total number of distinct rows within the step's range) by dividing 1 by RANGE_DENSITY and computes AVG_RANGE_ROWS (the average number of rows per distinct key value) by multiplying RANGE_ROWS by RANGE_DENSITY.

Updating Statistics

Statistics can be updated in a couple of ways. The first and most obvious is through the AUTO_UPDATE_STATISTICS database option. (You can turn this on via ALTER DATABASE, sp_dboption, or Enterprise Manager.) When statistics are generated automatically for a table of any size, SQL Server uses sampling (as opposed to scanning the entire table) to speed up the process. This works in the vast majority of cases but can sometimes lead to statistics that are less useful than they could be.

Closely related to automatic statistics updating is automatic statistics creation. This occurs when the AUTO_CREATE_STATISTICS database option has been enabled and you issue a query that filters on a nonindexed column (or one that is not left-to-right aligned with the filter criteria). SQL Server will automatically create a set of column statistics for you.

The second method of updating statistics is through the UPDATE STATISTICS command. UPDATE STATISTICS was the only way to update statistics prior to SQL Server 7.0. UPDATE STATISTICS can either use sampling, as happens with automatic updating, or it can do a full scan of the table, resulting in better statistics but likely taking longer.

The CREATE STATISTICS command performs a function similar to UPDATE STATISTICS. You use it to manually create column statistics. Once created, these statistics can be updated through automatic updating or via UPDATE STATISTICS, just as regular index statistics can.

SQL Server provides a few stored procedures to make creating and updating statistics easier. The sp_updatestats procedure runs UPDATE STATISTICS against all user-defined tables in the current database. Unlike the UPDATE STATISTICS command itself, though, sp_updatestats cannot issue a full scan of a table to build statistics—it always uses sampling. If you want full scan statistics, you have to use UPDATE STATISTICS.

The sp_createstats procedure can be similarly handy. It can automate the creation of column statistics for all eligible columns in all eligible tables in a database. Eligible columns include noncomputed columns with data types other than text, ntext, or image that do not already have column or first-column index statistics. Eligible tables include all user (nonsystem) tables. I'm not recommending that you run out and execute sp_createstats in each of your databases—it's unlikely that you'd need statistics on every column in a table. However, in the event that you do, sp_createstats can be a real timesaver.

The sp_autostats procedure allows you to control automatic statistics updating at the table and index levels. Rather than simply relying on the AUTO_UPDATE_STATISTICS database option, you can enable/disable auto stats generation at a more granular level. For example, if you run a nightly job on a large table to update its statistics using a full scan, you may want to disable automatic statistics updates for the table. Using sp_autostats, you can disable automatic statistics updates on this one table while leaving it enabled for the rest of the database (you can also use UPDATE STATIS-TICS...WITH NORECOMPUTE). Statistics updates on large tables, even those that use sampling, can take a while to run and can use significant CPU and I/O resources.

Keep in mind that the negative impact on performance of not having statistics or having out-of-date statistics almost always outweighs the performance benefits of avoiding automatic statistics updates/creation. You should disable auto update/create stats only when thorough testing has shown that there's no other way to achieve the performance or scalability you require.

Listing 12.9 shows a stored procedure that you can use to stay on top of statistics updates. It shows the statistics type, the last time it was updated, and a wealth of other information that you may find useful in managing index and column statistics.

Listing 12.9 The sp_showstatdate Procedure for Staying on Top of Statistics Updates

```
CREATE PROC sp_showstatdate @tabmask sysname='%',
    @indmask sysname='%'
AS
SELECT
  LEFT(CAST(USER_NAME(uid)+'.'+o.name AS sysname),30) AS TableName,
  LEFT(i.name,30) AS IndexName,
  CASE WHEN INDEXPROPERTY(o.id,i.name,'IsAutoStatistics')=1
        THEN 'AutoStatistics'
      WHEN INDEXPROPERTY(o.id,i.name,'IsStatistics')=1
        THEN 'Statistics'
  ELSE 'Index'
  END AS Type,
  STATS_DATE(o.id, i.indid) AS StatsUpdated,
  rowcnt,
  rowmodctr,
  ISNULL(CAST(rowmodctr/CAST(NULLIF(rowcnt,0) AS decimal(20,2))*100
      AS int),0) AS PercentModifiedRows,
  CASE i.status & 0x1000000
  WHEN 0 THEN 'No'
  ELSE 'Yes'
  END AS [NoRecompute?],
  i.status
FROM dbo.sysobjects o JOIN dbo.sysindexes i ON (o.id = i.id)
```

```
WHERE o.name LIKE @tabmask
  AND i.name LIKE @indmask
  AND OBJECTPROPERTY(o.id,'IsUserTable')=1
  AND i.indid BETWEEN 1 AND 254
ORDER BY TableName, IndexName
GO
USE pubs
GO
EXEC sp_showstatdate
```

(Results abridged)

TableName	IndexName	Type	StatsUpdated
dbo.authors	au_fname	Statistics	2000-07-02 19:42:04.487
dbo.authors	aunmind	Index	2000-06-30 20:54:56.737
dbo.authors	UPKCL_auidind	Index	2000-06-30 20:54:56.737
dbo.dtproperties	pk_dtproperties	Index	NULL
dbo.employee	employee_ind	Index	2000-06-30 20:54:45.280
dbo.employee	PK_emp_id	Index	2000-06-30 20:54:45.297

Selectivity Estimation

To correctly determine the relative cost of a query plan, the optimizer needs to be able to precisely estimate the number of rows returned by the query. As I mentioned earlier, this is known as selectivity, and it's crucial for the optimizer to be able to accurately estimate it.

Selectivity estimates come from comparing query criteria with the statistics for the index key or column they reference. Selectivity tells us whether to expect a single row or 10,000 rows for a given key value. It gives us an idea of how many rows correspond to the key or column value we're searching for. This, in turn, helps us determine what type of approach would be the most efficient for accessing those rows. Obviously, you take a different approach to access one row than you would for 10,000.

If the optimizer discovers that you don't have index or column statistics for a column in the query's filter criteria, it may automatically create column-level statistics for the column if you have the AUTO_CREATE_STATISTICS database option enabled. You'll incur the cost of creating the statistics the first time around, but subsequent queries should be sped up by the new stats.

Indexable Expressions

In other books and materials on SQL Server, you often see the discussion of index use in query plans couched in terms of "SARGs"—search arguments in a query that the optimizer can translate into a comparison between an index key and a value. There is, however, no such concept within the optimizer code itself. The term "SARG" is an anachronism from the old Sybase code base and Sybase training materials. The optimizer in all recent versions of SQL Server is far more sophisticated in terms of its ability to use an index to speed up a query than it was in older versions of the product. The optimizer's ability to use indexes is no longer constrained to simple expressions, nor is the decision of whether or not to use an index necessarily dependent on the form an expression may have. In other words, the actual expression used in a query predicate may be irrelevant depending on the indexes present, the optimizer's ability to ferret out column references within it, and the cost estimates produced by the optimizer. The term "SARG" has become less and less applicable, to the point that I think it's ready to be retired in favor of a more accurate and more generally encompassing term for "index friendly" query predicate expressions. A far more precise and accurate term (and the term used within the optimizer itself) is "indexable expression"—an expression that can be serviced with an index to provider faster access to the data returned by a query—so that's the term I'll use in this book.

For our purposes, an indexable expression is a clause in a query that the optimizer can potentially use in conjunction with an index to limit the results returned by the query. The optimizer attempts to identify indexable expressions in a query's criteria so that it can determine the best indexes to use to service the query.

Generally speaking, indexable expressions have the following form:

```
Column op Constant/Variable
```

(the terms can be reversed) where Column is a table column; op is one of the following operators: =, >=, <=, >, <, <>, !=, !>, !<, BETWEEN, and LIKE (some LIKE clauses can be translated into indexable expressions, and some can't); and Constant/Variable is a constant value, variable reference, or one of a handful of functions.

Operator Translation

Even though some of the operators mentioned above do not lend themselves to use with indexed lookups, the optimizer can translate them into expressions that do. For example, consider this query:

```
SELECT * FROM authors
WHERE au_lname != 'Greene'
```

Is the WHERE clause indexable? Yes. Look at the translation that occurs in this excerpt from the query plan:

```
SEEK:([authors].[au_lname] < 'Greene' OR
    [authors].[au_lname] > 'Greene')
```

The optimizer is smart enough to know that x != @parm is the same as x < @parm OR x > @parm and translates it accordingly. Since the two branches of the OR clause can be executed in parallel and merged, this affords the use of an index to service the WHERE criteria.

Now consider this query, which uses a LIKE expression:

```
SELECT * FROM authors
WHERE au_lname LIKE 'Gr%'
```

Is it indexable? Yes. Once again, the optimizer translates the WHERE clause criteria to something it finds more palatable:

```
SEEK:([authors].[au_lname] >= 'GQ' AND
    [authors].[au_lname] < 'GS')
```

Here's another:

```
SELECT * FROM authors
WHERE au_lname !> 'Greene'
```

Can the optimizer use an index to satisfy the query? Yes, it can. Here's an excerpt from the plan:

```
SEEK:([authors].[au_lname] <= 'Greene')
```

Here's one more query:

```
SELECT * FROM authors
WHERE au_lname !< 'Greene'
```

And here's its plan:

```
SEEK:([authors].[au_lname] >= 'Greene')
```

See the pattern? The optimizer attempts to translate seemingly nonindexable expressions into ones it can more easily service with indexes.

Indexable expressions can be joined together with AND to form compound clauses. The rule of thumb for identifying an indexable expression is that a clause can be serviced by an index if the optimizer can detect that it's a comparison between an index key value and a constant or variable. A common beginner's error is to involve a column in an expression when comparing it to a constant or variable. For the most part, this prevents the clause from being serviced by an index because the optimizer doesn't know what the expression actually evaluates to—it's not known until runtime. (There are exceptions to this—see the discussion below on folding for more information.) The trick, then, is to isolate the column in these types of expressions so that it's not modified or encapsulated in any way. Use commonsense algebra to put the modifiers in the clause on the value/constant side of the expression and leave the column itself unmodified.

If the optimizer is not able to identify an expression as an indexable expression, it is not able to use statistics to estimate the number of rows returned by the associated operator and must instead hazard a guess. It uses hard-coded "magic" numbers for these estimates, based on the comparison operator used. Table 12.3 summarizes the magic numbers the optimizer uses for each operator.

Folding

In certain limited circumstances, the optimizer is able to properly identify an indexable expression even when you wrap the column in the expression in a function or otherwise involve it in a subexpression. The process by which this occurs, folding, is an optimization over older versions of SQL Server in which the optimizer was unable to use an index to service a query clause when the table column was involved in an expression or buried in a function. Folding allows the optimizer to identity certain types of indexable expressions even when the column in the expression is involved in a subexpression

Table 12.3 Row Estimates for Nonindexable Expressions

Comparison Operator	Percentage of Rows Estimated
=	10
>	30
<	30
BETWEEN	10

or nestled in a function. Foldable expressions include some involving the DATEADD, ISNULL, and ROUND functions, certain forms of the LIKE predicate, and a few others. Consider the following query, for example:

```
SELECT *
FROM Orders
WHERE ISNULL(OrderDate,GETDATE())>'2003-04-06 19:55:00.000'
```

If the optimizer were unable to fold the expression involving the Order-Date column and the ISNULL function, it would be unable to use the Orders table's OrderDate index (whose key is the OrderDate column) to service this query. As it is, if you view the graphical showplan for this query in Query Analyzer, you'll see that the index is indeed used.

The rule of thumb here is still to avoid wrapping columns in expressions when you can. However, just be aware that there are situations when the optimizer can identify indexable expressions anyway.

Join Order and Type Selection

In addition to choosing indexes and indexable expressions, the optimizer also selects a join order and picks a join strategy for operators that require it. The selection of indexes and join strategy go hand in hand—indexes influence the types of join strategies that are viable, and the join strategy influences the types of indexes the optimizer needs to produce an efficient plan.

SQL Server supports three types of joins.

1. *Nested loop* works well with a smaller outer table and an index on the inner table.
2. *Merge* works well when both inputs are sorted on the joining column. (The optimizer can sort one of the inputs if necessary.)
3. *Hash* performs well in situations where there are no usable indexes. Usually, creating an index (so that a different join strategy can be chosen) will provide better performance.

The optimizer determines the join strategy to use to service a query. It evaluates the cost of each strategy and selects the one it thinks will cost the least. It reserves the right to reorder tables in the FROM clause if doing so will improve the performance of the query. You can always tell whether this has happened by inspecting the execution plan. The order of the tables in the execution plan is the order the optimizer thought would perform best.

You can override the optimizer's ability to determine join order by using the OPTION (FORCE ORDER) clause for a query, the SET FORCEPLAN ON session option, and join hints (e.g., INNER LOOP JOIN). Each of these forces the optimizer to join tables in the order specified by the FROM clause.

Note that forcing join order may have the side effect of also forcing a particular join strategy. For example, consider the query and its execution plan shown in Listing 12.10.

Listing 12.10 A Query with a Right-Outer Join and Its Execution Plan

(Query)

```
SELECT o.OrderId, p.ProductId
FROM [Order Details] o RIGHT JOIN Products p
ON (o.ProductId=p.ProductId)
```

(Execution plan)

```
StmtText
-------------------------------------------------------------------------
SELECT o.OrderId, p.ProductId
FROM [Order Details] o RIGHT JOIN Products p
ON (o.ProductId=p.ProductId)
  |--Nested Loops(Left Outer Join, OUTER REFERENCES:(p.ProductID))
       |--Index Scan(OBJECT:(Northwind.dbo.Products.SuppliersProducts AS p))
       |--Index Seek(OBJECT:(Northwind.dbo.[Order Details].ProductID AS o),
          SEEK:(o.ProductID=p.ProductID) ORDERED FORWARD)
```

Notice that the optimizer uses a nested loop join and that it reorders the tables (Products is listed first in the plan, even though Order Details is listed first in the FROM clause). Now let's force the join order by using the FORCE ORDER query hint and see what happens to the query plan (Listing 12.11).

Listing 12.11 Forcing the Join Order with the FORCE ORDER Hint

(Query)

```
SELECT o.OrderId, p.ProductId
FROM [Order Details] o RIGHT JOIN Products p ON
    (o.ProductId=p.ProductId)
OPTION(FORCE ORDER)
```

(Query plan)

```
StmtText
-------------------------------------------------------------------------
SELECT o.OrderId, p.ProductId
FROM [Order Details] o RIGHT JOIN Products p ON (o.ProductId=p.ProductId)
OPTION(FORCE ORDER)
 |--Merge Join(Right Outer Join, MANY-TO-MANY MERGE:(o.ProductID)=
    (p.ProductID), RESIDUAL:(o.ProductID=p.ProductID))
      |--Index Scan(OBJECT:(Northwind.dbo.[Order Details].
         ProductsOrder_Details AS o), ORDERED FORWARD)
      |--Clustered Index Scan(OBJECT:(Northwind.dbo.Products.
         PK_Products AS p), ORDERED FORWARD)
```

Since it can't reorder the tables, the optimizer switches to a merge join strategy. This is less efficient than letting the optimizer order the tables as it sees fit and join the tables using a nested loop.

Nested Loop Joins

Nested loop joins consist of a loop within a loop. A nested loop join designates one table in the join as the outer loop and the other as the inner loop. For each iteration of the outer loop, the entire inner loop is traversed. This works fine for small to medium-sized tables, but as the loops grow larger, this strategy becomes increasingly inefficient. The general process is as follows.

1. Find a row in the first table.
2. Use values from that row to find a row in the second table.
3. Repeat the process until there are no more rows in the first table that match the search criteria.

The optimizer evaluates at least four join combinations even if those combinations are not specified in the join predicate. It balances the cost of evaluating additional combinations with the need to keep down the overall cost of producing the query plan.

Nested loop joins perform much better than merge joins and hash joins when working with small to medium-sized amounts of data. The query optimizer uses nested loop joins if the outer input is quite small and the inner input is indexed and quite large. It orders the tables so that the smaller input is the outer table and requires a useful index on the inner table. The optimizer always uses the nested loop strategy with theta (nonequality) joins.

Merge Joins

Merge joins perform much more efficiently with large data sets than nested loop joins do. Both tables must be sorted on the merge column in order for the join to work. The optimizer usually chooses a merge join when working with large data sets that are already sorted on the join columns. The optimizer can use index trees to provide the sorted inputs and can also leverage the sort operations of GROUP BY, CUBE, and ORDER BY—the sorting needs to occur only once. If an input is not already sorted, the optimizer may opt to first sort it so that a merge join can be performed if it thinks a merge join is more efficient than a nested loop join. This happens very rarely and is denoted by the Sort operator in the query plan.

A merge join entails the following five steps.

1. Get the first input values from each table.
2. Compare them.
3. If the values are equal, return the rows.
4. If the values are not equal, toss the lower value and use the next input value from that table for the next comparison.
5. Repeat the process until all the rows from one of the tables have been processed.

The optimizer makes only one pass per table. The operation terminates after all the input values from one of the tables have been evaluated. Any values remaining in the other table are not processed.

The optimizer can perform a merge join operation for every type of relational join operation except CROSS JOIN and FULL JOIN. Merge operations can also be used to UNION tables together (since they must be sorted to eliminate duplicates).

Hash Joins

Hash joins are also more efficient with large data sets than nested loop joins are. Additionally, they work well with tables that are not sorted on the join column(s). The optimizer typically opts for a hash join when dealing with large inputs and when no index exists to join them or an index exists but is unusable.

SQL Server performs hash joins by hashing the rows from the smaller of the two tables (designated the build table) and inserting them into a hash table, then processing the larger table (the probe table) a row at a time and searching the hash table for matches. Because the smaller of the two tables supplies the values in the hash table, the table size is kept to a minimum, and because hashed values rather than real values are used, comparisons can be made between the tables very quickly.

Hash joins are a variation on the concept of hashed indexes that have been available in a handful of advanced DBMS products for several years. With hashed indexes, the hash table is stored permanently—it *is* the index. Data is hashed into slots that have the same hashing value. If the index has a unique contiguous key, what is known as a *minimal perfect hashing function* exists—every value hashes to its own slot and there are no gaps between slots in the index. If the index is unique but noncontiguous, the next best thing—a *perfect hashing function*—can exist wherein every value hashes to its own slot, but there are potentially gaps between them.

If the build and probe inputs are chosen incorrectly (e.g., because of inaccurate density estimates), the optimizer reverses them dynamically using a process called *role reversal*.

Hash join operations can service every type of relational join (including UNION and DIFFERENCE operations) except CROSS JOINs. Hashing can also be used to group data and remove duplicates (e.g., with vector aggregates—SUM(Quantity) GROUP BY ProductId). When it uses hashing in this fashion, the optimizer uses the same table for both the build and probe roles.

When join inputs are large and of similar size, a hash join performs comparably to a merge join. When join inputs are large but differ significantly in size, a hash join usually outperforms a merge join by a fair margin.

Subqueries and Join Alternatives

A subquery is a query nested within a larger one. Typically, a subquery supplies values for predicate operators (such as IN, ANY, and EXISTS) or a single value for a derived column or variable assignment. Subqueries can be used in many places, including a query's WHERE and HAVING clauses.

Understand that joins are not inherently better than subqueries. Often the optimizer will normalize a subquery into a join, but this doesn't mean that the subquery was an inefficient coding choice.

When attempting to rework a query to avoid the performance overhead of joins, remember that you can use table variables and temporary tables to store work data for further processing. For extremely complex queries, this may be the best alternative because it affords you more control over the optimization process. You can break the query into several steps and can control what executes when.

For simple to moderately complex queries, derived tables can provide a similar benefit in that they can allow you to serialize the order of query processing to some extent. Derived tables can work like parentheses in expression evaluation (and are, in fact, delimited with parentheses)—they can establish an order of evaluation. When you demote part of a complex SELECT to a derived table, against which you then apply the remainder of the SELECT, you're in effect saying, "Do this first, then hand its results to the outer SELECT." The optimizer isn't required to respect the order you supply—it can rearrange the tables in derived table expressions and can even discard the nesting in favor of a more efficient plan—but at least you have a syntactical mechanism for specifying the order you prefer. You will have to try the technique in specific situations to determine whether it provides the performance you require.

Logical and Physical Operators

Logical operators describe the relational operations used to process a query. They must be translated into physical operators in order to be executed. Physical operators describe what SQL Server must do to carry out the work (e.g., return the data) requested by the query. Often a logical operator maps to multiple physical operators. Execution plans consist of physical operators because these operators are what tell the LPE component within the server what it needs to do to carry out the work of the query. These physical operators are translated by the LPE component into OLE DB calls from the relational engine to the storage engine to perform the work requested by the query.

Each step in an execution plan corresponds to a physical operator. As I've said, execution plans consist of a series of physical operators. Query Analyzer's graphical execution plan displays these operations in the title area of its yellow popup hint windows. If a step has a logical operator in addition to the physical operator, it will also be displayed in the title area of the window to the right of the physical operator, separated by a slash. For the textual showplan, the PhysicalOp column stores the physical operator, while the LogicalOp column stores the logical operator for a step.

This is best understood by way of example. Consider the following query, which requests a relational inner join:

```
SELECT *
FROM Orders o JOIN [Order Details] d ON (o.OrderID = d.OrderID)
```

The optimizer chooses a merge join for it, though the query itself obviously doesn't ask for one. Relationally, the query is performing an inner join between the two tables. Here's an excerpt from its textual showplan:

```
PhysicalOp            LogicalOp             Argument
-------------------   -------------------   ------------------------------
Merge Join            Inner Join            MERGE:([o].[OrderID])=([d].[Or
Clustered Index Scan  Clustered Index Scan  OBJECT:([Northwind].[dbo].[Ord
Clustered Index Scan  Clustered Index Scan  OBJECT:([Northwind].[dbo].[Ord
```

Notice that the PhysicalOp column lists Merge Join as the operator. That's what happens behind the scenes to service the operation spelled out in the LogicalOp column: Inner Join. An inner join is what we requested via our query. The server chose a Merge Join as the physical operator to carry out our request.

Besides deciding which index to use and what join strategy to apply, the optimizer has additional decisions to make regarding other types of operations. The subsections below describe a few of them.

DISTINCT

When the optimizer encounters DISTINCT or UNION in a query, it must remove duplicates from the inputs before returning a result set. It has a couple of options here—it can sort the data to remove duplicates, or it can hash it. The optimizer may service the distinct or UNION logical operation by using a hash or sort physical operator. (Stream Aggregate—the same physical operator often used for GROUP BY queries—is also a popular choice here.)

GROUP BY

The optimizer can service GROUP BY queries by using plain sorts or by hashing. Again, the physical operator may be Hash or Sort, but the logical operator remains Aggregate or something similar. Also, as mentioned, Stream Aggregate is a popular choice for GROUP BY operations.

Because the optimizer may choose to perform a hash operation to group the data, the result set may not come back in sorted order. You can't rely on GROUP BY to automatically sort data. If you want the result set sorted, include an ORDER BY clause.

ORDER BY

Even with ORDER BY, the optimizer has a decision to make. Assuming no clustered index exists that has already sorted the data, the optimizer has to come up with a way to return the result set in the requested order. It can sort the data, as we'd naturally expect, or it can traverse the leaf level of an appropriately keyed nonclustered index. Which option the optimizer chooses depends on a number of factors. The biggest one is selectivity—how many rows will be returned by the query? Equally relevant is index covering—can the nonclustered index cover the query? If the number of rows is relatively low, it may be cheaper to use the nonclustered index than to sort the entire table. Likewise, if the index can cover the query, you've got the next best thing to having a second clustered index, and the optimizer will likely use it.

Spooling

The Spooling operator in a query plan indicates that the optimizer is saving the results from an intermediate query in a table for further processing. With a lazy spool, the work table is populated as needed. With an eager spool, the table is populated in one step. The optimizer favors lazy spools over eager spools because of the possibility that it may be able to avoid having to fill the work table completely based on logic deeper in the query plan. There are cases where eager spools are necessary—for example, to protect against the Halloween problem—but, generally, the optimizer prefers lazy spools because of their reduced overhead.

Spool operations can be performed on tables as well as indexes. The optimizer uses a rowcount spool when all it needs to know is whether a row exists.

Recap

Using indexes, statistics, and the submitted query text as input, the SQL Server query processor produces optimized execution plans that the server then carries out to access and return the requested data. The server can make use of clustered and nonclustered indexes as well as auto-generated and manually created statistics. It can use multiple indexes per table within a given query plan and can intersect and join indexes.

The query processor picks the plan with the lowest cost. Usually, this is driven by the estimated I/O for the plan, but there are other cost factors as well. The estimated I/O for each step in a plan is generally based on the estimated number of rows it will return for each execution and the estimated number of executions. Discrepancies between the estimated and actual row counts and executions can indicate inaccurate estimates, usually due to out-of-date statistics or statistics that are sampled with a sampling interval that is too low to accurately represent its base data.

The key to efficient query processing is providing the optimizer enough information to make informed decisions. Indexes, statistics, indexable expressions, constraints, and reusable query plans are essential for good query performance.

SQL Server provides several tools for helping you tune your queries. A wonderful tool for evaluating whether you have optimal indexes and statistics is the Index Tuning Wizard. You can supply it a trace load or an individual query, and it will suggest indexing and statistics changes that could make your code run more quickly. SQL Server's Profiler tool can show procedure recompilations and cache use information, as can Perfmon. Query Analyzer's graphical showplan can show specific information about plan estimates and step inputs.

Knowledge Measure

1. True or false: If you create a clustered index with a nonunique key, SQL Server automatically "uniquefies" it.
2. Provided an index exists on col, can the optimizer use it to service the WHERE clause predicate col <> 1?
3. Explain the difference between selectivity and cardinality.
4. What is the function of the bookmark lookup operator?
5. True or false: When an index is created, its fillfactor setting affects the number of rows stored on every page in the index's B-tree except the root page.
6. What is the maximum number of steps in an index's statistics histogram?
7. What column in sysindexes stores an index's statistics?
8. What DBCC command can you use to list the fragmentation for an index?
9. What stored procedure can you use to affect the types of locks SQL Server will use for a particular index?
10. What DBCC command can you use to list the statistics histogram for an index?

11. What does the term "covering index" refer to?

12. What sp_configure setting determines whether the query optimizer attempts to create a parallel execution plan on an SMP server?

13. True or false: A computed column that is nondeterministic cannot be indexed.

14. Explain what the term "density" refers to in terms of query optimization.

15. When we see an RID lock in the output of sp_lock, what does that immediately tell us about the referenced table's indexes?

16. Provided an index exists on col, can the WHERE clause predicate ISNULL(col,'')='foo' be serviced with an index?

CHAPTER 13

Transactions

I do not feel obliged to believe that the same God who has endowed us with sense, reason, and intellect has intended us to forgo their use.

—Galileo Galilei[1]

In this chapter, I'll update the coverage of SQL Server transactions that first appeared in my book *The Guru's Guide to Transact-SQL*. We'll build on the coverage that appeared in that book and update it for the current release of the product.

SQL Server's transaction management facilities help ensure the integrity and recoverability of the data stored in its databases. A transaction is a set of one or more database operations that are treated as a single unit—either they all occur or none of them do. As such, a transaction is a database's basic operational metric, its fundamental unit of work.

SQL Server transactions ensure data recoverability and consistency in spite of any hardware, operating system, application, or SQL Server errors that may occur. They ensure that multiple commands performed within a transaction are performed either completely or not at all, and that a single command that alters multiple rows changes either all of them or none of them.

The ACID Test

SQL Server transactions are often described as "having the ACID properties" or "passing the ACID test," where ACID is an acronym for atomic,

---

1. Galilei, Galileo. "Letter to the Grand Duchess Christina of Tuscany, 1615." In *Discoveries and Opinions of Galileo: Including the Starry Messenger*, trans. Stillman Drake. Baltimore: Anchor Books, 1957, pp. 177, 183.

consistent, isolated, and durable. Transactional adherence to the ACID tenets is commonplace in modern DBMSs and is a prerequisite for ensuring the safety and reliability of data.

Atomicity

A transaction is atomic if it's an all-or-nothing proposition. When the transaction succeeds, all of its changes are stored permanently; when it fails, they're completely reversed. So, for example, if a transaction includes ten DELETE commands and the last one fails, rolling back the transaction will reverse the previous nine. Likewise, if a single command attempts ten row deletions and one of them fails, the entire operation fails.

Consistency

A transaction is consistent if it ensures that its underlying data never appears in an interim or illogical state—that is, if it never appears to be inconsistent. So, the data affected by an UPDATE command that changes ten rows will never appear to the outside world in an intermediate state—all rows will appear in either their initial state or their final state. This prevents one user from inadvertently interfering with another user's work in progress. Consistency is usually implied by the other ACID properties.

Isolation

A transaction is isolated if it neither is impacted by nor impacts other concurrent transactions on the same data. The extent to which a transaction is isolated from other transactions is controlled by its transaction isolation level (TIL), specified via the SET TRANSACTION ISOLATION LEVEL command. These TILs range from no isolation at all—during which transactions can read uncommitted data and cannot exclusively lock resources—to serializable isolation—which locks the entire data set and prevents users from modifying it in any way until the transaction completes. (See the Transaction Isolation Levels section below for more information.) The trade-off with each isolation level is one of concurrency (concurrent access and modification of a data set by multiple users) versus consistency. The more airtight the isolation, the higher the degree of data consistency. The higher the consistency, the lower the concurrency. This is because SQL Server locks resources to ensure data consistency. More locks mean fewer simultaneous data modifications and a reduced accessibility overall.

Isolation prevents a transaction from retrieving illogical or incomplete snapshots of data currently under modification by another transaction. For example, if a transaction is inserting a number of rows into a table, isolation prevents other transactions from seeing those rows until the transaction is committed. SQL Server's TILs allow you to balance your data accessibility needs with your data integrity requirements.

Durability

A transaction is considered durable if it can complete despite a system failure, or, in the case of uncommitted transactions, if it can be completely reversed following a system failure. SQL Server's write-ahead logging and the database recovery process ensure that transactions committed but not yet stored in the database are written to the database following a system failure (rolled forward) and that transactions in progress are reversed (rolled back).

How SQL Server Transactions Work

SQL Server transactions are similar to command batches in that they usually consist of multiple Transact-SQL statements that are executed as a group. They differ in that a command batch is a client-side concept (it's a mechanism for sending groups of commands to the server), while a transaction is a server-side concept (it controls what SQL Server considers completed and in-progress work).

There's a many-to-many relationship between command batches and transactions. Command batches can contain multiple transactions, and a single transaction can span multiple batches. As a rule, you want to avoid transactions that span lengthy command batches because of the concurrency and performance problems that such transactions can cause.

Anytime a data modification occurs, SQL Server writes a record of the change to the transaction log before the change itself is performed. This is the reason SQL Server is described as having a write-ahead log—log records are written ahead of their corresponding data changes. Failing to do this could result in data changes that would not be rolled back if the server failed before the log record was written.

Modifications are never made directly to disk. Instead, SQL Server reads data pages into a buffer area as they're needed and changes them in memory. Before it changes a page in memory, the server ensures that the change is recorded in the transaction log. Since the transaction log is also cached, these changes are initially made in memory as well. Write-ahead logging ensures that the lazywriter process does not write modified data pages ("dirty" pages) to disk before their corresponding log records.

No permanent changes are made to a database until a transaction is committed. The exact timing of this varies based on the type of transaction. Once a transaction is committed, its changes are written to the database and cannot be rolled back.

Regardless of whether an operation is logged or nonlogged, terminating it before it has been committed results in the operation being rolled back completely. This is possible with nonlogged operations because page allocations are recorded in the transaction log.

In terms of transactions, triggers behave as though they were nested one level deep. If a transaction that contains a trigger is rolled back, so is the trigger. If the trigger is rolled back, so is any transaction that encompasses it.

Types of Transactions

SQL Server supports four basic types of transactions: automatic, implicit, user-defined, and distributed. Each has its own nuances, so I'll discuss each one separately.

Automatic Transactions

By default, each Transact-SQL command is its own transaction. These are known as automatic (or auto-commit) transactions. They are begun and committed by the server automatically. A DML command that's executed outside of a transaction (and while implicit transactions are disabled) is an example of an automatic transaction. You can think of an automatic transaction as a Transact-SQL statement that's ensconced between a BEGIN TRAN and a COMMIT TRAN. If the statement succeeds, it's committed. If not, it's rolled back.

Implicit Transactions

Implicit transactions are ANSI SQL-92–compliant automatic transactions. They're initiated automatically when any of several DDL or DML commands is executed. They continue until explicitly committed by the user. To toggle implicit transaction support, use the SET IMPLICIT_TRANSACTIONS command. By default, OLE DB and ODBC connections enable the ANSI_ DEFAULTS switch, which, in turn, enables implicit transactions. However, the connections then immediately disable implicit transactions because of the grief mismanaged transactions can cause applications. Enabling implicit transactions is like rigging your car doors to lock automatically every time you shut them. It costs more time than it saves, and, sooner or later, you're going to leave your keys in the ignition.

User-Defined Transactions

User-defined transactions are the chief means of managing transactions in SQL Server applications. A user-defined transaction is user-defined in that you control when it begins and when it ends. The BEGIN TRAN, COMMIT TRAN, and ROLLBACK TRAN commands are used to control user-defined transactions. Listing 13.1 offers an example.

Listing 13.1 A User-Defined Transaction

```
SELECT TOP 5 title_id, stor_id FROM sales ORDER BY
    title_id, stor_id
BEGIN TRAN
DELETE sales
SELECT TOP 5 title_id, stor_id FROM sales ORDER BY
    title_id, stor_id
GO
ROLLBACK TRAN
SELECT TOP 5 title_id, stor_id FROM sales ORDER BY
    title_id, stor_id

title_id stor_id
-------- -------
BU1032   6380
BU1032   8042
BU1032   8042
BU1111   8042
BU2075   7896

(5 row(s) affected)


(25 row(s) affected)
```

```
title_id stor_id
-------- -------

(0 row(s) affected)

title_id stor_id
-------- -------
BU1032   6380
BU1032   8042
BU1032   8042
BU1111   8042
BU2075   7896

(5 row(s) affected)
```

Distributed Transactions

Transactions that span multiple servers are known as distributed transactions. These transactions are administered by a central manager application that coordinates the activities of the involved servers. SQL Server can participate in distributed transactions coordinated by manager applications that support the X/Open XA specification for Distributed Transaction Processing, such as the Microsoft Distributed Transaction Coordinator (DTC). You can initiate a distributed transaction in Transact-SQL by using the BEGIN DISTRIBUTED TRANSACTION command.

Avoiding Transactions Altogether

Other than avoiding making database modifications, there's really no way to completely disable transaction logging. Some operations generate a minimum of log information, but there's no configuration option that turns off logging altogether.

Commands That Minimize Logging

The CREATE INDEX, BULK INSERT, TRUNCATE TABLE, SELECT... INTO, and WRITETEXT/UPDATETEXT commands minimize transaction logging by causing only page operations to be logged. (BULK INSERT can, depending on the circumstances, create regular detail log records.) Contrary to a popular misconception, these operations *are* logged—it's just that they don't generate *detail* transaction log information. That's why Books Online refers to them as *nonlogged* operations—they're nonlogged in that they don't generate row-level log records. I often refer to them as *minimally logged* operations.

Nonlogged operations tend to be much faster than fully logged operations. And since they generate page allocation log records, they can be rolled back (but not forward) just like other operations. The price you pay for using them is transaction log recovery. Nonlogged operations reduce the granularity of the information written to the transaction log, so they also impact the granularity of the recovery process. This is often quite acceptable, but it's something you should be aware of.

Transactions and Recovery Models

Naturally, the current recovery model affects transactions and transaction log management. The Simple recovery mode effectively truncates the transaction log at each system-generated checkpoint. The Bulk-Logged recovery model fully logs all operations except nonlogged operations. The Full recovery mode logs all operations, including those that would otherwise be nonlogged.

Read-Only and Single-User Databases

One obvious way to avoid logging as well as resource blocks and deadlocks in a database is by making the database read-only. Naturally, if the database can't be changed, there's no need for transaction logging or resource blocks. Making the database single-user even alleviates the need for read locks, avoiding the possibility of an application blocking itself.

Though reducing a database's accessibility in order to minimize transaction management issues might sound a little like not driving your car in order to keep it from breaking down, you sometimes see this in real applications. For example, it's fairly common for Decision Support System (DSS) applications to make use of read-only databases. These databases can be updated off-hours (e.g., overnight or on weekends), then returned to read-only status for use during normal working hours. Obviously, transaction management issues are greatly simplified when a database is only modifiable by one user at a time, is only changed *en masse,* or can't be changed at all.

Read-only databases can also be very functional as members of partitioned data banks. Sometimes an application can be spread across multiple databases—one containing static data that doesn't change much (and can therefore be set to read-only) and one containing more dynamic data that must submit to at least nominal transaction management.

Automatic Transaction Management

SQL Server provides a number of facilities for automating transaction management. The most prominent example of these is the automatic transaction (auto-commit) facility. As mentioned earlier, an automatic transaction is begun and committed or rolled back implicitly by the server. There's no need for explicit BEGIN TRAN or COMMIT/ROLLBACK TRAN statements. The server initiates a transaction when a modification command begins and, depending on the command's success, commits or rolls it back afterward. Automatic transaction mode is SQL Server's default mode but is disabled when implicit or user-defined transactions are enabled.

Implicit transactions offer another type of automated transaction management. Whenever certain commands (ALTER TABLE, FETCH, REVOKE, CREATE, GRANT, SELECT, DELETE, INSERT, TRUNCATE TABLE, DROP, OPEN, UPDATE) are executed, a transaction is automatically started. In a sense, implicit transactions offer an automated alternative to explicit transactions—a facility falling somewhere between auto-commit transactions and user-defined transactions in terms of functionality. These transactions are only semi-automated, though, since an explicit ROLLBACK TRAN or COMMIT TRAN is required to close them. Only the first part of the process is automated—the initiation of the transaction. Its termination must still be performed explicitly. Transact-SQL's SET IMPLICIT_TRANSACTIONS command is used to toggle implicit transaction mode.

SET XACT_ABORT toggles whether a transaction is aborted when a command raises a runtime error. The error can be a system-generated error condition or a user-generated one. It's essentially equivalent to checking @@ERROR after every statement and rolling back the transaction if an error is detected. Note that the command is a bit of misnomer. When XACT_ABORT is enabled and a runtime error occurs, not only is the current transaction aborted but the entire batch is as well. For example, consider the code in Listing 13.2.

Listing 13.2 Using XACT_ABORT When a Command Raises an Error

```
SET XACT_ABORT ON
SELECT TOP 5 au_lname, au_fname FROM authors ORDER BY
    au_lname, au_fname
BEGIN TRAN
DELETE authors
DELETE sales
SELECT TOP 5 au_lname, au_fname FROM authors ORDER BY
    au_lname, au_fname
ROLLBACK TRAN
PRINT 'End of batch -- never makes it here'
GO
SELECT TOP 5 au_lname, au_fname FROM authors ORDER BY
    au_lname, au_fname
SET XACT_ABORT ON
au_lname                                 au_fname
---------------------------------------- --------------------
Bennet                                   Abraham
Blotchet-Halls                           Reginald
Carson                                   Cheryl
DeFrance                                 Michel
del Castillo                             Innes

(5 row(s) affected)

Server: Msg 547, Level 16, State 1, Line 1
DELETE statement conflicted with COLUMN REFERENCE constraint
    'FK__titleauth__au_id__164452B1'. The conflict occurred in
    database 'pubs', table 'titleauthor', column 'au_id'.
au_lname                                 au_fname
---------------------------------------- --------------------
Bennet                                   Abraham
Blotchet-Halls                           Reginald
Carson                                   Cheryl
DeFrance                                 Michel
del Castillo                             Innes

(5 row(s) affected)
```

Execution never reaches the PRINT statement because the constraint violation generated by attempting to empty the authors table aborts the entire command batch (the statements before the GO). This is in spite of the fact that a ROLLBACK TRAN immediately precedes the PRINT.

The fact that the entire command batch is aborted is what makes checking @@ERROR after each data modification preferable to enabling SET XACT_ABORT. This is particularly true when calling a stored procedure within a transaction. If the procedure causes a runtime error, the statements following it in the command batch are aborted, affording no opportunity to handle the error condition.

Transaction Isolation Levels

SQL Server supports four TILs. As mentioned earlier, a transaction's isolation level controls how it impacts and is impacted by other transactions. The trade-off is always one of data consistency versus concurrency. Selecting a more restrictive TIL increases data consistency at the expense of accessibility. Selecting a less restrictive TIL increases concurrency at the expense of data consistency. The trick is to balance these opposing interests so that the needs of your application are met.

Use the SET TRANSACTION ISOLATION LEVEL command to set a transaction's isolation level. Valid TILs include READ UNCOMMITTED, READ COMMITTED, REPEATABLE READ, and SERIALIZABLE.

READ UNCOMMITTED

Specifying READ UNCOMMITTED is essentially the same as using the NOLOCK hint with every table referenced in a transaction. It is the least restrictive of SQL Server's four TILs. It permits dirty reads (reads of uncommitted changes by other transactions) and nonrepeatable reads (data that changes between reads during a transaction). To see how READ UNCOMMITTED permits dirty and nonrepeatable reads, run the queries shown in Listing 13.3 simultaneously.

Listing 13.3 Using READ UNCOMMITTED

```
-- Query 1

SELECT TOP 5 title_id, qty FROM sales ORDER BY title_id, stor_id
BEGIN TRAN
UPDATE sales SET qty=0
```

```
SELECT TOP 5 title_id, qty FROM sales ORDER BY title_id, stor_id
WAITFOR DELAY '00:00:05'
ROLLBACK TRAN
SELECT TOP 5 title_id, qty FROM sales ORDER BY title_id, stor_id

-- Query 2

SET TRANSACTION ISOLATION LEVEL READ UNCOMMITTED
PRINT 'Now you see it...'
SELECT TOP 5 title_id, qty FROM sales
WHERE qty=0
ORDER BY title_id, stor_id

IF @@ROWCOUNT>0 BEGIN
  WAITFOR DELAY '00:00:05'

  PRINT '...now you don''t'
  SELECT TOP 5 title_id, qty FROM sales
  WHERE qty=0
  ORDER BY title_id, stor_id
END

Now you see it...
title_id qty
-------- ------
BU1032   0
BU1032   0
BU1032   0
BU1111   0
BU2075   0

(5 row(s) affected)

...now you don't
title_id qty
-------- ------

(0 row(s) affected)
```

While the first query is running (you have five seconds), fire off the second one and you'll see that it's able to access the uncommitted data modifications of the first query. It then waits for the first transaction to finish, then attempts to read the same data again. Since the modifications were rolled back, the data has vanished, leaving the second query with a nonrepeatable read.

READ COMMITTED

READ COMMITTED is SQL Server's default TIL, so if you don't specify otherwise, you'll get READ COMMITTED. READ COMMITTED avoids dirty reads by initiating share locks on accessed data but permits changes to underlying data during the transaction, possibly resulting in nonrepeatable reads and/or phantom data. To see how this works, run the queries shown in Listing 13.4 simultaneously.

Listing 13.4 Using READ COMMITTED

```
-- Query 1

SET TRANSACTION ISOLATION LEVEL READ COMMITTED
BEGIN TRAN
PRINT 'Now you see it...'
SELECT TOP 5 title_id, qty FROM sales ORDER BY title_id, stor_id
WAITFOR DELAY '00:00:05'
PRINT '...now you don''t'
SELECT TOP 5 title_id, qty FROM sales ORDER BY title_id, stor_id
GO
ROLLBACK TRAN


-- Query 2

SET TRANSACTION ISOLATION LEVEL READ COMMITTED
UPDATE sales SET qty=6 WHERE qty=5

Now you see it...
title_id qty
-------- ------
BU1032   5
BU1032   10
BU1032   30
BU1111   25
BU2075   35
```

```
...now you don't
title_id qty
-------- ------
BU1032   6
BU1032   10
BU1032   30
BU1111   25
BU2075   35
```

As in the previous example, start the first query, then quickly run the second one simultaneously (you have five seconds).

In this example, the value of the qty column in the first row of the sales table changes between reads during the first query—a classic nonrepeatable read.

REPEATABLE READ

REPEATABLE READ initiates locks to prevent other users from changing the data a transaction accesses but doesn't prevent new rows from being inserted, possibly resulting in phantom rows appearing between reads during the transaction. Listing 13.5 provides an example. (As with the other examples, start the first query, then run the second one simultaneously—you have five seconds to start the second query.)

Listing 13.5 Using REPEATABLE READ

```
-- Query 1

SET TRANSACTION ISOLATION LEVEL REPEATABLE READ
BEGIN TRAN
PRINT 'Nothing up my sleeve...'
SELECT TOP 5 title_id, qty FROM sales ORDER BY qty
WAITFOR DELAY '00:00:05'
PRINT '...except this rabbit'
SELECT TOP 5 title_id, qty FROM sales ORDER BY qty
GO
ROLLBACK TRAN

-- Query 2

SET TRANSACTION ISOLATION LEVEL REPEATABLE READ
```

```
INSERT sales VALUES
    (6380,9999999,GETDATE(),2,'USG-Whenever','PS2091')

Nothing up my sleeve...
title_id qty
-------- ------
PS2091   3
BU1032   5
PS2091   10
MC2222   10
BU1032   10

...except this rabbit
title_id qty
-------- ------
PS2091   2
PS2091   3
BU1032   5
PS2091   10
MC2222   10
```

As you can see, a new row appears between the first and second reads of the sales table, even though REPEATABLE READ has been specified. Though REPEATABLE READ prevents changes to data it has already accessed, it doesn't prevent the addition of new data, thus introducing the possibility of phantom rows.

SERIALIZABLE

SERIALIZABLE prevents dirty reads and phantom rows by placing a range lock on the data it accesses. It is the most restrictive of SQL Server's four TILs. It's equivalent to using the HOLDLOCK hint with every table a transaction references. Listing 13.6 gives an example. (Delete the row you added in the previous example before running this code.)

Listing 13.6 Using SERIALIZABLE

```
-- Query 1

SET TRANSACTION ISOLATION LEVEL SERIALIZABLE
BEGIN TRAN
```

```
PRINT 'Nothing up my sleeve...'
SELECT TOP 5 title_id, qty FROM sales ORDER BY qty
WAITFOR DELAY '00:00:05'
PRINT '...or in my hat'
SELECT TOP 5 title_id, qty FROM sales ORDER BY qty
ROLLBACK TRAN


-- Query 2


BEGIN TRAN
SET TRANSACTION ISOLATION LEVEL SERIALIZABLE
-- This INSERT will be delayed until the
    first transaction completes
INSERT sales VALUES
    (6380,9999999,GETDATE(),2,'USG-Whenever','PS2091')
ROLLBACK TRAN


Nothing up my sleeve...
title_id qty
-------- ------
PS2091   3
BU1032   5
PS2091   10
MC2222   10
BU1032   10

...or in my hat
title_id qty
-------- ------
PS2091   3
BU1032   5
PS2091   10
MC2222   10
BU1032   10
```

In this example, the locks initiated by the SERIALIZABLE isolation level prevent the second query from running until after the first one finishes. While this provides airtight data consistency, it does so at a cost of greatly reduced concurrency.

Transaction Commands and Syntax

As I said earlier, the BEGIN TRAN, COMMIT TRAN, and ROLLBACK TRAN commands are used to manage transactions in Transact-SQL. (The sp_xxxx_xact system stored procedures are legacy code that was used in the past with DB-Library two-phase commit applications, and you should not use them.) The exact syntax used to begin a transaction is:

```
BEGIN TRAN[SACTION] [name|@TranNameVar]
```

To commit a transaction, use:

```
COMMIT TRAN[SACTION] [name|@TranNameVar]
```

And to roll back a transaction, use:

```
ROLLBACK TRAN[SACTION] [name|@TranNameVar]
```

You can also use the COMMIT WORK and ROLLBACK WORK commands in lieu of COMMIT TRANSACTION and ROLLBACK TRANSACTION, though you cannot use transaction names with them.

Nested Transactions

Transact-SQL allows you to nest transaction operations by issuing nested BEGIN TRAN commands. The @@TRANCOUNT automatic variable can be queried to determined the level of nesting—0 indicates no nesting, 1 indicates nesting one level deep, and so forth. Batches and stored procedures that are nesting sensitive should query @@TRANCOUNT when first executed and respond accordingly.

Though on the surface it appears otherwise, SQL Server doesn't support truly nested transactions. A COMMIT issued against any transaction except the outermost one doesn't commit any changes to disk—it merely decrements the @@TRANCOUNT automatic variable. A ROLLBACK, on the other hand, works regardless of the level at which it is issued, but it rolls back all transactions regardless of the nesting level. Though this is counterintuitive, there's a very good reason for it. If a nested COMMIT actually wrote changes permanently to disk, an outer ROLLBACK wouldn't be able to reverse those changes since they would already be recorded permanently. Likewise, if ROLLBACK didn't reverse all changes at all levels, calling it from within stored procedures and triggers would be vastly more complicated since the caller would have to check return values and the transaction nesting level when the routine returned in order to determine whether it needed to roll back pending transactions. Here's an example that illustrates some of the nuances of nested transactions (Listing 13.7).

Listing 13.7 Using Nested Transactions

```
SELECT 'Before BEGIN TRAN',@@TRANCOUNT
BEGIN TRAN
  SELECT 'After BEGIN TRAN',@@TRANCOUNT
  DELETE sales
  BEGIN TRAN nested
    SELECT 'After BEGIN TRAN nested',@@TRANCOUNT
    DELETE titleauthor
  COMMIT TRAN nested -- Does nothing except decrement @@TRANCOUNT
  SELECT 'After COMMIT TRAN nested',@@TRANCOUNT
GO-- When possible, it's a good idea to place ROLLBACK TRAN in a
  -- separate batch to prevent batch errors from leaving open
  -- transactions
ROLLBACK TRAN
SELECT 'After ROLLBACK TRAN',@@TRANCOUNT

SELECT TOP 5 au_id FROM titleauthor


----------------- -----------
Before BEGIN TRAN 0


----------------- -----------
After BEGIN TRAN 1


----------------------- -----------
After BEGIN TRAN nested 2


------------------------ -----------
After COMMIT TRAN nested 1


-------------------- -----------
After ROLLBACK TRAN 0
```

```
au_id
-----------
213-46-8915
409-56-7008
267-41-2394
724-80-9391
213-46-8915
```

In this example, we see that despite the nested COMMIT TRAN, the outer ROLLBACK still reverses the effects of the DELETE titleauthor command. Listing 13.8 shows another nested transaction example.

Listing 13.8 The Effects of ROLLBACK on a Nested Transaction

```
SELECT 'Before BEGIN TRAN',@@TRANCOUNT
BEGIN TRAN
  SELECT 'After BEGIN TRAN',@@TRANCOUNT
  DELETE sales
  BEGIN TRAN nested
    SELECT 'After BEGIN TRAN nested',@@TRANCOUNT
    DELETE titleauthor
  ROLLBACK TRAN
  SELECT 'After ROLLBACK TRAN',@@TRANCOUNT
IF @@TRANCOUNT>0 BEGIN
  COMMIT TRAN-- Never makes it here because of the ROLLBACK
  SELECT 'After COMMIT TRAN',@@TRANCOUNT
END

SELECT TOP 5 au_id FROM titleauthor

----------------- -----------
Before BEGIN TRAN 0


----------------- -----------
After BEGIN TRAN 1


----------------------- -----------
After BEGIN TRAN nested 2
```

```
------------------- -----------
After ROLLBACK TRAN 0

au_id
-----------
213-46-8915
409-56-7008
267-41-2394
724-80-9391
213-46-8915
```

In this example, execution never reaches the outer COMMIT TRAN because the ROLLBACK TRAN reverses all transactions currently in progress and sets @@TRANCOUNT to 0.

Note that we can't roll back the nested transaction. ROLLBACK can reverse a named transaction only when it's the outermost transaction. Attempting to roll back our nested transaction yields the following message:

```
Server: Msg 6401, Level 16, State 1, Line 10
Cannot roll back nested. No transaction or savepoint of that name
    was found.
```

The error message notwithstanding, the problem isn't that no transaction exists with the specified name. It's that ROLLBACK can only reference a transaction by name when it is also the outermost transaction. Here's an example that illustrates using ROLLBACK TRAN with transaction names (Listing 13.9).

Listing 13.9 Named Transactions and ROLLBACK

```
SELECT 'Before BEGIN TRAN main',@@TRANCOUNT
BEGIN TRAN main
  SELECT 'After BEGIN TRAN main',@@TRANCOUNT
  DELETE sales
  BEGIN TRAN nested
    SELECT 'After BEGIN TRAN nested',@@TRANCOUNT
    DELETE titleauthor
  ROLLBACK TRAN main
  SELECT 'After ROLLBACK TRAN main',@@TRANCOUNT
```

```
IF @@TRANCOUNT>0 BEGIN
  ROLLBACK TRAN  -- Never makes it here because of the
                 -- earlier ROLLBACK
  SELECT 'After ROLLBACK TRAN',@@TRANCOUNT
END

SELECT TOP 5 au_id FROM titleauthor


---------------------- -----------
Before BEGIN TRAN main 0


---------------------- -----------
After BEGIN TRAN main 1


---------------------- -----------
After BEGIN TRAN nested 2


---------------------- -----------
After ROLLBACK TRAN main 0

au_id
-----------
213-46-8915
409-56-7008
267-41-2394
724-80-9391
213-46-8915
```

Here, we named the outermost transaction main, then referenced it by name with ROLLBACK TRAN. Note that a transaction name is never required by ROLLBACK TRAN, regardless of whether the transaction is initiated with a name. For this reason, many developers avoid using transaction names with ROLLBACK altogether since they serve no real purpose. This is largely a matter of personal choice and works acceptably well either way so long as you understand it. Unless called with a save point (see below), ROLLBACK TRAN always rolls back all transactions and sets @@TRAN-COUNT to 0, regardless of the context in which it's called.

SAVE TRAN and Save Points

You can control how much work ROLLBACK reverses via the SAVE TRAN command. SAVE TRAN creates a save point to which you can roll back if you wish. Syntactically, you just pass the name of the save point to the ROLLBACK TRAN command. Listing 13.10 shows an example.

Listing 13.10 Setting a Save Point with SAVE TRAN

```
SELECT 'Before BEGIN TRAN main',@@TRANCOUNT
BEGIN TRAN main
  SELECT 'After BEGIN TRAN main',@@TRANCOUNT
  DELETE sales
  SAVE TRAN sales  -- Mark a save point
  SELECT 'After SAVE TRAN sales',@@TRANCOUNT
  -- @@TRANCOUNT is unchanged
  BEGIN TRAN nested
    SELECT 'After BEGIN TRAN nested',@@TRANCOUNT
    DELETE titleauthor
    SAVE TRAN titleauthor -- Mark a save point
    SELECT 'After SAVE TRAN titleauthor',@@TRANCOUNT
    -- @@TRANCOUNT is unchanged
  ROLLBACK TRAN sales
  SELECT 'After ROLLBACK TRAN sales',@@TRANCOUNT
  -- @@TRANCOUNT is unchanged
  SELECT TOP 5 au_id FROM titleauthor
IF @@TRANCOUNT>0 BEGIN
  ROLLBACK TRAN
  SELECT 'After ROLLBACK TRAN',@@TRANCOUNT
END

SELECT TOP 5 au_id FROM titleauthor


---------------------- -----------
Before BEGIN TRAN main 0


---------------------- -----------
After BEGIN TRAN main 1


---------------------- -----------
After SAVE TRAN sales 1
```

```
------------------------- -----------
After BEGIN TRAN nested 2



-------------------------- -----------
After SAVE TRAN titleauthor 2



-------------------------- -----------
After ROLLBACK TRAN sales 2

au_id
-----------
213-46-8915
409-56-7008
267-41-2394
724-80-9391
213-46-8915



------------------- -----------
After ROLLBACK TRAN 0

au_id
-----------
213-46-8915
409-56-7008
267-41-2394
724-80-9391
213-46-8915
```

SQL Server allows you to reuse a save point name if you wish, but if you do so, only the last save point is retained. Rolling back while using the save point name will roll the transaction back to the save point's last reference.

Accidental ROLLBACKs

Since ROLLBACK TRAN reverses all transactions in progress, it's important not to inadvertently nest calls to it. Once it has been called a single time, there's no need (nor are you allowed) to call it again until a new transaction is initiated. For example, consider the code in Listing 13.11.

Listing 13.11 ROLLBACK within a Nested Transaction

```
SELECT 'Before BEGIN TRAN',@@TRANCOUNT
BEGIN TRAN
  SELECT 'After BEGIN TRAN',@@TRANCOUNT
  DELETE sales
  BEGIN TRAN nested
    SELECT 'After BEGIN TRAN nested',@@TRANCOUNT
    DELETE titleauthor
  IF @@ROWCOUNT > 1000
    COMMIT TRAN nested
  ELSE BEGIN
    ROLLBACK TRAN -- Completely rolls back both transactions
    SELECT 'After ROLLBACK TRAN',@@TRANCOUNT
  END
  SELECT TOP 5 au_id FROM titleauthor
ROLLBACK TRAN -- This is an error
             -- there's no transaction to roll back
SELECT 'After ROLLBACK TRAN',@@TRANCOUNT

SELECT TOP 5 au_id FROM titleauthor

----------------- -----------
Before BEGIN TRAN 0


----------------- -----------
After BEGIN TRAN 1


------------------------ -----------
After BEGIN TRAN nested 2


-------------------- -----------
After ROLLBACK TRAN 0

au_id
-----------
213-46-8915
409-56-7008
267-41-2394
724-80-9391
213-46-8915
```

```
Server: Msg 3903, Level 16, State 1, Line 17
The ROLLBACK TRANSACTION request has no corresponding
BEGIN TRANSACTION.


------------------- -----------
After ROLLBACK TRAN 0

au_id
-----------
213-46-8915
409-56-7008
267-41-2394
724-80-9391
213-46-8915
```

Note the error message that's generated by the second ROLLBACK TRAN. Since the first ROLLBACK TRAN reverses both transactions, there's no transaction for the second to reverse. This situation is best handled by querying @@TRANCOUNT first, like this:

```
IF @@TRANCOUNT>0 BEGIN
   ROLLBACK TRAN
   SELECT 'After ROLLBACK TRAN',@@TRANCOUNT
END
```

Invalid T-SQL Syntax in Transactions

Some normally valid Transact-SQL syntax is prohibited while a transaction is active. For example, you can't use sp_dboption to change database options or call any other stored procedure that modifies the master database from within a transaction. Also, a number of Transact-SQL commands are illegal inside transactions: ALTER DATABASE, DROP DATABASE, RECONFIGURE, BACKUP LOG, DUMP TRANSACTION, RESTORE DATABASE, CREATE DATABASE, LOAD DATABASE, RESTORE LOG, DISK INIT, LOAD TRANSACTION, and UPDATE STATISTICS.

Debugging Transactions

Two DBCC commands come in very handy when debugging transaction-related problems. The first is DBCC OPENTRAN. It allows you to retrieve the oldest active transaction in a database. Since only the inactive portion of a log is backed up and truncated, a malevolent or zombie transaction can cause the log to fill prematurely. You can use DBCC OPENTRAN to identify the offending process so that it may be terminated if necessary. Listing 13.12 shows an example.

Listing 13.12 Using DBCC OPENTRAN

```
DBCC OPENTRAN(pubs)
Transaction information for database 'pubs'.

Oldest active transaction:
    SPID (server process ID) : 15
    UID (user ID) : 1
    Name            : user_transaction
    LSN             : (57:376:596)
    Start time      : Aug  5 1999  5:54:46:713AM
```

Another handy command for tracking down transaction-related problems is the DBCC LOG command. DBCC LOG lists the database transaction log. You can use it to look under the hood and see what operations are being carried out on your data. Listing 13.13 shows an example.

Listing 13.13 Using DBCC LOG

```
CREATE TABLE #logrecs
  (CurrentLSN varchar(30),
  Operation varchar(20),
  Context varchar(20),
  TransactionID varchar(20))

INSERT #logrecs
EXEC('DBCC LOG(''pubs'')')

SELECT * FROM #logrecs
GO
DROP TABLE #logrecs
```

(Results abridged)

CurrentLSN	Operation	Context	TransactionID
00000035:00000144:0001	LOP_BEGIN_CKPT	LCX_NULL	0000:00000000
00000035:00000145:0001	LOP_END_CKPT	LCX_NULL	0000:00000000
00000035:00000146:0001	LOP_MODIFY_ROW	LCX_SCHEMA_VERSION	0000:00000000
00000035:00000146:0002	LOP_BEGIN_XACT	LCX_NULL	0000:000020e0
00000035:00000146:0003	LOP_MARK_DDL	LCX_NULL	0000:000020e0
00000035:00000146:0004	LOP_COMMIT_XACT	LCX_NULL	0000:000020e0
00000035:00000147:0001	LOP_MODIFY_ROW	LCX_SCHEMA_VERSION	0000:00000000
00000035:00000147:0002	LOP_BEGIN_XACT	LCX_NULL	0000:000020e1
00000035:00000147:0003	LOP_MARK_DDL	LCX_NULL	0000:000020e1

No discussion of SQL Server transaction debugging would be complete without mentioning the @@TRANCOUNT automatic variable. Though we've already covered it elsewhere in this chapter, @@TRANCOUNT is a frequent target of PRINT statements and debugger watches because it reports the current transaction nesting level. When debugging complex nested transactions, it's common to insert SELECT or PRINT statements throughout the code to determine the current nesting level at various procedural junctures.

Finally, don't forget about Perfmon. It sports numerous objects and counters relating to transaction management and performance. In particular, the SQL Server:Databases object provides a wealth of transaction- and transaction log–related counters.

Optimizing Transactional Code

There are a number of general guidelines for writing efficient transaction-oriented T-SQL. Here are a few of them.

- Keep transactions as short as possible. Once you've determined what data modifications need to be made, initiate your transaction, perform those modifications, and then end the transaction as soon as possible. Try not to initiate transactions prematurely.
- Limit transactions to data modification statements when practical. Don't initiate a transaction while scanning data if you can avoid it. Though transactions certainly impact reading data as well as writing it (e.g., dirty and nonrepeatable reads, phantom rows, and so on), it's of-

ten possible to limit them to just those statements that modify data, especially if you do not need to reread data within a transaction.

- Don't require user input during a transaction. Doing so could allow a slow user to tie up server resources indefinitely. It could also cause the transaction log to fill prematurely since active transactions cannot be cleared out of it.

- Try to use optimistic concurrency control when possible. That is, rather than explicitly locking every object your application may change, allow the server to determine when a row has been changed by another user. You may find that this occurs so little in practice (perhaps the app is naturally partitioned, or, once entered, rows are rarely updated, and so on) as to be worth the risk in order to improve concurrency.

- Use nonlogged operations intelligently. As I've pointed out, non-logged operations impact the transaction log backup and recovery process. This may or may not be a showstopper, but when allowable, nonlogged operations can turbocharge an application. They can often reduce processing time for large amounts of data by orders of magnitude and virtually eliminate a number of common transaction management headaches. Just keep in mind that this increased performance sometimes comes at a cost.

- Try to use lower (less restrictive) TILs when possible. READ COMMITTED, the default, is suitable for most applications and will provide better concurrency than REPEATABLE READ or SERIALIZABLE.

- Attempt to keep the amount of data you change within a transaction to a minimum. Don't indiscriminately attempt to change millions of rows in a table and expect concurrency and resource utilization to magically take care of themselves. Database modifications require resources and locks, and these locks by definition impact other users. Unless your app is a single-user app, it pays to be mindful of operations that could negatively impact concurrency.

- Don't use implicit transactions unless you really need them, and even then watch them very closely. Because implicit transactions are initiated by nearly any primary Transact-SQL command (including SELECT), they can be started when you least expect them, potentially lowering concurrency and causing transaction log problems. It's nearly always better to manage transactions explicitly with BEGIN TRAN, COMMIT TRAN, and ROLLBACK TRAN than to use implicit transactions. When you manage transactions yourself, you know exactly when they're started and stopped—you have full control over what happens.

Recap

Transactions are SQL Server's basic unit of work. They ensure that a data modification operation is either carried out completely or not at all. Atomicity, consistency, isolation, and durability—the so-called ACID properties—characterize SQL Server transactions and help guard your data against incomplete or lost updates.

The current TIL governs transaction isolation. You set the current TIL via the SET TRANSACTION ISOLATION LEVEL command. Each TIL represents a trade-off between concurrency and consistency.

In this chapter, you became acquainted with SQL Server transactions and explored the various Transact-SQL commands that relate to transaction management. You learned about auto-commit and implicit transactions as well as user-defined and distributed transactions. You also explored some common transaction-related pitfalls and you learned methods for avoiding them.

Knowledge Measure

1. True or false: The Simple recovery model fully logs all operations except nonlogged operations such as BULK INSERT.
2. When COMMIT is executed from within a nested transaction, what percentage of the transaction's modifications is written to the transaction log?
3. When ROLLBACK is executed from within a nested transaction, what percentage of the transaction's modifications is rolled back?
4. True or false: SQL Server automatically rolls back a transaction that was initiated from an aborted Transact-SQL batch.
5. Is Transact-SQL's CREATE INDEX command a member of the list of nonlogged (or minimally logged) commands?
6. Describe the difference between a fully logged and minimally logged command.
7. What DBCC command reports the oldest active transaction for a database and the spid that initiated it?

8. If you were to write a trigger that saved the value of @@TRANCOUNT in a secondary table and you then caused the trigger to fire by executing a DML statement outside of a transaction against the trigger's underlying table, what value for @@TRANCOUNT would your trigger insert into the secondary table?

9. Describe the four ACID properties a transaction can exhibit.

10. Describe SQL Server's four transaction isolation levels.

CHAPTER 14

Cursors

I will not attack your doctrines nor your creeds if they accord liberty to me. If they hold thought to be dangerous—if they aver that doubt is a crime, then I attack them one and all, because they enslave the minds of men.

—Robert Green Ingersoll[1]

In this chapter, we'll update the coverage of cursors that first appeared in my book *The Guru's Guide to Transact-SQL*. We'll continue the discussion begun in that book regarding cursors and how to use them in SQL Server applications, and we'll update the information to cover the current release of the product.

Overview

A cursor is a mechanism for accessing the rows in a table or result set on a piecemeal basis—one at a time. They run counter to SQL Server's normal way of doing things by parceling result sets into individual rows; fetching a row from a cursor is analogous to returning a single row via a SELECT statement. Unlike a traditional result set, a cursor keeps track of its position automatically and provides a wealth of facilities for scrolling around in the underlying result set. Cursors also provide a handy means of updating the underlying result set in a positional fashion and of returning result set pointers via variables.

---

1. Ingersoll, Robert Green. "The Ghosts." In *Best of Robert Ingersoll: Selections from His Writings and Speeches,* ed. Roger E. Greeley. Amherst, NY: Prometheus Books, 1983, p. 34.

The advice I usually give people who are thinking about using cursors is not to. If you can solve a problem using Transact-SQL's many set-oriented tools, do so. It's rare (but not impossible) for a cursor-based solution to out-perform a set-based approach. SQL Server's standard result sets (also known as "firehose" cursors) have been used to solve a myriad of distinct kinds of computing problems for years—there aren't many conventional da-tabase challenges that actually *require* a cursor, though some are certainly more suited to cursors than to set handling.

On Cursors and ISAM Databases

People porting ISAM or local database applications to SQL Server are often tempted to perform shallow ports—to make no more changes than abso-lutely necessary to get the app working on the new DBMS. This usually in-volves shortcuts like replacing ISAM record navigation (e.g., ADO's Recordset.MoveNext) with Transact-SQL cursor loops. ISAM records and SQL Server cursors aren't synonymous, and any effort to treat an RDBMS like an ISAM product is likely to go down in flames.

Some time ago, I had the misfortune of assuming the task of porting an ISAM database application to a full-blown SQL Server app. I was trying to get the company to move to client/server RDBMS technology and after months of ambivalence they finally decided that they wanted to convert their flagship application from an ISAM product to SQL Server as a kind of proof-of-concept. Since, in spite of my best efforts, the intrinsic benefits of RDBMSs weren't apparent to them, I was inclined to accept the challenge in order to prove the viability of the technology. This was despite the fact that I would much rather have started with a new app than with an existing, vitally important product.

With my guardian angel in silent verbal assault, and without having in-vestigated the code much, I accepted the task, naively believing that the de-velopers had built the app in a reasonably relational and logical manner. Having nothing to suggest otherwise, I assumed that they were processing records in sets where possible in order to save time and code; even the puny local DBMS on which the app was built supported a fair amount of set-ori-ented access (including its own basic SQL dialect). Of course, I didn't ex-pect the code to be perfect, but I guess I assumed they'd used their tools more or less as they were intended to be used. In talking with the app's au-thors, that's certainly the impression they gave me, and I quickly rushed in where angels fear to tread.

After two to three weeks of wading through some of the worst application code I'd ever seen, of watching the application block *itself* from server resources due to its dreadful design, and of having one bowling ball after another roll out of the top of the proverbial closet and hit me in the head, I finally pulled the plug on the SQL Server conversion.

The app broke virtually every basic tenet of sensible database application design. It used application code to loop through tables rather than processing rows in sets. What minimal relational and data integrity it had was implemented in a hodge-podge of application code and database constraints and was far from airtight. It used a fatuous table-versioning scheme that had never been finished or fully implemented and gave no thought to consistent naming conventions or name casing, so database objects had arcane names that were impossible to remember and incongruous with one another. The same attribute in multiple tables often had different names, and different attributes among multiple tables often had the same name. Tables were de-normalized throughout the database, not for performance but because the developers didn't know any better. There'd been no attempt to provide for concurrency, and the app was by design (or by the lack of it) strictly a single-user contrivance. In short, it was a complete disaster from an architectural standpoint, and the fact that it had ever worked at all, even on the ISAM product, was more a testament to the developers' tenacity than to the robustness of the app.

So, shortly after this experience, I began rewriting the application. Of course, I could have taken the "easy" way out and merely performed a shallow port of the app to SQL Server, essentially turning the server into a glorified ISAM database server. I could have reused as much of the existing code as possible, regardless of how poorly designed it was. Every row-by-row access in the app could have been translated to an equivalent cursor operation on SQL Server. I could have used SQL Server in ways it was never intended to be used, and I could have refrained from fixing the many relational and other problems in the app, madly bolting the various disparate pieces together into a misshapen, software-borne Frankenstein. I could have done that—it certainly would have been faster in the short run and would have made management happier—but I just couldn't bring myself to do it. It's been my experience that there's usually an optimal way to build software, and all my instincts, training, and knowledge told me that this wasn't it.

Instead, it was apparent to me that the app would have to be redesigned from the ground up if it was to have a prayer of working properly on SQL Server or any other RDBMS. The acute need for a rewrite was as much due to the radical differences between ISAM products and RDBMSs as it was to poor design and coding in the application to begin with. The fact that software appears to work properly doesn't mean that it has been constructed properly any more than the fact that a house appears to be sound means that it won't fall into the ground the first time you try to build onto it. There is more to application design than whether the app meets immediate customer requirements. Making customers happy is paramount, but it should not result in the complete neglect of long-term concerns such as extensibility, interoperability, performance, scalability, concurrency, and supportability.

These may seem like technology-centric concerns, but customers care about these things, too, whether they know it or not. They're certainly affected by them indirectly, if not directly. A feature request that might seem trivial to the typical user—converting a single-user app to a multiuser app, for example—can be difficult if not impossible if the app was designed incorrectly to begin with. If the app's designer gave no thought to concurrency when building it, the app will likely have to be rewritten in order to accommodate multiple users. This rewrite translates into delayed releases and users having to wait on the features they need. Application design affects real people in real ways. Beauty is not in the eye of the beholder—it's in the eye of the designer.

The really ironic thing about the whole experience was that many of the problem application's design decisions didn't make any more sense on the ISAM database platform than they would have on SQL Server. It's just that SQL Server would have exposed many of these defects to the light of day. It would have forced the app to clean up its act or go elsewhere. Because of their emphasis on robustness and performance, RDBMSs tend to be less forgiving of application misbehavior than ISAM products. I don't lament this—I think it's a good thing. Developers shouldn't build shoddy applications regardless of the backend.

Porting an ISAM application to SQL Server is not a menial task, even for a properly designed application. Quickly performing a shallow port by doing things like replacing ISAM access with SQL Server cursors is almost never the right approach. It takes a good amount of moral fortitude and a stiff spine to say, "This port is going to take some work; the app will have to be redesigned or rewritten," but that's often the best approach. Reinventing the wheel is fine—even necessary—if the wheel you're "reinventing" was a square one to begin with. Do deep ports when moving applications to SQL Server; think of it as the foundation on which your applications should stand, not as just another service they use. Shallow ports are for those who, as Ron Soukup says, "believe that there's never time to do the port right but there's always time to do it over."[2]

---

2. Soukup, Ron. *Inside SQL Server 6.5*. Redmond, WA: Microsoft Press, 1998, p. 533.

Types of Cursors

There are four types of cursors supported by Transact-SQL: FORWARD_ ONLY, DYNAMIC, STATIC, and KEYSET. The primary differences between these types is in the ability to detect changes to their underlying data while the cursor is being traversed and in the resources (locks, tempdb space, and so on) they use.

Depending on the type of cursor you create, changes made to its underlying data may or may not be shown while traversing the cursor. In addition to new column values, these changes can affect which rows are returned by the cursor (membership) as well as the ordering of those rows. Also, opening the cursor may cause the entirety of its result set (or their keys) to be placed in a temporary table, possibly causing resource contention problems in tempdb. Table 14.1 summarizes the different cursor types and their attributes.

Table 14.1 The Types of Cursors Transact-SQL Supports and Their Attributes

Type	Scrollable	Membership/ Order	Column Values
FORWARD_ONLY (default)	No	Dynamic	Dynamic
DYNAMIC/SENSITIVE	Yes	Dynamic	Dynamic
STATIC/INSENSITIVE	Yes	Fixed	Fixed
KEYSET	Yes	Fixed	Dynamic

Forward-Only Cursors

A forward-only cursor (the default) returns rows sequentially from the database. It does not require space in tempdb, and changes made to the underlying data are visible as soon as they're reached. Listing 14.1 shows an example.

Listing 14.1 Using a Forward-Only Cursor

```
CREATE TABLE #temp (k1 int identity, c1 int NULL)

INSERT #temp DEFAULT VALUES
INSERT #temp DEFAULT VALUES
INSERT #temp DEFAULT VALUES
INSERT #temp DEFAULT VALUES
```

```
DECLARE c CURSOR FORWARD_ONLY
FOR SELECT k1, c1 FROM #temp

OPEN c

FETCH c

UPDATE #temp
SET c1=2
WHERE k1=3

FETCH c
FETCH c

SELECT * FROM #temp

CLOSE c
DEALLOCATE c
GO
DROP TABLE #temp
```

```
k1          c1
----------- -----------
1           NULL


k1          c1
----------- -----------
2           NULL


k1          c1
----------- -----------
3           2


k1          c1
----------- -----------
1           NULL
2           NULL
3           2
4           NULL
```

Dynamic Cursors

As with forward-only cursors, dynamic cursors reflect changes to their underlying rows as those rows are reached. No extra tempdb space is required. Unlike forward-only cursors, dynamic cursors are inherently scrollable—you aren't limited to accessing their rows sequentially. They're sometimes referred to as sensitive cursors because of their sensitivity to source data changes. Listing 14.2 shows an example.

Listing 14.2 Using a Dynamic Cursor

```
CREATE TABLE #temp (k1 int identity, c1 int NULL)

INSERT #temp DEFAULT VALUES
INSERT #temp DEFAULT VALUES
INSERT #temp DEFAULT VALUES
INSERT #temp DEFAULT VALUES

DECLARE c CURSOR DYNAMIC
FOR SELECT k1, c1 FROM #temp

OPEN c

FETCH c

UPDATE #temp
SET c1=2
WHERE k1=1

FETCH c
FETCH PRIOR FROM c

SELECT * FROM #temp

CLOSE c
DEALLOCATE c
GO
DROP TABLE #temp


k1          c1
----------- -----------
1           NULL
```

```
k1            c1
-----------   -----------
2             NULL

k1            c1
-----------   -----------
1             2

k1            c1
-----------   -----------
1             2
2             NULL
3             NULL
4             NULL
```

Here, we fetch a row, then update it, fetch another, and then refetch the first row. When we fetch the first row for the second time, we see the change made via the UPDATE, even though the UPDATE didn't use the cursor to make its change.

Static Cursors

A static cursor returns a read-only result set that's impervious to changes to the underlying data. It's the opposite of a dynamic cursor, though it's still completely scrollable. Once a static cursor is opened, changes made to its source data are not reflected by the cursor. This is because the entirety of its result set is copied to tempdb when it's first opened. Static cursors are sometimes called snapshot or insensitive cursors because they aren't sensitive to changes made to their source data. Listing 14.3 shows an example.

Listing 14.3 Using a Static Cursor

```
CREATE TABLE #temp (k1 int identity, c1 int NULL)

INSERT #temp DEFAULT VALUES
INSERT #temp DEFAULT VALUES
INSERT #temp DEFAULT VALUES
INSERT #temp DEFAULT VALUES

DECLARE c CURSOR STATIC
FOR SELECT k1, c1 FROM #temp
```

```
OPEN c  -- The entire result set is copied to tempdb

UPDATE #temp
SET c1=2
WHERE k1=1

FETCH c  -- This doesn't reflect the changed made by the UPDATE

SELECT * FROM #temp  -- But the change is indeed there

CLOSE c
DEALLOCATE c
GO
DROP TABLE #temp
```

```
k1            c1
-----------   -----------
1             NULL

k1            c1
-----------   -----------
1             2
2             NULL
3             NULL
4             NULL
```

Here, we open the cursor and immediately make a change to the first row in its underlying table. This change isn't reflected when we fetch that row from the cursor because the row is actually coming from tempdb. A subsequent SELECT from the underlying table shows the change to be intact even though it's not reflected by the cursor.

Keyset Cursors

Opening a keyset cursor returns a fully scrollable result set whose membership and order are fixed. Like forward-only and static cursors, changes to the values in its underlying data (except for keyset columns) are reflected when they're accessed; however, new row insertions are *not* reflected by the cursor. Similarly to a static cursor, the set of unique key values for the cursor's rows are copied to a table in tempdb (hence the term "keyset") when the cursor is opened. That's why membership in the cursor is fixed. If the underlying table doesn't have a primary or unique key, the entire set of candidate key columns is copied to the keyset table. Since changes to keyset columns aren't reflected by the cursor, failing to define a unique key of some type for the underlying data results in a keyset that doesn't reflect changes to *any* of its candidate key columns. Listing 14.4 shows a simple keyset example.

Listing 14.4 Using a Keyset Cursor

```
CREATE TABLE #temp (k1 int identity PRIMARY KEY, c1 int NULL)

INSERT #temp DEFAULT VALUES
INSERT #temp DEFAULT VALUES
INSERT #temp DEFAULT VALUES
INSERT #temp DEFAULT VALUES

DECLARE c CURSOR KEYSET
FOR SELECT k1, c1 FROM #temp

OPEN c  -- The keyset is copied to tempdb

UPDATE #temp
SET c1=2
WHERE k1=1

INSERT #temp VALUES (3) -- won't be visible to cursor
                        -- (can safely omit identity column)

FETCH c -- Change is visible
FETCH LAST FROM c -- New row isn't

SELECT * FROM #temp

CLOSE c
DEALLOCATE c
GO
DROP TABLE #temp


k1          c1
----------- -----------
1           2
```

```
k1            c1
-----------   -----------
4             NULL

k1            c1
-----------   -----------
1             2
2             NULL
3             NULL
4             NULL
5             3
```

Here, once the keyset cursor is opened, a change is made to its first row before the row is fetched from the cursor. Another row is then inserted into the underlying table. Once the routine begins fetching rows from the cursor, the first change we made shows up, but the new row doesn't. This is because membership in a keyset cursor doesn't change once it's opened.

Note the inclusion of a PRIMARY KEY constraint in the work table. Without it, changes to the table's c1 column aren't visible to the cursor, even though the cursor has an identity column. Why? Because, in and of themselves, identity columns aren't guaranteed to be unique. You could always use SET IDENTITY_INSERT to add duplicate identity values, or reset the identity seed to have the server add them for you. To ensure uniqueness, a PRIMARY KEY or UNIQUE KEY constraint is required. Without a unique key, the server copies the entirety of the candidate keys for each row to the keyset cursor's temporary table.

Appropriate Cursor Use

A word of advice: Use cursors only when you have to. That may seem a little simplistic or overly broad, but I think most seasoned Transact-SQL developers would agree that using cursors should be near the bottom of your list of coding techniques. Instead, try to find a solution that leverages Transact-SQL's ability to work with sets of data to solve your problems. That's what it was designed to do; that's what it does best. Though cursors are an easy concept for beginners to grasp, cursor overuse/misuse is a major source of performance problems with most RDBMSs, including SQL Server.

This isn't to say that cursor use is taboo or that all cursor users are headed for a fiery afterlife. If you program long enough in Transact-SQL, you'll use cursors sooner or later. Some kinds of development require them extensively. Like many things, your degree of success will depend largely on your mindset. *Use* cursors when it makes sense—just be careful not to *misuse* them.

Some examples of situations where cursor use is appropriate are dynamic queries, row-oriented operations, and scrollable forms. Dynamic queries build and execute Transact-SQL code at runtime. Row-oriented operations are multistatement routines that are too complex or otherwise unsuitable for single-statement operations such as SELECT or UPDATE. Scrollable forms typically feature a facility (sometimes listing multiple rows) that allows users to navigate within a result set. Scrollable cursors make setting up this functionality as straightforward as possible for the developer.

Dynamic Queries

Cursors come in handy with dynamic queries because they allow you to construct executable Transact-SQL code based on a result set. For example, suppose we want to construct a cross-tab (pivot table) over a series of values. Let's assume that there are three columns in the series—a key, a subkey, and the value column itself. We want a cross-tab featuring the keys on its x-axis and the subkeys on its y-axis, with the values listed at each intersection. Each key may have a different number of subkeys and these subkeys may or may not be consecutive. Listing 14.5 presents an approach that uses a cursor to construct dynamic T-SQL to render the cross-tab.

Listing 14.5 Using a Cursor to Render a Cross-Tab

```
CREATE TABLE #series
(key1 int,
  key2 int,
  value1 decimal(6,2) DEFAULT (
    (CASE (CAST(RAND()+.5 AS int)*-1) WHEN 0 THEN 1
    ELSE -1 END)*(CONVERT(int, RAND() * 100000) % 10000)*RAND()
    )
)

INSERT #series (key1, key2) VALUES (1,1)
INSERT #series (key1, key2) VALUES (1,2)
INSERT #series (key1, key2) VALUES (1,3)
```

```
INSERT #series (key1, key2) VALUES (1,4)
INSERT #series (key1, key2) VALUES (1,5)
INSERT #series (key1, key2) VALUES (1,6)
INSERT #series (key1, key2) VALUES (2,1)
INSERT #series (key1, key2) VALUES (2,2)
INSERT #series (key1, key2) VALUES (2,3)
INSERT #series (key1, key2) VALUES (2,4)
INSERT #series (key1, key2) VALUES (2,5)
INSERT #series (key1, key2) VALUES (2,6)
INSERT #series (key1, key2) VALUES (2,7)
INSERT #series (key1, key2) VALUES (3,1)
INSERT #series (key1, key2) VALUES (3,2)
INSERT #series (key1, key2) VALUES (3,3)

DECLARE s CURSOR
FOR
SELECT DISTINCT key2 FROM #series ORDER BY key2

DECLARE @key2 int, @key2str varchar(10), @sql varchar(8000)

OPEN s
FETCH s INTO @key2

SET @sql=''
WHILE (@@FETCH_STATUS=0) BEGIN
  SET @key2str=CAST(@key2 AS varchar)
  SET @sql=@sql+',SUM(CASE WHEN key2='+@key2str+' THEN value1
  ELSE NULL END) ['+@key2str+']'
  FETCH s INTO @key2
END

SET @sql='SELECT key1'+@sql+' FROM #series GROUP BY key1'
EXEC(@sql)

CLOSE s
DEALLOCATE s
DROP TABLE #series
```

key1	1	2	3	4	5	6	7
1	212.74	-1608.59	1825.29	690.48	1863.44	5302.54	NULL
2	-7531.42	1848.63	-3746.60	-54.37	-2263.63	-1014.01	5453.57
3	126.13	-10.41	205.35	NULL	NULL	NULL	NULL

To best understand how this works, it's instructive to examine the dynamic query itself. Here's what @sql looks like just prior to execution (Listing 14.6).

Listing 14.6 The Dynamic Query Text Just Prior to Execution

```
SELECT key1,SUM(CASE WHEN key2=1 THEN value1 ELSE NULL END) [1],
SUM(CASE WHEN key2=2 THEN value1 ELSE NULL END) [2],
SUM(CASE WHEN key2=3 THEN value1 ELSE NULL END) [3],
SUM(CASE WHEN key2=4 THEN value1 ELSE NULL END) [4],
SUM(CASE WHEN key2=5 THEN value1 ELSE NULL END) [5],
SUM(CASE WHEN key2=6 THEN value1 ELSE NULL END) [6],
SUM(CASE WHEN key2=7 THEN value1 ELSE NULL END) [7]
FROM #series GROUP BY key1
```

The cursor returns a row for each unique subkey in the series. Regardless of the key that contains it, if a subkey appears in the table, the cursor's SELECT DISTINCT returns an instance of it. The CASE statement that's constructed for each cross-tab column returns the value1 column when the subkey matches up with its column and returns NULL otherwise. The GROUP BY flattens the rows returned by the query such that each key appears exactly once. To better understand this, let's look at the cross-tab without the GROUP BY (Listing 14.7).

Listing 14.7 The Results of the Cross-Tab Query Minus the GROUP BY

key1	1	2	3	4	5	6	7
1	212.74	NULL	NULL	NULL	NULL	NULL	NULL
1	NULL	-1608.59	NULL	NULL	NULL	NULL	NULL
1	NULL	NULL	1825.29	NULL	NULL	NULL	NULL
1	NULL	NULL	NULL	690.48	NULL	NULL	NULL
1	NULL	NULL	NULL	NULL	5302.54	NULL	NULL
1	NULL	NULL	NULL	NULL	NULL	5302.54	NULL
2	-7531.42	NULL	NULL	NULL	NULL	NULL	NULL
2	NULL	1848.63	NULL	NULL	NULL	NULL	NULL
2	NULL	NULL	-3746.60	NULL	NULL	NULL	NULL
2	NULL	NULL	NULL	-54.37	NULL	NULL	NULL
2	NULL	NULL	NULL	NULL	-2263.63	NULL	NULL

2	NULL	NULL	NULL	NULL	NULL	−1014.01	NULL
2	NULL	NULL	NULL	NULL	NULL	NULL	5453.57
3	126.13	NULL	NULL	NULL	NULL	NULL	NULL
3	NULL	−10.41	NULL	NULL	NULL	NULL	NULL
3	NULL	NULL	205.35	NULL	NULL	NULL	NULL

Due to the characteristics of the original series data, only one subkey column in each key row has a value. The rest of the columns are set to NULL by their respective CASE expressions. The GROUP BY clause minimizes these NULLs, summarizing the pivot table such that each series value appears in its respective subkey column when present.

Row-Oriented Operations

Another good use of cursors is in row-oriented operations. A row-oriented operation is one that exceeds the capabilities of single-statement processing (e.g., SELECT). Some characteristic of it requires more power or more flexibility than a single-statement solution can provide. Listing 14.8 presents an example of a row-oriented operation that lists the source code for the triggers attached to each table in a database.

Listing 14.8 Using a Cursor in a Row-Oriented Operation

```
USE pubs
DECLARE objects CURSOR
FOR
SELECT name, deltrig, instrig, updtrig
FROM sysobjects WHERE type='U' AND deltrig+instrig+updtrig>0

DECLARE @objname sysname, @deltrig int, @instrig int, @updtrig int,
    @deltrigname sysname, @instrigname sysname, @updtrigname sysname

OPEN objects
FETCH objects INTO @objname, @deltrig, @instrig, @updtrig

WHILE (@@FETCH_STATUS=0) BEGIN
  PRINT 'Triggers for object: '+@objname
  SELECT @deltrigname=OBJECT_NAME(@deltrig),
    @instrigname=OBJECT_NAME(@instrig),
    @updtrigname=OBJECT_NAME(@updtrig)
```

```
    IF @deltrigname IS NOT NULL BEGIN
      PRINT 'Table: '+@objname+' Delete Trigger: '+@deltrigname
      EXEC sp_helptext @deltrigname
    END
    IF @instrigname IS NOT NULL BEGIN
      PRINT 'Table: '+@objname+' Insert Trigger: '+@instrigname
      EXEC sp_helptext @instrigname
    END
    IF @updtrigname IS NOT NULL BEGIN
      PRINT 'Table: '+@objname+' Update Trigger: '+@updtrigname
      EXEC sp_helptext @updtrigname
    END
    FETCH objects INTO @objname, @deltrig, @instrig, @updtrig
END


CLOSE objects
DEALLOCATE objects


Triggers for object: employee
Table: employee Insert Trigger: employee_insupd
Text
-------------------------------------------------------------------
CREATE TRIGGER employee_insupd
ON employee
FOR insert, UPDATE
AS
--Get the range of level for this job type from the jobs table.
declare @min_lvl tinyint,
  @max_lvl tinyint,
  @emp_lvl tinyint,
  @job_id smallint
select @min_lvl = min_lvl,
  @max_lvl = max_lvl,
  @emp_lvl = i.job_lvl,
  @job_id = i.job_id
from employee e, jobs j, inserted i
where e.emp_id = i.emp_id AND i.job_id = j.job_id
IF (@job_id = 1) and (@emp_lvl <> 10)
begin
  raiserror ('Job id 1 expects the default level of 10.',16,1)
  ROLLBACK TRANSACTION
end
ELSE
IF NOT (@emp_lvl BETWEEN @min_lvl AND @max_lvl)
```

```
begin
  raiserror ('The level for job_id:%d should be
    between %d and %d.',
    16, 1, @job_id, @min_lvl, @max_lvl)
  ROLLBACK TRANSACTION
end


Table: employee Update Trigger: employee_insupd
Text
------------------------------------------------------------------
CREATE TRIGGER employee_insupd
ON employee
FOR insert, UPDATE
AS
--Get the range of level for this job type from the jobs table.
declare @min_lvl tinyint,
  @max_lvl tinyint,
  @emp_lvl tinyint,
  @job_id smallint
select @min_lvl = min_lvl,
  @max_lvl = max_lvl,
  @emp_lvl = i.job_lvl,
  @job_id = i.job_id
from employee e, jobs j, inserted i
where e.emp_id = i.emp_id AND i.job_id = j.job_id
IF (@job_id = 1) and (@emp_lvl <> 10)
begin
  raiserror ('Job id 1 expects the default level of 10.',16,1)
  ROLLBACK TRANSACTION
end
ELSE
IF NOT (@emp_lvl BETWEEN @min_lvl AND @max_lvl)
begin
  raiserror ('The level for job_id:%d should be
    between %d and %d.',
    16, 1, @job_id, @min_lvl, @max_lvl)
  ROLLBACK TRANSACTION
end
```

Of course, we could query the syscomments table directly and join it with the sysobjects table to render the same information, but the result set wouldn't be formatted suitably. By iterating through the table one row at a time, we can format the output for each table and its triggers however we like.

Scrollable Forms

Whether you should use a cursor to service a scrollable form depends largely on how much data the form might require. Since Transact-SQL cursors reside on the server and only return fetched rows, they can save lots of time and resources when dealing with large result sets. You wouldn't want to return 100,000 rows over a network to a client application. On the other hand, cursors are unnecessary with smaller result sets and probably not worth the trouble. Other factors to consider when determining whether a cursor is appropriate for a scrollable form are whether or not the form is updateable and whether you want changes by other users to show up immediately. If the form is read-only or you're not concerned with showing changes by other users, you may be able to avoid using a cursor.

Transact-SQL Cursor Syntax

A number of commands and functions relate to cursors. Table 14.2 summarizes them. The following subsections cover these commands in more detail.

Table 14.2 Transact-SQL Cursor Commands and Functions

Command or Function	Purpose
DECLARE CURSOR	Defines a cursor
OPEN	Opens a cursor so that data may be retrieved from it
FETCH	Fetches a single row from the cursor
CLOSE	Closes the cursor, leaving intact the internal structures that service it
DEALLOCATE	Frees the cursor's internal structures
@@CURSOR_ROWS	Returns the number of rows exposed by the cursor
@@FETCH_STATUS	Indicates the success or failure of the last FETCH
CURSOR_STATUS	Reports status information for cursors and cursor variables

DECLARE CURSOR

DECLARE CURSOR defines cursors. There are two basic versions of the DECLARE CURSOR command—the ANSI/ISO SQL 92–compliant syntax and Transact-SQL's extended syntax. The ANSI/ISO syntax looks like this:

```
DECLARE name [INSENSITIVE][SCROLL] CURSOR
FOR select
[FOR {READ ONLY | UPDATE [OF column [,…n]]}]
```

Transact-SQL's extended syntax follows this form:

```
DECLARE name CURSOR
[LOCAL | GLOBAL]
[FORWARD_ONLY | SCROLL]
[STATIC | KEYSET | DYNAMIC | FAST_FORWARD]
[READ_ONLY | SCROLL_LOCKS | OPTIMISTIC]
[TYPE_WARNING]
FOR select
[FOR {READ ONLY | UPDATE [OF column [,…n]]}]
```

The *select* component of the command is a standard SELECT statement that defines what data the cursor returns. It is not permitted to contain the keywords COMPUTE [BY], FOR BROWSE, or INTO. The *select* component affects whether a cursor is read-only. For example, if you include the FOR UPDATE clause but specify a *select* that inherently prohibits updates (e.g., one that includes GROUP BY or DISTINCT), your cursor will be implicitly converted to a read-only (or static) cursor. The server converts cursors to static cursors that, by their very nature, cannot be updated. These types of automatic conversions are known as implicit cursor conversions. A number of criteria affect implicit cursor conversions; see Books Online for more information.

The corollary to this is that you don't have to specify FOR UPDATE in order to update a cursor if its SELECT statement is inherently updateable. Again, unless specified otherwise, the characteristics of the SELECT statement determine whether the cursor is updateable. Listing 14.9 shows an example.

Listing 14.9 Cursor Updatability

```
CREATE TABLE #temp (k1 int identity, c1 int NULL)

INSERT #temp DEFAULT VALUES
INSERT #temp DEFAULT VALUES
INSERT #temp DEFAULT VALUES
INSERT #temp DEFAULT VALUES

DECLARE c CURSOR
FOR SELECT k1, c1 FROM #temp

OPEN c
FETCH c
UPDATE #temp
SET c1=2
WHERE CURRENT OF c

SELECT * FROM #temp
CLOSE c
DEALLOCATE c
GO
DROP TABLE #temp


k1          c1
----------- -----------
1           NULL

k1          c1
----------- -----------
1           2
2           NULL
3           NULL
4           NULL
```

Even though this cursor isn't specifically defined as an updateable cursor, it's updateable by virtue of the fact that its SELECT statement is updateable—that is, the server can readily translate an update to the cursor into an update to a specific row in the underlying table.

If you specify the FOR UPDATE clause and include a column list, the column(s) you update must appear in that list. If you attempt to update a col-

umn not in the list using UPDATE's WHERE CURRENT OF clause, SQL
Server will reject the change and generate an error message (Listing 14.10).

Listing 14.10 Using FOR UPDATE to Determine Column Updatability

```
CREATE TABLE #temp (k1 int identity, c1 int NULL, c2 int NULL)

INSERT #temp DEFAULT VALUES
INSERT #temp DEFAULT VALUES
INSERT #temp DEFAULT VALUES
INSERT #temp DEFAULT VALUES

DECLARE c CURSOR
FOR SELECT k1, c1, c2 FROM #temp
FOR UPDATE OF c1

OPEN c
FETCH c

-- BAD T-SQL -- This UPDATE attempts to change a column
-- not in the FOR UPDATE OF list
UPDATE #temp
SET c2=2
WHERE CURRENT OF c


k1          c1          c2
----------- ----------- -----------
1           NULL        NULL

Server: Msg 16932, Level 16, State 1, Line 18
The cursor has a FOR UPDATE list and the requested column to be
updated is not in this list.
The statement has been terminated.
```

If DECLARE CURSOR's *select* statement references a variable, the variable is resolved when the cursor is declared, *not* when it's opened. This is significant in that you must assign values to variables before you declare a cursor
that uses them. You can't declare a cursor first, then assign a value to a variable that it depends on and expect the cursor to work properly. Listing 14.11
gives an example.

Listing 14.11 Using Variables with DECLARE CURSOR

```
-- In case these remain from the previous example
DEALLOCATE c
DROP TABLE #temp
GO


CREATE TABLE #temp (k1 int identity, c1 int NULL)

INSERT #temp DEFAULT VALUES
INSERT #temp DEFAULT VALUES
INSERT #temp DEFAULT VALUES
INSERT #temp DEFAULT VALUES

DECLARE @k1 int

DECLARE c CURSOR
FOR SELECT k1, c1 FROM #temp WHERE k1<@k1 -- Won't work
                                          -- @k1 is NULL here

SET @k1=3 -- Need to move this before the DECLARE CURSOR
OPEN c
FETCH c

UPDATE #temp
SET c1=2
WHERE CURRENT OF c

SELECT * FROM #temp
CLOSE c
DEALLOCATE c
GO
DROP TABLE #temp


k1          c1
----------- -----------


Server: Msg 16930, Level 16, State 1, Line 18
The requested row is not in the fetch buffer.
The statement has been terminated.
```

```
k1          c1
----------- -----------
1           NULL
2           NULL
3           NULL
4           NULL
```

Global vs. Local Cursors

A global cursor is visible outside the batch, stored procedure, or trigger that created it and persists until it's explicitly deallocated or until its host connection disconnects. A local cursor is visible only within the code module that created it unless it's returned via an output parameter. Local cursors are implicitly deallocated when they go out of scope.

For compatibility with earlier releases, SQL Server creates global cursors by default, but you can override the default behavior by explicitly specifying the GLOBAL or LOCAL keyword when you declare a cursor. Note that you can have global and local cursors with identical names, though this is a questionable coding practice. For example, the code in Listing 14.12 runs without error.

Listing 14.12 Local and Global Cursors with Identical Names

```
DECLARE Darryl CURSOR   -- My brother Darryl
LOCAL
FOR SELECT stor_id, title_id, qty FROM sales

DECLARE Darryl CURSOR   -- My other brother Darryl
GLOBAL
FOR SELECT au_lname, au_fname FROM authors

OPEN GLOBAL Darryl
OPEN Darryl

FETCH GLOBAL Darryl
FETCH Darryl

CLOSE GLOBAL Darryl
CLOSE Darryl
```

```
DEALLOCATE GLOBAL Darryl
DEALLOCATE Darryl


au_lname                                          au_fname
----------------------------------------    --------------------
White                                             Johnson

stor_id title_id qty
------- -------- ------
6380    BU1032   5
```

You can change whether SQL Server creates global cursors when the scope is unspecified via the sp_dboption system procedure (see the Configuring Cursors section on page 558 for more information).

OPEN

OPEN makes a cursor's rows accessible via FETCH. If the cursor is an IN-SENSITIVE or STATIC cursor, OPEN copies the entirety of its result set to a temporary table. If it's a KEYSET cursor, OPEN copies its set of unique key values (or the entirety of all candidate key columns if no unique key exists) to a temporary table. OPEN can indicate the scope of the cursor by including the optional GLOBAL keyword. If there is both a local and a global cursor with the same name (something you should avoid when possible), use GLOBAL to indicate the one you want to open. (The default to local cursor database option determines whether you get a global or local cursor when neither is explicitly specified. See the Configuring Cursors section on page 558 for more information.)

Use the @@CURSOR_ROWS automatic variable to determine how many rows are in the cursor. Listing 14.13 gives a simple OPEN example.

Listing 14.13 Using OPEN

```
CREATE TABLE #temp (k1 int identity PRIMARY KEY, c1 int NULL)

INSERT #temp DEFAULT VALUES
INSERT #temp DEFAULT VALUES
INSERT #temp DEFAULT VALUES
INSERT #temp DEFAULT VALUES
```

```
DECLARE GlobalCursor CURSOR STATIC  -- Declare a GLOBAL cursor
GLOBAL
FOR SELECT k1, c1 FROM #temp

DECLARE LocalCursor CURSOR STATIC -- Declare a LOCAL cursor
LOCAL
FOR SELECT k1, c1 FROM #temp WHERE k1<4  -- Only returns three rows

OPEN GLOBAL GlobalCursor
SELECT @@CURSOR_ROWS AS NumberOfGLOBALCursorRows

OPEN LocalCursor
SELECT @@CURSOR_ROWS AS NumberOfLOCALCursorRows

CLOSE GLOBAL GlobalCursor
DEALLOCATE GLOBAL GlobalCursor
CLOSE LocalCursor
DEALLOCATE LocalCursor
GO
DROP TABLE #temp


NumberOfGLOBALCursorRows
------------------------
4

NumberOfLOCALCursorRows
------------------------
3
```

For dynamic cursors, @@CURSOR_ROWS returns –1 since new row additions could change the number of rows returned by the cursor at any time. If the cursor is being populated asynchronously (see the Configuring Cursors section on page 558), @@CURSOR_ROWS returns a negative number whose absolute value indicates the number of rows currently in the cursor.

FETCH

FETCH is the means by which you retrieve data from a cursor. Think of it as a special SELECT that returns just one row from a predetermined result set. Typically, FETCH is called within a loop that uses @@FETCH_STATUS as its control variable, with each successive FETCH returning the cursor's next row.

Scrollable cursors (DYNAMIC, STATIC, and KEYSET cursors, or those declared using the SCROLL option) allow FETCH to retrieve rows other than the cursor's next row. In addition to retrieving the next row, scrollable cursors allow FETCH to retrieve a cursor's previous row, its first row, its last row, an absolute row number, and a row relative to the current row. Listing 14.14 provides a simple example.

Listing 14.14 Using FETCH

```
SET NOCOUNT ON
CREATE TABLE #cursortest (k1 int identity)

INSERT #cursortest DEFAULT VALUES
INSERT #cursortest DEFAULT VALUES
INSERT #cursortest DEFAULT VALUES
INSERT #cursortest DEFAULT VALUES
INSERT #cursortest DEFAULT VALUES
INSERT #cursortest DEFAULT VALUES
INSERT #cursortest DEFAULT VALUES
INSERT #cursortest DEFAULT VALUES
INSERT #cursortest DEFAULT VALUES
INSERT #cursortest DEFAULT VALUES

DECLARE c CURSOR SCROLL
FOR SELECT * FROM #cursortest

OPEN c

FETCH c -- Gets the first row
FETCH ABSOLUTE 4 FROM c -- Gets the fourth row
FETCH RELATIVE -1 FROM c -- Gets the third row
FETCH LAST FROM c -- Gets the last row
FETCH FIRST FROM c -- Gets the first row

CLOSE c
DEALLOCATE c
GO
DROP TABLE #cursortest
```

```
k1
-----------
1


k1
-----------
4


k1
-----------
3


k1
-----------
10


k1
-----------
1
```

FETCH can be used to return a result set of its own, but usually it's used to fill local variables with table data. FETCH's INTO clause allows retrieved values to be assigned to local variables, as demonstrated in Listing 14.15.

Listing 14.15 Using FETCH's INTO Clause

```
SET NOCOUNT ON
CREATE TABLE #cursortest (k1 int identity)

INSERT #cursortest DEFAULT VALUES
INSERT #cursortest DEFAULT VALUES
INSERT #cursortest DEFAULT VALUES
INSERT #cursortest DEFAULT VALUES
INSERT #cursortest DEFAULT VALUES
INSERT #cursortest DEFAULT VALUES
INSERT #cursortest DEFAULT VALUES
INSERT #cursortest DEFAULT VALUES
INSERT #cursortest DEFAULT VALUES
INSERT #cursortest DEFAULT VALUES
```

```
DECLARE c CURSOR SCROLL
FOR SELECT * FROM #cursortest

DECLARE @k int

OPEN c
FETCH c INTO @k
WHILE (@@FETCH_STATUS=0) BEGIN
  SELECT @k
  FETCH c INTO @k
END

CLOSE c
DEALLOCATE c
GO
DROP TABLE #cursortest
```

```
-----------
1


-----------
2


-----------
3


-----------
4


-----------
5


-----------
6


-----------
7
```

```
-----------
8


-----------
9


-----------
10
```

NEXT is the default fetch operation, so if you don't specify what type of fetch you want, you'll retrieve the cursor's next row. For fetch operations other than NEXT, the FROM keyword is required.

FETCH RELATIVE 0 can be used to refresh the current record. This allows you to accommodate changes made to the current row while the cursor is being traversed. Listing 14.16 shows an example.

Listing 14.16 Using FETCH RELATIVE 0

```
USE pubs
SET CURSOR_CLOSE_ON_COMMIT OFF
  -- In case it's been turned on previously
SET NOCOUNT ON

DECLARE c CURSOR SCROLL
FOR SELECT title_id, qty FROM sales ORDER BY qty

OPEN c


BEGIN TRAN  -- So that we can undo the changes we make

PRINT 'Before image'

FETCH c

UPDATE sales
SET qty=4
WHERE qty=3 -- We happen to know that only one row qualifies,
            -- the first one
```

```
PRINT 'After image'
FETCH RELATIVE 0 FROM c

ROLLBACK TRAN -- Reverse the UPDATE

CLOSE c
DEALLOCATE c


Before image
title_id qty
-------- ------
PS2091   3

After image
title_id qty
-------- ------
PS2091   4
```

CLOSE

CLOSE frees the current cursor result set and releases any locks being held by the cursor. (Prior to version 7.0, SQL Server retained *all* locks until the current transaction completed, including cursor locks. With 7.0 and later, cursor locks are handled independently of other kinds of locks.) The cursor's data structures themselves are left in place so that the cursor may be reopened if necessary. Specify the GLOBAL keyword to indicate that you're closing a global cursor.

DEALLOCATE

When you're finished with a cursor, you should always deallocate it. A cursor takes up space in the procedure cache that can be used for other things if you get rid of it when it's no longer needed. Even though deallocating a cursor automatically closes it, it's considered poor form to deallocate a cursor without first closing it with the CLOSE command.

Configuring Cursors

In addition to configuring cursors through declaration options, Transact-SQL also provides commands and configuration options that can modify cursor behavior as well. The sp_configure and sp_dboption procedures and the SET command can be used to configure how cursors are created and the way they behave once created.

Asynchronous Cursors

By default, SQL Server generates all keysets synchronously—that is, the call to OPEN doesn't return until the cursor's result set has been fully materialized. This may not be optimal for large data sets, and you can change it via the sp_configure 'cursor threshold' configuration option (cursor threshold is an advanced option; enable advanced options via sp_configure 'show advanced options' in order to access it). Here's an example that illustrates the difference rendering a cursor asynchronously can make (Listing 14.17).

Listing 14.17 Using Asynchronous Cursors

```
-- Turn on advanced options so that 'cursor threshold'
-- can be configured
EXEC sp_configure 'show advanced options',1
RECONFIGURE WITH OVERRIDE

USE northwind

DECLARE c CURSOR STATIC -- Force rows to be copied to tempdb
FOR SELECT OrderID, ProductID FROM [Order Details]

DECLARE @start datetime
SET @start=getdate()

-- First try it with a synchronous cursor
OPEN c

PRINT CHAR(13) -- Pretty up the display
SELECT DATEDIFF(ms,@start,getdate()) AS
  [Milliseconds elapsed for Synchronous cursor]

SELECT @@CURSOR_ROWS AS [Number of rows in Synchronous cursor]

CLOSE c

-- Now reconfigure 'cursor threshold' and force an asynch cursor
EXEC sp_configure 'cursor threshold', 1000
-- Asynchronous for cursors > 1000 rows
```

```
RECONFIGURE WITH OVERRIDE
PRINT CHAR(13) -- Pretty up the display

SET @start=getdate()
OPEN c -- Opens an asynch cursor since there are
       -- over 1000 rows in the table

-- OPEN comes back immediately because the cursor is
-- being populated asynchronously
SELECT DATEDIFF(ms,@start,getdate()) AS
   [Milliseconds elapsed for Asynchronous cursor]

SELECT @@CURSOR_ROWS AS [Number of rows in Asynchronous cursor]

CLOSE c

DEALLOCATE c
GO
EXEC sp_configure 'cursor threshold', -1 -- Back to synchronous
RECONFIGURE WITH OVERRIDE
```

```
DBCC execution completed. If DBCC printed error messages, contact
your system administrator.
Configuration option changed. Run the RECONFIGURE statement
to install.

Milliseconds elapsed for Synchronous cursor
-------------------------------------------
70

Number of rows in Synchronous cursor
------------------------------------
2155

DBCC execution completed. If DBCC printed error messages, contact
your system administrator.
Configuration option changed. Run the RECONFIGURE statement
to install.

Milliseconds elapsed for Asynchronous cursor
--------------------------------------------
0
```

```
Number of rows in Asynchronous cursor
-------------------------------------
-1

DBCC execution completed. If DBCC printed error messages, contact
your system administrator.
Configuration option changed. Run the RECONFIGURE statement
to install.
```

ANSI/ISO Automatic Cursor Closing

The ANSI/ISO SQL-92 specification calls for cursors to be closed automatically when a transaction is committed. This doesn't make a lot of sense for the types of apps where cursors would most often be used (those with scrollable forms, for example), so SQL Server doesn't comply with the standard out of the box. By default, a SQL Server cursor remains open until explicitly closed or until the connection that created it disconnects. To force SQL Server to close cursors when a transaction is committed, use the SET CURSOR_ CLOSE_ON_COMMIT command, as shown in Listing 14.18.

Listing 14.18 Closing a Cursor When a Transaction Is Committed

```
CREATE TABLE #temp (k1 int identity PRIMARY KEY, c1 int NULL)

INSERT #temp DEFAULT VALUES
INSERT #temp DEFAULT VALUES
INSERT #temp DEFAULT VALUES
INSERT #temp DEFAULT VALUES


DECLARE c CURSOR DYNAMIC
FOR SELECT k1, c1 FROM #temp

OPEN c

SET CURSOR_CLOSE_ON_COMMIT ON
BEGIN TRAN

UPDATE #temp
SET c1=2
WHERE k1=1
```

```
COMMIT TRAN

-- These FETCHes will fail because the cursor was closed by
-- the COMMIT
FETCH c
FETCH LAST FROM c

-- This CLOSE will fail because the cursor was closed by
-- the COMMIT
CLOSE c
DEALLOCATE c
GO
DROP TABLE #temp
SET CURSOR_CLOSE_ON_COMMIT OFF


Server: Msg 16917, Level 16, State 2, Line 0
Cursor is not open.
Server: Msg 16917, Level 16, State 2, Line 26
Cursor is not open.
Server: Msg 16917, Level 16, State 1, Line 29
Cursor is not open.
```

Contrary to Books Online, rolling back a transaction does *not* close up-dateable cursors when CLOSE_CURSOR_ON_COMMIT is disabled. The actual behavior following a ROLLBACK differs significantly from the documentation and more closely follows what happens when a transaction is committed. Basically, ROLLBACK doesn't close cursors unless CLOSE_ CURSOR_ON_COMMIT has been enabled. Listing 14.19 shows an example.

Listing 14.19 ROLLBACK and Cursor Closing

```
USE pubs
SET CURSOR_CLOSE_ON_COMMIT ON
BEGIN TRAN

DECLARE c CURSOR DYNAMIC
FOR SELECT qty FROM sales

OPEN c

FETCH c
```

```
SET qty=qty+1UPDATE sales
WHERE CURRENT OF c

ROLLBACK TRAN

-- These FETCHes will fail because the cursor was closed by
-- the ROLLBACK
FETCH c
FETCH LAST FROM c

-- This CLOSE will fail because the cursor was closed by
-- the ROLLBACK
CLOSE c
DEALLOCATE c
GO
SET CURSOR_CLOSE_ON_COMMIT OFF


qty
------
5

Server: Msg 16917, Level 16, State 2, Line 21
Cursor is not open.
Server: Msg 16917, Level 16, State 2, Line 22
Cursor is not open.
Server: Msg 16917, Level 16, State 1, Line 25
Cursor is not open.
```

Now let's disable CURSOR_CLOSE_ON_COMMIT and run the query again (Listing 14.20).

Listing 14.20 ROLLBACK and Cursor Closing Revisited

```
SET CURSOR_CLOSE_ON_COMMIT OFF
BEGIN TRAN

DECLARE c CURSOR DYNAMIC
FOR SELECT qty FROM sales FOR UPDATE OF qty

OPEN c
```

```
FETCH c

UPDATE sales
SET qty=qty+1
WHERE CURRENT OF c

ROLLBACK TRAN

-- These FETCHes will succeed because the cursor was left open
-- in spite of the ROLLBACK
FETCH c
FETCH LAST FROM c

-- This CLOSE will succeed because the cursor was left open
-- in spite of the ROLLBACK
CLOSE c
DEALLOCATE c


qty
------
5

qty
------
3

qty
------
30
```

Despite the fact that a transaction is rolled back while our dynamic cursor is open, the cursor is unaffected. This contradicts the way the server is documented to behave.

Defaulting to Global or Local Cursors

Out of the box, SQL Server creates global cursors by default. This is in keeping with previous versions of the server that did not support local cursors. If you'd like to change this, set the default to local cursor database option to true using sp_dboption.

Updating Cursors

The WHERE CURRENT OF clause of the UPDATE and DELETE commands allows you to update and delete rows via a cursor. An update or delete performed via a cursor is known as a positioned update or delete. Listing 14.21 shows an example.

Listing 14.21 Performing a Positioned Update and Delete

```
USE pubs
SET CURSOR_CLOSE_ON_COMMIT OFF

SET NOCOUNT ON
DECLARE c CURSOR DYNAMIC
FOR SELECT * FROM sales

OPEN c

FETCH c

BEGIN TRAN -- Start a transaction so we can reverse our changes

-- A positioned UPDATE
UPDATE sales SET qty=qty+1 WHERE CURRENT OF c

FETCH RELATIVE 0 FROM c

FETCH c

-- A positioned DELETE
DELETE sales WHERE CURRENT OF c

SELECT * FROM sales WHERE qty=3

ROLLBACK TRAN -- Throw away our changes

SELECT * FROM sales WHERE qty=3 -- The deleted row comes back

CLOSE c
DEALLOCATE c
```

```
stor_id ord_num  ord_date                 qty    payterms   title_id
------- --------  -----------------------  -----  ---------  --------
6380    6871      1994-09-14 00:00:00.000  5      Net 60     BU1032

stor_id ord_num  ord_date                 qty    payterms   title_id
------- --------  -----------------------  -----  ---------  --------
6380    6871      1994-09-14 00:00:00.000  6      Net 60     BU1032

stor_id ord_num  ord_date                 qty    payterms   title_id
------- --------  -----------------------  -----  ---------  --------
6380    722a      1994-09-13 00:00:00.000  3      Net 60     PS2091

stor_id ord_num  ord_date                 qty    payterms   title_id
------- --------  -----------------------  -----  ---------  --------

stor_id ord_num  ord_date                 qty    payterms   title_id
------- --------  -----------------------  -----  ---------  --------
6380    722a      1994-09-13 00:00:00.000  3      Net 60     PS2091
```

Cursor Variables

Transact-SQL allows you to define variables that contain pointers to cursors via its cursor data type. The OPEN, FETCH, CLOSE, and DEALLOCATE commands can reference cursor variables as well as cursor names. You can set up variables within stored procedures that store cursor definitions, and you can return a cursor created by a stored procedure via an output parameter. Several of SQL Server's own procedures use this capability to return results to their callers in an efficient, modular fashion (e.g., sp_cursor_list, sp_describe_cursor, sp_fulltext_tables_cursor, and so on). Note that you can't pass a cursor via an input parameter into a procedure—you can only return cursors via output parameters. You also cannot define table columns using the cursor data type—only variables are allowed—nor can you assign a cursor variable using the SELECT statement (as with scalar variables)—you must use SET.

Cursor output parameters represent an improvement over the traditional result set approach in that they give the caller more control over how to deal with the rows a procedure returns. You can process the cursor immediately if you want, treating it just like a traditional result set, or you can retain it for later use. Before the advent of cursor variables, the only way to achieve this same degree of flexibility was to trap the stored procedure's result set in a table, then process the table as needed. This worked okay for simple, small result sets but could be problematic with larger ones.

You can use the CURSOR_STATUS function to check a cursor output parameter to see whether it references an open cursor and to determine the number of rows it exposes. Here's an example that features cursor variables, output parameters, and the CURSOR_STATUS function (Listing 14.22).

Listing 14.22 Using Cursor Variables

```
CREATE PROC listsales_cur @title_id tid,
    @salescursor cursor varying OUT
AS
-- Declare a LOCAL cursor so it's automatically freed when it
-- goes out of scope
DECLARE c CURSOR DYNAMIC
LOCAL
FOR SELECT * FROM sales WHERE title_id LIKE @title_id

DECLARE @sc cursor    -- A local cursor variable
SET @sc=c             -- Now we have two references to the cursor

OPEN c

FETCH @sc

SET @salescursor=@sc -- Return the cursor via the output param
RETURN 0
GO

SET NOCOUNT ON
-- Define a local cursor variable to receive the output param
DECLARE @mycursor cursor

EXEC listsales_cur 'BU1032', @mycursor OUT -- Call the procedure

-- Make sure the returned cursor is open and has at least one row
IF (CURSOR_STATUS('variable','@mycursor')=1) BEGIN
  FETCH @mycursor
  WHILE (@@FETCH_STATUS=0) BEGIN
    FETCH @mycursor
  END
END
```

```
CLOSE @mycursor
DEALLOCATE @mycursor
```

```
stor_id ord_num  ord_date                   qty  payterms    title_id
------- -------- ------------------------    ---- ---------- --------
6380    6871     1994-09-14 00:00:00.000     5    Net 60      BU1032


stor_id ord_nu   ord_date                   qty  payterms    title_id
------- -------- ------------------------    ---- ---------- --------
8042    423LL930 1994-09-14 00:00:00.000     10   ON invoice BU1032


stor_id ord_num  ord_date                   qty  payterms    title_id
------- -------- ------------------------    ---- ---------- --------
8042    QA879.1  1999-06-24 19:13:26.230     30   Net 30      BU1032


stor_id ord_num  ord_date                   qty  payterms    title_id
------- -------- ------------------------    ---- ---------- --------
```

Notice the way the example code references the cursor using three different variables as well as its original name. For every command except DEALLOCATE, referencing a cursor variable is synonymous with referencing the cursor by name. If you open the cursor, regardless of whether you reference it using a cursor variable or the cursor name itself, the cursor is opened and you can fetch rows using any variable that references it. DEALLOCATE differs in that it doesn't actually deallocate the cursor unless it's the last reference to it. It does, however, prevent future access using the specified cursor identifier. So if you have a cursor named foo and a cursor variable named foovar to which foo has been assigned, deallocating foo will do nothing except prohibit access to the cursor via foo—foovar remains intact.

Cursor Stored Procedures

SQL Server provides a number of cursor-related stored procedures with which you should familiarize yourself if you expect to work with cursors much. Table 14.3 provides a brief list of them, along with a description of each.

Each of these returns its result via a cursor output parameter, so you'll need to supply a local cursor variable in order to process them.

Table 14.3 Stored Procedures Related to Cursors

Procedure	Function
sp_cursor_list	Returns a list of the cursors and their attributes that have been opened by a connection
sp_describe_cursor	Lists the attributes of an individual cursor
sp_describe_cursor_columns	Lists the columns (and their attributes) returned by a cursor
sp_describe_cursor_tables	Returns a list of the tables referenced by a cursor

Optimizing Cursor Performance

The best performance improvement technique for cursors is not to use them at all if you can avoid it. As I've said, SQL Server works much better with sets of data than with individual rows. It's a relational database, and single-row access has never been the strong suit of RDBMSs. That said, there are times when using a cursor is unavoidable, so here are a few tips for optimizing them.

- Don't use static/insensitive cursors unless you need them. Opening a static cursor causes all of its rows to be copied to a temporary table. That's why it's insensitive to changes—it's actually referencing a copy of the table in tempdb. Naturally, the larger the result set, the more likely declaring a static cursor over it will cause resource contention issues in tempdb.
- Don't use keyset cursors unless you really need them. As with static cursors, opening a keyset cursor creates a temporary table. Though this table contains only key values from the underlying table (unless no unique key exists), it can still be quite substantial when dealing with large result sets.
- Use the FAST_FORWARD cursor option in lieu of FORWARD_ONLY when working with unidirectional, read-only result sets. Using FAST_FORWARD defines a FORWARD_ONLY, READ_ONLY cursor with a number of internal performance optimizations.

- Define read-only cursors using the READ_ONLY keyword. This prevents you from making accidental changes and lets the server know that the cursor will not alter the rows it traverses.
- Be careful with modifying large numbers of rows via a cursor loop that's contained within a transaction. Depending on the transaction isolation level, those rows may remain locked until the transaction is committed or rolled back, possibly causing resource contention on the server.
- Consider using asynchronous cursors with large result sets in order to return control to the caller as quickly as possible. Asynchronous cursors are especially useful when returning a sizeable result set to a scrollable form because they allow the application to begin displaying rows almost immediately.
- Be careful with updating dynamic cursors, especially those constructed over tables with nonunique clustered index keys, because they can cause the "Halloween problem"—repetitive, erroneous updates of the same row or rows. Because SQL Server forces nonunique clustered index keys to be unique internally by suffixing them with a sequence number, it's possible that you could update a row's key to a value that already exists and force the server to append a suffix that would move it later in the result set. As you fetched through the remainder of the result set, you'd encounter the row again, and the process would repeat itself, resulting in an infinite loop. Listing 14.23 illustrates this problem.

Listing 14.23 The Halloween Problem

```
-- This code creates a cursor that exhibits the Halloween problem.
-- Don't run it unless you find infinite loops intriguing.
SET NOCOUNT ON
CREATE TABLE #temp (k1 int identity, c1 int NULL)
CREATE CLUSTERED INDEX c1 ON #temp(c1)

INSERT #temp VALUES (8)
INSERT #temp VALUES (6)
INSERT #temp VALUES (7)
INSERT #temp VALUES (5)
INSERT #temp VALUES (3)
INSERT #temp VALUES (0)
INSERT #temp VALUES (9)
```

```
DECLARE c CURSOR DYNAMIC
FOR SELECT k1, c1 FROM #temp

OPEN c

FETCH c

WHILE (@@FETCH_STATUS=0) BEGIN
  UPDATE #temp
  SET c1=c1+1
  WHERE CURRENT OF c
  FETCH c
  SELECT * FROM #temp ORDER BY k1
END


CLOSE c
DEALLOCATE c
GO
DROP TABLE #temp
```

Recap

Cursors are not the recommended way to solve most data access or update problems, and they can cause serious performance headaches when used improperly. Your first thought (before using Transact-SQL) when contemplating how to solve a problem you have seen should be to align your code with the way SQL Server was designed to work—that is, to access data in sets if at all possible. Resort to using cursors only after you've explored as many set-based alternatives as possible.

Knowledge Measure

1. True or false: When porting an ISAM application to SQL Server, you should attempt to change as little about the app as possible, particularly with respect to the way that data is accessed.
2. What WHERE clause element is used with an UPDATE or DELETE command to perform a positioned update or delete?

3. Is it possible to declare a variable in a stored procedure whose data type is cursor?

4. True or false: To return a cursor from a stored procedure, you must pass the cursor the procedure's return statement.

5. List the four types of cursors SQL Server supports.

6. In terms of resource utilization, what's the difference between DEALLOCATE CURSOR and CLOSE?

7. What mechanism does SQL Server use to store the data returned by a static cursor?

8. What automatic variable is typically used to control a loop that iterates through a cursor using FETCH?

9. What does the automatic variable @@CURSOR_ROWS return?

10. What function can you use to check the status of a cursor?

CHAPTER 15

ODSOLE

The surest way to corrupt a youth is to instruct him to hold in higher esteem those who think alike than those who think differently.

—Friedrich Nietzsche[1]

In this chapter, we'll talk about automating (i.e., controlling) COM components using SQL Server's Open Data Services Object Linking and Embedding (ODSOLE) facility. ODSOLE is implemented via Transact-SQL's sp_OA extended procedures (e.g., sp_OACreate, sp_OAMethod, and so on). We'll talk about how Automation works in general, then we'll explore several examples of it using the sp_OA procs.

This chapter updates my coverage of Automation via Transact-SQL and ODSOLE in previous books. As with my chapter on SQLXML, I decided in this book to both update the practical use information from my previous books and delve into architectural details that I've not covered before. People usually buy technical books to learn how to do something; I didn't feel comfortable discussing only abstract architectural details and omitting the practical application of those details. It's my belief that seeing how a design affects the practical use of a technology is a wonderful way to understand the design viscerally—to learn it, literally, inside out.

Overview

As I've mentioned, ODSOLE originally stood for Open Data Services Object Linking and Embedding, however, the meaning of the term "OLE" has

---

1. Nietzsche, Friedrich. "The Dawn." In *The Portable Nietzsche*, ed. Walter Kaufmann. New York: The Viking Press, 1954, p. 91.

changed over time and is no longer associated mainly with linking and embedding objects. The term "OLE Automation" itself has fallen out of favor, and now "Automation" is generally preferred.

Automation is a language-independent method of controlling and using COM objects. Lots of applications expose functionality via COM interfaces. Many of Microsoft's retail products, as well as many from other vendors, expose some type of functionality via COM objects. You can use those objects to manipulate the host application through an Automation controller—a facility that knows how to interact with the IDispatch COM interface. The most popular Automation controllers are Visual Basic and VBScript. SQL Server's ODSOLE facility is an Automation controller in its own right and is exposed via the sp_OA extended procedure you can call from Transact-SQL.

You can also create your own COM objects and access them from T-SQL using the ODSOLE facility. You can wrap functionality not available from T-SQL in a COM component and call it from within your T-SQL batches and stored procedures.

COM Objects and Threading Models

Before we get into working with COM objects from Transact-SQL via OD-SOLE, let's discuss a few basics regarding COM threading models and concurrency. Understanding how threading works with respect to ODSOLE and how object concurrency is managed will help us better understand how to use ODSOLE effectively and safely.

COM objects support two primary threading models: single-threaded apartment (STA, also known as "apartment-threaded") and multithreaded apartment (MTA, also known as "free-threaded"). Don't let the "apartment" concept confuse you or scare you away. The term helps define a conceptual framework that describes the relationships among threads, objects, and processes. An apartment is exactly what it sounds like—an area within a building. A building equates to a process in this analogy, so an apartment is simply a logical container within a process. It might contain multiple threads and/or objects, depending on the type of apartment, and a single process might have many individual apartments.

Each object and each thread can belong to only one apartment. Only the threads within an apartment can access the objects in that apartment directly; all other threads go through COM proxies of some sort. A thread establishes residence in an apartment (and optionally specifies the threading model it wants to use) through a call to a COM initialization function such as CoInitialize, CoInitializeEx, or OleInitialize.

In the STA model, an apartment has a single thread and can contain multiple objects. In the MTA model, an apartment can have multiple threads and multiple objects. A process can have multiple STAs but only one MTA. This one MTA can coexist with multiple STAs in the same process.

ODSOLE is implemented using the STA model. If you attach to SQL Server with a debugger and set a breakpoint on OleInitialize (in OLE32.DLL) before making your first sp_OA call, you'll see that the ODSOLE code calls OleInitialize. OleInitialize is hard-coded to use the STA model, hence, we can deduce that ODSOLE uses the STA model. (Once a thread has been initialized for a particular COM threading model it cannot be changed to a different one without first uninitializing COM.)

As I've mentioned, an out-of-process COM server (i.e., an executable) specifies its threading model via a COM initialization function call. CoInitializeEx is the only one of the three main COM initializers that permits the threading model to be specified; CoInitialize and OleInitialize both force the STA model. A call to either CoInitialize or OleInitialize ultimately results in a call to CoInitializeEx with STA hard-coded as the threading model. This means that SQL Server's call to OleInitialize results in a call to CoInitializeEx with a threading model specification of STA.

The threading model for an in-process COM server (a DLL) is not specified via a call to CoInitializeEx. Instead, it's specified via a registry key, like this:

```
HKEY_LOCAL_MACHINE\SOFTWARE\Classes\CLSID\InprocServer32\
ThreadingModel
```

The value of this key can be Apartment, Free, or Both. If the key is not found, STA is assumed.

As I've said, only the threads residing in the apartment in which a COM object was created can directly access the object. Other threads access the object through proxy objects. Given that only one thread resides in a given STA apartment, COM takes responsibility for synchronizing object access by other threads. It accomplishes this via Windows' messaging facilities. It creates a hidden window for each apartment and sets up proxies to post messages to the apartment owning an object in order to invoke it. The serialization of access to the object is managed through Windows' normal windows message queuing facilities. Methods on the object are called in response to messages posted to the apartment's hidden window. As messages are pulled out of the message queue (via PeekMessage and GetMessage) and dispatched (via DispatchMessage), the window procedure for the thread, which is implemented by COM, invokes the appropriate methods on the object. The process is reversed when the method call completes and results need to be returned to the calling thread. Messages are posted to the hidden window for the calling thread's apartment to provide the result(s) and indicate function completion. These messages are picked up by the calling thread, and it, in turn, returns through the proxy object method call, thus completing the method call on the object in the other apartment.

When a component is configured for the STA model, the objects it exposes are created on the SQL Server worker thread that called sp_OACreate. Other worker threads can't access these object instances. Given that sp_OA frees all created objects when a batch exits anyway (thus ensuring that all calls to a given object occur on the same physical thread), the use of STA by ODSOLE works out well.

When a component is configured for the MTA model, COM automatically starts a host MTA and instantiates the objects in it. When a component's threading model has been configured as both STA and MTA compatible, the object is created in the calling STA.

The Main STA

The first thread to initialize COM using the STA threading model becomes the main STA. This STA is required to remain alive until all COM work is completed because some in-process servers are always created in the context of the main STA.

OLE requires a single thread to be set up to respond to STA-related messages. ODSOLE handles this by creating a special thread for the express purpose of processing a message loop. This special thread is the first caller of OleInitialize and thus becomes the main STA for the SQL Server process.

Once created, the main STA is all but ignored by ODSOLE. Each worker thread that services sp_OA calls makes its own call to OleInitialize and increments the reference count on the main STA message thread. The main STA remains in existence until SQL Server is shut down or sp_OAStop is called.

Early Binding vs. Late Binding

An application can make use of COM objects through two basic means: through early binding or through late binding. When an application makes object references that are resolvable at compile-time, the object is considered early bound. To early bind an object in Visual Basic, you add a reference to the library containing the object during development, then Dim specific instances of it. To early bind an object in tools like Visual C++ and

Delphi, you import the object's type library and work with the interfaces it provides. In either case, you code directly to the interfaces exposed by the object as though they were interfaces you created yourself. The object itself may live on a completely separate machine and be accessed via Distributed COM (DCOM) or be marshaled by a transaction manager such as Microsoft Transaction Server or Component Services. Generally speaking, you don't care—you just code to the interface.

When references to an object aren't known until runtime, the object is late bound. You normally instantiate it via a call to CreateObject and store the object reference in a variant. Since the compiler didn't know what object you were referencing at compile-time, you may encounter bad method calls or nonexistent properties at runtime. That's the trade-off with late binding. It's more flexible in that you can decide at runtime what objects to create and can even instantiate objects that didn't exist on the development system, but it's more error prone—it's easy to make mistakes when you late bind objects because your development environment can't provide the same level of assistance it can when it knows the objects you're dealing with. Accessing COM objects via late binding is also slower than doing so via early binding, sometimes dramatically so. That said, late binding is all we have available to us from ODSOLE, so that's what we'll focus on in this chapter.

The sp_OA Procedures

Transact-SQL's Automation stored procedures are named using the convention sp_OA*Function*, where *Function* indicates what the procedure does (e.g., sp_OACreate creates COM objects, sp_OAMethod calls a method, sp_OAGetProperty and sp_OASetProperty get and set object properties, respectively, and so on). Each of the sp_OA procs except sp_OACreate expects an integer parameter containing a pointer to the previously created object. The sp_OACreate procedure, of course, creates the object, and so it expects an integer variable to be passed in as an output parameter to receive the reference to the object it creates. This integer actually references an internal wrapper object created by ODSOLE to encapsulate the COM object. This internal object contains a reference to the COM object as well as other housekeeping information.

Some sp_OA procs may support returning an output parameter from a COM method or property retrieval (e.g., sp_OAMethod or sp_OAGet-Property). If this parameter is not supplied, a single-column, single-row result set is returned. If the call returns an array, the output parameter is set to

NULL if it is supplied, and the array is translated into a result set. If the array is a single-dimensional array, a single row with the array elements as columns is returned. If the array is a two-dimensional array, it will be returned as a multirow result set. If the array has more than two dimensions, an error is returned.

sp_OACreate

As I've mentioned, you use sp_OACreate to instantiate a COM object. The call to sp_OACreate returns a pointer to an internal ODSOLE object that encapsulates the reference to the underlying COM object. When sp_OACreate is called, the following events occur.

1. The main STA is created if it does not already exist. You can see this from WinDbg by trapping calls to OleInitialize. If it already exists, the main STA thread's reference count is incremented.
2. TLS storage for the current worker thread is initialized. This storage is used for, among other things, tracking the objects created during the batch so they can be automatically released when the batch terminates.
3. OleInitialize is called for the current worker thread.
4. Two ODS event handlers, one for language events and one for RPC events, are set up to run when the batch completes. These handlers take care of automatically releasing created objects, calling CoUninitialize for the current worker thread, decrementing the reference count on the main STA, and performing other housekeeping work when the batch terminates.
5. The supplied object name is passed to the OLE API function CLSIDFromProgID in order to translate it from a ProgID to a COM class ID that can be instantiated via CoCreateInstance. A ProgID, or, programmatic identifier, is a string that identifies a COM object so that applications can access it by name. A ProgID can't be instantiated directly by COM, so in order to instantiate an object using its ProgID, we must translate its ProgID into its COM class ID using CLSIDFromProgID. If CLSIDFromProgID fails, ODSOLE assumes the string passed in is already a class ID and passes it to CLSIDFromString. If CLSIDFromString fails, an error is returned and the call to sp_OACreate fails.
6. The class ID derived from the supplied object name is passed into CoCreateInstance in order to create an instance of the COM object.

7. The QueryInterface COM method is called on the newly created object in order to return a reference to its implementation of the IDispatch interface. As I've mentioned, IDispatch is how late-binding clients interact with COM components. You could say that they early bind to the IDispatch interface.

8. At this stage, the object is ready for use by the other sp_OA procs, so the object reference is wrapped in an internal object, and a pointer to this internal object is returned in the sp_OACreate output parameter.

You can pass a context parameter into sp_OACreate. This parameter becomes the dwClsContext parameter to CoCreateInstance and determines the context in which an object is created. An object can be instantiated as an in-process server (in which case it runs in the same process as the caller—SQL Server—hence the term) or as an out-of-process server (in which case it runs in its own process), or the context parameter can be specified so as to support either context, with the actual context used varying based on whether the COM component resides in a DLL or EXE file. Creating a COM object out-of-process helps ensure that it cannot corrupt the SQL Server process or cause other types of stability problems.

sp_OAMethod

The sp_OAMethod procedure takes the previously created object reference as a parameter, along with a method name, an output parameter, and a variable list of input parameters. If an output parameter is supplied and the method doesn't return one, an error is returned. If an output parameter is supplied that is too small for the output value, an error is returned. If an output value is returned but an output parameter isn't supplied, a single-column, single-row result set is produced unless the return value is an array. And, as I mentioned earlier, if the return value is an array, a result set is returned.

When an RPC or language event calls sp_OAMethod, the following events occur.

1. The COM API function GetIDsOfNames is called to get the dispatch ID of the method being called. If this fails, sp_OAMethod fails.

2. A DISPPARAMS structure is populated with the parameters to be passed into the method.

3. The IDispatch::Invoke method is called to invoke the method. If this fails, its HRESULT is returned as the sp_OAMethod result.

sp_OASetProperty/sp_OAGetProperty

These procedures are very similar to sp_OAMethod. Setting/getting a property as opposed to calling a method is essentially the same operation when using late binding, so ODSOLE treats them very much the same. In fact, it has been my experience that you can usually use sp_OASetProperty or sp_OAGetProperty interchangeably with sp_OAMethod. GetIDsOfNames is called, as is IDispatch::Invoke. A bitmap parameter to IDispatch::Invoke indicates whether a property is being accessed or a method is being called; ODSOLE passes a mask that includes both switches because they are virtually indistinguishable when accessing an object via late binding.

sp_OAGetErrorInfo

This procedure returns the error information for the supplied object pointer or for the current worker thread. Typically, you'll check for a nonzero return from one of the other sp_OA calls, then call sp_OAGetErrorInfo to retrieve additional error information as appropriate.

sp_OADestroy

The procedure releases the reference to an object created via sp_OACreate. Once an object's reference has been released, it cannot be used in any further ODSOLE calls.

sp_OAStop

This shuts down OLE processing and stops the main STA thread. No additional sp_OA calls can be made until sp_OACreate is called again to create an object and restart the main STA thread.

Object Name Traversal

Similarly to Visual Basic, VBScript, and many other Automation-capable languages, ODSOLE allows you to use "dot notation" in method and property names to quickly traverse an object hierarchy. You can refer to the full path between a parent object and its children, their children, and so on, by separating the object names with periods in a property or method name string. Each intermediate term must refer to an object; the final term can refer to any exposed property or method. This means that instead of doing something like this:

```
-- Get a pointer to the SQLServer object's Databases collection
EXEC @hr = sp_OAGetProperty @srvobject, 'Databases', @object OUT
IF @hr <> 0 BEGIN
  EXEC sp_displayoaerrorinfo @srvobject, @hr
  GOTO FreeAll
END

-- Get a pointer from the Databases collection for the
-- specified database
EXEC @hr = sp_OAMethod @object, 'Item', @object OUT, @dbname
IF @hr <> 0 BEGIN
  EXEC sp_displayoaerrorinfo @object, @hr
  GOTO FreeAll
END
```

you can do this:

```
-- Get a pointer to the database
DECLARE @itemname varchar(255)
SET @itemname='Databases.Item("'+@dbname+'")'
EXEC @hr = sp_OAGetProperty @srvobject, @itemname, @object OUT
IF @hr <> 0 BEGIN
  EXEC sp_displayoaerrorinfo @srvobject, @hr
  GOTO FreeAll
END
```

The use of dot notation in the code above alleviates the need to first retrieve a pointer to the Databases collection, then make a separate call to get a specific item from it. The notation can be as deep as you need it to be; ODSOLE will traverse the method or property name and navigate to the leaf term as appropriate.

Named Parameters

As with Visual Basic and other Automation controllers, ODSOLE supports the notion of named parameters. These can be specified in method and property names (via dot notation) and can also be specified on the command line to an sp_OA extended proc. For the sp_OA procs, named parameters must come after the third parameter to the proc (named parameters before the fourth parameter are ignored) and will have their leading @ prefix stripped in the process. ODSOLE named parameters must follow the normal rules for Automation named parameters: Unnamed parameters must be specified before named parameters, and named parameters can be specified in any order.

Automating with ODSOLE

In the next few sections, we'll look at several examples that show how to automate COM objects using the sp_OA procs and ODSOLE. We'll walk through some basic examples that show how to access COM functionality that is probably already on your machine, then we'll explore automating SQL Server's Distributed Management Objects (SQL-DMO) from ODSOLE. We'll finish up with some esoteric coverage of implementing arrays in T-SQL using COM objects, using COM Interop and ODSOLE to access objects in the .NET Framework, and a few other odds and ends.

sp_checkspelling

Listing 15.1 illustrates a simple procedure that uses the sp_OA procedures to automate a COM object. The procedure instantiates the Microsoft Word Application object and calls its CheckSpelling method to check the spelling of a word you pass to the procedure.

Listing 15.1 Using sp_OA Procedures to Automate a COM Object

```
USE master
GO
IF (OBJECT_ID('sp_checkspelling') IS NOT NULL)
  DROP PROC sp_checkspelling
GO
CREATE PROC sp_checkspelling
  @word varchar(30),  -- Word to check
  @correct bit OUT  -- Returns whether word is correctly spelled
/*
Object: sp_checkspelling
Description: Checks the spelling of a word using the Microsoft Word
   Application Automation object
  Usage: sp_checkspelling
  @word varchar(128),   -- Word to check
```

```
    @correct bit OUT  -- Returns whether word is correctly spelled
    Returns: (None)
    $Author: Ken Henderson $. Email: khen@khen.com
    Example: EXEC sp_checkspelling 'asdf', @correct OUT
    Created: 2000-10-14.  $Modtime: 2001-01-13 $.
*/
AS
IF (@word='/?') GOTO Help
DECLARE @object int,  -- Work variable for instantiating
                      -- COM objects
   @hr int  -- Contains HRESULT returned by COM

-- Create a Word Application object
EXEC @hr=sp_OACreate 'Word.Application', @object OUT
IF (@hr <> 0) BEGIN
  EXEC sp_displayoaerrorinfo @object, @hr
  RETURN
END

-- Call its CheckSpelling method
EXEC @hr = sp_OAMethod @object, 'CheckSpelling', @correct OUT,
     @word
IF (@hr <> 0) BEGIN
  EXEC sp_displayoaerrorinfo @object, @hr
  RETURN @hr
END

-- Destroy it
EXEC @hr = sp_OADestroy @object
IF (@hr <> 0) BEGIN
  EXEC sp_displayoaerrorinfo @object, @hr
  RETURN @hr
END

RETURN 0

Help:

EXEC sp_usage @objectname='sp_checkspelling',
@desc='Checks the spelling of a word using the Microsoft Word
     Application Automation object',
@parameters='
  @word varchar(30),  -- Word to check
  @correct bit OUT  -- Returns whether word is correctly spelled
```

```
',
@author='Ken Henderson', @email='khen@khen.com',
@datecreated='20001014',@datelastchanged='20010113',
@example='EXEC sp_checkspelling ''asdf'', @correct OUT',
@returns='(None)'
RETURN -1
GO
```

The sp_checkspelling procedure exposes two parameters—the word whose spelling you wish to check and an output parameter to receive a 1 or 0 indicating whether the word is spelled correctly. A call to the procedure looks like this:

```
DECLARE @cor bit
EXEC sp_checkspelling 'asdf', @cor OUT
SELECT @cor
```

(Results)

```
----
0
```

There are three key elements of this procedure: the creation of the COM object, the method call, and the disposal of the object. Let's begin with the call to sp_OACreate. Calling sp_OACreate instantiates a COM object. Word.Application is a ProgID associated with Microsoft Word. How do we know to specify Word.Application here? Several ways—first, we could check the Word object interface as documented in MSDN. Second, we could fire up Visual Basic and add a Reference to the Microsoft Word Object Library to a project, then allow Visual Studio's Intellisense technology to show us the objects and methods available from Word. (You can do the same thing via Visual C++'s #import directive or Delphi's Project | Import Type Library option.) Third, we could simply check the system registry and scan for all the interfaces involving Microsoft Word. The registry, for example, tells us that Word.Application is Word's VersionIndependentProgID string. This means that instantiating Word.Application should work regardless of the version of Word that's installed.

We store the object handle that's returned by sp_OACreate in @object. This handle is then passed into sp_OAMethod when we call methods on the Word.Application interface. In this case, we call just one method, Check-

Spelling, and pass @word as the word to check spelling for and @correct to receive the 1 or 0 returned by the method.

When we're finished with the object, we destroy it through a call to sp_OADestroy. Again, we pass in the @object handle we received earlier from sp_OACreate.

This is what it's like to work with COM objects in Transact-SQL. As with many languages and technologies, you create the object, do some things with it, then clean up after yourself when you're done.

sp_vbscript_reg_ex

This next example we'll look at adds regular expression support to Transact-SQL. Regular expressions allow for wildcard and other types of string match tests. They are a common feature in programmers' editors (e.g., the Sequin SQL programming editor included on the CD accompanying this book supports regular expressions) and are exposed in a variety of APIs and languages. One facility that provides a nice regular expression evaluator is Microsoft's ActiveX scripting engine. It provides an object named RegExp that encapsulates basic regular expression pattern matching functionality. Listing 15.2 uses this object to perform a regular expression match from a stored procedure via Automation and ODSOLE.

Listing 15.2 Performing a Regular Expression Match from a Stored Procedure

```
USE master
GO
IF OBJECT_ID('dbo.sp_vbscript_reg_ex','P') IS NOT NULL
  DROP PROC dbo.sp_vbscript_reg_ex
GO
CREATE PROC dbo.sp_vbscript_reg_ex @pattern varchar(255),
    @matchstring varchar(8000)
AS
declare @obj int
declare @res int
declare @match bit
set @match=0
exec @res=sp_OACreate 'VBScript.RegExp',@obj OUT
IF (@res <> 0) BEGIN
  PRINT 'VBScript.RegExp Create failed'
  EXEC sp_DisplayOAErrorInfo @obj, @res
  RETURN
```

```
END
exec @res=sp_OASetProperty @obj, 'Pattern', @pattern
IF (@res <> 0) BEGIN
  PRINT 'Set Pattern failed'
  EXEC sp_DisplayOAErrorInfo @obj, @res
  RETURN
END
exec @res=sp_OASetProperty @obj, 'IgnoreCase', 1
IF (@res <> 0) BEGIN
  PRINT 'Set IgnoreCase failed'
  EXEC sp_DisplayOAErrorInfo @obj, @res
  RETURN
END
exec @res=sp_OAMethod @obj, 'Test',@match OUT, @matchstring
IF (@res <> 0) BEGIN
  PRINT 'Test call failed'
  EXEC sp_DisplayOAErrorInfo @obj, @res
  RETURN
END
exec @res=sp_OADestroy @obj
return @match
```

As you can see, there isn't much code to this routine. The procedure takes the following basic approach.

1. Instantiate the VBScript.RegExp object. As I've mentioned, RegExp encapsulates the ActiveX script regular expression facility.
2. Set the Pattern property of the RegExp object. This establishes the regular expression we intend to use.
3. Set the IgnoreCase property to true on the RegExp object. This provides for case-insensitive searches. Comment this out or control it via a parameter to the stored procedure if you want to perform case-sensitive matches.
4. Call the Test method on the RegExp object. Test checks a supplied string against the previously specified pattern to see whether they match and returns a Boolean indicating the result.
5. Destroy the object. Given that, as I've mentioned, ODSOLE frees allocated objects automatically, this isn't technically necessary, but it's still a good practice.

Listing 15.3 presents some more examples of calls to sp_vbscript_reg_ex.

Listing 15.3 Calling sp_vbscript_reg_ex

```
SET NOCOUNT ON
declare @res int

PRINT 'Check a basic wildcard pattern'
exec @res=sp_vbscript_reg_ex 'A.*C','AxxxxxxxxxxxxxxxxxxBC'
select @res

PRINT 'Check a word boundary (fails)'
exec @res=sp_vbscript_reg_ex 'es\b','These are the days'
select @res

PRINT 'Check a word boundary (succeeds)'
exec @res=sp_vbscript_reg_ex 'es\b','Would you like some fries
    with that?'
select @res

PRINT 'Check an either/or pattern'
exec @res=sp_vbscript_reg_ex 'good|great','Now is the time for all
    good men to come to'
select @res

PRINT 'Check an either/or pattern'
exec @res=sp_vbscript_reg_ex 'good|great','Goodness, gracious,
    great balls of fire!'
select @res

(Results)

Check a basic wildcard pattern

-----------
1

Check a word boundary (fails)

-----------
0
```

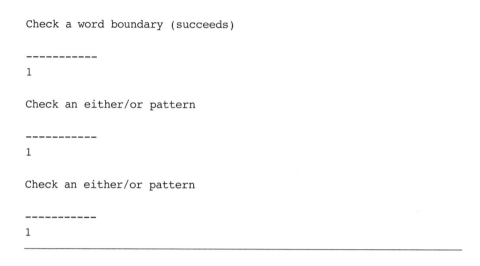

```
Check a word boundary (succeeds)

-----------
1

Check an either/or pattern

-----------
1

Check an either/or pattern

-----------
1
```

I've mainly focused on pattern matches that would be difficult if not impossible to do using standard T-SQL LIKE and PATINDEX wildcards. RegExp supports many other regular expression search terms. See the VB-Script documentation or MSDN for additional details.

Automating .NET Framework Classes via COM Interop

Another facility that provides a full-featured regular expression search engine is the .NET Framework. Given that the Framework also supports wrapping managed classes such that they can be accessed via COM, you can create managed objects that are accessible from T-SQL via ODSOLE.

Note that calling managed code from within SQL Server 2000 and earlier is unsupported by Microsoft. The ODSOLE facility and the .NET Framework have not been tested for interoperability with one another, so you may encounter problems that you won't be able to take to Microsoft Product Support Services.

That said, the vast functionality provided by the .NET Framework is hard to pass up, especially when it's so easy to get at using ODSOLE. In the sample code that follows, we'll create a managed class in C# that encapsulates the .NET Framework regular expression facility, then we'll publish and register this for use with COM via the .NET Framework's COM Interop technology so that we can access it from T-SQL via the sp_OA procs.

Let's begin with Listing 15.4, the source code to our managed class. (You can find the complete source to this example in the SQLRegExLib subfolder in the CH15 folder on the CD accompanying this book.)

Listing 15.4 The Source Code for SQLRegEx

```
using System;
using System.Text.RegularExpressions;

namespace SQLRegExLib
{
  public interface IRegEx
  {
    bool IsMatch(string Expression, string MatchString);
  }
  /// <summary>
  /// Summary description for Class1.
  /// </summary>
  public class SQLRegEx : IRegEx
  {
    public SQLRegEx()
    {
    }
    public bool IsMatch(string Expression, string MatchString)
    {
      Regex regex = new Regex(Expression,RegexOptions.Compiled |
          RegexOptions.IgnoreCase);
      if (null!=regex) return regex.IsMatch(MatchString);
      else throw new Exception("Unable to create Regex object");
    }
  }
}
```

This class exposes a single method, IsMatch, that takes two parameters: the pattern string and the string to search for a match. Inside the method, IsMatch creates an instance of the .NET Framework's Regex class, then calls its IsMatch method to determine whether the pattern and string match.

The key requirement that the class must meet in order to be accessible from COM is that it must be a public class. It must also implement a default (parameterless constructor). Additionally, though not required, this particular module also defines a public interface which the class then implements. Coding an explicit interface and implementing it in your public classes makes accessing those classes easier from COM.

To access this class via ODSOLE, follow these steps.

1. Create a new Windows Class Library project and add this class to it.
2. Compile the project to a DLL.
3. Copy the DLL to the binn folder under the SQL Server startup folder. Since we are not going to sign the assembly (the DLL) with a strong name and install it into the Global Assembly Cache, it must reside in the startup folder of its caller. Since we will be calling it via ODSOLE from SQL Server, the startup folder is the folder in which sqlservr.exe resides.
4. Register the assembly and its type library via the regasm.exe command line tool that comes with the .NET Framework. Registering a component and registering its type library are two distinct operations that you must complete separately. (See the regasm.exe help for details.) This will make the necessary entries in the system registry so that the class can be accessed from COM via its ProgID or class ID.
5. Call the sp_OA procedures to instantiate and manipulate the object, just like any other COM object.

When you register a managed class via regasm.exe, the main .NET Framework DLL, mscoree.DLL, is set up as the server for the COM object. This differs from unmanaged code in which the DLL that hosts the COM object functions as the server. With managed classes, the main .NET Framework DLL itself functions as the COM server, and the managed code assembly is referenced via the Assembly key under the object's entry in the system registry.

Listing 15.5 presents a stored procedure that wraps the calls to our managed code component once it's registered for use by COM.

Listing 15.5 Wrapping the Call to the Managed Code Component

```
USE master
GO
IF OBJECT_ID('dbo.sp_dotnet_reg_ex','P') IS NOT NULL
  DROP PROC dbo.sp_dotnet_reg_ex
GO
CREATE PROC dbo.sp_dotnet_reg_ex @pattern varchar(255),
    @matchstring varchar(8000)
AS
```

```
declare @obj int
declare @res int
declare @match bit
set @match=0
exec @res=sp_OACreate 'SQLRegExLib.SQLRegEx',@obj OUT
IF (@res <> 0) BEGIN
  EXEC sp_DisplayOAErrorInfo @obj, @res
  RETURN
END
exec @res=sp_OAMethod @obj, 'IsMatch',@match OUT, @pattern,
    @matchstring
IF (@res <> 0) BEGIN
  EXEC sp_DisplayOAErrorInfo @obj, @res
  RETURN
END
exec @res=sp_OADestroy @obj
return @match
```

This procedure works similarly to the procedure we created for the RegExp object we explored earlier and supports the same types of regular expressions.

Note that the virtual memory footprint of this version of the regular expression code is likely to be much larger than the RegExp-based code we built earlier. That's because you're not just loading the code for the SQL-RegEx component into the SQL Server process space; you're loading the .NET Framework, which the component requires, into that process space as well. As with loading any other type of large DLL, this could cause virtual memory address contention and fragmentation issues, as we discussed in Chapter 4.

Once again, this technique has not been tested by Microsoft and is not supported. I provide it here for instructional value only.

Using COM Objects in User-Defined Functions

While the ability to call a COM object via a stored procedure is certainly handy, I'm sure some of you are wondering whether you could wrap COM object functionality in a user-defined function for use in T-SQL queries. Wouldn't it be nice to be able to use a regular expression in a WHERE clause to filter a SELECT statement? Of course it would. Here's a function that demonstrates how to do that (Listing 15.6).

Listing 15.6 Using a Regular Expression to Filter a SELECT Statement

```
USE master
GO
exec sp_configure 'allow updates', 1
go
reconfigure with override
go
  DROP function system_function_schema.fn_regex
GO
CREATE FUNCTION
  system_function_schema.fn_regex(@pattern varchar(255),
      @matchstring varchar(8000))
RETURNS int
AS
BEGIN
declare @obj int
declare @res int
declare @match bit
set @match=0
exec @res=sp_OACreate 'VBScript.RegExp',@obj OUT
IF (@res <> 0) BEGIN
  RETURN NULL
END
exec @res=sp_OASetProperty @obj, 'Pattern', @pattern
IF (@res <> 0) BEGIN
  RETURN NULL
END
exec @res=sp_OASetProperty @obj, 'IgnoreCase', 1
IF (@res <> 0) BEGIN
  RETURN NULL
END
exec @res=sp_OAMethod @obj, 'Test',@match OUT, @matchstring
IF (@res <> 0) BEGIN
  RETURN NULL
END
exec @res=sp_OADestroy @obj
return @match
END
GO
exec sp_configure 'allow updates', 0
go
reconfigure with override
go
```

This code does several interesting things. First, note the use of the system_function_schema pseudo-user to create a system function. A system function is a function that's available from any database context without requiring a fully qualified name. As I documented in my book *The Guru's Guide to SQL Server Stored Procedures, XML, and HTML*, two steps are required in order to make a function a system function: It must be created in the master database with an owner of system_function_schema while allow updates is enabled, and its name must begin with fn_. I'm creating our regular expression function as a system function because it's naturally something that would be useful system-wide. It deserves to be a system function by virtue of its usefulness alone.

Second, note the fact that we call the sp_OA procs directly from our function. If you've done much UDF coding, you're probably aware of the fact that you can't call regular stored procedures from a UDF. Fortunately for us, although the sp_OA procs are prefixed with sp_, they're actually extended procedures, which you *can* call from a UDF. Equally fortunate is the fact that they aren't "spec procs"—extended procedures implemented internally by the server. Their entry points are in ODSOLE70.DLL, so they're callable from a UDF just like any other regular xproc.

The code in this function closely mirrors that of the stored proc we created earlier to access the VBScript RegExp object. We create the object, set some properties, then call the Test method to see whether we have a match.

As Listing 15.7 illustrates, once we've wrapped our regular expression functionality in a UDF, we can use it to filter a query.

Listing 15.7 Filtering a Query

```
use pubs
go
SELECT *
FROM authors
WHERE fn_regex('G.*',au_lname)<>0
```

(Results abridged)

```
au_id       au_lname                                au_fname
----------- --------------------------------------- ------------
213-46-8915 Green                                   Marjorie
527-72-3246 Greene                                  Morningstar
472-27-2349 Gringlesby                              Burt
998-72-3567 Ringer                                  Albert
```

```
899-46-2035 Ringer                              Anne
274-80-9391 Straight                            Dean
724-08-9931 Stringer                            Dirk
```

I'm sure you can think of other COM objects you might like to wrap in a UDF for use in queries. As you can see, it's not difficult to set up a system function to make the functionality in a COM object available across SQL Server.

Automating SQL-DMO by Using ODSOLE

Not surprisingly, a common use of the sp_OA procs is to automate COM objects exposed by SQL Server itself. Popular choices are the DTS object model and SQL-DMO. In this section, I'll present a couple of stored procedures that show how to automate the SQL-DMO COM objects using SQL Server's ODSOLE facility. Keep in mind that most DMO operations require a SQL Server connection, so stored procedures that control DMO objects via ODSOLE usually have to set up a loop-back connection. Loop-back connections can be problematic when they hold locks or attempt to access resources locked by the calling spid. You can run into situations where you effectively block yourself—your calling spid holds a lock on a resource that the loop-back connection you established for DMO work needs. This isn't that common, but it can happen. When it does, you can usually address the problem by managing your transactions more efficiently or by joining the parent transaction through calls to sp_getbindtoken and sp_bindsession.

sp_exporttable

The sp_exporttable procedure instantiates SQL Server's own SQL-DMO objects to export a table by name. It works analogously to the built-in BULK INSERT command, providing an interface to the Bulk Copy Program (BCP) API from Transact-SQL. Listing 15.8 shows the code.

Listing 15.8 The Code for the sp_exporttable Procedure

```
USE master
GO
IF (OBJECT_ID('sp_exporttable') IS NOT NULL)
  DROP PROC sp_exporttable
```

```
GO
CREATE PROC sp_exporttable
   @table sysname,                    -- Table to export
   @outputpath sysname=NULL,          -- Output directory, terminate with
                                      -- a "\"
   @outputname sysname=NULL,          -- Output file name (defaults to
                                      -- @table+'.BCP')
   @server sysname='(local)',         -- Name of server to connect to
   @username sysname='sa',            -- Name of user (defaults to 'sa')
   @password sysname=NULL,            -- User's password
   @trustedconnection bit=1           -- Use a trusted connection to
                                      -- connect to server
/*

Object: sp_exporttable
Description: Exports a table in a manner similar to BULK INSERT
   Usage: sp_exporttable
   @table sysname,                    -- Table to export
   @outputpath sysname=NULL,          -- Output directory, terminate with
                                      -- a '\'
   @outputname sysname=NULL,          -- Output filename (defaults to
                                      -- @table+'.BCP')
   @server sysname='(local)',         -- Name of server to connect to
   @username sysname='sa',            -- Name of user (defaults to 'sa')
   @password sysname=NULL,            -- User's password
   @trustedconnection bit=1           -- Use a trusted connection to
                                      -- connect to server
   Returns: Number of rows exported
   $Author: Ken Henderson $. Email: khen@khen.com
   Example: EXEC sp_exporttable 'authors', 'C:\TEMP\'
   Created: 1999-06-14.  $Modtime: 2000-12-01 $.
*/
AS
IF (@table='/?') OR (@outputpath IS NULL) GOTO Help
DECLARE @srvobject int,               -- Server object
   @object int,                       -- Work variable for instantiating
                                      -- COM objects
   @hr int,                           -- Contains HRESULT returned by COM
   @bcobject int,                     -- Stores pointer to BulkCopy object
   @TAB_DELIMITED int,                -- Will store a constant for
                                      -- tab-delimited output
   @logname sysname,                  -- Name of the log file
   @errname sysname,                  -- Name of the error file
   @dbname sysname,                   -- Name of the database
   @rowsexported int                  -- Number of rows exported
```

```
SET @TAB_DELIMITED=2 -- SQL-DMO constant for tab-delimited exports
SET @dbname=ISNULL(PARSENAME(@table,3),DB_NAME())
    -- Extract the DB name
SET @table=PARSENAME(@table,1)
    -- Remove extraneous stuff from table name
IF (@table IS NULL) BEGIN
   RAISERROR('Invalid table name.',16,1)
   GOTO Help
END
IF (RIGHT(@outputpath,1)<>'\')
   SET @outputpath=@outputpath+'\'      -- Append a "\" if necessary
SET @logname=@outputpath+@table+'.LOG' -- Construct log file name
SET @errname=@outputpath+@table+'.ERR' -- Construct error file name

IF (@outputname IS NULL)
   SET @outputname=@outputpath+@table+'.BCP' -- Construct output name
ELSE
   IF (CHARINDEX('\',@outputname)=0)
     SET @outputname=@outputpath+@outputname

-- Create a SQLServer object
EXEC @hr=sp_OACreate 'SQLDMO.SQLServer', @srvobject OUTPUT
IF (@hr <> 0) GOTO ServerError

-- Create a BulkCopy object
EXEC @hr=sp_OACreate 'SQLDMO.BulkCopy', @bcobject OUTPUT
IF (@hr <> 0) GOTO BCPError

-- Set BulkCopy's DataFilePath property to the output file name
EXEC @hr = sp_OASetProperty @bcobject, 'DataFilePath', @outputname
IF (@hr <> 0) GOTO BCPError

-- Tell BulkCopy to create tab-delimited files
EXEC @hr = sp_OASetProperty @bcobject, 'DataFileType',
    @TAB_DELIMITED
IF (@hr <> 0) GOTO BCPError

-- Set BulkCopy's LogFilePath property to the log file name
EXEC @hr = sp_OASetProperty @bcobject, 'LogFilePath', @logname
IF (@hr <> 0) GOTO BCPError

-- Set BulkCopy's ErrorFilePath property to the error file name
EXEC @hr = sp_OASetProperty @bcobject, 'ErrorFilePath', @errname
IF (@hr <> 0) GOTO BCPError
```

```
-- Connect to the server
IF (@trustedconnection=1) BEGIN
  EXEC @hr = sp_OASetProperty @srvobject, 'LoginSecure', 1
    IF (@hr <> 0) GOTO ServerError
  EXEC @hr = sp_OAMethod @srvobject, 'Connect', NULL, @server
END ELSE BEGIN
  IF (@password IS NOT NULL)
  EXEC @hr =sp_OAMethod @srvobject,'Connect',NULL,@server,
      @username, @password
    ELSE
      EXEC @hr = sp_OAMethod @srvobject, 'Connect', NULL,
          @server, @username
END
IF (@hr <> 0) GOTO ServerError

-- Get a pointer to the SQLServer object's Databases collection
EXEC @hr = sp_OAGetProperty @srvobject, 'Databases', @object OUT
IF (@hr <> 0) GOTO ServerError

-- Get a pointer from the Databases collection for the
-- specified database
EXEC @hr = sp_OAMethod @object, 'Item', @object OUT, @dbname
IF (@hr <> 0) GOTO Error

-- Get a pointer from the Database object's Tables collection
-- for the table
IF (OBJECTPROPERTY(OBJECT_ID(@table),'IsTable')=1) BEGIN
EXEC @hr = sp_OAMethod @object, 'Tables', @object OUT, @table
  IF (@hr <> 0) GOTO Error
END ELSE -- Get a pointer from the Database object's View
         -- collection for the view
IF (OBJECTPROPERTY(OBJECT_ID(@table),'IsView')=1) BEGIN
EXEC @hr = sp_OAMethod @object, 'Views', @object OUT, @table
  IF (@hr <> 0) GOTO Error
END ELSE BEGIN
  RAISERROR('Source object must be either a table or view.',16,1)
  RETURN -1
END

-- Call the object's ExportData method to export the table/view
-- using BulkCopy
EXEC @hr = sp_OAMethod @object, 'ExportData', @rowsexported OUT,
    @bcobject
IF (@hr <> 0) GOTO Error
```

```
EXEC sp_OADestroy @srvobject -- Dispose of the server object
EXEC sp_OADestroy @bcobject  -- Dispose of the bcp object
RETURN @rowsexported


Error:

EXEC sp_displayoaerrorinfo @object, @hr

GOTO ErrorCleanUp

BCPError:

EXEC sp_displayoaerrorinfo @bcobject, @hr

GOTO ErrorCleanUp

ServerError:

EXEC sp_displayoaerrorinfo @srvobject, @hr

GOTO ErrorCleanUp

ErrorCleanUp:

IF @srvobject IS NOT NULL
  EXEC sp_OADestroy @srvobject -- Dispose of the server object
IF @bcobject IS NOT NULL
  EXEC sp_OADestroy @bcobject  -- Dispose of the bcp object

RETURN -2

Help:

EXEC sp_usage @objectname='sp_exporttable',
@desc='Exports a table in a manner similar to BULK INSERT',
@parameters='
  @table sysname,              -- Table to export
  @outputpath sysname=NULL,    -- Output directory, terminate with
                               -- a ''\''
  @outputname sysname=NULL,    -- Output filename (defaults to
                               -- @table+''.BCP'')
  @server sysname=''(local)'', -- Name of server to connect to
  @username sysname=''sa'',    -- Name of user (defaults to ''sa'')
  @password sysname=NULL,      -- User''s password
  @trustedconnection bit=1     -- Use a trusted connection
```

```
',
@author='Ken Henderson', @email='khen@khen.com',
@datecreated='19990614',@datelastchanged='20001201',
@example='EXEC sp_exporttable ''authors'', ''C:\TEMP\''',
@returns='Number of rows exported'
RETURN -1
GO
```

The sp_exporttable proc follows the general plan of attack outlined below.

1. Create a SQLServer object. We'll use this object to connect to the server. Most DMO applications require a SQLServer object. We access the other objects on the server by drilling into the SQLServer object just as you do in Enterprise Manager.
2. Create a BulkCopy object. We'll use this object to export the table. Ultimately, we'll call the ExportData method of the specified table or view in order to bulk copy its contents to an operating system file. ExportData requires a BulkCopy object in order to do its work.
3. Set various properties on the BulkCopy object that will control the export.
4. Connect to the server using the SQLServer object.
5. Locate the table or view to be exported using nested object collections exposed by the SQLServer object.
6. Call the ExportData method of the view or table object, passing it the required BulkCopy object as a parameter.
7. Once the export finishes, dispose of the SQLServer and BulkCopy objects.

The comments in the stored procedure detail how it works—it's pretty straightforward. You run sp_exporttable using this syntax:

```
DECLARE @rc int
EXEC @rc=pubs..sp_exporttable @table='pubs..authors',
    @outputpath='c:\temp\'
SELECT RowsExported=@rc


RowsExported
------------
23
```

Note the use of the pubs.. prefix on the procedure call. Since sp_export-
table uses the OBJECTPROPERTY function (which does not work across
databases), in order for the procedure to work correctly with objects in other
databases, the database context must be temporarily changed to the correct
one for the object specified. Prefixing a system procedure call with a database
name temporarily changes the database context. The call above is the equivalent of:

```
USE pubs
GO
EXEC @rc=sp_exporttable @table='pubs..authors',
    @outputpath='c:\temp\'
GO
USE master — or some other database
GO
SELECT RowsExported=@rc
```

You may have noticed the calls to the sp_DisplayOAErrorInfo system
procedure in Listing 15.8. We use sp_DisplayOAErrorInfo to display more
verbose error information for error codes returned by the sp_OA procedures.
The sp_DisplayOAErrorInfo procedure calls sp_OAGetErrorInfo to extended error information for object Automation error codes.
sp_DisplayOAErrorInfo isn't created by default, but you can find it in Books
Online. It depends on sp_hexadecimal (also in Books Online) to convert binary values to hexadecimal strings. See the topic "OLE Automation Return
Codes and Error Information" in Books Online for the source code to both
procedures.

This example and several of the others in this chapter illustrate how to
use the sp_OA stored procedures to automate COM objects exposed by
SQL Server itself (SQL-DMO, in this case). The SQL-DMO objects provide much of Enterprise Manager's underlying functionality and are a
handy way to manage the server via program code.

The comments in sp_exporttable detail how it works. It does a number of
interesting things that are too extensive to get into here in detail. Using COM
Automation, the procedure is able to perform a fairly involved task with ease.
The amount of Transact-SQL code required to accomplish the task is no
more than that required by a comparable Delphi or Visual Basic program.

sp_generate_script

The sp_generate_script procedure generates Transact-SQL scripts for objects
in a database. It uses Automation to access SQL-DMO and calls the Script-

Transfer method on the SQL-DMO Transfer object to generate the script file. It originally appeared in my book *The Guru's Guide to Transact-SQL* and was updated in my follow-up to that book, *The Guru's Guide to SQL Server Stored Procedures, XML, and HTML*. I've updated it for this book to be a little more robust and a little more tolerant of some of the quirks in SQL-DMO.

You use sp_generate_script by passing it the name of the object you want to script. You can supply a mask with wildcards, if you like, or you can omit the name altogether and script the current database.

As I've said, sp_generate_script uses the SQL-DMO API to do its work. It creates DMO COM objects using sp_OACreate and calls methods on them using sp_OAMethod. Because DMO requires a connection to the server to do any type of scripting, you must pass login information into sp_generate_script so that it can instantiate a loop-back connection to the server using DMO method calls. Once the connection is established, the procedure finds the object or objects for which you're wanting to generate scripts and adds them to a DMO Transfer object so they can be written out to a disk file. If you opt to receive a result set (enabled by default), sp_generate_script calls xp_cmdshell to execute the operating system TYPE command to list the script file and return it as a result set.

The one quirk about the routine is that the DMO Transfer object generates a partial result set that cannot be disabled. You'll recall that I mentioned that if you call a method via sp_OAMethod that returns an output value without specifying an output parameter, ODSOLE will create a one-column, one-row result set containing the value for you. That's what occurs here. Because I'm not specifying an output parameter for the ScriptTransfer method call, DMO is creating a result set for the output value returned by the method—the text of the generated script. The reason I don't specify an output parameter here is that the method fails when a parameter is supplied that's not long enough to contain the entirety of the generated script. Given that the method doesn't accept parameters of type text, the largest output parameter I can supply is 8,000 characters long. If the script is longer than 8,000 characters (quite likely for even moderate-sized databases), the method fails and no script is generated. Therefore, I have no choice but to omit the output parameter (by specifying NULL in its place) and simply ignoring the result set fragments produced by ODSOLE.

The upshot of this is that whether you ask for a result set or not, you get a small one (actually three small ones—one for each call to ScriptTransfer) after every call to sp_generate_script. I've put a PRINT message in the code just after the final call to the Transfer object's ScriptTransfer method telling you to ignore this spurious output, but that's about all I can do. Fortunately, the output is completely harmless—the script is produced despite the message.

Listing 15.9 shows the sp_generate_script code.

Listing 15.9 The Code for the sp_generate_script Procedure

```
USE master
GO
IF OBJECT_ID('sp_generate_script','P') IS NOT NULL
  DROP PROC sp_generate_script
/*
  Object: sp_generate_script
Description: Generates a creation script for an object or
    collection of objects
  Usage: sp_generate_script [@objectname='Object name or mask
    (defaults to all object in current database)']
[,@outputname='Output file name' (Default: @objectname+'.SQL', or
    GENERATED_SCRIPT.SQL for entire database)]
[,@scriptoptions=bitmask specifying script generation options]
[,@resultset=bit specifying whether to generate a result set
[,@includeheaders=bit specifying whether to generate descriptive
    headers for scripts
[,@server='server name'][, @username='user name']
    [, @password='password'][, @trustedconnection=1]
  Returns: (None)
  $Author: Ken Henderson $. Email: khen@khen.com
  $Revision: 8.0 $
  Example: sp_generate_script @objectname='authors',
    @outputname='authors.sql'
  Created: 1998-04-01.  $Modtime: 2003-04-23 $.
  */
GO
CREATE PROC sp_generate_script
  @objectname sysname=NULL,   -- Object mask to copy
  @outputname sysname=NULL,   -- Output file to create (default:
                              -- 'GENERATED_SCRIPT.SQL')
  @scriptoptions int=NULL,    -- Options bitmask for Transfer
  @resultset bit=1,           -- Determines whether the script is
                              -- returned as a result set
  @trustedconnection bit=1,   -- Use a trusted connection to connect
                              -- to the server
  @IncludeHeaders bit=1,      -- Determines whether descriptive
                              -- headers are included with scripts
  @server sysname=@@SERVERNAME, -- server name (defaults to
                              -- @@SERVERNAME)
```

```
    @username sysname='sa',        -- Name of the user to connect as
                                   -- (defaults to 'sa')
    @password sysname=NULL         -- User's password
AS


-- SQLDMO_SCRIPT_TYPE vars
DECLARE @SQLDMOScript_Default int
DECLARE @SQLDMOScript_Drops int
DECLARE @SQLDMOScript_ObjectPermissions int
DECLARE @SQLDMOScript_PrimaryObject int
DECLARE @SQLDMOScript_ClusteredIndexes int
DECLARE @SQLDMOScript_Triggers int
DECLARE @SQLDMOScript_DatabasePermissions int
DECLARE @SQLDMOScript_Permissions int
DECLARE @SQLDMOScript_ToFileOnly int
DECLARE @SQLDMOScript_Bindings int
DECLARE @SQLDMOScript_AppendToFile int
DECLARE @SQLDMOScript_NoDRI int
DECLARE @SQLDMOScript_UDDTsToBaseType int
DECLARE @SQLDMOScript_IncludeIfNotExists int
DECLARE @SQLDMOScript_NonClusteredIndexes int
DECLARE @SQLDMOScript_Indexes int
DECLARE @SQLDMOScript_Aliases int
DECLARE @SQLDMOScript_NoCommandTerm int
DECLARE @SQLDMOScript_DRIIndexes int
DECLARE @SQLDMOScript_IncludeHeaders int
DECLARE @SQLDMOScript_OwnerQualify int
DECLARE @SQLDMOScript_TimestampToBinary int
DECLARE @SQLDMOScript_SortedData int
DECLARE @SQLDMOScript_SortedDataReorg int
DECLARE @SQLDMOScript_TransferDefault int
DECLARE @SQLDMOScript_DRI_NonClustered int
DECLARE @SQLDMOScript_DRI_Clustered int
DECLARE @SQLDMOScript_DRI_Checks int
DECLARE @SQLDMOScript_DRI_Defaults int
DECLARE @SQLDMOScript_DRI_UniqueKeys int
DECLARE @SQLDMOScript_DRI_ForeignKeys int
DECLARE @SQLDMOScript_DRI_PrimaryKey int
DECLARE @SQLDMOScript_DRI_AllKeys int
DECLARE @SQLDMOScript_DRI_AllConstraints int
DECLARE @SQLDMOScript_DRI_All int
DECLARE @SQLDMOScript_DRIWithNoCheck int
DECLARE @SQLDMOScript_NoIdentity int
DECLARE @SQLDMOScript_UseQuotedIdentifiers int
```

```
-- SQLDMO_SCRIPT2_TYPE vars
DECLARE @SQLDMOScript2_Default int
DECLARE @SQLDMOScript2_AnsiPadding int
DECLARE @SQLDMOScript2_AnsiFile int
DECLARE @SQLDMOScript2_UnicodeFile int
DECLARE @SQLDMOScript2_NonStop int
DECLARE @SQLDMOScript2_NoFG int
DECLARE @SQLDMOScript2_MarkTriggers int
DECLARE @SQLDMOScript2_OnlyUserTriggers int
DECLARE @SQLDMOScript2_EncryptPWD int
DECLARE @SQLDMOScript2_SeparateXPs int


-- SQLDMO_SCRIPT_TYPE values
SET @SQLDMOScript_Default = 4
SET @SQLDMOScript_Drops = 1
SET @SQLDMOScript_ObjectPermissions = 2
SET @SQLDMOScript_PrimaryObject = 4
SET @SQLDMOScript_ClusteredIndexes = 8
SET @SQLDMOScript_Triggers = 16
SET @SQLDMOScript_DatabasePermissions = 32
SET @SQLDMOScript_Permissions = 34
SET @SQLDMOScript_ToFileOnly = 64
SET @SQLDMOScript_Bindings = 128
SET @SQLDMOScript_AppendToFile = 256
SET @SQLDMOScript_NoDRI = 512
SET @SQLDMOScript_UDDTsToBaseType = 1024
SET @SQLDMOScript_IncludeIfNotExists = 4096
SET @SQLDMOScript_NonClusteredIndexes = 8192
SET @SQLDMOScript_Indexes = 73736
SET @SQLDMOScript_Aliases = 16384
SET @SQLDMOScript_NoCommandTerm = 32768
SET @SQLDMOScript_DRIIndexes = 65536
SET @SQLDMOScript_IncludeHeaders = 131072
SET @SQLDMOScript_OwnerQualify = 262144
SET @SQLDMOScript_TimestampToBinary = 524288
SET @SQLDMOScript_SortedData = 1048576
SET @SQLDMOScript_SortedDataReorg = 2097152
SET @SQLDMOScript_TransferDefault = 422143
SET @SQLDMOScript_DRI_NonClustered = 4194304
SET @SQLDMOScript_DRI_Clustered = 8388608
SET @SQLDMOScript_DRI_Checks = 16777216
SET @SQLDMOScript_DRI_Defaults = 33554432
SET @SQLDMOScript_DRI_UniqueKeys = 67108864
SET @SQLDMOScript_DRI_ForeignKeys = 134217728
```

```
SET @SQLDMOScript_DRI_PrimaryKey = 268435456
SET @SQLDMOScript_DRI_AllKeys = 469762048
SET @SQLDMOScript_DRI_AllConstraints = 520093696
SET @SQLDMOScript_DRI_All = 532676608
SET @SQLDMOScript_DRIWithNoCheck = 536870912
SET @SQLDMOScript_NoIdentity = 1073741824
SET @SQLDMOScript_UseQuotedIdentifiers = -1

-- SQLDMO_SCRIPT2_TYPE values
SET @SQLDMOScript2_Default = 0
SET @SQLDMOScript2_AnsiPadding = 1
SET @SQLDMOScript2_AnsiFile = 2
SET @SQLDMOScript2_UnicodeFile = 4
SET @SQLDMOScript2_NonStop = 8
SET @SQLDMOScript2_NoFG = 16
SET @SQLDMOScript2_MarkTriggers = 32
SET @SQLDMOScript2_OnlyUserTriggers = 64
SET @SQLDMOScript2_EncryptPWD = 128
SET @SQLDMOScript2_SeparateXPs = 256

DECLARE @dbname sysname,
    @srvobject int,  -- SQL Server object
    @object int,     -- Work variable for accessing COM objects
    @hr int,         -- Contains HRESULT returned by COM
    @tfobject int,   -- Stores pointer to Transfer object
    @res int

SET @res=0

IF (@objectname IS NOT NULL) AND (CHARINDEX('%',@objectname)=0)
      AND (CHARINDEX('_',@objectname)=0) BEGIN
   SET @dbname=ISNULL(PARSENAME(@objectname,3),DB_NAME())
       -- Extract the DB name; default to current

   SET @objectname=PARSENAME(@objectname,1)  -- Remove extraneous
                                             -- stuff from table name
   IF (@objectname IS NULL) BEGIN
     RAISERROR('Invalid object name.',16,1)
     RETURN -1
   END
   IF (@outputname IS NULL)
     SET @outputname=@objectname+'.SQL'
END ELSE BEGIN
     SET @dbname=DB_NAME()
```

```
    IF (@outputname IS NULL)
       SET @outputname='GENERATED_SCRIPT.SQL'
END


-- Create a SQLServer object
EXEC @hr=sp_OACreate 'SQLDMO.SQLServer', @srvobject OUTPUT
IF (@hr <> 0) BEGIN
  EXEC sp_displayoaerrorinfo @srvobject, @hr
  RETURN
END


-- Connect to the server
IF (@trustedconnection=1) BEGIN
  EXEC @hr = sp_OASetProperty @srvobject, 'LoginSecure', 1
  IF (@hr <> 0) BEGIN
    EXEC sp_displayoaerrorinfo @srvobject, @hr
    GOTO ServerError
  END
  EXEC @hr = sp_OAMethod @srvobject, 'Connect', NULL, @server
END
ELSE BEGIN
  IF (@password IS NOT NULL)
  BEGIN
    EXEC @hr = sp_OAMethod @srvobject, 'Connect', NULL, @server,
       @username, @password
  END
  ELSE BEGIN
    EXEC @hr = sp_OAMethod @srvobject, 'Connect', NULL, @server,
       @username
  END
END


IF (@hr <> 0) BEGIN
  EXEC sp_displayoaerrorinfo @srvobject, @hr
  GOTO ServerError
END


-- Create a Transfer object
EXEC @hr=sp_OACreate 'SQLDMO.Transfer', @tfobject OUTPUT
IF (@hr <> 0) BEGIN
  EXEC sp_displayoaerrorinfo @tfobject, @hr
  GOTO FreeSrv
END
```

```
-- Set Transfer's CopyData property
EXEC @hr = sp_OASetProperty @tfobject, 'CopyData', 0
IF (@hr <> 0) BEGIN
  EXEC sp_displayoaerrorinfo @tfobject, @hr
  GOTO FreeAll
END


-- Tell Transfer to copy the schema
EXEC @hr = sp_OASetProperty @tfobject, 'CopySchema', 1
IF (@hr <> 0) BEGIN
  EXEC sp_displayoaerrorinfo @tfobject, @hr
  GOTO FreeAll
END


IF (@objectname IS NULL) BEGIN  -- Get all objects in the database

  -- Tell Transfer to copy all objects
  EXEC @hr = sp_OASetProperty @tfobject, 'CopyAllObjects', 1
  IF (@hr <> 0) BEGIN
    EXEC sp_displayoaerrorinfo @tfobject, @hr
    GOTO FreeAll
  END

  -- Tell Transfer to get groups as well
  EXEC @hr = sp_OASetProperty @tfobject, 'IncludeGroups', 1
  IF (@hr <> 0) BEGIN
    EXEC sp_displayoaerrorinfo @tfobject, @hr
    GOTO FreeAll
  END

  -- Tell it to include users
  EXEC @hr = sp_OASetProperty @tfobject, 'IncludeUsers', 1
  IF (@hr <> 0) BEGIN
    EXEC sp_displayoaerrorinfo @tfobject, @hr
    GOTO FreeAll
  END

  -- Include object dependencies, too
  EXEC @hr = sp_OASetProperty @tfobject, 'IncludeDependencies', 1
  IF (@hr <> 0) BEGIN
    EXEC sp_displayoaerrorinfo @tfobject, @hr
    GOTO FreeAll
  END
```

```
   IF (@scriptoptions IS NULL) BEGIN
     SET @scriptoptions=@SQLDMOScript_OwnerQualify |
         @SQLDMOScript_Default | @SQLDMOScript_Triggers |
         @SQLDMOScript_Bindings | @SQLDMOScript_Permissions  |
         @SQLDMOScript_Indexes | @SQLDMOScript_DRI_Defaults --|
         @SQLDMOScript_NoDRI
      IF @includeheaders=1 SET @scriptoptions=@scriptoptions |
         @SQLDMOScript_IncludeHeaders
   END


END -- IF (@objectname IS NULL)
ELSE BEGIN
   DECLARE @obname sysname,
     @obtype varchar(2),
     @obowner sysname,
     @OBJECT_TYPES varchar(50),
     @obcode int

   -- Used to translate sysobjects.type into the bitmap that
   -- Transfer requires
   -- Don't change this string -- it serves as a translate table
   SET @OBJECT_TYPES='T     V   U   P       D  R  TR          FN TF IF '

   -- Find all the objects that match the supplied mask and add
   -- them to Transfer's list of objects to script
   DECLARE ObjectList CURSOR FOR
   SELECT name,CASE type WHEN 'TF' THEN 'FN' WHEN 'IF' THEN 'FN'
       ELSE type END AS type,USER_NAME(uid) FROM sysobjects
   WHERE (name LIKE @objectname)
     AND (CHARINDEX(type+' ',@OBJECT_TYPES)<>0)
     AND (OBJECTPROPERTY(id,'IsSystemTable')=0)
     AND (status>0)
   UNION ALL  -- Include user-defined data types
   SELECT name,'T',USER_NAME(uid)
   FROM SYSTYPES
   WHERE (usertype & 256)<>0
   AND (name LIKE @objectname)

   OPEN ObjectList

   FETCH ObjectList INTO @obname, @obtype, @obowner
   WHILE (@@FETCH_STATUS=0) BEGIN
     SET @obcode=POWER(2,(CHARINDEX(@obtype+' ',@OBJECT_TYPES)/3))
```

```
    EXEC @hr = sp_OAMethod @tfobject, 'AddObjectByName', NULL,
        @obname, @obcode, @obowner
    IF (@hr <> 0) BEGIN
      EXEC sp_displayoaerrorinfo @tfobject, @hr
      GOTO FreeAll
    END

    FETCH ObjectList INTO @obname, @obtype, @obowner  END
  CLOSE ObjectList
  DEALLOCATE ObjectList

  IF (@scriptoptions IS NULL)
    SET @scriptoptions=@SQLDMOScript_Default  -- Keep it simple
                        -- when not scripting the entire database
    IF @includeheaders=1 SET @scriptoptions=@scriptoptions |
        @SQLDMOScript_IncludeHeaders
END  -- ELSE IF (@objectname IS NULL)



-- Set Transfer's ScriptType property
EXEC @hr = sp_OASetProperty @tfobject, 'ScriptType', @scriptoptions
IF (@hr <> 0) BEGIN
  EXEC sp_displayoaerrorinfo @tfobject, @hr
  GOTO FreeAll
END

-- Set Transfer's Script2Type property
EXEC @hr = sp_OASetProperty @tfobject, 'Script2Type',
    @SQLDMOScript2_NoFG
IF (@hr <> 0) BEGIN
  EXEC sp_displayoaerrorinfo @tfobject, @hr
  GOTO FreeAll
END

-- Get a pointer to the database
DECLARE @itemname varchar(255)
SET @itemname='Databases.Item("'+@dbname+'")'
EXEC @hr = sp_OAGetProperty @srvobject, @itemname, @object OUT
IF @hr <> 0 BEGIN
  EXEC sp_displayoaerrorinfo @srvobject, @hr
  GOTO FreeAll
END
```

```
DECLARE @cmd varchar(8000)

-- Call the Database object's Transfer method to transfer the
-- schemas to the file
-- We begin by scripting the objects without DRI references, then
-- we script the PKs, then the FKs
EXEC @hr = sp_OAMethod @object, 'ScriptTransfer',NULL, @tfobject,
    2,@outputname
IF @hr <> 0 BEGIN
  EXEC sp_displayoaerrorinfo @object, @hr
  GOTO FreeAll
  END
-- Now get the PKs and UKs (append to the original script file)
-- We get the PKs and UKs separately from the tables themselves
-- because getting PKs sometimes also pulls FKs despite our not
-- having requested FKs
SET @scriptoptions=@SQLDMOScript_NoDRI |
    @SQLDMOScript_DRI_PrimaryKey | @SQLDMOScript_DRI_UniqueKeys |
    @SQLDMOScript_AppendToFile | @SQLDMOScript_OwnerQualify
IF @includeheaders=1 SET @scriptoptions=@scriptoptions |
    @SQLDMOScript_IncludeHeaders

-- Reset Transfer's ScriptType property
EXEC @hr = sp_OASetProperty @tfobject, 'ScriptType', @scriptoptions
IF (@hr <> 0) BEGIN
  EXEC sp_displayoaerrorinfo @tfobject, @hr
  GOTO FreeAll
END

EXEC @hr = sp_OAMethod @object, 'ScriptTransfer',NULL, @tfobject,
    2,@outputname
IF @hr <> 0 BEGIN
  EXEC sp_displayoaerrorinfo @object, @hr
  GOTO FreeAll
END

-- Now get the FKs (append to the original script file)
SET @scriptoptions=@SQLDMOScript_NoDRI |
    @SQLDMOScript_DRI_ForeignKeys | @SQLDMOScript_DRI_Checks |
    @SQLDMOScript_DRI_Defaults | @SQLDMOScript_AppendToFile |
    @SQLDMOScript_OwnerQualify
IF @includeheaders=1 SET @scriptoptions=@scriptoptions |
    @SQLDMOScript_IncludeHeaders
```

```
-- Reset Transfer's ScriptType property
EXEC @hr = sp_OASetProperty @tfobject, 'ScriptType', @scriptoptions
IF (@hr <> 0) BEGIN
  EXEC sp_displayoaerrorinfo @tfobject, @hr
  GOTO FreeAll
END

-- Generate the last section of the script
EXEC @hr = sp_OAMethod @object, 'ScriptTransfer',NULL, @tfobject,
    2,@outputname
IF @hr <> 0 BEGIN
  EXEC sp_displayoaerrorinfo @object, @hr
  GOTO FreeAll
END

IF (@resultset=1) BEGIN
  SET @cmd='TYPE "'+@outputname+'"'
  exec master.dbo.xp_cmdshell @cmd
END

GOTO FreeAll

ServerError:
SET @res=-1
RAISERROR ('Error generating script', 16, 1)

FreeAll:
EXEC sp_OADestroy @tfobject  -- For cleanliness

FreeSrv:
EXEC sp_OADestroy @srvobject

RETURN @res
GO
USE Northwind
GO
EXEC sp_generate_script  'Customers', @server='khenmp\ss2000'
```

(Results abridged)

```
Column1
-----------------------------------------------------------------
set quoted_identifier  OFF
GO
```

```
CREATE TABLE [Customers] (
  [CustomerID] [nchar] (5) COLLATE SQL_Latin1_General_CP1_CI_AS NO
  [CompanyName] [nvarchar] (40) COLLATE SQL_Latin1_General_CP1_CI_
  [ContactName] [nvarchar] (30) COLLATE SQL_Latin1_General_CP1_CI_
  [ContactTitle] [nvarchar] (30) COLLATE SQL_Latin1_General_CP1_CI
  [Address] [nvarchar] (60) COLLATE SQL_Latin1_General_CP1_CI_AS N
  [City] [nvarchar] (15) COLLATE SQL_Latin1_General_CP1_CI_AS NULL
  [Region] [nvarchar] (15) COLLATE SQL_Latin1_General_CP1_CI_AS NU
  [PostalCode] [nvarchar] (10) COLLATE SQL_Latin1_General_CP1_CI_A
  [Country] [nvarchar] (15) COLLATE SQL_Latin1_General_CP1_CI_AS N
  [Phone] [nvarchar] (24) COLLATE SQL_Latin1_General_CP1_CI_AS NUL
  [Fax] [nvarchar] (24) COLLATE SQL_Latin1_General_CP1_CI_AS NULL
  [rowguid]  uniqueidentifier ROWGUIDCOL  NOT NULL CONSTRAINT
  [DF__Customers__rowgu__0EF836A4] DEFAULT (newid()),
  CONSTRAINT [PK_Customers] PRIMARY KEY  CLUSTERED
  (
    [CustomerID]
  )  ON [PRIMARY]
) ON [PRIMARY]
GO


(1 row(s) affected)
```

**NOTE: Ignore the code displayed above. It's a remnant of the
SQL-DMO method used to produce the script file**
line

```
set quoted_identifier  OFF
GO


CREATE TABLE [Customers] (
  [CustomerID] [nchar] (5) COLLATE SQL_Latin1_General_CP1_CI_AS NO
  [CompanyName] [nvarchar] (40) COLLATE SQL_Latin1_General_CP1_CI_
  [ContactName] [nvarchar] (30) COLLATE SQL_Latin1_General_CP1_CI_
  [ContactTitle] [nvarchar] (30) COLLATE SQL_Latin1_General_CP1_CI
  [Address] [nvarchar] (60) COLLATE SQL_Latin1_General_CP1_CI_AS N
  [City] [nvarchar] (15) COLLATE SQL_Latin1_General_CP1_CI_AS NULL
  [Region] [nvarchar] (15) COLLATE SQL_Latin1_General_CP1_CI_AS NU
  [PostalCode] [nvarchar] (10) COLLATE SQL_Latin1_General_CP1_CI_A
  [Country] [nvarchar] (15) COLLATE SQL_Latin1_General_CP1_CI_AS N
  [Phone] [nvarchar] (24) COLLATE SQL_Latin1_General_CP1_CI_AS NUL
  [Fax] [nvarchar] (24) COLLATE SQL_Latin1_General_CP1_CI_AS NULL
  [rowguid]  uniqueidentifier ROWGUIDCOL  NOT NULL CONSTRAINT
```

```
[DF__Customers__rowgu__0EF836A4] DEFAULT (newid()),
CONSTRAINT [PK_Customers] PRIMARY KEY   CLUSTERED
(
   [CustomerID]
)  ON [PRIMARY]
) ON [PRIMARY]
GO
```

In the results section of the listing, everything above the PRINT message (bolded) is spurious output that you can safely ignore. The output below the message is the actual script. Here, I've scripted the Customers table from the Northwind database. I could just as easily have scripted the entire database or supplied a mask to generate a script or several at once.

The procedure begins by instantiating the DMO SQLServer and Transfer objects. DMO's SQLServer object is its root level access path—you use it to connect to the server and to access other objects on the server. The Transfer object encapsulates DMO's server-to-server or server-to-file object and data transfer facility. The sp_generate_script procedure uses it to generate SQL scripts.

If you've done any DMO programming, you may be wondering why I'm using a Transfer object instead of calling the Script method on individual objects. I do this in order to preserve object dependencies as much as possible. The Transfer object writes object schema information to the script in order of dependency based on the sysdepends table. Although this is not a completely reliable way to determine object dependency, it is better than nothing and is, unfortunately, all we have. Since it was originally intended to support transferring one database to another, the Transfer object has to be mindful of object creation order—otherwise CREATE statements for objects that depended on other objects will fail if the objects they require haven't already been created. Consider a foreign key constraint. If the Order Details table makes a foreign key reference to the Products table, the Products table must exist before the Order Details table can be created—the CREATE TABLE statement will fail if it doesn't. The Transfer object attempts to ensure this by checking object dependencies when it scripts out a database.

Because Transfer's object dependency detection can be faulty based on incorrect or missing information in sysdepends, sp_generate_script takes the additional step of breaking the generation process into three stages based on the general dependency of objects. The first stage scripts the requested objects without DRI of any kind. The second stage scripts the primary key and unique key constraints for the selected objects. And the third stage scripts the foreign key constraints for the specified objects. This allows the script to be reliably executed to recreate the database even if the dependency order reflected by sysdepends and used by DMO is incorrect.

Once the Transfer object is created, the procedure determines whether the user wants to script the entire database or only selected objects. This distinction is important because DMO attempts to list objects in order of dependency when scripting an entire database, as I've said. If only a subset of the objects in a database is to be scripted, the procedure opens a cursor on the sysobjects and systypes tables (via UNION ALL) and calls Transfer's AddObjectByName method to set them up to be scripted, one by one.

The procedure next uses the SQLServer object to locate the database housing the objects it needs to script. It finds this database by accessing the object's Databases collection. DMO objects often expose collections of other objects. Items in these collections can be accessed by name or by ordinal index. In the case of sp_generate_script, collection items are always accessed by name.

Once the procedure retrieves a pointer to the correct database, it calls that database's ScriptTransfer method, passing it the previously created Transfer object as a parameter. This generates a SQL script containing the objects we've specified.

The final step in the procedure is to return the script as a result set. Usually, the caller will expect to see the script immediately. If @resultset = 1 (the default), sp_generate_script calls xp_cmdshell to run the operating system TYPE command to list the file and return it as a result set. A useful variation of this would be to return a cursor pointer to the script, but that's an exercise I'll leave to the reader.

Using ODSOLE to Automate Custom Objects

In this section, I'll show you how to automate COM objects you create yourself. We'll walk through automating a library of Visual Basic functions that I've wrapped in a COM object named VBODSOLELib. Let's begin by looking at Listing 15.10, the Visual Basic source code for VBODSOLELib. (You can find the complete source code in the VBODSOLELib subfolder in the CH15 folder on the CD accompanying this book.)

Listing 15.10 The Source Code for VBODSOLELib

```
Option Explicit
Dim GlobalArray() As Variant
Dim lGlobalArraySize As Long


'String functions

Public Function VBInStrRev(strCheck As String, strMatch As String)
    As String
  VBInStrRev = InStrRev(strCheck, strMatch)
End Function

Public Function VBStrReverse(strIn As String) As String
  VBStrReverse = StrReverse(strIn)
End Function

Public Function VBFormat(vExpr As Variant, strFormat As String)
    As String
  VBFormat = Format(vExpr, strFormat)
End Function

Public Function VBHex(vExpr As Variant) As String
  VBHex = Hex(vExpr)
End Function

Public Function VBOct(vExpr As Variant) As String
  VBOct = Oct(vExpr)
End Function

Public Function VBLike(strMatch As String, strExpr As String)
    As Boolean
  VBLike = (strMatch Like strExpr)
End Function

Public Function VBScriptRegEx(strPattern As String, strMatch
    As String) As Long
  Dim regEx, Match, Matches
  Set regEx = CreateObject("VBScript.RegExp")
  regEx.Pattern = strPattern
  regEx.IgnoreCase = True
  Set Matches = regEx.Execute(strMatch)
```

```
      If Not IsEmpty(Matches) Then
        For Each Match In Matches
          VBScriptRegEx = Match.FirstIndex + 1 'Zero-based
          Exit For
        Next
      Else
        VBScriptRegEx = 0
      End If
    End Function


    Public Function VBScriptRegExTest(strPattern As String, strMatch
        As String) As Boolean
      Dim regEx, Match, Matches
      Set regEx = CreateObject("VBScript.RegExp")
      regEx.Pattern = strPattern
      regEx.IgnoreCase = True
      VBScriptRegExTest = regEx.Test(strMatch)
    End Function



    ' Misc

    Public Function VBShell(strCommandLine As String, Optional
        iWindowStyle As Variant) As Double
      VBShell = Shell(strCommandLine, IIf(IsMissing(iWindowStyle),
        vbNormalFocus, iWindowStyle))
    End Function

    ' Financial functions

    Public Function VBFV(nRate As Double, nPer As Double, nPmt
        As Double, Optional vPv As Variant, Optional vType As Variant)
      VBFV = FV(nRate, nPer, nPmt, IIf(IsMissing(vPv), 0, vPv),
        IIf(IsMissing(vType), 0, vType))
    End Function

    Public Function VBIPmt(nRate As Double, nPer As Double,
        nPmtPeriods As Double, nPV As Double, Optional vFv As
        Variant, Optional vType As Variant)
      VBIPmt = IPmt(nRate, nPer, nPmtPeriods, nPV,
        IIf(IsMissing(vFv), 0, vFv), IIf(IsMissing(vType), 0, vType))
    End Function

    Public Function VBNPer(nRate As Double, nPmt As Double, nPV
```

```
      As Double, Optional vFv As Variant, Optional vType As Variant)
    VBNPer = nPer(nRate, nPmt, nPV, IIf(IsMissing(vFv), 0, vFv),
      IIf(IsMissing(vType), 0, vType))
End Function

Public Function VBPmt(nRate As Double, nPer As Double, nPV
      As Double, Optional vFv As Variant, Optional vType As Variant)
    VBPmt = Pmt(nRate, nPer, nPV, IIf(IsMissing(vFv), 0, vFv),
      IIf(IsMissing(vType), 0, vType))
End Function

Public Function VBPPmt(nRate As Double, nPer As Double,
      nPmtPeriods As Double, nPV As Double, Optional vFv As Variant,
      Optional vType As Variant)
    VBPPmt = PPmt(nRate, nPer, nPmtPeriods, nPV,
      IIf(IsMissing(vFv), 0, vFv), IIf(IsMissing(vType), 0, vType))
End Function

Public Function VBPV(nRate As Double, nPer As Double, nPmt
      As Double, Optional vFv As Variant, Optional vType As Variant)
    VBPV = PV(nRate, nPer, nPmt, IIf(IsMissing(vFv), 0, vFv),
      IIf(IsMissing(vType), 0, vType))
End Function

' Routines

Public Sub VBAppActivate(strTitle As String, Optional bWait
      As Variant)
    AppActivate strTitle, IIf(IsMissing(bWait), False, bWait)
End Sub

Public Sub VBSendKeys(strKeys, Optional bWait As Variant)
    SendKeys strKeys, IIf(IsMissing(bWait), False, bWait)
End Sub

Public Sub VBAppActivateAndSendKeys(strTitle As String, strKeys
      As String, Optional bWait As Variant)
    AppActivate strTitle, IIf(IsMissing(bWait), False, bWait)
    SendKeys strKeys, IIf(IsMissing(bWait), False, bWait)
End Sub

Public Sub VBFileCopy(strSource As String, strDestination
      As String)
    FileCopy strSource, strDestination
```

```
End Sub

Public Sub VBFileErase(strFileName As String)
  Kill strFileName
End Sub

Public Sub VBMkDir(strDirName As String)
  MkDir strDirName
End Sub

Public Sub VBRmDir(strDirName As String)
  RmDir strDirName
End Sub
```

I won't go through all of these functions. You should already have a pretty good idea of how to access them from T-SQL using the sp_OA procs by now. Once you've registered the object's DLL via a call to regsvr32, you access it from T-SQL just as you would any other COM object and exactly as we have done in the other examples in this chapter.

Most of these functions do not exist in Transact-SQL, and you may find some of them quite useful. There are financial functions (e.g., VBIPmt, a function to compute the interest payment on an annuity), string manipulation functions (e.g., VBInStrRev, a reverse string search function), system functions (e.g., VBAppActivate; you will need to run SQL Server as a console app to use some of these), regular expression functions (e.g., VBScriptRegEx and VBScriptRegExTest), and many others. The VBODSOLELib subfolder on the CD includes several sample T-SQL scripts that demonstrate how to use these. Listing 15.11 shows an example that calls VBInStrRev.

Listing 15.11 Using VBInStrRev

```
declare @obj int
declare @hr int
declare @songs varchar(255)
set @songs='Sister Christian, Dance, Boys of Summer, The Dance'
declare @pos int
exec @hr=sp_OACreate 'VBODSOLE.VBODSOLELib', @obj OUT
IF (@hr <> 0) BEGIN
  EXEC sp_displayoaerrorinfo @obj, @hr
  RETURN
END
```

```
exec @hr=sp_OAMethod @obj, 'VBInStrRev', @pos OUT, @songs, 'Dance'
IF (@hr <> 0) BEGIN
  EXEC sp_displayoaerrorinfo @obj, @hr
  RETURN
END

select @pos

exec @hr=sp_OADestroy @obj
IF (@hr <> 0) BEGIN
  EXEC sp_displayoaerrorinfo @obj, @hr
  RETURN
END
```

(Results)

```
-----------
46
```

Arrays in T-SQL via COM Objects

One section of VBODSOLELib that I will cover in detail, however, is the set of VB array functions. These functions provide basic array services to Transact-SQL. In my last book, *The Guru's Guide to SQL Server Stored Procedures, XML, and HTML*, I added array support to Transact-SQL using xprocs and system functions. In this book, I'll take a different approach. I'll add array support to T-SQL via our VBODSOLELib COM object and some system functions. Let's start by looking at the array code from VBODSOLELib (Listing 15.12).

Listing 15.12 The Array Code from VBODSOLELib

```
Public Function VBCreateArray(lSize As Long) As Long
  Dim vArray()
  ReDim vArray(lSize)
  If IsEmpty(lGlobalArraySize) Then
    lGlobalArraySize = 0
  Else
    lGlobalArraySize = lGlobalArraySize + 1
  End If
  ReDim Preserve GlobalArray(lGlobalArraySize)
```

```
    GlobalArray(lGlobalArraySize) = vArray()
    VBCreateArray = lGlobalArraySize
End Function


Public Function VBGetArray(lGlobalIndex As Long, lIndex As Long)
    As Variant
  VBGetArray = GlobalArray(lGlobalIndex)(lIndex - 1)
End Function


Public Sub VBSetArray(lGlobalIndex As Long, lIndex As Long, vVal
    As Variant)
  GlobalArray(lGlobalIndex)(lIndex - 1) = vVal
End Sub


Public Sub VBDestroyArray(lGlobalIndex As Long)
  Set GlobalArray(lGlobalIndex) = Null
End Sub


Public Function VBCreateArraySplit(strIn As String, Optional
    strDelim As Variant) As Long
  If IsEmpty(lGlobalArraySize) Then
    lGlobalArraySize = 0
  Else
    lGlobalArraySize = lGlobalArraySize + 1
  End If
  ReDim Preserve GlobalArray(lGlobalArraySize)
  GlobalArray(lGlobalArraySize) = Split(strIn,
      IIf(IsMissing(strDelim), " ", strDelim))
    VBCreateArraySplit = lGlobalArraySize
End Function


Public Function VBArrayJoin(lGlobalIndex As Long, Optional
    strDelim As Variant) As String
  VBArrayJoin = Join(GlobalArray(lGlobalIndex),
      IIf(IsMissing(strDelim), " ", strDelim))
End Function


Public Function VBListArray(lGlobalIndex As Long) As Variant
  VBListArray = GlobalArray(lGlobalIndex)
End Function


Public Function VBArrayLen(lGlobalIndex As Long) As Long
  VBArrayLen = UBound(GlobalArray(lGlobalIndex))
End Function
```

This code presents eight functions:

- VBCreateArray—creates an array and returns a handle to it.
- VBGetArray—gets an array element.
- VBSetArray—sets an array element.
- VBDestroyArray—destroys an array.
- VBCreateArraySplit—creates an array by breaking a delimited string into elements.
- VBArrayJoin—returns the elements in an array as a delimited string.
- VBListArray—returns an array as a variant.
- VBArrayLen—returns the number of elements in an array.

The purpose of each of these should be pretty self-explanatory. Essentially, I've taken VB's base array functions and wrapped them in a COM object so that they're accessible from T-SQL. Listing 15.13 shows a sample script that demonstrates how to call them from T-SQL.

Listing 15.13 Calling Base Array Functions

```
declare @obj int
declare @hr int
declare @arr int
exec @hr=sp_oacreate 'VBODSOLE.VBODSOLELib', @obj OUT
IF (@hr <> 0) BEGIN
  EXEC sp_displayoaerrorinfo @obj, @hr
  RETURN
END


exec @hr=sp_oamethod @obj, 'VBCreateArray', @arr OUT, 10
IF (@hr <> 0) BEGIN
  EXEC sp_displayoaerrorinfo @obj, @hr
  Goto Cleanup
END


exec @hr=sp_oamethod @obj, 'VBSetArray', NULL, @arr, 3, 'foo'
IF (@hr <> 0) BEGIN
  EXEC sp_displayoaerrorinfo @obj, @hr
  Goto Cleanup
END


declare @val varchar(30)
exec @hr=sp_oamethod @obj, 'VBGetArray', @val OUT, @arr, 3
```

```
IF (@hr <> 0) BEGIN
  EXEC sp_displayoaerrorinfo @obj, @hr
  Goto Cleanup
END

SELECT @val

DECLARE @len int

exec @hr=sp_oamethod @obj, 'VBArrayLen', @len OUT, @arr
IF (@hr <> 0) BEGIN
  EXEC sp_displayoaerrorinfo @obj, @hr
  Goto Cleanup
END

SELECT @len

DECLARE @dummy int

exec @hr=sp_oamethod @obj, 'VBListArray', @dummy OUT, @arr
IF (@hr <> 0) BEGIN
  EXEC sp_displayoaerrorinfo @obj, @hr
  Goto Cleanup
END

Cleanup:

exec @hr=sp_oadestroy @obj
```

(Results abridged)

```
--------------------------------
foo


-----------
10

Column0      Column1      Column2      Column3
-----------  -----------  -----------  -----------
0            0            foo          0
```

There are a couple of interesting points to be made about this code. First, note the use of an integer index as the array's handle. Those of you who read my last book may be wondering why we're returning an index for the array handle rather than a pointer to the array itself as we did in the xproc array treatment in that book. The reason is that ODSOLE, in an attempt to help the developer, doesn't allow you to return an array type from an Automation method. If you return an array, ODSOLE automatically NULLs the output parameter that would have received the value and translates the array into a TDS result set. As I mentioned earlier, if the array is a single-dimensional array, you get a single row with a column for each element in the array. If the array has two dimensions, you'll get a multirow result set. And if the array has more than two dimensions or stores complex types such as structs, an error will be raised.

So, since we can't return an array from our COM methods without ODSOLE turning it into a result set, we allocate an "array of arrays"—an array of variants that each will store arrays—in the VBODSOLELib object. Each time a new array needs to be allocated, we ReDim this master array to include another slot, then allocate the new array at the new slot. In many ways, this master array resembles a two-dimensional array that supports jagged edges.

Once we successfully Dim a new array, we return the index to its slot in the class's master array. This index serves as the array's handle. Each time we access the array, we always index it in the master array using this handle.

Note that we use ODSOLE's propensity for translating arrays into result sets to our advantage in the VBListArray method. VBListArray doesn't actually list the array—it merely returns the variant containing the array. ODSOLE, on seeing this array return value, translates it into a result set, thus producing our list.

The ability to access this functionality via sp_OA calls is powerful enough, but as with my xproc array treatment, I've wrapped these sp_OA calls in system UDFs so they can be easily used across the server. Listing 15.14 presents the source to the script that sets up these UDFs.

Listing 15.14 The Array UDFs

```
USE master
GO
EXEC sp_configure 'allow updates',1
GO
RECONFIGURE WITH OVERRIDE
GO
```

```
DROP FUNCTION system_function_schema.fn_createobject,
             system_function_schema.fn_destroyobject,
             system_function_schema.fn_createarray,
             system_function_schema.fn_setarray,
             system_function_schema.fn_getarray,
             system_function_schema.fn_destroyarray,
             system_function_schema.fn_arraylen,
             system_function_schema.fn_listarray
GO
CREATE FUNCTION system_function_schema.fn_createobject()
RETURNS int
AS
BEGIN
  DECLARE @obj int
  DECLARE @hr int
  exec @hr=sp_OACreate 'VBODSOLE.VBODSOLELib', @obj OUT
  IF (@hr <> 0) BEGIN
    RETURN @hr
  END
  RETURN(@obj)
END
GO
CREATE FUNCTION system_function_schema.fn_destroyobject(@obj int)
RETURNS int
AS
BEGIN
  DECLARE @hr int
  exec @hr=sp_OADestroy @obj
  RETURN(@hr)
END
GO
CREATE FUNCTION system_function_schema.fn_createarray(@obj int,
    @size int)
RETURNS int
AS
BEGIN
  DECLARE @hr int
  DECLARE @hdl int
  exec @hr=sp_OAMethod @obj, 'VBCreateArray', @hdl OUT, @size
  IF (@hr <> 0) BEGIN
    RETURN @hr
  END
  RETURN(@hdl)
END
```

```
GO
CREATE FUNCTION system_function_schema.fn_destroyarray(@obj int,
    @hdl int)
RETURNS int
AS
BEGIN
DECLARE @hr int
exec @hr=sp_oamethod @obj, 'VBDestoryArray', NULL, @hdl
IF (@hr <> 0) BEGIN
  RETURN @hr
END
RETURN 0
END
GO
CREATE FUNCTION system_function_schema.fn_setarray(@obj int,
    @hdl int, @index int, @value sql_variant)
RETURNS int
AS
BEGIN
DECLARE @hr int
exec @hr=sp_OAMethod @obj, 'VBSetArray', NULL, @hdl, @index,
    @value
IF (@hr <> 0) BEGIN
  RETURN @hr
END
RETURN 0
END
GO
CREATE FUNCTION system_function_schema.fn_getarray(@obj int,
    @hdl int, @index int)
RETURNS sql_variant
AS
BEGIN
DECLARE @hr int, @valuestr varchar(8000)
exec @hr=sp_oamethod @obj, 'VBGetArray', @valuestr OUT, @hdl,
    @index
IF (@hr <> 0) BEGIN
  RETURN @hr
END
RETURN(@valuestr)
END
GO
CREATE FUNCTION system_function_schema.fn_arraylen(@obj int,
    @hdl int)
RETURNS int
```

```
AS
BEGIN
DECLARE @hr int, @len int
exec @hr=sp_oamethod @obj, 'VBArrayLen', @len OUT, @hdl
IF (@hr <> 0) BEGIN
  RETURN @hr
END
RETURN @len
END
GO
CREATE FUNCTION system_function_schema.fn_listarray(@obj int,
    @hdl int)
RETURNS @array TABLE (idx int, value sql_variant)
AS
BEGIN
  DECLARE @i int, @cnt int
  SET @cnt=fn_arraylen(@obj,@hdl)
  SET @i=1
  WHILE (@i<=@cnt) BEGIN
    INSERT @array VALUES (@i, fn_getarray(@obj,@hdl,@i))
    SET @i=@i+1
  END
  RETURN
END
GO
EXEC sp_configure 'allow updates',0
GO
RECONFIGURE WITH OVERRIDE
GO
```

By wrapping the sp_OA calls in system UDFs, we make these COM object–based array functions much easier to use. Listing 15.15 demonstrates how to use them.

Listing 15.15 Using the Array Functions

```
DECLARE @obj int, @hdl int, @siz int, @res int
SET @siz=1000

-- Create the array and return its handle and length
SET @obj=fn_createobject()
```

```
SET @hdl=fn_createarray(@obj,@siz)
SELECT @hdl, fn_arraylen(@obj,@hdl)

-- Set elements 1, 10, 998, and 1000
SELECT @res=fn_setarray(@obj,@hdl,1,'test1'),
@res=fn_setarray(@obj,@hdl,10,'test10'),
@res=fn_setarray(@obj,@hdl,998,'test998'),
@res=fn_setarray(@obj,@hdl,1000,'test1000')

-- Get element 10
SELECT fn_getarray(@obj,@hdl,10)

-- Get element 998
SELECT fn_getarray(@obj,@hdl,998)

-- List the array
SELECT * FROM ::fn_listarray(@obj, @hdl)
WHERE value IS NOT NULL

SET @res=fn_destroyarray(@obj,@hdl)
SET @res=fn_destroyobject(@obj)
```

(Results)

```
----------- -----------
1           1000


------------------------------------------------------------------
test10


------------------------------------------------------------------
test998

idx         value
----------- ------------------------------------------------------
1           test1
10          test10
998         test998
1000        test1000
```

As you can see, creating the array in the first place, then adding elements to it and retrieving those elements is extremely easy. Note that since these are functions, we can use them to process data in tables and views, as shown in Listing 15.16.

Listing 15.16 Using the Array Functions with Table/View Data

```
DECLARE @o int, @h int, @res int, @arraybase int

-- Create the object and the array
SET @o=fn_createobject()
SELECT @h=fn_createarray(@o,1000), @arraybase=10247

-- Load all the Order dates into it
SELECT @res=fn_setarray(@o,@h,OrderId-@arraybase,OrderDate)
FROM Northwind..orders

-- List an array element
SELECT idx+@arraybase AS OrderId, value AS OrderDate
FROM ::fn_listarray(@o,@h)
WHERE idx=10249-@arraybase

-- Destroy the array and the object
SET @res=fn_destroyarray(@o,@h)
SET @res=fn_destroyobject(@o)
```

(Results)

```
OrderId     OrderDate
----------- --------------------------------------------------------
10249       NULL
```

Here, we load the OrderDate column from the Northwind Orders table into our array using a SELECT statement and our fn_setarray function. Notice how we're able to load the entire table with a single SELECT statement. We then query the array like a table using the fn_listarray table-value function and filter the query using the array index.

As I'm sure you've surmised by now, there are numerous uses for an array-like facility in Transact-SQL. Even when coding in a set-oriented language, you still occasionally run into situations where an array is the right tool for the job. You can use the array code presented here to address those situations.

Recap

COM is a powerful and pervasive technology that enables applications to interoperate in a wide variety of ways. Thanks to ODSOLE, Transact-SQL can access COM object interfaces exposed by other applications and even by SQL Server itself. By combining the power of a relational database with the flexibility and ubiquity of Automation, you can build applications that are very powerful indeed.

SQL Server's ODSOLE facility uses late binding to interact with COM objects. This means that it makes calls to the IDispatch COM interface, similarly to traditional scripting languages such as VBScript and JScript.

ODSOLE makes use of the STA threading model. When first initialized, it creates the main STA if it has not already been created. In the STA model, access from other apartments is coordinated via Windows messages.

You create COM object instances from Transact-SQL using sp_OACreate, and you destroy them via sp_OADestroy. Any objects that aren't destroyed when the batch completes are automatically released by one of the two batch termination handlers ODSOLE sets up when an sp_OA proc is first called on a worker thread.

Knowledge Measure

1. What is the current preferred term for OLE Automation?
2. True or false: The sp_OA family of extended procedures are actually "spec procs"—their entry points do not reside in an external DLL.
3. What well-known COM interface does sp_OA use to invoke a method on a COM object?
4. How does ODSOLE react when an array value is returned from an sp_OA call?
5. True or false: It is not necessary to release COM object instances created by sp_OA calls because ODSOLE will release them for you automatically at the end of the current batch.
6. Describe, in general terms, the function of a process's main STA.

7. True or false: On SQL Server 2000 and earlier, using the sp_OA procedures to instantiate managed code classes that have been published as COM objects is not supported by Microsoft.
8. Explain a key difference between CoInitialize and CoInitializeEx.
9. Name the Windows API responsible for dispatching messages.
10. What must a T-SQL coder do in order to force a given COM component to attempt to start out-of-process?
11. True or false: The pointer returned by sp_OACreate is the address of the newly created COM object.
12. What object does the following dot notation refer to: 'Databases.Items("pubs")'?
13. What is the maximum number of MTAs that a single process can support?
14. What type of connection must a stored procedure establish if it wants to make most SQL-DMO calls against the server on which it's running?
15. When a managed class is compiled into a DLL assembly and registered for use with COM via the regasm.exe tool, what DLL is actually the host insofar as COM is concerned?
16. True or false: SQL-DMO determines object dependencies by examining the sysdepends table, which is not always a reliable and accurate source of such information.
17. What COM initialization function does ODSOLE call?
18. How is the threading model for an in-process COM server set by default?
19. True or false: Unlike Visual Basic, SQL Server's COM Automation facility does not support named parameters.
20. Is it possible to change the COM threading model of an existing thread without first uninitializing COM on that thread?
21. Describe how ODSOLE reacts when an output value is returned from an sp_OAMethod call but no output parameter is specified.
22. How would ODSOLE handle an array of structs returned from an sp_OAMethod call?
23. What well-known COM interface method does ODSOLE call in order to invoke a method on a COM object that has been late bound?
24. True or false: Given that their names start with sp_, the Transact-SQL parser does not allow the sp_OA procs to be called from UDFs because it mistakes them for regular stored procedures.
25. True or false: In order to be used by a COM client, a COM object created by exposing and registering a public managed class and interface must be installed into the Global Assembly Cache.

CHAPTER 16

Full-Text Search

I have never imputed to Nature a purpose or a goal, or anything that could be understood as anthropomorphic. What I see in Nature is a magnificent structure that we can comprehend only very imperfectly, and that must fill a thinking person with a feeling of humility. This is a genuinely religious feeling that has nothing to do with mysticism.

—Albert Einstein[1]

In this chapter, we'll talk about SQL Server's Full-Text Search (FTS) facility and the engine behind it, the Microsoft Search service. We'll talk about how FTS works and explore how you can use full-text queries to retrieve data using sophisticated search criteria.

Support for full-text searching was first added in SQL Server 7.0 and hasn't changed much since then. For data in SQL Server tables, FTS provides much of the functionality typically found in standalone indexing products such as the Microsoft Indexing Service (an operating system file-based search engine). It allows these tables to be searched using more sophisticated terms than is possible with standard Transact-SQL.

This chapter updates the coverage of FTS in my book *The Guru's Guide to Transact-SQL*. As with other chapters in this book where I've updated what I said on a particular topic in the past, I've tried to strike a balance between describing the architectural layout of the technology and providing up-to-date instruction on how to put it to practical use. Understanding how a technology works is the key to getting the most out of it. That said, throughout this book I've tried to get beyond the conceptual and show how to put what we know about a technology's design to work. I don't think there's a better way to solidify new learning than to put it to practical use.

---

1. Einstein, Albert, as quoted by Helen Dukas in *Albert Einstein, the Human Side.* Princeton, NJ: Princeton University Press, 1981, p. 39.

Overview

The ability to search character and text fields is nothing new in the world of SQL databases. For years, DBMSs have provided facilities for searching character strings and fields for other strings. However, these facilities are usually rudimentary at best. Prior to the advent of full-text search support, SQL Server's built-in text searching tools were more of the garden-variety type—just beyond ANSI-compliance, but nothing to write home about. You could perform equality tests using character strings (as with all data types), and you could search for a pattern within a string (using LIKE and PATINDEX), but you couldn't do anything sophisticated such as search by word proximity or inflectional usage.

The addition of native full-text indexing support changed this. Traditionally, database architects who wanted advanced text searching had to rely on database gateways, operating system files, and technologies external to SQL Server. That's no longer the case. The Microsoft Search service provides the functionality of a full-blown text search engine such as Microsoft Indexing Service within the SQL Server environment. It's used to build the metadata necessary to support full-text searching and to process full-text search queries. The service itself runs only on the server version of the Windows NT operating system family (Windows NT Server and Advanced Server, Windows 2000 Server and Advanced Server, Windows Server 2003, and so on) and can be accessed by SQL Server clients on Windows 9x, Windows ME, Windows 2000 Professional, and Windows XP.

Architectural Details

The data maintained by Microsoft Search—the full-text indexes and catalog information it uses to service queries—is not stored in regular system tables and can't be accessed directly from SQL Server. It's stored in operating system files and is accessible only by the service itself and by NT administrators. By default, these files are located in the FTDATA folder under your root SQL Server installation path. These files are *not* backed up by regular database backups, so you must back them up separately (and synchronize these backups with the backup of their corresponding metadata within SQL Server) if you want to protect them from catastrophic loss.

It's helpful to think of Microsoft Search as a *text* server in the same way that SQL Server is a *SQL* or *database* server—it receives queries and instructions related to full-text searching and returns results appropriately. Its one client is SQL Server, which is how you access it.

Communication between SQL Server and Microsoft Search occurs via a full-text provider. This provider resides in SQLFTQRY.DLL in the binn folder under your default SQL Server installation. SQLFTQRY provides both administration and full-text query services to SQL Server. The sp_fulltext_... system procedures interact with it via the undocumented DBCC CALL-FULLTEXT command to carry out administrative tasks related to full-text indexes and Microsoft Search. The call interface to DBCC CALLFULL-TEXT looks like this:

```
DBCC CALLFULLTEXT(funcid[,catid][,objid][,sub])
```

DBCC CALLFULLTEXT requires one parameter and supports three additional optional ones: funcid specifies what function to perform and what parameters are valid, catid is the full-text catalog ID, objid is the object ID of the affected object, and sub is the subfunction ID if there is one. Note that CALLFULLTEXT is only valid within a system stored procedure. This procedure must have its system bit set (using the undocumented procedure sp_MS_marksystemobject) and its name must begin with sp_fulltext_. Table 16.1 lists the supported functions.

Listing 16.1 shows an example of a procedure that calls DBCC CALL-FULLTEXT directly.

Listing 16.1 Calling DBCC CALLFULLTEXT

```
USE master
GO
IF OBJECT_ID('sp_fulltext_resource') IS NOT NULL
  DROP PROC sp_fulltext_resource
GO
CREATE PROC sp_fulltext_resource @value int -- value for
                                            -- 'resource_usage'
AS
  DBCC CALLFULLTEXT(13,@value) -- FTSetResource (@value)
  IF (@@error<>0) RETURN 1
  -- SUCCESS --
RETURN 0 -- sp_fulltext_resource
GO

EXEC sp_MS_marksystemobject 'sp_fulltext_resource'
EXEC sp_fulltext_resource 3
```

Table 16.1 DBCC CALLFULLTEXT Functions

funcid	sub	Function	Parameters
1		Creates a catalog	Catalog ID, path
2		Drops a catalog	Catalog ID
3		Populates a catalog	Catalog ID, 0=full, 1=incremental
4		Stops a catalog population	Catalog ID
5		Adds table for FT indexing	Catalog ID, Object ID
6		Removes table from FT indexing	Catalog ID, Object ID
7		Drops all catalogs	Database ID
8		Performs catalog cleanup	
9		Disables FT auto-propagation	Object ID
10		Enables FT auto-propagation	Catalog ID, Object ID
11		Starts FT auto-propagation	Catalog ID, Object ID
12	0	Starts a full crawl for a table	Catalog ID, Object ID
12	1	Starts an incremental population for a table	
12	2	Stops a full/incremental population (crawl) for a table	Catalog ID, Object ID
13		Specifies the level of CPU resources allocated to Microsoft Search	Resource value (1–5; 1=background, 5=dedicated; default: 3)
14		Sets the connection timeout for FT connections to SQL Server	Connection timeout value in seconds (1–32767)
15		Sets the data (query) timeout for FT requests to SQL Server	Data (query) timeout value in seconds (1–32767)
16		Recreates a catalog (drops first)	Catalog ID, path

As a rule, you shouldn't call DBCC CALLFULLTEXT in your own code. The function IDs and parameters listed above could change between releases (this actually happened between the 7.0 and 2000 releases of SQL Server), and you could do serious damage to your full-text installation by calling a destructive function by accident. There's no good reason not to use

Enterprise Manager and the sp_fulltext_... procedures to manage the Microsoft Search service and your full-text indexes. I document the above so that you can understand how SQL Server's full-text searching facility works. I don't recommend that you make use of DBCC CALLFULLTEXT in production code.

Regardless of the number of instances of SQL Server installed on a machine, there will be only one instance of Microsoft Search running at any given time. This lone instance handles full-text index management for all SQL Server instances on the machine.

Full-Text Searches on Non–SQL Server Data

Microsoft Search can search only SQL Server data. The full-text indexes you build cover SQL Server data exclusively—you can't use them to search operating system files. You can, however, make use of the Microsoft Indexing Service and the OLE DB provider it supplies for performing searches against operating system files. And, via a linked server or distributed query, you can access this provider from T-SQL and even use it in joins with regular full-text search queries against SQL Server objects. Using SQL Server's full-text search rowset and predicate functions coupled with linked server or OPENQUERY/OPENROWSET references that make use of the Microsoft OLE DB Provider for Indexing Service, you can combine the results from full-text queries within SQL Server with full-text searches against files outside of SQL Server.

Full-Text Searches on Binary Data

Because they can contain characters that are invalid in SQL Server character data types such as text, char, and nchar, data files from products such as Microsoft Word and Microsoft Excel cannot be stored in regular SQL Server character columns. Instead, they must be stored in image columns if you want to be able to store any byte value a file might contain and want to be able to store files larger than 8K (binary and varbinary columns can be used for files smaller than 8K).

SQL Server can create a full-text index over an image column and automatically recognize certain types of external data. It does this via file extension–based "filters." A filter simply identifies a particular type of binary data using a file extension. Normally, this file extension would be part of an external file name. However, within a SQL Server table, you associate a file extension with a particular image column value by setting up a column in the same table to contain the file extension for each row's binary data. You then supply this column name as the Document type column when you set up the table for full-text indexing in the Full-Text Indexing Wizard. (You can also specify this column via sp_fulltext_column's @type_colname parameter if you are creating the full-text index via stored procedures.)

Currently, SQL Server supports five filter types: .DOC (Microsoft Word), .XLS (Microsoft Excel), .PPT (Microsoft PowerPoint), .TXT (text files), and .HTM (Hypertext Markup Language). A table that stores binary file data using this technique can store a different format in each row. For example, you could have a Word document in one row, followed by an Excel document in another, and an HTML file in yet another. Each row's file extension column would identify the type of data it contained and direct Microsoft Search to use the appropriate filter.

Once an image type with the appropriate filter has been properly indexed, you can execute full-text queries over it just as you would any other type of column. The full-text indexes created over these types of columns are the same as those created over more traditional character columns.

TIP: Using a DTS package and a Read File transformation is an excellent way to load data from external sources such as Word documents and Excel spreadsheets into a SQL Server database so that it can be full-text indexed. A Read File transformation can load the contents of an operating system file into a column in a table. You set up a table that lists the file names to load, then configure the transformation to read the files listed in the table and post their contents to a column in the destination table. It's trivial to set up and allows you to easily load large numbers of files into a database table. See Chapter 20 on DTS for more information on Read File transformations.

Setting Up Full-Text Indexes

Setting up full-text indexes is not a one-step process. With increased flexibility often comes increased complexity. Assuming the Microsoft Search service is started, the process required to set up a specific table column so that it can be searched with full-text search syntax such as the CONTAINS predicate and the FREETEXTTABLE rowset function includes six steps.

1. Full-text indexing must be enabled in the host database.
2. Full-text catalogs must be created for the database.
3. Full-text indexing must then be enabled for the host table and associated with a full-text catalog.

4. The column is then added to the table's full-text index.
5. This full-text index is then activated.
6. The full-text catalog must then be populated. This population can be a full or incremental population. Of course, the initial population of a full-text index is always a full population. Subsequent populations can be incremental if the table contains a timestamp column and if its metadata hasn't changed since the last population. You can also enable change tracking such that changes to an indexed column are recorded and the full-text index is updated as they occur, or on demand, or based on a schedule. To enable change tracking for a specific table, right-click the table in Enterprise Manager and select Change Tracking from the Full-Text Index Table menu. (You can also enable change tracking by passing start_change_tracking in sp_fulltext_table's @action parameter.)

As with most SQL Server administrative tasks, the best tool for creating full-text indexes is Enterprise Manager. The process required is too tedious to do by hand frequently. That said, it's instructive to set up full-text indexes using Transact-SQL because you get a better feel for what's going on behind the scenes and how the whole facility works than you do by clicking through a wizard in Enterprise Manager. Listing 16.2 shows some sample code that illustrates how to set up a full-text search column using nothing but Transact-SQL. (I've numbered the steps in the code to correspond to the previous list.)

Listing 16.2 Setting Up a Full-Text Search Column

```
USE pubs
DECLARE @tablename sysname, @catalogname sysname,
    @indexname sysname, @columnname sysname

SET @tablename='pub_info'
SET @catalogname='pubsCatalog'
SET @indexname='UPKCL_pubinfo'
SET @columnname='pr_info'

-- STEP 1: Enable FTS for the database
EXEC sp_fulltext_database  'enable'

-- STEP 2: Create a full-text catalog
EXEC sp_fulltext_catalog @catalogname, 'create'
```

```
-- STEP 3: Create a full-text index for the table
EXEC sp_fulltext_table @tablename,'create',@catalogname,@indexname

-- STEP 4: Add the column to it
EXEC sp_fulltext_column @tablename, @columnname, 'add'

-- STEP 5: Activate the newly created FT index
EXEC sp_fulltext_table @tablename,'activate'

-- STEP 6: Populate the newly created FT catalog
EXEC sp_fulltext_catalog @catalogname, 'start_full'
```

This code sets up full-text indexing on the pr_info column in pubs.pub_info. This is a text column, so it's a good candidate for full-text indexing. For simplicity's sake, the routine makes a number of assumptions that may not be valid in the real world. For example, it doesn't check to see whether the full-text catalog exists before attempting to create it. If the catalog already exists, the statement and the batch will fail. The same is true of the full-text index on the pub_info table. Each table can have just one full-text index. Attempting to create a second full-text index or recreate an existing one results in an error. The routine in Listing 16.2 serves merely to demonstrate the basics of setting up full-text indexing using Transact-SQL.

Much of the information that we need to check before calling the full-text stored procedures can be accessed via metadata functions. For example, you can use the FULLTEXTCATALOGPROPERTY function to determine whether a given catalog exists. (The function returns NULL when passed a nonexistent name.) You can determine whether a table has a full-text index via the OBJECTPROPERTY function and whether a column has been added to a full-text index by using the COLUMNPROPERTY function. Listing 16.3 presents a stored procedure that makes use of these functions and a few others to set up a column for full-text indexing in a much more reliable fashion. It's significantly more robust than the example in Listing 16.2 and much safer to use in the real world.

Listing 16.3 A Stored Procedure to Set Up a Full-Text Column

```
USE master
GO
IF OBJECT_ID('sp_enable_fulltext') IS NOT NULL
  DROP PROC sp_enable_fulltext
```

```
GO
CREATE PROC sp_enable_fulltext @tablename sysname,
    @columnname sysname=NULL, @catalogname sysname=NULL,
    @startserver varchar(3)='NO'
/*

Object: sp_enable_fulltext
Description: Enables full-text indexing for a specified column
  Usage: sp_enable_fulltext @tablename=name of host table,
    @columnname=column to set up, [,@catalogname=name of full-text
    catalog to use (Default: DB_NAME()+"Catalog")]
    [,@startsrever=YES|NO specifies whether to start the
    Microsoft Search service on this machine prior to setting up
    the column (Default: YES)]
  Returns: (None)
  Created by: Ken Henderson. Email: khen@khen.com
  Example: EXEC sp_enable_fulltext "pubs..pub_info","pr_info",
    DEFAULT,"YES"
  Created: 1999-06-14.  Last changed: 1999-07-14.

*/
AS
SET NOCOUNT ON

IF (@tablename='/?') OR (@columnname IS NULL) OR
    (OBJECT_ID(@tablename) IS NULL) GOTO Help

IF (FULLTEXTSERVICEPROPERTY('IsFulltextInstalled')=0)
    BEGIN -- Search engine's not installed
  RAISERROR('The Microsoft Search service is not installed on
      server %s',16,10,@@SERVERNAME)
  RETURN -1
END

DECLARE @catalogstatus int, @indexname sysname

IF (UPPER(@startserver)='YES')
  EXEC master..xp_cmdshell 'NET START mssearch', no_output

IF (@catalogname IS NULL)
  SET @catalogname=DB_NAME()+'Catalog'

CREATE TABLE #indexes ( -- Used to located a unique index for use
                        -- with FTS
```

```
Qualifier          sysname NULL,
Owner              sysname NULL,
TableName          sysname NULL,
NonUnique          smallint NULL,
IndexQualifier     sysname NULL,
IndexName          sysname NULL,
Type               smallint NULL,
PositionInIndex    smallint NULL,
ColumnName         sysname NULL,
Collation          char(1) NULL,
Cardinality        int NULL,
Pages              int NULL,
FilterCondition    sysname NULL)

INSERT #indexes
EXEC sp_statistics @tablename

SELECT @indexname=IndexName FROM #indexes WHERE NonUnique=0
    -- Get a unique index on the table (gets LAST if multiple)

DROP TABLE #indexes

IF (@indexname IS NULL) BEGIN -- If no unique indexes, abort
  RAISERROR('No suitable unique index found on table %s',16,
      10,@tablename)
  RETURN -1
END

IF (DATABASEPROPERTY(DB_NAME(),'IsFulltextEnabled')<>1)
    -- Enable FTS for the database
  EXEC sp_fulltext_database  'enable'

SET @catalogstatus=FULLTEXTCATALOGPROPERTY(@catalogname,
    'PopulateStatus')

IF (@catalogstatus IS NULL) -- Doesn't yet exist
  EXEC sp_fulltext_catalog @catalogname, 'create'
ELSE IF (@catalogstatus IN (0,1,3,4,6,7)) -- Population in
    progress, Throttled, Recovering, Incremental Population in
    Progress or Updating Index
  EXEC sp_fulltext_catalog @catalogname, 'stop'

IF (OBJECTPROPERTY(OBJECT_ID(@tablename),
    'TableHasActiveFullTextIndex')=0) -- Create full-text index
                                      -- if not already present
```

```
    EXEC sp_fulltext_table @tablename,'create',@catalogname,
        @indexname
ELSE
    EXEC sp_fulltext_table @tablename,'deactivate'  -- Deactivate it
                                        -- so we can make changes to it

IF (COLUMNPROPERTY(OBJECT_ID(@tablename),@columnname,
    'IsFulltextIndexed')=0) BEGIN -- Add the column to the index
    EXEC sp_fulltext_column @tablename, @columnname, 'add'
    PRINT 'Successfully added a full-text index for '+@tablename+
        '.'+@columnname+' in database '+DB_NAME()
END ELSE
    PRINT 'Column '+@columnname+' in table '+DB_NAME()+'.'+
        @tablename+' is already full-text indexed'

EXEC sp_fulltext_table @tablename,'activate'

EXEC sp_fulltext_catalog @catalogname, 'start_full'
RETURN 0

Help:
EXEC sp_usage @objectname='sp_enable_fulltext',@desc='Enables
    full-text indexing for a specified column',
@parameters='@tablename=name of host table, @columnname=column
    to set up,
[,@catalogname=name of full-text catalog to use (Default:
    DB_NAME()+"Catalog")][,@startsrever=YES|NO specifies whether
    to start the Microsoft Search service on this machine prior to
    setting up the column (Default: YES)]',
@author='Ken Henderson', @email='khen@khen.com',
@datecreated='19990614',@datelastchanged='19990714',
@example='EXEC sp_enable_fulltext "pubs..pub_info","pr_info",
    DEFAULT,"YES"'
RETURN -1

sp_enable_fulltext 'pub_info','pr_info'

Successfully added a full-text index for pub_info.pr_info
in database pubs
```

This procedure does a number of interesting things. It begins by check-ing to see whether the Microsoft Search service has been installed. If it hasn't, the procedure aborts immediately. Next, it uses xp_cmdshell to start the Microsoft Search service if asked to do so. (The command has no effect if the service is already running.) This is done via the NET START mssearch operating system command. NET START is the Windows NT command syntax for starting a service, and mssearch is the internal name of the Microsoft Search service. (You can also start the service via Enterprise Manager, the Services applet in the Windows NT Control Panel, and the SQL Server Service Manager.)

The procedure next retrieves a unique key table index for the specified table. Adding a full-text index to a table requires a unique key index. Here, the procedure traps the output of sp_statistics (which lists a table's indexes) in a temporary table via INSERT...EXEC, then scans that table for a unique index on the table. If it doesn't find one, it aborts immediately.

Next, the procedure checks to see whether the database is enabled for full-text indexing. If not, the procedure enables it. The code next checks the status of the full-text catalog. If it's nonexistent, the routine creates it. If it's active, it shuts down the catalog so that changes can be made to it.

Once the full-text catalog is in place, the routine creates a full-text index for the table after checking with OBJECTPROPERTY to ensure that a full-text index doesn't already exist. This is where the unique index that the routine located earlier is used.

After the full-text index has been set up, the routine adds the specified column to it. The procedure takes the name of the column that was passed into it and adds it to the table's full-text index using sp_fulltext_column. This tells the server that you want to build an index to track advanced search information for the specified column but doesn't actually activate the index or populate it with data. That comes next.

The routine finishes by calling sp_fulltext_table and sp_fulltext_catalog to activate the new full-text index and populate it with data. Once these processes complete, you can begin using full-text predicates and rowset functions that reference the newly indexed column.

Full-Text Predicates

A predicate is a logical construct that returns TRUE or NOT TRUE. (I'll avoid FALSE here because of the issues related to three-value logic.) In SQL, these usually take the form of functions and reside in the WHERE clause. LIKE and EXISTS are examples of WHERE clause predicates.

When full-text searching is enabled, two additional predicates are available in Transact-SQL: CONTAINS and FREETEXT. CONTAINS provides support for both exact and inexact string matches, searches based on word proximity, word inflection searches, and weighted searches. FREETEXT, by contrast, is used to find words or phrases with the same basic *meaning* as those in the search term.

Before we begin exploring these functions via code, let's enable full-text searching on the Employees table in the Northwind database. Employees includes a Notes text column that's ideal for full-text searching. You can use the sp_enable_fulltext procedure discussed above to set it up, like so:

```
EXEC northwind..sp_enable_fulltext 'Employees','notes'
```

This should create the necessary metadata and indexing information to allow the full-text search functions to work properly.

The CONTAINS Predicate

CONTAINS locates rows that contain a word or words or variations of them. It can perform exact and inexact word locations, word proximity searches, and inflectional searches. You can think of it as the LIKE predicate on steroids. Listing 16.4 presents an example that uses CONTAINS to find all the people in the Employees table whose Notes fields mention the word "English."

Listing 16.4 Using CONTAINS

```
SELECT LastName, FirstName, Notes
FROM EMPLOYEES
WHERE CONTAINS(Notes,'English')
```

(Results abridged)

```
LastName             FirstName   Notes
-------------------  ----------  --------------------------------
Peacock              Margaret    Margaret holds a BA in English lit
Dodsworth            Anne        Anne has a BA degree in English fr
King                 Robert      ...completing his degree in English
```

Note that since we're searching all the full-text index columns in Employees (there's only one), we could have substituted ° for the column name and achieved the same result, like this:

```
SELECT LastName, FirstName, Notes
FROM EMPLOYEES
WHERE CONTAINS(*,'English')
```

CONTAINS supports word proximity searches as well. Listing 16.5 shows a refinement of the last example that narrows the employees listed to those whose Notes fields contain the word "degree" located near the word "English."

Listing 16.5 Refining a Search

```
SELECT LastName, FirstName, Notes
FROM EMPLOYEES
WHERE CONTAINS(*,'degree NEAR English')
```

(Results abridged)

```
LastName              FirstName  Notes
--------------------  ---------- ----------------------------------
Dodsworth             Anne       Anne has a BA degree in English fr
King                  Robert     ...completing his degree in English
```

This time, only two rows are listed because Margaret Peacock's Notes field doesn't contain the word "degree" at all. Note that the tilde character (~) is synonymous with NEAR, so we could rewrite the beginning of Listing 16.5 like this:

```
SELECT LastName, FirstName, Notes
FROM EMPLOYEES
WHERE CONTAINS(*,'degree ~ English')
```

The search condition string also supports Boolean expressions, as shown in Listing 16.6.

Listing 16.6 Searching with Boolean Expressions

```
SELECT LastName, FirstName, Notes
FROM EMPLOYEES
WHERE CONTAINS(Notes,'English OR German')
```

(Results abridged)

LastName	FirstName	Notes
Peacock	Margaret	Margaret holds a BA in English lit
Dodsworth	Anne	Anne has a BA degree in English fr
Fuller	Andrew	...and reads German
King	Robert	...completing his degree in English

This query returns those rows containing the words "English" or "German." The exact or relative positions of the words are unimportant—if either of the words appear anywhere in the Notes column, the row is returned.

In this use, CONTAINS behaves similarly to LIKE, but there's one important difference—CONTAINS is sensitive to word boundaries; LIKE isn't. For example, here's the query rewritten to use LIKE:

```
SELECT LastName, FirstName, Notes
FROM EMPLOYEES
WHERE Notes LIKE '%English%'
OR Notes LIKE '%German%'
```

It looks similar, but this query doesn't really ask the same question as the CONTAINS query. It will find matches with variations of the search words and even with words that happen to contain them (e.g., Germantown, Englishman, Germanic, Burgerman, and so on). The CONTAINS query, by contrast, is word-savvy—it knows the difference between English and Englishman and is smart enough to return only what you ask for.

CONTAINS also supports prefix-based wildcards. Unfortunately, they're more like operating system wildcards than standard SQL wildcards. Listing 16.7 shows an example.

Listing 16.7 Searching with Wildcards

```
SELECT LastName, FirstName, Notes
FROM EMPLOYEES
WHERE CONTAINS(*,'"psy*" OR "chem*"')
```

(Result abridged)

```
LastName              FirstName  Notes
-------------------   ---------- ------------------------------------
Leverling             Janet      Janet has a BS degree in chemistry
Davolio               Nancy      Education includes a BA in psychol
Callahan              Laura      Laura received a BA in psychology
```

This query locates all rows with Notes fields containing words that begin with "psy" or "chem." Note that neither single-character wildcards nor wildcards that appear at the start of a search term are supported.

Quotes are used within the condition string to delineate search strings from one another. When wildcards and multiple terms are present in the search criteria string, quotes are required; omitting them will cause the query to fail.

A really powerful aspect of CONTAINS is its support for inflectional searches. The ability to search based on word forms is a potent and often very useful addition to the Transact-SQL repertoire. Listing 16.8 illustrates how to search for the forms of a word.

Listing 16.8 Searching for Forms of a Word

```
SELECT LastName, FirstName, Notes
FROM EMPLOYEES
WHERE CONTAINS(*,'FORMSOF(INFLECTIONAL,complete)')
```

(Results abridged)

```
LastName              FirstName  Notes
-------------------   ---------- ------------------------------------
Leverling             Janet      ...completed a certificate program
Davolio               Nancy      ...She also completed "The Art of t
King                  Robert     ...completing his degree in English
```

```
Buchanan              Steven      ...has completed the courses
Callahan              Laura       ...completed a course in business F
```

You can use the FORMSOF clause to locate the different tenses of a verb as well as the singular and plural forms of a noun. In this case, the code finds five rows that contain forms of the word "complete" including "completed" and "completing."

The FREETEXT Predicate

FREETEXT is useful for locating rows containing words that have the same basic meaning as those in a search string. Unlike CONTAINS, FREETEXT allows you to specify a series of terms that are then weighted internally and matched with values in the full-text column(s). Listing 16.9 presents an example that locates employees with college degrees, especially bachelor's degrees.

Listing 16.9 Using FREETEXT

```
SELECT LastName, FirstName, Notes
FROM EMPLOYEES
WHERE FREETEXT(Notes,'BA BTS BS BSC degree')
```

(Results abridged)

```
LastName              FirstName   Notes
-------------------   ----------  -----------------------------------
Leverling             Janet       Janet has a BS degree in chemistry
Davolio               Nancy       Education includes a BA in psychol
Peacock               Margaret    Margaret holds a BA in English lit
Dodsworth             Anne        Anne has a BA degree in English fr
Fuller                Andrew      Andrew received his BTS commercial
King                  Robert      Robert King [completed] his degree
Buchanan              Steven      Steven Buchanan graduated with a B
Callahan              Laura       Laura received a BA in psychology
```

Here, any row containing any of the terms or similar words are returned. As with CONTAINS, * is used to signify all full-text indexed columns in the table.

Rowset Functions

Transact-SQL defines a special class of functions called rowset functions that can be used in place of tables in the FROM clauses of queries. Rowset functions return result sets in a fashion similar to a derived table and can be joined with real tables, summarized, grouped, and so on. There are two rowset functions related to full-text searching: CONTAINSTABLE and FREETEXTTABLE. These are rowset versions of the predicates discussed earlier in the chapter. Rather than being used in the WHERE clause, these functions typically appear in the FROM clause of a SELECT statement. They return a result set consisting of index key values and row rankings.

The CONTAINSTABLE Rowset Function

Despite the fact that it's a rowset function rather than a predicate, the CONTAINSTABLE function works very similarly to CONTAINS, as its name would suggest. It supports the same search string criteria as CONTAINS and requires one parameter—the name of the underlying table—in addition to those required by the predicate. Listing 16.10 presents an example that uses CONTAINSTABLE to produce a list of key values and search rankings.

Listing 16.10 Using CONTAINSTABLE

```
SELECT *
FROM CONTAINSTABLE(Employees,*,'English OR French OR Italian
    OR German OR Flemish')
ORDER BY RANK DESC
```

(Results)

KEY	RANK
8	64
2	64
4	48
7	48
9	48
6	32
5	32

CONTAINSTABLE returns two columns: the key value of the row from the underlying table and a ranking of each row. In this example, we use the RANK column to sequence the rows logically such that higher rankings are listed first. The key value can be used to join back to the original table in order to translate the key into something a bit more meaningful, as you'll see in a moment.

The rankings returned by the RANK column can be tailored to your needs by using the ISABOUT function of the search criteria string, as shown in Listing 16.11.

Listing 16.11 Using ISABOUT

```
SELECT *
FROM CONTAINSTABLE(Employees,*,'ISABOUT(English weight(.8),
    French weight(.1), Italian weight(.2), German weight(.4),
    Flemish weight(0.0))')
ORDER BY RANK DESC
```

(Results)

KEY	RANK
9	85
2	54
4	47
7	47
8	7
6	3
5	3

In this example, weights are assigned for each language skill specifically indicated by an employee's Notes entry, ranging from 0.0 for Flemish to 0.8 for English. Valid weights range from 0.0 to 1.0. As in the previous example, we use the RANK column to sequence the rows such that higher rankings are listed first. ISABOUT is also available with the CONTAINS predicate but has no effect since its only purpose is to alter the RANK column, which is not used by the predicate.

To generate results that are truly meaningful, you need to join the result set returned by CONTAINSTABLE with its underlying table. The key values and rankings returned by the function itself aren't terribly useful without some correlation to the original data. Listing 16.12 presents an example.

Listing 16.12 Joining the Result Set with Its Underlying Table

```
SELECT R.RANK, E.LastName, E.FirstName, E.Notes
FROM Employees AS E JOIN
CONTAINSTABLE(Employees,*,'ISABOUT(English weight(.8),
    French weight(.1), Italian weight(.2), German weight(.4),
    Flemish weight(0.0))') AS R ON (E.EmployeeId=R.[KEY])
ORDER BY R.RANK DESC
```

(Results abridged)

```
RANK          LastName    FirstName   Notes
-----------   ----------  ----------  -------------------------------
85            Dodsworth   Anne        ...is fluent in French and German.
54            Fuller      Andrew      ...fluent in French and Italian ... G
47            Peacock     Margaret    Margaret holds a BA in English l
47            King        Robert      ...before completing his degree in
7             Callahan    Laura       ...reads and writes French
3             Suyama      Michael     ...can read and write French, Port
3             Buchanan    Steven      ...is fluent in French
```

A simple inner join using the Employees table's EmployeeID column and the KEY column from the CONTAINSTABLE function is all that's required to link the two tables. KEY contains the value of the EmployeeID column in the rows returned by CONTAINSTABLE, so this makes sense.

As with the earlier examples, this query sequences its result set using the RANK column returned by CONTAINSTABLE. Note the use of brackets ([]) around the reference to the KEY column returned by CONTAINSTABLE. Inexplicably, SQL Server uses KEY as a column name for CONTAINSTABLE even though it's a reserved word. This necessitates surrounding it with brackets (or double quotes if the QUOTED_IDENTIFIER setting is enabled) any time you reference it directly.

To see the effect of the rank weighting, let's revise the query to use the default ranking returned by Microsoft Search (Listing 16.13).

Listing 16.13 Using the Default Ranking

```
SELECT R.RANK, E.LastName, E.FirstName, E.Notes
FROM Employees AS E JOIN
CONTAINSTABLE(Employees,*,'English OR French OR Italian OR German
    OR Flemish') AS R ON (E.EmployeeId=R.[KEY])
ORDER BY R.RANK DESC
```

(Results abridged)

```
RANK        LastName    FirstName   Notes
----------- ----------- ----------- -------------------------------
64          Fuller      Andrew      ...fluent in French and Italian ... G
64          Callahan    Laura       ...reads and writes French
48          Peacock     Margaret    Margaret holds a BA in English l
48          King        Robert      ...before completing his degree in
48          Dodsworth   Anne        ...is fluent in French and German.
32          Suyama      Michael     ...can read and write French, Port
32          Buchanan    Steven      ...is fluent in French
```

As you can see, the custom weighting we supplied makes a noticeable difference. It changes much of the order in which the rows are listed.

The FREETEXTTABLE Rowset Function

As with its predicate cousin, FREETEXTTABLE locates rows containing words with the same basic meaning as those specified in the search criteria. The format of its search criteria string is open-ended ("free") and has no specific syntax. The search engine extracts each word from the string and assigns it a weight, then locates rows accordingly. Listing 16.14 performs the earlier search that locates employees with bachelor's degrees but is rewritten to use FREETEXTTABLE.

Listing 16.14 Using FREETEXTTABLE

```
SELECT R.RANK, E.LastName, E.FirstName, E.Notes
FROM Employees AS E JOIN
FREETEXTTABLE(Employees,*,'BA BTS BS BCS degree') AS R ON
    (E.EmployeeId=R.[KEY])
ORDER BY R.RANK DESC
```

(Results)

```
RANK          LastName               FirstName   Notes
-----------   --------------------   ----------  ----------------------
24            Leverling              Janet       Janet has a BS degree
10            Fuller                 Andrew      Andrew received his BT
16            Dodsworth              Anne        Anne has a BA degree i
8             Peacock                Margaret    Margaret holds a BA in
8             Callahan               Laura       Laura received a BA in
8             Davolio                Nancy       Education includes a B
8             King                   Robert      Robert King completing
8             Buchanan               Steven      with a BSC degree in 1
```

With such a broad criteria string, the query returns all but one row in the Employees table. Each of these has some form of one of the words listed in the search criteria string.

Recap

SQL Server's FTS facility is a potent tool that provides most of the functionality of standalone file-based search engines. Enabling columns for text searching is nontrivial and you should use Enterprise Manager or the sp_enable_fulltext stored procedure (included in this chapter) to set them up. Once a column has been set up for full-text searches, the CONTAINS and FREETEXT predicates, as well as the CONTAINSTABLE and FREE-TEXTTABLE rowset functions, become available for use. They offer a powerful alternative to commonplace search implements such as LIKE and PATINDEX.

Knowledge Measure

1. What's the name of the DLL that SQL Server uses to interact with the Microsoft Search engine?
2. What undocumented DBCC command is used by the sp_fulltext... procedures to interact with the Microsoft Search service?

3. True or false: SQL Server's FTS facility can be installed on Windows 2000 Server but not on Windows 2000 Professional.
4. Name the two new predicate functions you can use on tables that have been full-text indexed.
5. What's the maximum number of full-text indexes a single table can have?
6. Is it possible to query both full-text indexed data and files that have been indexed by the Microsoft Indexing Service from the same T-SQL query?
7. Name the two new rowset functions you can use with tables that have been full-text indexed.
8. What T-SQL function can you call to determine whether SQL Server's FTS facility has been installed?
9. True or false: Full-text indexes are stored in the sysfulltextindexes system table.
10. Is it possible to configure the amount of time the Microsoft Search service will wait on a connection to SQL Server to complete before timing out?

PART III

Data Services

CHAPTER 17

Server Federations

*I am convinced that a vivid consciousness of the primary importance
of moral principles for the betterment and ennoblement of life
does not need the idea of a lawgiver, especially a lawgiver who
works on the basis of reward and punishment.*

—Albert Einstein[1]

A SQL Server federation is a group of SQL Servers that have had a distributed partitioned view spread horizontally across them. Each server in the federation stores only part of the view's underlying data. Each has the full view definition and can use its metadata to determine the actual server that stores the physical data a query against the partitioned view seeks. In this way, the group of servers acts as a loose federation of SQL Servers. In terms of scalability, it allows an organization to "scale out" horizontally rather than (or in addition to) scaling up to a more powerful server machine.

You create a federation of SQL Servers by creating a distributed partitioned view that spans them. In this chapter, we'll talk about partitioned views (both local and distributed), then discuss how to create distributed partitioned views. We'll explore performance issues associated with partitioned views and delve into a few execution plans. This updates the coverage of partitioned views in my last book, *The Guru's Guide to SQL Server Stored Procedures, XML, and HTML.*

Partitioned Views

Simply put, a partitioned view is a view that unions tables together that serve as partitions—or sections—of a larger set of data. For example, a partitioned

---

1. Einstein, Albert. Letter to M. Berkowitz, October 25, 1950. Reprinted in *The Expanded Quotable Einstein*, ed. Alice Calaprice. Princeton, NJ: Princeton University Press, 2000, p. 216.

view over the activity on a Web site might union together separate tables for each month of the year. Each of these tables would store the activity data for a particular month. By unioning them together, the partitioned view would allow them to be treated as a single table while still keeping their sizes manageable.

There are two types of partitioned views—local partitioned views (LPVs) and distributed partitioned views (DPVs). An LPV is a view in which all the underlying tables reside on the same SQL Server instance. A DPV is a view in which they live on separate instances. These instances don't have to be on different machines, but usually they are. Spreading a DPV across multiple machines helps "scale out" large SQL Server implementations. It can effectively bring the processing power and resources of many machines together to process a single query.

A partitioned view is a normal view object that unions together tables with certain attributes. It is characterized by tables with the same structure that are combined to provide a unified view of a set of data but are segmented on a clearly defined "partitioning column." This partitioning column is set up using a CHECK constraint. In addition to doing what CHECK constraints always do—namely, controlling the type of data a column will accept—the partitioning column of an LPV or a DPV provides a means for the SQL Server query optimizer to be able to determine which partition a given column value resides in as it creates a query plan. This allows it to eliminate searches for the other partitions from the query plan when optimizing a query that includes the partitioning column.

This is best understood by way of example (Listing 17.1).

Listing 17.1 A Basic Partitioned View

```
CREATE TABLE CustomersUS (
   CustomerID nchar (5) NOT NULL,
   CompanyName nvarchar (40) NOT NULL ,
   ContactName nvarchar (30) NULL ,
   ContactTitle nvarchar (30) NULL ,
   Address nvarchar (60) NULL ,
   City nvarchar (15) NULL ,
   Region nvarchar (15) NULL ,
   PostalCode nvarchar (10) NULL ,
   Country nvarchar (15) NOT NULL CHECK (Country='US'),
   Phone nvarchar (24) NULL ,
   Fax nvarchar (24) NULL,
CONSTRAINT PK_CustUS PRIMARY KEY (Country, CustomerID)
)
```

```
CREATE TABLE CustomersUK (
  CustomerID nchar (5) NOT NULL,
  CompanyName nvarchar (40) NOT NULL ,
  ContactName nvarchar (30) NULL ,
  ContactTitle nvarchar (30) NULL ,
  Address nvarchar (60) NULL ,
  City nvarchar (15) NULL ,
  Region nvarchar (15) NULL ,
  PostalCode nvarchar (10) NULL ,
  Country nvarchar (15) NOT NULL CHECK (Country='UK'),
  Phone nvarchar (24) NULL ,
  Fax nvarchar (24) NULL,
CONSTRAINT PK_CustUK PRIMARY KEY (Country, CustomerID)
)

CREATE TABLE CustomersFrance (
  CustomerID nchar (5) NOT NULL,
  CompanyName nvarchar (40) NOT NULL ,
  ContactName nvarchar (30) NULL ,
  ContactTitle nvarchar (30) NULL ,
  Address nvarchar (60) NULL ,
  City nvarchar (15) NULL ,
  Region nvarchar (15) NULL ,
  PostalCode nvarchar (10) NULL ,
  Country nvarchar (15) NOT NULL CHECK (Country='France'),
  Phone nvarchar (24) NULL ,
  Fax nvarchar (24) NULL,
CONSTRAINT PK_CustFR PRIMARY KEY (Country, CustomerID)
)

GO

DROP VIEW CustomersV
GO

CREATE VIEW CustomersV
AS
SELECT * FROM dbo.CustomersUS
UNION ALL
SELECT * FROM dbo.CustomersUK
UNION ALL
SELECT * FROM dbo.CustomersFrance
GO
```

As you can see, we create three tables to store partitions, or slices, of a customer table. We then union those tables back together using a partitioned view. What's the point? Why not store the data as a single table? There are two advantages to using this approach: (1) By segmenting the customer data, we keep the tables more manageable—the individual partitions will be a fraction of the size of the entire customer table; and (2) SQL Server's query optimizer can recognize partitioned views and automatically determine the right underlying table to query based on the filter criteria and the CHECK constraint on the partitioning column. For example, have a look at the execution plan of the following query:

```
SELECT * FROM dbo.Customersv WHERE Country='US'
```

(Results abridged)

```
StmtText
-----------------------------------------------------------------
SELECT CompanyName=CompanyName FROM dbo.CustomersV WHERE Country=@
  |--Compute Scalar(DEFINE:(CustomersUS.CompanyName=CustomersUS.Co
     |--Clustered Index Scan(OBJECT:(Northwind.dbo.CustomersUS.P
```

Even though we reference the view in our query, the optimizer figures out that the data we're requesting could only reside in one of the view's underlying tables, so it queries that table directly and omits the others from the query plan. It uses the WHERE clause criteria and the partitioning column in each table (its primary key) to make this determination.

There are a number of requirements that a view and its base tables must meet in order for the view to be a partitioned view in the first place and for the optimizer to be able to optimize queries against it in this way. The number and significance of these requirements have, in fact, discouraged many users from taking advantage of partitioned views, especially LPVs. Whether you use them is a judgment call you'll have to make; you can read up on the requirements and limitations associated with partitioned views in Books Online. Regarding the optimizer's ability to use the partitioning column to identify the correct base table to search for data, it has been my experience that the partitioning column should be the leftmost in the primary key. This bears further examination. Consider the partitioned view and query shown in Listing 17.2.

Listing 17.2 A Partitioning Column/Primary Key Mismatch

```
CREATE TABLE Orders1996 (
  OrderID int PRIMARY KEY NOT NULL ,
```

```
    CustomerID nchar (5) NULL ,
    EmployeeID int NULL ,
    OrderDate datetime NOT NULL CHECK (Year(OrderDate)=1996),
    OrderYear int NOT NULL CHECK (OrderYear=1996),
    RequiredDate datetime NULL ,
    ShippedDate datetime NULL ,
    ShipVia int NULL
)
GO


CREATE TABLE Orders1997 (
    OrderID int PRIMARY KEY NOT NULL ,
    CustomerID nchar (5) NULL ,
    EmployeeID int NULL ,
    OrderDate datetime NOT NULL CHECK (Year(OrderDate)=1997),
    OrderYear int NOT NULL CHECK (OrderYear=1997),
    RequiredDate datetime NULL ,
    ShippedDate datetime NULL ,
    ShipVia int NULL
)
GO


CREATE TABLE Orders1998 (
    OrderID int PRIMARY KEY NOT NULL ,
    CustomerID nchar (5) NULL ,
    EmployeeID int NULL ,
    OrderDate datetime NOT NULL CHECK (Year(OrderDate)=1998),
    OrderYear int NOT NULL CHECK (OrderYear=1998),
    RequiredDate datetime NULL ,
    ShippedDate datetime NULL ,
    ShipVia int NULL
)
GO


CREATE VIEW OrdersV
AS
SELECT * FROM Orders1996
UNION ALL
SELECT * FROM Orders1997
UNION ALL
SELECT * FROM Orders1998
GO


SELECT * FROM OrdersV WHERE OrderYear=1997
```

Will the optimizer be able to narrow its search to just the Orders1997 partition? Let's look at the execution plan:

(Results abridged)

```
-----------------------------------------------------------------
Executes    StmtText
----------  -----------------------------------------------------
1           SELECT * FROM [OrdersV] WHERE [OrderYear]=@1
1             |--Concatenation
1                  |--Filter(WHERE:(STARTUP EXPR(Convert([@1])=199
0                  |     |--Clustered Index Scan(OBJECT:([Northwind
1                  |--Filter(WHERE:(STARTUP EXPR(Convert([@1])=199
1                  |     |--Clustered Index Scan(OBJECT:([Northwind
1                  |--Filter(WHERE:(STARTUP EXPR(Convert([@1])=199
0                        |--Clustered Index Scan(OBJECT:([Northwind
```

At first glance, it might appear that even though we're querying data from only one of the partitions, the query plan includes searches for all three of them—but have a closer look. Note the Executes column. It indicates the number of times the corresponding query step was executed. In this case, it tells us that only one of the tables is actually searched. The other two have a 0 in their Executes column. This means that even though the partition could not be eliminated at compile-time, the server was able to get rid of it at runtime. Runtime partition elimination is a very handy feature that allows a plan to be used with a greater number of input parameters than one in which partitions are eliminated when a plan is first compiled. When a partition is eliminated at compile-time, it can service only user queries that end up querying the same partition. With runtime partition elimination, the plan can be used for any potential parameter value, regardless of the partition it eventually routes to.

Despite the fact that runtime partition elimination generally leads to better plan reuse, you may be wondering why the optimizer doesn't eliminate the unneeded partitions at compile-time. In order to get the optimizer to eliminate the unused partitions at compile-time, we need to include all the columns from the primary key in the query's filter criteria. Listing 17.3 shows such a revision and its resultant execution plan.

Listing 17.3 Matching Up the Partitioning Column and Primary Key to Eliminate Partitions from the Execution Plan

```
SELECT * FROM OrdersV WHERE OrderYear=1997 AND OrderID=1000
```

(Results abridged)

```
StmtText
------------------------------------------------------------------
SELECT * FROM OrdersV WHERE OrderYear=@1 AND OrderID=@2
|-Compute Scalar(DEFINE:(Orders1997.OrderID=Orders1997.OrderID, Or
  |-Clustered Index Scan(OBJECT:(Northwind.dbo.Orders1997.PK_Order
```

Now we see compile-time partition elimination. Not only is the partitioning column included in its host table's primary key but all the columns in the primary key are included in the query's search criteria as well. In this case, merely matching query columns to primary key columns left to right wasn't enough to achieve the compile-time partition elimination we were striving for—the query had to include *all* the columns in the primary key or the optimizer produced an inefficient plan. Listing 17.4 presents a variation on our partitioned view and query that demonstrates the same concept.

Listing 17.4 Adding a Column to the Primary Key to Prevent Compile-Time Partition Elimination

```
CREATE TABLE Orders1996 (
  OrderID int NOT NULL ,
  CustomerID nchar (5) NOT NULL ,
  EmployeeID int NULL ,
  OrderDate datetime NOT NULL CHECK (Year(OrderDate)=1996),
  OrderYear int NOT NULL DEFAULT 1996 CHECK (OrderYear=1996),
  RequiredDate datetime NULL ,
  ShippedDate datetime NULL ,
  ShipVia int NULL,
  CONSTRAINT PK_Orders1996
  PRIMARY KEY (OrderYear, OrderID, CustomerId)
)
GO

CREATE TABLE Orders1997 (
  OrderID int NOT NULL ,
  CustomerID nchar (5) NOT NULL ,
  EmployeeID int NULL ,
  OrderDate datetime NOT NULL CHECK (Year(OrderDate)=1997),
  OrderYear int NOT NULL DEFAULT 1997 CHECK (OrderYear=1997),
  RequiredDate datetime NULL ,
  ShippedDate datetime NULL ,
  ShipVia int NULL,
```

```
    CONSTRAINT PK_Orders1997
    PRIMARY KEY (OrderYear, OrderID, CustomerId)
)
GO

CREATE TABLE Orders1998 (
  OrderID int NOT NULL ,
  CustomerID nchar (5) NOT NULL ,
  EmployeeID int NULL ,
  OrderDate datetime NOT NULL CHECK (Year(OrderDate)=1998),
  OrderYear int NOT NULL DEFAULT 1998 CHECK (OrderYear=1998),
  RequiredDate datetime NULL ,
  ShippedDate datetime NULL ,
  ShipVia int NULL,
  CONSTRAINT PK_Orders1998
  PRIMARY KEY (OrderYear, OrderID, CustomerId)
)
GO

CREATE VIEW OrdersV
AS
SELECT * FROM Orders1996
UNION ALL
SELECT * FROM Orders1997
UNION ALL
SELECT * FROM Orders1998
GO

SELECT * FROM OrdersV WHERE OrderYear=1997 AND OrderID=1000
```

(Results abridged)

```
-------------------------------------------------------------------
Executes    StmtText
----------  -------------------------------------------------------
1           SELECT * FROM [OrdersV] WHERE [OrderYear]=@1 AND [Orde
1             |--Concatenation
1                  |--Filter(WHERE:(STARTUP EXPR(Convert([@1])=199
0                  |      |--Clustered Index Seek(OBJECT:([Northwind
1                  |--Filter(WHERE:(STARTUP EXPR(Convert([@1])=199
1                  |      |--Clustered Index Seek(OBJECT:([Northwind
1                  |--Filter(WHERE:(STARTUP EXPR(Convert([@1])=199
0                         |--Clustered Index Seek(OBJECT:([Northwind
-------------------------------------------------------------------
```

Here, we've added the CustomerID column to each partition's primary key, but we haven't changed the query to include this new column in its search criteria. The result is a plan in which the optimizer eliminates the unneeded partitions at runtime rather than at compile-time (note the Executes column). Let's see what happens when we add the CustomerID to the query's search criteria (Listing 17.5).

Listing 17.5 Adding CustomerID to the Search Criteria to Facilitate Compile-Time Elimination

```
SELECT * FROM OrdersV
WHERE OrderYear=1997 AND OrderID=1000 AND CustomerID = 'AAAAA'

StmtText
-------------------------------------------------------------------
SELECT * FROM OrdersV WHERE OrderYear=@1 AND OrderID=@2 AND Custom
 |-Compute Scalar(DEFINE:(Orders1997.OrderID=Orders1997.OrderID, O
  |-Clustered Index Scan(OBJECT:(Northwind.dbo.Orders1997.PK_Order
```

Once again, we're seeing compile-time partition elimination because we've matched the query criteria with the primary columns of the partitioned view one-to-one. In this case, we achieved the compile-time partition elimination by adding columns to the search criteria. We could just as easily have removed columns from the primary key of each partition.

As the very first example in this section illustrated, it's not a requirement that you must always filter by the entire primary key in order to get an efficient execution plan when querying a partitioned view. Just be aware that this may be necessary in order to force the optimizer to eliminate partitions at compile-time rather than runtime.

BETWEEN and Partitioned View Queries

In addition to the primary key–partition column relationship, another thing to watch out for with partitioned views is the use of theta (nonequality) operators. Even if the operators in the partitioning CHECK constraint and the query match exactly, the optimizer may be unable to correctly identify the partition to search when theta operators are used. This means that it may have to search all partitions and concatenate the results. For example, consider the partitioned view and query shown in Listing 17.6.

Listing 17.6 A Query That Features a BETWEEN Predicate against a Partitioned View

```
CREATE TABLE CustomersUS (
  CustomerID nchar (5) NOT NULL,
  CompanyName nvarchar (40) NOT NULL ,
  ContactName nvarchar (30) NULL ,
  ContactTitle nvarchar (30) NULL ,
  Address nvarchar (60) NULL ,
  City nvarchar (15) NULL ,
  Region nvarchar (15) NULL ,
  PostalCode nvarchar (10) NULL ,
  Country nvarchar (15) NOT NULL CHECK (Country='US'),
  Phone nvarchar (24) NULL ,
  Fax nvarchar (24) NULL,
PRIMARY KEY (Country, CustomerID)
)

CREATE TABLE CustomersUK (
  CustomerID nchar (5) NOT NULL,
  CompanyName nvarchar (40) NOT NULL ,
  ContactName nvarchar (30) NULL ,
  ContactTitle nvarchar (30) NULL ,
  Address nvarchar (60) NULL ,
  City nvarchar (15) NULL ,
  Region nvarchar (15) NULL ,
  PostalCode nvarchar (10) NULL ,
  Country nvarchar (15) NOT NULL CHECK (Country='UK'),
  Phone nvarchar (24) NULL ,
  Fax nvarchar (24) NULL,
PRIMARY KEY (Country, CustomerID)
)

CREATE TABLE CustomersFrance (
  CustomerID nchar (5) NOT NULL,
  CompanyName nvarchar (40) NOT NULL ,
  ContactName nvarchar (30) NULL ,
  ContactTitle nvarchar (30) NULL ,
  Address nvarchar (60) NULL ,
  City nvarchar (15) NULL ,
  Region nvarchar (15) NULL ,
  PostalCode nvarchar (10) NULL ,
  Country nvarchar (15) NOT NULL CHECK (Country='France'),
  Phone nvarchar (24) NULL ,
  Fax nvarchar (24) NULL,
```

```
PRIMARY KEY (Country, CustomerID)
)

GO

DROP VIEW CustomersV
GO

CREATE VIEW CustomersV
AS
SELECT * FROM dbo.CustomersUS
UNION ALL
SELECT * FROM dbo.CustomersUK
UNION ALL
SELECT * FROM dbo.CustomersFrance
GO

SELECT * FROM dbo.CustomersV WHERE Country BETWEEN 'UK' AND 'US'
```

Even though the view's partitioning column is each underlying table's primary key and even though the query filter criteria and the partitioning CHECK constraint match exactly, here's the execution plan we get:

(Results abridged)

```
Executes  StmtText
--------- ----------------------------------------------------------
1         SELECT * FROM [dbo].[CustomersV] WHERE [Country]>=@1 AND
1         |--Concatenation
1             |--Filter(WHERE:(STARTUP EXPR(Convert([@1])<='US'
1             |    |--Clustered Index Seek(OBJECT:([Northwind].
1             |--Filter(WHERE:(STARTUP EXPR(Convert([@1])<='UK'
1             |    |--Clustered Index Seek(OBJECT:([Northwind].
1             |--Filter(WHERE:(STARTUP EXPR(Convert([@1])<='Fra
0                 |--Clustered Index Seek(OBJECT:([Northwind].
```

The CustomersFrance base table is mentioned in the plan even though it's not logically possible that CustomersFrance contains the data we're seeking. Note, however, that CustomersFrance is not actually searched (its Clustered Index Seek operator has 0 executions). Once again, the optimizer has generated a plan that eliminates unneeded partitions at runtime. This is a more flexible and generally more useful plan than one in which they are eliminated when the plan is initially compiled.

Distributed Partitioned Views

A DPV is a partitioned view whose base tables are scattered across a federation (a group) of autonomous servers. These remote base tables are accessed via linked server definitions. To set up a DPV, follow these steps.

1. Create linked server definitions for the servers on which the remote tables you want to access reside.
2. Enable the lazy schema validation server option for each linked server. This option cannot be set using the Linked Server Properties dialog in Enterprise Manager, so you must use sp_serveroption.
3. Create a partitioned view that references the remote partitions using four part names.
4. Repeat these steps on each of the linked servers referenced by the partitioned view. Doing this will allow you to load-balance your SQL Server environment by routing users to different versions of the same view.

Listing 17.7 shows our earlier partitioned view converted to a DPV.

Listing 17.7 A Distributed Partitioned View in the Wild

```
CREATE VIEW OrdersV
AS
SELECT * FROM Orders1996
UNION ALL
SELECT * FROM HOMER.Northwind.dbo.Orders1997
UNION ALL
SELECT * FROM MARGE.Northwind.dbo.Orders1998
GO

SELECT CustomerID FROM OrdersV WHERE OrderYear=1997 AND
    OrderID=1000
(Results abridged)
StmtText
----------------------------------------------------------------------
SELECT CustomerID=CustomerID FROM OrdersV WHERE OrderYear=@1 AND OrderID=@2
  |-Compute Scalar(DEFINE:(HOMER.Northwind.dbo.Orders1997.CustomerID=HOMER.nort
    |-Remote Query(SOURCE:(HOMER),QUERY:(SELECT Col1024 FROM (SELECT Tbl1003.
      "OrderID" Col1023,Tbl1003."CustomerID" Col1024,Tbl1003."OrderYear" Col1027
      FROM "northwind"."dbo"."Orders1997" Tbl1003) Qry1031 WHERE Col1023=(1000)))
```

As you can see, given that we've properly matched up the query's filter criteria with the partitioned view's primary key, the optimizer correctly focuses the search on just one of the partitions. Since that partition resides on a linked server, the optimizer adds a Remote Query step to the plan and sends the query to the remote server. Note that the WHERE clause of the remote query (bolded) does not include the partition column even though the original query does. This is because it isn't needed. Once the correct partition has been identified, the partition column itself isn't needed to locate the data in the remote table. By virtue of the CHECK constraint, the optimizer knows that Orders1997 contains data for only one partition, 1997.

Recap

You create a server federation by creating a partitioned view that's distributed across a group of servers. These servers refer to one another via regular linked server references.

SQL Server imposes a number of restrictions on partitioned views, but once those restrictions are met, the query optimizer on each server in the federation handles eliminating unnecessary partitions (either at compile-time or at runtime) so that these partitions are not needlessly scanned for matching rows.

Knowledge Measure

1. True or false: If you view the execution plan for a query against a partitioned view and see unnecessary partitions listed in the plan, you have probably discovered a bug and should call Microsoft.
2. What does an Executes column of 0 for a given query plan step indicate?
3. True or false: In order to ensure maximum query performance, the CHECK constraints that define the partition column for a partitioned view must not overlap.
4. Describe the purpose of the partitioning column in a partitioned view.

5. True or false: The SQL Server query optimizer can eliminate un-needed partitions from a query against a partitioned view at compile-time as well as at runtime.

6. True or false: Although it may be possible to force the optimizer to eliminate unneeded partitions at compile-time rather than at runt-ime, it is generally better to allow it to remove them at runtime.

7. True or false: To set up a DPV, you must disable the lazy schema val-idation option.

CHAPTER 18

SQLXML

The key to everything is happiness. Do what you can to be happy in this world. Life is short—too short to do otherwise. The deferred gratification you mention so often is more deferred than gratifying.

—H. W. Kenton

NOTE: This chapter assumes that you're running, at a minimum, SQL Server 2000 with SQLXML 3.0. The SQLXML Web releases have changed and enhanced SQL Server's XML functionality significantly. For the sake of staying current with the technology, I'm covering the latest version of SQLXML rather than the version that shipped with the original release of SQL Server 2000.

This chapter updates the coverage of SQLXML in my last book, *The Guru's Guide to SQL Server Stored Procedures, XML, and HTML*. That book was written before Web Release 1 (the update to SQL Server 2000's original SQLXML functionality) had shipped. As of this writing, SQLXML 3.0 (which would be the equivalent of Web Release 3 had Microsoft not changed the naming scheme) has shipped, and Yukon, the next version of SQL Server, is about to go into beta test.

This chapter will also get more into how the SQLXML technologies are designed and how they fit together from an architectural standpoint. As with the rest of the book, my intent here is to get beyond the "how to" and into the "why" behind how SQL Server's technologies work.

I must confess that I was conflicted when I sat down to write this chapter. I wrestled with whether to update the SQLXML coverage in my last book, which was more focused on the practical application of SQLXML but which I felt really needed updating, or to write something completely new on just the architectural aspects of SQLXML, with little or no discussion of how to apply them in practice. Ultimately, I decided to do both things. In keeping with the chief purpose of this book, I decided to cover the architectural aspects of SQLXML, and, in order to stay up with the current state of SQL Server's XML family of technologies, I decided to update the coverage of SQLXML in my last book from the standpoint of practical use. So, this chapter updates what I had to say previously about SQLXML and also delves into the SQLXML architecture in ways I've not done before.

Overview

With the popularity and ubiquity of XML, it's no surprise that SQL Server has extensive support for working with it. Like most modern DBMSs, SQL Server regularly needs to work with and store data that may have originated in XML. Without this built-in support, getting XML to and from SQL Server would require the application developer to translate XML data before sending it to SQL Server and again after receiving it back. Obviously, this could quickly become very tedious given the pervasiveness of the language.

SQL Server is an XML-enabled DBMS. This means that it can read and write XML data. It can return data from databases in XML format, and it can read and update data stored in XML documents. As Table 18.1 illustrates,

Table 18.1 SQL Server's XML Features

Feature	Purpose
FOR XML	An extension to the SELECT command that allows result sets to be returned as XML
OPENXML	Allows reading and writing of data in XML documents
XPath queries	Allows SQL Server databases to be queried using XPath syntax
Schemas	Supports XSD and XDR mapping schemas and XPath queries against them
SOAP support	Allows clients to access SQL Server's functionality as a Web service
Updategrams	XML templates through which data modifications can be applied to a database
Managed classes	Classes that expose the functionality of SQLXML inside the .NET Framework
XML Bulk Load	A high-speed facility for loading XML data into a SQL Server database

out of the box, SQL Server's XML features can be broken down into eight general categories.

We'll explore each of these in this chapter and discuss how they work and how they interoperate.

MSXML

SQL Server uses Microsoft's XML parser, MSXML, to load XML data, so we'll begin our discussion there. There are two basic ways to parse XML data using MSXML: using the Document Object Model (DOM) or using the Simple API for XML (SAX). Both DOM and SAX are W3C standards. The DOM method involves parsing the XML document and loading it into a tree structure in memory. The entire document is materialized and stored in memory when processed this way. An XML document parsed via DOM is known as a DOM document (or just "DOM" for short). XML parsers provide a variety of ways to manipulate DOM documents. Listing 18.1 shows a short Visual Basic app that demonstrates parsing an XML document via DOM and querying it for a particular node set. (You can find the source code to this app in the CH18\msxmltest subfolder on the CD accompanying this book.)

Listing 18.1

```
Private Sub Command1_Click()

  Dim bstrDoc As String

  bstrDoc = "<Songs> " & _
            "<Song>One More Day</Song>" & _
            "<Song>Hard Habit to Break</Song>" & _
            "<Song>Forever</Song>" & _
            "<Song>Boys of Summer</Song>" & _
            "<Song>Cherish</Song>" & _
            "<Song>Dance</Song>" & _
            "<Song>I Will Always Love You</Song>" & _
        "</Songs>"

  Dim xmlDoc As New DOMDocument30

  If Len(Text1.Text) = 0 Then
    Text1.Text = bstrDoc
  End If
```

```
If Not xmlDoc.loadXML(Text1.Text) Then
  MsgBox "Error loading document"
Else
  Dim oNodes As IXMLDOMNodeList
  Dim oNode As IXMLDOMNode

  If Len(Text2.Text) = 0 Then
    Text2.Text = "//Song"
  End If
  Set oNodes = xmlDoc.selectNodes(Text2.Text)

  For Each oNode In oNodes
    If Not (oNode Is Nothing) Then
      sName = oNode.nodeName
      sData = oNode.xml
      MsgBox "Node <" + sName + ">:" _
          + vbNewLine + vbTab + sData + vbNewLine
    End If
  Next

  Set xmlDoc = Nothing
  End If
End Sub
```

We begin by instantiating a DOMDocument object, then call its loadXML method to parse the XML document and load it into the DOM tree. We call its selectNodes method to query it via XPath. The selectNodes method returns a node list object, which we then iterate through using For Each. In this case, we display each node name followed by its contents via VB's Msg-Box function. We're able to access and manipulate the document as though it were an object because that's exactly what it is—parsing an XML document via DOM turns the document into a memory object that you can then work with just as you would any other object.

SAX, by contrast, is an event-driven API. You process an XML document via SAX by configuring your application to respond to SAX events. As the SAX processor reads through an XML document, it raises events each time it encounters something the calling application should know about, such as an element starting or ending, an attribute starting or ending, and so on. It passes the relevant data about the event to the application's handler for the event. The application can then decide what to do in response—it could store the event data in some type of tree structure, as is the case with DOM processing; it could ignore the event; it could search the event data for something in particular; or it could take some other action. Once the event is handled, the SAX processor continues reading the document. At no point does it persist the document in memory as DOM does. It's really just a parsing mechanism to which an application can attach its own functionality. In fact, SAX is the underlying parsing mechanism for MSXML's DOM processor. Microsoft's DOM implementation sets up SAX event handlers that simply store the data handed to them by the SAX engine in a DOM tree.

As you've probably surmised by now, SAX consumes far less memory than DOM does. That said, it's also much more trouble to set up and use. By persisting documents in memory, the DOM API makes working with XML documents as easy as working with any other kind of object.

SQL Server uses MSXML and the DOM to process documents you load via sp_xml_preparedocument. It restricts the virtual memory MSXML can use for DOM processing to one-eighth of the physical memory on the machine or 500MB, whichever is less. In actual practice, it's highly unlikely that MSXML would be able to access 500MB of virtual memory, even on a machine with 4GB of physical memory. The reason for this is that, by default, SQL Server reserves most of the user mode address space for use by its buffer pool. You'll recall that we talked about the MemToLeave space in Chapter 11 and noted that the non–thread stack portion defaults to 256MB on SQL Server 2000. This means that, by default, MSXML won't be able to use more than 256MB of memory—and probably considerably less given that other things are also allocated from this region—regardless of the amount of physical memory on the machine.

The reason MSXML is limited to no more than 500MB of virtual memory use regardless of the amount of memory on the machine is that SQL Server calls the GlobalMemoryStatus Win32 API function to determine the amount of available physical memory. GlobalMemoryStatus populates a MEMORYSTATUS structure with information about the status of memory use on the machine. On machines with more than 4GB of physical memory, GlobalMemoryStatus can return incorrect information, so Windows returns a -1 to indicate an overflow. The Win32 API function GlobalMemoryStatusEx exists to address this shortcoming, but SQLXML does not call it. You can see this for yourself by working through the following exercise.

Exercise 18.1   Determining How MSXML Computes Its Memory Ceiling

1. Restart your SQL Server, preferably from a console since we will be attaching to it with WinDbg. This should be a test or development system, and, ideally, you should be its only user.
2. Start Query Analyzer and connect to your SQL Server.
3. Attach to SQL Server using WinDbg. (Press F6 and select sqlservr.exe from the list of running tasks; if you have multiple instances, be sure to select the right one.)
4. At the WinDbg command prompt, add the following breakpoint:

```
bp kernel32!GlobalMemoryStatus
```

5. Once the breakpoint is added, type g and hit Enter to allow SQL Server to run.
6. Next, return to Query Analyzer and run the following query:

```
declare @doc varchar(8000)
set @doc='
<Songs>
  <Song name="She''s Like the Wind" artist="Patrick Swayze"/>
  <Song name="Hard to Say I''m Sorry" artist="Chicago"/>
  <Song name="She Loves Me" artist="Chicago"/>
  <Song name="I Can''t Make You Love Me" artist="Bonnie Raitt"/>
  <Song name="Heart of the Matter" artist="Don Henley"/>
  <Song name="Almost Like a Song" artist="Ronnie Milsap"/>
  <Song name="I''ll Be Over You" artist="Toto"/>
</Songs>
'

declare @hDoc int
exec sp_xml_preparedocument @hDoc OUT, @doc
```

7. The first time you parse an XML document using sp_xml_preparedocument, SQLXML calls GlobalMemoryStatus to retrieve the amount of physical memory in the machine, then calls an undocumented function exported by MSXML to restrict the amount of virtual memory it may allocate. (I had you restart your server so that we'd be sure to go down this code path.) This undocumented MSXML function is exported by ordinal rather than by name from the MSXML*n*.DLL and was added to MSXML expressly for use by SQL Server.
8. At this point, Query Analyzer should appear to be hung because your breakpoint has been hit in WinDbg and SQL Server has been stopped. Switch back to WinDbg and type kv at the command prompt to dump the call stack of the current thread. Your stack should look something like this (I've omitted everything but the function names):

```
KERNEL32!GlobalMemoryStatus (FPO: [Non-Fpo])
sqlservr!CXMLLoadLibrary::DoLoad+0x1b5
sqlservr!CXMLDocsList::Load+0x58
sqlservr!CXMLDocsList::LoadXMLDocument+0x1b
sqlservr!SpXmlPrepareDocument+0x423
sqlservr!CSpecProc::ExecuteSpecial+0x334
sqlservr!CXProc::Execute+0xa3
sqlservr!CSQLSource::Execute+0x3c0
sqlservr!CStmtExec::XretLocalExec+0x14d
sqlservr!CStmtExec::XretExecute+0x31a
sqlservr!CMsqlExecContext::ExecuteStmts+0x3b9
sqlservr!CMsqlExecContext::Execute+0x1b6
sqlservr!CSQLSource::Execute+0x357
sqlservr!language_exec+0x3e1
```

9. You'll recall from Chapter 3 that we discovered that the entry point
   for T-SQL batch execution within SQL Server is language_exec. You
   can see the call to language_exec at the bottom of this stack—this
   was called when you submitted the T-SQL batch to the server to run.
   Working upward from the bottom, we can see the call to SpXmlPrepareDocument, the internal "spec proc" (an extended procedure implemented internally by the server rather than in an external DLL)
   responsible for implementing the sp_xml_preparedocument xproc.
   We can see from there that SpXmlPrepareDocument calls LoadXML-
   Document, LoadXMLDocument calls a method named Load, Load
   calls a method named DoLoad, and DoLoad calls GlobalMemoryStatus. So, that's how we know how MSXML computes the amount of
   physical memory in the machine, and, knowing the limitations of this
   function, that's how we know the maximum amount of virtual memory MSXML can use.
10. Type q and hit Enter to quit WinDbg. You will have to restart your SQL
    Server.

FOR XML

Despite MSXML's power and ease of use, SQL Server doesn't leverage
MSXML in all of its XML features. It doesn't use it to implement server-
side FOR XML queries, for example, even though it's trivial to construct a
DOM document programmatically and return it as text. MSXML has facilities that make this quite easy. For example, Listing 18.2 presents a Visual
Basic app that executes a query via ADO and constructs a DOM document
on-the-fly based on the results it returns.

Listing 18.2

```
Private Sub Command1_Click()

  Dim xmlDoc As New DOMDocument30
  Dim oRootNode As IXMLDOMNode

  Set oRootNode = xmlDoc.createElement("Root")

  Set xmlDoc.documentElement = oRootNode

  Dim oAttr As IXMLDOMAttribute
  Dim oNode As IXMLDOMNode

  Dim oConn As New ADODB.Connection
  Dim oComm As New ADODB.Command
  Dim oRs As New ADODB.Recordset

  oConn.Open (Text3.Text)
  oComm.ActiveConnection = oConn

  oComm.CommandText = Text1.Text
  Set oRs = oComm.Execute

  Dim oField As ADODB.Field

  While Not oRs.EOF
    Set oNode = xmlDoc.createElement("Row")
    For Each oField In oRs.Fields
      Set oAttr = xmlDoc.createAttribute(oField.Name)
      oAttr.Value = oField.Value
      oNode.Attributes.setNamedItem oAttr
    Next
    oRootNode.appendChild oNode
    oRs.MoveNext
  Wend

  oConn.Close

  Text2.Text = xmlDoc.xml

  Set xmlDoc = Nothing
  Set oRs = Nothing
  Set oComm = Nothing
  Set oConn = Nothing
End Sub
```

As you can see, translating a result set to XML doesn't require much code. The ADO Recordset object even supports being streamed directly to an XML document (via its Save method), so if you don't need complete control over the conversion process, you might be able to get away with even less code than in my example.

As I've said, SQL Server doesn't use MSXML or build a DOM document in order to return a result set as XML. Why is that? And how do we know that it doesn't use MSXML to process server-side FOR XML queries? I'll answer both questions in just a moment.

The answer to the first question should be pretty obvious. Building a DOM from a result set before returning it as text would require SQL Server to persist the entire result set in memory. Given that the memory footprint of the DOM version of an XML document is roughly three to five times as large as the document itself, this doesn't paint a pretty resource usage picture. If they had to first be persisted entirely in memory before being returned to the client, even moderately large FOR XML result sets could use huge amounts of virtual memory (or run into the MSXML memory ceiling and therefore be too large to generate).

To answer the second question, let's again have a look at SQL Server under a debugger.

Exercise 18.2 Determining Whether Server-Side FOR XML Uses MSXML

1. Restart your SQL Server, preferably from a console since we will be attaching to it with WinDbg. This should be a test or development system, and, ideally, you should be its only user.
2. Start Query Analyzer and connect to your SQL Server.
3. Attach to SQL Server using WinDbg. (Press F6 and select sqlservr.exe from the list of running tasks; if you have multiple instances, be sure to select the right one.) Once the WinDbg command prompt appears, type g and press Enter so that SQL Server can continue to run.
4. Back in Query Analyzer, run a FOR XML query of some type:

```
SELECT * FROM (
SELECT 'Summer Dream' as Song
UNION
SELECT 'Summer Snow'
UNION
SELECT 'Crazy For You'
) s FOR XML AUTO
```

This query unions some SELECT statements together, then queries the union as a derived table using a FOR XML clause.

5. After you run the query, switch back to WinDbg. You will likely see some ModLoad messages in the WinDbg command window. WinDbg displays a ModLoad message whenever a module is loaded into the process being debugged. If MSXMLn.DLL were being used to service your FOR XML query, you'd see a ModLoad message for it. As you've noticed, there isn't one. MSXML isn't used to service FOR XML queries.

6. If you've done much debugging, you may be speculating that perhaps the MSXML DLL is already loaded; hence, we wouldn't see a ModLoad message for it when we ran our FOR XML query. That's easy enough to check. Hit Ctrl+Break in the debugger, then type lm in the command window and hit Enter. The lm command lists the modules currently loaded into the process space. Do you see MSXMLn.DLL in the list? Unless you've been interacting with SQL Server's other XML features since you recycled your server, it should not be there. Type g in the command window and press Enter so that SQL Server can continue to run.

7. As a final test, let's force MSXMLn.DLL to load by parsing an XML document. Reload the query from Exercise 18.1 above in Query Analyzer and run it. You should see a ModLoad message for MSXML's DLL in the WinDbg command window.

8. Hit Ctrl+Break again to stop WinDbg, then type q and hit Enter to stop debugging. You will need to restart your SQL Server.

So, based on all this, we can conclude that SQL Server generates its own XML when it processes a server-side FOR XML query. There is no memory-efficient mechanism in MSXML to assist with this, so it is not used.

Using FOR XML

As you saw in Exercise 18.2, you can append FOR XML AUTO to the end of a SELECT statement in order to cause the result to be returned as an XML document fragment. Transact-SQL's FOR XML syntax is much richer than this, though—it supports several options that extend its usefulness in numerous ways. In this section, we'll discuss a few of these and work through examples that illustrate them.

SELECT...FOR XML (Server-Side)

As I'm sure you've already surmised, you can retrieve XML data from SQL Server by using the FOR XML option of the SELECT command. FOR XML causes SELECT to return query results as an XML stream rather than a traditional rowset. On the server-side, this stream can have one of three formats: RAW, AUTO, or EXPLICIT. The basic FOR XML syntax looks like this:

```
SELECT column list
FROM table list
WHERE filter criteria
FOR XML RAW | AUTO | EXPLICIT [, XMLDATA] [, ELEMENTS]
    [, BINARY BASE64]
```

RAW returns column values as attributes and wraps each row in a generic row element. AUTO returns column values as attributes and wraps each row in an element named after the table from which it came.[1] EXPLICIT lets you completely control the format of the XML returned by a query.

XMLDATA causes an XML-Data schema to be returned for the document being retrieved. ELEMENTS causes the columns in XML AUTO data to be returned as elements rather than attributes. BINARY BASE64 specifies that binary data is to be returned using BASE64 encoding.

I'll discuss these options in more detail in just a moment. Also note that there are client-side specific options available with FOR XML queries that aren't available in server-side queries. We'll talk about those in just a moment, too.

RAW Mode

RAW mode is the simplest of the three basic FOR XML modes. It performs a very basic translation of the result set into XML. Listing 18.3 shows an example.

Listing 18.3

```
SELECT CustomerId, CompanyName
FROM Customers FOR XML RAW
```

(Results abridged)

```
XML_F52E2B61-18A1-11d1-B105-00805F49916B
```

---

1. There's actually more to this than simply naming each row after the table, view, or UDF that produced it. SQL Server uses a set of heuristics to decide what the actual element names are with FOR XML AUTO.

```
------------------------------------------------------------------
<row CustomerId="ALFKI" CompanyName="Alfreds Futterkiste"/><row Cu
CompanyName="Ana Trujillo Emparedados y helados"/><row CustomerId=
CompanyName="Antonio Moreno Taquería"/><row CustomerId="AROUT" Com
Horn"/><row CustomerId="BERGS" CompanyName="Berglunds snabbköp"/><
CustomerId="BLAUS" CompanyName="Blauer See Delikatessen"/><row Cus
CompanyName="Blondesddsl p_re et fils"/><row CustomerId="WELLI"
CompanyName="Wellington Importadora"/><row CustomerId="WHITC" Comp
Clover Markets"/><row CustomerId="WILMK" CompanyName="Wilman Kala"
CustomerId="WOLZA"
CompanyName="Wolski Zajazd"/>
```

Each column becomes an attribute in the result set, and each row becomes an element with the generic name of row.

As I've mentioned before, the XML that's returned by FOR XML is not well formed because it lacks a root element. It's technically an XML fragment and must include a root element in order to be usable by an XML parser. From the client side, you can set an ADO Command object's xml root property in order to automatically generate a root node when you execute a FOR XML query.

AUTO Mode

FOR XML AUTO gives you more control than RAW mode over the XML fragment that's produced. To begin with, each row in the result set is named after the table, view, or table-valued UDF that produced it. For example, Listing 18.4 shows a basic FOR XML AUTO query.

Listing 18.4

```
SELECT CustomerId, CompanyName
FROM Customers FOR XML AUTO
```

(Results abridged)

```
XML_F52E2B61-18A1-11d1-B105-00805F49916B
------------------------------------------------------------------
<Customers CustomerId="ALFKI" CompanyName="Alfreds Futterkiste"/><
CustomerId="ANATR" CompanyName="Ana Trujillo Emparedados y helados
CustomerId="ANTON" CompanyName="Antonio Moreno Taquería"/><Custome
```

```
CustomerId="AROUT" CompanyName="Around the Horn"/><Customers Custo
CompanyName="Vins et alcools Chevalier"/><Customers CustomerId="WA
CompanyName="Wartian Herkku"/><Customers CustomerId="WELLI" Compan
Importadora"/><Customers CustomerId="WHITC" CompanyName="White Clo
Markets"/><Customers CustomerId="WILMK" CompanyName="Wilman Kala"/
CustomerId="WOLZA"
CompanyName="Wolski Zajazd"/>
```

Notice that each row is named after the table from whence it came: Customers. For results with more than one row, this amounts to having more than one top-level (root) element in the fragment, which isn't allowed in XML.

One big difference between AUTO and RAW mode is the way in which joins are handled. In RAW mode, a simple one-to-one translation occurs between columns in the result set and attributes in the XML fragment. Each row becomes an element in the fragment named row. These elements are technically empty themselves—they contain no values or subelements, only attributes. Think of attributes as specifying characteristics of an element, while data and subelements compose its contents. In AUTO mode, each row is named after the source from which it came, and the rows from joined tables are nested within one another. Listing 18.5 presents an example.

Listing 18.5

```
SELECT Customers.CustomerID, CompanyName, OrderId
FROM Customers JOIN Orders
ON (Customers.CustomerId=Orders.CustomerId)
FOR XML AUTO
```

(Results abridged and formatted)

```
XML_F52E2B61-18A1-11d1-B105-00805F49916B
-----------------------------------------------------------------
<Customers CustomerID="ALFKI" CompanyName="Alfreds Futterkiste">
  <Orders OrderId="10643"/><Orders OrderId="10692"/>
  <Orders OrderId="10702"/><Orders OrderId="10835"/>
  <Orders OrderId="10952"/><Orders OrderId="11011"/>
</Customers>
<Customers CustomerID="ANATR" CompanyName="Ana Trujillo Emparedado
  <Orders OrderId="10308"/><Orders OrderId="10625"/>
  <Orders OrderId="10759"/><Orders OrderId="10926"/></Customers>
```

```
<Customers CustomerID="FRANR" CompanyName="France restauration">
  <Orders OrderId="10671"/><Orders OrderId="10860"/>
  <Orders OrderId="10971"/>
</Customers>
```

I've formatted the XML fragment to make it easier to read—if you run the query yourself from Query Analyzer, you'll see an unformatted stream of XML text.

Note the way in which the Orders for each customer are contained within each Customer element. As I said, AUTO mode nests the rows returned by joins. Note my use of the full table name in the join criterion. Why didn't I use a table alias? Because AUTO mode uses the table aliases you specify to name the elements it returns. If you use shortened monikers for a table, its elements will have that name in the resulting XML fragment. While useful in traditional Transact-SQL, this makes the fragment difficult to read if the alias isn't sufficiently descriptive.

ELEMENTS Option

The ELEMENTS option of the FOR XML AUTO clause causes AUTO mode to return nested elements instead of attributes. Depending on your business needs, element-centric mapping may be preferable to the default attribute-centric mapping. Listing 18.6 gives an example of a FOR XML query that returns elements instead of attributes.

Listing 18.6

```
SELECT CustomerID, CompanyName
FROM Customers
FOR XML AUTO, ELEMENTS

(Results abridged and formatted)

XML_F52E2B61-18A1-11d1-B105-00805F49916B
-----------------------------------------------------------------
<Customers>
  <CustomerID>ALFKI</CustomerID>
  <CompanyName>Alfreds Futterkiste</CompanyName>
</Customers>
```

```
<Customers>
  <CustomerID>ANATR</CustomerID>
  <CompanyName>Ana Trujillo Emparedados y helados</CompanyName>
</Customers>
<Customers>
  <CustomerID>ANTON</CustomerID>
  <CompanyName>Antonio Moreno Taquería</CompanyName>
</Customers>
<Customers>
  <CustomerID>AROUT</CustomerID>
  <CompanyName>Around the Horn</CompanyName>
</Customers>
<Customers>
  <CustomerID>WILMK</CustomerID>
  <CompanyName>Wilman Kala</CompanyName>
</Customers>
<Customers>
  <CustomerID>WOLZA</CustomerID>
  <CompanyName>Wolski  Zajazd</CompanyName>
</Customers>
```

Notice that the ELEMENTS option has caused what were being returned as attributes of the Customers element to instead be returned as subelements. Each attribute is now a pair of element tags that enclose the value from a column in the table.

NOTE: Currently, AUTO mode does not support GROUP BY or aggregate functions. The heuristics it uses to determine element names are incompatible with these constructs, so you cannot use them in AUTO mode queries. Additionally, FOR XML itself is incompatible with COMPUTE, so you can't use it in FOR XML queries of any kind.

EXPLICIT Mode

If you need more control over the XML than FOR XML produces, EXPLICIT mode is more flexible (and therefore more complicated to use) than either RAW mode or AUTO mode. EXPLICIT mode queries define XML documents in terms of a "universal table"—a mechanism for returning a result set from SQL Server that *describes* what you want the document to look like, rather than composing the document itself. A universal table is just a

SQL Server result set with special column headings that tell the server how to produce an XML document from your data. Think of it as a set-oriented method of making an API call and passing parameters to it. You use the facilities available in Transact-SQL to make the call and pass it parameters.

A universal table consists of one column for each table column that you want to return in the XML fragment, plus two additional columns: Tag and Parent. Tag is a positive integer that uniquely identifies each tag that is to be returned by the document; Parent establishes parent-child relationships between tags.

The other columns in a universal table—the ones that correspond to the data you want to include in the XML fragment—have special names that actually consist of multiple segments delimited by exclamation points (!). These special column names pass muster with SQL Server's parser and provide specific instructions regarding the XML fragment to produce. They have the following format:

```
Element!Tag!Attribute!Directive
```

We'll see some examples of these shortly.

The first thing you need to do to build an EXPLICIT mode query is to determine the layout of the XML document you want to end up with. Once you know this, you can work backward from there to build a universal table that will produce the desired format. For example, let's say we want a simple customer list based on the Northwind Customers table that returns the customer ID as an attribute and the company name as an element. The XML fragment we're after might look like this:

```
<Customers CustomerId="ALFKI">Alfreds Futterkiste</Customers>
```

Listing 18.7 shows a Transact-SQL query that returns a universal table that specifies this layout.

Listing 18.7

```
SELECT 1 AS Tag,
NULL AS Parent,
CustomerId AS [Customers!1!CustomerId],
CompanyName AS [Customers!1]
FROM Customers
```

(Results abridged)

```
Tag     Parent    Customers!1!CustomerId Customers!1
------  --------  --------------------- ---------------------------
1       NULL      ALFKI                 Alfreds Futterkiste
1       NULL      ANATR                 Ana Trujillo Emparedados y
1       NULL      ANTON                 Antonio Moreno Taquería
```

The first two columns are the extra columns I mentioned earlier. Tag specifies an identifier for the tag we want to produce. Since we want to produce only one element per row, we hard-code this to 1. The same is true of Parent—there's only one element and a top-level element doesn't have a parent, so we return NULL for Parent in every row.

Since we want to return the customer ID as an attribute, we specify an attribute name in the heading of column 3 (bolded). And since we want to return CompanyName as an element rather than an attribute, we omit the attribute name in column 4.

By itself, this table accomplishes nothing. We have to add FOR XML EXPLICIT to the end of it in order for the odd column names to have any special meaning. Add FOR XML EXPLICIT to the query and run it from Query Analyzer. Listing 18.8 shows what you should see.

Listing 18.8

```
SELECT 1 AS Tag,
NULL AS Parent,
CustomerId AS [Customers!1!CustomerId],
CompanyName AS [Customers!1]
FROM Customers
FOR XML EXPLICIT
```

(Results abridged and formatted)

```
XML_F52E2B61-18A1-11d1-B105-00805F49916B
-----------------------------------------------------------------
<Customers CustomerId="ALFKI">Alfreds Futterkiste</Customers>
<Customers CustomerId="ANATR">Ana Trujillo Emparedados y helados
  </Customers>
<Customers CustomerId="WHITC">White Clover Markets</Customers>
<Customers CustomerId="WILMK">Wilman Kala</Customers>
<Customers CustomerId="WOLZA">Wolski Zajazd</Customers>
```

Table 18.2 EXPLICIT Mode Directives

Value	Function
element	Causes data in the column to be encoded and represented as a subelement
xml	Causes data to be represented as a subelement without encoding it
xmltext	Retrieves data from an overflow column and appends it to the document
cdata	Causes data in the column to be represented as a CDATA section in the resulting document
hide	Hides (omits) a column that appears in the universal table from the resulting XML fragment
id, idref, and idrefs	In conjunction with XMLDATA, can establish relationships between elements across multiple XML fragments

As you can see, each CustomerId value is returned as an attribute, and each CompanyName is returned as the element data for the Customers element, just as we specified.

Directives

The fourth part of the multivalued column headings supported by EXPLICIT mode queries is the directive segment. You use it to further control how data is represented in the resulting XML fragment. As Table 18.2 illustrates, the directive segment supports eight values.

Of these, element is the most frequently used. It causes data to be rendered as a subelement rather than an attribute. For example, let's say that, in addition to CustomerId and CompanyName, we wanted to return ContactName in our XML fragment and we wanted it to be a subelement rather than an attribute. Listing 18.9 shows how the query would look.

Listing 18.9

```
SELECT 1 AS Tag,
NULL AS Parent,
CustomerId AS [Customers!1!CustomerId],
```

```
CompanyName AS [Customers!1],
ContactName AS [Customers!1!ContactName!element]
FROM Customers
FOR XML EXPLICIT
```

(Results abridged and formatted)

```
XML_F52E2B61-18A1-11d1-B105-00805F49916B
-----------------------------------------------------------------
<Customers CustomerId="ALFKI">Alfreds Futterkiste
  <ContactName>Maria Anders</ContactName>
</Customers>
<Customers CustomerId="ANATR">Ana Trujillo Emparedados y
  <ContactName>Ana Trujillo</ContactName>
</Customers>
<Customers CustomerId="ANTON">Antonio Moreno Taquería
  <ContactName>Antonio Moreno</ContactName>
</Customers>
<Customers CustomerId="AROUT">Around the Horn
  <ContactName>Thomas Hardy</ContactName>
</Customers>
<Customers CustomerId="BERGS">Berglunds snabbköp
  <ContactName>Christina Berglund</ContactName>
</Customers>
<Customers CustomerId="WILMK">Wilman Kala
  <ContactName>Matti Karttunen</ContactName>
</Customers>
<Customers CustomerId="WOLZA">Wolski  Zajazd
  <ContactName>Zbyszek Piestrzeniewicz</ContactName>
</Customers>
```

As you can see, ContactName is nested within each Customers element as a subelement. The elements directive encodes the data it returns. We can retrieve the same data by using the xml directive without encoding, as shown in Listing 18.10.

Listing 18.10

```
SELECT 1 AS Tag,
NULL AS Parent,
CustomerId AS [Customers!1!CustomerId],
CompanyName AS [Customers!1],
```

```
ContactName AS [Customers!1!ContactName!xml]
FROM Customers
FOR XML EXPLICIT
```

The xml directive (bolded) causes the column to be returned without encoding any special characters it contains.

Establishing Data Relationships

Thus far, we've been listing the data from a single table, so our EXPLICT queries haven't been terribly complex. That would still be true even if we queried multiple tables as long as we didn't mind repeating the data from each table in each top-level element in the XML fragment. Just as the column values from joined tables are often repeated in the result sets of Transact-SQL queries, we could create an XML fragment that contained data from multiple tables repeated in each element. However, that wouldn't be the most efficient way to represent the data in XML. Remember: XML supports hierarchical relationships between elements. You can establish these hierarchies by using EXPLICIT mode queries and T-SQL UNIONs. Listing 18.11 provides an example.

Listing 18.11

```
SELECT 1 AS Tag,
NULL AS Parent,
CustomerId AS [Customers!1!CustomerId],
CompanyName AS [Customers!1],
NULL AS [Orders!2!OrderId],
NULL AS [Orders!2!OrderDate!element]
FROM Customers
UNION
SELECT 2 AS Tag,
1 AS Parent,
CustomerId,
NULL,
OrderId,
OrderDate
FROM Orders
ORDER BY [Customers!1!CustomerId], [Orders!2!OrderDate!element]
FOR XML EXPLICIT
```

This query does several interesting things. First, it links the Customers and Orders tables using the CustomerId column they share. Notice the third column in each SELECT statement—it returns the CustomerId column from each table. The Tag and Parent columns establish the details of the relationship between the two tables. The Tag and Parent values in the second query link it to the first. They establish that Order records are children of Customer records. Lastly, note the ORDER BY clause. It arranges the elements in the table in a sensible fashion—first by CustomerId and second by the OrderDate of each Order. Listing 18.12 shows the result set.

Listing 18.12

(Results abridged and formatted)

```
XML_F52E2B61-18A1-11d1-B105-00805F49916B
-----------------------------------------------------------------
<Customers CustomerId="ALFKI">Alfreds Futterkiste
  <Orders OrderId="10643">
    <OrderDate>1997-08-25T00:00:00</OrderDate>
  </Orders>
  <Orders OrderId="10692">
    <OrderDate>1997-10-03T00:00:00</OrderDate>
  </Orders>
  <Orders OrderId="10702">
    <OrderDate>1997-10-13T00:00:00</OrderDate>
  </Orders>
  <Orders OrderId="10835">
    <OrderDate>1998-01-15T00:00:00</OrderDate>
  </Orders>
  <Orders OrderId="10952">
    <OrderDate>1998-03-16T00:00:00</OrderDate>
  </Orders>
  <Orders OrderId="11011">
    <OrderDate>1998-04-09T00:00:00</OrderDate>
  </Orders>
</Customers>
<Customers CustomerId="ANATR">Ana Trujillo Emparedados y helados
  <Orders OrderId="10308">
    <OrderDate>1996-09-18T00:00:00</OrderDate>
  </Orders>
  <Orders OrderId="10625">
    <OrderDate>1997-08-08T00:00:00</OrderDate>
```

```
</Orders>
<Orders OrderId="10759">
  <OrderDate>1997-11-28T00:00:00</OrderDate>
</Orders>
<Orders OrderId="10926">
  <OrderDate>1998-03-04T00:00:00</OrderDate>
</Orders>
</Customers>
```

As you can see, each customer's orders are nested within its element.

The hide Directive

The hide directive omits a column you've included in the universal table from the resulting XML document. One use of this functionality is to order the result by a column that you don't want to include in the XML fragment. When you aren't using UNION to merge tables, this isn't a problem because you can order by any column you choose. However, the presence of UNION in a query requires order by columns to exist in the result set. The hide directive gives you a way to satisfy this requirement without being forced to return data you don't want to. Listing 18.13 shows an example.

Listing 18.13

```
SELECT 1 AS Tag,
NULL AS Parent,
CustomerId AS [Customers!1!CustomerId],
CompanyName AS [Customers!1],
PostalCode AS [Customers!1!PostalCode!hide],
NULL AS [Orders!2!OrderId],
NULL AS [Orders!2!OrderDate!element]
FROM Customers
UNION
SELECT 2 AS Tag,
1 AS Parent,
CustomerId,
NULL,
NULL,
OrderId,
OrderDate
FROM Orders
```

```
ORDER BY [Customers!1!CustomerId], [Orders!2!OrderDate!element],
[Customers!1!PostalCode!hide]
FOR XML EXPLICIT
```

Notice the hide directive (bolded) that's included in the column 5 heading. It allows the column to be specified in the ORDER BY clause without actually appearing in the resulting XML fragment.

The cdata Directive

CDATA sections may appear anywhere in an XML document that character data may appear. A CDATA section is used to escape characters that would otherwise be recognized as markup (e.g., <, >, /, and so on). Thus CDATA sections allow you to include sections in an XML document that might otherwise confuse the parser. To render a CDATA section from an EXPLICIT mode query, include the cdata directive, as demonstrated in Listing 18.14.

Listing 18.14

```
SELECT 1 AS Tag,
NULL AS Parent,
CustomerId AS [Customers!1!CustomerId],
CompanyName AS [Customers!1],
Fax AS [Customers!1!!cdata]
FROM Customers
FOR XML EXPLICIT
```

(Results abridged and formatted)

```
XML_F52E2B61-18A1-11d1-B105-00805F49916B
----------------------------------------------------------------
<Customers CustomerId="ALFKI">Alfreds Futterkiste
  <![CDATA[030-0076545]]>
</Customers>
<Customers CustomerId="ANATR">Ana Trujillo Emparedados y helados
  <![CDATA[(5) 555-3745]]>
</Customers>
<Customers CustomerId="ANTON">Antonio Moreno Taquería
</Customers>
<Customers CustomerId="AROUT">Around the Horn
  <![CDATA[(171) 555-6750]]>
```

```
</Customers>
<Customers CustomerId="BERGS">Berglunds snabbköp
  <![CDATA[0921-12 34 67]]>
</Customers>
```

As you can see, each value in the Fax column is returned as a CDATA section in the XML fragment. Note the omission of the attribute name in the cdata column heading (bolded). This is because attribute names aren't allowed for CDATA sections. Again, they represent escaped document segments, so the XML parser doesn't process any attribute or element names they may contain.

The id, idref, and idrefs Directives

The ID, IDREF, and IDFREFS data types can be used to represent relational data in an XML document. Set up in a DTD or XML-Data schema, they establish relationships between elements. They're handy in situations where you need to exchange complex data and want to minimize the amount of data duplication in the document.

EXPLICIT mode queries can use the id, idref, and idrefs directives to specify relational fields in an XML document. Naturally, this approach works only if a schema is used to define the document and identify the columns used to establish links between entities. FOR XML's XMLDATA option provides a means of generating an inline schema for its XML fragment. In conjunction with the id directives, it can identify relational fields in the XML fragment. Listing 18.15 gives an example.

Listing 18.15

```
SELECT 1 AS Tag,
       NULL AS Parent,
       CustomerId AS [Customers!1!CustomerId!id],
       CompanyName AS [Customers!1!CompanyName],
       NULL AS [Orders!2!OrderID],
       NULL AS [Orders!2!CustomerId!idref]
FROM Customers
UNION
SELECT 2,
       NULL,
       NULL,
       NULL,
```

```
        OrderID,
        CustomerId
FROM Orders
ORDER BY [Orders!2!OrderID]
FOR XML EXPLICIT, XMLDATA
```

(Results abridged and formatted)

```
XML_F52E2B61-18A1-11d1-B105-00805F49916B
-------------------------------------------------------------------
<Schema name="Schema2" xmlns="urn:schemas-microsoft-com:xml-data"
xmlns:dt="urn:schemas-microsoft-com:datatypes">
  <ElementType name="Customers" content="mixed" model="open">
    <AttributeType name="CustomerId" dt:type="id"/>
    <AttributeType name="CompanyName" dt:type="string"/>
    <attribute type="CustomerId"/>
    <attribute type="CompanyName"/>
  </ElementType>
  <ElementType name="Orders" content="mixed" model="open">
    <AttributeType name="OrderID" dt:type="i4"/>
    <AttributeType name="CustomerId" dt:type="idref"/>
    <attribute type="OrderID"/>
    <attribute type="CustomerId"/>
  </ElementType>
</Schema>
<Customers xmlns="x-schema:#Schema2" CustomerId="ALFKI"
  CompanyName="Alfreds Futterkiste"/>
<Customers xmlns="x-schema:#Schema2" CustomerId="ANATR"
  CompanyName="Ana Trujillo Emparedados y helados"/>
<Customers xmlns="x-schema:#Schema2" CustomerId="ANTON"
  CompanyName="Antonio Moreno Taquería"/>
<Customers xmlns="x-schema:#Schema2" CustomerId="AROUT"
  CompanyName="Around the Horn"/>
<Orders xmlns="x-schema:#Schema2" OrderID="10248"
    CustomerId="VINET"/>
<Orders xmlns="x-schema:#Schema2" OrderID="10249"
    CustomerId="TOMSP"/>
<Orders xmlns="x-schema:#Schema2" OrderID="10250"
    CustomerId="HANAR"/>
<Orders xmlns="x-schema:#Schema2" OrderID="10251"
    CustomerId="VICTE"/>
<Orders xmlns="x-schema:#Schema2" OrderID="10252"
    CustomerId="SUPRD"/>
<Orders xmlns="x-schema:#Schema2" OrderID="10253"
    CustomerId="HANAR"/>
```

```
<Orders xmlns="x-schema:#Schema2" OrderID="10254"
    CustomerId="CHOPS"/>
<Orders xmlns="x-schema:#Schema2" OrderID="10255"
    CustomerId="RICSU"/>
```

Note the use of the id and idref directives in the CustomerId columns of the Customers and Orders tables (bolded). These directives link the two tables by using the CustomerId column they share.

If you examine the XML fragment returned by the query, you'll see that it starts off with the XML-Data schema that the XMLDATA directive created. This schema is then referenced in the XML fragment that follows.

SELECT...FOR XML (Client-Side)

SQLXML also supports the notion of offloading to the client the work of translating a result set into XML. This functionality is accessible via the SQLXML managed classes, XML templates, a virtual directory configuration switch, and the SQLXMLOLEDB provider. Because it requires the least amount of setup, I'll cover client-side FOR XML using SQLXMLOLEDB here. The underlying technology is the same regardless of the mechanism used.

SQLXMLOLEDB serves as a layer between a client (or middle-tier) app and SQL Server's native SQLOLEDB provider. The Data Source property of the SQLXMLOLEDB provider specifies the OLE DB provider through which it executes queries; currently only SQLOLEDB is allowed.

SQLXMLOLEDB is not a rowset provider. In order to use it from ADO, you must access it via ADO's stream mode. I'll show you some code in just a minute that illustrates this.

You perform client-side FOR XML processing using SQLXMLOLEDB by following these general steps.

1. Connect using an ADO connection string that specifies SQLXMLOLEDB as the provider.
2. Set the ClientSideXML property of your ADO Command object to True.
3. Create and open an ADO stream object and associate it with your Command object's Output Stream property.
4. Execute a FOR XML EXPLICIT, FOR XML RAW, or FOR XML NESTED Transact-SQL query via your Command object, specifying the adExecuteStream option in your call to Execute.

Listing 18.16 illustrates. (You can find the source code for this app in the CH18\forxml_clientside subfolder on this book's CD.)

Listing 18.16

```
Private Sub Command1_Click()
  Dim oConn As New ADODB.Connection
  Dim oComm As New ADODB.Command

  Dim stOutput As New ADODB.Stream
  stOutput.Open

  oConn.Open (Text3.Text)
  oComm.ActiveConnection = oConn
  oComm.Properties("ClientSideXML") = "True"
  If Len(Text1.Text) = 0 Then
    Text1.Text = _
      "select * from pubs..authors FOR XML NESTED"
  End If
  oComm.CommandText = Text1.Text
  oComm.Properties("Output Stream") = stOutput
  oComm.Properties("xml root") = "Root"
  oComm.Execute , , adExecuteStream

  Text2.Text = stOutput.ReadText(adReadAll)

  stOutput.Close
  oConn.Close

  Set oComm = Nothing
  Set oConn = Nothing
End Sub
```

As you can see, most of the action here revolves around the ADO Command object. We set its ClientSideXML property to True and its Output Stream property to an ADO stream object we created before callings its Execute method.

Note the use of the FOR XML NESTED clause. The NESTED option is specific to client-side FOR XML processing—you can't use it in server-side queries. It's very much like FOR XML AUTO but has some minor differences. For example, when a FOR XML NESTED query references a view, the names of the view's underlying base tables are used in the generated XML. The same is true for table aliases—their base names are used in the XML that's produced. Using FOR XML AUTO in a client-side FOR XML query causes the query to be processed on the server rather than the client, so use NESTED when you want similar functionality to FOR XML AUTO on the client.

Given our previous investigation into whether MSXML is involved in the production of server-side XML (Exercise 18.2), you might be wondering whether it's used by SQLXML's client-side FOR XML processing. It isn't. Again, you can attach a debugger (in this case, to the forxml_clientside app) to see this for yourself. You *will* see SQLXML*n*.DLL loaded into the app's process space the first time you run the query. This DLL is where the SQLXMLOLEDB provider resides and is where SQLXML's client-side FOR XML processing occurs.

OPENXML

OPENXML is a built-in Transact-SQL function that can return an XML document as a rowset. In conjunction with sp_xml_preparedocument and sp_xml_removedocument, OPENXML allows you to break down (or shred) nonrelational XML documents into relational pieces that can be inserted into tables.

I suppose we should begin the investigation of how OPENXML works by determining where it's implemented. Does it reside in a separate DLL (SQLXML*n*.DLL, perhaps?) or is it implemented completely within the SQL Server executable?

The most expedient way to determine this is to run SQL Server under a debugger, stop it in the middle of an OPENXML call, and inspect the call stack. That would tell us in what module it was implemented. Since we don't know the name of the classes or functions that implement OPENXML, we can't easily set a breakpoint to accomplish this. Instead, we will have to just be quick and/or lucky enough to stop the debugger in the right place if we want to use this approach to find out the module in which OPENXML is implemented. This is really easier said than done. Even with complicated documents, OPENXML returns fairly quickly, so breaking in with a debugger while it's in progress could prove pretty elusive.

Another way to accomplish the same thing would be to force OPENXML to error and have a breakpoint set up in advance to stop in SQL Server's standard error reporting routine. From years of working with the product and seeing my share of access violations and stack dumps, I know that ex_raise is a central error-reporting routine for the server. Not all errors go through ex_raise, but many of them do, so it's worth setting a breakpoint in ex_raise and forcing OPENXML to error to see whether we can get a call stack and ascertain where OPENXML is implemented. Exercise 18.3 will take you through the process of doing exactly that.

Exercise 18.3   Determining Where OPENXML Is Implemented

1. Restart your SQL Server, preferably from a console since we will be attaching to it with WinDbg. This should be a test or development system, and, ideally, you should be its only user.
2. Start Query Analyzer and connect to your SQL Server.
3. Attach to SQL Server using WinDbg. (Press F6 and select sqlservr.exe from the list of running tasks; if you have multiple instances, be sure to select the right one.)
4. Once the WinDbg command prompt appears, set a breakpoint in ex_raise:

```
bp sqlservr!ex_raise
```

5. Type g and press Enter so that SQL Server can continue to run.
6. Back in Query Analyzer, run this query:

```
declare @hDoc int
set @hdoc=8675309  -- force a bogus handle
select * from openxml(@hdoc,'/',1)
```

7. Query Analyzer should appear to hang because the breakpoint you set in WinDbg has been hit. Switch back to WinDbg and type kv at the command prompt and press Enter. This will dump the call stack. Your stack should look something like this (I've removed everything but the function names):

```
sqlservr!ex_raise
sqlservr!CXMLDocsList::XMLMapFromHandle+0x3f
sqlservr!COpenXMLRange::GetRowset+0x14d
sqlservr!CQScanRmtScan::OpenConnection+0x141
sqlservr!CQScanRmtBase::Open+0x18
sqlservr!CQueryScan::Startup+0x10d
sqlservr!CStmtQuery::ErsqExecuteQuery+0x26b
sqlservr!CStmtSelect::XretExecute+0x229
sqlservr!CMsqlExecContext::ExecuteStmts+0x3b9
sqlservr!CMsqlExecContext::Execute+0x1b6
sqlservr!CSQLSource::Execute+0x357
sqlservr!language_exec+0x3e1
```

```
sqlservr!process_commands+0x10e
UMS!ProcessWorkRequests+0x272
UMS!ThreadStartRoutine+0x98 (FPO: [EBP 0x00bd6878] [1,0,4])
MSVCRT!_beginthread+0xce
KERNEL32!BaseThreadStart+0x52 (FPO: [Non-Fpo])
```

8. This call stack tells us a couple of things. First, it tells us that OPENXML is implemented directly by the server itself. It resides in sqlservr.exe, SQL Server's executable. Second, it tells us that a class named COpenXMLRange is responsible for producing the rowset that the T-SQL OPENXML function returns.

9. Type q and hit Enter to stop debugging. You will need to restart your SQL Server.

By reviewing this call stack, we can deduce how OPENXML works. It comes into the server via a language or RPC event (our code obviously came into the server as a language event—note the language_exec entry in the call stack) and eventually results in a call to the GetRowset method of the COpenXML-Range class. We can assume that GetRowset accesses the DOM document previously created via the call to sp_xml_preparedocument and turns it into a two-dimensional matrix that can be returned as a rowset, thus finishing up the work of the OPENXML function.

Now that we know the name of the class and method behind OPENXML, we could set a new breakpoint in COpenXMLRange::GetRowset, pass a valid document handle into OPENXML, and step through the disassembly for the method when the breakpoint is hit. However, we've got a pretty good idea of how OPENXML works; there's little to be learned about OPENXML's architecture from stepping through the disassembly at this point.

Using OPENXML

Books Online documents how to use OPENXML pretty well, so I'll try not to repeat that information here. Listing 18.17 shows a basic example of how to use OPENXML.

Listing 18.17

```
DECLARE @hDoc int
EXEC sp_xml_preparedocument @hDoc output,
'<songs>
  <song><name>Somebody to Love</name></song>
```

```
    <song><name>These Are the Days of Our Lives</name></song>
    <song><name>Bicycle Race</name></song>
    <song><name>Who Wants to Live Forever</name></song>
    <song><name>I Want to Break Free</name></song>
    <song><name>Friends Will Be Friends</name></song>
</songs>'
SELECT * FROM OPENXML(@hdoc, '/songs/song', 2) WITH
    (name varchar(80))
EXEC sp_xml_removedocument @hDoc
```

(Results)

```
name
------------------------------------------------------------------
Somebody to Love
These Are the Days of Our Lives
Bicycle Race
Who Wants to Live Forever
I Want to Break Free
Friends Will Be Friends
```

To use OPENXML, follow these basic steps.

1. Call sp_xml_preparedocument to load the XML document into memory. MSXML's DOM parser is called to translate the document into a tree of nodes that you can then access with an XPath query. A pointer to this tree is returned by the procedure as an integer.
2. Issue a SELECT statement from OPENXML, passing in the handle you received in step 1.
3. Include XPath syntax in the call to OPENXML in order to specify exactly which nodes you want to access.
4. Optionally include a WITH clause that maps the XML document into a specific table schema. This can be a full table schema as well as a reference to a table itself.

OPENXML is extremely flexible, so several of these steps have variations and alternatives, but this is the basic process you follow to shred and use an XML document with OPENXML.

Listing 18.18 presents a variation of the earlier query that employs a table to define the schema used to map the document.

Listing 18.18

```
USE tempdb
GO
create table songs (name varchar(80))
go
DECLARE @hDoc int
EXEC sp_xml_preparedocument @hDoc output,
'<songs>
  <song><name>Somebody to Love</name></song>
  <song><name>These Are the Days of Our Lives</name></song>
  <song><name>Bicycle Race</name></song>
  <song><name>Who Wants to Live Forever</name></song>
  <song><name>I Want to Break Free</name></song>
  <song><name>Friends Will Be Friends</name></song>
</songs>'
SELECT * FROM OPENXML(@hdoc, '/songs/song', 2) WITH songs
EXEC sp_xml_removedocument @hDoc
GO
DROP TABLE songs
```

(Results)

```
name
-------------------------------------------------------------------
Somebody to Love
These Are the Days of Our Lives
Bicycle Race
Who Wants to Live Forever
I Want to Break Free
Friends Will Be Friends
```

You can also use the WITH clause to set up detailed mappings between the XML document and the tables in your database, as shown in Listing 18.19.

Listing 18.19

```
DECLARE @hDoc int
EXEC sp_xml_preparedocument @hDoc output,
'<songs>
  <artist name="Johnny Hartman">
  <song> <name>It Was Almost Like a Song</name></song>
```

```
<song> <name>I See Your Face Before Me</name></song>
<song> <name>For All We Know</name></song>
<song> <name>Easy Living</name></song>
</artist>
<artist name="Harry Connick, Jr.">
<song> <name>Sonny Cried</name></song>
<song> <name>A Nightingale Sang in Berkeley Square</name></song>
<song> <name>Heavenly</name></song>
<song> <name>You Didn''t Know Me When</name></song>
</artist>
</songs>'
SELECT * FROM OPENXML(@hdoc, '/songs/artist/song', 2)
WITH (artist varchar(30) '../@name',
      song varchar(50) 'name')
EXEC sp_xml_removedocument @hDoc
```

(Results)

```
artist                           song
-------------------------        ---------------------------------------
Johnny Hartman                   It Was Almost Like a Song
Johnny Hartman                   I See Your Face Before Me
Johnny Hartman                   For All We Know
Johnny Hartman                   Easy Living
Harry Connick, Jr.               Sonny Cried
Harry Connick, Jr.               A Nightingale Sang in Berkeley Square
Harry Connick, Jr.               Heavenly
Harry Connick, Jr.               You Didn't Know Me When
```

Note that attribute references are prefixed with the @ symbol. In Listing 18.19, we supply an XPath query that navigates the tree down to the song element, then reference an attribute called name in song's parent element, artist. For the second column, we retrieve a child element of song that's also called name.

Listing 18.20 offers another example.

Listing 18.20

```
DECLARE @hDoc int
EXEC sp_xml_preparedocument @hDoc output,
'<songs>
```

```
    <artist> <name>Johnny Hartman</name>
    <song> <name>It Was Almost Like a Song</name></song>
    <song> <name>I See Your Face Before Me</name></song>
    <song> <name>For All We Know</name></song>
    <song> <name>Easy Living</name></song>
    </artist>
    <artist> <name>Harry Connick, Jr.</name>
    <song> <name>Sonny Cried</name></song>
    <song> <name>A Nightingale Sang in Berkeley Square</name></song>
    <song> <name>Heavenly</name></song>
    <song> <name>You Didn''t Know Me When</name></song>
    </artist>
</songs>'
SELECT * FROM OPENXML(@hdoc, '/songs/artist/name', 2)
WITH (artist varchar(30) '.',
      song varchar(50) '../song/name')
EXEC sp_xml_removedocument @hDoc
```

(Results)

```
artist                          song
------------------------       -------------------------------------
Johnny Hartman                  It Was Almost Like a Song
Harry Connick, Jr.              Sonny Cried
```

Notice that we get only two rows. Why is that? It's due to the fact that our XPath pattern navigated to the artist/name node, of which there are only two. In addition to getting each artist's name element, we also grabbed the name of its first song element. In the previous query, the XPath pattern navigated us to the song element, of which there were eight, then referenced each song's parent node (its artist) via the XPath ".." designator.

Note the use in the above query of the XPath "." specifier. This merely references the current element. We need it here because we are changing the name of the current element from name to artist. Keep this technique in mind when you want to rename an element you're returning via OPENXML.

The flags Parameter

OPENXML's flags parameter allows you to specify whether OPENXML should process the document in an attribute-centric fashion, an element-centric fashion, or some combination of the two. Thus far, we've been specifying 2 for the flags parameter, which specifies element-centric mapping. Listing 18.21 shows an example of attribute-centric mapping.

Listing 18.21

```
DECLARE @hDoc int
EXEC sp_xml_preparedocument @hDoc output,
'<songs>
  <artist name="Johnny Hartman">
  <song name="It Was Almost Like a Song"/>
  <song name="I See Your Face Before Me"/>
  <song name="For All We Know"/>
  <song name="Easy Living"/>
  </artist>
  <artist name="Harry Connick, Jr.">
  <song name="Sonny Cried"/>
  <song name="A Nightingale Sang in Berkeley Square"/>
  <song name="Heavenly"/>
  <song name="You Didn''t Know Me When"/>
  </artist>
</songs>'
SELECT * FROM OPENXML(@hdoc, '/songs/artist/song', 1)
WITH (artist varchar(30) '../@name',
      song varchar(50) '@name')
EXEC sp_xml_removedocument @hDoc
```

(Results)

artist	song
Johnny Hartman	It Was Almost Like a Song
Johnny Hartman	I See Your Face Before Me
Johnny Hartman	For All We Know
Johnny Hartman	Easy Living
Harry Connick, Jr.	Sonny Cried
Harry Connick, Jr.	A Nightingale Sang in Berkeley Square
Harry Connick, Jr.	Heavenly
Harry Connick, Jr.	You Didn't Know Me When

Edge Table Format

You can completely omit OPENXML's WITH clause in order to retrieve a portion of an XML document in "edge table format"—essentially a two-dimensional representation of the XML tree. Listing 18.22 provides an example.

Listing 18.22

```
DECLARE @hDoc int
EXEC sp_xml_preparedocument @hDoc output,
'<songs>
  <artist name="Johnny Hartman">
  <song> <name>It Was Almost Like a Song</name></song>
  <song> <name>I See Your Face Before Me</name></song>
  <song> <name>For All We Know</name></song>
  <song> <name>Easy Living</name></song>
  </artist>
  <artist name="Harry Connick, Jr.">
  <song> <name>Sonny Cried</name></song>
  <song> <name>A Nightingale Sang in Berkeley Square</name></song>
  <song> <name>Heavenly</name></song>
  <song> <name>You Didn''t Know Me When</name></song>
  </artist>
</songs>'
SELECT * FROM OPENXML(@hdoc, '/songs/artist/song', 2)
EXEC sp_xml_removedocument @hDoc
```

(Results abridged)

id	parentid	nodetype	localname
4	2	1	song
5	4	1	name
22	5	3	#text
6	2	1	song
7	6	1	name
23	7	3	#text
8	2	1	song
9	8	1	name
24	9	3	#text
10	2	1	song
11	10	1	name
25	11	3	#text
14	12	1	song

15	14	1	name
26	15	3	#text
16	12	1	song
17	16	1	name
27	17	3	#text
18	12	1	song
19	18	1	name
28	19	3	#text
20	12	1	song
21	20	1	name
29	21	3	#text

Inserting Data with OPENXML

Given that it's a rowset function, it's natural that you'd want to insert the results of a SELECT against OPENXML into another table. There are a couple of ways to approach this. First, you could execute a separate pass against the XML document for each piece of it you wanted to extract. You would execute an INSERT...SELECT FROM OPENXML for each table you wanted to insert rows into, grabbing a different section of the XML document with each pass, as demonstrated in Listing 18.23.

Listing 18.23

```
USE tempdb
GO
CREATE TABLE Artists
(ArtistId varchar(5),
  Name varchar(30))
GO
CREATE TABLE Songs
(ArtistId varchar(5),
  SongId int,
  Name varchar(50))
GO

DECLARE @hDoc int
EXEC sp_xml_preparedocument @hDoc output,
'<songs>
  <artist id="JHART" name="Johnny Hartman">
  <song id="1" name="It Was Almost Like a Song"/>
  <song id="2" name="I See Your Face Before Me"/>
  <song id="3" name="For All We Know"/>
```

```
        <song id="4" name="Easy Living"/>
    </artist>
    <artist id="HCONN" name="Harry Connick, Jr.">
    <song id="1" name="Sonny Cried"/>
    <song id="2" name="A Nightingale Sang in Berkeley Square"/>
    <song id="3" name="Heavenly"/>
    <song id="4" name="You Didn''t Know Me When"/>
    </artist>
</songs>'
INSERT Artists (ArtistId, Name)
SELECT id,name
FROM OPENXML(@hdoc, '/songs/artist', 1)
WITH (id varchar(5) '@id',
      name varchar(30) '@name')

INSERT Songs (ArtistId, SongId, Name)
SELECT artistid, id,name
FROM OPENXML(@hdoc, '/songs/artist/song', 1)
WITH (artistid varchar(5) '../@id',
      id int '@id',
      name varchar(50) '@name')
EXEC sp_xml_removedocument @hDoc
GO
SELECT * FROM Artists
SELECT * FROM Songs
GO
DROP TABLE Artists, Songs
```

(Results)

```
ArtistId Name
-------- ------------------------------
JHART    Johnny Hartman
HCONN    Harry Connick, Jr.

ArtistId SongId      Name
-------- ----------- ---------------------------------------------
JHART    1           It Was Almost Like a Song
JHART    2           I See Your Face Before Me
JHART    3           For All We Know
JHART    4           Easy Living
HCONN    1           Sonny Cried
HCONN    2           A Nightingale Sang in Berkeley Square
HCONN    3           Heavenly
HCONN    4           You Didn't Know Me When
```

As you can see, we make a separate call to OPENXML for each table. The tables are normalized; the XML document is not, so we shred it into multiple tables. Listing 18.24 shows another way to accomplish the same thing that doesn't require multiple calls to OPENXML.

Listing 18.24

```
USE tempdb
GO
CREATE TABLE Artists
(ArtistId varchar(5),
  Name varchar(30))
GO
CREATE TABLE Songs
(ArtistId varchar(5),
  SongId int,
  Name varchar(50))
GO
CREATE VIEW ArtistSongs AS
SELECT a.ArtistId,
       a.Name AS ArtistName,
       s.SongId,
       s.Name as SongName
FROM Artists a JOIN Songs s
ON (a.ArtistId=s.ArtistId)
GO
CREATE TRIGGER ArtistSongsInsert ON ArtistSongs INSTEAD OF
     INSERT AS
INSERT Artists
SELECT DISTINCT ArtistId, ArtistName FROM inserted
INSERT Songs
SELECT ArtistId, SongId, SongName FROM inserted
GO

DECLARE @hDoc int
EXEC sp_xml_preparedocument @hDoc output,
'<songs>
  <artist id="JHART" name="Johnny Hartman">
  <song id="1" name="It Was Almost Like a Song"/>
  <song id="2" name="I See Your Face Before Me"/>
  <song id="3" name="For All We Know"/>
  <song id="4" name="Easy Living"/>
  </artist>
  <artist id="HCONN" name="Harry Connick, Jr.">
```

```
      <song id="1" name="Sonny Cried"/>
      <song id="2" name="A Nightingale Sang in Berkeley Square"/>
      <song id="3" name="Heavenly"/>
      <song id="4" name="You Didn''t Know Me When"/>
      </artist>
</songs>'
INSERT ArtistSongs (ArtistId, ArtistName, SongId, SongName)
SELECT artistid, artistname, songid, songname
FROM OPENXML(@hdoc, '/songs/artist/song', 1)
WITH (artistid varchar(5) '../@id',
      artistname varchar(30) '../@name',
      songid int '@id',
      songname varchar(50) '@name')

EXEC sp_xml_removedocument @hDoc
GO
SELECT * FROM Artists
SELECT * FROM Songs
GO
DROP VIEW ArtistSongs
GO
DROP TABLE Artists, Songs
```

(Results)

```
ArtistId Name
-------- -------------------------------
HCONN    Harry Connick, Jr.
JHART    Johnny Hartman

ArtistId SongId      Name
-------- ----------- ----------------------------------------------
JHART    1           It Was Almost Like a Song
JHART    2           I See Your Face Before Me
JHART    3           For All We Know
JHART    4           Easy Living
HCONN    1           Sonny Cried
HCONN    2           A Nightingale Sang in Berkeley Square
HCONN    3           Heavenly
HCONN    4           You Didn't Know Me When
```

This technique uses a view and an INSTEAD OF trigger to alleviate the need for two passes with OPENXML. We use a view to simulate the denormalized layout of the XML document, then set up an INSTEAD OF trigger to allow us to insert the data in the XML document "into" this view. The trigger performs the actual work of shredding, only it does so much more efficiently than calling OPENXML twice. It makes two passes over the logical inserted table and splits the columns contained therein (which mirror those of the view) into two separate tables.

Accessing SQL Server over HTTP

To get started accessing SQL Server via HTTP, you should set up an IIS virtual directory using the Configure IIS Support menu option in the SQLXML program folder. Of course, you can retrieve XML data from SQL Server without setting up a virtual directory (e.g., by using ADO or OLE DB); I'm referring exclusively to retrieving XML data from SQL Server via HTTP.

Configuring a virtual directory allows you to work with SQL Server's XML features via HTTP. You use a virtual directory to establish a link between a SQL Server database and a segment of a URL. It provides a navigation path from the root directory on your Web server to a database on your SQL Server.

SQL Server's ability to publish data over HTTP is made possible through SQLISAPI, an Internet Server API (ISAPI) extension that ships with the product. SQLISAPI uses SQLOLEDB, SQL Server's native OLE DB provider, to access the database associated with a virtual directory and return results to the client.

Client applications have four methods of requesting data from SQL Server over HTTP. These can be broken down into two broad types: those more suitable for private intranet access because of security concerns, and those safe to use on the public Internet.

Private Intranet

1. Post an XML query template to SQLISAPI.
2. Send a SELECT...FOR XML query string in a URL.

Public Internet

3. Specify a server-side XML schema in a virtual root.
4. Specify a server-side XML query template in a virtual root.

Due to their open-ended nature, methods 1 and 2 could pose security risks over the public Internet but are perfectly valid on corporate or private intranets. Normally, Web applications use server-side schemas and query templates to make XML data accessible to the outside world in a controlled fashion.

Configuring a Virtual Directory

Load the Configure IIS Support utility in the SQLXML folder under Start | Programs. You should see the IIS servers configured on the current machine. Click the plus sign to the left of your server name to expand it. (If your server isn't listed—for example, if it's a remote server—right-click the IIS Virtual Directory Manager node and select Connect to connect to your server.) To add a new virtual directory, right-click the Default Web Site node and select New | Virtual Directory. You should then see the New Virtual Directory Properties dialog.

Specifying a Virtual Directory Name and Path

The Virtual Directory Name entry box is where you specify the name of the new virtual directory. This is the name that users will include in a URL to access the data exposed by the virtual directory, so it's important to make it descriptive. A common convention is to name virtual directories after the databases they reference. To work through the rest of the examples in the chapter, specify Northwind as the name of the new virtual directory.

Though Local Path will sometimes not be used, it's required nonetheless. In a normal ASP or HTML application, this would be the path where the source files themselves reside. In SQLISAPI applications, this folder does not necessarily need to contain anything, but it must exist nevertheless. On NTFS partitions, you must also make sure that users have at least read access to this folder in order to use the virtual directory. You configure which user account will be used to access the application (and thus will need access to the folder) in the dialog's Security page.

Click the Security tab to select the authentication mode you'd like to use. You can use a specific user account, Windows Integrated Authentication, or Basic (clear text) Authentication. Select the option that matches your usage scenario most closely; Windows Integrated Authentication will likely be the best choice for working through the demos in this chapter.

Next, click the Data Source page tab. This is where you set the SQL Server and the database that the virtual directory references. Select your SQL Server from the list and specify Northwind as the database name.

Go to the Virtual Names table and set up two virtual names, templates and schemas. Create two folders under Northwind named Templates and Schemas so that each of these virtual names can have its own local folder. Set the type for schemas to schema and the type for templates to template.

Each of these provides a navigation path from a URL to the files in its local folder. We'll use them later.

The last dialog page we're concerned with is the Settings page. Click it, then make sure every checkbox on it is checked. We want to allow all of these options so that we may test them later in the chapter. The subsections below provide brief descriptions of each of the options on the Settings page.

Allow sql=... or template=... or URL queries

When this option is enabled, you can execute queries posted to a URL (via an HTTP GET or POST command) as sql= or template= parameters. URL queries allow users to specify a complete Transact-SQL query via a URL. Special characters are replaced with placeholders, but, essentially, the query is sent to the server as is, and its results are returned over HTTP. Note that this option allows users to execute arbitrary queries against the virtual root and database, so you shouldn't enable it for anything but intranet use. Go ahead and enable it for now so that we can try it out later.

Selecting this option disables the Allow template=... containing update-grams only option because you can always post XML templates with up-dategrams when this option is selected. The Allow template=... containing updategrams only option permits XML templates (that contain only update-grams) to be posted to a URL. Since this disallows SQL and XPath queries from existing in a template, it provides some limited security.

Template queries are by far the most popular method of retrieving XML data from SQL Server over HTTP. XML documents that store query tem-plates—generic parameterized queries with placeholders for parameters—reside on the server and provide a controlled access to the underlying data. The results from template queries are returned over HTTP to the user.

Allow XPath

When Allow XPath is enabled, users can use a subset of the XPath language to retrieve data from SQL Server based on an annotated schema. Annotated schemas are stored on a Web server as XML documents and map XML ele-ments and attributes to the data in the database referenced by a virtual di-rectory. XPath queries allow the user to specify the data defined in an annotated schema to return.

Allow POST

HTTP supports the notion of sending data to a Web server via its POST com-mand. When Allow POST is enabled, you can post a query template (usually implemented as a hidden form field on a Web page) to a Web server via HTTP. This causes the query to be executed and returns the results back to the client.

As I mentioned earlier, the open-endedness of this usually limits its use to private intranets. Malicious users could form their own templates and post them over HTTP to retrieve data to which they aren't supposed to have access or, worse yet, make changes to it.

Run on the client

This option specifies that XML formatting (e.g., FOR XML) is to be done on the client side. Enabling this option allows you to offload to the client the work of translating a rowset into XML for HTTP queries.

Expose runtime errors as HTTP error

This option controls whether query errors in an XML template are returned in the HTTP header or as part of the generated XML document. When this option is enabled and a query in a template fails, HTTP error 512 is returned and error descriptions are returned in the HTTP header. When it's disabled and a template query fails, the HTTP success code, 200, is returned, and the error descriptions are returned as processing instructions inside the XML document.

Enable all the options on the Settings page except the last two described above and click OK to create your new virtual directory.

TIP: A handy option on the Advanced tab is Disable caching of mapping schemas. Normally, mapping schemas are cached in memory the first time they're used and accessed from the cache thereafter. While developing a mapping schema, you'll likely want to disable this so that the schema will be reloaded each time you test it.

URL Queries

The facility that permits SQL Server to be queried via HTTP resides in SQLXML's ISAPI extension DLL, SQLIS*n*.DLL, commonly referred to as SQLISAPI. Although the Configure IIS Support tool provides a default, you can configure the exact extension DLL uses when you set up a virtual directory for use by HTTP queries.

If you attach to IIS (the executable name is inetinfo.exe) with WinDbg prior to running any HTTP queries, you'll see ModLoad messages for SQLIS*n*.DLL as well as one or two other DLLs. An ISAPI extension DLL is not loaded until the first time it's called.

Architecturally, here's what happens when you execute a basic URL query.

1. You supply the query as a URL in a Web browser.
2. It travels from your browser to the Web server as an HTTP GET request.
3. The virtual directory specified in your query indicates which extension DLL should be called to process the URL. IIS loads the appropriate extension and passes your query to it.
4. SQLIS*n*.DLL, the SQLISAPI extension DLL, gathers the connection, authentication, and database information from the specified virtual directory entry, connects to the appropriate SQL Server and database, and runs the specified query. If the query was passed as a plain T-SQL query, it comes into the server as a language event. If it was passed as a template query, it comes in as an RPC event.
5. The server gathers the requested data and returns it to SQLIS*n*.DLL.
6. The ISAPI extension returns the result data to the Web server, which then, in turn, sends it to the client browser that requested it. Thus, the original HTTP GET request is completed.

Using URL Queries

The easiest way to test the virtual directory you built earlier is to submit a URL query that uses it from an XML-enabled browser such as Internet Explorer. URL queries take this form:

```
http://localhost/Northwind?sql=SELECT+*+FROM+
Customers+FOR+XML+AUTO &root=Customers
```

NOTE: As with all URLs, the URL listed above should be typed on one line. Page width restrictions may force some of the URLs listed in this book to span multiple lines, but a URL should always be typed on a single line.

Here, localhost is the name of the Web server. It could just as easily be a fully qualified DNS domain name such as http://www.khen.com. Northwind is the virtual directory name we created earlier.

A question mark separates the URL from its parameters. Multiple parameters are separated by ampersands. The first parameter we pass here is named sql. It specifies the query to run. The second parameter specifies the name of the root element for the XML document that will be returned. By definition, you get just one of these per document. Failure to specify a root element results in an error if your query returns more than one top-level element.

To see how this works, submit the URL shown in Listing 18.25 from your Web browser. (Be sure to change localhost to the correct name of your Web server if it resides on a different machine).

Listing 18.25

```
http://localhost/Northwind?sql=SELECT+*+FROM+Customers+WHERE
+CustomerId='ALFKI'+FOR+XML+AUTO
```

(Results)

```
<Customers CustomerID="ALFKI" CompanyName="Alfreds Futterkiste"
ContactName="Maria Anders" ContactTitle="Sales Representative"
Address="Obere Str. 57" City="Berlin" PostalCode="12209"
Country="Germany" Phone="030-0074321" Fax="030-0076545" />
```

Notice that we left off the root element specification. Look at what happens when we bring back more than one row (Listing 18.26).

Listing 18.26

```
http://localhost/Northwind?sql=SELECT+*+FROM+Customers+
WHERE+CustomerId='ALFKI'+OR+CustomerId='ANATR'+FOR+XML+AUTO
```

(Results abridged)

```
The XML page cannot be displayed
Only one top level element is allowed in an XML document.
Line 1, Position 243
```

Since we're returning multiple top-level elements (two, to be exact), our XML document has two root elements named Customers, which, of course, isn't allowed since it isn't well-formed XML. To remedy the situation, we need to specify a root element. This element can be named anything—it serves only to wrap the rows returned by FOR XML so that we have a well-formed document. Listing 18.27 shows an example.

Listing 18.27

```
http://localhost/Northwind?sql=SELECT+*+FROM+Customers+WHERE
+CustomerId='ALFKI'+OR+CustomerId='ANATR'+FOR+XML+AUTO
&root=CustomerList
```

(Results)

```
<?xml version="1.0" encoding="utf-8" ?>
<CustomerList>
  <Customers CustomerID="ALFKI" CompanyName="Alfreds Futterkiste"
    ContactName="Maria Anders" ContactTitle="Sales Representative"
    Address="Obere Str. 57" City="Berlin" PostalCode="12209"
    Country="Germany" Phone="030-0074321" Fax="030-0076545" />
  <Customers CustomerID="ANATR" CompanyName=
    "Ana Trujillo Emparedados y helados" ContactName="Ana Trujillo"
    ContactTitle="Owner" Address="Avda. de la Constitución 2222"
    City="México D.F." PostalCode="05021" Country="Mexico"
    Phone="(5) 555-4729" Fax="(5) 555-3745" />
</CustomerList>
```

You can also supply the root element yourself as part of the sql parameter, as shown in Listing 18.28.

Listing 18.28

```
http://localhost/Northwind?sql=SELECT+'<CustomerList>';
SELECT+*+FROM+Customers+WHERE+CustomerId='ALFKI'+OR
+CustomerId='ANATR'+FOR+XML+AUTO;
SELECT+'</CustomerList>';
```

(Results formatted)

```
<CustomerList>
  <Customers CustomerID="ALFKI" CompanyName="Alfreds Futterkiste"
    ContactName="Maria Anders" ContactTitle="Sales Representative"
    Address="Obere Str. 57" City="Berlin" PostalCode="12209"
    Country="Germany" Phone="030-0074321" Fax="030-0076545" />
  <Customers CustomerID="ANATR" CompanyName=
    "Ana Trujillo Emparedados y helados" ContactName="Ana Trujillo"
    ContactTitle="Owner" Address="Avda. de la Constitución 2222"
    City="México D.F." PostalCode="05021" Country="Mexico"
    Phone="(5) 555-4729" Fax="(5) 555-3745" />
</CustomerList>
```

The sql parameter of this URL actually contains three queries. The first one generates an opening tag for the root element. The second is the query itself, and the third generates a closing tag for the root element. We separate the individual queries with semicolons.

As you can see, FOR XML returns XML document fragments, so you'll need to provide a root element in order to produce a well-formed document.

Special Characters

Certain characters that are perfectly valid in Transact-SQL can cause problems in URL queries because they have special meanings within a URL. You've already noticed that we're using the plus symbol (+) to signify a space character. Obviously, this precludes the direct use of + in the query itself. Instead, you must encode characters that have special meaning within a URL query so that SQLISAPI can properly translate them before passing on the query to SQL Server. Encoding a special character amounts to specifying a percent sign (%) followed by the character's ASCII value in hexadecimal. Table 18.3 lists the special characters recognized by SQLISAPI and their corresponding values.

Here's a URL query that illustrates how to encode special characters.

```
http://localhost/Northwind?sql=SELECT+'<CustomerList>';SELECT
  +*+FROM+Customers+ WHERE+CustomerId+LIKE+'A%25'+FOR+XML+AUTO;
  SELECT+'</CustomerList>';
```

This query specifies a LIKE predicate that includes an encoded percent sign (%), Transact-SQL's wildcard symbol. Hexadecimal 25 (decimal 37) is the ASCII value of the percent sign, so we encode it as %25.

Table 18.3 Special Characters and Their Hexadecimal Values

Character	Hexadecimal Value
+	2B
&	26
?	3F
%	25
/	2F
#	23

Style Sheets

In addition to the sql and root parameters, a URL query can also include the xsl parameter in order to specify an XML style sheet to use to translate the XML document that's returned by the query into a different format. The most common use of this feature is to translate the document into HTML. This allows you to view the document using browsers that aren't XML aware and gives you more control over the display of the document in those that are. Here's a URL query that includes the xsl parameter:

```
http://localhost/Northwind?sql=SELECT+CustomerId,+CompanyName+FROM
    +Customers+FOR+XML+AUTO&root=CustomerList&xsl=CustomerList.xsl
```

Listing 18.29 shows the XSL style sheet it references and the output produced.

Listing 18.29

```
<?xml version="1.0"?>
<xsl:stylesheet xmlns:xsl="http://www.w3.org/1999/XSL/Transform"
      version="1.0">
  <xsl:template match="/">
    <HTML>
      <BODY>
        <TABLE border="1">
          <TR>
            <TD><B>Customer ID</B></TD>
            <TD><B>Company Name</B></TD>
```

```
          </TR>
          <xsl:for-each select="CustomerList/Customers">
            <TR>
              <TD>
              <xsl:value-of select="@CustomerId"/>
              </TD>
              <TD>
              <xsl:value-of select="@CompanyName"/>
              </TD>
            </TR>
          </xsl:for-each>
        </TABLE>
      </BODY>
    </HTML>
  </xsl:template>
</xsl:stylesheet>
```

(Results abridged)

Customer ID	Company Name
ALFKI	Alfreds Futterkiste
ANATR	Ana Trujillo Emparedados y helados
ANTON	Antonio Moreno TaquerÃa
AROUT	Around the Horn
BERGS	Berglunds snabbkÃ¶p
BLAUS	Blauer See Delikatessen
BLONP	Blondesddsl pÃ¨re et fils
WARTH	Wartian Herkku
WELLI	Wellington Importadora
WHITC	White Clover Markets
WILMK	Wilman Kala
WOLZA	Wolski Zajazd

Content Type

By default, SQLISAPI returns the results of a URL query with the appropriate type specified in the header so that a browser can properly render it. When FOR XML is used in the query, this is text/xml unless the xsl attribute specifies a style sheet that translates the XML document into HTML. In that case, text/html is returned.

You can force the content type using the contenttype URL query parameter, like this:

```
http://localhost/Northwind?sql=SELECT+CustomerId,+CompanyName+FROM
    +Customers+FOR+XML+AUTO&root=CustomerList&xsl=CustomerList.xsl
    &contenttype=text/xml
```

Here, we've specified the style sheet from the previous example in order to cause the content type to default to text/html. Then we override this default by specifying a contenttype parameter of text/xml. The result is an XML document containing the translated result set, as shown in Listing 18.30.

Listing 18.30

```
<HTML>
  <BODY>
    <TABLE border="1">
      <TR>
        <TD>
          <B>Customer ID</B>
        </TD>
        <TD>
          <B>Company Name</B>
        </TD>
      </TR>
      <TR>
        <TD>ALFKI</TD>
        <TD>Alfreds Futterkiste</TD>
      </TR>
      <TR>
        <TD>ANATR</TD>
        <TD>Ana Trujillo Emparedados y helados</TD>
      </TR>
      <TR>
        <TD>WILMK</TD>
        <TD>Wilman Kala</TD>
      </TR>
      <TR>
        <TD>WOLZA</TD>
        <TD>Wolski Zajazd</TD>
      </TR>
```

```
    </TABLE>
  </BODY>
</HTML>
```

So, even though the document consists of well-formed HTML, it's rendered as an XML document because we've forced the content type.

Non-XML Results

Being able to specify the content type comes in particularly handy when working with XML fragments in an XML-aware browser. As I mentioned earlier, executing a FOR XML query with no root element results in an error. You can, however, work around this by forcing the content to HTML, like this:

```
http://localhost/Northwind?sql=SELECT+*+FROM+Customers+WHERE+
    CustomerId='ALFKI'+OR+CustomerId='ANATR'+FOR+XML+AUTO
    &contenttype=text/html
```

If you load this URL in a browser, you'll probably see a blank page because most browsers ignore tags that they don't understand. However, you can view the source of the Web page and you'll see an XML fragment returned as you'd expect. This would be handy in situations where you're communicating with SQLISAPI using HTTP from outside of a browser—from an application of some sort. You could return the XML fragment to the client, then use client-side logic to apply a root element and/or process the XML further.

SQLISAPI also allows you to omit the FOR XML clause in order to return a single column from a table, view, or table-valued function as a plain text stream, as shown in Listing 18.31.

Listing 18.31

```
http://localhost/Northwind?sql=SELECT+CAST(CustomerId+AS+
    char(10))+AS+CustomerId+FROM+Customers+ORDER+BY+CustomerId
    &contenttype=text/html
```

(Results)

```
ALFKI ANATR ANTON AROUT BERGS BLAUS BLONP BOLID BONAP BOTTM BSBEV
CACTU CENTC CHOPS COMMI CONSH DRACD DUMON EASTC ERNSH FAMIA FISSA
FOLIG FOLKO FRANK FRANR FRANS FURIB GALED GODOS GOURL GREAL GROSR
HANAR HILAA HUNGC HUNGO ISLAT KOENE LACOR LAMAI LAUGB LAZYK LEHMS
LETSS LILAS LINOD LONEP MAGAA MAISD MEREP MORGK NORTS OCEAN OLDWO
OTTIK PARIS PERIC PICCO PRINI QUEDE QUEEN QUICK RANCH RATTC REGGC
RICAR RICSU ROMEY SANTG SAVEA SEVES SIMOB SPECD SPLIR SUPRD THEBI
THECR TOMSP TORTU TRADH TRAIH VAFFE VICTE VINET WANDK WARTH WELLI
WHITC WILMK WOLZA
```

Note that SQLISAPI doesn't support returning multicolumn results this way. That said, this is still a handy way to quickly return a simple data list.

Stored Procedures

You can execute stored procedures via URL queries just as you can other types of Transact-SQL queries. Of course, this procedure needs to return its result using FOR XML if you intend to process it as XML in the browser or on the client side. The stored procedure in Listing 18.32 illustrates.

Listing 18.32

```
CREATE PROC ListCustomersXML
@CustomerId varchar(10)='%',
@CompanyName varchar(80)='%'
AS
SELECT CustomerId, CompanyName
FROM Customers
WHERE CustomerId LIKE @CustomerId
AND CompanyName LIKE @CompanyName
FOR XML AUTO
```

Once your procedure correctly returns results in XML format, you can call it from a URL query using the Transact-SQL EXEC command. Listing 18.33 shows an example of a URL query that calls a stored procedure using EXEC.

Listing 18.33

```
http://localhost/Northwind?sql=EXEC+ListCustomersXML
    +@CustomerId='A%25',@CompanyName='An%25'&root=CustomerList
```

(Results)

```
<?xml version="1.0" encoding="utf-8" ?>
<CustomerList>
  <Customers CustomerId="ANATR" CompanyName="Ana Trujillo
      Emparedados y helados" />
  <Customers CustomerId="ANTON" CompanyName="Antonio Moreno
      Taquería" />
</CustomerList>
```

Notice that we specify the Transact-SQL wildcard character "%" by using its encoded equivalent, %25. This is necessary, as I said earlier, because % has special meaning in a URL query.

TIP: You can also use the ODBC CALL syntax to call a stored procedure from a URL query. This executes the procedures via an RPC event on the server, which is generally faster and more efficient than normal T-SQL language events. On high-volume Web sites, the small difference in performance this makes can add up quickly.
Here are a couple of URL queries that use the ODBC CALL syntax:

```
http://localhost/Northwind?sql={CALL+ListCustomersXML}+
    &root=CustomerList
```

```
http://localhost/Northwind?sql={CALL+ListCustomersXML('ALFKI')}+
    &root=CustomerList
```

If you submit one of these URLs from your Web browser while you have a Profiler trace running that includes the RPC:Starting event, you should see an RPC:Starting event for the procedure. This indicates that the procedure is being called via the more efficient RPC mechanism rather than via a language event.
See the Template Queries section below for more information on making RPCs from SQLXML.

Template Queries

A safer and more widely used technique for retrieving data over HTTP is to use server-side XML templates that encapsulate Transact-SQL queries. Because these templates are stored on the Web server and referenced via a virtual name, the end users never see the source code. The templates are XML documents based on the XML-SQL namespace and function as a mechanism for translating a URL into a query that SQL Server can process. As with plain URL queries, results from template queries are returned as either XML or HTML.

Listing 18.34 shows a simple XML query template.

Listing 18.34

```
<?xml version='1.0' ?>
<CustomerList xmlns:sql='urn:schemas-microsoft-com:xml-sql'>
  <sql:query>
    SELECT CustomerId, CompanyName
    FROM Customers
    FOR XML AUTO
  </sql:query>
</CustomerList>
```

Note the use of the sql namespace prefix with the query itself. This is made possible by the namespace reference on the second line of the template (bolded).

Here we're merely returning two columns from the Northwind Customers table, as we've done several times in this chapter. We include FOR XML AUTO to return the data as XML. The URL shown in Listing 18.35 uses the template, along with the data it returns.

Listing 18.35

```
http://localhost/Northwind/templates/CustomerList.XML
```

(Results abridged)

```
<?xml version="1.0" ?>
<CustomerList xmlns:sql="urn:schemas-microsoft-com:xml-sql">
```

```
<Customers CustomerId="ALFKI" CompanyName=
   "Alfreds Futterkiste" />
<Customers CustomerId="VAFFE" CompanyName="Vaffeljernet" />
<Customers CustomerId="VICTE" CompanyName=
   "Victuailles en stock" />
<Customers CustomerId="VINET" CompanyName=
   "Vins et alcools Chevalier" />
<Customers CustomerId="WARTH" CompanyName="Wartian Herkku" />
<Customers CustomerId="WELLI" CompanyName=
   "Wellington Importadora" />
<Customers CustomerId="WHITC" CompanyName=
   "White Clover Markets" />
<Customers CustomerId="WILMK" CompanyName="Wilman Kala" />
<Customers CustomerId="WOLZA" CompanyName="Wolski Zajazd" />
</CustomerList>
```

Notice that we're using the templates virtual name that we created under the Northwind virtual directory earlier.

Parameterized Templates

You can also create parameterized XML query templates that permit the user to supply parameters to the query when it's executed. You define parameters in the header of the template, which is contained in its sql:header element. Each parameter is defined using the sql:param tag and can include an optional default value. Listing 18.36 presents an example.

Listing 18.36

```
<?xml version='1.0' ?>
<CustomerList xmlns:sql='urn:schemas-microsoft-com:xml-sql'>
  <sql:header>
    <sql:param name='CustomerId'>%</sql:param>
  </sql:header>
  <sql:query>
    SELECT CustomerId, CompanyName
    FROM Customers
    WHERE CustomerId LIKE @CustomerId
    FOR XML AUTO
  </sql:query>
</CustomerList>
```

Note the use of sql:param to define the parameter. Here, we give the parameter a default value of % since we're using it in a LIKE predicate in the query. This means that we list all customers if no value is specified for the parameter.

Note that SQLISAPI is smart enough to submit a template query to the server as an RPC when you define query parameters. It binds the parameters you specify in the template as RPC parameters and sends the query to SQL Server using RPC API calls. This is more efficient than using T-SQL language events and should result in better performance, particularly on systems with high throughput.

Listing 18.37 gives an example of a URL that specifies a parameterized template query, along with its results.

Listing 18.37

```
http://localhost/Northwind/Templates/CustomerList2.XML?
  CustomerId=A%25
```

(Results)

```
<?xml version="1.0" ?>
<CustomerList xmlns:sql="urn:schemas-microsoft-com:xml-sql">
  <Customers CustomerId="ALFKI" CompanyName=
    "Alfreds Futterkiste" />
  <Customers CustomerId="ANATR" CompanyName=
    "Ana Trujillo Emparedados y helados" />
  <Customers CustomerId="ANTON" CompanyName=
    "Antonio Moreno Taquería" />
  <Customers CustomerId="AROUT" CompanyName="Around the Horn" />
</CustomerList>
```

Style Sheets

As with regular URL queries, you can specify a style sheet to apply to a template query. You can do this in the template itself or in the URL that accesses it. Here's an example of a URL that applies a style sheet to a template query:

```
http://localhost/Northwind/Templates/CustomerList3.XML
  ?xsl=Templates/CustomerList3.xsl&contenttype=text/html
```

Note the use of the contenttype parameter to force the output to be treated as HTML (bolded). We do this because we know that the style sheet we're applying translates the XML returned by SQL Server into an HTML table.

We include the relative path from the virtual directory to the style sheet because it's not automatically located in the Templates folder even though the XML document is located there. The path specifications for a template query and its parameters are separate from one another.

As I've mentioned, the XML-SQL namespace also supports specifying the style sheet in the template itself. Listing 18.38 shows a template that specifies a style sheet.

Listing 18.38

```
<?xml version='1.0' ?>
<CustomerList xmlns:sql='urn:schemas-microsoft-com:xml-sql'
    sql:xsl='CustomerList3.xsl'>
  <sql:query>
    SELECT CustomerId, CompanyName
    FROM Customers
    FOR XML AUTO
  </sql:query>
</CustomerList>
```

The style sheet referenced by the template appears in Listing 18.39.

Listing 18.39

```
<?xml version="1.0"?>
<xsl:stylesheet xmlns:xsl="http://www.w3.org/1999/XSL/Transform"
    version="1.0">
  <xsl:template match="/">
    <HTML>
      <BODY>
        <TABLE border="1">
          <TR>
            <TD><I>Customer ID</I></TD>
            <TD><I>Company Name</I></TD>
          </TR>
          <xsl:for-each select="CustomerList/Customers">
            <TR>
              <TD><B>
```

```
            <xsl:value-of select="@CustomerId"/>
            </B></TD>
            <TD>
            <xsl:value-of select="@CompanyName"/>
            </TD>
          </TR>
        </xsl:for-each>
      </TABLE>
    </BODY>
  </HTML>
  </xsl:template>
</xsl:stylesheet>
```

Listing 18.40 shows a URL that uses the template and the style sheet shown in the previous two listings, along with the results it produces.

Listing 18.40

```
http://localhost/Northwind/Templates/CustomerList4.XML?
    contenttype=text/html
```

(Results abridged)

Customer ID	Company Name
ALFKI	Alfreds Futterkiste
ANATR	Ana Trujillo Emparedados y helados
ANTON	Antonio Moreno TaquerÃa
AROUT	Around the Horn
VICTE	Victuailles en stock
VINET	Vins et alcools Chevalier
WARTH	Wartian Herkku
WELLI	Wellington Importadora
WHITC	White Clover Markets
WILMK	Wilman Kala
WOLZA	Wolski Zajazd

Note that, once again, we specify the contenttype parameter in order to force the output to be treated as HTML. This is necessary because XML-aware browsers such as Internet Explorer automatically treat the output returned by XML templates as text/xml. Since the HTML we're returning is also well-formed XML, the browser doesn't know to render it as HTML unless we tell it to. That's what the contenttype specification is for—it causes the browser to render the output of the template query as it would any other HTML document.

TIP: While developing XML templates and similar documents that you then test in a Web browser, you may run into problems with the browser caching old versions of documents, even when you click the Refresh button or hit the Refresh key (F5). In Internet Explorer, you can press Ctrl+F5 to cause a document to be completely reloaded, even if the browser doesn't think it needs to be. Usually, this resolves problems with an old version persisting in memory after you've changed the one on disk.

You can also disable the caching of templates for a given virtual directory by selecting the Disable caching of templates option on the Advanced page of the Properties dialog for the virtual directory. I almost always disable all caching while developing templates and other XML documents.

Applying Style Sheets on the Client

If the client is XML-enabled, you can also apply style sheets to template queries on the client side. This offloads a bit of the work of the server but requires a separate roundtrip to download the style sheet to the client. If the client is not XML-enabled, the style sheet will be ignored, making this approach more suitable to situations where you know for certain whether your clients are XML-enabled, such as with private intranet or corporate applications.

The template in Listing 18.41 specifies a client-side style sheet translation.

Listing 18.41

```
<?xml version='1.0' ?>
<?xml-stylesheet type='text/xsl' href='CustomerList3.xsl'?>
<CustomerList xmlns:sql='urn:schemas-microsoft-com:xml-sql'>
  <sql:query>
    SELECT CustomerId, CompanyName
    FROM Customers
    FOR XML AUTO
  </sql:query>
</CustomerList>
```

Note the xml-stylesheet specification at the top of the document (bolded). This tells the client-side XML processor to download the style sheet specified in the href attribute and apply it to the XML document rendered by the template. Listing 18.42 shows the URL and results.

Listing 18.42

```
http://localhost/Northwind/Templates/CustomerList5.XML?
    contenttype=text/html
```

(Results abridged)

Customer ID	Company Name
ALFKI	Alfreds Futterkiste
ANATR	Ana Trujillo Emparedados y helados
ANTON	Antonio Moreno TaquerÃa
AROUT	Around the Horn
VICTE	Victuailles en stock
VINET	Vins et alcools Chevalier
WARTH	Wartian Herkku
WELLI	Wellington Importadora
WHITC	White Clover Markets
WILMK	Wilman Kala
WOLZA	Wolski Zajazd

Client-Side Templates

As I mentioned earlier, it's far more popular (and safer) to store templates on your Web server and route users to them via virtual names. That said, there are times when allowing the user the flexibility to specify templates on the client side is very useful. Specifying client-side templates in HTML or in an application alleviates the necessity to set up in advance the templates or the virtual names that reference them. While this is certainly easier from an administration standpoint, it's potentially unsafe on the public Internet because it allows clients to specify the code they run against your SQL Server. Use of this technique should probably be limited to private intranets and corporate networks.

Listing 18.43 presents a Web page that embeds a client-side template.

Listing 18.43

```
<HTML>
  <HEAD>
    <TITLE>Customer List</TITLE>
  </HEAD>
  <BODY>
    <FORM action='http://localhost/Northwind' method='POST'>
      <B>Customer ID Number</B>
      <INPUT type=text name=CustomerId value='AAAAA'>
      <INPUT type=hidden name=xsl value=Templates/CustomerList2.xsl>
      <INPUT type=hidden name=template value='
      <CustomerList xmlns:sql="urn:schemas-microsoft-com:xml-sql">
        <sql:header>
          <sql:param name="CustomerId">%</sql:param>
        </sql:header>
        <sql:query>
          SELECT CompanyName, ContactName
          FROM Customers
          WHERE CustomerId LIKE @CustomerId
          FOR XML AUTO
        </sql:query>
      </CustomerList>
      '>
      <P><input type='submit'>
    </FORM>
  </BODY>
</HTML>
```

The client-side template (bolded) is embedded as a hidden field in the Web page. If you open this page in a Web browser, you should see an entry box for a Customer ID and a submit button. Entering a customer ID or mask and clicking Submit Query will post the template to the Web server. SQLISAPI will then extract the query contained in the template and run it against SQL Server's Northwind database (because of the template's virtual directory reference). The CustomerList2.xsl style sheet will then be applied to translate the XML document that SQL Server returns into HTML, and the result will be returned to the client. Listing 18.44 shows an example.

Listing 18.44

Customer ID Number | A% |

| Submit Query |

(Results)

Company Name	Contact Name
Alfreds Futterkiste	Maria Anders
Ana Trujillo Emparedados y helados	Ana Trujillo
Antonio Moreno TaquerÃa	Antonio Moreno
Around the Horn	Thomas Hardy

As with server-side templates, client-side templates are sent to SQL Server using an RPC.

Mapping Schemas

XML schemas are XML documents that define the type of data that other XML documents may contain. They are a replacement for the old DTD technology originally employed for that purpose and are easier to use and more flexible because they consist of XML themselves.

By their very nature, schemas also define document exchange formats. Since they define what a document may and may not contain, companies wishing to exchange XML data need to agree on a common schema definition in order to do so. XML schemas allow companies with disparate business needs and cultures to exchange data seamlessly.

A mapping schema is a special type of schema that maps data between an XML document and a relational table. A mapping schema can be used to create an XML view of a SQL Server table. In that sense, a mapping schema is similar to a SQL Server view object that returns an XML-centric view of the underlying SQL Server table or view object.

Work on the final XML Schema standard was still under way when SQL Server 2000 shipped. At that time, Microsoft, along with several other companies, proposed that a subset of the W3C XML-Data syntax be used to define schemas for document interchange. SQL Server's original XML schema support was based on XML-Data Reduced (XDR), an XML-Data subset that can be used to define schemas. Since then, the XML Schema standard has been finalized, and SQLXML has been enhanced to support it. XML Schema is now the preferred method of building schemas for use by SQLXML. It is more flexible and has more features than the original XDR schema support in SQLXML. I'll cover SQLXML's XDR and XML Schema support in the next two sections.

XDR Mapping Schemas

Let's begin our coverage of XDR mapping schemas with an example (Listing 18.45).

Listing 18.45

```
<?xml version="1.0"?>
<Schema name="NorthwindProducts"
  xmlns="urn:schemas-microsoft-com:xml-data"
  xmlns:dt="urn:schemas-microsoft-com:datatypes">

  <ElementType name="Description" dt:type="string"/>
  <ElementType name="Price" dt:type="fixed.19.4"/>

  <ElementType name="Product" model="closed">
    <AttributeType name="ProductCode" dt:type="string"/>
    <attribute type="ProductCode" required="yes"/>
    <element type="Description" minOccurs="1" maxOccurs="1"/>
    <element type="Price" minOccurs="1" maxOccurs="1"/>
  </ElementType>

  <ElementType name="Category" model="closed">
    <AttributeType name="CategoryID" dt:type="string"/>
    <AttributeType name="CategoryName" dt:type="string"/>
    <attribute type="CategoryID" required="yes"/>
```

```
    <attribute type="CategoryName" required="yes"/>
    <element type="Product" minOccurs="1" maxOccurs="*"/>
  </ElementType>

  <ElementType name="Catalog" model="closed">
    <element type="Category" minOccurs="1" maxOccurs="1"/>
  </ElementType>

</Schema>
```

This schema defines how a product catalog might look. (We're using the sample tables and data from the Northwind database.) It uses the datatypes namespace (bolded) to define the valid data types for elements and attributes in the document. Every place you see dt: in the listing is a reference to the datatypes namespace. The use of the closed model guarantees that only elements that exist in the schema can be used in a document based on it.

Listing 18.46 shows an XML document that uses ProductCat.xdr.

Listing 18.46

```
<?xml version="1.0"?>
<Catalog xmlns=
  "x-schema:http://localhost/ProductsCat.xdr">
  <Category CategoryID="1" CategoryName="Beverages">
    <Product ProductCode="1">
      <Description>Chai</Description>
      <Price>18</Price>
    </Product>
    <Product ProductCode="2">
      <Description>Chang</Description>
      <Price>19</Price>
    </Product>
  </Category>
  <Category CategoryID="2" CategoryName="Condiments">
    <Product ProductCode="3">
      <Description>Aniseed Syrup</Description>
      <Price>10</Price>
    </Product>
  </Category>
</Catalog>
```

If you copy both of these files to the root folder of your Web server and type the following URL:

```
http://localhost/ProductsCat.xml
```

into your browser, you should see this output:

```
<?xml version="1.0" ?>
<Catalog xmlns="x-schema:http://localhost/ProductsCat.xdr">
<Category CategoryID="1" CategoryName="Beverages">
  <Product ProductCode="1">
    <Description>Chai</Description>
    <Price>18</Price>
  </Product>
  <Product ProductCode="2">
    <Description>Chang</Description>
    <Price>19</Price>
  </Product>
</Category>
<Category CategoryID="2" CategoryName="Condiments">
  <Product ProductCode="3">
    <Description>Aniseed Syrup</Description>
    <Price>10</Price>
  </Product>
</Category>
</Catalog>
```

You've already seen that XML data can be extracted and formatted in a variety of ways. One of the challenges in exchanging data using XML is this flexibility. Mapping schemas help overcome this challenge. They allow us to return data from a database in a particular format. They allow us to map columns and tables to attributes and elements.

The easiest way to use an XDR schema to map data returned by SQL Server into XML entities is to assume the default mapping returned by SQL Server. That is, every table becomes an element, and every column becomes an attribute. Listing 18.47 presents an XDR schema that does that.

Listing 18.47

```
<?xml version="1.0"?>
<Schema name="customers"
  xmlns="urn:schemas-microsoft-com:xml-data">
```

```
    <ElementType name="Customers">
      <AttributeType name="CustomerId"/>
      <AttributeType name="CompanyName"/>
    </ElementType>
</Schema>
```

Here, we retrieve only two columns, each of them from the Customers table. If you store this XDR schema under a virtual directory on your Web server and retrieve it via a URL, you'll see a simple XML document with the data from the Northwind Customers table in an attribute-centric mapping.

You use XML-Data's ElementType to map a column in a table to an element in the resulting XML document, as demonstrated in Listing 18.48.

Listing 18.48

```
<?xml version="1.0"?>
<Schema name="customers"
  xmlns="urn:schemas-microsoft-com:xml-data">
  <ElementType name="Customers">
    <ElementType name="CustomerId" content="textOnly"/>
    <ElementType name="CompanyName" content="textOnly"/>
  </ElementType>
</Schema>
```

Note the use of the content="textOnly" attribute with each element. In conjunction with the ElementType element, this maps a column to an element in the resulting XML document. Note that the elements corresponding to each column are actually empty—they contain attributes only, no data.

Annotated XDR Schemas

An annotated schema is a mapping schema with special annotations (from the XML-SQL namespace) that link elements and attributes with tables and columns. The code in Listing 18.49 uses our familiar Customer list example.

Listing 18.49

```
<?xml version="1.0"?>
<Schema name="customers"
```

```
xmlns="urn:schemas-microsoft-com:xml-data">
xmlns:sql="urn:schemas-microsoft-com:xml-sql">
<ElementType name="Customer" sql:relation="Customers">
  <AttributeType name="CustomerNumber" sql:field="CustomerId"/>
  <AttributeType name="Name" sql:field="CompanyName"/>
</ElementType>
</Schema>
```

First, note the reference to the XML-SQL namespace at the top of the schema. Since we'll be referencing it later in the schema, we begin with a reference to XML-SQL so that we can use the sql: namespace shorthand for it later. Next, notice the sql:relation attribute of the first ElementType element. It establishes that the Customer element in the resulting document relates to the Customers table in the database referenced by the virtual directory. This allows you to call the element whatever you want. Last, notice the sql:field references. They establish, for example, that the Customer-Number element refers to the CustomerId column in the referenced table. Things get more complicated when multiple tables are involved, but you get the picture—an annotated schema allows you to establish granular mappings between document entities and database entities.

XSD Mapping Schemas

Similarly to XDR, you can also construct XML views using annotated XML Schema Definition (XSD) language. This is, in fact, the preferable way to build annotated schemas because XDR was an interim technology that preceded the finalization of the XML Schema standard, as I mentioned earlier. In this section, we'll talk about the various ways to construct annotated XSD mapping schemas and walk through a few examples.

Just as we did with XDR, let's begin our discussion of XSD mapping schemas with an example (Listing 18.50).

Listing 18.50

```
<xsd:schema xmlns:xsd="http://www.w3.org/2001/XMLSchema"
           xmlns:sql="urn:schemas-microsoft-com:mapping-schema">
  <xsd:element name="Customers" >
    <xsd:complexType>
      <xsd:attribute name="CustomerID" type="xsd:string" />
      <xsd:attribute name="CompanyName" type="xsd:string" />
```

```
      <xsd:attribute name="ContactName" type="xsd:string" />
    </xsd:complexType>
  </xsd:element>
</xsd:schema>
```

Note the reference to the XSD namespace, http://www.w3.org/2001/XMLSchema. We alias this to xsd (the alias name is arbitrary—it serves merely as shorthand to distinguish XSD elements and attributes from those of other namespaces), then prefix XSD elements/attributes in the schema with xsd:.

SQLXML's mapping schema namespace is defined at urn:schemas-microsoft-com:mapping-schema. We use this namespace to map elements and attributes in the schema to tables and columns in a database. We've defined this namespace with an alias of sql, so we'll use a prefix of sql: when referring to elements and attributes in SQLXML's mapping schema namespace.

Default Mapping

The schema above uses default mapping to associate complex XSD types with tables/views of the same name and attributes with same-named columns. Note the absence of any reference to the sql namespace (once it's defined). We're not using it because we're not explicitly mapping any elements or attributes to tables or columns. You can construct a template like the following to query this XML view using an XPath expression:

```
<ROOT xmlns:sql="urn:schemas-microsoft-com:xml-sql">
  <sql:xpath-query mapping-schema="Customers.xsd">
    /Customers
  </sql:xpath-query>
</ROOT>
```

Follow these steps to query the XML view in Listing 18.50 by using the above template from your browser.

1. Save the XML view as Customers.XSD in the templates folder you created under the Northwind virtual directory earlier.
2. Save the template above as CustomersT.XML in the same folder.
3. Go to the following URL in your browser:

```
http://localhost/Northwind/templates/CustomersT.XML
```

Explicit Mapping

A mapping schema can also specify explicit relationships between XSD elements and attributes and SQL Server tables and columns. This is done by using the SQLXML mapped schema namespace I mentioned above. Specifically, we'll make use of sql:field and sql:relation to establish these relationships, as shown in Listing 18.51.

Listing 18.51

```
<xsd:schema xmlns:xsd="http://www.w3.org/2001/XMLSchema"
            xmlns:sql="urn:schemas-microsoft-com:mapping-schema">
  <xsd:element name="Cust" sql:relation="Customers" >
    <xsd:complexType>
      <xsd:sequence>
        <xsd:element name="CustNo"
                     sql:field="CustomerId"
                     type="xsd:integer" />
        <xsd:element name="Contact"
                     sql:field="ContactName"
                     type="xsd:string" />
        <xsd:element name="Company"
                     sql:field="CompanyName"
                     type="xsd:string" />
      </xsd:sequence>
    </xsd:complexType>
  </xsd:element>
</xsd:schema>
```

Note the use of sql:relation to establish the mapping between the Cust document element and the Customers database table and the use of the sql:field notation to establish mappings between document elements and table columns. Because each table column is annotated as an element, each column in the Customers table will become a separate element in the resulting XML document. You can also map table columns to attributes, as demonstrated in Listing 18.52.

Listing 18.52

```
<xsd:schema xmlns:xsd="http://www.w3.org/2001/XMLSchema"
            xmlns:sql="urn:schemas-microsoft-com:mapping-schema">
  <xsd:element name="Cust" sql:relation="Customers" >
```

```
    <xsd:complexType>
      <xsd:attribute name="CustNo" sql:field="CustomerId"
          type="xsd:integer" />
      <xsd:attribute name="Contact" sql:field="ContactName"
          type="xsd:string" />
      <xsd:attribute name="Company" sql:field="CompanyName"
          type="xsd:string" />
    </xsd:complexType>
  </xsd:element>
</xsd:schema>
```

Here, we leave out the complexType element (because we don't need it—we're not defining nested elements) and simply map each table column to an attribute in the XSD using sql:field.

Relationships

You can use the sql:relationship annotation to establish a relationship between two elements. You define an empty sql:relationship element and include parent, parent-key, child, and child-key attributes to define the relationship between the two elements. Relationships defined this way can be named or unnamed. For elements mapped to tables and columns in a SQL Server database, this is similar to joining the tables; the parent/child and parent-key/child-key matchups supply the join criteria. Listing 18.53 shows an example (from EmpOrders.XSD in the CH18 subfolder on the CD accompanying this book).

Listing 18.53

```
<xsd:schema xmlns:xsd="http://www.w3.org/2001/XMLSchema"
            xmlns:sql="urn:schemas-microsoft-com:mapping-schema">

  <xsd:element name="Employee" sql:relation="Employees"
      type="EmployeeType" />
    <xsd:complexType name="EmployeeType" >
      <xsd:sequence>
        <xsd:element name="Order"
                    sql:relation="Orders">
          <xsd:annotation>
            <xsd:appinfo>
              <sql:relationship
                parent="Employees"
```

```
                  parent-key="EmployeeID"
                  child="Orders"
                  child-key="EmployeeID" />
             </xsd:appinfo>
          </xsd:annotation>
          <xsd:complexType>
             <xsd:attribute name="OrderID" type="xsd:integer" />
             <xsd:attribute name="EmployeeID" type="xsd:integer" />
          </xsd:complexType>
        </xsd:element>
      </xsd:sequence>
        <xsd:attribute name="EmployeeID"   type="xsd:integer" />
        <xsd:attribute name="LastName"  type="xsd:string" />
    </xsd:complexType>
</xsd:schema>
```

In this schema, we establish a relationship between the Employee and Order elements using the EmployeeID attribute. Again, this is accomplished via the notational attributes provided by Microsoft's mapping-schema namespace.

sql:inverse

You can use the sql:inverse annotation to invert a relationship established with sql:relationship. Why would you want to do that? SQLXML's updategram logic interprets the schema in order to determine the tables being updated by an updategram. (We'll cover updategrams in the next section.) The parent-child relationships established with sql:relationship determine the order in which row deletions and inserts occur. If you specify the sql:relationship notation such that the parent-child relationship between the tables is the inverse of the underlying primary key/foreign key relationship, the attempted insert or delete operation will fail due to key violations. You can set the sql:inverse attribute to 1 (or true) in the sql:relationship element in order to flip the relationship so that this doesn't happen.

The usefulness of the sql:inverse notation is limited to updategrams. There's no point in inversing a regular mapping schema. Listing 18.54 presents an example of a mapping schema that puts the sql:inverse annotation attribute to good use. (You can find this in OrderDetails.XSD in the CH18 folder on the CD accompanying this book.)

Listing 18.54

```
<xsd:schema xmlns:xsd="http://www.w3.org/2001/XMLSchema"
            xmlns:sql="urn:schemas-microsoft-com:mapping-schema">

  <xsd:element name="OrderDetails" sql:relation="[Order Details]"
      type="OrderDetailsType" />
    <xsd:complexType name="OrderDetailsType" >
      <xsd:sequence>
        <xsd:element name="Order"
                    sql:relation="Orders">
          <xsd:annotation>
            <xsd:appinfo>
              <sql:relationship
                parent="[Order Details]"
                parent-key="OrderID"
                child="Orders"
                child-key="OrderID"
               inverse="true" />
            </xsd:appinfo>
          </xsd:annotation>
          <xsd:complexType>
            <xsd:attribute name="OrderID" type="xsd:integer" />
            <xsd:attribute name="EmployeeID" type="xsd:integer" />
          </xsd:complexType>
        </xsd:element>
      </xsd:sequence>
      <xsd:attribute name="ProductID"   type="xsd:integer" />
      <xsd:attribute name="Qty" sql:field="Quantity" type="xsd:integer" />
    </xsd:complexType>
</xsd:schema>
```

Note the use of square brackets around the Order Details table name. These are required in the mapping schema for SQL Server table names that contain spaces.

sql:mapped

You can use the sql:mapped annotation to control whether an attribute or element is mapped to a database object. When the default mapping is used, every element and attribute in a mapping schema maps to a database object. If you have a schema in which you have elements or attributes that you do not want to map to database objects, you can set the sql:mapped annotation to 0 (or false) in an XSD element or attribute specification. The sql:mapped annotation is especially useful in situations where the schema can't be changed or is being used to validate other XML data and contains elements or attributes that do not have analogues in your database. Listing 18.55 uses sql:mapped to include an element in a mapping schema that is not mapped to a database object.

Listing 18.55

```
<xsd:schema xmlns:xsd="http://www.w3.org/2001/XMLSchema"
            xmlns:sql="urn:schemas-microsoft-com:mapping-schema">

  <xsd:element name="Employee" sql:relation="Employees"
     type="EmployeeType" />
   <xsd:complexType name="EmployeeType" >
     <xsd:sequence>
       <xsd:element name="Order"
                    sql:relation="Orders">
         <xsd:annotation>
           <xsd:appinfo>
             <sql:relationship
               parent="Employees"
               parent-key="EmployeeID"
               child="Orders"
               child-key="EmployeeID" />
           </xsd:appinfo>
         </xsd:annotation>
         <xsd:complexType>
           <xsd:attribute name="OrderID" type="xsd:integer" />
           <xsd:attribute name="EmployeeID" type="xsd:integer" />
         </xsd:complexType>
       </xsd:element>
     </xsd:sequence>
     <xsd:attribute name="EmployeeID"   type="xsd:integer" />
     <xsd:attribute name="LastName"  type="xsd:string" />
     <xsd:attribute name="Level" type="xsd:integer"
          sql:mapped="0" />
   </xsd:complexType>
</xsd:schema>
```

Note the inclusion of the Level attribute in the Employee element. Because it contains a sql:mapped annotation that is set to false, it is not mapped to a database object.

sql:limit-field and sql:limit-value

Similarly to the way you can filter XML views using XPath expressions, you can also filter them based on values returned from the database using the sql:limit-field and sql:limit-value annotations. The sql:limit-field annotation specifies the filter column from the database; sql:limit-value specifies the value to filter it by. Note that sql:limit-value is actually optional—if it isn't supplied, NULL is assumed. Listing 18.56 shows an example of a mapping schema that filters based on the value of a column in the database.

Listing 18.56

```
<xsd:schema xmlns:xsd="http://www.w3.org/2001/XMLSchema"
            xmlns:sql="urn:schemas-microsoft-com:mapping-schema">

  <xsd:element name="Employee" sql:relation="Employees"
      type="EmployeeType" />
    <xsd:complexType name="EmployeeType" >
      <xsd:sequence>
        <xsd:element name="Order"
                     sql:relation="Orders">
          <xsd:annotation>
            <xsd:appinfo>
              <sql:relationship
                parent="Employees"
                parent-key="EmployeeID"
                child="Orders"
                child-key="EmployeeID" />
            </xsd:appinfo>
          </xsd:annotation>
          <xsd:complexType>
            <xsd:attribute name="OrderID" type="xsd:integer" />
            <xsd:attribute name="EmployeeID" type="xsd:integer" />
          </xsd:complexType>
        </xsd:element>
      </xsd:sequence>
      <xsd:attribute name="EmployeeID"
        type="xsd:integer"
        sql:limit-field="EmployeeID"
```

```
        sql:limit-value="3"/>
      <xsd:attribute name="LastName"  type="xsd:string" />
    </xsd:complexType>

</xsd:schema>
```

This schema filters the XML document based on the EmployeeID column in the database. Only those rows with an EmployeeID of 3 are returned in the document. If you submit a URL query against this mapping schema using the following template:

```
<ROOT xmlns:sql="urn:schemas-microsoft-com:xml-sql">
  <sql:xpath-query mapping-schema="EmpOrders_Filtered.XSD">
    /Employee
  </sql:xpath-query>
</ROOT>
```

you'll see a document that looks something like this in your browser (results abridged):

```
<ROOT xmlns:sql="urn:schemas-microsoft-com:xml-sql">
  <Employee EmployeeID="3" LastName="Leverling">
  <Order EmployeeID="3" OrderID="10251" />
  <Order EmployeeID="3" OrderID="10253" />
  <Order EmployeeID="3" OrderID="10256" />
  <Order EmployeeID="3" OrderID="10266" />
  <Order EmployeeID="3" OrderID="10273" />
  <Order EmployeeID="3" OrderID="10283" />
  <Order EmployeeID="3" OrderID="10309" />
  <Order EmployeeID="3" OrderID="10321" />
  <Order EmployeeID="3" OrderID="10330" />
  <Order EmployeeID="3" OrderID="10332" />
  <Order EmployeeID="3" OrderID="10346" />
  <Order EmployeeID="3" OrderID="10352" />
...
</ROOT>
```

sql:key-fields

You use the sql:key-fields annotation to identify the key columns in a table to which an XML view is mapped. The sql:key-fields annotation is usually required in mapping schemas in order to ensure that proper nesting occurs in the resulting XML document. This is because the key columns of the underlying table are used to nest the document. This makes the XML that's produced sensitive to the order of the underlying data. If the key columns of the underlying data can't be determined, the generated XML might be formed incorrectly. You should always specify either sql:key-fields or elements that map directly to tables in the database. Listing 18.57 offers an example of a mapping schema that uses sql:key-fields (from EmpOrders_ KeyFields.XSD in the CH18 folder on the CD accompanying this book).

Listing 18.57

```
<xsd:schema xmlns:xsd="http://www.w3.org/2001/XMLSchema"
            xmlns:sql="urn:schemas-microsoft-com:mapping-schema">

  <xsd:element name="Employee"
  sql:relation="Employees"
  type="EmployeeType"
  sql:key-fields="EmployeeID"/>
    <xsd:complexType name="EmployeeType" >
      <xsd:sequence>
        <xsd:element name="Order"
                     sql:relation="Orders">
          <xsd:annotation>
            <xsd:appinfo>
              <sql:relationship
                parent="Employees"
                parent-key="EmployeeID"
                child="Orders"
                child-key="EmployeeID" />
            </xsd:appinfo>
          </xsd:annotation>
          <xsd:complexType>
            <xsd:attribute name="OrderID" type="xsd:integer" />
            <xsd:attribute name="EmployeeID" type="xsd:integer" />
          </xsd:complexType>
        </xsd:element>
      </xsd:sequence>
        <xsd:attribute name="LastName"  type="xsd:string" />
        <xsd:attribute name="FirstName" type="xsd:string" />
    </xsd:complexType>
</xsd:schema>
```

Note that we haven't mapped the EmployeeID column in the Employees table. Without this column, we don't have a column with which we can join the Orders table. Including it in the sql:key-fields annotation allows us to leave it unmapped but still establish the relationship between the two tables.

Updategrams

Thus far, we've looked at how data can be retrieved from SQL Server in XML format, but we haven't talked about how to update SQL Server data using XML. Updategrams provide an XML-based method of updating data in a SQL Server database. They are basically templates with special attributes and elements that allow you to specify the data you want to update and how you want to update it. An updategram contains a before image and an after image of the data you want to change. You submit updategrams to SQL Server in much the same way as you submit templates. All the execution mechanisms available with templates work equally well with updategrams. You can POST updategrams via HTTP, save updategrams to files and execute them via URLs, and execute updategrams directly via ADO and OLE DB.

How They Work

Updategrams are based on the xml-updategram namespace. You reference this namespace via the xmlns:updg qualifier. Each updategram contains at least one sync element. This sync element contains the data changes you wish to make in the form of before and after elements. The before element contains the before image of the data you wish to change. Normally, it will also contain a primary key or candidate key reference so that SQL Server will be able to locate the row you wish to change. Note that only one row can be selected for update by the before element. If the elements and attributes included in the before element identify more than one row, you'll receive an error message.

For row deletions, an updategram will have a before image but no after image. For insertions, it will have an after image but no before image. And, of course, for updates, an updategram will have both a before image and an after image. Listing 18.58 provides an example.

Listing 18.58

```
<?xml version="1.0"?>
<employeeupdate xmlns:updg=
    "urn:schemas-microsoft-com:xml-updategram">
  <updg:sync>
    <updg:before>
      <Employees EmployeeID="4"/>
    </updg:before>
    <updg:after>
      <Employees City="Scotts Valley" Region="CA"/>
    </updg:after>
  </updg:sync>
</employeeupdate>
```

In this example, we change the City and Region columns for Employee 4 in the Northwind Employees table. The EmployeeID attribute in the before element identifies the row to change, and the City and Region attributes in the after element identify which columns to change and what values to assign them.

Each batch of updates within a sync element is considered a transaction. Either all the updates in the sync element succeed or none of them do. You can include multiple sync elements to break updates into multiple transactions.

Mapping Data

Of course, in sending data to the server for updates, deletions, and insertions via XML, we need a means of linking values in the XML document to columns in the target database table. SQL Server sports two facilities for doing this: default mapping and mapping schemas.

Default Mapping

Naturally, the easiest way to map data in an updategram to columns in the target table is to use the default mapping (also known as intrinsic mapping). With default mapping, a before or after element's top-level tag is assumed to refer to the target database table, and each subelement or attribute it contains refers to a column of the same name in the table.

Here's an example that shows how to map the OrderID column in the Orders table:

```
<Orders OrderID="10248"/>
```

This example maps XML attributes to table columns. You could also map subelements to table columns, like this:

```
<Orders>
  <OrderID>10248</OrderID>
</Orders>
```

You need not select either attribute-centric or element-centric mapping. You can freely mix them within a given before or after element, as shown below:

```
<Orders OrderID="10248">
  <ShipCity>Reims</ShipCity>
</Orders>
```

Use the four-digit hexadecimal UCS-2 code for characters in table names that are illegal in XML elements (e.g., spaces). For example, to reference the Northwind Order Details table, do this:

```
<Order_x0020_Details OrderID="10248"/>
```

Mapping Schemas

You can also use XDR and XSD mapping schemas to map data in an updategram to tables and columns in a database. You use a sync's updg:mapping-schema attribute to specify the mapping schema for an updategram. Listing 18.59 shows an example that specifies an updategram for the Orders table.

Listing 18.59

```
<?xml version="1.0"?>
<orderupdate xmlns:updg=
    "urn:schemas-microsoft-com:xml-updategram">
  <updg:sync updg:mapping-schema="OrderSchema.xml">
    <updg:before>
```

```
      <Order OID="10248"/>
    </updg:before>
    <updg:after>
      <Order City="Reims"/>
    </updg:after>
  </updg:sync>
</orderupdate>
```

Listing 18.60 shows its XDR mapping schema.

Listing 18.60

```
<?xml version="1.0"?>
<Schema xmlns="urn:schemas-microsoft-com:xml-data"
        xmlns:sql="urn:schemas-microsoft-com:xml-sql">
  <ElementType name="Order" sql:relation="Orders">
    <AttributeType name="OID"/>
    <AttributeType name="City"/>
    <attribute type="OID" sql:field="OrderID"/>
    <attribute type="City" sql:field="ShipCity"/>
  </ElementType>
</Schema>
```

Listing 18.61 shows its XSD mapping schema.

Listing 18.61

```
<xsd:schema xmlns:xsd="http://www.w3.org/2001/XMLSchema"
            xmlns:sql="urn:schemas-microsoft-com:mapping-schema">
  <xsd:element name="Order" sql:relation="Orders" >
    <xsd:complexType>
      <xsd:attribute name="OID" sql:field="OrderId"
          type="xsd:integer" />
      <xsd:attribute name="City" sql:field="ShipCity"
          type="xsd:string" />
    </xsd:complexType>
  </xsd:element>
</xsd:schema>
```

As you can see, a mapping schema maps the layout of the XML document to the Northwind Orders table. See the Mapping Schemas section earlier in the chapter for more information on building XML mapping schemas.

NULLs

It's common to represent missing or inapplicable data as NULL in a database. To represent or retrieve NULL data in an updategram, you use the sync element's nullvalue attribute to specify a placeholder for NULL. This placeholder is then used everywhere in the updategram that you need to specify a NULL value, as demonstrated in Listing 18.62.

Listing 18.62

```
<?xml version="1.0"?>
<employeeupdate xmlns:updg=
    "urn:schemas-microsoft-com:xml-updategram">
  <updg:sync updg:nullvalue="NONE">
    <updg:before>
      <Orders OrderID="10248"/>
    </updg:before>
    <updg:after>
      <Orders ShipCity="Reims" ShipRegion="NONE"
        ShipName="NONE"/>
    </updg:after>
  </updg:sync>
</employeeupdate>
```

As you can see, we define a placeholder for NULL named NONE. We then use this placeholder to assign a NULL value to the ShipRegion and ShipName columns.

Parameters

Curiously, parameters work a little differently with updategrams than with templates. Rather than using at (@) symbols to denote updategram parameters, you use dollar ($) symbols, as shown in Listing 18.63.

Listing 18.63

```
<?xml version="1.0"?>
<orderupdate xmlns:updg=
    "urn:schemas-microsoft-com:xml-updategram">
  <updg:header>
    <updg:param name="OrderID"/>
    <updg:param name="ShipCity"/>
  </updg:header>
  <updg:sync>
    <updg:before>
      <Orders OrderID="$OrderID"/>
    </updg:before>
    <updg:after>
      <Orders ShipCity="$ShipCity"/>
    </updg:after>
  </updg:sync>
</orderupdate>
```

This nuance has interesting implications for passing currency values as parameters. To pass a currency parameter value to a table column (e.g., the Freight column in the Orders table), you must map the data using a mapping schema.

NULL Parameters

In order to pass a parameter with a NULL value to an updategram, include the nullvalue placeholder attribute in the updategram's header element. You can then pass this placeholder value into the updategram to signify a NULL parameter value. This is similar to the way you specify a NULL value for a column in an updategram, the difference being that you specify nullvalue within the sync element for column values but within the header element for parameters. Listing 18.64 shows an example.

Listing 18.64

```
<?xml version="1.0"?>
<orderupdate xmlns:updg=
    "urn:schemas-microsoft-com:xml-updategram">
  <updg:header nullvalue="NONE">
    <updg:param name="OrderID"/>
```

```
<updg:param name="ShipCity"/>
</updg:header>
  <updg:sync>
    <updg:before>
      <Orders OrderID="$OrderID"/>
    </updg:before>
    <updg:after>
      <Orders ShipCity="$ShipCity"/>
    </updg:after>
  </updg:sync>
</orderupdate>
```

This updategram accepts two parameters. Passing a value of NONE will cause the ShipCity column to be set to NULL for the specified order.

Note that we don't include the xml-updategram (updg:) qualifier when specifying the nullvalue placeholder for parameters in the updategram's header.

Multiple Rows

I mentioned earlier that each before element can identify at most one row. This means that to update multiple rows, you must include an element for each row you wish to change.

The id Attribute

When you specify multiple subelements within your before and after elements, SQL Server requires that you provide a means of matching each before element with its corresponding after element. One way to do this is through the id attribute. The id attribute allows you to specify a unique string value that you can use to match a before element with an after element. Listing 18.65 gives an example.

Listing 18.65

```
<?xml version="1.0"?>
<orderupdate xmlns:updg=
    "urn:schemas-microsoft-com:xml-updategram">
  <updg:sync>
    <updg:before>
```

```
       <Orders updg:id="ID1" OrderID="10248"/>
       <Orders updg:id="ID2" OrderID="10249"/>
     </updg:before>
     <updg:after>
       <Orders updg:id="ID2" ShipCity="Munster"/>
       <Orders updg:id="ID1" ShipCity="Reims"/>
     </updg:after>
   </updg:sync>
</orderupdate>
```

Here, we use the updg:id attribute to match up subelements in the before and after elements. Even though these subelements are specified out
of sequence, SQL Server is able to apply the updates to the correct rows.

Multiple before and after Elements

Another way to do this is to specify multiple before and after elements rather
than multiple subelements. For each row you want to change, you specify a
separate before/after element pair, as demonstrated in Listing 18.66.

Listing 18.66

```
<?xml version="1.0"?>
<orderupdate xmlns:updg=
    "urn:schemas-microsoft-com:xml-updategram">
  <updg:sync>
    <updg:before>
      <Orders OrderID="10248"/>
    </updg:before>
    <updg:after>
      <Orders ShipCity="Reims"/>
    </updg:after>
    <updg:before>
      <Orders OrderID="10249"/>
    </updg:before>
    <updg:after>
      <Orders ShipCity="Munster"/>
    </updg:after>
  </updg:sync>
</orderupdate>
```

As you can see, this updategram updates two rows. It includes a separate before/after element pair for each update.

Results

The result returned to a client application that executes an updategram is normally an XML document containing the empty root element specified in the updategram. For example, we would expect to see this result returned by the orderupdate updategram:

```
<?xml version="1.0"?>
<orderupdate xmlns:updg=
    "urn:schemas-microsoft-com:xml-updategram">
</orderupdate>
```

Any errors that occur during updategram execution are returned as <?MSSQLError> elements within the updategram's root element.

Identity Column Values

In real applications, you often need to be able to retrieve an identity value that's generated by SQL Server for one table and insert it into another. This is especially true when you need to insert data into a table whose primary key is an identity column and a table that references this primary key via a foreign key constraint. Take the example of inserting orders in the Northwind Orders and Order Details tables. As its name suggests, Order Details stores detail information for the orders in the Orders table. Part of Order Details' primary key is the Orders table's OrderID column. When we insert a new row into the Orders table, we need to be able to retrieve that value and insert it into the Order Details table.

From Transact-SQL, we'd usually handle this situation with an INSTEAD OF insert trigger or a stored procedure. To handle it with an updategram, we use the at-identity attribute. Similarly to the id attribute, at-identity serves as a placeholder—everywhere we use its value in the updategram, SQL Server supplies the identity value for the corresponding table. (Each table can have just one identity column.) Listing 18.67 shows an example.

Listing 18.67

```
<?xml version="1.0"?>
<orderinsert xmlns:updg=
```

```
    "urn:schemas-microsoft-com:xml-updategram">
  <updg:sync>
   <updg:before>
   </updg:before>
   <updg:after>
    <Orders updg:at-identity="ID" ShipCity="Reims"/>
    <Order_x0020_Details OrderID="ID" ProductID="11"
     UnitPrice="$16.00" Quantity="12"/>
    <Order_x0020_Details OrderID="ID" ProductID="42"
     UnitPrice="$9.80" Quantity="10"/>
   </updg:after>
  </updg:sync>
</orderinsert>
```

Here, we use the string "ID" to signify the identity column in the Orders table. Once the string is assigned, we can use it in the insertions for the
Order Details table.

In addition to being able to use an identity column value elsewhere in
an updategram, it's quite likely that you'll want to be able to return it to the
client. To do this, use the after element's returnid attribute and specify the
at-identity placeholder as its value, as shown in Listing 18.68.

Listing 18.68

```
<?xml version="1.0"?>
<orderinsert xmlns:updg=
    "urn:schemas-microsoft-com:xml-updategram">
  <updg:sync>
   <updg:before>
   </updg:before>
   <updg:after updg:returnid="ID">
    <Orders updg:at-identity="ID" ShipCity="Reims"/>
    <Order_x0020_Details OrderID="ID" ProductID="11"
     UnitPrice="$16.00" Quantity="12"/>
    <Order_x0020_Details OrderID="ID" ProductID="42"
     UnitPrice="$9.80" Quantity="10"/>
   </updg:after>
  </updg:sync>
</orderinsert>
```

Executing this updategram will return an XML document that looks like this:

```
<?xml version="1.0"?>
<orderinsert xmlns:updg=
    "urn:schemas-microsoft-com:xml-updategram">
  <returnid>
    <ID>10248</ID>
  </returnid>
</orderinsert>
```

Globally Unique Identifiers

It's not unusual to see Globally Unique Identifiers (GUIDs) used as key values across a partitioned view or other distributed system. (These are stored in columns of type uniqueidentifier.) Normally, you use the Transact-SQL NEWID() function to generate new uniqueidentifiers. The updategram equivalent of NEWID() is the guid attribute. You can specify the guid attribute to generate a GUID for use elsewhere in a sync element. As with id, nullvalue, and the other attributes presented in this section, the guid attribute establishes a placeholder that you can then supply to other elements and attributes in the updategram in order to use the generated GUID. Listing 18.69 presents an example.

Listing 18.69

```
<orderinsert>
  xmlns:updg="urn:schemas-microsoft-com:xml-updategram">
  <updg:sync>
    <updg:before>
    </updg:before>
    <updg:after>
      <Orders updg:guid="GUID">
        <OrderID>GUID</OrderID>
        <ShipCity>Reims</ShipCity>
      </Orders>
      <Order_x0020_Details OrderID="GUID" ProductID="11"
        UnitPrice="$16.00" Quantity="12"/>
      <Order_x0020_Details OrderID="GUID" ProductID="42"
        UnitPrice="$9.80" Quantity="10"/>
    </updg:after>
  </updg:sync>
</orderinsert>
```

XML Bulk Load

As we saw in the earlier discussions of updategrams and OPENXML, inserting XML data into a SQL Server database is relatively easy. However, both of these methods of loading data have one serious drawback: They're not suitable for loading large amounts of data. In the same way that using the Transact-SQL INSERT statement is suboptimal for loading large numbers of rows, using updategrams and OPENXML to load large volumes of XML data into SQL Server is slow and resource intensive.

SQLXML provides a facility intended specifically to address this problem. Called the XML Bulk Load component, it is a COM component you can call from OLE Automation–capable languages and tools such as Visual Basic, Delphi, and even Transact-SQL. It presents an object-oriented interface to loading XML data in bulk in a manner similar to the Transact-SQL BULK INSERT command.

Architecturally, XML Bulk Load is an in-process COM component named SQLXMLBulkLoad that resides in a DLL named XBLKLD*n*.DLL. When it bulk loads data to SQL Server, it does so via the bulk load interface of SQL Server's SQLOLEDB native OLE DB provider. If you have a Profiler trace running while the bulk load is occurring, you'll see an INSERT BULK language event show up in the trace. INSERT BULK is indicative of a special TDS packet type designed especially for bulk loading data. It's neither a true language event nor an RPC event; instead, it is a distinct type of data packet that bulk load facilities send to the server when they want to initiate a bulk copy operation.

Using the Component

The first step in using the XML Bulk Load component is to define a mapping schema that maps the XML data you're importing to tables and columns in your database. When the component loads your XML data, it will read it as a stream and use the mapping schema to decide where the data goes in the database.

The mapping schema determines the scope of each row added by the Bulk Load component. As the closing tag for each row is read, its corresponding data is written to the database.

You access the Bulk Load component itself via the SQLXMLBulkLoad interface on the SQLXMLBulkLoad COM object. The first step in using it is to connect to the database using an OLE DB connection string or by setting its ConnectionCommand property to an existing ADO Command object. The second step is to call its Execute method. The VBScript code in Listing 18.70 illustrates.

Listing 18.70

```
Set objBulkLoad = CreateObject("SQLXMLBulkLoad.SQLXMLBulkLoad")
objBulkLoad.ConnectionString = _
  "provider=SQLOLEDB;data source=KUFNATHE;database=Northwind;" & _
  "Integrated Security=SSPI;"
objBulkLoad.Execute "d:\xml\OrdersSchema.xml",
    "d:\xml\OrdersData.xml"
Set objBulkLoad = Nothing
```

You can also specify an XML stream (rather than a file) to load, making cross-DBMS data transfers (from platforms that feature XML support) fairly easy.

XML Fragments

Setting the XMLFragment property to True allows the Bulk Load component to load data from an XML fragment (an XML document with no root element, similar to the type returned by Transact-SQL's FOR XML extension). Listing 18.71 shows an example.

Listing 18.71

```
Set objBulkLoad = CreateObject("SQLXMLBulkLoad.SQLXMLBulkLoad")
objBulkLoad.ConnectionString = _
  "provider=SQLOLEDB;data source=KUFNATHE;database=Northwind;" & _
  "Integrated Security=SSPI;"
objBulkLoad.XMLFragment = True
objBulkLoad.Execute "d:\xml\OrdersSchema.xml",
    "d:\xml\OrdersData.xml"
Set objBulkLoad = Nothing
```

Enforcing Constraints

By default, the XML Bulk Load component does not enforce check and referential integrity constraints. Enforcing constraints as data is loaded slows down the process significantly, so the component doesn't enforce them unless you tell it to. For example, you might want to do that when you're loading data directly into production tables and you want to ensure that the integrity of your data is not compromised. To cause the component to enforce your constraints as it loads data, set the CheckConstraints property to True, as shown in Listing 18.72.

Listing 18.72

```
Set objBulkLoad = CreateObject("SQLXMLBulkLoad.SQLXMLBulkLoad")
objBulkLoad.ConnectionString = _
  "provider=SQLOLEDB;data source=KUFNATHE;database=Northwind;" & _
  "Integrated Security=SSPI;"
objBulkLoad.CheckConstraints = True
objBulkLoad.Execute "d:\xml\OrdersSchema.xml",
    "d:\xml\OrdersData.xml"
Set objBulkLoad = Nothing
```

Duplicate Keys

Normally you'd want to stop a bulk load process when you encounter a duplicate key. Usually this means you've got unexpected data values or data corruption of some type and you need to look at the source data before proceeding. There are, however, exceptions. Say, for example, that you get a daily data feed from an external source that contains the entirety of a table. Each day, a few new rows show up, but, for the most part, the data in the XML document already exists in your table. Your interest is in loading the new rows, but the external source that provides you the data may not know which rows you have and which ones you don't. They may provide data to lots of companies—what your particular database contains may be unknown to them.

In this situation, you can set the IgnoreDuplicateKeys property before the load, and the component will ignore the duplicate key values it encounters. The bulk load won't halt when it encounters a duplicate key—it will simply ignore the row containing the duplicate key, and the rows with nond-uplicate keys will be loaded as you'd expect. Listing 18.73 shows an example.

Listing 18.73

```
Set objBulkLoad = CreateObject("SQLXMLBulkLoad.SQLXMLBulkLoad")
objBulkLoad.ConnectionString = _
    "provider=SQLOLEDB;data source=KUFNATHE;database=Northwind;" & _
    "Integrated Security=SSPI;"
objBulkLoad.IgnoreDuplicateKeys = True
objBulkLoad.Execute "d:\xml\OrdersSchema.xml",
    "d:\xml\OrdersData.xml"
Set objBulkLoad = Nothing
```

When IgnoreDuplicateKeys is set to True, inserts that would cause a duplicate key will still fail, but the bulk load process will not halt. The re-mainder of the rows will be processed as though no error occurred.

IDENTITY Columns

SQLXMLBulkLoad's KeepIdentity property is True by default. This means that values for identity columns in your XML data will be loaded into the database rather than being generated on-the-fly by SQL Server. Normally, this is what you'd want, but you can set KeepIdentity to False if you'd rather have SQL Server generate these values.

There are a couple of caveats regarding the KeepIdentity property. First, when KeepIdentity is set to True, SQL Server uses SET IDENTITY_ IN-SERT to enable identity value insertion into the target table. SET IDENTITY_ INSERT has specific permissions requirements—execute permission de-faults to the sysadmin role, the db_owner and db_ddladmin fixed database roles, and the table owner. This means that a user who does not own the tar-get table and who also is not a sysadmin, db_owner, or DDL administrator will likely have trouble loading data with the XML Bulk Load component. Merely having bulkadmin rights is not enough.

Another caveat is that you would normally want to preserve identity val-ues when bulk loading data into a table with dependent tables. Allowing these values to be regenerated by the server could be disastrous—you could break parent-child relationships between tables with no hope of recon-structing them. If a parent table's primary key is its identity column and

KeepIdentity is set to False when you load it, you may not be able to resynchronize it with the data you load for its child table. Fortunately, KeepIdentity is enabled by default, so normally this isn't a concern, but be sure you know what you're doing if you choose to set it to False.

Listing 18.74 illustrates setting the KeepIdentity property.

Listing 18.74

```
Set objBulkLoad = CreateObject("SQLXMLBulkLoad.SQLXMLBulkLoad")
objBulkLoad.ConnectionString = _
  "provider=SQLOLEDB;data source=KUFNATHE;database=Northwind;" & _
  "Integrated Security=SSPI;"
objBulkLoad.KeepIdentity = False
objBulkLoad.Execute "d:\xml\OrdersSchema.xml",
    "d:\xml\OrdersData.xml"
Set objBulkLoad = Nothing
```

Another thing to keep in mind is that KeepIdentity is a very binary option—either it's on or it's not. The value you give it affects every object into which XML Bulk Load inserts rows within a given bulk load. You can't retain identity values for some tables and allow SQL Server to generate them for others.

NULL Values

For a column not mapped in the schema, the column's default value is inserted. If the column doesn't have a default, NULL is inserted. If the column doesn't allow NULLs, the bulk load halts with an error message.

The KeepNulls property allows you to tell the bulk load facility to insert a NULL value rather than a column's default when the column is not mapped in the schema. Listing 18.75 demonstrates.

Listing 18.75

```
Set objBulkLoad = CreateObject("SQLXMLBulkLoad.SQLXMLBulkLoad")
objBulkLoad.ConnectionString = _
  "provider=SQLOLEDB;data source=KUFNATHE;database=Northwind;" & _
  "Integrated Security=SSPI;"
objBulkLoad.KeepNulls = True
```

```
objBulkLoad.Execute "d:\xml\OrdersSchema.xml",
    "d:\xml\OrdersData.xml"
Set objBulkLoad = Nothing
```

Table Locks

As with SQL Server's other bulk load facilities, you can configure SQLXM-LBulkLoad to lock the target table before it begins loading data into it. This is more efficient and faster than using more granular locks but has the disadvantage of preventing other users from accessing the table while the bulk load runs. To force a table lock during an XML bulk load, set the ForceTableLock property to True, as shown in Listing 18.76.

Listing 18.76

```
Set objBulkLoad = CreateObject("SQLXMLBulkLoad.SQLXMLBulkLoad")
objBulkLoad.ConnectionString = _
    "provider=SQLOLEDB;data source=KUFNATHE;database=Northwind;" & _
    "Integrated Security=SSPI;"
objBulkLoad.ForceTableLock = True
objBulkLoad.Execute "d:\xml\OrdersSchema.xml",
    "d:\xml\OrdersData.xml"
Set objBulkLoad = Nothing
```

Transactions

By default, XML bulk load operations are not transactional—that is, if an error occurs during the load process, the rows loaded up to that point will remain in the database. This is the fastest way to do things, but it has the disadvantage of possibly leaving a table in a partially loaded state. To force a bulk load operation to be handled as a single transaction, set SQLXML-BulkLoad's Transaction property to True before calling Execute.

When Transaction is True, all inserts are cached in a temporary file before being loaded onto SQL Server. You can control where this file is written by setting the TempFilePath property. TempFilePath has no meaning unless Transaction is True. If TempFilePath is not otherwise set, it defaults to the folder specified by the TEMP environmental variable on the server.

I should point out that bulk loading data within a transaction is much slower than loading it outside of one. That's why the component doesn't load data within a transaction by default. Also note that you can't bulk load binary XML data from within a transaction.

Listing 18.77 illustrates a transactional bulk load.

Listing 18.77

```
Set objBulkLoad = CreateObject("SQLXMLBulkLoad.SQLXMLBulkLoad")
objBulkLoad.ConnectionString = _
  "provider=SQLOLEDB;data source=KUFNATHE;database=Northwind;" & _
  "Integrated Security=SSPI;"
objBulkLoad.Transaction = True
objBulkLoad.TempFilePath = "c:\temp\xmlswap"
objBulkLoad.Execute "d:\xml\OrdersSchema.xml",
    "d:\xml\OrdersData.xml"
Set objBulkLoad = Nothing
```

In this example, SQLXMLBulkLoad establishes its own connection to the server over OLE DB, so it operates within its own transaction context. If an error occurs during the bulk load, the component rolls back its own transaction.

When SQLXMLBulkLoad uses an existing OLE DB connection via its ConnectionCommand property, the transaction context belongs to that connection and is controlled by the client application. When the bulk load completes, the client application must explicitly commit or roll back the transaction. Listing 18.78 shows an example.

Listing 18.78

```
On Error Resume Next
Err.Clear
Set objCmd = CreateObject("ADODB.Command")
objCmd.ActiveConnection= _
  "provider=SQLOLEDB;data source=KUFNATHE;database=Northwind;" & _
  "Integrated Security=SSPI;"
Set objBulkLoad = CreateObject("SQLXMLBulkLoad.SQLXMLBulkLoad")
objBulkLoad.Transaction = True
objBulkLoad.ConnectionCommand = objCmd
objBulkLoad.Execute "d:\xml\OrdersSchema.xml",
    "d:\xml\OrdersData.xml"
```

```
If Err.Number = 0 Then
  objCmd.ActiveConnection.CommitTrans
Else
  objCmd.ActiveConnection.RollbackTrans
End If
Set objBulkLoad = Nothing
Set objCmd = Nothing
```

Note that when using the ConnectionCommand property, Transaction is required—it must be set to True.

Errors

The XML Bulk Copy component supports logging error messages to a file via its ErrorLogFile property. This file is an XML document itself that lists any errors that occurred during the bulk load. Listing 18.79 demonstrates how to use this property.

Listing 18.79

```
Set objBulkLoad = CreateObject("SQLXMLBulkLoad.SQLXMLBulkLoad")
objBulkLoad.ConnectionString = _
  "provider=SQLOLEDB;data source=KUFNATHE;database=Northwind;" & _
  "Integrated Security=SSPI;"
objBulkLoad.ErrorLogFile = "c:\temp\xmlswap\errors.xml"
objBulkLoad.Execute "d:\xml\OrdersSchema.xml",
    "d:\xml\OrdersData.xml"
Set objBulkLoad = Nothing
```

The file you specify will contain a Record element for each error that occurred during the last bulk load. The most recent error message will be listed first.

Generating Database Schemas

In addition to loading data into existing tables, the XML Bulk Copy component can also create target tables for you if they do not already exist, or drop and recreate them if they do exist. To create nonexistent tables, set the component's SchemaGen property to True, as shown in Listing 18.80.

Listing 18.80

```
Set objBulkLoad = CreateObject("SQLXMLBulkLoad.SQLXMLBulkLoad")
objBulkLoad.ConnectionString = _
  "provider=SQLOLEDB;data source=KUFNATHE;database=Northwind;" & _
  "Integrated Security=SSPI;"
objBulkLoad.SchemaGen = True
objBulkLoad.Execute "d:\xml\OrdersSchema.xml",
    "d:\xml\OrdersData.xml"
Set objBulkLoad = Nothing
```

Since SchemaGen is set to True, any tables in the schema that don't already exist will be created when the bulk load starts. For tables that already exist, data is simply loaded into them as it would normally be.

If you set the BulkLoad property of the component to False, no data is loaded. So, if SchemaGen is set to True but BulkLoad is False, you'll get empty tables for those in the mapping schema that did not already exist in the database, but you'll get no data. Listing 18.81 presents an example.

Listing 18.81

```
Set objBulkLoad = CreateObject("SQLXMLBulkLoad.SQLXMLBulkLoad")
objBulkLoad.ConnectionString = _
  "provider=SQLOLEDB;data source=KUFNATHE;database=Northwind;" & _
  "Integrated Security=SSPI;"
objBulkLoad.SchemaGen = True
objBulkLoad.BulkLoad = False
objBulkLoad.Execute "d:\xml\OrdersSchema.xml",
    "d:\xml\OrdersData.xml"
Set objBulkLoad = Nothing
```

When XML Bulk Load creates tables, it uses the information in the mapping schema to define the columns in each table. The sql:datatype annotation defines column data types, and the dt:type attribute further defines column type information. To define a primary key within the mapping schema, set a column's dt:type attribute to id and set the SGUseID property of the XML Bulk Load component to True. The mapping schema in Listing 18.82 illustrates.

Listing 18.82

```
<ElementType name="Orders" sql:relation="Orders">
  <AttributeType name="OrderID" sql:datatype="int" dt:type="id"/>
  <AttributeType name="ShipCity" sql:datatype="nvarchar(30)"/>

  <attribute type="OrderID" sql:field="OrderID"/>
  <attribute type="ShipCity" sql:field="ShipCity"/>
</ElementType>
```

Listing 18.83 shows some VBScript code that sets the SGUseID property so that a primary key will automatically be defined for the table that's created on the server.

Listing 18.83

```
Set objBulkLoad = CreateObject("SQLXMLBulkLoad.SQLXMLBulkLoad")
objBulkLoad.ConnectionString = _
  "provider=SQLOLEDB;data source=KUFNATHE;database=Northwind;" & _
  "Integrated Security=SSPI;"
objBulkLoad.SchemaGen = True
objBulkLoad.SGUseID = True
objBulkLoad.Execute "d:\xml\OrdersSchema.xml",
    "d:\xml\OrdersData.xml"
Set objBulkLoad = Nothing
```

Here's the Transact-SQL that results when the bulk load executes:

```
CREATE TABLE Orders
(
  OrderID int NOT NULL,
  ShipCity nvarchar(30) NULL,
  PRIMARY KEY CLUSTERED (OrderID)
)
```

In addition to being able to create new tables from those in the mapping schema, SQLXMLBulkLoad can also drop and recreate tables. Set the SGDropTables property to True to cause the component to drop and recreate the tables mapped in the schema, as shown in Listing 18.84.

Listing 18.84

```
Set objBulkLoad = CreateObject("SQLXMLBulkLoad.SQLXMLBulkLoad")
objBulkLoad.ConnectionString = _
   "provider=SQLOLEDB;data source=KUFNATHE;database=Northwind;" & _
   "Integrated Security=SSPI;"
objBulkLoad.SchemaGen = True
objBulkLoad.SGDropTables = True
objBulkLoad.Execute "d:\xml\OrdersSchema.xml",
    "d:\xml\OrdersData.xml"
Set objBulkLoad = Nothing
```

Managed Classes

SQLXML provides managed code classes that allow you to retrieve XML data from SQL Server (you can translate the data to XML on the server or at the client). These classes have analogues in the .NET Framework itself but are more geared toward SQLXML and exposing its unique functionality in managed code applications. The SQLXML classes reside in an assembly named Microsoft.Data.SqlXml, and, as with any managed code assembly, they can be accessed from apps written in any CLR-compliant language, including C#, VB.NET, Delphi.NET, and others.

The SqlXmlCommand, SqlXmlParameter, and SqlXmlAdapter classes are the key managed code classes in the SqlXml assembly. As I've mentioned, these are similar to their similarly named counterparts in the .NET Framework. SqlXmlCommand is used to execute T-SQL commands or SQL Server procedural objects and optionally return their results as XML. SqlXmlParameter is used to set up parameterized queries. SqlXmlAdapter is used to process the results from a SqlXmlCommand execution. If the underlying data source supports modification, changes can be made at the client and posted back to the server using diffgrams, specialized updategram-like templates used by the .NET Framework to encapsulate data modifications.

The best way to understand how these classes interoperate in a real application is to build one. The C# example code in the next example demonstrates how to use each of the main SQLXML managed classes to execute a stored procedure and process its result set. Let's begin with the source code for the stored procedure (Listing 18.85).

Listing 18.85

```
USE Northwind
GO
DROP PROC ListCustomers
GO
CREATE PROC ListCustomers @CustomerID nvarchar(10)='%'
AS
PRINT '@CustomerID = ' +@CustomerID

SELECT *
FROM Customers
WHERE CustomerID LIKE @CustomerID

RAISERROR('%d Customers', 1,1, @@ROWCOUNT)
GO
EXEC ListCustomers N'ALFKI'
```

This stored proc takes a single parameter, a customer ID mask, and lists all the rows from the Northwind Customers table that match it. Listing 18.86 shows the C# code that uses SQLXML managed classes to execute the stored proc. (You can find this code in the CH18\managed_classes subfolder on the CD accompanying this book.)

Listing 18.86

```
using System;
using Microsoft.Data.SqlXml;
using System.IO;
using System.Xml;
class CmdExample
{
  static string strConn = "Provider=SQLOLEDB;Data Source='(local)';
      database=Northwind; Integrated Security=SSPI";
  public static int CmdExampleWriteXML()
  {
    XmlReader Reader;
    SqlXmlParameter Param;
    XmlTextWriter TxtWriter;

    //Create a new SqlXmlCommand instance
    SqlXmlCommand Cmd = new SqlXmlCommand(strConn);
```

```
    //Set it up to call our stored proc
    Cmd.CommandText = "EXEC ListCustomersXML ?";

    //Create a parameter and give it a value
    Param = Cmd.CreateParameter();
    Param.Value = "ALFKI";

    //Execute the proc
    Reader = Cmd.ExecuteXmlReader();

    //Create a new XmlTextWriter instance
    //to write to the console
    TxtWriter = new XmlTextWriter(Console.Out);

    //Move to the root element
    Reader.MoveToContent();

    //Write the document to the console
    TxtWriter.WriteNode(Reader, false);

    //Flush the writer and close the reader
    TxtWriter.Flush();
    Reader.Close();

    return 0;
  }
  public static int Main(String[] args)
  {
    CmdExampleWriteXML();
    return 0;
  }
}
```

Note the reference to the Microsoft.Data.SqlXml assembly. You will have to add a reference to this assembly in the Visual Studio .NET IDE (or on the csc.exe command line) in order to compile and link this code.

Let's walk through how this code works. We begin by instantiating a new SqlXmlCommand and passing it our connection string. We then set its CommandText property to call a stored procedure with a replaceable parameter. Next, we create a SqlXmlParameter instance and assign its Value property in order to supply a value for the stored procedure's parameter.

Once the SqlXmlCommand object is properly set up, we call its ExecuteXmlReader method. This returns an XmlReader instance that we can use to process the stored proc's results. We then create an XmlTextWriter object so that we can write out the XML returned by the SqlXmlCommand object. We follow up by moving to the start of the document itself (via the MoveToContent call), then write the entire document to the console via the TxtWriter.WriteNode call. We then conclude by flushing the XmlTextWriter object and closing the XmlReader object that was originally returned by the call to SqlXmlCommand.ExecuteXmlReader.

If you've done much programming with the .NET Framework's ADO.NET and XML classes, this code probably looks very familiar to you. All three SQLXML managed classes have counterparts in the .NET Framework itself. The metaphors are the same. They return compatible types with the base .NET Framework classes where it makes sense and can be used interchangeably with them. Their purpose is to extend the ADO.NET classes to include functionality that's specific to SQLXML, not replace them or offer an alternative to them.

SQLXML Web Service (SOAP) Support

SQLXML's Web service support allows you to expose SQL Server as a Web service. This allows stored procedures, other procedural objects, and query templates to be executed as though they were methods exposed by a traditional SOAP-based Web service. SQLXML provides the plumbing necessary to access SQL Server data using SOAP from any platform or client that can make SOAP requests.

The advantage of this, of course, is that you don't need SQL Server client software to run queries and access SQL Server objects. This means that applications on client platforms not directly supported by SQL Server (e.g., Linux) can submit queries and retrieve results from SQL Server via SQLXML and its SOAP facility.

You set up SQL Server to masquerade as a Web service by configuring a SOAP virtual name in the IIS Virtual Directory Management tool. (You can find this under the SQLXML | Configure IIS menu option under Start | Programs.) A SOAP virtual name is simply a folder associated with an IIS virtual directory name whose type has been set to soap. You can specify whatever service name you like in the Web Service Name text box; the conventional name is soap. Once this virtual name is set up, you configure specific SQL Server objects to be exposed by the Web service by clicking the Configure button on the Virtual Names tab and selecting the object name, the format of the XML to produce on the middle tier (via SQLISAPI), and the manner in which to expose the object: as a collection of XML elements, as a single Dataset object, or as a collection of Datasets. As the exercise we'll go through in just a moment illustrates, you can expose a given server object multiple times and in multiple ways, providing client applications with a wealth of ways to communicate with SQL Server over SOAP.

Architecturally, SQLXML's SOAP capabilities are provided by its ISAPI extension, SQLISAPI. These capabilities are an extension of the virtual directory concept that you configure in order to access the server via URL queries and templates. The SOAP virtual name that you set up provides access to SQLXML's Web service facility via a URL. It allows any client application that can communicate over SOAP with this URL to access SQL Server objects just as it would any other Web service. Java applications, traditional ADO applications, and, of course, .NET applications can access SQL Server procedural objects and XML templates without using traditional SQL Server client software or communicating over TDS.

In this next exercise, we'll walk through exposing SQL Server as a Web service and then consuming that service in a C# application. We'll set up the SOAP virtual name, then we'll configure a SQL Server procedure object to be exposed as a collection of Web service methods. Finally, we'll build a small application to consume the service and demonstrate how to interact with it.

Exercise 18.4   Building and Consuming a SQLXML Web Service

1. Under the \inetpub\wwwroot\Northwind folder that you created earlier, create a folder named Soap.
2. Start the IIS Virtual Directory Management for SQLXML tool that you used to configure the Northwind virtual folder earlier.
3. Go to the Virtual Names tab and add a new virtual name with a Name, Type, and Web Service Name of soap. Set the path to the folder you created in step 1.
4. Save the virtual name configuration. At this point, the Configure button should be enabled. Click it to begin exposing specific procedural objects and templates via the Web service.
5. Click the ellipsis button to the right of the SP/Template text box and select the ListCustomers stored procedure from the list.
6. Name the method ListCustomers and set its row format to Raw and its output format to XML objects, then click OK.

7. Repeat the process and name the new method ListCustomersAs-Dataset (you will be referencing the ListCustomers stored procedure). Set its output type to Single dataset, then click OK.

8. Repeat the process again and name the new method ListCustomersAs-Datasets. Set its output type to Dataset objects, then click OK. You've just exposed the ListCustomers stored procedure as three different Web service methods using three different output formats. Note that procedural objects you set up this way must not return XML themselves (i.e., they must not use the Transact-SQL FOR XML option) because XML formatting is handled exclusively at the middle tier by SQLISAPI when using the SQLXML Web service facility.

9. Start a new C# Windows application project in Visual Studio .NET. The app we'll build will allow you to invoke the SQLXML Web service facility to execute the ListCustomers stored proc using a specified CustomerID mask.

10. Add a single TextBox control to the upper-left corner of the default form to serve as the entry box for the CustomerID mask.

11. Add a Button control to the right of the TextBox control to be used to execute the Web service method.

12. Add three RadioButton controls to the right of the button to specify which Web method we want to execute. Name the first rbXMLElements, the second rbDataset, and the third rbDatasetObjects. Set the Text property of each control to a brief description of its corresponding Web method (e.g., the Text property for rbXMLElements should be something like "XML Elements").

13. Add a ListBox control below the other controls on the form. This will be used to display the output from the Web service methods we call. Dock the ListBox control to the bottom of the form and be sure it is sized to occupy most of the form.

14. Make sure your instance of IIS is running and accessible. As with the other Web-oriented examples in this chapter, I'm assuming that you have your own instance of IIS and that it's running on the local machine.

15. Right-click your solution in the Solution Explorer and select Add Web Reference. In the URL for the Web reference, type the following:

```
http://localhost/Northwind/soap?wsdl
```

This URL refers by name to the virtual directory you created earlier, then to the soap virtual name you created under it, and finally to the Web Services Description Language (WSDL) functionality provided by SQLISAPI. As I mentioned earlier, a question mark in a URL denotes the start of the URL's parameters, so wsdl is being passed as a parameter into the SQLISAPI extension DLL. Like XML and SOAP, WSDL is its own W3C standard and describes, in XML, Web services as a set of end points operating on messages containing either procedural or document-oriented information. You can learn more about WSDL by visiting this link on the W3C Web site: http://www.w3.org/TR/wsdl.

16. Once you've added the Web reference, the localhost Web service will be available for use within your application. A proxy class is created under your application folder that knows how to communicate with the Web service you referenced. To your code, this proxy class looks identical to the actual Web service. When you make calls to this class, they are transparently marshaled to the Web service itself, which might reside on some other machine located elsewhere on the local intranet or on the public Internet. You'll recall from Chapter 6 that I described Windows' RPC facility as working the very same way. Web services are really just an extension of this concept. You work and interoperate with local classes and methods; the plumbing behind the scenes handles getting data to and from the actual implementation of the service without your app even being aware of the fact that it is dealing with any sort of remote resource.

17. Double-click the Button control you added earlier and add to it the code in Listing 18.87.

Listing 18.87

```
int iReturn = 0;
object result;
object[] results;
System.Xml.XmlElement resultElement;
System.Data.DataSet resultDS;
localhost.soap proxy = new localhost.soap();
proxy.Credentials=System.Net.CredentialCache.DefaultCredentials;

// Return ListCustomers as XMLElements
if (rbXMLElements.Checked)
{
  listBox1.Items.Add("Executing ListCustomers...");
  listBox1.Items.Add("");

  results = proxy.ListCustomers(textBox1.Text);

  for (int j=0; j<results.Length; j++)
  {
    localhost.SqlMessage errorMessage;
    result= results[j];
```

```
        if (result.GetType().IsPrimitive)
        {
          listBox1.Items.Add(
            string.Format("ListCustomers return value: {0}", result));
        }
        if (result is System.Xml.XmlElement)
        {
          resultElement = (System.Xml.XmlElement) results[j];
          listBox1.Items.Add(resultElement.OuterXml);
        }
        else if (result is localhost.SqlMessage) {
          errorMessage = (localhost.SqlMessage) results[j];
          listBox1.Items.Add(errorMessage.Message);
          listBox1.Items.Add(errorMessage.Source);
        }
      }
      listBox1.Items.Add("");
    }
    // Return ListCustomers as Dataset objects
    else if (rbDatasetObjects.Checked)
    {
      listBox1.Items.Add("Executing ListCustomersAsDatasets...");
      listBox1.Items.Add("");
      results = proxy.ListCustomersAsDatasets(textBox1.Text);

      for (int j=0; j<results.Length; j++)
      {
        localhost.SqlMessage errorMessage;
        result= results[j];

        if (result.GetType().IsPrimitive)
        {
          listBox1.Items.Add(
            string.Format("ListCustomers return value: {0}", result));
        }
        if (result is System.Data.DataSet)
        {
          resultDS = (System.Data.DataSet) results[j];
          listBox1.Items.Add("DataSet " +resultDS.GetXml());
        }
        else if (result is localhost.SqlMessage)
        {
          errorMessage = (localhost.SqlMessage) results[j];
          listBox1.Items.Add("Message " +errorMessage.Message);
```

```
        listBox1.Items.Add(errorMessage.Source);
    }
  }
  listBox1.Items.Add("");
}
// Return ListCustomers as Dataset
else if (rbDataset.Checked)
{
  listBox1.Items.Add("Executing ListCustomersAsDataset...");
  listBox1.Items.Add("");
  resultDS = proxy.ListCustomersAsDataset(textBox1.Text,
      out iReturn);
  listBox1.Items.Add(resultDS.GetXml());
  listBox1.Items.Add(
    string.Format("ListCustomers return value: {0}", iReturn));
  listBox1.Items.Add("");
}
```

18. This code can be divided into three major routines—one each for the three Web service methods we call. Study the code for each type of output format and compare and contrast their similarities and differences. Note the use of reflection in the code to determine what type of object we receive back from Web service calls in situations where multiple types are possible.

19. Compile and run the app. Try all three output formats and try different CustomerID masks. Each time you click your Button control, the following things happen.

   a. Your code makes a method call to a proxy class Visual Studio .NET added to your project when you added the Web reference to the SQLXML SOAP Web service you set up for Northwind.

   b. The .NET Web service code translates your method call into a SOAP call and passes it across the network to the specified host. In this case, your Web service host probably resides on the same machine, but the architecture allows it to reside anywhere on the local intranet or public Internet.

   c. The SQLXML ISAPI extension receives your SOAP call and translates it into a call to the ListCustomers stored procedure in the database referenced by your IIS virtual directory, Northwind.

   d. SQL Server runs the procedure and returns its results as a rowset to SQLISAPI.

   e. SQLISAPI translates the rowset to the appropriate XML format and object based on the way the Web service method you called was configured, then returns it via SOAP to the .NET Framework Web service code running on your client machine.

f. The .NET Framework Web services code translates the SOAP it receives into the appropriate objects and result codes and returns them to your application.

g. Your app then uses additional method calls to extract the returned information as text and writes that text to the ListBox control.

So, there you have it, a basic runthrough of how to use SQLXML's SOAP facilities to access SQL Server via SOAP. As I've said, an obvious application of this technology is to permit SQL Server to play in the Web service space—to interoperate with other Web services without requiring the installation of proprietary client software or the use of supported operating systems. Thanks to SQLXML's Web service facility, anyone who can speak SOAP can access SQL Server. SQLXML's Web service support is a welcome and very powerful addition to the SQL Server technology family.

SQLXML Limitations

SQL Server's XML support has some fundamental limitations that make it difficult to use in certain situations. In this section, we'll explore a couple of these and look at ways to work around them.

sp_xml_concat

Given that sp_xml_preparedocument accepts document text of virtually any length (up to 2GB), you'd think that SQL Server's XML facilities would be able to handle long documents just fine—but that's not the case. Although sp_xml_preparedocument's xmltext parameter accepts text as well as varchar parameters, Transact-SQL doesn't support local text *variables*. About the closest you can get to a local text variable in Transact-SQL is to set up a procedure with a text *parameter*. However, this parameter cannot be assigned to nor can it be the recipient of the text data returned by the READTEXT command. About the only thing you can do with it is insert it into a table.

The problem is painfully obvious when you try to store a large XML document in a table and process it with sp_xml_preparedocument. Once the document is loaded into the table, how do you extract it in order to pass it into sp_xml_preparedocument? Unfortunately, there's no easy way to do so. Since we can't declare local text variables, about the only thing we can do is break the document into multiple 8,000-byte varchar variables and use parameter concatenation when we call sp_xml_preparedocument. This is a ridiculously difficult task, so I've written a stored procedure to do it for you.

It's called sp_xml_concat, and you can use it to process large XML documents stored in a table in a text, varchar, or char column.

The sp_xml_concat procedure takes three parameters: the names of the
table and column in which the document resides and an output parameter
that returns the document handle as generated by sp_xml_preparedocument.
You can take the handle that's returned by sp_xml_concat and use it with
OPENXML and sp_xml_unpreparedocument.

The table parameter can be either an actual table or view name or a
Transact-SQL query wrapped in parentheses that will function as a derived
table. The ability to specify a derived table allows you to filter the table that
the procedure sees. So, if you want to process a specific row in the table or
otherwise restrict the procedure's view of the table, you can do so using a
derived table expression.

Listing 18.88 shows the full source code for sp_xml_concat.

Listing 18.88

```
USE master
GO
IF OBJECT_ID('sp_xml_concat','P') IS NOT NULL
  DROP PROC sp_xml_concat
GO
CREATE PROC sp_xml_concat
  @hdl int OUT,
  @table sysname,
  @column sysname
AS
EXEC('
SET TEXTSIZE 4000
DECLARE
  @cnt int,
  @c nvarchar(4000)
DECLARE
  @declare varchar(8000),
  @assign varchar(8000),
  @concat varchar(8000)

SELECT @c = CONVERT(nvarchar(4000),'+@column+') FROM '+@table+'

SELECT @declare = ''DECLARE'',
       @concat = '''''''''''''''''''''''''''''',
       @assign = '''''',
       @cnt = 0
```

```
WHILE (LEN(@c) > 0) BEGIN
  SELECT @declare = @declare + '' @c''+CAST(@cnt as nvarchar(15))
      +''nvarchar(4000),'',
    @assign = @assign + ''SELECT @c''+CONVERT(nvarchar(15),@cnt)
        +''= SUBSTRING(' + @column+',''+ CONVERT(nvarchar(15),
      1+@cnt*4000)+ '', 4000) FROM '+@table+' '',
    @concat = @concat + ''+@c''+CONVERT(nvarchar(15),@cnt)
  SET @cnt = @cnt+1
  SELECT @c = CONVERT(nvarchar(4000),SUBSTRING('+@column+',
    1+@cnt*4000,4000)) FROM '+@table+'
END

IF (@cnt = 0) SET @declare = ''''
ELSE SET @declare = SUBSTRING(@declare,1,LEN(@declare)-1)

SET @concat = @concat + ''+'''''''''''''

EXEC(@declare+'' ''+@assign+'' ''+
''EXEC(
''''DECLARE @hdl_doc int
  EXEC sp_xml_preparedocument @hdl_doc OUT, ''+@concat+''
    DECLARE hdlcursor CURSOR GLOBAL FOR SELECT @hdl_doc AS
      DocHandle'''')''
)
')
OPEN hdlcursor
FETCH hdlcursor INTO @hdl
DEALLOCATE hdlcursor
GO
```

This procedure dynamically generates the necessary DECLARE and SELECT statements to break up a large text column into nvarchar(4000) pieces (e.g., DECLARE @c1 nvarchar(4000) SELECT @c1= ...). As it does this, it also generates a concatenation expression that includes all of these variables (e.g., @c1+@c2+@c3, ...). Since the EXEC() function supports concatenation of strings up to 2GB in size, we pass this concatenation expression into it dynamically and allow EXEC() to perform the concatenation on-the-fly. This basically reconstructs the document that we extracted from the table. This concatenated string is then passed into sp_xml_preparedocument for processing. The end result is a document handle that you can use with OPENXML. Listing 18.89 shows an example.

(You'll find the full test query in the CH18 subfolder on the CD accompanying this book.)

Listing 18.89

(Code abridged)

```
USE Northwind
GO
CREATE TABLE xmldoc
(id int identity,
  doc text)
INSERT xmldoc VALUES('<Customers>
<Customer CustomerID="VINET" ContactName="Paul Henriot">
  <Order CustomerID="VINET" EmployeeID="5" OrderDate=
      "1996-07-04T00:00:00">
    <OrderDetail OrderID="10248" ProductID="11" Quantity="12"/>
    <OrderDetail OrderID="10248" ProductID="42" Quantity="10"/>
// More code lines here...
  </Order>
</Customer>
<Customer CustomerID="LILAS" ContactName="Carlos GOnzlez">
  <Order CustomerID="LILAS" EmployeeID="3" OrderDate=
      "1996-08-16T00:00:00">
    <OrderDetail OrderID="10283" ProductID="72" Quantity="3"/>
  </Order>
</Customer>
</Customers>')

DECLARE @hdl int
EXEC sp_xml_concat @hdl OUT, '(SELECT doc FROM xmldoc WHERE id=1)
    a', 'doc'

SELECT * FROM OPENXML(@hdl, '/Customers/Customer') WITH
    (CustomerID nvarchar(50))

EXEC sp_xml_removedocument @hdl
SELECT DATALENGTH(doc) from xmldoc
GO
DROP TABLE xmldoc
```

(Results)

```
CustomerID
-------------------------------------------------
VINET
LILAS


-----------
36061
```

Although I've abridged the XML document in the test query, the one on the CD is over 36,000 bytes in size, as you can see from the result of the DATALENGTH() query at the end of the test code.

We pass a derived table expression into sp_xml_concat along with the column name we want to extract, and the procedure does the rest. It's able to extract the nodes we're searching for, even though one of them is near the end of a fairly large document.

sp_run_xml_proc

Another limitation of SQL Server's XML support exists because XML results are not returned as traditional rowsets. Returning XML results as streams has many advantages, but one of the disadvantages is that you can't call a stored procedure that returns an XML result using a four-part name or OPENQUERY() and get a useful result. The result set you'll get will be an unrecognizable binary result set because SQL Server's linked server architecture doesn't support XML streams.

You'll run into similar limitations if you try to insert the result of a FOR XML query into a table or attempt to trap it in a variable—SQL Server simply won't let you do either of these. Why? Because the XML documents returned by SQL Server are not traditional rowsets.

To work around this, I've written a stored procedure named sp_run_xml_proc. You can use it to call linked server stored procedures (it needs to reside on the linked server) that return XML documents as well as local XML procedures whose results you'd like to store in a table or trap in a variable. This procedure does its magic by opening its own connection into the server (it assumes Windows Authentication is being used) and running your procedure. Once your procedure completes, sp_run_xml_proc processes the XML stream it returns using SQL-DMO calls, then translates it into a traditional rowset and returns that rowset. This result set can be inserted into a table or processed further just like any other result set. Listing 18.90 presents the source code for sp_run_xml_proc.

Listing 18.90

```
USE master
GO
IF OBJECT_ID('sp_run_xml_proc','P') IS NOT NULL
  DROP PROC sp_run_xml_proc
GO
CREATE PROC sp_run_xml_proc
  @procname sysname  -- Proc to run
AS

DECLARE @dbname sysname,
  @sqlobject int,   -- SQL Server object
  @object int,   -- Work variable for accessing COM objects
  @hr int,   -- Contains HRESULT returned by COM
  @results int,   -- QueryResults object
  @msgs varchar(8000)   -- Query messages

IF (@procname='/?') GOTO Help

-- Create a SQLServer object
EXEC @hr=sp_OACreate 'SQLDMO.SQLServer', @sqlobject OUT
IF (@hr <> 0) BEGIN
  EXEC sp_displayoaerrorinfo @sqlobject, @hr
  RETURN
END

-- Set SQLServer object to use a trusted connection
EXEC @hr = sp_OASetProperty @sqlobject, 'LoginSecure', 1
IF (@hr <> 0) BEGIN
  EXEC sp_displayoaerrorinfo @sqlobject, @hr
  RETURN
END

-- Turn off ODBC prefixes on messages
EXEC @hr = sp_OASetProperty @sqlobject, 'ODBCPrefix', 0
IF (@hr <> 0) BEGIN
  EXEC sp_displayoaerrorinfo @sqlobject, @hr
  RETURN
END

-- Open a new connection (assumes a trusted connection)
EXEC @hr = sp_OAMethod @sqlobject, 'Connect', NULL, @@SERVERNAME
IF (@hr <> 0) BEGIN
```

```
    EXEC sp_displayoaerrorinfo @sqlobject, @hr
    RETURN
END

-- Get a pointer to the SQLServer object's Databases collection
EXEC @hr = sp_OAGetProperty @sqlobject, 'Databases', @object OUT
IF @hr <> 0 BEGIN
  EXEC sp_displayoaerrorinfo @sqlobject, @hr
  RETURN
END

-- Get a pointer from the Databases collection for the
-- current database
SET @dbname=DB_NAME()
EXEC @hr = sp_OAMethod @object, 'Item', @object OUT, @dbname
IF @hr <> 0 BEGIN
  EXEC sp_displayoaerrorinfo @object, @hr
  RETURN
END

-- Call the Database object's ExecuteWithResultsAndMessages2
-- method to run the proc
EXEC @hr = sp_OAMethod @object, 'ExecuteWithResultsAndMessages2',
    @results OUT, @procname, @msgs OUT
IF @hr <> 0 BEGIN
  EXEC sp_displayoaerrorinfo @object, @hr
  RETURN
END

-- Display any messages returned by the proc
PRINT @msgs

DECLARE @rows int, @cols int, @x int, @y int, @col varchar(8000),
    @row varchar(8000)

-- Call the QueryResult object's Rows method to get the number of
-- rows in the result set
EXEC @hr = sp_OAMethod @results, 'Rows',@rows OUT
IF @hr <> 0 BEGIN
  EXEC sp_displayoaerrorinfo @object, @hr
  RETURN
END

-- Call the QueryResult object's Columns method to get the number
-- of columns in the result set
```

```
EXEC @hr = sp_OAMethod @results, 'Columns',@cols OUT
IF @hr <> 0 BEGIN
  EXEC sp_displayoaerrorinfo @object, @hr
  RETURN
END

DECLARE @table TABLE (XMLText varchar(8000))

-- Retrieve the result set column-by-column using the
-- GetColumnString method
SET @y=1
WHILE (@y<=@rows) BEGIN
  SET @x=1
  SET @row=''
  WHILE (@x<=@cols) BEGIN
      EXEC @hr = sp_OAMethod @results, 'GetColumnString',
          @col OUT, @y, @x
      IF @hr <> 0 BEGIN
        EXEC sp_displayoaerrorinfo @object, @hr
        RETURN
      END
    SET @row=@row+@col+' '
    SET @x=@x+1
  END
  INSERT @table VALUES (@row)
  SET @y=@y+1
END

SELECT * FROM @table

EXEC sp_OADestroy @sqlobject    -- For cleanliness

RETURN 0

Help:
PRINT 'You must specify a procedure name to run'
RETURN -1

GO
```

Although the prospect of having to open a separate connection into the server in order to translate the document is not particularly exciting, it is unfortunately the only way to do this without resorting to client-side processing—at least for now. The test code in Listing 18.91 shows how to use sp_run_xml_proc.

Listing 18.91

```
USE pubs
GO
DROP PROC testxml
GO
CREATE PROC testxml as
PRINT 'a message here'
SELECT * FROM pubs..authors FOR XML AUTO
GO
EXEC [TUK\PHRIP].pubs.dbo.sp_run_xml_proc 'testxml'
```

(Results abridged)

```
a message here
XMLText
------------------------------------------------------------------
<pubs..authors au_id="172-32-1176" au_lname="White" au_fname="John
<pubs..authors au_id="672-71-3249" au_lname="Yokomoto" au_fname="A
```

Although I've clipped the resulting document considerably, if you run this code from Query Analyzer (replace the linked server reference in the example with your own), you'll see that the entire document is returned as a result set. You can then insert this result set into a table using INSERT…EXEC for further processing. For example, you could use this technique to assign the document that's returned to a variable (up to the first 8,000 bytes) or to change it in some way using Transact-SQL. And once the document is modified to your satisfaction, you could call sp_xml_concat (listed earlier in the chapter) to return a document handle for it so that you can query it with OPENXML. Listing 18.92 does just that.

Listing 18.92

```
SET NOCOUNT ON
GO
USE pubs
```

```
GO
DROP PROC testxml
GO
CREATE PROC testxml as
SELECT au_lname, au_fname FROM authors FOR XML AUTO
GO


CREATE TABLE #XMLText1
(XMLText varchar(8000))
GO


-- Insert the XML document into a table
-- using sp_run_xml_proc
INSERT #XMLText1
EXEC sp_run_xml_proc 'testxml'


-- Put the document in a variable
-- and add a root element
DECLARE @doc varchar(8000)
SET @doc=''
SELECT @doc=@doc+XMLText FROM #XMLText1
SET @doc='<root>'+@doc+'</root>'


-- Put the document back in a table
-- so that we can pass it into sp_xml_concat
SELECT @doc AS XMLText INTO #XMLText2


GO
DECLARE @hdl int
EXEC sp_xml_concat @hdl OUT, '#XMLText2', 'XMLText'
SELECT * FROM OPENXML(@hdl, '/root/authors') WITH
    (au_lname nvarchar(40))
EXEC sp_xml_removedocument @hdl
GO
DROP TABLE #XMLText1, #XMLText2
```

After the document is returned by sp_run_xml_proc and stored in a table, we load it into a variable, wrap it in a root element and store it in a second table so that we may pass it into sp_xml_concat. Once sp_xml_concat returns, we pass the document handle it returns into OPENXML and extract part of the document:

(Results abridged)

```
au_lname
----------------------------------------
Bennet
Blotchet-Halls
Carson
DeFrance
...
Ringer
Ringer
Smith
Straight
Stringer
White
Yokomoto
```

So, using sp_xml_concat and sp_run_xml_proc in conjunction with SQL Server's built-in XML tools, we're able to run the entire XML processing gamut. We start with an XML fragment returned by FOR XML AUTO, then we store this in a table, retrieve it from the table, wrap it in a root node, and pass it into OPENXML in order to extract a small portion of the original document as a rowset. You should find that these two procedures enhance SQL Server's own XML abilities significantly.

Recap

SQLXML provides a veritable treasure trove of XML-enabled features for SQL Server. You can parse and load XML documents, query them using XPath syntax, query database objects using XPath, and construct templates and mapping schemas to query data. You can use OPENXML, updategrams, and XML Bulk Load to load data into SQL Server via XML, and you can use FOR XML to return SQL Server data as XML. You can access SQL Server via HTTP and SOAP, and you can return XML data to the client via both SQLOLEDB and SQLXMLOLEDB. You can translate a rowset to XML on the server as well as on the client, and you can control the format the generated XML takes through a variety of mechanisms. And when you run into a couple of the more significant limitations in the SQLXML technologies, you can use the sp_xml_concat and sp_run_xml_proc stored procedures presented in this chapter to work around them.

Knowledge Measure

1. What XML parser does SQL Server's XML features use?
2. True or false: The NESTED option can be used only in client-side FOR XML.
3. What extended stored procedure is used to prepare an XML document for use by OPENXML?
4. What's the theoretical maximum amount of memory that SQLXML will allow MSXML to use from the SQL Server process space?
5. True or false: There is currently no way to disable template caching for a given SQLISAPI virtual directory.
6. Describe the use of the sql:mapping attribute from Microsoft's mapping-schema namespace.
7. Why is the maximum mentioned in question 4 only a theoretical maximum? What other factors could prevent MSXML from reaching its maximum memory allocation ceiling?
8. What XML support file must you first define before bulk loading an XML document into a SQL Server database?
9. What does sql:relationship establish for two tables?
10. Is it possible to change the name of the ISAPI extension DLL associated with a given virtual directory, or must all SQLISAPI-configured virtual directories use the same ISAPI extension?
11. Explain the way that URL queries are handled by SQLXML.
12. True or false: You can return traditional rowsets from SQLXMLOLEDB just as you can from any other OLE DB provider.
13. What Win32 API does SQLXML call in order to compute the amount of physical memory in the machine?
14. Name the two major APIs that MSXML provides for parsing XML documents.
15. Approximately how much larger in memory is a DOM document than the underlying XML document?
16. Describe what a "spec proc" is.
17. What internal spec proc is responsible for implementing the sp_xml_preparedocument extended procedure?

18. What two properties must be set on the ADO Command object in order to allow for client-side FOR XML processing?

19. What method of the ADO Recordset object can persist a recordset as XML?

20. What does the acronym "SAX" stand for in XML parlance?

21. When a standard Transact-SQL query is executed via a URL query, what type of event does it come into SQL Server as?

22. What's the name of the OLE DB provider that implements client-side FOR XML functionality and in what DLL does it reside?

23. Does SQLXML use MSXML to return XML results from server-side FOR XML queries?

24. True or false: SQLXML no longer supports XDR schemas.

25. What component should you use to load XML data into SQL Server in the fastest possible manner?

26. True or false: SQLISAPI does not support returning non-XML data from SQL Server.

27. Is it possible to configure a virtual directory such that FOR XML queries are processed on the client side by default?

28. Approximately how much larger than the actual document is the in-memory representation of an XML document stored by SQLXML for use with OPENXML?

29. True or false: SQLXML does not support inserting new data via OPENXML because OPENXML returns a read-only rowset.

30. What mapping-schema notational attribute should you use with the xsd:relationship attribute if you are using a mapping schema with an updategram and the mapping schema relates two tables in reverse order?

31. Name the central SQL Server error-reporting routine in which we set a breakpoint in this chapter.

32. Describe a scenario in which it would make sense to use a mapping schema with an updategram.

33. What lone value can SQLXMLOLEDB's Data Source parameter have?

34. True or false: The SAX parser is built around the notion of persisting a document in memory in a tree structure so that it is readily accessible to the rest of the application.

CHAPTER 19

Notification Services

You can't lead from the middle of the pack.

—Kenneth E. Routen

Unless you've been living in a cave, you've likely noticed the trend toward notification-based data delivery. Even now, you can go to Web sites and subscribe to weather notifications, traffic reports, sports scores, and a host of other notification-based data. Once subscribed, the data can "follow" you around—being simultaneously pushed to you via e-mail, pager messages, cell phone text messages, instance messaging, and so on. These types of apps are taking over the world and are a major focus of Microsoft's .NET initiative.

Notification Services was developed to provide an enterprise-level platform for creating robust, scalable, and full-featured notification apps that use SQL Server as their data store. It leverages the power of the .NET Framework (most of Notification Services is written in managed code), the scalability and stability of SQL Server, and the configurability and flexibility of XML to provide a first-class toolset for developing custom notification applications. We'll explore Notification Services in the first part of this chapter, then finish up by building a notification application.

How It Works

First, let's get some terminology straight: As the name suggests, Notification Services is not just a single service. It is a platform and set of supporting tools that help you produce notification applications. A key component of a notification application is a Windows service that Notification Services provides for you, but it does not constitute the entire application.

Unlike SQL Server proper, you don't install Notification Services, then build notification applications that connect to it with client software. Instead, you design a notification application using the tools provided by Notification Services, and they in turn generate your application. So, the term "Notification Services" can be a bit nebulous, especially if you think of it in terms of how SQL Server works. I think the most accurate way to view Notification Services is as a collection of services and tools designed to help you build rich, scalable notification applications.

A Notification Services application does not run inside the SQL Server process, nor does it even have to run on the same machine. Technically, it's a SQL Server client, just like any other application. Notification Services applications use SQL Server as a data store in much the same way that products like Systems Management Server and Microsoft Exchange can.

A Notification Services application typically has three components: a Windows Service, a set of SQL Server databases to serve as the data store, and a subscription management application. Notification Services generates the first two components for you and provides sample applications that you can reuse to at least get a head start on the third.

Each Notification Services application is hosted by a Notification Services instance. A Notification Services instance consists of three things: an entry in the registry under HKLM\Software\Microsoft\Notification Services\Instances, a SQL Server database that stores instance-related data (e.g., the subscribers table), and a Windows service that performs the actual work of matching up events with subscriptions and producing notifications. A single instance can host multiple applications, but it's common to see a one-to-one correspondence between instances and applications.

An example of a situation in which you might want to have multiple applications hosted by a single instance is when you have several related notification applications that need to share a common list of subscribers. Rather than have separate instances where a user would have to be set up as a subscriber independently in each one, hosting all the apps in a single instance allows a user to be set up just once in order to subscribe to notifications from any of the applications.

NSControl

The entry point to building and managing Notification Services applications is a utility called NSControl. It's a command line application that plays the same general role in Notification Services that Enterprise Manager plays in SQL Server—you build, administer, and control Notification Services apps with NSControl. For example, to create the SQL Server databases used by a notification application, you call NSControl Create. To register a new Notification Services instance, you call NSControl Register. We'll cover this in more detail later in the chapter.

The Instance and Application Databases

Each Notification Services application depends on at least two SQL Server databases. When you generate a new notification application using NSControl Create, these databases are created for you. One is set aside for the instance to use; the other is used by the application itself. If an instance supports multiple applications, there will be just one instance database and perhaps many application databases. An application can make use of other databases, but in a typical configuration there's just one application-specific database and one instance database.

The instance database will always end with a suffix of NSMain. An application database will always be both prefixed and suffixed with the name you specified for the application in the application configuration file. We'll talk more about the application configuration file in just a moment.

These databases contain a bevy of stored procedures, system tables, and other support objects. With only two exceptions that I know of, the names of these objects will always be prefixed with NS. The subscriptions view in the application database has the name *AppName*Subscriptions, where *AppName* is the name of the application, and the notification UDF in the instance database is named *ClassName*Notify, where *ClassName* is the name of the notification class to which the UDF corresponds. All other Notification Services objects in the instance and application databases are prefixed with NS.

The Configuration Files

A moment ago I mentioned the configuration files used to construct a Notification Services application. You may be wondering exactly what they are and how they're used. I'll start by giving you an overview of each one; we'll explore them in more depth when we build our own notification application later in the chapter.

There are two configuration files used to define a Notification Services application: the instance configuration file and the application definition file. The instance configuration file defines the instance and references the applications it hosts. The application definition file defines an individual application. If an instance hosts multiple applications, you will have just one instance configuration file and multiple application definition files.

The instance configuration file is commonly named appConfig.XML (e.g., in the Sample applications) but can actually have any name. I prefer in-stConfig.XML because the file doesn't define a single application but rather relates to an entire instance. This file is an XML document that must conform to the ConfigurationFileSchema.XSD XML schema. (You can find this file in the XML Schemas subfolder under your Notification Services root installation folder.) The instance configuration file configures the instance and determines how its Windows service runs.

The instance configuration file contains an entry that references the application definition file for each application it hosts. It also contains nodes referencing the SQL Server that will host the instance, as well as the delivery protocols and delivery channels the instance supports. For tasks for which NSControl requires a configuration file to be supplied, you will need to supply only the instance configuration file name. Since it contains references to the definition files for the applications hosted by the instance, NSControl can access them without requiring you to supply their names on the command line.

The application definition file is also an XML document. It conforms to the ApplicationDefinitionFileSchema.XSD XML schema, also located in the XML Schemas subfolder under your Notification Services root installation folder. It defines an individual Notification Services application and lays out the structure of the events and subscriptions the application accepts as input, as well as the notifications it produces as output. We'll walk through an example of an application definition file when we build our sample app later in the chapter.

Understand that these configuration files are used only by NSControl. They provide configuration details for specific NSControl tasks, such as creating the instance and application databases or updating an instance's configuration. They are not referenced by the instance service once it has been created. Once passed into NSControl, the configuration information provided by these files is materialized into objects and table entries in the instance and application databases—they are not referenced thereafter by the event collection process, by the generator, or during the distribution process. You should not delete them, of course, because you may decide to change a configuration detail after an app has been created and registered (in which case, you'd pass the appropriate configuration file into NSControl Update). However, be aware that these files just serve as inputs to the NSControl utility—nothing more.

NSService.exe

NSService.exe is the Notification Services executable that runs as the Windows service in a notification application. Every Notification Services application for a given release of the product uses the same copy of NSService.exe. (In that sense, a Notification Services instance equates to an instance of this executable.) When an instance is registered as a service, NSService.exe is listed as the executable, with the name of the instance passed on its command line. Once started, NSService.exe takes this instance name and looks up the host SQL Server using the registry key. Since it can determine the name of the instance database using the instance name, it then has all it needs to access the SQL Server objects it requires to monitor for events and turn those events into notifications.

Note that you don't have to run NSService.exe as a service. Similarly to SQL Server's replication agents, NSService.exe can also be executed as a command line utility. There's no good reason for doing this; I mention it only for completeness and to give you a sense of how all the pieces fit together. You can run NSService.exe from the command line like this:

```
nsservice InstanceName -a
```

where *InstanceName* is the name of your instance. Of course, the executable will either need to be on your path or you'll need to be in the folder where it resides when you run this command. (The default location is \Program Files\Microsoft SQL Server Notification Services\v2.0.2114.0\Bin, where v2.0.2114.0 is the version of Notification Services you have installed.)

WARNING: Again, I mention how to run NSService.exe from the command line only for completeness. I don't suggest that you run it this way in any sort of production scenario. I could foresee problems if you were to run NSInstance.exe from the command line at the same time it was already running as a service, with both processes referencing the same Notification Services instance.

The main purpose of NSService.exe is to match event data with subscriptions and produce notifications. NSService.exe provides a notification engine—a facility capable of collecting events, matching those events with subscriptions, and turning those matches into notifications to subscribers. You hook your own code into this engine through the following mechanisms:

- Instance configuration and application definition files
- Transact-SQL triggers, queries, and stored procedures
- Managed code components such as custom event providers and custom delivery protocols
- XML style sheets

We'll discuss each of these in more detail later in the chapter.

Notification Services provides an extensible foundation onto which you can build a rich set of custom functionality. It provides the engine and mechanisms for turning events and subscriptions into notifications. You turn this generic notification generation engine into a custom application by hooking your own functionality into the appropriate places using well-defined interfaces and standard APIs.

Notification Application Components

Three key components carry out the work of a Notification Services application: event providers, the generator, and the distributor. Event providers handle collecting events. The generator matches those events with subscriptions and generates raw notifications. The distribution process takes these raw notifications and turns them into notifications suitable for delivery to subscribers.

Event Providers

As I've said, event providers collect events of interest to a Notification Services application. For example, an event provider might collect sports scores for use in a sports notification application or temperature readings in a weather notification application. You can have multiple event providers for a single notification application.

An event provider can be either hosted or nonhosted. A hosted event provider is a DLL or assembly that implements the IEventProvider or IScheduledEventProvider interfaces. This type of provider runs within the NSService.exe process.

Hosted event providers come in two varieties: scheduled and continuous. A scheduled event provider is invoked on a schedule that you specify when you create the application with NSControl Create. A continuous event provider is started when the notification application starts and runs until it is shut down.

A nonhosted, or independent, event provider runs outside of Notification Services. It may be a separate executable, or it may run within another process such as IIS. It uses one of the following APIs for submitting events into the system.

1. For XML data, an independent provider can create an Event-Loader object and write events from the XML data into the application database.

2. A provider can also call special stored procedures provided by Notification Services in the application database in order to submit events. The application that we'll build later in the chapter uses this technique from within a T-SQL trigger to generate Notification Services events.

3. A managed-code provider can create Event objects directly, add them to an EventCollector object, and submit them as a batch to the system.

4. A provider can use COM objects and methods to submit events. Notification Services uses COM Interop to expose its managed code classes as COM interfaces.

The Generator

In contrast to event providers, you can have just one generator per application. The generator matches subscriptions with events and produces notifications. The rules by which a match between a subscription and an event is found are called match rules and consist of Transact-SQL statements that you define in the application definition file.

The process by which matches are detected and notifications are generated can be more complex than simply matching subscriptions to events. Notifications can be generated based on a schedule defined by a subscription and can also make use of historical data.

The generator produces "raw" notifications that must be put through the distribution process in order to be turned into something suitable for delivery to subscribers. I've often wished that a term other than "notification" was used in the Notification Services docs for these pubescent notification items. Perhaps "prenotification" or "raw notification" or even "message" would be better. Whatever the case, just understand that the output from the generation process must still be processed by the distributor before it can be sent to subscribers.

When an application supports scheduled subscriptions and the generator processes those subscriptions, it processes only the subscriptions due for evaluation at a particular point in time. This provision keeps the generator from needlessly evaluating subscriptions that cannot be filled because their scheduled time interval or runtime has not passed.

An application that needs to use historical data to determine whether a subscription and event match can do so through the use of supplemental tables called chronicle tables. Basically, a chronicle table is a special table defined by the application that logs historical data (i.e., that chronicles it, hence the term) for later use by the notification generation process. For example, you might use a chronicle table to record a stock issue's price fluctuation over time so that you can avoid repeatedly generating notifications as the price rises above and falls below a subscription's price threshold throughout the trading day.

Match Rules

As I've said, the events that the generator translates into raw notifications are matched with subscriptions through the use of match rules. Match rules are T-SQL SELECT statements specified in the application definition file. The generator supports three rule types.

1. *Event chronicle rules* log historical event information in supplemental tables. As I've mentioned, chronicles help provide historical context to the generation process. Chronicle rules are fired first by the generator.
2. *Subscription event rules* generate notifications for event-based subscriptions. They are fired after the event chronicle rules when a related event batch is available and can also interact with chronicle tables.
3. *Scheduled subscription rules* generate notifications for scheduled subscriptions. They fire after the event chronicle rules for related subscriptions fire. They can also interact with chronicle tables.

The Quantum

The quantum time period you specify in the QuantumDuration node of the application definition file controls how often the generator wakes up and fires rules. This time period is specified in standard ISO 8601 XML Schema time format and can range from a few seconds to as long as necessary. Obviously, a shorter quantum period causes the generator to fire more often and the requisite load on the system to be heavier. A longer quantum period lightens the load on the system but causes notifications to take longer to be generated and, hence, to be delivered to subscribers. If unspecified, the quantum period defaults to one minute.

The Notification Function

Notifications are generated by means of a notification function, a SQL Server UDF that's created for you by Notification Services in the application database for each notification class (type of notification) you define in the application definition file. If you define just one notification class, you'll have just one notification function. Each notification UDF is named after its corresponding notification class and has the suffix Notify appended to it. This function is used within the SELECT statement of a match rule to generate notifications. It pulls this off by calling an extended procedure that opens a loop-back connection into the host SQL Server and inserts notifications via a call to the NSInsertNotification*N* stored procedure. (A loop-back connection is necessary because xprocs cannot otherwise run queries against SQL Server.) This xproc is named xp_NSNotify_*version*, where *version* is your Notification Services version.

Because the columns in the match rule's T-SQL SELECT statement set are passed into the UDF, it is called for each row in the result set. (When a UDF used in a SELECT statement is not passed any columns, it is called just once for the entire statement.) The interaction between the UDF and notification generation is best understood by way of example. We'll discuss match rules in more depth later in the chapter, but here's a sample rule that demonstrates the use of the UDF to produce notifications (Listing 19.1).

Listing 19.1

```
SELECT dbo.BNSInfoNotify(s.SubscriberId,
                         s.DeviceName,
                         s.SubscriberLocale,
                         p.ID,
                         p.Product,
                         p.OpenedBy)
FROM BNSEvents e, BNSSubscriptions s, BNS..Bugs p
WHERE e.ID = p.ID
AND p.Product = s.Product
```

Note the use of the BNSInfoNotify function. It calls the notification xproc. The SELECT statement isn't as interested in the return value of the function as it is in the function's side effect. Because the UDF calls an xproc, it's able to modify other tables on the server within the context of the SELECT statement. Normally, this isn't allowed in a UDF. Basically, the UDF allows the match rule to avoid having to open a cursor on the SELECT statement that matches events with subscriptions and call NSInsertNotification*N* for each one separately. By taking this approach, Notification Services lessens the match rule coding burden on the developer.

This is the same approach taken by the xp_exec extended procedure in my last book, *The Guru's Guide to SQL Server Stored Procedures, XML, and HTML*. As I pointed out in that book, because of the numerous restrictions on what you can do from within a SQL Server UDF, calling an xproc that uses a loop-back connection to run custom T-SQL code is about the only means of doing a number of useful things from within a UDF, including using a SELECT statement to drive parameterized calls to a stored procedure, which is what the notification UDF does. The notification UDF takes the same approach demonstrated by the xp_exec example code: It uses an xproc to open a loop-back connection into the server and runs code that would normally not be allowed from within a UDF (stored procedure calls) based on values passed in from the SELECT statement.

This technique is not unlike the facility provided by DTS's Data Driven Query (DDQ) task. A DDQ task executes parameterized queries based on data fed to it by another DTS task (which may well be a SELECT statement or stored procedure call).

Unlike xp_exec, the notification xproc does not support the notion of joining the caller's transactional context. Why is that? Shouldn't the xproc join the caller's transactional context in order to guarantee that it will not be blocked by it? The reason the notification xproc doesn't do this is simple: SQL Server doesn't support it. As I pointed out in the discussion of xp_exec in my last book, an xproc cannot join its caller's transactional context when called from a UDF. Given that the xp_NSNotify xproc wasn't intended to be called from anywhere except a UDF, it wouldn't have made sense for it to provide any support for binding to the calling spid's transactional space.

Despite the fact that it's about the only way to do what the Notification Services developers were obviously trying to accomplish, the fact that a separate connection is initiated from within a UDF raises some interesting issues. For one thing, given that separate spids could theoretically be going after the same resources, scenarios could exist where the notification xproc could be blocked by its caller. Given that the transactional context in which match rules run is controlled exclusively by NSService.exe, this is unlikely. The user would probably have to code some UDF tricks of his or her own into the match rule in order to change the transactional environment to the extent that the xproc could be blocked. It would have to find a way to take out and hold locks on the same tables NSInsertNotification*N* accesses to insert new notifications. I can't imagine this happening except in a very contrived situation.

A far more likely scenario is that the loop-back connection could fail. I've seen this actually occur with xp_exec and the undocumented xp_execresultset xproc that ships with SQL Server. (As of SQL Server 2000 Service Pack 3, this is no longer an xproc.) When a client uses a trusted connection to connect to SQL Server, if the domain controller is unreachable and sufficient credentials information isn't cached on the local machine, the connection will receive the infamous "cannot generate SSPI context" error. SSPI is the Security Support Provider Interface, and the error indicates that it can't complete the necessary security operations to successfully delegate the client's security token to SQL Server, often because it can't reach the domain controller. Thanks to cached credentials, you can usually resolve this (at least until the next reboot) by reconnecting to the network or otherwise making the domain controller accessible.

If access to the domain controller is tenuous, calls to the notification xproc could fail even though NSService.exe is connected to SQL Server and continues to run without problems. NSService.exe makes use of connection pooling, so it's not as likely to need to initiate a new connection to the server once it's running. The notification xproc, on the other hand, may indeed initiate a new connection and may fail if the domain controller is unreachable. A common scenario in which I might expect to see this is when running Notification Services on a laptop. If the laptop normally logs into a domain controller and is rebooted after being disconnected from the network, you may run into problems with generating notifications due to SSPI context generation failures. If so, the system event log will indicate the failed call and the reason for it.

Given that NSInsertNotification$N$ issues a simple INSERT statement to insert a new notification, another way to accomplish the same thing as the xproc loop-back technique would be to use an INSTEAD OF trigger on a view or placeholder table. The match rule would insert into this view or placeholder table, and the trigger would handle translating the inserted rows into INSERT(s) into the appropriate underlying tables. This is the technique shown in my last book, where I presented an alternate way to shred XML documents through the use of an INSTEAD OF trigger.

Although the UDF/xproc technique used by Notification Services lessens the coding burden on the person writing the match rules for a notification application, I'm not sure that it makes it more scalable than, say, using a cursor over the match rule result. As I mentioned in Chapter 10, invoking an xproc of any kind, regardless of whether it initiates a loop-back connection, takes the worker thread associated with the calling spid "off" of the scheduler. In other words, the thread becomes unusable to the scheduler for processing work requests by other spids. Because the scheduler doesn't know whether the xproc will yield often enough, it must assume that it will not and must ignore its host worker thread in terms of carrying out work requests until the xproc completes.

If you use the STRESS.CMD utility discussed earlier in this book to instantiate, say, 255 connections to execute an xproc that simply calls Windows' Sleep API function in order to pause the calling thread for 30 seconds, you won't be able to establish a new connection to your server while the xprocs run. Moreover, any other connections currently executing queries may find themselves starved because they have yielded a worker thread that an xproc has taken over. So, right off the bat, calling an xproc has a negative impact on SQL Server scalability because it forces a worker thread to be dedicated to a given spid rather than being shared by perhaps many of them as it normally would be.

Add to this the fact that, for each row in the match result set, the xproc initiates a new SQL Server connection, and you could well encounter scalability issues with this approach. In a system that may process thousands or even millions of notifications using a single match rule invocation, you might see thousands or millions of new SQL Server connections being made and dropped *during one instance of the generator firing*. Worse yet, if the system is extremely busy or has a limited number of available worker threads (e.g., due to xprocs taking them over), the notification function's xproc may not be able to immediately establish a loop-back connection and may block while it waits on one. Obviously, the system impact caused by these loop-back connections could be very significant, depending on the number and frequency of them.

The INSTEAD OF trigger approach I mentioned earlier doesn't have this caveat, nor would simply opening a cursor over the match result set and invoking the NSInsertNotification*N* stored procedure for each row. Of course, cursors can have their own performance and scalability issues, but they will, at least, not cause a spid to commandeer a worker thread, nor will they cause connection thrashing.

Distributors

As I said earlier, notifications produced by the generator are generated in a raw format and need to be formatted and packaged in order to be distributed as end user notifications. That's where the distributor comes in. The distributor takes the raw notifications produced by the generator and translates them into formatted notifications that can be sent out over a delivery protocol. XML style sheets are commonly used to translate raw notifications into files suitable for delivery to subscribers.

Once the generator finishes creating a batch of raw notifications, the distributor reads the subscriber data in the batch and determines the type of formatting required. The distributor then formats each raw notification and sends it to a delivery service (e.g., SMTP) using a delivery channel as defined in the instance configuration file.

Formatting Messages

When you set up a notification class in an application definition file, you specify how the class is to be formatted. As I've mentioned, a common method of transforming raw notifications into something that can be sent to subscribers is to use an XML style sheet. To use Notification Services' built-in XSL-based formatter, specify XsltFormatter as the ContentFormatter node's ClassName in your application definition file. Of course, you must also create the style sheet and specify the location and name of the file in the ContentFormatter node.

You must set up a content formatter for every combination of device and locale. An application that supports multiple locales and multiple delivery devices must set up a content formatter for each combination of them.

Notification Services provides one content formatter for you out of the box, the XsltFormatter content formatter. Given the flexibility and power of the XML style sheet language, this will be the only content formatter that many apps will ever need. As we saw in Chapter 8, an XML style sheet can produce a wide variety of output from a single XML data source. You have looping, conditional logic, and user-defined functions at your disposal, so there isn't much you can't do.

That said, you may run into situations where you need or want to construct a custom content formatter. If so, Notification Services allows you to build custom content formatters by implementing the IContentFormatter interface. You specify this content formatter and any parameters it requires in the NotificationClasses section of your application definition file.

Delivering Notifications

NSService.exe does not handle the ultimate delivery of notifications—it leaves that to delivery services such as SMTP. It delivers notifications to these services via delivery channels, which you define in the instance configuration file. A delivery channel packages the notifications it receives into a protocol packet and sends them on to the specified delivery service. For example, for SMTP, a delivery channel would package notifications using the SMTP delivery protocol and deliver them to the specified SMTP or Exchange server, and the server would, in turn, deliver them to subscribers. Notification Services supports the following standard delivery protocols.

- The SMTP protocol—supports sending notifications to SMTP or Exchange servers.
- The file protocol—supports placing notifications in an operating system file that can be picked up by other processes for further distribution. This protocol is also handy for debugging notification applications.

Note that you can also create your own custom delivery protocols. To create a custom delivery protocol, a class must implement either the IDeliveryProtocol interface or the IHttpProtocolProvider interface. IDeliveryProtocol is the base custom delivery protocol interface. Notification Services provides the IHttpProtocolProvider interface to make it easier to build custom HTTP-based delivery protocols. Most of the plumbing required to deal with HTTP is provided for you; you simply provide code to format the envelope and process the response. You can use the IHttpProtocolProvider to provide notifications via HTTP-based protocols such as SOAP, SMS, and .NET Alerts.

Digest and Multicast Notifications

Beyond standard message-based notifications, Notification Services also allows notifications for a particular subscriber to be grouped together and sent as a single notification via a facility known as digest notifications. It also allows a single notification to be sent to multiple subscribers through a facility known as multicast delivery. Digest notifications help keep subscribers from being pummeled by notifications, and multicast delivery allows for greater scalability by reusing a single notification for multiple subscribers rather than sending it separately for each one.

Subscribers and Subscriptions

As I said at the outset, Notification Services applications consist of three major components: the Windows service executable, the SQL Server data store, and the subscription management application. Of these, the first two are either provided or generated for you by Notification Services. The third, the subscription management application, you must build yourself.

In a notification application, the subscription management application is responsible for setting up subscribers, subscriber devices, and subscriptions. It can be a Web app or a standard Windows app, but it must be able to use the Notification Services object model to manage subscriptions and related information. Although most of the work of the object model that's related to subscription management is actually carried out by stored procedures in either the instance database or the application database, I don't suggest that you call these procedures directly because they are undocumented.

As I mentioned earlier, subscription-related information is stored in the application database, while subscriber-related information resides in the instance database. This arrangement allows a subscriber to subscribe to notifications from multiple applications without having to be set up separately in each one. You're not required to supply a specific database name when working with the Notification Services object model. Based on the instance and application names you supply, it knows the database in which to locate a particular type of object.

Later in this chapter, we'll build a complete Notification Services application, including a subscription management application. You'll get to see firsthand how the typical subscription management application interacts with the Notification Services object model.

The Sample Apps

Notification Services ships with a set of sample applications that you can copy and customize for use with your own notification applications. You can use the CopySample utility to copy a sample app to a new application, complete with its own IIS virtual directory and project-specific environment variables.

These sample apps demonstrate how to use a Makefile project in Visual Studio .NET to integrate a custom build process into the Visual Studio IDE. Each sample solution consists of two projects. One is the subscription management application, which is a regular ASP.NET application; the other is a VC++ Makefile project named AppDefinition, which encapsulates the collection of configuration files, CMD files, XSLT style sheets, and other support files used to create and register the sample notification application.

A VC++ Makefile project allows you to wire in your own custom commands for the Build, Clean, and Rebuild commands in the Visual Studio IDE. The Notification Services sample projects leverage this to call custom CMD files that handle each of these operations for the AppDefinition project. The result is a custom build solution that's fairly well integrated with the Visual Studio IDE. When you right-click the AppDefinition project in the Visual Studio Solution Explorer and select Build, you're actually calling a CMD file that runs NSControl. Its output is collected in the output window, and it is, for all intents and purposes, a part of the IDE itself.

CMD File Tricks

While I'm on the subject of CMD files and the sample apps, I should mention that the CMD files that ship with the Notification Services samples are a great way to learn about NSControl and about the Notification Services application creation process in general. Several of these CMD files feature clever tricks to get the most out of Windows' CMD file syntax. I think these are worth mentioning in the interest of understanding how the samples work and, indirectly, how NSControl works. If you can read the sample CMD files that ship with the product, you are well on your way to knowing how to use NSControl to create and manage a Notification Services application. Table 19.1 lists some of the more interesting CMD file syntax I've discovered in these files and what it does.

Building Your Own Notification Application

In this section, we'll build a Notification Services application from scratch. The app we'll build will be a Bug Notification Service (BNS)—it will notify subscribers when new product bugs are entered into a SQL Server table and when changes are made to them. Events will be generated via a trigger on the Bugs table in a custom database (outside of Notification Services), and notifications will be delivered over SMTP. We'll build all the pieces of the application, including the subscription management app. I'm assuming for the purposes of this exercise that you have SQL Server, Notification Services, and an SMTP server (the Windows NT product family ships with an SMTP server) all installed on the same machine. If your SMTP server is running, stop it for the time being so that no actual e-mails are sent out as a result of our example application.

The Notification Services Development Process

The typical Notification Services application development cycle goes like this.

1. Create the instance configuration file and the application definition file.
2. Use NSControl Create to generate the instance and application databases using the configuration files.
3. Grant access rights to the new databases to the appropriate users.

Table 19.1 CMD File Tricks Used by the Notification Services Sample Apps

Syntax	Function
if %ERRORLEVEL% GEQ 1 popd & goto Error	This tests the ERRORLEVEL environment variable to see whether it's greater than or equal to 1 and, if so, changes to the previous directory (pushed onto the directory "stack" via the pushd command) and jumps to the Error label.
exit /B 1	This exits the current command file and sets the ERRORLEVEL environment variable in the process.
del %TEMP%\Grant-Permissions.out > nul 2>&1	This command deletes the specified file and redirects the output of that command to the nul device in order to keep it from being displayed. It also redirects stderr (the OS pipe errors are written to by default) to stdout, so that error messages are also redirected to the nul device.
start /wait cmd.exe /c call GrantPermissions.cmd	This command starts a new window (which is visible to the user) so that osql (which is called by GrantPermissions.cmd) can prompt for any passwords it needs.
@if "%_echo%" == "" echo off	This tests to see whether the _echo environment variable has been set and turns off command echoing if not. This is handy for debugging—you can turn command echoing on or off without editing the CMD file itself.
setlocal	This makes environment variable changes local to the current CMD file until endlocal is executed. Normally, changing an environment variable in a CMD file also changes it in the current CMD.EXE session.
echo.	This writes a blank line to the console—handy for keeping the output produced by a CMD file readable.
set SqlServer=%SqlServer:"=%	This syntax removes the character that precedes the equal sign (a double quote, in this case) from the environment variable. You can specify any character you like here, and CMD.EXE will strip it from the environment variable before making the assignment. Note that this technique isn't limited to set statements—you can use it anywhere that you reference an environment variable.

4. Use NSControl Register to register the new instance and its corresponding Windows service.
5. Use NSControl Enable to enable the new instance and application.
6. Use NET START or the Services application to start the new service. At this point, you have a running instance of the server-side portion of your app.
7. Create the subscription management application and begin entering subscriptions and events to test your new notification application.

Creating the Configuration Files

Let's start by building the instance configuration file. We'll use a bare-bones configuration to keep the concepts from being lost in the details. Listing 19.2 shows the one we'll use for the BNS app. (You can find this code in the instConfig.XML file in the CH19\bns\svc subfolder on the CD accompanying this book.)

Listing 19.2

```
<?xml version="1.0" encoding="utf-8"?>
<NotificationServicesInstance xmlns:xsd=
    "http://www.w3.org/2001/XMLSchema" xmlns:xsi=
    "http://www.w3.org/2001/XMLSchema-instance" xmlns=
    "http://www.microsoft.com/MicrosoftNotificationServices/
    ConfigurationFileSchema">
  <InstanceName>BNSInstance</InstanceName>
  <SqlServerSystem>%Server_Instance%</SqlServerSystem>
  <Applications>
    <Application>
      <ApplicationName>BNS</ApplicationName>
      <BaseDirectoryPath>%BasePath%</BaseDirectoryPath>
      <ApplicationDefinitionFilePath>appADF.xml
          </ApplicationDefinitionFilePath>
      <Parameters>
        <Parameter>
          <Name>Server_Instance</Name>
          <Value>%Server_Instance%</Value>
        </Parameter>
        <Parameter>
          <Name>SystemName</Name>
          <Value>%COMPUTERNAME%</Value>
```

```
        </Parameter>
        <Parameter>
          <Name>BasePath</Name>
          <Value>%BasePath%</Value>
        </Parameter>
      </Parameters>
    </Application>
  </Applications>
  <DeliveryChannels>
    <DeliveryChannel>
      <DeliveryChannelName>EmailChannel</DeliveryChannelName>
      <ProtocolName>SMTP</ProtocolName>
    </DeliveryChannel>
  </DeliveryChannels>
</NotificationServicesInstance>
```

I've bolded the two values in the file that you'll need to customize to your specific configuration. You can specify values for them by setting up environment variables before calling NSControl or by passing them on the NSControl command line. We'll pass them on the command line when we call NSControl in just a moment.

The first parameter, the SqlServerSystem node, is the machine name and SQL Server instance (separated by a backslash) that will host your notification application. The second entry, BaseDirectoryPath, is the base path for the configuration files, XML style sheets, and other support files that will be used to create the application.

This configuration file references a single application, BNS, and a single delivery channel, the EmailChannel, which uses the built-in SMTP delivery protocol. Note the Parameters node within the BNS Application node. This defines the parameters to pass into the application definition file. Unlike the instance configuration file, the application definition file cannot retrieve parameters from the environment or from the NSControl command line. In this case, we simply pass on the parameters originally passed into the instance configuration file (along with the COMPUTERNAME environment variable). In other scenarios, you might have more sophisticated parameter needs.

Let's now turn to the application definition file, appADF.XML, shown in Listing 19.3. (You can find this file in the CH19\bns\svc subfolder on the CD accompanying this book.)

Listing 19.3

```xml
<?xml version="1.0" encoding="utf-8" ?>
<Application xmlns:xsd="http://www.w3.org/2001/XMLSchema"
    xmlns:xsi="http://www.w3.org/2001/XMLSchema-instance"
    xmlns="http://www.microsoft.com/MicrosoftNotificationServices/
    ApplicationDefinitionFileSchema">
  <EventClasses>
    <EventClass>
      <EventClassName>BNSEvents</EventClassName>
      <Schema>
        <Field>
          <FieldName>ID</FieldName>
          <FieldType>integer</FieldType>
          <FieldTypeMods>not null</FieldTypeMods>
        </Field>
      </Schema>
    </EventClass>
  </EventClasses>


  <SubscriptionClasses>
    <SubscriptionClass>
      <SubscriptionClassName>BNSSubscriptions
          </SubscriptionClassName>
      <Schema>
        <Field>
          <FieldName>DeviceName</FieldName>
          <FieldType>nvarchar(255)</FieldType>
          <FieldTypeMods>not null</FieldTypeMods>
        </Field>
        <Field>
          <FieldName>SubscriberLocale</FieldName>
          <FieldType>nvarchar(10)</FieldType>
          <FieldTypeMods>not null</FieldTypeMods>
        </Field>
        <Field>
          <FieldName>Product</FieldName>
          <FieldType>nvarchar(30)</FieldType>
          <FieldTypeMods>not null</FieldTypeMods>
        </Field>
        <Field>
          <FieldName>ID</FieldName>
          <FieldType>nvarchar(15)</FieldType>
          <FieldTypeMods>not null</FieldTypeMods>
```

```
      </Field>
      <Field>
        <FieldName>OpenedBy</FieldName>
        <FieldType>nvarchar(30)</FieldType>
        <FieldTypeMods>not null</FieldTypeMods>
      </Field>
      <Field>
        <FieldName>AssignedTo</FieldName>
        <FieldType>nvarchar(30)</FieldType>
        <FieldTypeMods>not null</FieldTypeMods>
      </Field>
    </Schema>
    <EventRules>
      <EventRule>
        <RuleName>BNSSubscriptionsRule</RuleName>
        <Action>
          SELECT dbo.BNSInfoNotify(s.SubscriberId,
                                   s.DeviceName,
                                   s.SubscriberLocale,
                                   p.ID,
                                   p.Product,
                                   p.OpenedBy,
                                   p.AssignedTo,
                                   p.Description,
                                   p.DateChanged,
                                   p.Pri,
                                   p.Sev)
          FROM BNSEvents e, BNSSubscriptions s, BNS..Bugs p
          WHERE e.ID = p.ID
            AND p.Product = s.Product
            AND p.OpenedBy LIKE s.OpenedBy
            AND p.AssignedTo LIKE s.AssignedTo
            AND p.ID LIKE s.ID
        </Action>
        <EventClassName>BNSEvents</EventClassName>
      </EventRule>
    </EventRules>
  </SubscriptionClass>
</SubscriptionClasses>
<NotificationClasses>
  <NotificationClass>
    <NotificationClassName>BNSInfo</NotificationClassName>
    <Schema>
      <Fields>
```

```
              <Field>
                <FieldName>ID</FieldName>
                <FieldType>int</FieldType>
              </Field>
              <Field>
                <FieldName>Product</FieldName>
                <FieldType>nvarchar(30)</FieldType>
              </Field>
              <Field>
                <FieldName>OpenedBy</FieldName>
                <FieldType>nvarchar(30)</FieldType>
              </Field>
              <Field>
                <FieldName>AssignedTo</FieldName>
                <FieldType>nvarchar(30)</FieldType>
              </Field>
              <Field>
                <FieldName>Description</FieldName>
                <FieldType>nvarchar(80)</FieldType>
              </Field>
              <Field>
                <FieldName>DateChanged</FieldName>
                <FieldType>datetime</FieldType>
              </Field>
              <Field>
                <FieldName>Pri</FieldName>
                <FieldType>int</FieldType>
              </Field>
              <Field>
                <FieldName>Sev</FieldName>
                <FieldType>integer</FieldType>
              </Field>
            </Fields>
          </Schema>
          <ContentFormatter>
            <ClassName>XsltFormatter</ClassName>
            <Arguments>
              <Argument>
                <Name>XsltBaseDirectoryPath</Name>
                <Value>%BasePath%</Value>
              </Argument>
              <Argument>
                <Name>XsltFileName</Name>
                <Value>BNSInfo.xslt</Value>
```

```xml
          </Argument>
        </Arguments>
      </ContentFormatter>
      <Protocols>
        <Protocol>
          <ProtocolName>SMTP</ProtocolName>
          <Fields>
            <Field>
              <FieldName>Subject</FieldName>
              <SqlExpression>'Bug Change Notification'
                  </SqlExpression>
            </Field>
            <Field>
              <FieldName>BodyFormat</FieldName>
              <SqlExpression>'html'</SqlExpression>
            </Field>
            <Field>
              <FieldName>From</FieldName>
              <SqlExpression>'bns@yourcompany.com'</SqlExpression>
            </Field>
            <Field>
              <FieldName>Priority</FieldName>
              <SqlExpression>'Normal'</SqlExpression>
            </Field>
            <Field>
              <FieldName>To</FieldName>
              <SqlExpression>DeviceAddress</SqlExpression>
            </Field>
          </Fields>
        </Protocol>
      </Protocols>
    </NotificationClass>
  </NotificationClasses>
  <Providers>
    <NonHostedProvider>
      <ProviderName>SQLTriggerEventProvider</ProviderName>
    </NonHostedProvider>
  </Providers>
  <Generator>
    <SystemName>%SystemName%</SystemName>
  </Generator>
  <Distributors>
    <Distributor>
      <SystemName>%SystemName%</SystemName>
```

```
    <QuantumDuration>PT5S</QuantumDuration>
  </Distributor>
</Distributors>
<ApplicationExecutionSettings>
  <QuantumDuration>PT5S</QuantumDuration>
  <Vacuum>
    <RetentionAge>P3DT00H00M00S</RetentionAge>
    <VacuumSchedule>
      <Schedule>
        <StartTime>23:00:00</StartTime>
        <Duration>P0DT02H00M00S</Duration>
      </Schedule>
      <Schedule>
        <StartTime>03:00:00</StartTime>
        <Duration>P0DT02H00M00S</Duration>
      </Schedule>
    </VacuumSchedule>
  </Vacuum>
</ApplicationExecutionSettings>
</Application>
```

I've bolded the parameters that are passed in from the instance configuration file. As I mentioned earlier, you never pass the application definition file directly to NSControl. When NSControl requires a configuration file, you pass the instance configuration file, and it, in turn, references the application definition files for the applications it hosts.

The SystemName node in the Generator and Distributor sections refers to the machine name that's hosting your notification application. The XsltBaseDirectoryPath node refers to the path that contains the XML style sheets that the XSLT content formatter is to use.

As its name suggests, an application definition file defines the behavior of a notification application. The event class nodes determine what an event looks like. The subscription and notification class nodes determine what subscriptions and notifications look like, respectively. The generator and distributor sections determine how the generator and distributor run and what they do, respectively. The providers section tells us what type of event provider we're using. In this case, we're providing events via SQL Server triggers, as I mentioned earlier. The vacuum section determines how often obsolete data (e.g., delivered notifications) is removed from the system. Since event and notification data will continue to accrue and grow over time in your databases, it's essential that vacuuming runs regularly.

WARNING: The sample applications that ship with Notification Services do not include vacuum sections in their application definition files, so if you use the CopySample utility to copy one of them so that you can customize it for your own use, your new app won't have a vacuum section in its application definition file by default and won't vacuum obsolete data. You can add a vacuum section to the application definition file before creating your application with NSControl Create, or you can add it afterward and use NSControl Update to apply the change. You can also invoke vacuuming manually by running the NSVacuum stored procedure. Users who vacuum old data must belong to the NSVacuum role.

Note the way that the match rule is constructed in the EventRules section. Its join clause looks like this:

```
WHERE e.ID = p.ID
  AND p.Product = s.Product
  AND p.OpenedBy LIKE s.OpenedBy
  AND p.AssignedTo LIKE s.AssignedTo
  AND p.ID LIKE s.ID
```

The use of LIKE in the query predicates allows wildcards to be used in place of actual values in the subscription definition. So, the OpenedBy, AssignedTo, and ID (the bug ID) columns are effectively optional. If they are unspecified in the subscription management application, the GUI can plug them with a value of "%" in order to cause them to be effectively ignored for purposes of filtering the query. This probably isn't the best strategy in terms of effective index use, but it does allow the match rule to be somewhat dynamic. I'll show you an alternate way of constructing dynamic matching rules later in the chapter.

Creating Your Custom Database

The only other thing that we need to do before running NSControl to create, register, and enable the notification application is create the custom database that stores the Bugs table. As I mentioned earlier, this table will have a trigger on it that will generate a notification every time a new bug is added or changed. Listing 19.4 presents a T-SQL script to create the BNS database. (You can find this code in the CreateBNS.SQL script in the \CH19\ bns\svc subfolder on the CD accompanying this book.)

Listing 19.4

```
USE master
GO
IF (DB_ID('BNS') IS NOT NULL)
  DROP DATABASE BNS
GO

CREATE DATABASE BNS
GO

USE BNS
GO

IF ('BNS'<>DB_NAME()) RAISERROR('Database create failed.
    Aborting.',25,1) WITH LOG
GO

CREATE TABLE Bugs (
  ID            int,
  Product       nvarchar(30),
  OpenedBy      nvarchar(30),
  AssignedTo    nvarchar(30),
  Description   nvarchar(80),
  DateChanged   datetime,
  Pri           int,
  Sev           int,
  Status        int,
  BugText       text,
  Repro         text
primary key (ID))
GO
CREATE TRIGGER BugTrigger ON Bugs
FOR INSERT, UPDATE
AS
BEGIN
  DECLARE @EventBatchId bigint

  -- Open the event batch
  EXEC BNSInstanceBNS..NSEventBeginBatchBNSEvents
    @ProviderName = N'SQLTriggerEventProvider',
    @EventBatchId = @EventBatchId OUTPUT

  DECLARE @BugID integer
```

```
DECLARE NewBugCursor CURSOR
LOCAL FAST_FORWARD
FOR Select ID from inserted

OPEN NewBugCursor

FETCH NEXT FROM NewBugCursor INTO @BugId
WHILE @@FETCH_STATUS = 0
BEGIN
  -- Write an event to the batch
  EXEC BNSInstanceBNS..NSEventWriteBNSEvents
    @EventBatchId,
    @BugId

  FETCH NEXT FROM NewBugCursor INTO @BugId
END

CLOSE NewBugCursor
DEALLOCATE NewBugCursor

-- Close the event batch
EXEC BNSInstanceBNS..NSEventFlushBatchBNSEvents @EventBatchId

END
GO

EXECUTE sp_grantdbaccess guest
GO
```

This script creates a new database, BNS, then creates a Bugs table in it for storing bug entries. It then creates a trigger over the table that fires on an INSERT or UPDATE operation against the table and generates notifications accordingly. Run the script to create the BNS database, then we'll get started building the notification application. (If you see warning messages regarding missing objects and the inability to set up dependency information in sysdepends, ignore them.)

Creating the Instance and Application Databases

Once you've built the BNS database, add the Notification Services bin folder to the system path so that we can call NSControl without fully qualifying its

location. This folder should be at \Program Files\Microsoft SQL Server Notification Services\vN.N.N.N\bin on the drive on which you installed Notification Services.

After you've added the bin folder to the system path, open a command
window and change to the CH19\bns\svc subfolder on the CD accompanying this book. Once there, run NSControl to create the instance and application databases using this command line (type this on a single line):

```
nscontrol create -in instConfig.xml Server_Instance=YourServer\
YourSSInstance BasePath=D:\CH19\bns\svc
```

Server_Instance and BasePath are parameters being passed into the instance configuration file. As I mentioned earlier, Server_Instance is your
machine name and SQL Server instance name, separated by a backslash.
BasePath is the folder where the configuration files, XML style sheets, and
other supporting files reside for the instance. Replace each of these values
with the appropriate values for your system when you run NSControl.

Registering the Instance

Once the instance and application databases are created, you're ready to
register the instance. Although you can register the instance without also
registering its Windows service, there's no point in doing that in our scenario, so we'll register both at the same time. Use NSControl to register the
instance like this (type this on a single line):

```
nscontrol register -name BNSInstance -server YourServer\
YourSSInstance -service -serviceusername YourSvcUser
-servicepassword YourSvcPwd
```

Replace YourServer\YourSSInstance with the name of the machine and
SQL Server instance that is hosting your notification application. For purposes of this exercise, I'm assuming that your SQL Server and Notification
Services app will reside on the same machine. Replace YourSvcUser and
YourSvcPwd with the user name and password, respectively, of the NT account that you want NSService.exe to run under. It's common for users to
create a special account just for this purpose. If you do that, be sure that it
has the proper access rights by following the instructions laid out in the
"NS$instance_name Service Account Security" topic in Notification Ser-
vices Books Online.

Enabling the Instance

Once an instance has been registered, you must enable it in order for it to begin generating notifications. You can selectively enable and disable parts of an application—for example, you could enable event collection but not the generator. In our case, we want to enable the entire application, so we'll simply pass the instance name on the command line to NSControl:

```
nscontrol enable -n BNSInstance
```

(It has been my experience that the -name parameter can usually be abbreviated -n.)

You can enable the instance before or after you start the Windows service. If you enable it before you've started the service (as we just have), you'll see that some of the components of the application show a pending state after NSControl Enable runs. That's nothing to worry about. They'll come online once the service is started, which we'll do next.

Starting the Service

You can start your new notification service using Windows' Services application or via NET START. Given that I'm an old-fashioned sort of guy, I usually use NET START, like this:

```
NET START NS$BNSInstance
```

Once the service is started, it's officially ready to begin delivering notifications. Now all we have to do is create a subscription management application and begin entering subscriptions and events to test out our new notification application.

Building the Subscription Management Application

As I mentioned earlier, you can use the CopySample utility to duplicate one of the sample apps that ships with Notification Services so that you can customize it for your own use. We're not going to do that in this exercise. Instead, we'll build a new subscription management app from scratch in Visual Basic .NET. The app will be a traditional Windows app rather than the more common ASP.NET application because I want to illustrate what's involved with interacting with the Notification Services object model with as little clutter as possible. Building a subscription management app as a traditional Windows app isn't the most practical approach because, by default, the app needs to run on the same machine as your notification application. When the subscription app is an ASP.NET app, this is not a big problem—regardless of where the users of the app reside, the app itself runs on the IIS server, which can easily share its host machine with a notification application. However, when the subscription management application is a Windows app, the app runs in the context of whatever user machine executes it. By default, a user would have to run the app on the same machine that hosts your notification application in order for it to work properly.

It's possible to access the Notification Services object model remotely using COM Interop and DCOM, but, as a rule, you'll probably want to build your subscription management apps as ASP.NET apps to keep things simple and to keep from mixing COM and managed code classes unless absolutely necessary. The app presented here isn't intended for production use.

As I've said, I didn't build the subscription management app we'll use in this example as an ASP.NET app because I wanted to keep the example as simple as possible. There are nuances and idiosyncrasies associated with connectionless (Web-based) apps that you don't have with traditional Windows apps, and my purpose here is not to provide a subscription app that you can immediately drop into place in a production system but rather to demonstrate how easy it is to interact with and use the Notification Services object model.

I should also mention that I used Visual Basic .NET here rather than C# because I think a fair number of SQL Server practitioners are Visual Basic people rather than C, C++, or C# coders. Personally, I much prefer C# to Visual Basic of any flavor and would much rather use it. However, given that all the Notification Services sample apps except the Flight sample are written in C# and given that, as I've said, most SQL Server people are likely to prefer Visual Basic, I've built the subscription app we'll look at in Visual Basic .NET. Most of the code in this app could easily be reused in an ASP.NET application written in Visual Basic .NET with little or no changes. All of the sample subscription management apps that ship with Notification Services are ASP.NET apps, so you can reference them for ideas on how to implement your own ASP.NET-based subscription management app.

The Notification Services sample apps make use of a common utility class that's stored in NSUtility.cs. This class makes interacting with the Notification Services object model even easier than it already is and is used extensively by the sample apps. Given that our subscription app is written in Visual Basic and given that you can't use a C# module in a Visual Basic .NET project without first compiling it to an assembly, I've translated a fair number of the functions in NSUtility.cs into Visual Basic .NET. You're welcome to extract these functions from the source code we're about to explore and use them in your own Visual Basic .NET–based subscription management applications.

The first thing you must do in order to allow a managed code app to interact with the Notification Services object model is add a reference to the Microsoft.SqlServer.NotificationServices assembly to your project. If you load the BNSSubscribe solution into Visual Studio .NET, you'll see that it does indeed reference this assembly.

So, without further ado, let's look at the source code for BNSSubscribe (Listing 19.5), the subscription management application for the BNS. Given that much of the source for the app was generated by Visual Studio .NET, I won't take you through all of it. We'll just explore the code that I wrote to implement the app and hit the high points of how it works. (You can find this code in the Form1.vb file in the \CH19\bns\BNSSubscribe subfolder on the CD accompanying this book. Due to VB's prehistoric predilection for line-orientated coding, some of this code doesn't format well on the printed page; see the source code file itself for a much more readable listing.)

Listing 19.5

```
Private Function CreateDataSource
        (ByVal subscriptionEnumeration As _SubscriptionEnumeration)
        As DataSet
    Dim ds As DataSet = New DataSet()
    Dim dt As DataTable = New DataTable("Subscriptions")
    ds.Tables.Add(dt)

    Dim dr As DataRow

    dt.Columns.Add(New DataColumn("SubscriptionId",
        System.Type.GetType("System.Int32")))
    dt.Columns.Add(New DataColumn("Product", System.Type.GetType
        ("System.String")))
    dt.Columns.Add(New DataColumn("ID", System.Type.GetType
        ("System.String")))
    dt.Columns.Add(New DataColumn("OpenedBy", System.Type.GetType
        ("System.String")))
    dt.Columns.Add(New DataColumn("AssignedTo",
        System.Type.GetType("System.String")))

    Dim subscription As Subscription
    For Each subscription In subscriptionEnumeration
      dr = dt.NewRow()
```

```
      Dim i As Integer
      Dim name As String
      For i = 0 To dt.Columns.Count - 1
        name = dt.Columns(i).ColumnName

        If (0 = String.Compare(name, "SubscriptionId", True))
            Then
          dr(name) = subscription.SubscriptionId
        Else
          dr(name) = subscription(name)
        End If
      Next
      dt.Rows.Add(dr)
      Next


      Return ds
End Function

Public Sub UpdateGrid(ByVal userName As String)
  Dim subscriptionEnumeration As SubscriptionEnumeration
  subscriptionEnumeration = New SubscriptionEnumeration
      (application, subscriptionClassName, userName)

  dgSubscriptions.SetDataBinding(CreateDataSource
      (subscriptionEnumeration), "Subscriptions")
End Sub

Public Function GetDeliveryChannel(ByVal protocolName As
      String) As String
  Dim deliveryChannelEnumeration As DeliveryChannelEnumeration
      = New DeliveryChannelEnumeration(instance)

  Dim deliveryChannel As IDeliveryChannel
  For Each deliveryChannel In deliveryChannelEnumeration
    If deliveryChannel.ProtocolName = protocolName Then
      Return deliveryChannel.DeliveryChannelName
    End If
  Next
  Return Nothing
End Function

Public Function GetSubscriberDeviceName(ByVal subscriberId As
      String) As String
  Dim subscriberDeviceName As String = Nothing
```

```vbnet
    Dim subDeviceEnumeration As SubscriberDeviceEnumeration
    subDeviceEnumeration = New SubscriberDeviceEnumeration
        (instance, subscriberId)

    If Not subDeviceEnumeration Is Nothing Then
      Dim subscriberDevice As SubscriberDevice
      For Each subscriberDevice In subDeviceEnumeration
        subscriberDeviceName = subscriberDevice.DeviceName
      Next
    End If


    Return subscriberDeviceName
End Function

Private Sub AddSubscriber(ByVal subscriberId As String, ByVal
    protocolName As String, ByVal emailaddress As String)
  Try
    Dim subscriber As Subscriber = New Subscriber(instance)

    subscriber.SubscriberId = subscriberId

    subscriber.Add()

    Dim subscriberDevice As SubscriberDevice =
        New SubscriberDevice(instance)

    Dim deliveryChannelName As String =
        GetDeliveryChannel(protocolName)

    subscriberDevice.SubscriberId = subscriberId
    subscriberDevice.DeviceTypeName = protocolName
    subscriberDevice.DeviceName = "myDevice"
    subscriberDevice.DeviceAddress = emailaddress
    subscriberDevice.DeliveryChannelName = deliveryChannelName

    subscriberDevice.Add()
  Catch ex As NSException
    If (NSEventEnum.DuplicateSubscriber <> ex.ErrorCode) Then
      Throw (ex)
    End If
  End Try
End Sub
```

```vb
Public Function AddSubscription(ByVal subscriberId As String, _
                    ByVal subscriptionClassName As String, _
                    ByVal subscriptionFields As Hashtable, _
                    ByVal dateTimeStart As String, _
                    ByVal recurrence As String)

    Dim subscription As Subscription = New Subscription
        (application, subscriptionClassName)
    subscription.SubscriberId = subscriberId

    Dim entry As DictionaryEntry
    For Each entry In subscriptionFields
      Dim fieldName As String = entry.Key
      Dim fieldValue As Object = entry.Value
      subscription(fieldName) = fieldValue
    Next

    If subscription.HasTimedRule Then
      subscription.ScheduleStart = dateTimeStart
      subscription.ScheduleRecurrence = recurrence
    End If

    Return subscription.Add()
End Function

Private Sub DeleteSubscription(ByVal subscriberId As String,
      ByVal subscriptionClassName As String,
      ByVal subscriptionIdString As String)
    Dim subscriptionEnumeration As SubscriptionEnumeration =
        New SubscriptionEnumeration(application,
        subscriptionClassName, subscriberId)

    Dim subscription As Subscription = subscriptionEnumeration
        (subscriptionIdString)

    subscription.Delete()
End Sub

Private Sub AddSub(ByVal Product As String,
      ByVal Bug As String, ByVal OpenedBy As String,
      ByVal AssignedTo As String)
    Dim subscriberDeviceName As String = Nothing
    Dim subscriptionId As String = Nothing
    Dim subscriptionFields As Hashtable = Nothing
    Dim bugmask As String = "%"
```

```vb
    Dim openedbymask As String = "%"
    Dim assignedtomask As String = "%"

    Try
      Try
        If 0 <> OpenedBy.Length Then openedbymask =
            tbOpenedBy.Text
        If 0 <> AssignedTo.Length Then assignedtomask =
            tbAssignedTo.Text
        If 0 <> Bug.Length Then bugmask =
            Int32.Parse(tbBug.Text).ToString()
      Catch ex As Exception
        Throw New Exception("Invalid Bug ID specified.", ex)
      End Try

      AddSubscriber(userName, "SMTP", tbEmail.Text)

      subscriberDeviceName = GetSubscriberDeviceName(userName)

      subscriptionFields = New Hashtable()

      subscriptionFields.Add("DeviceName", subscriberDeviceName)
      subscriptionFields.Add("SubscriberLocale", "en-US")
      subscriptionFields.Add("Product", Product)
      subscriptionFields.Add("ID", bugmask)
      subscriptionFields.Add("OpenedBy", openedbymask)
      subscriptionFields.Add("AssignedTo", assignedtomask)

      subscriptionId = AddSubscription(userName,
          subscriptionClassName, subscriptionFields,
          Nothing, Nothing)

      UpdateGrid(userName)

      sbMsg.Text = "Subscription successfully added."
    Catch ex As Exception
      sbMsg.Text = "Cannot add subscription: " + ex.Message
    End Try
End Sub

Private Sub btAdd_Click(ByVal sender As System.Object,
    ByVal e As System.EventArgs) Handles btAdd.Click
  AddSub(cbProduct.SelectedItem, tbBug.Text, tbOpenedBy.Text,
      tbAssignedTo.Text)
End Sub
```

```
Private Sub btDelete_Click(ByVal sender As System.Object,
    ByVal e As System.EventArgs) Handles btDelete.Click
  If (-1 = dgSubscriptions.CurrentRowIndex) Then Exit Sub
  Dim subscriptionIdString As String =
      dgSubscriptions.Item(dgSubscriptions.CurrentCell)

  Try
    DeleteSubscription(userName, subscriptionClassName,
        subscriptionIdString)

    sbMsg.Text = "Subscription deleted"

    UpdateGrid(userName)
  Catch ex As Exception
    sbMsg.Text = "Cannot delete the subscription: " +
        ex.Message
  End Try
End Sub
End Class
```

Let's walk through the main elements of this application. First, in the form class's constructor, I instantiate NSInstance and NSApplication objects. I've not included the constructor code here because most of it was generated by Visual Studio .NET, but here are the specific lines that instantiate these objects:

```
instance = New NSInstance(instanceName)
application = New NSApplication(instance, applicationName)
```

The instance and application variables are members of the form class, so they are accessible to all of its methods. Once created, we can use them when we make other calls to the Notification Services object model.

Once these objects are created, we retrieve the subscriptions for the current user and update the grid at the bottom of the form that lists them. The UpdateGrid method is responsible for carrying this work out. As you can see from the source code listing, it creates a new SubscriptionEnumeration object, then passes it to a method named CreateDataSource to create a data source (a DataSet object, in this case) that's suitable for use with a DataGrid control. We pass in the current user name (which we retrieved at application startup via System.Security.Principal.WindowsIdentity.GetCurrent.Name) to UpdateGrid, and it uses this to filter the subscriptions it enumerates.

The next code of interest is the btAdd_Click and AddSub methods. This code runs when the user clicks the Add button in the GUI to add a subscription. The btAdd_Click method calls AddSub, and AddSub carries out the real work of adding the subscription. It begins by adding the subscriber (in case he or she hasn't already been added), then retrieves the subscriber's delivery device and adds the subscription. As I mentioned earlier, the GUI supplies wildcard values for subscription fields that are left blank. This allows them to be effectively optional when the match rule runs.

The last segment of code that we'll look at is the btDelete_Click method. Obviously, this code runs when the user selects a subscription definition in the DataGrid and clicks the Delete button to delete it. It calls the DeleteSubscription method, which I've translated from the NSUtility.cs C# source file that ships with the Notification Services sample apps.

The rest of the code in this source module is support code for the app's two main functions: adding and deleting subscriptions. A subscription management app could obviously provide much more functionality than this, but you need at least these two functions in any subscription management app you build.

Testing Notifications

Let's use BNSSubscribe to add a subscription so that we can test our notification application. Run the app now from the \CH19\bns\BNSSubscribe\bin subfolder and add a subscription for bugs filed against the Sequin product. (If we were going to allow notifications to actually be delivered, we'd need to change the e-mail address field to a valid address; don't worry about that for now.) Leave the other entry fields blank and click the Add button to add the subscription. Once the subscription adds successfully, start Query Analyzer and run the following query:

```
USE BNS
GO
INSERT INTO Bugs
VALUES(1, 'Sequin', '','','', getdate(), 1, 1, 1, '','')
```

Once you've executed this query, open Windows Explorer and navigate to the pickup folder for your SMTP server. On the Windows NT family, this is located at \Inetpub\mailroot\pickup. After a few seconds, you should see a file with an extension of .eml show up in this folder. If your SMTP server is running, it will pick up this file and attempt to send it to the recipient.

Congratulations—you've just generated your first notification with Notification Services!

Possible Improvements

As you might guess, there are a number of ways we could improve this application and make it more suitable for production use. For one thing, as I've mentioned, the subscription management app should probably be a Web app if the software is going to be used in a production scenario. For another, you could enable digest notifications in order to keep subscribers from being pummeled by notifications in the event that lots of bug entries are suddenly added or changed. Setting up digest notifications would group all of the notifications in a notification batch for each subscriber into a single e-mail, perhaps substantially reducing the number of notification e-mails they receive.

Dynamic Match Rules

Another useful improvement to this application would be to open up the match rule specification so that a user could specify more sophisticated subscription criteria. As I mentioned earlier, the use of wildcards to make columns optional in a match rule query is not the most efficient approach in terms of index usage. Using a plain "%" wildcard virtually guarantees a table scan. (You'll see a clustered index scan if a clustered index exists on the table, but they are semantically and functionally equivalent.) A better approach would be to completely eliminate columns the user doesn't want to filter the subscription by from the query. However, given that the same match rule is used for all subscribers, this isn't an easy task.

One method for doing this would be to set up a dynamic match rule using some T-SQL tricks I've demonstrated in previous books. Basically, the dynamic match rule technique works like this.

1. Instead of merely allowing values to be supplied for a fixed set of subscription filter fields, the GUI presents a query builder–type interface that allows a subscriber to create any type of query against the underlying data (the Bugs table, in our case) that he or she desires. The query builder supports the notion of logical connectors (AND, OR, NOT) and permits any field in the underlying table to serve as part of the subscription criteria.
2. When the user clicks the Add button in the GUI to add the subscription to the application database, the GUI creates a SQL Server view

object behind the scenes that encapsulates the specified subscription criteria. Each view returns all the columns in the underlying table for all rows that match the custom criteria supplied by the user. The GUI then adds the subscription to the application database using this view name as its lone criterion.

3. When the match rule runs, it generates a dynamic T-SQL query that takes the names of the views previously built by the GUI and concatenates them into a minimum number of large UNION ALL queries. Each of these dynamic queries is less than 8,000 bytes in length due to the limitations of the varchar data type. Each one is used to generate notifications just as a normal match rule SELECT is. The end result is that the custom subscription criteria specified in each subscription is used to drive the notification process without requiring the use of a cursor or other inefficient mechanism.

This is best understood by way of example, such as Listing 19.6. (You can find this code in the dynamic_filter.sql script in the \CH19\bns\svc subfolder on the CD accompanying this book.)

Listing 19.6

```
DECLARE @strQry varchar(8000)  -- dynamic query str
DECLARE @strLastView varchar(128)  -- track last view processed
DECLARE @nViewNameLen int  -- max view name length
DECLARE @nMaxViewsPerQuery int  -- total # of views we can handle
                               -- for each dynamic query
DECLARE @nViewQryLen int  -- total str space per view
DECLARE @strSelectFrag varchar(30)  -- portion of query for
                                    -- SELECT stmt
DECLARE @strUnionFrag varchar(30)  -- portion of query for UNION
DECLARE @nNumViews int  -- total # of views to process

SET @strSelectFrag='SELECT * FROM '  -- SELECT fragment of
                                     -- dynamic query
SET @strUnionFrag=' UNION ALL '  -- UNION fragment of dynamic query
SET @nViewNameLen=7  -- names have form V###### - allows
                     -- for 999,999 views

SET @nViewQryLen=@nViewNameLen+
   DATALENGTH(@strSelectFrag)+DATALENGTH(@strUnionFrag)

SET @nMaxViewsPerQuery=8000 / @nViewQryLen
```

```
SET @strQry=''

SELECT @nNumViews=COUNT(*)
FROM sysobjects
WHERE type='V'
AND name LIKE 'V%'

SET @strLastView=''

SET ROWCOUNT @nMaxViewsPerQuery

-- drop table matchtable
-- select * into matchtable from authors where 0=1

WHILE (@nNumViews>0) BEGIN

  SELECT @strQry=@strQry+
        @strSelectFrag+
        cast(name as varchar(128))+
        @strUnionFrag,
        @strLastView=cast(name as varchar(128))
  FROM sysobjects
  WHERE type='V'
  AND name LIKE 'V%'
  AND name > @strLastView
  ORDER BY name

  -- Remove last UNION ALL
  SET @strQry=LEFT(@strQry,DATALENGTH(@strQry)-
        DATALENGTH(@strUnionFrag))

SET ROWCOUNT 0
  INSERT matchtable
  EXEC(@strQry)
SET ROWCOUNT @nMaxViewsPerQuery

  SET @nNumViews=@nNumViews-@nMaxViewsPerQuery
  SET @strQry=''

END

SET ROWCOUNT 0
```

The salient code here is within the WHILE loop. It uses a couple of interesting techniques to avoid using a cursor and to query as many of the subscription criteria views at once as possible. First, it uses the concatenation trick I first demonstrated in my book *The Guru's Guide to Transact-SQL* to build a dynamic T-SQL string that SELECTs from as many criteria views at once as possible. Second, it sets @strLastView to the final view name it processes with each iteration so that it can keep track of which view names remain to be processed. Given that our dynamic query string is limited to 8,000 characters, we calculate the number of criteria views we can process with each iteration, then use SET ROWCOUNT to limit the number of view names we see within the loop to this number. That's the purpose of the @MaxViewsPerQuery variable. Because we know that a variable that's assigned the value from a column in a result set with multiple rows retains the value from the last row, we can assign @strLastView in the same SELECT statement that we use to build our dynamic query string, then use it in subsequent iterations of the code to pick up where we left off.

The INSERT statement above is a placeholder for the SELECT statement that's normally used in a matching rule. I insert the results from the dynamic filter into this table to make the code easy to test. Obviously, we'd call the notification function to generate raw notifications using the dynamic filter views if we were going to make use of this in our application. For example, we might change our match rule query to look something like this:

```
EXEC('SELECT dbo.BNSInfoNotify(b.SubscriberId,
    s.DeviceName,
    s.SubscriberLocale,
    b.ID,
    b.Product,
    b.OpenedBy,
    b.AssignedTo,
    b.Description,
    b.DateChanged,
    b.Pri,
    b.Sev)
FROM BNSSubscriptions e JOIN ('+@strQry+') b ON
    (e.SubscriberId=b.SubscriberId)')
```

We'd then execute it for each iteration of the WHILE loop. The result would be notification generations based on the criteria specified in the views.

This is just a prototype of how you could implement dynamic match rules with Notification Services. In my own testing, it's quite fast and seems fully functional. You can use the create_views.sql and dynamic_filter.sql scripts in the CH19\bns\svc subfolder on the CD accompanying this book to experiment with this technique.

Of course, this type of mechanism isn't really justified when the underlying data has only a few columns in the first place, as is the case with our Bugs table. However, envision a situation where you have hundreds of columns in the underlying data. Using the wildcard trick to allow columns to be omitted from the subscription criteria may not be suitable from a performance standpoint. It may also be too restrictive in terms of search criteria—users may want more flexibility than merely specifying simple search criteria for a fixed set of fields. In that scenario, a dynamic match rule mechanism like the one just demonstrated would likely be not only more efficient than the wildcard approach but also much more flexible. You could even create a supplemental table to allow users to associate names or descriptions with their criteria views that they could then use to reference the view for later reuse . In other words, you'd be allowing them to create named, reusable queries that were encapsulated as view objects and capable of generating notifications through a modified version of the standard Notification Services match rule, as demonstrated above.

Recap

Notification Services provides a flexible, extensible, and scalable platform for creating notification applications. It provides most of the plumbing necessary to build these types of applications; you supply custom code as necessary to implement the functionality you need.

There are three main components in any Notification Services application: the Windows service, the SQL Server data store, and the subscription management application. Notification Services provides the tools to automatically produce the SQL Server data store and the Windows service and provides sample applications that you can copy and customize to create your own subscription management applications.

Within the Windows service, NSService.exe, three main tasks are carried out to produce subscriber notifications. The event collector process is responsible for collecting events of interest to the application. The generator is responsible for matching these events with subscriptions and generating raw notifications. The distributor is responsible for transforming these raw messages into notifications and delivering them to delivery channels to be sent to subscribers.

Notification Services provides a rich object framework with which you can construct notification applications. Interfaces are provided for implementing custom event providers, delivery channels, and content formatters. Objects are provided for managing subscribers, subscriber devices, subscriptions, and various other Notification Services elements. Between this model and the XML configuration files and style sheets supported by the product, you have a fully programmable solution that can be customized to meet your needs.

Knowledge Measure

1. What element in a notification application is responsible for translating raw notifications into notification messages suitable for sending to subscribers?
2. What is the maximum number of generator processes a single instance of a Notification Services application can support?
3. True or false: Because the Notification Services Windows service is a managed code executable, custom event collectors are required to be managed code assemblies that run within the context of this executable's process.
4. What is the name of the executable that serves as the Windows service within a Notification Services application?
5. True or false: Unlike instance configuration files, application definition files cannot directly access environment variables for use as parameters.
6. Which task usually comes first in the Notification Services development cycle: registering the Windows service or creating the instance and application databases?
7. Describe the function of NSControl Enable.
8. Name the lone content formatter that ships with Notification Services.
9. When the notification function is called from within a matching rule, what happens behind the scenes?
10. Why is it a good idea to implement a subscription management application as a Web application rather than a Windows application if possible?
11. True or false: Once an instance has been registered, its configuration file is not used directly by the instance's Windows service.

12. True or false: You use regsvr32.exe to register a new notification application instance.

13. Which XML configuration file—the instance configuration file or the application definition file—lists the delivery channels available for application use?

14. Is it possible to run the Windows service executable as a regular console application?

15. Describe the purpose of chronicle tables.

16. Name the process within a Notification Services application that's used to get rid of obsolete event and notification data.

17. Name the three types of Notification Services components for which you can develop custom code by implementing predefined interfaces.

18. What does the quantum period specified in the application definition file control?

19. Describe the scalability benefit of using multicast delivery.

20. True or false: Notification Services subscription management applications must be developed in C# due to their dependence on the NSUtility.cs class file, which has not, as yet, been translated into any other CLR-compliant language.

CHAPTER 20

Data Transformation Services

Character is what you do when no one's looking.

—Kenneth E. Routen

Data Transformation Services (DTS) is one of the most exciting technologies to be added to SQL Server in years. In times past, you would have had to go to a third-party product (and probably an expensive one at that) to get the type of functionality that DTS provides right in the SQL Server box. Speaking as both a veteran coder and a long-time SQL Server practitioner, DTS appears to be a well-designed, powerful addition to the SQL Server family. It features a sleek interface that is high on functionality and low on distraction. The DTS user experience is intuitive and well thought out—it is what all visual designer-type apps should be: easy to use, extensible, and fully functional.

DTS showcases key Microsoft technologies such as COM, ATL, OLE DB, and, of course, SQL Server. The DTS Designer is based on an extensible object model, which allows it to be extended with COM components. The DTS object model itself is accessible via COM Automation, so you can programmatically control DTS packages and transformations in any language that is capable of COM Automation (e.g., Visual Basic).

It should come as no surprise that DTS is able to transfer data between a source and a destination. Given this and the fact that its underlying data architecture is based on OLE DB, it shouldn't be surprising that you can transfer data from one OLE DB provider to another. The source and destination can be flat files, client/server databases, mainframe databases, and so on. The whole point of DTS is to make moving data from Point A to Point B as easy as possible, so it's fitting that it offers a myriad of options for doing exactly that.

I'm not going to bore you with step-by-step instructions for building lots of different types of DTS packages or for transferring data between providers. The Import/Export Wizard and the DTS Designer are intuitive enough that you shouldn't need a book for that. You drop some connections onto the DTS Designer workspace, link these connections with transformation tasks and precedence constraints, and away you go. Building a basic package is so simple that you shouldn't need to consult Books Online to figure out how to do it, let alone a third-party book. The DTS Designer is best experienced by simply diving in and building a few packages of your own. An excellent way to get a jump start on this is to use the DTS Import/Export Wizard and allow it to build a package for you, then load the resulting package into the DTS Designer.

I'm also not going to fill these pages with screenshot after screenshot of the DTS Designer. I once made the mistake of buying a SQL Server programming book only to discover that the coverage of many topics, DTS included, consisted mostly of screenshots. Frequently, the author put two screenshots on one page, with just a line or two of explanatory text between them. I don't think you need a book to see what the DTS Designer looks like—you can fire it up for yourself right from Enterprise Manager. And although it might help make this book seem a bit heftier, I don't think you bought it to look at screen prints of something you can readily view on your PC.

So we'll talk about the basic elements of DTS packages, we'll delve into how DTS is put together from an architectural standpoint, we'll discuss a few of the fringe elements of DTS programming and applications, and then we'll walk through a sample DTS application. You'll learn about some of DTS's strengths and weaknesses, and you'll hopefully gain a fresh perspective into some of the innovative ways in which you can put DTS to use.

Overview

Architecturally, DTS is composed of the following pieces:

- OLE DB providers. (Technically speaking, these aren't part of DTS, but they are integral to using it. OLE DB is the means by which DTS retrieves and stores data.)
- A multiphase data pump that you can use to set up sophisticated data transformations.
- A graphical designer that is based on an extensible COM-based object model. The key elements in this model are packages and tasks. In order to serve as a custom DTS task, a COM component must implement the CustomTask interface defined in the Microsoft

DTSPackage Object Library. This component must run in-process in order to be used in the DTS Designer, but it can run out-of-process when used programmatically.

- A set of programmable COM objects that provide a means of creating, manipulating, and executing DTS packages. Objects for working directly with the DTS data pump and data-driven query facility are also provided, as well as an Application object for managing DTS application-level settings.
- A collection of tools such as the DTS Import/Export Wizard, dtsrun, and dtsrunui for creating and executing packages.
- The DTS Query Designer, a graphical T-SQL query generator.

To use DTS to transfer or transform data, you create a package consisting of connections, task steps, and precedence constraints. DTS tasks range from simple data transformations to complex ActiveX and T-SQL scripts. Because you have COM at your disposal from an ActiveX script, you can carry out a wide variety of tasks from within a DTS package.

Packages

The fundamental element of a DTS application is the package. You can create a package in one of two ways: via the DTS Import/Export Wizard or the DTS Designer. A package can be stored in SQL Server, in the Metadata Repository, as Visual Basic code (this is a one-way operation—you cannot load packages saved as VB into the DTS Designer), or in a COM structured storage file.

NOTE: As of this writing, if you want to enable the ability to save packages to the repository, you must right-click the Data Transformation Services node in Enterprise Manager, select the Properties option, and check the Enable Save To Meta Data Services checkbox. Until this option is enabled, Meta Data Services will not appear as an option in the package save dialog box.

When you choose the SQL Server storage option, the DTS Designer calls an undocumented stored procedure named sp_add_dtspackage to store the package in msdb. The package is passed as an image data type to the procedure and stored in a table named sysdtspackages. You can view the list of packages saved to sysdtspackages via the Local Packages node located under the Data Transformation Services node in Enterprise Manager.

COM structured storage files resemble file systems in many ways. They provide a means of persisting COM objects to disk. Storing a DTS package on disk as a COM structured storage file allows you to easily transport it via other mediums such as e-mail and CD-ROM.

A DTS package consists of Connection objects (references to OLE DB providers), tasks, transformations, steps, and precedence constraints. The precedence constraints control the package's workflow—the flow of data through it. (You can also control package workflow using ActiveX scripts, as we'll discuss in just a moment.) The transformations specify whether and how data is converted and formatted as it is transferred from a source to a destination. Connection objects provide the ends of a transformation process—the sender and the receiver of the data being transformed and transferred from one location to another.

Connections

The connections supported by DTS consist of OLE DB data sources. Because an OLE DB provider exists that supports ODBC data sources, you can also use ODBC data sources with DTS. Examples of the kinds of data you can access with DTS through OLE DB include the following.

- SQL Server databases (via SQLOLEDB, the native SQL Server OLE DB provider)
- Other RDBMS backends such as Oracle, Sybase, and DB2
- Nonrelational stores such as Active Directory, Indexing Service, Site Server, and Exchange Server
- Text files—delimited as well as fixed-format
- HTML
- Access, Excel, and Visual FoxPro
- dBase and Paradox
- Other backends accessible via ODBC

Tasks

A task is an atomic work item. Each task in a DTS package defines a part of the data transformation process and is executed as a single step. Out of the box, DTS provides a number of task objects you can use to build complex data transformation applications. Examples of the types of things you can do include the following.

- Data copying between disparate OLE DB providers. You can load data from one type of data source into another type of destination. For example, you can copy data from an Oracle database into a SQL Server database or vice versa. You can transfer nonrelational as well as relational data, and you can use DTS's Bulk Load functionality to set up high-speed data loads from text files into SQL Server databases.
- Complex data transformations. You can map columns from a data source to a data destination and specify how the data is to be transformed as it is copied. You can use ActiveX scripts to manipulate the data in transit, and you can specify one-to-many, many-to-one, and other unusual relationships between source and destination data.
- Nested packages. Using the Execute Package task, you can set up one package to call another, adjust its global variables, and so on.
- Message transmittal. DTS provides facilities for sending e-mail based on package step completion status and for interacting with Message Queue in order to transmit messages between packages.
- T-SQL and ActiveX script execution. You can execute T-SQL and ActiveX scripts of your choosing as package steps. The T-SQL statements you execute can be ad hoc queries as well as stored procedure calls and can be generated using the DTS Query Designer. The ActiveX scripts you build can be any ActiveX script language. VBScript and JScript are available by default on any SQL Server installation.
- Database object duplication. You can transfer tables, views, stored procedures, user-defined functions, defaults, rules, and user-defined data types from one SQL Server database to another. DTS can even optionally script the entire operation for you as a series of T-SQL scripts and BCP data files.

The Multiphase Data Pump

Much of the real functionality of DTS is encapsulated in its multiphase data pump. It's the engine behind the Transform Data task, the Data Driven Query task, and the Parallel Data Pump task. As you might expect, the main purpose of the pump is to move and transform data between data sources.

The data pump goes through six basic steps or phases during the transformation of data from one source to another. These phases can be exposed as events to which you can attach scripting code in order to customize the behavior of the data pump. Note that the row transformation phase is the only data pump phase to which you can attach code by default. In order to make the other phases visible to your package and scripting code, you must enable multiphase pump display in the DTS Designer by right-clicking the Data Transformation Services node in Enterprise Manager and checking the Show multi-phase pump in DTS Designer option. Once the multiphase pump has been fully exposed in the Designer, you can attach ActiveX script code to phase events to customize the behavior of the pump. As I've said, the data pump goes through six basic phases when transforming data.

1. Presource phase—this step occurs before any rows are actually read from the source data. This is a good place to create header rows or carry out other preparatory work prior to the start of the row transformation process.

2. Row transform phase—this is the default data pump phase and is the step where each row is read from the source data and optionally transformed.

3. Post–row transform phase—this step occurs after the row transform phase has completed and is itself composed of three subphases.
   a. On Transform Failure—this phase is executed when an error occurs during row transformation. Note that any errors generated during this phase do not count toward the maximum number of errors specified in the Options page for the transformation. You can use script code to detect errors during this phase and respond accordingly. Based on what happens in this step, one of the two following substeps then executes.
   b. On Insert Success—this phase occurs when a row is successfully inserted into the destination rowset. (Understand that no data is actually written to the destination at this point—the writes are to the destination rowset, a cache that will later be written to the destination.)
   c. On Insert Failure—this phase is executed when the insertion of a transformed row into the destination rowset fails. This error does not count toward the maximum specified in the Options page for the transformation.

4. Batch complete phase—this phase occurs whenever the number of rows inserted into the destination rowset equals the batch size specified in the Options page for the transformation. It also occurs when

all the rows in the source data have been processed and there is at least one row in the destination rowset. When this phase occurs, the pump writes the rows in the destination rowset to the destination table. Depending on whether you've configured the package to use transactions, an error during this phase may result in only some of the rows being written to the destination. This phase executes on completion of a batch, regardless of whether it's successfully written to the destination. Note that it may not execute in some circumstances, such as when the insertion of each source row into the destination rowset fails. In that scenario, there's no batch to write to the destination because the destination rowset is empty.

5. Postsource phase—this is the corollary to the presource phase and allows you to hook up script code that performs some task after all rows have been transformed. You can still access the destination data at this point, so you could use this phase to write out summary rows or further interact with the destination data in some way.

6. Pump complete phase—this phase occurs after all processing is complete, just before the pump shuts down. Although you no longer have access to either source or destination data at this point, you still have the full ActiveX scripting environment at your disposal to do things such as write audit or log records, interact with the file system, and so on.

You attach script code to the other phases in a data pump transformation just as you would normally attach it to the row transform phase: You click the Transformations tab, then select the phase to which you want to attach code in the Phases filter combo box and click the New button to set it up. Select the ActiveX script option in the Create New Transformation dialog, then click the Properties button in the Transformation Options dialog in order to add your scripting code. Configure the source and destination columns as appropriate and save the transformation. When you run the package, the code you attached to the specified pump phase will execute as appropriate.

To experiment with this a bit, load the MultiphaseDataPumpExample.DTS package from the CH20 folder on the CD accompanying this book into the DTS Designer. This is a basic package that simply copies a table from the pubs database to the Northwind database. I've hooked ActiveX script code to each of the pump phase events so that you can see how these work. Set your connection properties as appropriate, then run the package. You should see a dialog box displayed for each event. Note that some events occur more than others—for example, you should see close to two dozen Insert Success events—one for each row copied from the source to the destination.

NOTE: All of the example packages mentioned in this chapter use "(local)" when referring to a SQL Server. If the server on which you'll be testing these packages is a named instance, you can create a client configuration alias named "(local)" in order to avoid having to modify the example packages before running them.

If you bring up the options dialog for each of the ActiveX transformations, you'll see a Phases tab that allows you to specify which phase(s) the code is to be associated with. By default, this is the same as the phase selected in the Phase filter combo box when the transformation was first created. You'll note that the last two items in the dialog are reversed in terms of when they execute: the pump complete event actually occurs after the post-source event.

The Bulk Insert Task

Aside from the multiphase data pump, the other key DTS mechanism for loading data is the Bulk Insert task. The Bulk Insert task basically exposes the functionality of the T-SQL BULK INSERT command via a graphical interface and internally calls it to load data into the server. The fact that BULK INSERT is the actual mechanism used to load data into the server brings with it a couple of important considerations. First, the path to the source file must be specified in relation to the target SQL Server. So, if you're using a Bulk Insert task to copy a file from a client machine to a remote SQL Server, you must specify a UNC path to the file, and the account under which SQL Server is running must have access to the file (e.g., Local-System won't work because LocalSystem has no network rights). Second, you'll see much better performance if the file you're loading resides on the same machine as the SQL Server instance. Internally, the T-SQL BULK INSERT command is implemented by a COM object that runs inside SQL Server. If the file being loaded resides on the SQL Server machine, the COM object simply opens it and reads it as a local file. If the file resides elsewhere on the network, you may find that network bandwidth limitations throttle the speed of your bulk load, just as they would with any other bulk load facility such as bcp.exe or the BULK INSERT command itself.

Note that you cannot use a Bulk Insert task to load data directly from one SQL Server database table into another. The source for a Bulk Insert task must be an operating system file. That said, you can enable high-speed bulk copy processing with normal Transform Data tasks via the task option Use fast load (which is enabled by default).

Also note that Bulk Insert tasks do not support the types of ActiveX script transformations supported by the more ubiquitous Transform Data task. Because Bulk Insert calls the T-SQL BULK INSERT command, its functionality is more limited than that of the Transform Data task.

You can load the sample package BulkInsertExample.DTS from the CH20 folder on the CD accompanying this book to experiment with Bulk Insert tasks. I encourage you to start a Profiler trace before executing the package so that you can see the T-SQL code being sent to the server.

The Data Driven Query Task

In a simpler world, basic DML would be sufficient to transfer data between two sources. Data transformation would consist mostly of one-to-one column copies, and you'd rarely need to employ any sort of complex logic to determine how and whether data should be copied from one place to another. In the real world, however, complex logic is often behind the methods used to move data from place to place, and stored procedures and custom queries are often necessary to get the job done. The Data Driven Query task exists for these types of situations. If you have a data transformation need wherein you require more functionality than simply inserting rows into a destination table, a Data Driven Query task may fit the bill. For garden-variety data load operations, the Transform Data task and the Bulk Insert task are preferable to a Data Driven Query because they are highly optimized for inserts. You should use a Data Driven Query task instead of one of these only when your needs exceed their capabilities.

A Data Driven Query task works by allowing you to set up alternate insert, update, and delete queries to be executed for each row in the source data. These queries can be simple SQL queries or they can be stored procedure calls or complex SQL batches. Each query can have replaceable parameters, to which the Data Driven Query task can assign the values from the source data as they are read for each row.

When you set up a Data Driven Query task, you configure a binding table. It's important to understand the purpose of the binding table and how it's used by the task. Basically, the binding table is a placeholder—a mechanism for defining the destination rowset into which to place data from the source rowset. The queries you set up determine where the data actually goes. They can reference the binding table or a different table or tables altogether.

Understand that these queries are placeholders only—you can execute an UPDATE from your insert query, a DELETE from your update query, and so forth. Listing 20.1 shows an example of a typical update query.

Listing 20.1

```
UPDATE authors_new
SET au_lname=?,
au_fname =?,
phone=?,
address=?,
city=?,
state=?,
zip=?,
contract=1
WHERE au_id=?
```

Here, we're updating the columns in a copy of the pubs..authors table with values from the source data with the exception of the contract column, which we force to 1 for updates.

Once you've configured your insert, update, and delete queries, you set up an ActiveX script to determine which of these gets called as data is processed. The return value from the script determines which query gets executed. You can check for the existence/nonexistence of rows, use a switch statement to return a different script result based on a column in the source data, branch based on global variables, and so on—basically you have full control over which of your queries gets executed. Listing 20.2 demonstrates how a Data Driven Query ActiveX script might look.

Listing 20.2

```
Function Main()

  DTSDestination("au_id") = DTSSource("au_id")
  DTSDestination("au_lname") = DTSSource("au_lname")
  DTSDestination("au_fname") = DTSSource("au_fname")
  DTSDestination("phone") = DTSSource("phone")
  DTSDestination("address") = DTSSource("address")
  DTSDestination("city") = DTSSource("city")
  DTSDestination("state") = DTSSource("state")
```

```
   DTSDestination("zip") = DTSSource("zip")
   DTSDestination("contract") = DTSSource("contract")

   Select Case Trim(DTSSource("state"))
   Case "CA"
     Main = DTSTransformstat_InsertQuery
   Case "OR"
     Main = DTSTransformstat_UpdateQuery
   Case "KS"
     Main = DTSTransformstat_DeleteQuery
   Case Else
     Main = DTSTransformstat_SkipRow
   End Select
End Function
```

Here, we branch based on the value of the state column in the source data. For California customers, we always do an insert. For Oregon customers, we always do an update. For Kansas customers, we always do a delete. And for everyone else, we do nothing—we skip the source row. As I said, the insert, update, delete, and select query placeholders are just that: placeholders. The actual queries you execute could do anything you please—for example, they might all do inserts into the destination, albeit in different ways. You can use the four selections you have inside the Data Driven Query task to divide the queries you need to run into up to four groups. And, of course, the SQL code or stored procedure you call can branch further based on values it receives from the source data.

You can explore the Data Driven Query task by loading the DataDrivenQueryExample.DTS package from the CH20 folder on the CD accompanying this book. Again, collecting a Profiler trace while the package runs can be a handy way to see what's going on behind the scenes on the server as each row in the source data is transformed.

ActiveX Transformations

Earlier, I mentioned that DTS provides several mechanisms for employing ActiveX script code to enhance package functionality. One of the ways you can use ActiveX code to enhance the functionality of a DTS package is through ActiveX transformations. ActiveX transformations give you complete control over the mapping of source columns to destination columns in a data transformation. You can concatenate multiple source columns into a single destination column, and you can break a single source column into multiple destination columns. You can assign a destination column using no source columns at all (usually the source data comes from global variables or lookups in this scenario); you can transform a source column without using a destination column (usually a global variable is the target of the transformation in this case); and you can perform transformations where you have neither source nor destination columns (e.g., to manipulate global variables or external objects via the FileSystemObject or ADO).

This is best understood by way of example. The sample ActiveX script in Listing 20.3 combines the address, city, state, and zip columns from the pubs..authors table into a single destination column.

Listing 20.3

```
Function Main()
  DTSDestination("address") = DTSSource("address") & " " _
    & DTSSource("city") _
    & ", "+DTSSource("state") & " " &DTSSource("zip")
  Main = DTSTransformStat_OK
End Function
```

Note the use of the built-in DTSSource and DTSDestination objects. Since an ActiveX transformation script is executed for each row in the source data, DTSSource will always refer to whatever the current row in the source is, and DTSDestination will always refer to the current row in the destination. You can find the source to this package in the file ActiveXTransformationExample.DTS in the CH20 folder on the CD accompanying this book.

Other Types of Transformations

I said at the beginning of the chapter that I wouldn't bore you with every single DTS feature and usage detail. You can glean most of these yourself by reading through Books Online and by building a few packages. That said, a few of the more esoteric features bear mentioning. One is the WriteFile transformation. A WriteFile transformation allows you to take two source columns—one supplying a file name and the other supplying the file's data—and transform them into an external text file for each row in the source table. The text file can be written in ANSI, UNICODE, or OEM format. The WriteFileExample.DTS package in the CH20 folder on the CD accompanying this book demonstrates how to use a WriteFile task to transform the pubs..pub_info table into a series of text files.

Similarly, a Read File task can be used to load the contents of a series of text files on disk into a destination column. In this scenario, you have just one source and one destination column. The source column specifies the name of the file to load, and the destination column specifies the target column for the file's contents. The ReadFileExample.DTS package in the CH20 folder on the CD accompanying this book demonstrates how to use a Read File task to load the text files created by the WriteFileExample.DTS package into a copy of the pubs..pub_info table.

In both examples, we use the pub_id column of the pub_info table to name the input or output file. Since pub_id is the primary key for the table, this ensures that we don't run into file name collisions in the file system.

Lookup Queries

Although I don't recommend you use lookup queries extensively, I feel obligated to cover them and explain how they work. Essentially, a lookup query is a parameterized subquery that you can set up to be called to look up data values. (A lookup query can actually do things besides look up data values and perform other types of work for each value in the source data.) Using a lookup query is similar to opening a cursor on a table in T-SQL and calling a stored procedure or executing a subquery for each row in the cursor. You usually execute a lookup query during a transformation of some type. A lookup query can be a stored procedure call or a plain SQL query. A typical lookup query might resemble the following:

```
SELECT    phone
FROM      authors
WHERE     (au_id = ?)
```

You set up lookup queries on the Lookups tab of your transformation task. If the task supports lookup queries, you'll see a Lookups tab in the dialog. Each lookup query has a name, a source connection, a cache setting, and a query associated with it. The cache setting allows you to configure the number of values returned by the lookup that are cached for reuse. This is especially useful when you are transforming a relatively large number of rows and the number of rows in the lookup table is relatively small.

You reference lookup queries by using the DTSLookups global function. A typical reference to a lookup query in an ActiveX transformation might look like this:

```
DTSDestination("phone") =
  DTSLookups("phone").Execute(DTSSource("au_id"))
```

Here, we pass the DTSLookups function the name of the lookup we want, then call the Execute method on that lookup object, passing it the parameter required by its parameterized query.

It's possible for a lookup query to return zero rows. When that happens, the Execute method will return an empty variant. You can test for this in your script using the VBScript IsEmpty function, as shown in Listing 20.4.

Listing 20.4

```
Dim Phone
Phone = DTSLookups("phone").Execute(DTSSource("au_id"))
If IsEmpty(Phone) Then
  DTSDestination("phone")="None"
Else
  DTSDestination("phone")=Phone
End If
```

It's also possible for a lookup query to return multiple rows. While you only have access to the first row returned, you can use an ORDER BY clause in your lookup query to ensure that the first row returned is the one you want. You can also detect when multiple rows are returned by inspecting the LastRowCount property of the lookup object returned by DTSLookups, as shown in Listing 20.5.

Listing 20.5

```
Dim c
c=DTSLookups("phone").LastRowCount
If  c > 1 Then
  MsgBox "Warning: " & c & " lookup matches found"
End If
```

You can explore lookup queries further by loading into the DTS Designer the LookupQueryExample.DTS package in the CH20 folder on the CD accompanying this book. Double-click the Transform Data task and check out its Lookups page. In this example, we copy the authors listed in the pubs..titleauthor table to a new table in the Northwind database. We take the au_id column from titleauthor and pass it to a series of lookup queries to retrieve various columns from the authors table. No columns from titleauthor are actually copied to the destination except for the au_id column.

Workflow Properties

You can control the behavior of each part of a package's workflow by adjusting its workflow properties. I won't go through all of these, but some of them are very handy to know about, especially when building more complex packages. You bring up the Workflow Properties dialog by right-clicking a package step and selecting Workflow Properties from the popup menu.

Close connection on completion Property

The Close connection on completion option instructs DTS to close the connection associated with a task after it has completed. This is useful in the following circumstances.

- There are a limited number of connections available on a data source and you need to be conservative with them.
- The cost of maintaining an open connection is unacceptably high.
- You need to free the locks an open connection is holding on resources (e.g., local disk files).
- You need to refresh the metadata the connection caches when it's opened.

Execute on main package thread Property

By default, DTS is multithreaded and will execute tasks in parallel. You can control the maximum number of tasks executed in parallel via the Package Properties dialog. Some COM components, however, are not free-threaded and do not support parallel execution of tasks (e.g., custom tasks created with VB are exclusively apartment-threaded, as are some OLE DB providers).

Although the DTS Designer will automatically set this option for you for tasks that it detects require it, you must set it yourself for associated tasks—tasks that have a dependency on the apartment-threaded task must also run on the main package thread (e.g., an ActiveX Script task or a Dynamic Properties task that makes changes to the apartment-threaded task, or an Execute Package task that executes a package containing an apartment-threaded task). If you run into a situation where you must use such a component in a DTS package, you can enable the Execute on main package thread workflow option to ensure that you can access the component safely.

Step priority Property

Each thread DTS creates to execute tasks has a Normal thread priority by default. You can adjust this for a particular task in order to increase or lessen its priority in relation to the other tasks in the package. This causes DTS to call the Win32 API SetThreadPriority to adjust the thread's priority in relation to the other worker threads. (Recall that we discussed SetThreadPriority in Chapter 3.) Normally, you shouldn't need to adjust a task's priority, but this ability can come in handy when you have CPU-intensive tasks that you need to execute as quickly as possible, even at the expense of other work in the package.

DTS and Transactions

Normally, each modification within a DTS package is committed as it's made. The Use transactions package property controls whether the package initiates a transaction when executed. And although this property defaults to true, you must also enable the Join transaction if present workflow property for a step in order to actually queue changes to a transaction. Since this workflow property is false by default, changes made within a package are normally committed as soon as they're made.

You can configure a package to log its changes in a transaction by:

- Enabling the Use transactions package property (which is true by default) and
- Enabling the Join transaction if present workflow property for each step that you want to participate in the transaction

In order for the transaction to start successfully, the following conditions must be true.

- MSDTC must be available on the machine. (Because a distributed transaction is required in order for multiple connections to participate, DTS always attempts to start a distributed transaction regardless of the number of connections in a package.)
- The data sources involved must support transactions (e.g., SQL Server and Oracle support transactions; a dBase file does not).
- The steps you are attempting to enlist in the transaction must be supported task types (e.g., the Bulk Insert task is supported; the Execute Process task is not).

Note that because configuring a package step to join a transaction causes its associated connections to be enlisted in the transaction, any other tasks that use those same connections will also be enlisted in the transaction, even if they do not have the Join transaction if present option enabled. To avoid this, use separate connections for tasks that you want to enlist in transactions and those that you don't.

You can control whether a package step commits the current transaction on success or rolls it back on failure through the Commit transaction on successful completion of this step and Rollback transaction on failure workflow options, respectively. You can also control whether successfully executing the package as a whole commits the open transaction via the Commit on successful package completion package property.

A package you execute from within another package via an Execute Package task inherits its calling package's transactional context if the Execute Package task that called it has joined its parent package's transaction. This changes the transactional semantics within the child package considerably. For one thing, no package transaction is initiated, even if the child package has enabled the Use transactions option and has steps with the Join transaction if present option enabled. For another, the Commit transaction on successful completion of this step and Commit on successful package completion options are ignored. No commit is performed within the child package, regardless of these settings. Note, however, that a rollback within a child package *will* roll back the parent package's transaction.

You can experiment with DTS and transactions by loading up the TransactionExample.DTS package located in the CH20 folder on the CD accompanying this book. This package performs two data transformations between pubs and Northwind, creating two new tables and populating each with data.

In particular, try stopping and disabling the Microsoft Distributed Transaction Coordinator to see how this affects the ability of the package to run.

Controlling Package Workflow through Scripting

I mentioned earlier that you can control the workflow of a package by using ActiveX script code. An obvious need for this type of functionality is in implementing loops within a package. There are multiple ways to go about this. I'll walk you through a few of them, and you can decide which of them best meets your needs.

Looping by Using a Separate Package

The easiest way to implement looping behavior within a DTS package is to put the steps that you want to execute repetitively in a separate package and use a simple ActiveX script to execute it as many times as necessary. Listing 20.6 shows an example of an ActiveX Script task that loops a set number of times, executing a second package with each iteration. (You can find this code in the outer.dts sample package in the CH20 folder on the CD accompanying this book.)

Listing 20.6

```
Function Main()
  Dim oPkg
  Set oPkg=CreateObject("DTS.Package")
  oPkg.LoadFromStorageFile "inner.dts", ""
  For x=1 TO 5
    oPkg.Execute
  Next
  Main = DTSTaskExecResult_Success
End Function
```

Note that because this code doesn't rely on the DTS runtime environment, you could run it as a standalone VBScript (minus the function result, of course). It simply creates a DTS package object, loads a package from a structured storage file, then executes it five times. We don't explicitly free the object (by setting oPkg to Nothing) because the script runtime environment will do that for us. See the VBScript file, loop.vbs, in the CH20 folder on the CD accompanying this book for any example of a standalone VB-Script that executes a package repetitively.

Looping by Using ExecutionStatus

Another way to control package workflow from within an ActiveX script and to effect a type of looping behavior is to set the ExecutionStatus of an already executed step back to DTSStepExecStat_Waiting. This will cause the step to execute again, producing a type of repetitive loop within the package. Since you can decide whether to change the ExecutionStatus property based on the logical condition of your choosing, you have all the tools you need to construct a logical loop, just as you might typically build in a more traditional programming environment.

There are a couple of distinct approaches for using ExecutionStatus to implement a loop within a DTS package. The easiest and most flexible is to associate an ActiveX script with a package step via the Workflow Properties dialog. We use the Steps collection of the current package to locate the step to repeat, then set its ExecutionStatus to DTSStepExecStat_Waiting.

This approach is better than the approach that we'll discuss in a moment because it doesn't require ActiveX Script tasks to be set aside for the sole purpose of implementing looping behavior. By piggybacking an ActiveX script onto an already existing package step through a Workflow Properties association, we alleviate the need for separate components just to set up our loop, and we allow any step to be the loop initializer, worker, or controller.

Another advantage of this approach is that we can control whether the step to which we've associated our ActiveX script executes based on the looping condition. For example, we might not want the step to execute until the loop completes. Because we're associating an ActiveX script with the step's workflow, we can return DTSStepScriptResult_DontExecuteTask from the ActiveX script to prevent the step from executing.

Listing 20.7 offers an example of a DTS package loop implemented via ActiveX script workflow associations. (You can find this on the CD accompanying this book in the file CH20\LoopExample.dts—see the Loop1 example code.)

Listing 20.7

Step 1:

```
'****************************************************************
'  Initialize the loop control variable
'****************************************************************

Function Main()
  DTSGlobalVariables("foo").Value=0
  MsgBox "Loop1:  Initialize"
  Main = DTSTaskExecResult_Success
End Function
```

Step 2:

```
'****************************************************************
' Perform loop work
'****************************************************************

Function Main()
  MsgBox "Loop1:  Work"
  Main = DTSTaskExecResult_Success
End Function
```

Step 3:

```
'****************************************************************
'  Check the loop variable and repeat the step as appropriate
'****************************************************************

Function Main()
  Dim oPkg
  DTSGlobalVariables("foo").Value = _
  DTSGlobalVariables("foo").Value + 1

  If DTSGlobalVariables("foo").Value < 5 Then
    MsgBox "Loop1:  " & DTSGlobalVariables("foo").Value
    Set oPkg = DTSGlobalVariables.Parent

    oPkg.Steps("DTSStep_DTSActiveScriptTask_6").ExecutionStatus = _
      DTSStepExecStat_Waiting

    Main = DTSStepScriptResult_DontExecuteTask
```

```
    Else
      Main = DTSStepScriptResult_ExecuteTask
    End If

End Function
```

As I've said, there are multiple ways to use ExecutionStatus to construct a looping mechanism in a DTS package. Another method for doing this makes use of ActiveX Script tasks to implement the looping code. This technique works as described below.

1. You set up a package with a step that you want to execute repeatedly.
2. You link an ActiveX Script task step to this step using a precedence constraint. This constraint can be any of the three stock workflow constraints: On Success, On Completion, or On Failure, depending on what you're actually trying to accomplish. You'd likely use the first two when implementing a basic loop; you might use an On Failure constraint when implementing retry logic.
3. In the ActiveX script code, you check a logical condition that determines whether to repeat the initial step (assuming you don't want to loop indefinitely) and set the ExecutionStatus of the step to DTSStepExecStat_Waiting if so.

This is best understood by seeing the code itself, so Listing 20.8 presents the ActiveX source code from a package that demonstrates this technique. (You can find this on the CD accompanying this book in the file CH20\LoopExample.dts—see the Loop2 example code.)

Listing 20.8

Step 1:

```
'****************************************************************
'   Initialize the loop control variable
'****************************************************************

Function Main()
  DTSGlobalVariables("bar").Value=0
  MsgBox "Loop2:  Initialize"
  Main = DTSTaskExecResult_Success
End Function
```

Step 2:

```
'****************************************************************
' Perform loop work
'****************************************************************

Function Main()
  MsgBox "Loop2:  Work"
  Main = DTSTaskExecResult_Success
End Function
```

Step 3:

```
'****************************************************************
'  Check the loop variable and repeat the step as appropriate
'****************************************************************

Function Main()

  DTSGlobalVariables("bar").Value=DTSGlobalVari-
ables("bar").Value+1
  If DTSGlobalVariables("bar").Value<5 Then
    MsgBox "Loop2:  " & DTSGlobalVariables("bar").Value
    Dim oPkg
    Set oPkg = DTSGlobalVariables.Parent
    oPkg.Steps("DTSStep_DTSActiveScriptTask_1").ExecutionStatus _
       = DTSStepExecStat_Waiting
  End If
  Main = DTSTaskExecResult_Success
End Function
```

Here, we have a package comprised of three steps. In the first step, we use an ActiveX script to initialize our loop control variable, a global variable named bar. In step 2, we carry out the work that we want to execute repeatedly. In step 3, we increment our control variable and check to see whether it's less than 5, and, if so, change the ExecutionStatus of the step 2 ActiveX task to DTSStepExecStat_Waiting. This will cause the second step to execute again, which will lead back to step 3, at which time we'll again increment and evaluate the loop control variable to determine whether to continue the loop or proceed with the rest of the package.

Some people prefer this approach to the first one I presented because the ActiveX code that implements the loop is more readily accessible in the

DTS Designer. With the first approach, this code is somewhat hidden through a workflow properties association.

Note the use of the DTSGlobalVariables.Parent member to obtain a reference to the currently running package. This is conceptually equivalent to "this" in C++ and C#, "Me" in VB, and "Self" in Object Pascal. It's the conventional way to acquire a reference to the currently executing package from an ActiveX script within that package.

Also note the use of the step name as the index for the Steps collection. You can obtain the name of a step by right-clicking it, selecting Workflow Properties, and clicking on the Options page (the step name is listed at the top of the page). Object collection access in VB code is typically done using either the ordinal index of a collection member or its name. Here, we use the name for the sake of readability.

Implementing a loop by using either one of the ExecutionStatus techniques is more flexible than the execute package approach for the obvious reason that you don't need to first place the steps you want to repeat in a separate package. You can set up complex conditional tests to determine whether the loop continues and can even do so from multiple steps. An example of where you might check the loop condition from multiple steps and set ExecutionStatus accordingly is when implementing retry logic. For example, you might need to execute a number of steps to determine the validity of data you're in the process of loading, and you might construct your package such that the failure of any of these steps requires the process to be restarted. If so, you can use ActiveX scripts to check for these failure conditions from multiple package steps and assign ExecutionStatus as appropriate when any of them fail.

Implementing Conditional Execution

As you've probably already surmised, you can also use ActiveX script associations to implement conditional execution. In the first ExecutionStatus looping example above, we return DTSStepScriptResult_DontExecuteTask from the ActiveX script associated with a step's workflow when we don't want the step to execute and DTSStepScriptResult_ExecuteTask when we do. You can use this same technique to conditionally execute a step based on any criteria you can evaluate from an ActiveX script.

Note that you can also use ActiveX script associations to implement retry logic. In addition to returning DTSStepScriptResult_ExecuteTask and DTSStepScriptResult_DontExecuteTask from a workflow ActiveX script, you can also return DTSStepScriptResult_RetryLater in order to cause the step to be reexecuted at some later point during package execution.

Conditional Execution with ExecutionStatus and ActiveX Script Tasks

You can use a variation of the ActiveX Script task looping technique to implement conditional execution of package steps. Say, for example, that when a given condition is true, you want to execute a specified series of package steps, otherwise you want to skip them. One way to do this is to check for the condition in an ActiveX task that precedes the series in question and set the ExecutionStatus of the first step in the series to DTSStepExecStat_Inactive if you do not want to execute it. Deactivating a step has the effect of causing it and the steps that follow it not to execute. Listing 20.9 presents some VBScript code to illustrate.

Listing 20.9

```
Function Main()
  Dim oPkg
  Set oPkg = DTSGlobalVariables.Parent
  If DTSGlobalVariables("bFoo") Then
    oPkg.Steps("DTSStep_DTSCreateProcessTask_1") _
        .ExecutionStatus = DTSStepExecStat_Waiting
  Else
    oPkg.Steps("DTSStep_DTSCreateProcessTask_1") _
        .ExecutionStatus = DTSStepExecStat_Inactive
  End If
  Main = DTSTaskExecResult_Success
End Function
```

Assuming that DTSStep_DTSCreateProcessTask_1 follows the ActiveX Script task that executes this code, it (and the steps that follow it) will execute only if the global variable bFoo is set to true on entrance to this step.

Conditional Execution with Task Success/Failure

Another way to implement conditional execution is to check a control variable and return DTSTaskExecResult_Failure when you want to prevent execution of the steps that follow a particular ActiveX task (assuming that these steps have been linked with On Success precedence constraints). Listing 20.10 illustrates.

Listing 20.10

```
Function Main()
  If DTSGlobalVariables("bFoo") Then
    Main = DTSTaskExecResult_Success
  Else
    Main = DTSTaskExecResult_Failure
  End If
End Function
```

Here, we check a global variable and return a task result based on its value. This technique isn't as clean as the other techniques because it can cause errors to be reported by the DTS package execution engine. Of course, you could ignore these error messages, but by using one of the other techniques instead you avoid the error messages altogether.

Parameterized DTS Packages

A natural thing to want to do with a DTS package is to parameterize it so that, for example, it can work with different data sources/destinations than the ones it referenced when it was originally built. Things like global variable values, connection properties, object names, and the like are natural targets for parameterization.

There are a couple of ways to parameterize DTS packages. The first is to use a Dynamic Properties task. A Dynamic Properties task allows you to set the value of any property in a package from one of six sources:

1. A global variable from the package
2. A value in an INI file
3. An environment variable
4. A T-SQL query (only the first column of the first row in the query result set is used)
5. A data file
6. A constant

Given that you can supply values for global variables when you execute a package (e.g., using the dtsrunui utility or an ExecutePackage task within another package), a common practice is to assign global variables to package properties using a Dynamic Properties task, then assign those variables' values at runtime. Using global variables in this way provides a layer of abstraction between the mechanism supplying the parameter values and the dynamic method used to assign property values within the package. This allows you to easily change the method of executing the package without losing the dynamic nature of the package.

Another way to parameterize a DTS package is via ActiveX script code. It's often less trouble to modify package properties using script code than it is to set up a Dynamic Properties task. Also, understand that you can't insert global variables into the middle of a property using a Dynamic Properties task—either you assign the whole property or you don't assign any of it. Using script code or Automation code from outside the package, you have more control over changing property values at runtime and can use global variables to help you do so in any way you see fit.

Exercise 20.1   A Parameterized Package

To gain a better understanding of how a package can be parameterized, load the ParamExample.DTS package from the CH20 folder on the CD accompanying this book into the DTS Designer. This package will copy a table of your choosing from a specified source server and database to a specified destination server and database.

1. Double-click the Dynamic Properties task named Get Params.
2. Double-click each of the entries in the Change list to see what properties they're being used to assign. What you should see is that global variables are being used to assign the key connection properties for the TransferObject task.
3. Exit the Dynamic Properties dialog and right-click the DTS Designer canvas. Select Package Properties from the content menu.
4. Click the Global Variables tab in the property dialog. There you should see six global variables defined: one each for the source server, database, and table and the destination server, database, and table.
5. Start the dtsrunui utility. In the DTS Run dialog, change the Location field to Structured Storage File, then select the ParamExample.DTS package that you previously viewed in the DTS Designer by clicking the ellipsis button to the right of the File name: text box.
6. Key ParamExample for the package name, then click the Advanced button to display a dialog that will allow you to set global variable values for the package before executing it.
7. Configure values for the source server, database, and table as well as the destination server, database, and table. The pubs and Northwind databases are fine for use here.

8. Click OK to close the Advanced DTS Run dialog, then click the Run button to run the package with your parameterized values. You should see the package run and copy the specified object from the source to the destination you specified.

The DSO Rowset Provider

Another one of the cooler things you can do with a DTS package is query it with an OLE DB provider. You can flag a step of a package as a DSO rowset provider, then query the package from T-SQL using OPENROWSET and the DTSPackageDSO OLE DB provider. This allows you, for example, to expose the result of a transformation as a rowset that can be queried via T-SQL. This means, of course, that one package can serve as the data source for another package because you can obviously set up T-SQL queries as the data source in a transformation within a package. It also means that you can offload complex data processing to a DTS package, then invoke the transformation from within a T-SQL query or stored procedure. Here's an example of a T-SQL query that retrieves the results of a transformation task as a result set:

```
SELECT *
FROM OPENROWSET('DTSPackageDSO', '/FD:\CH20\DSORowsetExample.dts',
'SELECT * ')
```

The two parameters the DTSPackageDSO provider supports are the dtsrun-like command line parameters and the query text. You can specify dtsrun command line parameters to identify the source and location of the package. In the example above, I'm referencing a package stored as a COM structured storage file.

Note the absence of anything resembling a table name in the query text passed into OPENROWSET. This is because the referenced package has just one step that's been flagged as a DSO rowset provider. If multiple steps are flagged this way, specify the step name in the query text to identify the one that you want to query, like this:

```
SELECT *
FROM OPENROWSET('DTSPackageDSO',
'/FD: \CH20\DSORowsetExample.dts',
'SELECT * FROM DTSStep_DTSDataPumpTask_1')
```

Note that a step that's been flagged as a DSO rowset provider won't actually execute when you run the package. It's reserved strictly for providing data and is ignored by the package execution engine. You can experiment with a DSO rowset provider task by querying the DSORowsetExample.DTS package (in the CH20 folder on the CD accompanying this book) from Query Analyzer using the sample T-SQL script, DSORowsetExample.SQL. You will likely want to first load the package into the DTS Designer so that you can configure connection properties and so forth.

Using DTS to Transform Replication Subscriptions

We'll discuss SQL Server's replication facilities in more detail in Chapters 21 through 23. For now, let's explore how you can use a DTS package to transform published data as it is provided to subscribers. You're probably familiar with the basic concept of a replication publisher—a server or machine that provides data to subscribers, the data consumers in a replication scenario. In addition to being able to use T-SQL to manipulate data as it's being published to subscribers, you can also create DTS packages that perform sophisticated transformations of the data en route. The package used to transform a subscription can reside at the distributor or at individual subscribers and can be used to partition as well as transform published data.

To create a transformable subscription, you begin by creating a transformable publication.

1. Create a new snapshot or transactional publication by using the Create Publication wizard. Be sure the Show advanced options in this wizard checkbox is selected.
2. Do not enable the publication to be updatable in the wizard (immediate or queued). Updatable publications and transformable subscriptions are mutually exclusive.
3. Click Yes on the Transform Published Data page in the Create Publication wizard.
4. Finish creating the publication by selecting the articles, snapshot options, and so forth in the Create Publication wizard.

Once the transformable publication is created, you're ready to set up the transformation itself. You do this via the Transform Published Data wizard.

1. Right-click the transformable publication and select Properties. On the Subscriptions page in the Publication Properties dialog, click the Transformations button.

2. You will be prompted for the name of the publication to transform. Accept the default and click Next.

3. You'll next select a destination for the transformation. If you intend to have more than one subscriber for the publication, configure a destination that is representative of your intended subscribers as a whole, then click Next.

4. Define the transformations for your data in the next dialog. Click the ellipsis button to the right of each article to display the Column Mappings and Transformations dialog. Here, you can make simple one-to-one column mapping assignments, or you can define sophisticated ActiveX transformations.

5. You'll next configure where the DTS package will be physically located. You can locate the package at the distributor or on the subscriber.

6. You finish by naming the package. The package will be stored in msdb..sysdtspackages on the server you chose in the previous step. You can't store subscription transformation packages in COM Structured Storage File format or in the Meta Data Services repository.

7. Click the Finish button to create the transformation package.

8. Click OK to exit the Publication Properties dialog.

When you subscribe to a transformable subscription, you will be prompted for the name of the package to use to transform the subscription. Note that you can have multiple transform packages for each publication. You can use this ability to transform and partition data differently for each subscriber.

How It Works

The DTS package created by the Transform Published Data wizard consists of at least four objects: for each article, a Connection object, an Execute SQL task, and a Data Driven Query task; plus a Connection object used by all the articles to provide data to the subscriber. The Execute SQL task selects the rows from the source article in order to provide data to the Data Driven Query task. A Data Driven Query task is always used in lieu of a Transform Data or Bulk Insert task when creating transformable subscriptions. It can perform straight column-to-column copies or more sophisticated transformations using ActiveX script code that you supply, as we just discussed.

You can open transformation packages in the DTS Designer just as you would any other local SQL Server package. To do so, connect to the distributor or subscriber (depending on where you stored the package) from

Enterprise Manager, then click the Local Packages node under Data Transformation Services. In the list on the right, double-click the package you defined in the Transform Published Data wizard in order to open it.

In order to retrieve data from the publication, a DTS transformation package will contain a Connection object that references the SQL Server Replication OLE DB Provider for DTS for each article in the publication. If you display the Properties dialog for one of these Connection objects, then click the Properties button, you'll find the list of columns being published by the article on the All tab of the Data Link Properties dialog. This provider is designed for the exclusive use of transformable packages and is not available from the default DTS Designer Connection palette.

Custom Tasks

As I mentioned earlier, DTS is based on an extensible COM model. One of the benefits of this is that you can create your own custom tasks as COM objects and install them into the DTS Designer. There are a couple of ways to go about this: You can create a custom task object from scratch in a language capable of implementing COM interfaces, or you can customize one of the sample custom task components included with SQL Server. Depending on your needs, either of these approaches can be a viable method of extending DTS, so I'll show you how to do it both ways.

Creating a New Custom Task

All DTS task objects implement the DTS CustomTask interface. Any custom task that you build will also need to implement this interface. In terms of interface implementation, there's no difference between built-in tasks and custom tasks that you create—DTS's built-in tasks are just COM components that, at a minimum, implement the CustomTask interface. A custom task can also implement other interfaces, such as CustomTaskUI (for components that define their own user interfaces), but we'll focus on the CustomTask interface in our discussions here because it is what allows a COM component to serve as a custom DTS task.

In this next exercise, we'll create a custom task in Visual Basic that can execute T-SQL scripts. You may be wondering why we'd need such a component given the existence of the built-in Execute SQL task. The reason is simple: While Execute SQL can execute T-SQL scripts, it has no mechanism for handling large amounts of variable script output. That is, if you execute a script that returns multiple result sets interlaced with PRINT and RAISER-ROR statement output, you have no way to retrieve that output from an Execute SQL task as you can with tools like Query Analyzer and osql.

In actuality, our new custom task will merely call a script execution utility that is specified via a property. osql is a good choice here, but you could just as well call ISQL or some other script execution utility. Let's go ahead and build the component, then we'll talk some more about what it can do and how it does it.

Exercise 20.2   Creating a Custom DTS Task in Visual Basic

1. Start Visual Basic (the steps that follow assume VB6; VB.NET should work as well, though the steps will likely differ some) and start a new ActiveX DLL project from the New Project dialog box. Although the DTS runtime environment (e.g., dtsrun) can make use of custom tasks implemented as out-of-process components (i.e., EXEs), a custom task must be defined as an in-process component if you want to use it with the DTS Designer.

2. From the Project menu, display the Project Properties dialog box and change the Project Name to ExecuteSQLScript. Make sure Startup Object is set to "(None)," Threading Model is set to "Apartment Threaded," and Project Compatibility is selected on the Component tab, then click OK.

3. VB names your new class Class1 by default. In the Properties Window, change this to clsExecuteSQLScript. Also make sure that the Instancing property is set to "5—Multiuse."

4. Click the References option on the Project menu and select Microsoft DTSPackage Object Library from the list of available references. This will import the DTSPackage COM type library into your project and make the interfaces it exposes available to you.

5. In the code window, make sure that "(General)" and "(Declarations)" are selected in the two combo boxes, then type the following into the editor:

   ```
   Implements DTS.CustomTask
   ```

   This tells VB that your new component will implement the DTS CustomTask interface (which is defined in the DTSPackage Object Library). The VB IDE will then make the methods exposed by the CustomTask interface available to you in the code editor.

6. Change the left combo box in the code editor to reference the CustomTask interface. The editor should immediately insert an empty CustomTask_Properties Get method.

7. Add the following line to the CustomTask_Properties Get method:

```
Set CustomTask_Properties = Nothing
```

Although you can implement your own property editor for your new component, setting this property to Nothing instructs DTS to provide a default property editor for you.

8. In the right combo box, select each of the other methods exposed by the CustomTask interface. The VB editor will insert empty placeholder methods for each one.

9. Add the following two lines at the top of your source code file:

```
Dim m_bstrName As String
Dim m_bstrDescription As String
```

We'll use these two member variables to cache the new component's name and description.

10. Add the following line to the Let function for the CustomTask_Description property:

```
m_bstrDescription = RHS
```

This assigns the RHS parameter (which is passed into the function when the Description property is assigned) to the member variable we set up earlier.

11. Add the following line to the Get function for the CustomTask_Description property:

```
CustomTask_Description = m_bstrDescription
```

This causes the value of the m_bstrDescription member variable to be returned whenever the Description property is queried for its value.

12. Set up the Name property similarly to the Description property—code its Let and Get functions so that they assign and retrieve the m_bstrName member variable we defined earlier.

13. You'll notice that the property Let and Get methods defined by the CustomTask interface are private by default. This is because they refer to properties of the base DTS custom task, not to your custom task. You'll need to define public properties in order for them to be visible to a DTS package. Create two new methods (shown in Listing 20.11) to expose the Description property from your custom task.

Listing 20.11

```
Public Property Get Description() As String
  Description = m_bstrDescription
End Property
```

```
Public Property Let Description(ByVal RHS As String)
  m_bstrDescription = RHS
End Property
```

Don't create similar methods for the Name property because we don't want to allow it to be changed in the DTS Designer. The Designer will auto-generate a name for the task when you drop it onto the design sheet. In keeping with the way the Designer was intended to work, you should not allow the name to be changed, so there's no point in exposing it via a public property.

14. At this point, you have a complete custom DTS task object and could compile it to a DLL and register it in the DTS Designer if you liked. The component doesn't yet do anything, so we won't do that just yet.

15. Add the member variables shown in Listing 20.12 to the top of your source code file.

Listing 20.12

```
Private m_bstrScriptUtility As String
Private m_bstrServerInstance As String
Private m_bstrAuthString As String
Private m_bstrScriptToExecute As String
Private m_bstrOutputFileName As String
Private m_lTimeout As Long
Private m_bTerminateOnTimeout As Boolean
```

The function of each of these should be pretty obvious, but I'll provide a brief description for most of them anyway. The m_bstrScriptUtility member will store the command line to the script utility. As you'll see in just a moment, it supports the use of replaceable parameters that are actually defined by other properties. The m_bstrServerInstance member stores the SQL Server name and instance (separated by a backslash) to which we want to connect. The m_bstrAuthString member stores the authentication string we want to pass to the script utility. In the case of osql, this might be "-E" (use a trusted connection) or "-U user -P password" (for SQL Server authentication). The m_bstrScriptToExecute member stores the name of the script we want to execute. Note that this could also be a SQL query string if the script utility supports having a query string passed directly on its command line (as osql does). The m_bstrOutputFileName member stores the name of the output file the script utility is to create. If the utility directly supports trapping its output in a file and having the name of that file passed on the command line, you can use this member to supply it. If the utility does not directly support an output file name but writes its output to the console, you can change the script utility to execute the command processor (e.g., CMD.EXE on the Windows NT family of operating systems) and use redirection to route the output to this file. You have to execute the script utility via the command processor in this situation because the command processor is the facility by which console redirection occurs. See the CustomTaskVB_TimeoutExample.DTS package in the CH20\Custom-TaskVB subfolder on the CD accompanying this book for an example of this technique.

16. Set up public Let and Get functions for each of these, being careful to use the proper data types as you do. Feel free to copy and paste some of the existing Let and Get methods in order to speed this up.

17. In this next step, we'll define the custom task's Execute method and the plumbing it requires. Because we need to be able to shell to a script utility and pause execution until it either completes or times out, we can't use the VB Shell function (which executes asynchronously) and must instead call the Win32 CreateProcess function. Recall that we discussed CreateProcess in Chapter 3; it's the Win32 API by which one process can start another. You use Declare Function to import a function that resides in a DLL (as all Win32 API functions do) into a VB program. We need to import several of these, so we'll be adding several Declare Function statements in the code editor. Add the code shown in Listing 20.13 to the top of your source code module.

Listing 20.13

```
Private Type PROCESS_INFORMATION
  hProcess As Long
  hThread As Long
  dwProcessId As Long
  dwThreadId As Long
End Type

Private Type STARTUPINFO
  cb As Long
  lpReserved As String
  lpDesktop As String
  lpTitle As String
  dwX As Long
```

```
      dwY As Long
      dwXSize As Long
      dwYSize As Long
      dwXCountChars As Long
      dwYCountChars As Long
      dwFillAttribute As Long
      dwFlags As Long
      wShowWindow As Integer
      cbReserved2 As Integer
      lpReserved2 As Long
      hStdInput As Long
      hStdOutput As Long
      hStdError As Long
   End Type

   Private Declare Function CreateProcess Lib "kernel32" _
      Alias "CreateProcessA" _
      (ByVal lpApplicationName As String, _
      ByVal lpCommandLine As String, _
      lpProcessAttributes As Any, _
      lpThreadAttributes As Any, _
      ByVal bInheritHandles As Long, _
      ByVal dwCreationFlags As Long, _
      lpEnvironment As Any, _
      ByVal lpCurrentDirectory As String, _
      lpStartupInfo As STARTUPINFO, _
      lpProcessInformation As PROCESS_INFORMATION) As Long

   Private Declare Function TerminateProcess Lib "kernel32" _
      (ByVal hProcess As Long, _
      ByVal uExitCode As Long) As Long

   Private Declare Function WaitForSingleObject Lib "kernel32" _
      (ByVal hHandle As Long, ByVal dwMilliseconds As Long) As Long

   Private Declare Function CloseHandle Lib "kernel32" (ByVal _
      hObject As Long) As Long

   Private Declare Function GetLastError Lib "kernel32" () As Long

   Private Const CREATE_DEFAULT_ERROR_MODE = &H4000000
   Private Const WAIT_TIMEOUT = &H102&
   Private Const INFINITE = -1&
```

      This imports the CreateProcess, TerminateProcess, WaitForSingle-Object, CloseHandle, and GetLastError Win32 API functions, along with the structures and constants they require.

18. Now that we've imported the Win32 functions we need, we're ready to code the Execute method itself. Add the code shown in Listing 20.14 to the CustomTask_Execute method.

Listing 20.14

```
Dim pi As PROCESS_INFORMATION
Dim si As STARTUPINFO
Dim lRes As Long

Dim bstrCmdLine As String

' Replace script cmd line tokens
bstrCmdLine = m_bstrScriptUtility
bstrCmdLine = Replace(bstrCmdLine, "%server_instance%", _
    m_bstrServerInstance)
bstrCmdLine = Replace(bstrCmdLine, "%auth_string%", _
    m_bstrAuthString)
bstrCmdLine = Replace(bstrCmdLine, "%script%", _
    m_bstrScriptToExecute)
bstrCmdLine = Replace(bstrCmdLine, "%output%", _
    m_bstrOutputFileName)

' Initialize STARTUPINFO struct
si.cb = Len(si)

' Start the process
Dim bstrNull As String

lRes = CreateProcess(bstrNull, _
                     bstrCmdLine, _
                     ByVal 0&, _
                     ByVal 0&, _
                     0&, _
                     CREATE_DEFAULT_ERROR_MODE, _
                     ByVal 0&, _
                     bstrNull, _
                     si, _
                     pi)
```

```
If lRes <> 0 Then

  Dim lTimeout As Long
  If 0 = m_lTimeout Then
    lTimeout = INFINITE
  Else
    lTimeout = m_lTimeout * 1000
  End If

  ' Wait on the process to complete or time out
  lRes = WaitForSingleObject(pi.hProcess, lTimeout)

  ' If we timed out, log a message
  If WAIT_TIMEOUT = lRes Then
    If Not pPackageLog Is Nothing Then
      pPackageLog.WriteTaskRecord 50001, Me.Description & ": _
          Script execution timed out"
    End If
    If m_bTerminateOnTimeout Then
      lRes = TerminateProcess(pi.hProcess, -1&)
      If 0 = lRes Then
        pPackageLog.WriteTaskRecord 50002,Me.Description& _
            ": Script termination failed"
      End If
    End If
  End If

  Call CloseHandle(pi.hThread)
  Call CloseHandle(pi.hProcess)

  pTaskResult = DTSTaskExecResult_Success

Else
  Dim lLastError As Long

  ' Get the last error from Windows
  lLastError = GetLastError()

  Dim oPkgEvent As DTS.PackageEvents
  Set oPkgEvent = pPackageEvents

  Dim bCancel As Boolean
  bCancel = True
```

```
' Call the OnError event handler
oPkgEvent.OnError Me.Description, lLastError, bstrCmdLine, _
    "CreateProcess failed", "", 0, "", bCancel
If bCancel Then
    pTaskResult = DTSTaskExecResult_Failure
Else
    pTaskResult = DTSTaskExecResult_Success
End If

End If
```

---

19. This code performs the work of actually executing the script utility. It begins by dimming the PROCESS_INFORMATION and STARTUPINFO structures required by CreateProcess. STARTUPINFO supplies parameters to the process creation, and PROCESS_INFORMATION will be populated with handles and process/thread IDs pertinent to the new process once it's created.

20. The code next replaces several hard-coded tokens in the script utility command line. In order to allow you to easily configure the command line parameters for the script execution utility using DTS global variables, Dynamic Property tasks, Automation code, and the like, the component is set up to store the major parts of the script utility command line in separate properties, which it then uses to build the command line it executes by replacing tokens you specify with their appropriate values when the Execute method is called. For example, assume you have the following script utility command line:

```
OSQL %auth_string% -S%server_instance% -i%script% -o%output%
```

When you execute the step, the Execute method will replace %auth_string% with the value of m_bstrAuthString, %server_instance% with m_bstrServerInstance, %script% with m_bstrScriptToExecute, and %output% with m_bstrOutputFileName. Setting up Execute to work this way allows you to place the parameters wherever you'd like in the command line and allows them to be easily changed via global variables, Dynamic Property tasks, and similar mechanisms without forcing you to rebuild the command line string for the script utility from within the host package (e.g., via an ActiveX script).

21. Execute next calls CreateProcess to start the script utility. It then calls WaitForSingleObject to wait on the script utility to complete. If the Timeout property is nonzero, Execute passes a timeout value into WaitForSingleObject so that the wait can time out; otherwise, Execute waits indefinitely on the script utility to complete.

22. If the TerminateOnTimeout property is set to true and WaitForSingleObject times out while waiting on the script utility, Execute calls TerminateProcess to terminate the utility.

23. Note the call to the WriteTaskRecord method of the PackageLog object. PackageLog is a member of the DTS object model and provides a means of writing to a package's log. In this case, we silently record information that should not cause the task to fail and does not need to be immediately reported to the user.

24. When CreateProcess fails, it returns 0. We check for this and call the OnError package event if it occurs. Note the use of the Me identifier to refer to the current task object.

25. Once CreateProcess has been called and has either succeeded or failed, we return the appropriate step result from the custom task. This allows DTS to detect whether we successfully ran the script utility.

26. Now that you've finished coding the ExecuteSQLScript task, let's install your new component into the DTS Designer so that you can use it in a package. Begin by compiling the component into a DLL file via the File | Make menu option.

27. Next, create a new DTS package by right-clicking the Data Transformation Services node in Enterprise Manager and selecting New Package. Select the Task | Register Custom Task menu option from within the DTS Designer. Click the ellipsis next to the Task location text box and locate your custom task's DLL file.

28. Supply a meaningful description for your component in the Task description text box. The DTS Designer appends ": undefined" to whatever you supply here when it creates a default description for a new instance of your task object in a package, so use something that easily identifies the component. I'm using "Execute SQL Script Task."

29. Click OK to close the Register Custom Task dialog and register your new component with the DTS Designer. You should see it appear in the task palette.

30. You can now use your new component in a DTS package, so go ahead and drag it onto the design sheet. You should see displayed the default property dialog that DTS constructs for you based on the public properties exposed by your component.

31. You can experiment further with your new custom task by loading the CustomTaskVBExample.DTS and CustomTaskVB_TimeoutExample.DTS packages from the CH20\CustomTaskVB subfolder on the CD accompanying this book. CustomTaskVBExample executes a simple script via OSQL.EXE using an ExecuteSQLScript custom task. CustomTaskVB_TimeoutExample executes a query string (rather than a script) and times out if the query takes longer than five seconds to execute. It also executes the script utility via the CMD.EXE command processor and uses redirection to route the output to the output file.

Creating a New Custom Task Based on a Sample Task

Another method for creating a custom DTS task is to customize one of the sample tasks that ship with SQL Server. In the next exercise, I'll walk you through customizing the DTSSampleTask custom task that's included in the DTS example code that comes with SQL Server. You can find the code for this task in the …\80\Tools\DevTools\Samples\dts\CustomTasks\DTSTask subfolder under your SQL Server installation path. (This is the default location; you may have to unzip the DTS samples in order to see this folder.) This sample task implements the same essential functionality as the Execute Process task: You provide a process command line to execute, and the task calls the Win32 CreateProcess API to execute it, optionally waiting on it to complete and/or timing out and terminating it as appropriate.

NOTE: DTSSampleTask is a COM component written in C++. Customizing it involves modifying Interface Definition Language (IDL) as well as C++. If you aren't pretty comfortable with both of these languages, you should probably skip this exercise.

Exercise 20.3   Creating a New Custom Task by Using a Sample Task

1. Load the dtstask project (from the DTSTask subfolder, mentioned above) into the Visual C++ IDE. (The instructions that follow assume VC6, but VC7 should work as well, though the steps will likely differ some.) You may want to copy the subfolder to a different location in order to avoid modifying the original sample task code.
2. We'll begin with the dtstask.idl file. This file contains the IDL code that defines the custom task component's COM interface. The MIDL compiler uses this file to produce other files that are ultimately compiled along with the component's other source files to build the custom task DLL.
3. You should see property attribute specifications for the ProcessCommandLine property near the middle of the file. Delete the four lines that define the ProcessCommandLine property.
4. Insert the lines shown in Listing 20.15 in place of the ones you deleted and renumber the properties that follow them accordingly.

Listing 20.15

```
[id(15), propget, helpstring("Command line of script _
    execution utility (e.g., OSQL.EXE). Specify %script% for _
    script file name placeholder and %output% for output _
    file name.")]
```

```
HRESULT ScriptExecutionUtility([out, retval] BSTR *pRetVal);
[id(15), propput]
HRESULT ScriptExecutionUtility([in] BSTR NewValue);

[id(16), propget, helpstring("UNC File name of the script _
    to execute")]
HRESULT ScriptToExecute([out, retval] BSTR *pRetVal);
[id(16), propput]
HRESULT ScriptToExecute([in] BSTR NewValue);

[id(17), propget, helpstring("UNC File name of the output _
    file to create")]
HRESULT OutputFileToCreate([out, retval] BSTR *pRetVal);
[id(17), propput]
HRESULT OutputFileToCreate([in] BSTR NewValue);
```

This will define three new properties: ScriptExecutionUtility, Script-ToExecute, and OutputFileToCreate. Be sure to renumber the properties that follow these so that you end up with unique IDs for each property.

5. Change the custom task's help string at the bottom of dtstask.idl, which currently reads "DTS Sample Task: Create process," to "DTS ExecuteScript Task."

6. The next file we'll change is the task.h header file. This file defines the interface to the class that implements our custom task object. Remove all references to m_bstrCommandLine and ProcessCommandLine in this file. Be sure to remove the entirety of the get and put method declarations in IDTSSampleTask for ProcessCommandLine.

7. Add the following lines to the CTask constructor:

```
m_bstrScriptExecutionUtility = SysAllocString(L"");
m_bstrScriptToExecute = SysAllocString(L"");
m_bstrOutputFileToCreate = SysAllocString(L"");
```

8. Add the following lines to the CTask destructor:

```
if (m_bstrScriptExecutionUtility)
  SysFreeString(m_bstrScriptExecutionUtility);
if (m_bstrScriptToExecute)
  SysFreeString(m_bstrScriptToExecute);
if (m_bstrOutputFileToCreate)
  SysFreeString(m_bstrOutputFileToCreate);
```

9. Add the method declarations in Listing 20.16 to IDTSSampleTask.

Listing 20.16

```
STDMETHOD(get_ScriptExecutionUtility)(
    /* [retval][out] */ BSTR   *pRetVal);

STDMETHOD(put_ScriptExecutionUtility)(
    /* [in] */ BSTR NewValue);

STDMETHOD(get_ScriptToExecute)(
    /* [retval][out] */ BSTR   *pRetVal);

STDMETHOD(put_ScriptToExecute)(
    /* [in] */ BSTR NewValue);

STDMETHOD(get_OutputFileToCreate)(
    /* [retval][out] */ BSTR   *pRetVal);

STDMETHOD(put_OutputFileToCreate)(
    /* [in] */ BSTR NewValue);
```

10. Change the private BSTR member declarations in IDTSSampleTask to look like this:

```
BSTR m_bstrName, m_bstrDescription, m_bstrScriptExecutionUtility,
    m_bstrScriptToExecute, m_bstrOutputFileToCreate;
```

    This will define the private member variables we'll use to cache the values of our new properties.

11. The last file we'll modify is task.cpp, the module responsible for implementing our custom task. Find the get and put methods for Process-CommandLine and remove them. In their place, add the code shown in Listing 20.17.

Listing 20.17

```
STDMETHODIMP CTask::get_ScriptExecutionUtility(
    /* [retval][out] */ BSTR   *pRetVal)
{
  if (!pRetVal)
    return E_POINTER;
  *pRetVal = SysAllocString(m_bstrScriptExecutionUtility);
  if (!*pRetVal)
```

```
        return E_OUTOFMEMORY;
    return NOERROR;
}



STDMETHODIMP CTask::put_ScriptExecutionUtility(
        /* [in] */ BSTR NewValue)
{
    if (m_bstrScriptExecutionUtility)
        SysFreeString(m_bstrScriptExecutionUtility);
    m_bstrScriptExecutionUtility = SysAllocString(NewValue);
    if (!m_bstrScriptExecutionUtility)
        return E_OUTOFMEMORY;
    return NOERROR;
}

STDMETHODIMP CTask::get_ScriptToExecute(
        /* [retval][out] */ BSTR  *pRetVal)
{
    if (!pRetVal)
        return E_POINTER;
    *pRetVal = SysAllocString(m_bstrScriptToExecute);
    if (!*pRetVal)
        return E_OUTOFMEMORY;
    return NOERROR;
}



STDMETHODIMP CTask::put_ScriptToExecute(
        /* [in] */ BSTR NewValue)
{
    if (m_bstrScriptToExecute)
        SysFreeString(m_bstrScriptToExecute);
    m_bstrScriptToExecute = SysAllocString(NewValue);
    if (!m_bstrScriptToExecute)
        return E_OUTOFMEMORY;
    return NOERROR;
}

STDMETHODIMP CTask::get_OutputFileToCreate(
        /* [retval][out] */ BSTR  *pRetVal)
{
    if (!pRetVal)
        return E_POINTER;
```

```
  *pRetVal = SysAllocString(m_bstrOutputFileToCreate);
  if (!*pRetVal)
    return E_OUTOFMEMORY;
  return NOERROR;
}


STDMETHODIMP CTask::put_OutputFileToCreate(
     /* [in] */ BSTR NewValue)
{
  if (m_bstrOutputFileToCreate)
    SysFreeString(m_bstrOutputFileToCreate);
  m_bstrOutputFileToCreate = SysAllocString(NewValue);
  if (!m_bstrOutputFileToCreate)
    return E_OUTOFMEMORY;
  return NOERROR;
}
```

These methods will provide the plumbing necessary to set and get values for our new properties.

12. The last thing we need to do to customize this task for our own use is modify the Execute method to call our script execution utility. Without belaboring this, I'll just present the code here, and you can read through it to see how it works. The main difference between it and the original Execute method is that it replaces predefined string tokens in the script utility command line with the values of m_bstrScriptToExecute and m_bstrOutputFileToCreate as appropriate. As with the Custom-TaskVB example, this provides flexibility in setting up the script utility command line and allows you to supply the name of the script to execute and the output file name to create using global variables, Dynamic Properties tasks, and similar package facilities. It also fixes a bug in the original sample task code that ships with SQL Server that caused two handles (a thread handle and a process handle) to be leaked with each call to Execute. Replace the original Execute method with the one provided in Listing 20.18.

Listing 20.18

```
STDMETHODIMP CTask::Execute(
     /* [in] */ IDispatch  *pPackage,
     /* [in] */ IDispatch  *pPackageEvents,
     /* [in] */ IDispatch  *pPackageLog,
     /* [out][in] */ LONG  *pTaskResult)
```

```
{
    //**************************************************************
    //NOTE: This sample does not properly SetErrorInfo. You should
    //implement ISupportErrorInfo
    //and properly call SetErrorInfo on failures.
    //**************************************************************
    USES_CONVERSION;

    HRESULT hr = NOERROR;

    //Validate and initialize return value and output
    //parameter pointers.
    *pTaskResult = DTSTaskExecResult_Failure; //Assume failure

    //*** BEGIN_METHOD_CODE ***

    PROCESS_INFORMATION    procInfo;
    STARTUPINFO    startupInfo;
    DWORD    dwTimeout;
    LPTSTR    szScriptExecutionUtility;
    LPTSTR    szScriptToExecute;
    LPTSTR    szOutputFileToCreate;
    TCHAR szCmd[0x1000];
    TCHAR szCmd2[0x1000];
    const TCHAR *SCRIPT = _T("%script%");
    const TCHAR *OUTPUT = _T("%output%");

    memset(&startupInfo, 0, sizeof(startupInfo));
    memset(&procInfo, 0, sizeof(procInfo));
    startupInfo.cb = sizeof(STARTUPINFO);

    szScriptExecutionUtility = OLE2T(m_bstrScriptExecutionUtility);
    szScriptToExecute = OLE2T(m_bstrScriptToExecute);
    szOutputFileToCreate = OLE2T(m_bstrOutputFileToCreate);

    //Replace SCRIPT and OUTPUT tokens
    TCHAR *p=_tcsstr(szScriptExecutionUtility,SCRIPT);
    TCHAR *q=_tcsstr(szScriptExecutionUtility,OUTPUT);
    if ((p) || (q)) {
      if ((q) && (p) && (p<q)) {  //Got script and output,
                                  //script first
        //Replace script token
        _tcsncpy(szCmd,szScriptExecutionUtility,
        p-szScriptExecutionUtility);
```

```
  szCmd[p-szScriptExecutionUtility]=_T('\0');
  _tcscat(szCmd,szScriptToExecute);
  _tcscat(szCmd,p+_tcslen(SCRIPT));

  //Replace output token
  q=_tcsstr(szCmd,OUTPUT);
  _tcsncpy(szCmd2,szCmd,q-szCmd);
  szCmd2[q-szCmd]=_T('\0');
  _tcscat(szCmd2,szOutputFileToCreate);
  _tcscat(szCmd2,q+_tcslen(OUTPUT));

  _tcscpy(szCmd,szCmd2);
}
else if ((q) && (p) && (p>q)) {  //Got script and output,
                                 //output first
  //Replace output token
  _tcsncpy(szCmd,szScriptExecutionUtility,
      q-szScriptExecutionUtility);
  szCmd[q-szScriptExecutionUtility]=_T('\0');
  _tcscat(szCmd,szOutputFileToCreate);
  _tcscat(szCmd,q+_tcslen(OUTPUT));

  //Replace script token
  p=_tcsstr(szCmd,OUTPUT);
  _tcsncpy(szCmd2,szCmd,p-szCmd);
  szCmd2[p-szCmd]=_T('\0');
  _tcscat(szCmd2,szScriptToExecute);
  _tcscat(szCmd2,p+_tcslen(SCRIPT));

  _tcscpy(szCmd,szCmd2);
}
else if ((q) && (!p)) { //Got output and no script
  //Replace output token
  _tcsncpy(szCmd,szScriptExecutionUtility,q-szScriptExecutionUtility);
  szCmd[q-szScriptExecutionUtility]=_T('\0');
  _tcscat(szCmd,szOutputFileToCreate);
  _tcscat(szCmd,q+_tcslen(OUTPUT));

}
else {  //Got script and no output
  //Replace script token
  _tcsncpy(szCmd,szScriptExecutionUtility,
  p-szScriptExecutionUtility);
```

```
    szCmd[p-szScriptExecutionUtility]=_T('\0');
    _tcscat(szCmd,szScriptToExecute);
    _tcscat(szCmd,p+_tcslen(SCRIPT));

  }

}
else
  _tcscpy(szCmd,szScriptExecutionUtility);


//Create process from command line
if (!CreateProcess(NULL, szCmd, NULL, NULL, FALSE,
    CREATE_DEFAULT_ERROR_MODE, NULL, NULL, &startupInfo,
    &procInfo))
  return E_UNEXPECTED;

if (m_lTimeout == 0)  //No timeout
  dwTimeout = INFINITE;
else
  dwTimeout = 1000 * m_lTimeout;

if (WAIT_TIMEOUT != WaitForSingleObject
    (procInfo.hProcess, dwTimeout))
{
  //Process terminated
  DWORD dwExitCode;
  if (!GetExitCodeProcess(procInfo.hProcess, &dwExitCode))
    return E_UNEXPECTED;

  if (dwExitCode == (DWORD)m_lSuccessReturnCode)  //If exit code
                   // matches the desired value it is a success
    *pTaskResult = DTSTaskExecResult_Success; //Assume failure
}
else
{
  if (m_bTerminateProcessAfterTimeout)  //Blow the process if
              //that is what the user wants. *Not* the default.
    TerminateProcess(procInfo.hProcess, (UINT)-1);
  if (m_bFailPackageOnTimeout) {  //We error this ::Execute if
              //timeout instead of just failing task if that
              //is what the user wants.
    CloseHandle(procInfo.hProcess);
    CloseHandle(procInfo.hThread);
```

```
        return HRESULT_FROM_WIN32(ERROR_TIMEOUT);   //This is like
                                                     //a cancel.

    }
}

CloseHandle(procInfo.hProcess);
CloseHandle(procInfo.hThread);
return hr;
}
```

13. You're now ready to compile this component into a DLL and register it in the DTS Designer. Hit F7 to build the project. Once dtstask.DLL is created, register it in the DTS Designer via the Task | Register Custom Task menu option, just as you registered the ExecuteSQLScript.DLL custom task DLL (dtstask.DLL is created in the ReleaseUMinDependency folder by default). As before, you can supply a description for the custom task when you register it. I'm using "Execute Script Task."

14. Once the new component is registered in the DTS Designer, you can drag it onto the design sheet and configure it for use in the package. As with the Execute SQL Script Task that we created in the previous exercise, you can use token strings in the script utility command line in order to specify where you want the ScriptToExecute and OutputFileToCreate properties to be inserted. For example, you might set the ScriptExecutionUtility property to something like this:

```
OSQL -S. -E -i%script% -o%output%
```

When the task is executed and its Execute method is called, %script% will be replaced with the current value of the ScriptToExecute property, and %output% will be replaced with the current value of the OutputFileToCreate property. Since these properties can be assigned using global variables, Dynamic Properties tasks, and similar mechanisms, this capability allows you to dynamically replace parts of the script utility command line without having to rebuild the command line in its entirety through script code or something similar.

15. You can experiment further with the ExecuteScript custom task by loading the CustomTaskExample.DTS package from the CH20\CustomTask subfolder on the CD accompanying this book into the DTS Designer and running and modifying it.

Debugging Custom Task Components

Debugging a custom task component is much like debugging any other type of DLL (again, I recommend you build custom task components as DLLs so they can be used in the DTS Designer), but I can offer some pointers to make your life easier if you ever need to do this. I've seen newsgroup postings where people were jumping through lots of hoops (often unnecessarily) in order to debug a custom DTS task. Here are some general guidelines that may make this more intuitive should you ever need to do it.

1. Keep in mind that you don't debug a DLL directly, you debug its host executable. I've seen people advising the uninitiated to attempt to debug directly from Visual Basic or Visual C++ by setting up Enterprise Manager as the "host application" insofar as the IDE debugger is concerned. While this can be made to work, it's overly complicated. There's an easier way: Simply start your host process as you normally would, then attach your debugger to that process. In the case of Enterprise Manager, this will be MMC.EXE, the application under which SEM runs. In the case of dtsrun, this, of course, is dtsrun.exe. And in the case of a standalone application that is accessing the DTS object model via COM Automation, you would attach your debugger to the application itself. Both the VC++ debugger and WinDbg, the standalone debugger we've been using throughout this book, support the ability to attach to a running process.

2. Use a debug build of your component if possible. Debugging with optimized code can be difficult if not impossible because optimizing compilers can rearrange and even eliminate the machine code that corresponds to individual source code lines. The custom task we just created supports two different debug build configurations. You can access them from the VC6 IDE via the Build | Set Active Configuration menu item.

3. Be sure to generate debug symbols for your component. This is the default for debug builds in VC++, and you can enable it for VB projects by checking the Create Symbolic Debug Info checkbox in the Project Properties | Compile dialog.

4. Before you attach to the host app with your debugger, be sure your symbol and source paths are set correctly in the debugger. You'll probably need to add the path containing the PDB generated by VB or VC++ to your symbol path, and you may need to add the path containing your component's source code to the debugger's source path.

5. Once you've attached to your host application, check to see whether your component's DLL is already loaded and whether the debugger has located its symbol file. In WinDbg, you can do this using the lm command, which lists the currently loaded modules, along with the

symbol path for each one if the symbol file has been located and loaded. If your component hasn't yet been loaded, do whatever is necessary in the host application to cause it to load—you won't be able to reference its symbols (e.g., to set breakpoints) until it has been loaded. If you see your component DLL loaded, but its symbols haven't yet been loaded, make sure the symbol file is on the debugger's symbol path, then instruct the debugger to attempt to reload the symbols for your component. (You won't be able to fully debug your component until its symbols load successfully.) Different debuggers have different commands for doing this; you use the .reload -f command in WinDbg to force a symbol reload.

6. You should be able to reference methods in your component by using normal Class::method syntax, even for components created in VB. For example, if your component class in VB is named clsExecuteSQL-Script, you can set a breakpoint in its Execute method by referencing the clsExecuteSQLScript::CustomTask_Execute symbol.

Provided that your symbol and source paths are set correctly, you should be able to debug your component just as you would any other DLL. Let's walk through a simple exercise in which we use the WinDbg standalone debugger to debug a custom task you've created.

Exercise 20.4 Debugging a Custom Task

1. Compile your custom task to a DLL file and make sure symbolic debugging information is created so that a PDB file is generated. You enable this in Visual Basic by selecting the Create Symbolic Debug Info option on the Compile tab in the Project Properties dialog.
2. Start the DTS Designer and install your custom task into it if you've not already done so.
3. Start WinDbg and set its symbol and source paths (on the File menu) to the folder(s) containing the PDB file corresponding to your DLL and its source code, respectively.
4. From WinDbg, attach to the Enterprise Manager's host app, MMC.EXE. (Press F6 to see the list of running processes.)
5. Set a breakpoint in the Execute method of your custom task's class. For example, if your class is named clsExecuteSQLScript and your Execute method is named CustomTask_Execute, you might enter this command in WinDbg to set the breakpoint:

```
bp clsExecuteSQLScript::CustomTask_Execute
```

This breakpoint will cause execution to stop when the task is executed.

6. Type g and hit Enter to allow MMC to continue to run.

7. Switch back to the DTS Designer and drop an instance of your custom task onto the design sheet.

8. Right-click your custom task object and select Execute. This should trigger your breakpoint in WinDbg and stop execution. (You'll have to use Alt+Tab to get back to WinDbg—the Designer will probably appear to hang.)

9. You should now see the source code module containing your custom task's Execute method loaded in WinDbg, and you should be able to step through it by pressing F10. You can set up watches, examine the call stack and registers, view local variables, and so on as you step through your code. This can be immensely helpful in tracking down obscure bugs in custom DTS tasks.

10. When you're ready for the Designer to resume running, type g and press Enter in the WinDbg command window. When you detach from MMC.EXE, you'll likely notice that it disappears altogether. Unless you're on Windows XP or later, detaching from a process to which you've attached "invasively" (invasive attachment is the default and is necessary to set breakpoints) automatically terminates the process that was being debugged.

Setting Up a Test Harness

Another technique for debugging custom tasks is to create a simple VB app that programmatically creates a package containing your custom task (or opens a package containing a reference to it) and executes it. You can then code the app to touch specific parts of the package, execute specified steps that you want to check out, and so on. You can step through the app itself under a debugger and interactively view package properties, step into your custom task code, and so on. Without ever leaving VB, you can do many of the things you could do using a standalone debugger and attaching to MMC or dtsrun.

Controlling DTS through Automation

In my opinion, the real power of DTS is in its programmability. The DTS Designer is elegant enough that practically anyone can use it and be productive with it. However, more sophisticated data transformations often require direct access to the DTS object model from custom programs. You'll need to be able to configure and control what occurs and when it happens using custom application code, just as you do with other types of SQL Server applications.

Getting into a detailed discussion of the DTS object model is beyond the scope of this book. Several books have already been written on this subject, and I don't have the space or time to do it justice here. As I said at the outset, it's not my intent to explore every nook and cranny of SQL Server's DTS technology in this one chapter. I want you to understand the functionality that's available to you and how it works from an architectural standpoint, but I can't get into as many details as I might like. That said, no discussion of DTS would be complete without at least touching on the programmability of the technology, so we'll delve into it a bit in this next section.

I'll finish up this chapter by introducing you to some DTS applications that demonstrate how to program the DTS object model in order to control DTS packages and workflow from a standalone application. This is a good way to close out the exploration of DTS because it codifies many of the concepts we've been discussing.

A Simple DTS Automation App

Let's begin by looking at the source code for the first application, shown in Listing 20.19. (You can find the complete source for this application in the CH20\Automation subfolder on the CD accompanying this book.)

Listing 20.19

```
Dim g_oPkg As DTS.Package2
Dim g_bInited

Function TaskName(Descrip As String) As String
  Dim oTask As DTS.Task
  TaskName = "NotFound"
  For Each oTask In g_oPkg.Tasks
    If oTask.Description = Descrip Then
      TaskName = oTask.Name
      Exit For
    End If
  Next
End Function
```

```
Private Sub Command1_Click()
  Dim oPkg As New DTS.Package2
  If (g_bInited) Then
    g_oPkg.UnInitialize
    Set g_oPkg = Nothing
    g_bInited = False
  End If
  Set g_oPkg = oPkg
  oPkg.LoadFromStorageFile App.Path & "\" & Text1.Text, ""

  lbGlobals.Clear
  Dim oGlobal As DTS.GlobalVariable2
  For Each oGlobal In oPkg.GlobalVariables
    lbGlobals.AddItem (oGlobal.Name & "=" & oGlobal.Value)
  Next

  lbSteps.Clear
  Dim oStep As DTS.Step2
  For Each oStep In oPkg.Steps
    lbSteps.AddItem (oStep.Name)
  Next

  lbTasks.Clear
  Dim oTask As DTS.Task
  For Each oTask In oPkg.Tasks
    lbTasks.AddItem (oTask.Description)
  Next

  g_bInited = True

End Sub

Private Sub Command2_Click()
  If (g_bInited) And (Len(Text2.Text) <> 0) Then
    g_oPkg.SaveToStorageFile App.Path & "\" & Text2.Text
  End If
End Sub

Private Sub Command3_Click()
  If (g_bInited) And (lbSteps.ListIndex <> -1) Then
    Dim oStep As DTS.Step2
    Set oStep = g_oPkg.Steps(lbSteps.List(lbSteps.ListIndex))
    oStep.Execute
  End If
```

```
End Sub

Private Sub Form_Load()
  g_bInited = False
End Sub
```

This application does several interesting things. It begins by allowing you to load a DTS package that's been saved in COM structured format into memory. You can load any package you choose; I've provided a sample package to get you started. When the package loads, the VB application iterates through its global variables, steps, and tasks and lists them in ListBox controls on the form. Each of these is stored in a collection, so a simple For Each loop does the trick.

The app also allows you to select an individual step in the Step list box and execute it. We look up the Step object using its name, then simply call its Execute method.

You can also save the package to a COM structured file. You can save it to the same file from which it was loaded, or you can pick a different one.

As you can see, the key to manipulating a DTS package via Automation code is creating a Package or Package2 object. Once you've done that, everything else is a matter of accessing properties, methods, and events off that object.

DTSPkgGuru

The last app we'll look at in this chapter is a little more involved than most of the others we've explored. First of all, it's written in managed code—C#, to be exact. I wrote it in managed code to demonstrate how to automate the DTS object model from managed code. It's not that different from unmanaged code, but there are some nuances and things you should be aware of.

The name of the app is DTSPkgGuru. It exists to allow you to edit packages outside the DTS Designer. Specifically, it's designed to allow you to automate a series of changes to a package without losing the design sheet layout of the package.

It's common to want to perform a series of changes to a package via Automation code. Doing so can be much faster and much more precise than making the changes by hand in the DTS Designer. For example, if you need to change the timeout period for a hundred Execute Process tasks (and you didn't have the foresight to assign the timeout using a Dynamic Properties task), it's much faster to open the package via Automation code and loop through the package's Task objects, making the changes you need to make as you go. Once you're finished, you call one of the Save methods on the DTS Package object to resave the modified package.

An annoying limitation of this approach is that the package's layout information is lost when it is saved via Automation code. Even if you add no objects and change properties only on existing objects, saving the package via Automation resets the design sheet layout. If you then reopen the package in the DTS Designer, you'll likely see a layout that's very different from the one you may have spent hours getting just right. The only facility by which you can modify a package and save it without losing the design sheet layout is the DTS Designer itself. All the time spent getting the visual layout the way you want it is wasted once you save the package via Automation code.

I've tried working around this limitation by using a variety of techniques (including passing the pVarPersistStgOfHost parameter of the DTS.Package Save methods) with no success. As far as I know, there is no way to save a package via Automation code without losing the design sheet layout.

So, to address this, I wrote DTSPkgGuru. It opens a package via Automation, allows you to build a queue of changes to the package, then sends those changes to the DTS Designer. Since there is no documented means of automating the DTS Designer via standard COM Automation, DTSPkgGuru controls the Designer by sending keystrokes to it to carry out the package changes you specify.

DTSPkgGuru also allows you to save a set of changes as a tab-delimited text file and reload it later. You can also save all the properties in a package to a tab-delimited text file. These two features allow you to easily perform global find and replace operations or other complex package changes using the text editor of your choice, then load the text file in DTSPkgGuru and apply the changes to your package in the DTS Designer.

In order to use DTSPkgGuru to automate package changes, you must meet two basic requirements.

1. Your package must be saved as a COM structured storage file. Someday I may add the ability to load packages from msdb..sysdtspackages or from the repository (feel free to change the code to do this yourself if you like), but for now DTSPkgGuru can load only packages saved as COM structured storage files. That doesn't mean you can't use the tool to modify a package stored elsewhere. If you want to modify a package that's been saved to the repository, for example, just load it into the DTS Designer and save it out to a COM structured storage file. DTSPkgGuru requires that the package be a COM structured storage file in order to load it, but the app can

automate the changes to any package you can load into the DTS Designer.

2. In case you haven't already guessed, the second requirement is that you must load your package into the DTS Designer before invoking DTSPkgGuru. Since it controls the Designer via the keyboard, the app is expecting the package to already be loaded when it runs. Again, the package itself can be stored in any format or location supported by the Designer. As long as the package is loaded into the Designer, DTSPkgGuru can help you automate changes to it.

You can find the executable and source code for DTSPkgGuru in the CH20\DTSPkgGuru subfolder on the CD accompanying this book. Before we examine the source code, let me give a brief rundown of how to use the tool. I will resist the temptation here to show a screenshot of the tool because I've managed to make it through this entire chapter without using any screenshots (no mean feat when you consider we're discussing technology that revolves around a visual designer), and I don't want to slip up now. That said, you may want to load a package into the DTS Designer (once you do, save it as a COM structured stored file if necessary), then run the DTSPkgGuru executable in order to follow along. Make sure you have only one copy of Enterprise Manager running. We use the window title to locate Enterprise Manager when we prepare to take over the keyboard, so having multiple copies running could make it difficult to find the correct app to automate.

1. You begin by clicking the Open button to load a package into DTSP-kgGuru. Again, the package must be saved in COM structured storage format.

2. You should see all the package items and their properties displayed in the DTSPkgGuru GUI. The package components are in the tree view on the left; the properties are in the grid on the right.

3. You set up changes to your package by making them in the GUI and adding them to the change list at the bottom of the DTSPkgGuru main form. To do this, click a property in the grid on the right of the form. You'll see its value displayed in a text box at the top of the screen. Make your change in this text box, then click the Add change button. This will add your change to the change list at the bottom of the form. Repeat this process for every change you'd like to make.

4. When you're ready to send your changes over to the DTS Designer, click the Send changes button. This will switch the active window context to Enterprise Manager (where DTS Designer should already

be running with your package loaded), then automatically supply the keystrokes necessary to make the changes you've queued up.

5. Once the changes complete, you can use Alt+Tab to return to DTSPkgGuru or continue to work with your package in the DTS Designer.

6. You can save your change list to a tab-delimited text file for later retrieval by right-clicking it and selecting the Save option. You can also save all the properties in the package to a tab-delimited text file by clicking the Save all button. These options use the same file format, so you can load a text file created by either into the change list at the bottom of the form by right-clicking it and selecting Load. Given that these are normal tab-delimited text files, you can load them into a text editor of your choosing and make whatever changes are required, then reload them into the DTSPkgGuru GUI and apply them to the DTS Designer.

DTSPkgGuru is able to make the changes you request to your package thanks to the Disconnected Edit facility. There are a couple of caveats that come with using this facility. First, much of the Designer's normal validation code is bypassed when in Disconnected Edit mode. Changing a property to an invalid or incorrect value via Disconnected Edit can have catastrophic consequences. Second, the properties you change via Disconnected Edit that are displayed in the design sheet (e.g., task descriptions) will not be immediately reflected in the design sheet display after DTSPkgGuru runs. They have, however, been made—the fact that they aren't reflected immediately is due to the way the Designer itself works. It does not refresh its display after changes are made via Disconnected Edit, regardless of whether you make those changes yourself or allow DTSPkgGuru to do it.

Another thing to be aware of when using DTSPkgGuru is that some properties cannot be modified. For example, the package ID and version ID for a package are read-only and can't be changed. DTSPkgGuru attempts to help you with this by not allowing you to enter changes for read-only properties and by prefixing read-only properties with a comment marker when streaming all properties to a text file (via the Save all button). However, it can't stop you from adding read-only properties to a change list manually by editing a text file and loading it into the DTSPkgGuru GUI. Given that you can stream both the entire property list as well as individual change lists as text files, you have the ability to put whatever property changes you want into the file via a text editor. Be advised that if you add a read-only property to this list, your change won't succeed, and the changes that follow it in the list will also likely fail because the DTS Designer will be in a different state than DTSPkgGuru is expecting.

So, all that said, let's have a look at the DTSPkgGuru code. Again, you can find it in the CH20\DTSPkgGuru subfolder on the CD accompanying this book. I won't include all the source code to DTSPkgGuru here given that much of it is automatically generated by the Visual Studio .NET IDE. Instead, let's have a look at the parts of the code that I wrote (Listing 20.20).

Listing 20.20

```
DTS.Package2Class pkg;

private void btOpen_Click(object sender, System.EventArgs e)
{
  if (DialogResult.OK!=od_dts.ShowDialog()) return;
  tbFileName.Text=od_dts.FileName;
  pkg = new DTS.Package2Class();
  object dummy=new object();
  pkg.LoadFromStorageFile(tbFileName.Text,"",null,null,null,
      ref dummy);
  TreeNode noderoot;
  TreeNode nodeparent;
  TreeNode nodechild;
  btAddChange.Enabled=false;
  btSave.Enabled=false;
  btSend.Enabled=false;
  tvItems.BeginUpdate();
  lvProperties.BeginUpdate();
  lvChanges.BeginUpdate();
  try
  {
    tvItems.Nodes.Clear();
    lvProperties.Items.Clear();
    lvChanges.Items.Clear();
    noderoot=tvItems.Nodes.Add(pkg.Name);
    noderoot.Tag=pkg;
    nodeparent=noderoot.Nodes.Add("Connections");
    foreach (DTS.Connection conn  in pkg.Connections)
    {
      nodechild=nodeparent.Nodes.Add(conn.Name);
      nodechild.Tag=conn;
    }
    nodeparent=noderoot.Nodes.Add("Tasks");
    foreach (DTS.Task task in pkg.Tasks)
    {
```

```
      nodechild=nodeparent.Nodes.Add(task.Name);
      nodechild.Tag=task;
    }
    nodeparent=noderoot.Nodes.Add("Steps");
    foreach (DTS.Step step in pkg.Steps)
    {
      nodechild=nodeparent.Nodes.Add(step.Name);
      nodechild.Tag=step;
    }
    nodeparent=noderoot.Nodes.Add("Global Variables");
    foreach (DTS.GlobalVariable var in pkg.GlobalVariables)
    {
      nodechild=nodeparent.Nodes.Add(var.Name);
      nodechild.Tag=var;
    }
    tvItems.ExpandAll();
    btSave.Enabled=true;
  }
  finally
  {
    tvItems.EndUpdate();
    lvProperties.EndUpdate();
    lvChanges.EndUpdate();
  }
}

private void tvItems_AfterSelect(object sender,
    System.Windows.Forms.TreeViewEventArgs e)
{
  tbChange.Text="";
  btAddChange.Enabled=false;
  lvProperties.BeginUpdate();
  try
  {
    lvProperties.Items.Clear();
    if ((null==pkg) ||
      (null==tvItems.SelectedNode) ||
      (null==tvItems.SelectedNode.Tag))
      return;
    DTS.Properties props=null;
    if (tvItems.SelectedNode.Tag is DTS.Package)
      props = (tvItems.SelectedNode.Tag as DTS.Package).
          Properties;
    else if (tvItems.SelectedNode.Tag is DTS.Connection)
```

```
            props = (tvItems.SelectedNode.Tag as DTS.Connection).
               Properties;
         else if (tvItems.SelectedNode.Tag is DTS.Task)
           props = (tvItems.SelectedNode.Tag as DTS.Task).
               Properties;
         else if (tvItems.SelectedNode.Tag is DTS.Step)
           props = (tvItems.SelectedNode.Tag as DTS.Step).
               Properties;
         else if (tvItems.SelectedNode.Tag is DTS.GlobalVariable)
           props = (tvItems.SelectedNode.Tag as DTS.GlobalVariable).
               Properties;

         foreach (DTS.Property prop in props)
         {
           ListViewItem lvitem = lvProperties.Items.Add(prop.Name);
           lvitem.SubItems.Add(prop.Value as string);
           lvitem.Tag=tvItems.SelectedNode.Tag;
           if (!prop.Set)
             lvitem.ImageIndex=1;   //readonly property
         }
       }
       finally
       {
         lvProperties.EndUpdate();
       }
     }

     private void lvProperties_SelectedIndexChanged(object sender,
         System.EventArgs e)
     {
       if ((null==lvProperties.SelectedItems) ||
         (0==lvProperties.SelectedItems.Count))
         return;
       if (1!=lvProperties.SelectedItems[0].ImageIndex)
       {
         btAddChange.Enabled=true;
         tbChange.ReadOnly=false;
       }
       else
       {
         btAddChange.Enabled=false;
         tbChange.ReadOnly=true;
       }
```

```
      //See if this item is already in the change list
      foreach (ListViewItem lvitem in lvChanges.Items)
      {
        if (lvitem.Tag.Equals(lvProperties.SelectedItems[0]))
        {
          tbChange.Text=lvitem.SubItems[3].Text;
          return;
        }
      }
      tbChange.Text=lvProperties.SelectedItems[0].SubItems[1].Text;
    }

    private void btAddChange_Click(object sender,
        System.EventArgs e)
    {
      if ((null==lvProperties.SelectedItems) ||
        (0==lvProperties.SelectedItems.Count)
        )
        return;
      foreach (ListViewItem lvi in lvChanges.Items)
      {
        if (lvi.Tag.Equals(lvProperties.SelectedItems[0]))
        {
          lvChanges.Items.Remove(lvi);
          break;
        }
      }

      ListViewItem lvitem = lvChanges.Items.Add(tvItems.
          SelectedNode.Text);
      lvitem.SubItems.Add(lvProperties.SelectedItems[0].
          SubItems[0].Text);
      lvitem.SubItems.Add(lvProperties.SelectedItems[0].
          SubItems[1].Text);
      lvitem.SubItems.Add(tbChange.Text);
      lvitem.Tag=lvProperties.SelectedItems[0];
      btSend.Enabled=true;
    }
    // Clear changes
    private void menuItem1_Click(object sender, System.
        EventArgs e)
    {
```

```
        lvChanges.Items.Clear();
        btSend.Enabled=false;
}

//Translate keys that confuse SendKeys
string ReplaceSpecialKeys(string instring)
{
    if (null==instring) return string.Empty;
    instring=instring.Replace("{","\\{").Replace("}","\\}").
        Replace("%","{%}").Replace("^","{^}").Replace("+","{+}");
    return instring.Replace("\\{","{{}").Replace("\\}","{}}");
}

private void btSend_Click(object sender, System.EventArgs e)
{
    foreach (ListViewItem lvitem in lvChanges.Items)
    {
        lvitem.Checked=false;
    }

    int hWnd=Win32.FindWindow(null,
        "SQL Server Enterprise Manager");
    if (Win32.SetForegroundWindow(hWnd))
    {
        lvChanges.BeginUpdate();
        try
        {
            string Keys;
            Keys="%pd";
            SendKeys.SendWait(Keys);
            foreach (ListViewItem lvitem in lvChanges.Items)
            {
                Keys="";
                if ((lvitem.Tag as ListViewItem).Tag is DTS.Connection)
                    Keys+="c";
                else if ((lvitem.Tag as ListViewItem).Tag is DTS.Task)
                    Keys+="t";
                else if ((lvitem.Tag as ListViewItem).Tag is DTS.Step)
                    Keys+="s";
                else if ((lvitem.Tag as ListViewItem).Tag is
                    DTS.GlobalVariable)
                    Keys+="g";
                SendKeys.SendWait(Keys);
                if (0!=Keys.Length) //Not package properties
```

```
          {
            Keys="{RIGHT}{DOWN}";
            SendKeys.SendWait(Keys);
            Keys=lvitem.Text;  //item name
            SendKeys.SendWait(Keys);
          }
          Keys="{TAB}{DOWN}";
          SendKeys.SendWait(Keys);
          Keys=lvitem.SubItems[1].Text;  //prop name
          SendKeys.SendWait(Keys);
          Keys="{ENTER}";
          SendKeys.SendWait(Keys);
          Keys="{TAB}";
          SendKeys.SendWait(Keys);
          Keys=ReplaceSpecialKeys(lvitem.SubItems[3].Text);
          SendKeys.SendWait(Keys);
          Keys="{ENTER}";
          SendKeys.SendWait(Keys);
          Keys="+{TAB}{HOME}";
          SendKeys.SendWait(Keys);
          lvitem.Checked=true;
        }
        Keys="%c"; //Close the Disconnected Edit dialog
        SendKeys.SendWait(Keys);
      }
      finally
      {
        lvChanges.EndUpdate();
      }
    }
    else MessageBox.Show("Could not find Enterprise Manager
        window");
}

TreeNode FindNode(TreeNodeCollection nodes, string
    searchstring)
{
  TreeNode result=null;
  foreach (TreeNode tvitem in nodes)
  {
    if (0!=tvitem.Nodes.Count)
      result=FindNode(tvitem.Nodes,searchstring);
    if (null==result)
    {
```

```
        if (tvitem.Text.ToLower()==searchstring.ToLower())
        {
          result = tvitem;
          break;
        }
      }
      else break;
    }
    return result;
  }


  //Replace chars with escape equivalents (for storage in
  //txt file)
  string NoEscapeChars(object inobj)
  {
    string instring = inobj as string;
    if (null==instring) return string.Empty;
    return instring.Replace("\n\r","\\n\\r").Replace("\n","\\n").
        Replace("\r","\\r").Replace("\t","\\t");
  }


  //Change escape chars to actual chars (for load from txt file)
  string ReplaceEscapeChars(object inobj)
  {
    string instring = inobj as string;
    if (null==instring) return string.Empty;
    return instring.Replace("\\n\\r","\n\r").Replace("\\n","\n").
        Replace("\\r","\r").Replace("\\t","\t");
  }
  // Load change list
  private void menuItem2_Click(object sender,
      System.EventArgs e)
  {
    if (DialogResult.OK!=od_TXT.ShowDialog()) return;
    lvChanges.Items.Clear();
    StreamReader f = File.OpenText(od_TXT.FileName);
    tvItems.BeginUpdate();
    lvProperties.BeginUpdate();
    lvChanges.BeginUpdate();
    try
    {
      string linein;
      while (null!=(linein = f.ReadLine()))
      {
```

```csharp
if (linein[0]==';') //Comment
  continue;
string[] args=linein.Split('\t');
ListViewItem lvitem = new ListViewItem();
//Break up the input line on tab
foreach (string arg in args)
{
  if (0==lvitem.Text.Length)
    lvitem.Text=arg;
  else
    lvitem.SubItems.Add(ReplaceEscapeChars(arg));
}

//Find the parent item (task, step, etc.)
TreeNode parentnode=null;
parentnode=FindNode(tvItems.Nodes,lvitem.SubItems[0].
    Text);
if (null==parentnode)
{
  MessageBox.Show("Unable to locate item " +
      lvitem.SubItems[0].Text);
  return;
}
tvItems.SelectedNode=parentnode;

//Find the parent property
ListViewItem propitem=null;
foreach (ListViewItem lvi in lvProperties.Items)
{
  if (lvi.Text.ToLower()==lvitem.SubItems[1].
      Text.ToLower())
  {
    propitem = lvi;
    break;
  }
}
if (null==propitem)
{
  MessageBox.Show("Unable to locate property " +
      lvitem.SubItems[1].Text);
  return;
}
lvitem.Tag=propitem;
```

```
          lvChanges.Items.Add(lvitem);
          btSend.Enabled=true;


        }
      }
      finally
      {
        f.Close();
        tvItems.EndUpdate();
        lvProperties.EndUpdate();
        lvChanges.EndUpdate();
      }


    }
    //Save change list
    private void menuItem3_Click(object sender,
        System.EventArgs e)
    {
      if (DialogResult.OK!=sd_TXT.ShowDialog()) return;
      StreamWriter f = File.CreateText(sd_TXT.FileName);
      try
      {
        f.WriteLine(";ItemName\tPropertyName\tOldValue\tNewValue");
        foreach (ListViewItem lvitem in lvChanges.Items)
        {
          f.WriteLine("{0}\t{1}\t{2}\t{3}",lvitem.Text,lvitem.
              SubItems[1].Text,lvitem.SubItems[2].Text,lvitem.
              SubItems[3].Text);
        }
        od_TXT.FileName=sd_TXT.FileName;
      }
      finally
      {
        f.Close();
      }
    }


    private void btSave_Click(object sender,
        System.EventArgs e)
    {
      if (DialogResult.OK!=sd_TXT.ShowDialog()) return;
      StreamWriter f = File.CreateText(sd_TXT.FileName);
      try
```

```
{
  f.WriteLine(";ItemName\tPropertyName\tOldValue\tNewValue");
  foreach (DTS.Property prop in pkg.Properties)
  {
    f.WriteLine("{0}{1}\t{2}\t{3}\t{4}",prop.Set?"":";",
        pkg.Name,prop.Name,NoEscapeChars(prop.Value),
        NoEscapeChars(prop.Value));
  }
  foreach (DTS.Connection conn in pkg.Connections)
  {
    foreach (DTS.Property prop in conn.Properties)
    {
      f.WriteLine("{0}{1}\t{2}\t{3}\t{4}",prop.Set?"":";",
          conn.Name,prop.Name,NoEscapeChars(prop.Value),
          NoEscapeChars(prop.Value));
    }
  }
  foreach (DTS.Task task in pkg.Tasks)
  {
    foreach (DTS.Property prop in task.Properties)
    {
      f.WriteLine("{0}{1}\t{2}\t{3}\t{4}",prop.Set?"":";",
          task.Name,prop.Name,NoEscapeChars(prop.Value),
          NoEscapeChars(prop.Value));
    }
  }
  foreach (DTS.Step step in pkg.Steps)
  {
    foreach (DTS.Property prop in step.Properties)
    {
      f.WriteLine("{0}{1}\t{2}\t{3}\t{4}",prop.Set?"":";",
          step.Name,prop.Name,NoEscapeChars(prop.Value),
          NoEscapeChars(prop.Value));
    }
  }
  foreach (DTS.GlobalVariable var in pkg.GlobalVariables)
  {
    foreach (DTS.Property prop in var.Properties)
    {
      f.WriteLine("{0}{1}\t{2}\t{3}\t{4}",prop.Set?"":";",
          var.Name,prop.Name,NoEscapeChars(prop.Value),
          NoEscapeChars(prop.Value));
```

```
      }
    }
  }
  finally
  {
    f.Close();
  }
}
```

I'll walk through the code step by step and point out what I consider to be its more noteworthy elements. I'll just hit the high points rather than boring you with a line-by-line discussion. I've bolded the methods we'll talk about in the listing above.

1. In order for DTSPkgGuru to make calls against the DTS Package object model, a reference to the DTS Package COM object library must first be added to the project. This is accomplished by selecting Add Reference in the Visual Studio .NET IDE and choosing the COM tab in the dialog. Managed code apps can make use of COM objects through COM Interop—a set of services and APIs that make working with COM objects and exposing managed classes to COM easier. (Note the reference to the System.Runtime.InteropServices assembly at the top of the DTSPkgGuru.cs source file.) The DTS Package object library is listed on the COM tab just as it's listed in Visual Basic 6.

2. Next, the code that's behind the btOpen button handles opening a package and populating the GUI with the package's items and properties. This code works very much like the VB code we looked at in the last example app—we simply iterate through the appropriate collections and populate each GUI element accordingly. Note the use of the Tag property to keep track of the DTS package item to which a given tree node corresponds. This allows us to use reflection when we get ready to send the change list over to the DTS Designer in order to determine which branch in the Disconnected Edit tree view we need to select. For example, we'll select a different branch based on whether we're making a change to a Connection object versus a Task object.

3. The code behind the tree view's AfterSelect event allows us to populate the property grid based on the package component selected in the tree view. Each time the selection changes, we rebuild the property list.

4. The code behind the property list view's SelectedIndexChanged event allows us to (a) determine whether the property is editable and change the appropriate GUI elements accordingly, and (b) display the modified value for a property (if there is one) in the text box at the top of the form.

5. The code behind the click event for the btAddChange button adds an entry to the change list view at the bottom of the form. An entry in the list consists of the object name, the property name, the old value of the property, and the new value. The old value isn't actually used for anything and is included in the list just for display purposes.

6. The code behind the click event for the btSend button handles switching the input focus to Enterprise Manager and sending in the necessary keystrokes to carry out the changes in the change list. We use the .NET Framework's SendKeys class and send the keystrokes for each change in several individual calls. We begin by displaying the Disconnected Edit dialog, then we send in the keys for each change. Once we've finished, we close the Disconnected Edit dialog. Again, because the changes are automated entirely through keystrokes, DTSPkgGuru can help you modify any package you can load into the Designer, regardless of where it's stored. It needs a COM structured file format package for its own GUI enumeration, but it can make changes to any type of package.

7. The code behind the btSave button's click event writes all the components in the package and their properties to a tab-delimited text file. Since the file format is intentionally the same as that for the change list, this code writes the current value for each property twice to the file: once for the old value and once for the new value. You can change the new value via a text editor and reload the file in the DTSPkgGuru GUI in order to use this list as a change list. The list is also a handy tool for saving a package to disk as a text file. Just as you can save a package as VB code in the DTS Designer, you can use this facility to get a bird's-eye view of your package and its contents. Since the file is a standard tab-delimited file, you could even import it into a table via DTS for further analysis or store it in a version control system so that you can detect changes to a package over time and compare one version with another using text differencing tools such as WinDiff and the Visual SourceSafe diff tool.

So, that's DTSPkgGuru. I encourage you to study the source code, run the utility, and even allow it to make some changes to packages you've loaded into the DTS Designer. If you end up needing to make a number of automated changes to a package, you may even find that DTSPkgGuru comes in quite handy.

Recap

DTS is a welcome and powerful addition to the SQL Server technology family. It provides a wealth of data transformation and workflow management facilities that rival those in third-party products. In many ways, DTS is a self-contained visual programming environment—you can use it to build lots of different types of applications, even those not directly related to transforming data.

The primary means of data transport within a DTS package is the multiphase data pump. This component allows data to be moved from one OLE DB provider to another. It's the engine behind the Transform Data task, the Data Driven Query task, and the Parallel Data Pump task. You can also use Bulk Insert tasks to move data from a text file into SQL Server. DTS provides a number of mechanisms for moving data around flexibly and quickly.

A DTS package is extensively programmable. You can execute ActiveX scripts at practically any stage in a transformation. You can hook specific scripts to specific data pump phases, and you can also associate them with individual workflow items. Given that you can access practically anything via ActiveX scripting (e.g., COM objects, ADO, the file system, the Windows API, and so on), the ways in which you can apply the power afforded you by DTS are virtually limitless.

Knowledge Measure

1. In what format should you store a DTS package that you'd like to send via e-mail to a colleague?
2. What single DTS component is the engine behind the Transform Data task, the Data Driven Query task, and the Parallel Data Pump task?
3. True or false: You must define the package to be used in a transformable replication subscription using the DTS Designer and must use a Data Driven Query task to refer to published articles.

4. What DTS task can you use to retrieve values from an INI file and assign them to global variables?

5. True or false: Conditionally executing a given task line in a DTS package requires the use of an ActiveX Script task.

6. What interface must a COM object implement in order to serve as a custom DTS task?

7. Describe the function of precedence constraints in a DTS package.

8. How can you detect that a lookup query has returned multiple rows?

9. What DTS task should you use to execute another process?

10. Describe a scenario in which a Data Driven Query task would be preferable to either a Transform Data task or a Bulk Insert task.

11. How many stock queries can you associate with a single Data Driven Query task?

12. When a nested package is joined to the transaction context of its caller, what happens when the child package commits the transaction?

13. Can you set up ActiveX transformations for a Bulk Insert task?

14. What step must you first take in order to be able to save DTS packages in the Meta Data Services repository?

15. When a DTS package is stored locally on a SQL Server, into what database and table is it saved?

16. What OLE DB provider is used to query a DTS package from Transact-SQL?

17. What OLE DB provider is used to query publication data for a transformable subscription?

18. Which data pump phase occurs first, the postsource phase or the pump complete phase?

19. True or false: In order to use the high-speed bulk copy facilities provided by an OLE DB data source, you must enable the Use fast load option in a Transform Data task—it is not enabled by default.

20. True or false: While an Execute SQL task can execute regular T-SQL scripts with embedded batch terminators, it does not provide a mechanism for retrieving irregular or multirowset output.

21. Why is using the Disconnected Edit facility to change property values in a DTS package potentially dangerous?

22. What T-SQL command is called by the Bulk Insert task?

23. What option must you enable in order to show multiphase data pump options in the DTS Designer?

24. What annoying side effect occurs when you save a DTS package using Automation code?

25. True or false: DTS supports direct connections to HTML data sources.

26. Explain the purpose of the Close connection on completion workflow option.

27. What method of the DTS Package object can an application call in order to load a package directly from a structured storage file?

28. True or false: Because the DTS Package object library is a COM library, you cannot use the foreach construct in managed code languages such as C# or VB.NET to iterate through a collection exposed by the library.

29. True or false: Even if there is only one Connection object in the package, the Microsoft Distributed Transaction Coordinator must be available in order for a DTS package to queue data modifications in a transaction.

30. True or false: Although you may have other ActiveX script languages installed on the machine on which the DTS Designer is running, you may use only VBScript and JScript when coding ActiveX scripts for DTS packages.

31. Once you've created a new project, what must you do to use the DTS Package object library in a managed code application?

32. Describe a situation in which it would be appropriate to enable the Execute on main package thread workflow option.

33. When a child package that has its Use transactions property enabled is executed via an Execute Package task from a package that has already started a transaction and the Execute Package task is enlisted in that transaction, does the child package initiate a nested transaction?

34. True or false: Due to the lack of IDispatch support in the COM Interop facility provided by the .NET Framework, it is impossible to open a DTS package in a managed code app using the DTS Package object library.

35. Describe the way in which the WriteFile transformation works.

Snapshot Replication

There's a difference between volatility and agility. Volatility is random change—change for the sake of change. It has no real purpose. Agility is change to adapt to the obstacles that impede our progress toward our goals and to dodge the slings and arrows the world hurls our way.

—H. W. Kenton

In this chapter and the next two, we'll delve into how SQL Server replication works. This book isn't about replication per se, so we don't have the time or space to get into the subject in the breadth or depth we might like. The chapters on replication in this book will not walk you through setting up replication or administering it; you won't find any screenshots of the Enterprise Manager Replication wizards in these pages. The Replication wizards are simple enough to use that you shouldn't need the help of a book for that, anyway. Moreover, Books Online covers the basic setup and management of replication quite well; what you can't figure out from the Enterprise Manager wizards is covered pretty well there.

This book will also not take you through the many idiosyncrasies of replication or caveats and exceptions that seem to have attached themselves to every single feature within it. Again, Books Online does a pretty fair job of that, and the aim of this book isn't to merely regurgitate Books Online.

This chapter assumes that you've read what Books Online has to say about replication and that you're familiar with basic replication terms such as distributor, publisher, agent, snapshot, article, and so forth. If you haven't yet read through the coverage of replication in Books Online, now would be a good time to do that.

As with the other topics covered in this book, our mission here is to explore replication from an architectural standpoint and answer the fundamental question, *How does it work?* How does it do what it does? You may have a basic understanding of *what* snapshot replication does, but do you know *how* it does it? That's the subject of this chapter.

Overview

Snapshot replication consists of taking a copy of an object on the publisher and transferring it to a subscriber. The transmittal of the replicated data is an all-or-nothing proposition: Although you can filter a snapshot horizontally as well as vertically to limit the data it captures, there's no support in snapshot replication for propagating incremental changes. You use transactional or merge replication for that.

SQL Server implements snapshot replication via the Snapshot Agent and the Distribution Agent. The Snapshot Agent takes care of creating the data and schema snapshot that will be propagated to subscribers. The Distribution Agent handles taking the snapshot and applying it to subscribers.

The Snapshot Agent

As with all replication agents, the Snapshot Agent is a console mode application that uses ODBC to communicate with SQL Server. The executables for SQL Server's replication agents reside in the 80\COM subfolder under the Microsoft SQL Server folder. When you set up a snapshot publication, SQL Server creates a SQL Server Agent job that runs the Snapshot Agent. You can view this job by opening the appropriate entry under the Agents\Snapshot Agents node in the Replication Monitor on the distributor (or via the Jobs node under Management\SQL Server Agent) in Enterprise Manager. Each snapshot job consists of several steps, one of which is to run snapshot.exe, the executable for the Snapshot Agent. The job step that actually runs the Snapshot Agent is configured as being of type Replication Snapshot, which tells SQL Server Agent to run snapshot.exe when it executes the step.

You can explore the Replication Snapshot job step to see what parameters are passed to snapshot.exe by default. Depending on how you've set up your snapshot publication, the parameters you see should look something like the following:

```
-Publisher [TUK\PHRIP] -PublisherDB [pubs] -Distributor
   [TUK\PHRIP] -Publication [pubs_sales] -DistributorSecurityMode 1
```

Note that you can run snapshot.exe independently of SQL Server Agent. Exercise 21.1 takes you through doing just that.

Exercise 21.1   Running a Replication Agent from the Command Line

1. Start Enterprise Manager from your distributor machine and use the Create Publication wizard to create a snapshot publication if you haven't already done so. When you set up a snapshot publication via the Create Publication wizard, Enterprise Manager calls the sp_addpublication and sp_addpublication_snapshot stored procedures to create it, as shown in Listing 21.1.

Listing 21.1

```
exec sp_addpublication @publication = N'pubs_titles',
    @restricted = N'false', @sync_method = N'native',
    @repl_freq = N'snapshot', @description = N'Snapshot
    publication of pubs database from Publisher TUK\PHRIP.',
    @status = N'inactive', @allow_push = N'true', @allow_pull =
    N'true', @allow_anonymous = N'true', @enabled_for_internet =
    N'false', @independent_agent = N'true', @immediate_sync =
    N'true', @allow_sync_tran = N'false', @autogen_sync_procs =
    N'true', @retention = 336, @allow_queued_tran = N'false',
    @snapshot_in_defaultfolder = N'true', @compress_snapshot =
    N'false', @ftp_port = 21, @allow_dts = N'false',
    @allow_subscription_copy = N'false', @add_to_active_directory =
    N'false'
exec sp_addpublication_snapshot @publication = N'pubs_titles',
    @frequency_type = 8, @frequency_interval = 64,
    @frequency_relative_interval = 0, @frequency_recurrence_factor
    = 1, @frequency_subday = 1, @frequency_subday_interval = 0,
    @active_start_date = 0, @active_end_date = 99991231,
    @active_start_time_of_day = 10600, @active_end_time_of_day = 0
```

2. Open the Snapshot Agent entry corresponding to the publication under the Agents\Snapshot Agents node in Replication Monitor in Enterprise Manager.
3. Double-click the job step named Run Agent.
4. Select the text in the Command window and copy it to the clipboard (Ctrl+C).

5. Close the job step editor and the agent properties dialog in Enterprise Manager.

6. Open a command window on your distributor and change to the 80\COM subfolder under the Microsoft SQL Server folder.

7. Type snapshot followed by a space on the command line, then paste the clipboard contents onto the command line (e.g., Alt+Space, E, P).

8. Hit Enter to run the agent from the command line. You should see output like that shown in Listing 21.2.

Listing 21.2

```
Microsoft SQL Server Snapshot Agent 8.00.194
Copyright (c) 2000 Microsoft Corporation

Generating schema script for article 'titles'
Bulk copying snapshot data for article 'titles'
Bulk copied snapshot data for article 'titles' (18 rows).
Inserted schema command for article 'titles' into the
distribution database
Inserted index creation command for article 'titles' into the
distribution database.
Inserted bcp command for article 'titles' into the distribution
database.
A snapshot of 1 article(s) was generated.

The process finished. Use CTRL+C to close this window.
```

9. The snapshot has been generated from the command line just as it normally is from SQL Server Agent. This is a handy thing to do when you're having trouble getting a snapshot to generate properly. You can run it from the command line to see its output appear in a console window rather than having to view system tables in the distribution database.

10. Note that you can direct the agent's output to a text file via the -Output filename parameter. Simply add -Output followed by the name of the output file you want to create to the agent command line and restart it to try this out. If the file you specify already exists, it will be appended to; if it does not exist, it will be created.

The Snapshot Agent creates files containing the data and schema for a publication's articles under the snapshot folder. By default, this folder is located under the ReplData folder under the root folder of your distributor's SQL Server installation but can be changed via the Publication Properties dialog in Enterprise Manager. Each publication gets its own snapshot folder. This folder name is composed of the name of the server, instance, and database from which the publication is publishing data as well as the name of the publication itself. Under each publication snapshot folder, there are two subfolders: unc and FTP. The unc path is the container for UNC path-based publication snapshots. The FTP subfolder is the container for FTP-based publication snapshots. Unless you explicitly enable a publication to be distributed over FTP, you should find its snapshots in a subfolder under the unc path.

Each generated snapshot gets its own subfolder under either unc or FTP. The name of this subfolder consists of the current date and time when the snapshot was generated. This subfolder contains the actual snapshot files themselves.

If you configure a publication to generate its snapshot in an alternate location (via the Publication Properties dialog) and you do not disable the generation in the normal snapshot folder, the snapshot will actually be written to both folders. If you enable the publication to be distributed via FTP, you can specify the relative path that an FTP client will use to access the files.

The snapshot files themselves are a mix of BCP data and Transact-SQL scripts. The data is saved in BCP format and has a file extension of .bcp. If you configured the publication for distribution only to other SQL Servers and did not allow it to be transformed via DTS, this file is written in BCP's native format (because this is generally faster); otherwise, character format is used. The other files (e.g., .sch, .dri, .trg, .idx, and so on) contain the Transact-SQL necessary to create each article's object, its declarative referential integrity, its triggers, and its indexes, as appropriate.

Besides storing the data for a table, the BCP files created by the Snapshot Agent also store the data returned by view objects. Just as you can use the BCP utility to write the results of a query against a view to a file, the Snapshot Agent will create a snapshot of the data returned by a view as though the view contained the data itself.

When the Snapshot Agent runs, it determines whether any new subscriptions have been added since the last time it ran. If no new subscriptions have been created, the agent doesn't need to create new scripts or data files. However, if a publication was created with the option to generate its snapshot immediately, the Snapshot Agent will create a new snapshot for it each time the agent runs.

Note that the Snapshot Agent is used to generate snapshots not only for snapshot replication but also for transactional and merge replication. Regardless of the type of replication, an initial snapshot is needed in order to seed a subscriber with data.

Once a snapshot has been generated for a publication, either the Distribution Agent (for snapshot and transactional replication) or the Merge Agent (for merge replication) picks it up and distributes it to subscribers. You can also take the files from the snapshot folder and transfer them to the subscriber manually. This is often done when setting up a remote subscriber for the first time that has a low-bandwidth connection to the distributor. By putting the initial snapshot on, say, a CD, you allow the site to be set up more quickly than if it had to wait on the snapshot to be transferred over a slow WAN link.

Duties of the Snapshot and Distribution Agents

As I've mentioned, the work of snapshot replication is divided between the Snapshot Agent and the Distribution Agent. In this next section, we'll cover the work each of these carries out separately.

Snapshot Agent Tasks

The Snapshot Agent begins by connecting from the distributor to the publisher and setting a share lock on each of the tables included in a publication's articles. These locks help guarantee a consistent view of the data by preventing changes to the data until they are released. Naturally, this means that you'd normally want to run the Snapshot Agent during times when not being able to change the data in published articles isn't a problem for your users.

As it works, the Snapshot Agent keeps a record of what it's doing in the MSsnapshot_history table. If you list the MSsnapshot_history table, you'll see log records similar to those we saw when we ran the agent from the command prompt. You can adjust the verbosity of the agent via its OutputVerboseLevel parameter. This affects the level of detail written to MSsnapshot_history (and to the console if you are running the agent from the command line). MSsnapshot_history is a good place to start if you run into problems with a snapshot and want to narrow down where the problem is occurring. You can access the information in MSsnapshot_history by simply querying the table, or from Enterprise Manager by selecting the publication under the Replication Monitor node, then double-clicking its Snapshot Agent (every snapshot publication will have its own Snapshot Agent) and selecting Session Details from the Snapshot Agent History dialog. Listing 21.3 shows an example of what you might find in the MSsnapshot_history table.

Listing 21.3

(Abridged)

```
runs start_time             dur comments
---- ----------------------- --- ----------------------------
1    2003-03-25 15:39:57.977 0   Starting agent.
1    2003-03-25 15:39:59.870 0   Initializing
3    2003-03-25 15:39:59.870 1   Connecting to Publisher 'TUK
3    2003-03-25 15:39:59.870 3   Generating schema script for
3    2003-03-25 15:39:59.870 4   Locking published tables whi
3    2003-03-25 15:39:59.870 4   Bulk copying snapshot data f
3    2003-03-25 15:39:59.870 5   Bulk copied snapshot data fo
3    2003-03-25 15:39:59.870 6   Posting snapshot commands in
2    2003-03-25 15:39:59.870 7   A snapshot of 1 article(s) w
```

After locking the objects it intends to take a snapshot of, the agent next connects over the network from the publisher to the distributor (if they are on separate machines) and saves the schema for each article in the publication to its own file in the snapshot folder on the distributor (the location of the snapshot folder can be changed, as I mentioned earlier). Each schema file will have the extension .sch and will contain the T-SQL statements necessary to create an article's object. If you opted to include indexes, triggers, or referential integrity when you added an article to the publication (clustered indexes are included by default in the Create Publication wizard), the Snapshot Agent will save the T-SQL commands necessary to create these objects in a separate file for each article, each with its own file extension.

The Snapshot Agent next writes the data itself to the snapshot folder. As I said earlier, each data file is written in BCP format (either native or character mode, depending on whether the publication allows heterogeneous subscribers and whether it is being transformed via DTS) and has the extension .bcp. The data and schema files represent a synchronization set—files that record the state of an object as it existed at a given point in time—for each article in the publication.

The agent next adds rows to the distribution database's MSrepl_commands table indicating the location of the synchronization set and specifying any pre- or postapplication scripts.

When you set up a snapshot publication, you can specify custom T-SQL scripts to run before and/or after the snapshot is applied at a subscriber. When you specify one of these scripts, the Snapshot Agent copies it to the

Table 21.1 The Structure of the MSrepl_commands Table

Name	Type
publisher_database_id	int
xact_seqno	varbinary(16)
type	int
article_id	int
originator_id	int
command_id	int
partial_command	bit
command	varbinary(1024)

snapshot folder so that the Distribution Agent can run it when applying the snapshot and adds a row to MSrepl_commands for it.

MSrepl_commands plays a key role in both snapshot and transactional replication. It has the structure shown in Table 21.1.

You can use the sp_browsereplcmds stored procedure to list MSrepl_commands. It forms a dynamic T-SQL query based on the parameters you give it and calls an undocumented stored procedure, xp_printstatements, to run the query (via a loop-back connection) and return the table in a human-readable format.

A more efficient way to list the snapshot-related commands in MSrepl_commands is simply to query it with T-SQL yourself, casting the command column in the process. (Note that this doesn't always work for other types of replication commands, such as transactional- or merge-related commands—use sp_browsereplcmds when in doubt). Although command is defined as a varbinary(1024), you can cast it to an nvarchar(512) to return many commands in a human-readable format without need of either sp_browsereplcmds or xp_printstatements. Listing 21.4 presents an example.

Listing 21.4

```
USE distribution
GO
SELECT
publisher_database_id,
xact_seqno,
```

```
type,
article_id,
originator_id,
command_id,
partial_command,
CAST(command AS nvarchar(512)) AS command
FROM msrepl_commands
```

(Results abridged)

```
pub xact_seqno       type         art orig comm part command
--- --------------   -----------  --- ---- ---- ---- ----------------
1   0x000000070000  -2147483598  1   0    1    0    \\TUK\C$\Program
1   0x000000070000  -2147483597  1   0    2    0
1   0x000000070000  -2147483641  0   0    3    0    \\TUK\C$\Program
1   0x000000070000  -2147483646  1   0    4    0    \\TUK\C$\Program
1   0x000000070000  -2147483646  1   0    5    0    \\TUK\C$\Program
1   0x000000070000  -2147483645  1   0    6    0    sync -t"titles"
1   0x000000070000  -2147483596  1   0    7    0
```

You'll typically see multiple rows in MSrepl_commands for each snapshot. Note that each snapshot in MSrepl_commands gets its own xact_seqno value, so you can use this value to distinguish the commands for one snapshot from those of another.

The Snapshot Agent also adds rows to the MSrepl_transactions table. These entries reference the subscriber synchronization task.

Once it has completed generating the snapshot and updating the appropriate replication system tables, the Snapshot Agent releases the share locks it took out earlier and adds its final log entries to the MSsnapshot_history table.

You can view generated snapshots from Enterprise Manager by right-clicking a snapshot publication in the Replication\Publications folder and selecting Explore the Latest Snapshot Folder from the menu. Enterprise Manager will open the latest snapshot folder for the publication in Windows Explorer so that you can browse the files it contains. This would be useful, for example, if you intended to copy the files to another medium, such as a CD, for transfer to a subscriber.

Distribution Agent Tasks

The Distribution Agent handles the task of moving the schema and data files from a snapshot to a subscriber. It begins this task by connecting from the server where it is running to the distributor. For push subscriptions, the Distribution Agent usually runs on the distributor; for pull subscriptions, it usually runs on the subscriber.

The agent next reads MSrepl_commands and MSrepl_transactions to retrieve the location of the synchronization sets it will transfer and the subscriber synchronization commands. The rows it reads from these tables were added earlier by the Snapshot Agent.

Finally, the Distribution Agent applies the snapshot to the subscriber by creating the necessary objects and loading the data contained in each synchronization set in the snapshot. It handles data type conversions as necessary for non–SQL Server and down-level subscribers. It synchronizes all the articles in the publication and preserves the transactional and referential integrity of the affected objects in the subscription database, provided that the subscriber has the capability to do so.

The Distribution Agent can apply a snapshot when a subscription is first created or based on a schedule you define when you create a publication. If you set up a snapshot to be applied on a schedule, keep in mind that the schedule is based on the system time on the machine on which the Distribution Agent is running. If it's running on the distributor, the schedule will be based on the system time of the distributor machine. If it's running on a subscriber (e.g., as it would be with a pull subscription), the schedule is based on the system time of the subscriber machine.

Updatable Subscriptions

By default, data replicated via snapshot replication is not updatable at the subscriber—that is, you can't make changes at the subscriber and have them propagate to the publisher or to other subscribers. However, you can *enable* a snapshot publication such that it is updatable at the subscriber. You have three options for doing so: immediate updating subscribers, queued updating subscribers, and immediate updating subscribers with queued updating as a fallback.

Immediate Updating

Immediate updating subscribers work by initiating a distributed transaction with the publisher using Microsoft Distributed Transaction Coordinator. The update is carried out using the two-phase commit (2PC) protocol—either the change occurs on both the subscriber and the publisher or it occurs on neither of them.

Of course, this option requires that the publisher be available to the subscriber when the change needs to be made. The 2PC to the publisher occurs automatically (via a trigger on the replicated table), so the subscriber makes changes to the table without making any special provision for the fact that a distributed transaction is actually being initiated behind the scenes.

When you publish a table via snapshot replication and allow it to be updated, SQL Server adds a uniqueidentifier column to it named msrepl_tran_version. This column is used in the filter criteria for subsequent updates and deletes. Because this column is added to the table (and you won't normally be inserting values into it), inserts on the publisher or subscriber must include a column list.

SQL Server restricts the tables you can publish via snapshot replication and update on the subscriber to those that already have at least one unique key. Although you can publish a table via snapshot replication that does not have a primary key, it cannot be a part of a publication that allows the subscriber to update it.

On the subscriber, updatable tables received via snapshot replication have three triggers automatically created for them, one each for insert, update, and delete operations. Each of these triggers requires that it be the first trigger to execute for its specified operation. They enforce this through use of the undocumented TriggerInsertOrder, TriggerUpdateOrder, and Trigger-DeleteOrder OBJECTPROPERTY strings. I'm not sure why they don't use the documented ExecIsFirstInsertTrigger, ExecIsFirstUpdateTrigger, and ExecIsFirstDeleteTrigger properties instead, but these undocumented properties appear to work similarly.

Once each trigger has ensured that it is executing in the proper sequence, it calls a stored procedure to carry out the update on the publisher. It passes this procedure the values for each column in the table and a bitmap indicating which ones were actually changed. (It derives this bitmap from the COLUMNS_UPDATED function.) If multiple rows are being changed by the DML operation that fired the trigger, it opens a cursor on the appropriate deleted and/or inserted table and calls the stored procedure once for each row being altered.

This stored procedure uses the table's primary key and the GUID stored in the uniqueidentifier column to ensure that it updates the correct row. It also makes use of the supplied bitmap to determine which column(s) to change. To keep things simple, it assigns a column's value back to itself if the column was not changed by the original DML operation on the subscriber. Unfortunately, this will cause other triggers on the table that use the

COLUMNS_UPDATED or IF UPDATE syntax to think that each column in the table has changed regardless of whether it actually has.

The data modification is sent to the publisher using SQL Server's normal linked server facility and invokes the Microsoft Distributed Transaction Coordinator as necessary. If the change succeeds on the publisher, the trigger allows the change to proceed on the subscriber; otherwise it is rolled back.

Subscriber applications need to allow for the possibility that an update may fail on the publisher. This could be due to several reasons including a possible conflict with updates from other subscribers or the publisher itself. Often, the correct course of action is simply to wait a few seconds and retry the update.

Once an update is successfully applied to the publisher, other subscribers receive it at the time of the next snapshot refresh. Because it requires only that the updating subscriber and the publisher participate in the transaction, this approach is less resource-intensive than the typical distributed transaction approach wherein all recipients of the data must participate in the same distributed transaction.

Queued Updating

A publication enabled for queued updating works much the same as one enabled for immediate updating—triggers on the subscriber enable changes to be propagated to the publisher, which then propagates them to the other subscribers. The difference, of course, is that these changes are stored in a queue until they can be sent to the publisher. By default, this queue is a SQL Server table creatively named MSreplication_queue, but the queue can also be implemented via Microsoft Message Queuing (MSMQ). You can change a publication initially set up to use MSreplication_ queue to use MSMQ via the Updatable tab in the Publication Properties dialog in Enterprise Manager.

When a subscriber changes a snapshot replication table enabled for queued updates, a trigger fires and adds an entry to the queue signaling the update. If the queue is MSreplication_queue, this amounts to a row being added to the table for each row changed in the replicated table. If the queue is implemented using MSMQ, the updates will be stored in a queue on the distributor. If the distributor is unreachable, MSMQ will queue the updates on the subscriber until it can reach the distributor.

The Queue Reader Agent reads the queue and applies the stored changes to the publisher. If MSreplication_queue is being used, the agent reads the queued changes directly from the table. If MSMQ is being used, the agent reads the changes from the queue on the distributor.

If conflicts are detected, they're resolved according to the conflict resolution policy established when the publication was first created. Consequently, compensating commands may be generated to roll back a transaction to a subscriber, but they will be sent only to the originating subscriber, not to all subscribers of the publication.

Immediate Updating with Queued Updating as Failover

Contrary to what you might infer from the loquacious name, configuring a publication to allow immediate updating on the subscriber with queued updating as a failover *does not* cause queued updating to be enabled automatically when immediate updating fails (e.g., because the subscriber cannot connect to the publisher). You must enable the failover manually, and, once you do, you cannot switch back to immediate updating mode until the subscriber and publisher can communicate and the Queue Reader Agent has applied all queued updates.

Queued updating is not automatically enabled with this option because there may be easy resolutions to communications difficulties between a subscriber and the publisher. It may be preferable to resolve those issues rather than to have updates automatically begin queuing to a table or MSMQ store.

Remote Agent Activation

I've mentioned that the Distribution Agent can be run on a server other than the default if you choose. You can do this via remote agent activation. Running the Distribution Agent remotely amounts to either running it on the subscriber for push subscriptions or running it on the distributor for pull subscriptions. Normally, the Distribution Agent runs on the distributor for push subscriptions and on the subscriber for pull subscriptions. You can change its default location when you set up a subscription. This is something to consider when you want to offload some of the work of the distributor to subscribers when processing push subscriptions, especially large numbers of them. Given that the agent runs on the subscriber by default with pull subscriptions, this isn't an issue unless you have push subscriptions. If so, you may want to configure the agent to run on subscriber machines in order to lessen the load on the distributor.

Remote agent activation uses DCOM to run an agent on another machine. You must have DCOM permissions properly configured in order to use remote agent activation. Failing to do so could cause the synchronization between the distributor and a subscriber to fail. Note that you can't use remote agent activation with Win9x subscribers.

Replication Cleanup

One of the tasks you have to provide for in an environment intended for long-term use is cleanup. An architecture that does not perform system cleanup and handle as much of its own system maintenance as possible can present administration headaches down the road. When replication is first enabled, SQL Server creates five canned SQL Server Agent jobs to help keep replication humming along and to aid it in cleaning up after itself. Table 21.2 summarizes these jobs.

Each of these maintenance tasks helps replication continue to run well over the long-term and reduces the administrative burden on those managing the replication installation. For example, the distribution cleanup job deletes the files associated with a snapshot once the snapshot has been applied to all subscribers. Of course, if a snapshot publication supports anonymous subscribers or was defined with the option to create the first snapshot immediately, at least one copy of the snapshot files must be retained.

Table 21.2 Replication Maintenance Jobs

Job	Purpose
Agent history cleanup	Ages and clears out replication agent history from the distribution database
Distribution cleanup	Clears replicated transactions from the distribution database
Expired subscription cleanup	Detects and deletes expired subscriptions from published databases
Reinitialize subscriptions having data validation failures	Reinitializes all subscriptions that experienced data validation failures
Replication agents checkup	Detects replication agents that have "gone silent" (that are not actively logging history)

Recap

Snapshot replication is used for copying whole objects from a publisher to a subscriber. Although a snapshot can be filtered, snapshot replication has no facility for sending incremental changes to subscribers.

SQL Server implements snapshot replication via the Snapshot and Distribution Agents. The Snapshot Agent handles creating the snapshot, which consists of BCP data files and T-SQL scripts. The Distribution Agent takes the snapshot and applies it to subscribers. All along the way, both agents access and update replication system tables in the distribution database.

Knowledge Measure

1. In what format does the Snapshot Agent save data from tables published as articles in a snapshot publication?
2. True or false: Although similar to SQL Server Agent, the Snapshot Agent is installed as its own Windows service when you enable replication and does not make use of SQL Server Agent.
3. What agent is responsible for delivering the snapshots created by the Snapshot Agent to subscribers?
4. When a view object is included in a snapshot publication, does the Snapshot Agent write out the data returned by the view or only its schema?
5. What system stored procedure can be used to list the MSrepl_ commands table?
6. True or false: Although a replication agent can be executed as a console application, it does not actually carry out any work when run from the command line.
7. Name one of the five tasks that SQL Server sets up when replication is first enabled in order to help the system maintain itself.
8. Identify two scenarios in which the Snapshot Agent will automatically write data files in BCP character mode format rather than native format.
9. True or false: Though it is possible to update tables on a subscriber that have been received as part of a snapshot publication, there is no supported way to propagate these changes to the publisher so that they can be sent to other subscribers.

10. The command column in the MSrepl_commands table is stored as a varbinary(1024). What must one do in order to translate snapshot-related commands in this column into human-readable text?

11. What type of column is added to snapshot replication tables that are part of publications enabled for immediate updating?

12. What is the name of the table in which the Snapshot Agent records its progress as it creates a snapshot?

13. Define the term *synchronization set*.

14. What's the creative name of the table used for queuing updates when SQL Server provides the store for queued updates?

15. True or false: The Snapshot Agent is also used in transactional replication to create an initial snapshot of data that is published for transactional replication.

16. What agent command line parameter can you specify to change the verbosity level of the Snapshot Agent?

17. When MSMQ provides the queue for queued updates, where does the queue reside?

18. True or false: Every snapshot publication gets its own instance of the Snapshot Agent.

19. True or false: When a snapshot publication is configured to be distributed on a schedule, the date and time at which the snapshot is applied is always based on the system time of the distributor machine, never that of a subscriber.

20. True or false: Triggers are used to initiate 2PC operations when the immediate updating option is used with a snapshot publication.

CHAPTER 22

Transactional Replication

> *Whenever someone tells me that adopting their beliefs*
> *could give me the same type of life they have, I tell them*
> *that that's exactly what I'm afraid of.*
>
> —H. W. Kenton

Transactional replication is by far the most widely used form of SQL Server replication. It combines a good deal of functionality with reasonably simple configuration and administration. It's more full-featured than snapshot replication but much easier to set up and manage than merge replication.

One mistake I often see people make when deciding which type of replication to go with is not realizing that both snapshot replication and transactional replication offer immediate and queued updating subscriptions. People somehow get the idea that merge replication is the only replication type that supports bidirectional data replication. That's not the case, as should have been obvious from our discussion in the last chapter regarding updating subscribers and snapshot replication. Transactional replication offers the same updatability that snapshot replication provides. Additionally, it offers a publication model that is practical to use in situations where you need to regularly apply incremental updates from a publisher to subscribers.

Overview

SQL Server implements transactional replication via the Snapshot Agent, the Log Reader Agent, and the Distribution Agent. As with snapshot replication, the Snapshot Agent prepares the initial snapshot of a transactional publication. The Log Reader Agent scans the transaction log on the publisher and detects the changes made to the data after the snapshot has been taken and records them in the distribution database. (With concurrent snapshot processing, the Log Reader Agent can actually log changes made during the snapshot generation, as we'll discuss below.) The Distribution Agent reads the changes recorded in the distribution database and applies them to subscribers.

The MSrepl_commands Table

Each modification to a published table causes the Log Reader Agent to write at least one row to MSrepl_commands. Unlike snapshot replication, you can't simply cast the command column in MSrepl_commands as an nvarchar(512) and return human-readable text for transactional replication commands, so you'll want to use sp_browsereplcmds instead.

Understand that, just as a single T-SQL command may cause multiple entries to be written to the transaction log, so can a single T-SQL command cause the Log Reader Agent to write multiple entries to MSrepl_commands. If you have, say, a T-SQL UPDATE statement that affects 10,000 rows, you'll get at least 10,000 entries in MSrepl_commands. The same is true for DELETE commands—if a single T-SQL DELETE command deletes 10,000 rows, the Log Reader Agent will add at least 10,000 rows to MSrepl_commands. For each row in a transactional publication table article that's modified by a T-SQL command, you'll see at least one entry in MSrepl_commands.

Each modification to a uniquely constrained column in a transactional publication table article will result in at least *two* rows being written to MSrepl_commands for each changed row: a DELETE command or stored procedure call, followed by an INSERT command or stored procedure call. As far as transactional replication is concerned, a uniquely constrained column is any column that is part of a unique index key or clustered index key, even if the clustered index is not a unique clustered index. (SQL Server adds a special "uniqueifier" to nonunique clustered index keys in order to make them unique so they can be used as row locators in nonclustered indexes.) An update to an indexed view or to a table on which an indexed view is based will also cause at least two rows to be written to MSrepl_commands for each modified row.

Because of this, a single DML statement against a table that has been published with transactional replication may cause significant log activity not only in the original database but also in the distribution database and in the destination database on subscribers. For this reason, transactional replication probably isn't your best choice when you want to replicate the entirety of a database and all the activity on it to another machine. You'd likely be better off using something like log shipping in that scenario.

NOTE: You can configure log shipping and replication to work together. Specifically, you can configure transactional replication such that it interoperates with log shipping to provide a warm standby server if the publisher fails.

You have two options for integrating log shipping and transactional replication: synchronous mode and semisynchronous mode. To enable synchronous mode, you set the sync with backup option on the publishing database via the sp_replicationdboption stored procedure. Once in synchronous mode, the Log Reader Agent will ignore change records in the transaction log until they have been backed up. This ensures that no subscriber can get ahead of the distributor. This way, if the publisher fails, we can be certain that no subscriber will have data not on the standby server. Naturally, this increases the latency between the time a change is made on the publisher and the time is propagated to subscribers from what is usually a few seconds to what might be several minutes.

To enable semisynchronous mode you simply set up log shipping as you normally would and allow transactional replication to behave as it does by default. In this mode, it is possible for the standby server and subscribers to be out of sync, but the latency between changes on the publisher and their propagation to subscribers is not tied to the log shipping interval, usually somewhere between two and ten minutes.

The sp_replcmds Procedure

The Log Reader Agent uses the extended procedure sp_replcmds (implemented internally by SQL Server) to retrieve the log records produced by DML statements in the published database's transaction log. Each publisher database participating in transactional replication will have just one Log Reader Agent regardless of how many transactional publications it contains.

The first client that calls sp_replcmds for a database is considered the log reader for that database until it disconnects. Other clients attempting to run sp_replcmds before the first client disconnects will receive an error stating that "Another log reader is replicating the database."

One reason that only one Log Reader Agent is permitted for each database is that scanning the log for changes can impact performance. Each time the Log Reader Agent invokes sp_replcmds, it causes log reader code within the SQL Server process to scan the published database's transaction log for changes that need to be replicated. When it does this, the Log Reader Agent changes the typical sequential method SQL Server uses to access the log into something more random. While the server is writing new entries to the end of the transaction log as changes are made to the database, the Log Reader Agent may be reading a different section of the log in order to write replication commands to MSrepl_commands and MSrepl_transactions. This can cause resource contention for the transaction log and impact the performance of the server as a whole.

The Article Cache

SQL Server maintains a global cache of article metadata known as the article cache. This cache stores metadata from sysarticles and syscolumns for each replicated article. When the log reader code within the server needs the metadata for a particular article, it consults this cache. If the article is already in the cache, the log reader code retrieves the required information from the cache. If the article isn't in the cache, it accesses sysarticles and syscolumns directly and retrieves the information it needs, then adds that information to the cache.

You can check for the existence of the article cache via the undocumented DBCC RESOURCE command. See my previous books, *The Guru's Guide to Transact-SQL* and *The Guru's Guide to SQL Server Stored Procedures, XML, and HTML* for more information on DBCC RESOURCE. This command will return the address within the server process of the article cache. To see this for yourself, run the following from Query Analyzer:

```
DBCC TRACEON(3604) -- route the output to the client
DBCC RESOURCE
DBCC TRACEOFF(3604)
```

Once DBCC RESOURCE returns, search its output for the string article_cache. This member of the global resource structure contains the address of the replication article cache.

The article_cache member of the global resource structure contains a pointer to a linked list of replicated database objects. A member in each list item indicates which SRV_PROC structure is the current log reader for the corresponding database. When a connection calls sp_replcmds, the server assigns its SRV_PROC pointer to the appropriate item in the database object list (provided another connection has not already done so). As long as this SRV_PROC pointer is nonzero, another connection cannot successfully run sp_replcmds for that particular database. When the connection currently assigned as a database's log reader disconnects, an ODS predisconnect handler resets the SRV_PROC pointer in the appropriate database object so that another connection can then assume the log reader role.

sp_replcmds Parameters

The @maxtrans parameter specifies the number of transactions about which sp_replcmds should return information. You can adjust the value the Log Reader Agent passes in for @maxtrans by creating a custom agent profile. To do that, follow these steps.

1. Start Enterprise Manager and expand the Replication Monitor node on your replication distributor.
2. Expand the Agents node and click Log Reader Agents.
3. Find your Log Reader Agent in the list on the right and double-click it.
4. Click the Agent Profile button, then click New Profile.
5. Give the new profile a name, then change its ReadBatchSize to the value you'd like passed in for @maxtrans. Setting this value to 1 is a common troubleshooting step. (If unspecified, @maxtrans actually defaults to 1.)
6. Back in the Agent Profile dialog, click the radio button next to your new profile in order to select it, then click OK.

Note that although Books Online documents just one parameter for sp_replcmds, the procedure actually supports several parameters. If you capture a Profiler trace while the Log Reader Agent is running, you'll find that besides the documented @maxtrans parameter, two additional integer parameters are regularly passed in. In my cursory tests, their values appear never to change (they're always 0 and -1), but it's worth noting that there's more here than meets the eye.

Another point worth mentioning is that the parameters you see in Profiler differ from those shown in the Log Reader Agent's output. To see this for yourself, create a transactional replication publication and enable an output file for the Log Reader Agent. (Specify the -Output filename command line parameter to set up an agent output file, as we discussed in Chapter 21.) You should see output file entries like this for the calls to sp_replcmds:

```
Publisher: {call sp_replcmds (500, 0)}
```

The same call yields the following in Profiler:

```
RPC:Starting  exec sp_replcmds 500, 0, -1
```

This, of course, begs the question as to what the -1 sent in for the third parameter indicates. In my testing, the value of this parameter varies based on the release of SQL Server installed. For releases prior to SQL Server 2000 Service Pack 1, the parameter is not passed, so we might infer, given that the actual value of the parameter doesn't appear to change, that the -1 parameter indicates the release of SQL Server is at least SQL Server 2000 Service Pack 1. Regardless of whether Profiler indicates that the parameter is passed, it is recorded as 0 in the agent output if it is logged at all.

Other parameters can be passed to sp_replcmds depending on the circumstances. These aren't important to our use of transactional replication since we don't call sp_replcmds directly.

The sp_repldone Procedure

Once the Log Reader Agent finishes calling sp_replcmds and writing new entries to MSrepl_commands and MSrepl_transactions, it calls sp_repldone to indicate that the specified log records have been successfully replicated (to the distributor). This allows SQL Server to purge the log records as necessary. (Log records for transactional replication articles cannot be purged until the articles are successfully replicated to the distributor.)

Note that you shouldn't execute sp_repldone manually. Doing so can invalidate the order and consistency of replicated transactions. If you run into an emergency situation where your transaction log is overflowing because replicated transactions refuse to be purged (and you're certain they've been sent to the distributor), calling sp_repldone manually might be an appropriate step, but you should do so only when instructed to by Microsoft or a Microsoft support partner. Instead, let the Log Reader Agent decide when to execute sp_repldone. I mention it here so that you'll know why you may occasionally see it in Log Reader Agent output and Profiler traces.

Update Stored Procedures

The format of the actual commands the Log Reader Agent places in MSrepl_ commands varies based on how a particular article is set up. You can customize the way that DML commands are passed to subscribers for each table article in a publication. To do this, click the ellipsis button next to the table article in the Articles tab of the Publication Properties dialog. Select the Commands tab in the Table Article Properties dialog to configure the format of the commands sent to the subscriber. You have four options.

1. You can clear the Replace… checkboxes in order to cause the Log Reader to write plain INSERT, UPDATE, or DELETE statements to MSrepl_commands. If you are publishing for SQL Server subscribers only, it's better and more efficient to use stored procedures to carry out these operations, so SQL Server gives you three options for doing so.

2. If your publication is limited to SQL Server subscribers, you'll notice that the checkboxes to use stored procedures instead of INSERT, UPDATE, and DELETE commands are checked by default. You have three options for specifying how the Distribution Agent will call these procedures on the subscriber: CALL, MCALL, and XCALL syntax. Each calling convention provides a slightly different mechanism for calling a DML stored procedure and affords flexibility to those designing replication topologies. By default, the insert and delete procedures are called using CALL syntax, and the update procedure is invoked using MCALL syntax. For an insert, the CALL syntax specifies that the procedure accepts values for each of the table's columns as parameters. For a delete, CALL specifies that the procedure accepts values for the table's primary key column(s) as parameters. For an update, MCALL specifies that the procedure must accept new values for all the article's columns, followed by the original values of its primary key column(s).

3. As I've mentioned, an update procedure for a SQL Server–only publication is called using MCALL syntax by default. MCALL syntax specifies that an update procedure will be passed the updated values for all the columns in an article, followed by the original values of the primary key column(s) and a bitmap indicating which columns have actually changed. By indicating which columns have changed, SQL Server allows the stored proc to avoid writing unchanged values to a database and needlessly generating log records, running constraint code, and firing triggers.

4. The last option for calling these routines is to use XCALL syntax. XCALL syntax specifies that an update procedure will be passed the original value of every column in the article followed by the new value for every column in it. Having the original column values allows you to more easily implement optimistic concurrency controls that detect changes to an article on the subscriber by other users.

NOTE: One thing to watch out for here is malformed procedure names in the stored proc calls generated by the Log Reader Agent. As of this writing, allowing the Log Reader Agent to generate CALL, MCALL, or XCALL syntax for a table article whose name contains a space produces malformed commands in MSrepl_commands. This is because the names of the update procedures are based on the name of the table article, and the Log Reader Agent doesn't properly wrap the procedure name in either quotes or square brackets, so syntax like this gets into MSrepl_commands:

```
{CALL sp_MSupd_Order Details (NULL,NULL,NULL,24,NULL,10248,
    11,0x08)}
```

Note the space between sp_MSupd_Order and Details. The proper syntax is:

```
{CALL [sp_MSupd_Order Details] (NULL,NULL,NULL,48,NULL,10248,
    11,0x08)}
```

You can work around this by placing square brackets or quotes around the stored proc names in the Table Article Properties dialog when you specify the calling convention to use.

Regardless of whether you use CALL, MCALL, or XCALL syntax, the Distribution Agent sends the appropriate stored proc calls to each subscriber as an RPC event. The MCALL and XCALL conventions are really just variations on the ODBC CALL syntax, which allows you to invoke stored procedures using SQL Server's RPC facility. (You'll recall that we discussed RPC in Chapter 6.) MCALL and XCALL just specify what types of parameters to pass into a DML procedure; they both ultimately result in the procedure being invoked using ODBC's RPC CALL syntax.

Concurrent Snapshot Processing

By default, SQL Server places shared locks on the table articles in a transactional publication while the initial snapshot is being created. This ensures transactional consistency for the snapshot but prevents updates from being made to the tables while the snapshot is being generated.

Transactional replication offers an option to work around this limitation known as concurrent snapshot processing. Note that the option is available only when a publication is limited to SQL Server 7.0 and later subscribers. When concurrent snapshot processing is enabled for a transactional publication, the Snapshot Agent will place a shared lock on the table articles in the publication as it always does. It will then add an entry to the transaction log indicating that a transactional snapshot was started and release the shared locks on the table articles. At this point, snapshot generation continues, and changes can be made to the published tables. Normally, the shared locks taken out during concurrent snapshot processing are very brief in duration, usually not lasting more than a few seconds.

Once the snapshot generation completes, the Snapshot Agent writes a second record to the transaction log indicating that it has finished. The Log Reader Agent then reads the transactions from the log that occurred between the time the snapshot was started and when it was completed and writes the appropriate commands to the distribution database to reconcile the generated snapshot with the present state of the table.

Naturally, this requires the Log Reader Agent to participate in completing the snapshot process since it handles collecting the changes that occur during the snapshot generation and writing them to the distribution database. In order for the snapshot to be consistent from a transactional standpoint, the Log Reader Agent must detect the changes that occurred between the start of the snapshot generation and its conclusion and write them to the distribution database. In fact, if the Log Reader Agent is unable to run, the Distribution Agent will be unable to apply the snapshot to subscribers and will return an error indicating that the snapshot is not available.

When the Distribution Agent applies a concurrent snapshot to a subscriber, it applies not only the initial snapshot files generated by the Snapshot Agent but also the commands the Log Reader Agent wrote to the distribution database in order to reconcile the snapshot. While the Distribution Agent does this, it locks the tables contained in the publication on the subscriber in order to ensure that they are transactionally consistent once the snapshot has been applied. This reconciliation process is not unlike the recovery process that a database goes through when SQL Server first starts.

Note that you can't use UPDATETEXT on a column in a table for which a concurrent snapshot is being generated. If you attempt to do so, you'll receive a 7137 error, "UPDATETEXT is not allowed because the column is being processed by a concurrent snapshot. . . ." Once the snapshot completes, you can again execute UPDATETEXT statements against the column.

Because a concurrent snapshot consists of a series of BCP files followed by INSERT and DELETE statements, the subscription database may be in an inconsistent state while the snapshot is being applied. If you've defined constraints on the subscriber tables being updated by the snapshot, these may erroneously indicate integrity or business rule violations while the snapshot is being applied. Although the concurrent snapshot is applied as a single transaction (which keeps users from seeing the data in an inconsistent state), your business logic code may still detect bogus rule violations. To keep this from happening, set the NOT FOR REPLICATION option for all constraints and identity columns on the subscriber that may be impacted by the application of a concurrent snapshot. Note that you don't need to set the NOT FOR REPLICATION option for foreign key constraints, check constraints, and triggers because these are disabled during the application of a concurrent snapshot and will be reenabled afterward.

You should expect performance to be impacted somewhat on the publisher during the generation of a concurrent snapshot. Even though updates to published tables are allowed, the overhead of the snapshot generation itself, coupled with the overhead of the Log Reader Agent reading changes from the transaction log and writing them to the distributor, can have a noticeable effect on performance, especially if the publisher and distributor are on the same machine. As with regular snapshots, you should schedule concurrent snapshots to run during periods of low system activity (e.g., at night or during off-hours).

Note that replication can fail if you enable concurrent snapshot processing for a publication containing a table with a primary key or unique constraint not contained in the clustered index and modifications to the clustering key occur during snapshot processing. To prevent this, don't enable concurrent snapshot processing on publications containing a table with a primary key or unique constraint not contained in its clustered index unless you can ensure that the clustered index columns will not be modified during snapshot processing.

When publishing to subscribers running on SQL Server 7.0, the distributor must be running on SQL Server 2000 or later, and using concurrent snapshots requires using push subscriptions to push the data out to them. Using a push subscription causes the Distribution Agent to run at the distributor, whereas a pull subscription would cause it to run at the SQL Server 7.0 subscriber where concurrent snapshot processing is not available.

Due to the many restrictions and caveats associated with concurrent snapshot processing, it's not enabled by default. However, you can edit the properties for a transactional publication after it has been created and enable it via the Snapshot tab of the Publication Properties dialog.

Updatable Subscriptions

By default, data replicated via transactional replication is not updatable at the subscriber—that is, you can't make changes at the subscriber and have them propagate to the publisher or to other subscribers. However, you can *enable* a transactional publication such that it is updatable at the subscriber. You have three options for doing so: immediate updating subscribers, queued updating subscribers, and immediate updating subscribers with queued updating as a fallback.

Immediate Updating

Immediate updating subscribers work by initiating a distributed transaction with the publisher using Microsoft Distributed Transaction Coordinator. The update is carried out using the two-phase commit (2PC) protocol—either the change occurs on both the subscriber and the publisher or it occurs on neither of them.

Of course, this option requires the publisher to be available to the subscriber when the change needs to be made. The 2PC to the publisher occurs automatically (via a trigger on the replicated table), so the subscriber makes changes to the table without making any special provision for the fact that a distributed transaction is actually being initiated behind the scenes.

When you publish a table via transactional replication and allow it to be updated, SQL Server adds a uniqueidentifier column to it named msrepl_tran_version. This column is used in subsequent updates and deletes to locate the correct row(s) to change. Because this column is added to the table (and you won't normally be inserting values into it), inserts on the publisher or subscriber must include a column list.

On the subscriber, updatable tables received via transactional replication have three triggers automatically created for them, one each for insert, update, and delete operations. Each of these triggers requires that it be the first trigger to execute for its specified operation. They enforce this through use of the undocumented TriggerInsertOrder, TriggerUpdateOrder, and TriggerDeleteOrder OBJECTPROPERTY strings. I'm not sure why they don't use the documented ExecIsFirstInsertTrigger, ExecIsFirstUpdateTrigger, and ExecIsFirstDeleteTrigger properties instead, but these undocumented properties appear to work similarly.

Once each trigger has ensured that it is executing in the proper sequence, it calls a stored procedure to carry out the update on the publisher. It passes this procedure the values for each column in the table and a bitmap indicating which ones were actually changed. (It derives this bitmap from the COLUMNS_UPDATED function.) If multiple rows are being changed by the DML operation that fired the trigger, it opens a cursor on the appropriate deleted and/or inserted table and calls the stored procedure once for each row being altered.

This stored procedure uses the table's primary key and the GUID stored in the uniqueidentifier column to ensure that it updates the correct row. It also makes use of the supplied bitmap to determine which column(s) to change. To keep things simple, it assigns a column's value back to itself if the column was not changed by the original DML operation on the subscriber. Unfortunately, this will cause other triggers on the table that use the COLUMNS_UPDATED or IF UPDATE syntax to think that each column in the table has changed regardless of whether it actually has.

The data modification is sent to the publisher using SQL Server's normal linked server facility and invokes the Microsoft Distributed Transaction Coordinator as necessary. If the change succeeds on the publisher, the trigger allows the change to proceed on the subscriber; otherwise, it is rolled back.

Subscriber applications need to allow for the possibility that an update may fail on the publisher. This could be due to several reasons including a possible conflict with updates from other subscribers or the publisher itself. Often, the correct course of action is simply to wait a few seconds and retry the update.

Once an update is successfully applied to the publisher, other subscribers receive it at the time of the next snapshot refresh. Because it requires only that the updating subscriber and the publisher participate in the transaction, this approach is less resource-intensive than the typical distributed transaction approach wherein all recipients of the data must participate in the same distributed transaction.

Queued Updating

A publication enabled for queued updating works much the same as one enabled for immediate updating—triggers on the subscriber enable changes to be propagated to the publisher, which then propagates them to the other subscribers. The difference, of course, is that these changes are stored in a queue until they can be sent to the publisher. By default, this queue is a SQL Server table creatively named MSreplication_queue, but the queue can also be implemented via Microsoft Message Queuing (MSMQ). You can change a publication initially set up to use MSreplication_queue to use MSMQ via the Updatable tab in the Publication Properties dialog in Enterprise Manager.

When a subscriber changes a transactional replication table enabled for queued updates, a trigger fires and adds an entry to the queue signaling the update. If the queue is MSreplication_queue, this amounts to a row being added to the table for each row changed in the replicated table. If the queue is implemented using MSMQ, the updates will be stored in a queue on the distributor. If the distributor is unreachable, MSMQ will queue the updates on the subscriber until it can reach the distributor.

The Queue Reader Agent reads the queue and applies the stored changes to the publisher. If MSreplication_queue is being used, the agent reads the queued changes directly from the table. If MSMQ is being used, the agent reads the changes from the queue on the distributor.

If conflicts are detected, they're resolved according to the conflict resolution policy established when the publication was first created. Consequently, compensating commands may be generated to roll back a transaction to a subscriber, but they will be sent only to the originating subscriber, not to all subscribers of the publication.

Immediate Updating with Queued Updating as Failover

Contrary to what you might infer from the loquacious name, configuring a publication to allow immediate updating on the subscriber with queued updating as a failover *does not* cause queued updating to be enabled automatically when immediate updating fails (e.g., because the subscriber cannot connect to the publisher). You must enable the failover manually, and, once you do, you cannot switch back to immediate updating mode until the subscriber and publisher can communicate and the Queue Reader Agent has applied all queued updates.

Queued updating is not automatically enabled with this option because there may be easy resolutions to communications difficulties between a subscriber and the publisher. It may be preferable to resolve those issues rather than to have updates automatically begin queuing to a table or MSMQ store.

Validating Replicated Data

As with snapshot and merge replication, SQL Server can validate data replicated via a transactional replication publication. You can choose to verify merely that the publication tables on the subscriber and the publisher have the same number of rows, or you can verify checksums or binary checksums of the data in the tables. When you use checksum validation, the server compares a 32-bit cyclic redundancy check (CRC) for each table article on the publisher and subscriber. Because this CRC is computed on a column-by-column basis, the precise column order for an article can vary between the publisher and subscriber without affecting the comparison. Data from text and image columns is not included in the comparison.

To validate replicated data, follow these steps.

1. Expand the Publishers node under the Replication Monitor in Enterprise Manager at the distributor and select the publisher of the publication you want to validate.
2. In the list of publications on the right, find the publication you want to validate and right-click it. Select Validate Subscriptions.
3. In the Validate Subscriptions dialog, select the subscriptions you want to validate. (The subscription list may be empty if you have only anonymous pull subscriptions—select Validate all subscriptions if that's the case.)
4. Click the Validate Options button to specify the type of validation to do. You can choose to compute a "fast" row count (based on cached information) or to retrieve an actual row count for each table via a T-SQL query. You can opt to compare checksums or, if both the publisher and subscriber are running SQL Server 2000 or later, binary checksums.
5. Click OK once you've chosen your validation options, then click OK in the Validate Subscriptions dialog to validate your data.

This results in the sp_article_validation stored procedure being called on the publisher. Then sp_article_validation calls sp_replpostcmd to post a call to sp_table_validation into the distribution database. This call includes the row count and/or checksum values from the publisher table so that they can be compared with those on the subscribers. The Distribution Agent then picks up the call to sp_table_validation and runs it on the subscriber. If the validation fails, sp_table_validation raises errors via the T-SQL RAISERROR command, causing them to be logged in the MSdistribution_history and MSrepl_errors tables in the distribution database.

To see this firsthand, let's work though a simple exercise to force a data validation failure.

Exercise 22.1   Validating a Transactional Publication

1. Create a transaction publication for the Northwind Customers table. Enable anonymous subscriptions for it and accept the defaults for the rest of the settings.
2. Create an anonymous subscription for your new publication. Set its target database to be the pubs database.

3. Check for the Northwind Customers table to be replicated to your pubs database. Once it's there, proceed to step 4.

4. Update one of the columns in the Customers table in pubs such that it differs from the publisher's version of the table.

5. Connect to the distributor from Enterprise Manager. In the Replication Monitor node in the Enterprise Manager tree, expand the Publishers subnode, find your publisher, and click it.

6. Right-click the publication in the list on the right and select Validate Subscriptions.

7. Leave the Validate all subscriptions radio button selected and click the Validation Options button.

8. Click the Compare checksums to verify row data option and the This subscriber is a server running SQL Server 2000, use a binary checksum option, then click OK.

9. Click OK to begin the data validation process.

10. After the Distribution Agent next runs, double-click it in the Agents\Distribution Agents list under Replication Monitor on the distributor to display its agent history. Click the Session Details button to list details for the sessions listed in the agent history.

11. You should see an entry indicating that data validation may have failed for the table article in question. You can click the Error Details button to view additional information about the failure. Click Close to exit the Session Details dialog, then click Close again to exit the Distribution Agent History dialog.

12. You can also view the errors directly from the tables in the distribution database. To do this, execute the following queries from Query Analyzer:

```
SELECT * FROM distribution..MSdistribution_history
SELECT * FROM distribution..MSrepl_errors
```

where distribution is the name of your distribution database. You should see entries in both tables indicating potential data validation problems.

You can configure replication alerts to notify you when a data validation fails, and you can also reinitialize the affected subscription(s) automatically. To set up either one of these, follow the steps below.

1. Click the Replication Alerts node under the Replication Monitor on the distributor.

2. Right-click the Subscriber has failed validation entry in the list on the right and select Properties.

3. In the General tab in the Properties dialog, click the Enabled checkbox to enable the alert. You can configure specific operators on the Response tab.
4. If you want to automatically reinitialize a subscription that has failed validation, click the Execute job checkbox on the Response tab and select the Reinitialize subscriptions having data validation failures job in the drop-down box to the right of it.
5. Click OK to save the alert.

Note that immediate updating subscribers can cause data validation to fail between the time a change is made on the subscriber and the time it is propagated to the publisher. Naturally, during the period of time the two copies of the published article do not match, a data validation will fail. The only sure way to avoid this is not to make changes on the subscriber during the validation process.

Note that checksum validations are not supported with publications where DTS is used to transform the data because transformation implies different data values at the publisher and subscriber, so the checksum values would not likely match.

Also, row count validation is not supported for articles configured as DTS horizontal partitions because the filter criteria for the partition is saved with the DTS package; it's not in a view on the publisher as is the case with regular replication filters.

You also can't validate subscriptions published to heterogeneous subscribers for obvious reasons—the SQL Server stored procedures used to carry out the validation will not likely exist on these subscribers.

Skipping Errors

You can skip errors in transactional replication via the -SkipErrors command line parameter available with the Distribution Agent and the Log Reader Agent. Normally, when these agents are running in continuous mode and encounter an error, the distribution process is aborted. You can use this parameter to specify a colon-delimited list of error numbers that you do not want to interfere with replication. When the agent encounters one of the errors in your list, it will simply log the error in MSrepl_errors and continue running. For an example of how this functionality can be put to good use, see the "Continue on data consistency errors" profile for the Distribution Agent.

Cleanup

One of the stock SQL Server Agent jobs added when replication is installed is the Distribution clean up task. Once all subscribers have received replicated transactions, the sp_MSdistribution_cleanup stored procedure is called to remove delivered transactions from the distribution database. The amount of time delivered transactions remain in the distribution database is known as the retention period and defaults to 72 hours for transactional replication. You can change the retention period for a distributor by following these steps.

1. Right-click the Replication node in Enterprise Manager on the distributor and select Configure Publishing, Subscribers, and Distribution from the menu.
2. On the Distributor tab, select the distribution database and click the Properties button.
3. You can set the minimum and maximum retention in hours or days via the dialog's Transaction retention section.

If you coordinate the retention period you specify with the backup interval of your subscriber destination databases, you can ensure that the data required to recover a subscriber destination database is available within the distribution database. This can make recovering a failed subscriber database fairly trivial because the subscriber can simply reload its last backup, then synchronize with the publisher and be brought immediately up to date.

Recap

Transactional replication strikes a nice balance between enhanced functionality and straightforward administration. It provides more flexible and full-featured replication options than snapshot replication affords but is much easier to set up and manage than merge replication.

Architecturally, transactional replication is implemented by three agents—the Snapshot Agent, the Log Reader Agent, and the Distribution Agent—as well as by code implemented internally by SQL Server. The Snapshot Agent creates the initial snapshot for a transactional publication, just as it does with snapshot publications. The Log Reader Agent then reads changes made to the publication's database and writes change information for published articles to the MSrepl_commands and MSrepl_transactions tables in the distribution database. The Distribution Agent then picks up these changes and applies them at subscribers.

Knowledge Measure

1. True or false: Of the three replication types, merge replication is the only type that allows subscribers to update replicated data.
2. What extended stored procedure, implemented internally by SQL Server, does the Log Reader Agent call in order to retrieve changes from the transaction log for a published database?
3. What's the default retention period for transactional replication?
4. True or false: Although the Snapshot Agent places shared locks on table articles when it begins creating the snapshot for a transactional publication, the publication can be configured to allow changes to these objects while the snapshot is being created.
5. What table in the distribution database is used to store replication commands the Distribution Agent is to carry out on subscribers?
6. What table in the distribution database stores replication-related error information?
7. What table in the distribution database stores history information for the Distribution Agent?
8. Is it possible to configure a replication alert such that subscriptions that fail validation can be automatically reinitialized?
9. What stored procedure is called on the subscriber to validate a table article?
10. Define *retention period*.
11. What stored procedure must one call in order to set the sync with backup option for a database?
12. Is it possible for multiple Log Reader Agents to execute concurrently for the same published database?
13. What internal extended procedure can the Log Reader Agent call to indicate that it has completed processing a set of change records from the transaction log?
14. One of the three calling conventions you can use to call update procedures used with transactional replication is the CALL syntax. Name the other two and explain how they differ.
15. What does the @maxtrans parameter for sp_replcmds specify?

16. True or false: Log shipping and transactional replication are mutually exclusive—because they both read the transaction log of a published database, you cannot use them together.

17. True or false: In order for an immediate updating transactional replication subscriber to fail over to queued mode, you must manually enable the failover.

18. Is it possible for a SQL Server 7.0 subscriber to initiate a pull subscription for a concurrent snapshot?

19. Assume that I issue a T-SQL UPDATE statement against a published table article that changes 100 of its rows. At a minimum, what number of new entries should I see in MSrepl_commands on the distributor?

20. What's the simplest way to change the retention period for a distributor?

CHAPTER 23

Merge Replication

I've never liked the word "tolerate." Saying you tolerate someone else's culture or beliefs is like saying you put up with the guy who keeps a messy yard because the government says you have to, but you'd gladly evict him if the opportunity presented itself. We shouldn't just tolerate other cultures—we should celebrate them. Inasmuch as we want our own culture to be respected and well thought of, we should respect and enjoy the cultures of other people.

—H. W. Kenton

Although both transactional replication and snapshot replication support the notion of bidirectional data updates, they do not offer as much power and flexibility as merge replication offers. While they both support subscriber-side updates as well as queued updating, they were not designed from the ground up for these tasks—they are essentially data transfer mechanisms that also provide a nice set of data update functionality. Snapshot and transactional replication were not designed to be used in environments where subscribers are frequently disconnected or where subscribers update data as much as or more than the publisher. They also cannot publish data directly to SQL Server CE subscribers. That said, merge replication is much more difficult to set up and manage, does not guarantee transactional consistency, and may not perform as well as transactional replication in simple bidirectional scenarios. It is also the relative new kid on the block, having first appeared in SQL Server 7.0.

As I said in Chapter 21, I'm not going to try to cover every single idiosyncrasy of merge replication or how to administer it in this chapter. This chapter is about *how merge replication works*. Books Online provides good coverage of the many nuances and details of how to set up and manage merge replication, just as it does the other types of replication.

Overview

SQL Server implements merge replication via the Snapshot Agent and the Merge Agent. As with snapshot and transactional replication, the Snapshot Agent is responsible for creating the initial snapshot of the data that will be distributed by the publisher. Once it creates the initial snapshot, the Snapshot Agent creates synchronization jobs on the publisher and builds replication-specific system tables, stored procedures, and triggers. Subscriber-side system objects are created when the snapshot is first applied to the subscriber.

Note that a merge subscription table can subscribe to only one publication at a time. If you attempt to subscribe from a single subscriber table to an article in two different publications, one of the Merge Agents will fail when the initial snapshot is applied.

The Distribution Agent is not used in merge replication. The functions normally performed by the Distribution Agent in snapshot and transactional replication are handled by the Merge Agent in merge replication. The distribution database is also not used much in merge replication. Its main function is to support agent logging and history—no data is stored in it for forwarding to and from subscribers. Each publisher/subscriber database maintains its own store-and-forward tables. Because the role of the distributor is so limited with merge replication, it's not unusual for the distributor to reside on the same server as the publisher.

The Merge Agent is responsible for taking the initial snapshot and applying it to subscribers. Once the snapshot is applied, the Merge Agent is responsible for collecting the incremental changes made after the snapshot was taken, applying them to subscribers, and uploading changes made at subscribers to the publisher. This process is known as synchronization. For push subscriptions, the Merge Agent runs on the distributor. For pull subscriptions, it runs on the subscriber. As with the Distribution Agent used for snapshot and transactional replication, you can change the machine on which the Merge Agent runs via remote agent activation.

As with the other replication agents, the Merge Agent is an ODBC console application. Normally it runs via SQL Server Agent, but you can also run it from the command line. Its executable file is replmerge.exe. If you check its thread count in Perfmon or attach a debugger and dump its thread stacks, you'll see that it's a multithreaded application.

The Merge Agent applies changes to a publisher or subscriber by calling the stored procedures generated by the Snapshot Agent. There are separate stored procedures for inserting, updating, and deleting rows. Typically, these procedures are named sp_upd_*GUID*, sp_ins_*GUID*, and sp_del_*GUID*, where *GUID* is the uniqueidentifier article ID (from the artid column in sysmergearticles) for the corresponding article. These are invoked via RPC.

The Merge Agent is able to detect changed data on the publisher and subscribers because special triggers record data changes to published tables in merge system tables on the publisher or subscriber as they occur. Each time a row is inserted or updated, the change is recorded in MSmerge_contents. Each time a row is deleted, a trigger records it in MSmerge_tombstone. Together, these tables serve the same purpose in merge replication that the MSrepl_commands table serves in snapshot and transactional replication. You can use the rowguid column in each of them to join back to the original publishing table. By examining these tables, along with the MSmerge_genhistory and MSmerge_info tables, the Merge Agent is able to determine which rows to send to the other party in the synchronization operation.

When you publish a table as an article in a merge publication it must have a uniqueidentifier column that has been flagged with the ROWGUIDCOL property and that has a unique index on it. If such a column does not exist, one named rowguidcol will be added automatically and a unique index will be built for it. This column stores a GUID value. A GUID is guaranteed to be unique among all the networked computers in the world. This allows a particular row to be identified uniquely across multiple publisher and subscriber machines.

It's worth mentioning here that the publisher and subscribers in a merge replication scenario are pretty much equal partners. Unlike snapshot and transactional replication, where the publisher is clearly preeminent, because merge replication is designed for bidirectional replication, most of the key system tables that exist on the publisher also exist on subscribers. For example, a merge subscriber logs changes to published articles in its own MSmerge_contents and MSmerge_tombstone tables just as the publisher does. It has an MSmerge_genhistory table that is structured identically to the one on the publisher. It tracks sent and received generations in its own MSmerge_replinfo table exactly as the publisher does. The one exception to this symmetry is the set of conflict tables. Every published article has its own conflict table. When a conflict is resolved, the details of the resolution are logged in the conflict table. Since conflict resolution always occurs from the vantage point of the publisher, only the publisher maintains conflict tables. Other than this, the system tables and processes for transmitting changed data are virtually the same on the subscriber as on the publisher in a merge replication implementation.

Conflict Resolution

Merge replication provides an elaborate and extensible conflict resolution system. To begin with, you can specify what actually constitutes a conflict—a change made to the same article row by two different parties in the merge replication scenario, or a change made to the same article column in the same row by two different parties. If you employ column-based conflict detection, two parties in the replication scenario can change different columns in the same row without causing a conflict. If you employ row-based conflict detection, changes made by two different parties to the same row cause a conflict that must be resolved.

Merge replication detects conflicts by inspecting rowguidcol values, generations, lineage values, and, in the case of column-based detection, the colvl column in the MSmerge_contents table. We'll talk more about rowguidcol and generation values in just a moment; let's talk about the role of the lineage and colvl columns now. The lineage column exists in both the MSmerge_contents and MSmerge_tombstone tables and is a varbinary(249). A lineage value provides a history of changes to a row and consists of publisher and subscriber nickname/version number pairs that have been involved in previous changes to the row. The colvl column tracks similar information for individual columns and is a varbinary(2048). It's used when column-based conflict detection is employed.

The system provides a default conflict resolver (the publisher wins all conflicts with a subscriber; higher-priority subscribers win conflicts with lower-priority subscribers) as well as several others you can use depending on your business needs. For example, you can stipulate that the first or last publisher/subscriber to make a change wins. You can specify that the minimum or maximum of two conflicting values wins. You can also create your own conflict resolvers either as COM objects or as stored procedures. You can list the currently installed resolvers using the sp_enumcustomresolvers stored procedure.

When a publisher and subscriber are synchronized, the changes made on the subscriber are uploaded to the publisher first, then the changes on the publisher are downloaded to the subscriber. This allows for early conflict detection since conflict resolution always occurs from the vantage point of the publisher and the default conflict resolver stipulates that the publisher wins all conflicts.

During the synchronization process, deletes are processed first, followed by inserts and updates. This means that changes recorded in the subscriber's MSmerge_tombstone table are uploaded to the publisher when the synchronization process first begins. After deletes are uploaded, inserts and updates are then applied. As I said above, these are logged in MSmerge_contents on the publisher and subscribers.

Each time a publisher is synchronized with one of its subscribers, it effectively takes ownership of the changes made by the subscriber to the published data. If the subscriber made changes that did not conflict with those on the publisher (or if a conflict resolver is being used that allows the subscriber to win), the changes are applied to the publisher. When the publisher then synchronizes with other subscribers, these changes are applied to the subscribers provided there are no conflicts. If there are conflicts, they are resolved, and changes are made to the publisher or subscriber accordingly.

If a publisher synchronizes with a lower-priority subscriber and receives a change from it that is later reversed when the publisher synchronizes with a higher-priority subscriber, the data on the lower-priority subscriber will differ from both the publisher and the higher-priority subscriber until the Merge Agent runs to synchronize it again. This means that it's entirely possible for different versions of the same row to exist at different places in a replication scenario temporarily, even after all subscribers have been synchronized once. Eventually, all parties will end up with the same data, but it may take multiple synchronizations for that to occur.

Generations

Each row tracked in MSmerge_contents and MSmerge_tombstone is assigned a generation number. A generation is a simple integer column that functions as a sort of logical clock that enables the Merge Agent to determine when a change was made to a row and how the time of that change relates to changes to the same row made by other parties in the replication scenario. An integer rather than a datetime value is used because it avoids having any sort of dependency on synchronized clocks between sites and is more resilient to common intersite issues such as time zone differences.

Only one row is maintained in MSmerge_contents for each row inserted or updated in a table. Each time a row is updated, its generation number is updated in MSmerge_contents with the current generation number as specified in MSmerge_genhistory. Each time the Merge Agent synchronizes the article with the publisher/subscriber, it updates the MSmerge_replinfo table to indicate the last generation that was sent and received (via calls to the sp_MSsetlastsentgen and sp_MSsetlastrecgen procedures, respectively), then calls sp_MSupdategenhistory to update MSmerge_genhistory to the next generation number for each article for which it retrieves changes.

A generation permits the changes against different articles to be organized into separate batches or groups. This might lead you to believe that generation numbers are unique to each article in a publication and serve as a sort of secondary key to the article ID, but that's not the case. Generation numbers are not reused across articles; they are global (across the MSmerge_genhistory table) in scope. When the system needs a new generation number for an article that does not yet have a generation number in MSmerge_genhistory (for example, when the first row is inserted into the table), it simply takes the maximum generation number in MSmerge_genhistory and adds 1 to it. Two articles in the same publication will not share a generation number or use the same generation number. Each article has its own current generation number, which is maintained in MSmerge_ genhistory. This allows for flexibly applying changes to the other party in a merge synchronization and allows the changes to different articles to be tracked separately.

The current generation number for a published database is incremented by Merge Agent runs. Until the Merge Agent runs, changes made to a particular article use the current generation number for that article when they're recorded in MSmerge_comments and MSmerge_tombstone.

To understand how merge generations work, let's walk through an example. Let's say that TableA and TableB are published in two separate merge publications and that they are the only two tables published from a given database. A couple of rows in TableA are updated, and these rows are recorded in MSmerge_contents with the current (maximum) generation for TableA found in MSmerge_genhistory, which is 2. The Merge Agent then runs, retrieves the updated rows from MSmerge_contents, and updates MSmerge_genhistory's maximum generation number for TableA to 4 because 3 is the maximum generation value used by any article in the table. Later, a row in TableB is updated. It records its modified rows in MSmerge_contents using the current generation for TableB, which is generation 3. The Merge Agent runs again, picks up the new modifications, and updates MSmerge_genhistory to use generation number 5 for TableB because 4 is the maximum generation value on file in the table. At this point, the current generation for TableA is 4 and the current generation for TableB is 5. If we then update another row in TableA, that change will be recorded in MS-merge_contents using generation 4. When the Merge Agent runs and retrieves the changes made to TableA, it will set the current generation value for TableA to 6 because 5 is the highest generation value currently on file. So changes to TableA can be found under generations 2, 4, and 6; changes to TableB will be found under generations 3 and 5. Each time the Merge Agent sets the current value for a given article, it also sets the high-water mark for the next generation number that must be produced, regardless of the article.

In certain circumstances, the generation number for a row can be set to 0, independent of the generation number for its article recorded in MS-merge_genhistory. One example is when a row is updated at a publisher but deleted at a subscriber. Assuming the default conflict resolution strategy (where the publisher always wins), the update on the publisher will conflict with the delete on the subscriber, forcing the delete on the subscriber to have to be reversed. What happens in that scenario is that the row is reinserted at the subscriber, and an entry is made in the subscriber's MSmerge_contents table for that row, with a generation of 0. The row in the subscriber's MS-merge_tombstone table is deleted, and the subscriber behaves as though the deletion never occurred. The conflict is logged in the publisher's MSmerge_delete_conflicts table with a reason_text value along the lines of, "The same row was updated at 'TUK\PHRIP.Northwind' and deleted at 'TUK\PHRIP.testrepl'. The resolver chose the update as the winner."

Filtering

As with other types of replication, you can filter merge replication vertically as well as horizontally. Horizontal (or row) filters are implemented via an SQL WHERE clause and limit the rows a publication includes based on user-specified criteria. Vertical (or column) filters limit the columns that a publication includes.

When you define a column filter, a view is created that includes only the requested columns. This view will have a name of the form *publication_article*_VIEW and will reside in the publication database. The object ID of this view, rather than that of the base object, will be stored in the sysmergearticles sync_objid column and will be queried for new rows by the Merge Agent.

On the subscriber side of the equation, the sync_objid column in sys-mergearticles will contain the ID of the base object. The filtering effect is accomplished by the custom stored procedures (generated by the Snapshot Agent), which exclude columns that were not included in the filter.

When you create a row filter, a similar process occurs. A view is created in the publication database with a name of the form *publication_article_VIEW*. It selects rows from the associated table article that match the filter expression (WHERE clause criteria) you specified when you defined the filter. Here's what a typical vertical filter view looks like:

```
create view [Northwind_Huck_Photech_VIEW] as
select  [Huck_Photech].*  from [dbo].[ Huck_Photech] [Huck_Photech]
where ( (id>1) )
and ({ fn ISPALUSER('256ABC83-6C4D-49AF-8456-766443672303') } = 1)
```

In this case, the filter is based on the id column in the table, so a WHERE clause is generated that restricts the rows returned to those matching a particular set of id values (bolded). Additionally, the view invokes the ISPALUSER function (using ODBC escape syntax) to ensure that the user accessing the view is on the publication access list for the publication. (The GUID passed into ISPALUSER corresponds to the pubid value for the publication stored in sysmergearticles.)

As with a vertical filter view, the object ID for a horizontal filter view is stored in the sync_objid column in the sysmergearticles table. On the subscriber, the object ID of the table article itself is used.

If the subscriber inserts a row that violates a horizontal filter, the Merge Agent will delete it the next time the subscriber synchronizes with the publisher. It will place the deleted row in the MSmerge_tombstone table on the subscriber and will set MSmerge_tombstone.reason to "System delete."

Optimizing Synchronization

SQL Server supports a special optimization for publications with horizontal filters that allows the publisher to keep track of which rows go into and out of a filter partition on a published table. If you have a horizontally filtered publication where the filter column or columns are frequently changed, you may want to enable this optimization (available via the Optimize Synchronization option in the Create Publication Wizard) because it can drastically reduce the amount of data sent to subscribers. Consider the situation where you horizontally filter a table based on the ZipCode column. When the zip code is changed for a particular row in the table, the partition the table corresponds to changes as well. By default, the Merge Agent has no way to know which partition the newly changed row once belonged in, so it doesn't know which subscribers to send the updated row to. It must therefore send the update to all of them, wasting bandwidth and network resources along the way. By enabling the Optimize Synchronization option, you provide the Merge Agent a means of determining the previous values for the filter columns. This allows it to determine which subscriber(s) need the updated row.

Keep in mind that this requires extra storage on the publisher. The exact amount of additional space will vary based on the size of the filter columns. If the filter columns are 50 bytes in size and you have 100,000 rows, you'll need 5MB of additional space to use the Optimize Synchronization option. Given the tremendous bandwidth savings this can provide, this is usually a good trade-off.

Dynamic Filters

A dynamic filter is a special type of horizontal filter that uses a nondeterministic T-SQL function such as HOST_NAME or SUSER_SNAME as part of its filter criteria. The dynamic filter can contain a direct reference to the nondeterministic function, or it can contain a reference to a user-defined function that either contains a reference to a nondeterministic function or accepts one as a parameter. The idea is that the filter criteria should return different rows based on the subscriber that's connecting.

When you create a publication containing a dynamic filter, you have the option of having the system validate that the value of the nondeterministic function(s) you're using to restrict the rows sent to a subscriber doesn't change between synchronizations. This helps ensure that data is partitioned consistently with each synchronization. For example, if you used the HOST_NAME function to set up a dynamic filter and a subscriber machine's computer name changed at some point after rows had been delivered to the subscriber by the Merge Agent, the subscription would need to be reinitialized because the rows currently on the subscriber would fall outside the dynamic filter. Due to the existence of the filter, it would be impossible for the Merge Agent to update those same rows with changes from the publisher.

Join Filters

A join filter allows a row filter to be extended from one published table to another. After supplying a horizontal filter for one table in the publication, you can extend the filter to another table in the publication by setting up a join filter (basically consisting of a T-SQL JOIN clause) that relates the first table to the second one. This will cause the second table to be filtered by the join condition you've set up—only rows that match the join condition will be supplied to subscribers.

You can relate multiple tables in this fashion, essentially filtering all the tables based on the horizontal filter criteria for the first table combined with the join conditions you specify for the other tables. The relationships you establish between these tables are enforced during synchronization and allow you to set up complex relationships between published articles.

Dynamic Snapshots

By default, when you set up a dynamic filter, the Merge Agent applies the initial snapshot to the subscriber one row at a time in order to make sure that each row matches the filter criteria (the filter criteria aren't resolved until synchronization). Naturally, this can take awhile with large amounts of data. You can greatly speed up the application of the initial snapshot by creating a dynamic snapshot. A dynamic snapshot allows you to prepare a set of BCP data files that are filtered in advance by values for SUSER_SNAME and HOST_NAME that you specify. In other words, if you have a subscriber whose Merge Agent will be connecting as a given user in order to synchronize a dynamically filtered publication, you can create the snapshot for this particular subscriber in advance and store it in its own folder. Then, when the subscriber's Merge Agent connects to synchronize with the publisher, it can insert data at normal bulk copy speed rather than inserting rows one at a time.

To create and apply a dynamic snapshot, follow these steps.

1. Create a dynamically filtered publication and generate its default snapshot.
2. Create a dynamic snapshot job via the Create Dynamic Snapshot Job wizard. (You can access this wizard by right-clicking a publication under the Databases\YourDatabase\Publications node in Enterprise Manager.)
3. Create a pull subscription and specify the snapshot location that you supplied to the Create Dynamic Snapshot Job wizard. Check the checkbox indicating that this is a dynamic snapshot.

Keep in mind that dynamic snapshot jobs cannot be administered via Replication Monitor. Although all replication jobs are managed by SQL Server Agent, most of them can also be administered by Replication Monitor. Dynamic snapshot jobs are an exception. Instead, you'll want to use Management\SQL Server Agent\Jobs to manage dynamic snapshot jobs.

Identity Range Management

One of the common problems you often face with typical replication scenarios is managing identity ranges on the publisher and subscriber effectively. If multiple parties can insert new rows, how do we keep their identity values from colliding?

There are several solutions to this problem. One that I've used in the past is to set up odd-even/negative-positive identity values. For example, say that you have a simple implementation with a publisher and a single subscriber. You could seed the publisher's identity value at 1 and increment it by 1 with each row insertion, and you could set the subscriber's seed value to –1 (remember, SQL Server's int data type is signed) and increment it by –1 with each new row. Now let's say you have four machines in your implementation—a publisher and three subscribers. Here, you could seed the first machine at 1 and increment it by 2 with each new row (resulting in odd identity values); the second machine could be seeded at 2 and incremented by 2 (resulting in even values); the third machine could be seeded at –1 and incremented by –2 with each new row (resulting in negative odd values); and the fourth machine could be seeded at –2 and incremented by –2 (resulting in negative even values). You can expand this to more machines by breaking up each identity range into smaller pieces. You get the basic idea—you can come up with numerous creative ways to keep identity values from colliding between publishers and subscribers just by using a few tricks with the identity column's seed and increment values.

Another way to manage identity values in replication scenarios is to use the NOT FOR REPLICATION option when you define your identity column and either set up compatible identity ranges on the publisher and subscribers or set identity values programmatically. Normally, when an identity value is inserted directly via an INSERT statement while SET IDENTITY INSERT is enabled, the identity seed is reset. Enabling NOT FOR REPLICATION gives replication agents a waiver in regard to identity reseeding—that is, when a replication agent inserts a value into an identity column that was created with the NOT FOR REPLICATION option, the identity value is not reseeded. This allows replication to do what it must do in order to ship data from place to place within the topology—that is, to insert, update, and delete data—without inhibiting the normal use of identity columns either at the publisher or at subscribers.

If you go the NOT FOR REPLICATION route, you should also create a CHECK constraint on your articles in order to ensure that the identity values on each participant in the replication scenario do not overlap. Because you are assuming the responsibility of managing these values yourself, you must ensure that they're assigned and managed logically and consistently.

Still another option for avoiding problems with identity value collisions in replication scenarios is not to use an identity column at all (or avoid publishing it). If an identity column is not actually needed at the subscriber, you may be able to use a vertical filter to omit it from the publication. If the column is part of the table's primary key, you cannot omit it using a filter, so you may want to look at identifying a different column or columns as your primary key if that's possible and reasonable in your scenario. For example, the rowguidcol added by merge replication makes a decent primary key (although, at 16 bytes of storage, it's a little larger than ideal). Or you may be able to use some other column or combination of columns. The bottom line is that if you can avoid publishing the identity value in the first place, you avoid the possibility of identity value collisions between the publisher and subscribers and can still potentially take advantage of SQL Server's ability to automatically generate identity values on the publisher if you decide to simply filter it out of the publication rather than drop it from the table.

The best way to manage identity values in replication scenarios is to let SQL Server do it for you. For merge publications (where bidirectional modification is assumed) and transactional and snapshot publication with queued updating subscribers enabled, SQL Server can manage identity ranges on the publisher and subscribers. When you add an article to the publication, you can click the ellipsis button on the Specify Articles page of the Create Publication Wizard to display the Table Article Properties dialog. You can then click the Identity Range tab to set up SQL Server's automatic identity range management.

You can set three key values in this dialog. The first is the identity range size at the publisher. The second is the identity range size at subscribers. Both of these default to 100; you can set them to something higher or lower if you wish. The last value is the threshold at which to assign a new range. Via the appropriate replication agent, SQL Server will automatically assign a compatible range of identity values on the publisher and on each subscriber. No party in the replication scenario will start off with overlapping ranges. Then, as rows are inserted into the table at each site and changes are synchronized between the publisher and subscribers, the identity range will be checked to see how full it is. When it reaches the threshold specified in the Table Article Properties dialog, a new range will be created for it, and its identity seed will be set to the start of this new range.

We use a threshold rather than the end value of the range because synchronization may not be scheduled often enough to keep the table from running out of values in the range. Therefore, we try to leave a reasonably sized buffer at the end of the range so that we can create a new range before we run out of values, provided that we synchronize often enough. If you run out of values in a managed identity value range, you'll see a message like this:

```
Server: Msg 548, Level 16, State 2, Line 1
The identity range managed by replication is full and must be
updated by a replication agent. The INSERT conflict occurred in
database 'Northwind', table 'Huck_Photech', column 'id'.
Sp_adjustpublisheridentityrange can be called to get a new
identity range.
The statement has been terminated.
```

As the message says, you can call sp_adjustpublisheridentityrange (or just allow synchronization to occur) to alleviate this problem. Note that you call sp_adjustpublisheridentityrange regardless of whether the problem actually exists on the publisher or on one of the subscribers.

You should be able to adjust the range sizes, threshold, and synchronization schedule to prevent this error from occurring. You can check the details of a managed identity range by inspecting the MSrepl_identity_range table.

Recap

Merge replication is considerably more difficult to set up and manage than transactional or snapshot replication, but it offers several features that they don't offer. It's not necessarily the best choice in every scenario where you need bidirectional data replication (transactional replication is often quite adequate), but merge replication offers more flexibility than snapshot or transactional replication, especially for disconnect users and SQL Server CE subscribers.

The system offers a bevy of mechanisms for detecting and dealing with conflicts. You can control what is considered a conflict in the first place and who wins when a conflict is detected.

Knowledge Measure

1. True or false: You can manage dynamic snapshot jobs from the Replication Monitor in Enterprise Manager.
2. By default, who wins a conflict between a publisher and a high-priority subscriber?
3. True or false: In a typical merge scenario, no more than one synchronization run should be required to synchronize subscriber and publisher data, regardless of the number of subscribers.
4. Why does a dynamic snapshot provide a performance boost for dynamically filtered publications?
5. Describe what is stored in a lineage value.
6. What table does merge replication use to queue deleted rows?
7. In what table does merge replication track the last sent and received generations?
8. True or false: Merge replication is the only type of replication that can publish to heterogeneous subscribers such as Microsoft Access.
9. True or false: Merge replication is the only type of replication that can publish to SQL Server CE subscribers.
10. When applying an update to a subscriber, does the Merge Agent call a stored procedure or invoke the T-SQL UPDATE command?
11. True or false: The Merge Agent is a single-threaded application.
12. What is the name of the uniqueidentifier column that merge replication will automatically add to a table article if it does not already have one?
13. Describe the usage of the colvl column in MSmerge_contents.
14. True or false: The Distribution Agent is responsible for transferring updates from a merge subscriber to the publisher.
15. True or false: In merge replication, a trigger updates the GUID column in a row each time it's changed.
16. What type of filter is the SUSER_SNAME T-SQL function typically used with?
17. Describe the function of the sp_enumcustomresolvers stored procedure.
18. When NOT FOR REPLICATION is *not* specified for an identity column and a connection inserts a value into the column (while SET IDENTITY_INSERT is enabled), what happens to the identity seed?
19. What's the best way to avoid identity value collisions between a publisher and subscribers or between multiple subscribers?
20. In what release of SQL Server did merge replication first appear?

21. Describe the function of a join filter.

22. True or false: During the synchronization process, deletes are processed first, followed by inserts and updates.

23. True or false: During the synchronization process, changes from the publisher are downloaded to the subscribers first, then their changes are uploaded in sequence to the publisher.

24. What role does the distribution database play in merge replication?

25. Is it possible to resolve conflicts by using a stored procedure?

PART IV

Undocumented SQL Server

CHAPTER 24

Finding Undocumented Features

To a great designer, not applying knowledge is tantamount to not having obtained the knowledge in the first place.

—Steve McConnell[1]

I dedicated a chapter in each of my last two SQL Server books to exposing undocumented features in the product. In each book, I provided lists of undocumented stored procedures, extended procedures, functions, trace flags, command syntax, and product features. In keeping with the spirit of this book—which is that how something works is at least as important as putting it to practical use—I'm not going to do that in this book. Instead, I'm going to show you how to find these undocumented features for yourself.

It's my hope that by pointing out these features, particularly those in Transact-SQL—the facility users go through to reach the server—I will encourage these features either to be documented or to be made completely inaccessible to users. It's my belief that SQL Server has an inordinate number of these hidden goodies. It appears to have far more of these types of things than similar products. Perhaps that's because it has so many more features than other similar products; perhaps that's because it relies too much on undocumented functionality.

Many of these undocumented features are robust enough for important parts of the product such as replication or the Index Tuning Wizard to depend on them, so the argument that they aren't suitable for use by end users just doesn't ring true. Some are used to implement fringe features of the product and very well might not be suitable for more general use, so I can understand why they're undocumented. Some trace flags can be downright

---

1. McConnell, Steve. *After the Gold Rush.* Redmond, WA: Microsoft Press, 1999, p. 27.

dangerous if used improperly, for example, so I've always been wary of listing many of them. Generally, I list only those undocumented features I consider to be safe to use or so generally applicable that I feel compelled to mention them.

I think some undocumented features are undocumented simply because they fell through the cracks. There are so many features in SQL Server in general and in Transact-SQL in particular that I wonder if perhaps some of them were inadvertently left out of the product documentation. Take the TriggerInsertOrder, TriggerDeleteOrder, and TriggerUpdateOrder OBJECT-PROPERTY property names, for example. I don't know why they aren't documented. For that matter, I don't know why they exist. Replication triggers use them to ensure that a trigger is the first one executed for a particular type of DML operation. The documented ExecIsFirstInsertTrigger, ExecIsFirstUpdateTrigger, and ExecIsFirstDeleteTrigger property names could be used to return the same information—there's really no need for these undocumented property names in the first place. And, even if there were, what would be the harm in documenting them so long as users understood that, other than the first or last trigger for a particular DML operation, trigger order execution is undocumented and can't be depended on in any fashion?

Regardless of the reason a feature may be undocumented, knowing about it and knowing what it does tells us more about the product. I think that's an especially worthwhile endeavor in a book whose whole purpose is to explore how the product works. Knowing about a product's undocumented features and why they exist gives you better insight into how it is designed. You get a better feel for where its limitations are and how its designers intended it to be used. These are all good things, irrespective of whether you ever actually make use of any undocumented features.

So, all that said, let me repeat the disclaimer from my previous books: Use undocumented features at your own risk. By leaving product features undocumented, a vendor reserves the right to change them at any time. A hot fix release, security patch, service pack, or new product version could change or eliminate undocumented functionality that you or your code has come to depend on. Moreover, an undocumented feature you make use of may not have been tested as thoroughly as the rest of the product (it's unusual for test teams to develop test suites for undocumented features) and may not work reliably in all situations. Many times, using an undocumented feature isn't even the best tool for the job and may even be completely superfluous (e.g., TriggerInsertOrder). The euphoria that comes from discovering an undocumented xproc and putting it to immediate use in production code quickly subsides when it crashes your server with an access violation. And from a product support perspective, assume undocumented means unsupported—you can't expect a vendor to support functionality it has intentionally left out of a product's documented feature set. The bottom line is: It's best not to use undocumented features unless absolutely necessary.

Now that I've got that out of my system, let's proceed with the discussion of how to find undocumented SQL Server features. Finding these is surprisingly easy; you will likely be astonished at just how much hidden functionality is right under your nose.

NOTE: I have it on good authority that Microsoft intends to remove much of the access to undocumented features in the next release of SQL Server. That's probably a good move; however, for now, those features are still there and readily accessible, so we'll explore how to get at them in order to better understand how the product works.

The syscomments Gold Mine

A bountiful source of undocumented features, commands, functions, and syntax can be found in the syscomments system table. The syscomments table is where the source code to every procedural object—every stored procedure, trigger, view, user-defined function, default, and rule object—in a database is stored. Each database has its own copy of this table. I'm especially fond of the syscomments tables in master, msdb, and the replication distribution databases. I've also found undocumented features hiding in replication-generated stored procedures, views, and triggers in publication or subscription databases.

Undocumented DBCC Commands

I've found a gold mine of undocumented commands by snooping around in master..syscomments. For example, to find all the DBCC commands (on a case-insensitive server) called by procedural objects in master, we might run this T-SQL command:

```
SELECT OBJECT_NAME(id),
SUBSTRING(text,PATINDEX('%dbcc%',text),50) as text
FROM master..syscomments
WHERE PATINDEX('%dbcc%',text)<>0
```

Undocumented Trace Flags

To find just the DBCC TRACEON calls (and thereby find references to undocumented trace flags), we might run this query:

```
SELECT OBJECT_NAME(id),
SUBSTRING(text,PATINDEX('%traceon%',text),50) as text
FROM master..syscomments
WHERE PATINDEX('%traceon%',text)<>0
```

Other Undocumented Goodies in syscomments

Some of the procedural objects in master, msdb, and distribution helpfully divulge whether they make use of undocumented features by including the word "undocumented" or the words "DO NOT DOCUMENT" somewhere in their text. I've found these to be especially useful. You can find them by using a query like this:

```
SELECT OBJECT_NAME(id),
SUBSTRING(text,PATINDEX('%document%',text),50) as text
FROM master..syscomments
WHERE PATINDEX('%document%',text)<>0
```

Goodies in sysobjects

The sysobjects system table exists in every database and contains a row for every object in the database. If you have some idea of the name or type of an undocumented object, you can check for its existence in Enterprise Manager's navigation tree and in Query Analyzer's Object Browser. You can also query sysobjects directly to get this information, which is where Enterprise Manager and Query Analyzer ultimately get it. The code below queries sysobjects directly for simplicity's sake.

Undocumented Extended Procedures

Extended procedures must reside in the master database and are usually prefixed with xp_. Here's a sysobjects query that returns the name of the extended procedures registered in the master database:

```
SELECT LEFT(name, 30)
FROM master..sysobjects
WHERE TYPE='X'
```

Note that some of these procedures have prefixes of sp_ rather than the more traditional xp_. Also, some are implemented internally by the server rather than in external DLLs. Extended procedures implemented internally by SQL Server are known as special procedures (spec procs for short). You can list the spec procs registered in master via a query like this:

```
SELECT OBJECT_NAME(c.id)
FROM master..syscomments c JOIN master..sysobjects o ON
    (c.id=o.id)
WHERE o.type='X'
AND c.text NOT LIKE '%.dll%' OR c.text IS NULL
```

The name of the DLL containing a regular xproc will be listed in the xproc's text column in syscomments. Since a spec proc doesn't reside in a DLL, its entry in syscomments will contain something besides a DLL name. The query above lists the xprocs entries in syscomments where this is the case.

Knowing about the existence of an extended procedure is one thing; knowing how to use it is another. Many xprocs are called by regular procedural objects such as stored procedures and user-defined functions. Here's a T-SQL query that will list all the extended procedures whose names begin with xp_ that are called by objects in master:

```
SELECT OBJECT_NAME(id),
SUBSTRING(text,PATINDEX('%xp_%',text),50) as text
FROM master..syscomments
WHERE text LIKE '%xp\_%' ESCAPE '\'
```

(I've used an ESCAPE character here to help eliminate false hits due to the fact that "_" is a wildcard character.)

Undocumented Functions

Another favorite hiding place for undocumented functionality is in undocumented user-defined functions. Some of these are user objects; some are system functions. System functions begin with the prefix fn_ and are owned by the system_function_schema pseudo-user. You can find out which of these exist in a particular database via a simple query against the appropriate sysobjects table. It's rare for other objects besides functions to have names that begin with fn_, so it's usually safe just to search on the name prefix alone. Here's a query that will return all the objects that begin with fn_ from master..sysobjects. Since it's possible to create an undefined function not owned by system_function_schema, I haven't limited the search to a particular owner.

```
SELECT LEFT(name, 30)
FROM master..sysobjects
WHERE LEFT(name, 3) = 'fn_'
```

As with extended procedures, knowing about the existence of a function doesn't imply knowing how to use it. Here's a query that shows all the procedural objects in master that reference objects whose names begin with fn_:

```
SELECT OBJECT_NAME(id), SUBSTRING(text,PATINDEX('%fn_%',text),50)
    as text
FROM master..syscomments
WHERE text LIKE '%fn\_%' ESCAPE '\'
```

Of course, this query (and all the others in this chapter that work similarly) can yield false hits due to extraneous string matches in the text in syscomments. Obviously, you'll have to examine the results you get from these queries and eliminate the false matches they return.

Scripting Undocumented and System Objects

Enterprise Manager disables the Generate SQL Script menu item for objects marked as system objects (those whose system bit has been set via a call to sp_MS_marksystemobject). You can still double-click a system object in Enterprise Manager to display its source, but you can't edit it. The obvious intent here is to prevent people from accidentally modifying important internal objects. The Properties dialog for stored procedures and similar objects is a pain to use, and I rarely subject myself to trying to view or edit the source to procedural objects with it. It's a modal dialog (and, therefore, doesn't have a maximize button), and it's also missing a resize grip in its lower right corner, something every self-respecting resizable form should have. So rather than deal with the inadequacies of Enterprise Manager, I usually prefer to script stored procedures to a file, then use another tool to view or edit them. Unfortunately, Enterprise Manager's attempt to protect me from myself hampers this a bit when dealing with system procedures. If I can't easily generate a script and I don't want to use Enterprise Manager's limited Stored Procedure Properties dialog, how can I quickly view or edit the text of a system stored procedure? Thankfully, Query Analyzer doesn't have the same concern for my well-being that Enterprise Manager does. Its Object Browser allows me to generate a script for any unencrypted object on my server, including system objects. So, when I need to view or edit procedural objects—especially system objects—using a capable editor, I use Query Analyzer.

Of course, another way to list the source for a system procedural object is to use the sp_helptext procedure. You can use sp_helptext to return the source for any unencrypted procedural object in a database.

The Profiler Treasure Trove

An excellent way to learn about undocumented feature use in SQL Server is to use Profiler to record the execution of stored procedures and batches on the server, especially by tools included with SQL Server. A couple of my favorites are Enterprise Manager and the Index Tuning Wizard. The replication agents also occasionally reveal some hidden goodies.

Examining a Profiler trace captured while these tools run can yield interesting details about the way the server works. For example, while watching a Profiler trace during an Index Tuning Wizard run, I discovered that the wizard creates what are known as "hypothetical" indexes—statistics-only indexes used to determine whether a different indexing strategy would improve the performance of a given query or workload. (You can check to see whether an index is a hypothetical index via the IsHypothetical INDEXPROPERTY property name.) The Index Tuning Wizard builds these by calling CREATE INDEX using an undocumented WITH option: statistics_only. This tells us some things about how the server works. For example, if I didn't already know it, this would have told me that the optimizer doesn't look at data when it decides whether to use an index—it looks only at the statistics for an index when optimizing a query plan. It tells us how the wizard can evaluate so many different kinds of indexes in such a (relatively) short period of time: It creates test indexes without any data. So we learn something about the Index Tuning Wizard as well as SQL Server from the discovery of this undocumented feature.

Profiler also comes in handy in figuring out how undocumented xprocs and functions are used. SQL-DMO and Enterprise Manager use undocumented xprocs and functions extensively; capturing a Profiler trace while you run Enterprise Manager through its paces can turn up all sorts of hidden features.

One peculiar thing I've discovered about Profiler traces, though, is that the tool is apparently hard-coded to hide lines that contain the text "-- sp_password." Given that this text would be displayed for SP:StmtStarting/StmtCompleted events for the sp_password system procedure, the intent seems to be to keep Profiler traces from recording password changes. That said, the rudimentary way in which this has been implemented would allow a hacker to cover her or his tracks by appending "-- sp_password" to any line in a T-SQL batch or stored procedure she or he did not want to show up in a trace.

Snooping around in the Installation Scripts

Another good source of undocumented information is the set of installation scripts that ship with SQL Server. You can find these scripts in the Install folder under your root SQL Server installation. You can conduct the same sorts of searches against these scripts that we used with syscomments to find undocumented trace flags, DBCC commands, stored procedures, user-defined functions, and the like. For example, I discovered how to create my own INFORMATION_SCHEMA views (and documented the process in my last book) by examining ansiview.sql. I figured out how to create my own system functions by examining instdist.sql. There's a wealth of undocumented information to be had by examining the scripts that ship with the product, especially with respect to creating objects. We know that the server is somehow creating many of these via Transact-SQL. If we want to use the same functionality or just want to better understand how the server works, the installation scripts are good places to start.

DLL Imports

A final place to check for undocumented features is the SQL Server executable's import table. Every Windows executable has an import table. For each of the DLLs that the executable requires to load, this table lists the functions that it has explicitly referenced. By examining this table, you can learn about undocumented functions the executable may be calling. Once you have a function name, you can use a debugger to set a breakpoint and see when it's called.

A good example of this is the OPENDS60.DLL that ships with SQL Server. This DLL implements the Open Data Services API that the server uses internally and that is used to construct extended procedures. If you look at the import table for sqlservr.exe, the SQL Server executable, you'll see that it imports a large number of functions from OPENDS60.DLL, many of them undocumented. If you were to attach a debugger to sqlservr.exe and set breakpoints for these functions, you could likely determine in what circumstances they were used. This might help narrow down exactly what they do and how and why the server calls them.

Recap

Don't use undocumented features unless there's absolutely no other way. Your best strategy here is not to use them at all unless instructed to by Microsoft. Use your investigation into the undocumented features in SQL Server as a means of getting to know the product better, not a treasure hunt for nifty routines you can drop untested onto production systems.

Knowledge Measure

1. Cite three reasons you shouldn't use undocumented SQL Server features.

DTSDIAG

> *A few times over the years I've faced dire situations that tempted me to return to my former faith. Times of trial and despair are hard on anyone, and my former faith provided just the right crutch to avoid facing reality and ascribe something that was truly unjust or wrong to some higher purpose. But each time I've faced this down—each time I've withstood the temptation—I've found myself stronger and better able to handle the storms of life than before. Freeing oneself from a mental dependence on errant faith is a lot like giving up an addiction—there are powerful temptations to lapse back into the former habits, but the momentary dulling of the senses that comes from falling off the wagon is never worth the high cost.*
>
> —H. W. Kenton

I will close out this book by introducing you to a diagnostic application that you may find useful in your own work. It's based on SQL Server's DTS technology and makes use of the DTS object model. It demonstrates the kind of power an application can wield by bringing together the technologies on which SQL Server is based. If you haven't yet read Chapter 20 on DTS, you might want to before proceeding.

The name of the application is DTSDIAG. Its purpose in life is to collect diagnostic data from SQL Server. It can simultaneously collect Perfmon/Sysmon counters; a SQLDIAG report; the application, system, and security event logs; a Profiler trace; and the output of a blocking detection script (as defined in Microsoft Knowledge Base articles 251004, "INF: How to Monitor SQL Server 7.0 Blocking," and 271509, "INF: How to Monitor SQL Server 2000 Blocking").

DTSDIAG consists of a standalone Visual Basic application, four DTS packages, and some miscellaneous command line tools and scripts that it executes to gather the desired diagnostic data. The VB app allows you to specify the version of SQL Server to connect to, as well as the authentication information to use. Once the collection process has been started by clicking the Start button in the app, you can stop it by clicking the Stop button.

I've often found the need for a tool such as this when diagnosing SQL Server issues. Many times, expecting someone to collect Perfmon, Profiler, and the other types of diagnostics that I typically like to look at when investigating an issue turns out to be too much to ask. Often, the person I'm trying to assist simply can't get all the diagnostic collections going at once. Sometimes they can collect the right diagnostics, but they collect them at the wrong times or at different times. DTSDIAG alleviates this by allowing me to configure which diagnostics I need before sending the tool out to a target machine. I set up the types of data I want to collect in an INI file, then have the DTSDIAG executable and support files copied onto the target machine and executed. The only data supplied at the collection site is the name of the server/instance (and version) to connect to and the supporting authentication information. This makes the diagnostic collection process as foolproof as possible while still allowing it to be configured as necessary.

So, now that you know what the app does, let's have a look at its source code. I've already mentioned that diagnostic collection is started/stopped via the Start/Stop button in the DTSDIAG application. Here's the VB code attached to that button (Listing 25.1).

Listing 25.1

```
Private Sub btStartStop_Click()
If Not bRunning Then
  bRunning = True
  btStartStop.Caption = "Stop"
  ExecutePackage "dtsdiag_template.dts", "dtsdiag.dts",
      App.Path + "\dtsdiag.log"

Else
  btStartStop.Enabled = False
  ExecutePackage "dtsdiag_shutdown_template.dts",
      "dtsdiag_shutdown.dts", App.Path + "\dtsdiag_shutdown.log"
  ExecutePackage "dtsdiag_cleanup_template.dts",
      "dtsdiag_cleanup.dts", App.Path + "\dtsdiag_cleanup.log"
  bRunning = False
```

```
    btStartStop.Caption = "Start"
    btStartStop.Enabled = True
End If
End Sub
```

We use the same button for starting and stopping collection and merely change the button's caption based on what state we're in. When we start collection, we call a subroutine named ExecutePackage in order to run the dtsdiag_template.dts package. ExecutePackage saves dtsdiag_template.dts as dtsdiag.dts (I'll explain why in a moment) and runs it.

When we stop collecting, we run two packages: dtsdiag_shutdown_template.dts and dtsdiag_cleanup_template.dts. As with dtsdiag_template.dts, these packages are saved as new packages without the _template suffix and executed.

Certain diagnostics such as the SQLDIAG report and the system event logs can be collected when DTSDIAG is started up or when it is shut down or at both occasions. Whether and when these diagnostics are collected is specified in the DTSDIAG.INI file. The dtsdiag_shutdown_template.dts package exists to collect diagnostics that have been configured for collection during shutdown. The dtsdiag_cleanup_template.dts package exists to remove the stored procedures and other remnants from the collection process once DTSDIAG is stopped. It also checks for the existence of KILL.EXE, a utility from the Windows NT 4/2000 Resource Kit that can terminate other processes, and attempts to kill instances of osql, the utility DTSDIAG uses to collect much of its diagnostic data.

DTSDIAG's configuration file, DTSDIAG.INI, has a very simple format, as shown in Listing 25.2.

Listing 25.2

```
[DTSDIAG]
SQLDiag=1
SQLDiagStartup=0
SQLDiagShutdown=1
EventLogs=1
EventLogsStartup=0
EventLogsShutdown=1
Profiler=1
ProfilerEvents=76,75,92,94,93,95,16,22,21,33,67,55,79,80,61,69,25,
59,60,27,58,14,15,81,17,10,11,35,36,37,19,50,12,13
```

```
Perfmon=1
BlockingScript=1
BlockerLatch=0
BlockerFast=1
MaxTraceFileSize=100
MaxPerfmonLogSize=256
PerfmonPollingInterval=5
ProfilerPollingInterval=5
BlockingPollingInterval=120
Counter0=\MSSQL$%s:Buffer Manager\Buffer cache hit ratio
Counter1=\MSSQL$%s:Buffer Manager\Buffer cache hit ratio base
Counter2=\MSSQL$%s:Buffer Manager\Page lookups/sec
...
```

The format of the file should be pretty self-explanatory. Each type of diagnostic has its own Boolean switch. For example, if the Profiler value is set to 1, we attempt to collect a Profiler trace; otherwise, we don't.

Some of the settings in the file serve as options for the collection process. For example, ProfilerEvents contains a comma-delimited list of events (see sp_trace_setevent in Books Online for the master event number list) to capture in the Profiler trace. The Counter$N$ entries contain the list of Perfmon/Sysmon counters to collect. The BlockerLatch and BlockerFast options contain parameter switches for the blocking detection script (again, as outlined in Knowledge Base articles 251004 and 271509).

The key routine in DTSDIAG.EXE is the ExecutePackage method. Let's look at the code (Listing 25.3), then I'll walk you through what it does and how it does it.

Listing 25.3

```
Private Sub ExecutePackage(SrcName As String, TargName As String,
    LogName As String)
  Dim oPkg                As DTS.Package
  Dim oTask               As DTS.Task
  Dim oCreateProcessTask  As DTS.CreateProcessTask
  Set oPkg = New DTS.Package
  oPkg.LoadFromStorageFile SrcName, ""
  oPkg.LogFileName = LogName

  For Each oTask In oPkg.Tasks
```

```
    If 0 <> InStr(1, oTask.Name, "CreateProcess",
        vbTextCompare) Then
      Set oCreateProcessTask = oTask.CustomTask
      oCreateProcessTask.ProcessCommandLine =
          TranslateVars(oCreateProcessTask.ProcessCommandLine)
    End If
  Next

  Dim oFs
  Set oFs = CreateObject("Scripting.FileSystemObject")

  If oFs.FileExists(TargName) Then
    Kill TargName    'Delete in advance so the file won't grow
                     'ad infinitum
  End If

  Set oFs = Nothing

  oPkg.SaveToStorageFile TargName
  oPkg.Execute
  oPkg.UnInitialize
  Set oPkg = Nothing
End Sub
```

The routine begins by instantiating a DTS Package object. Although Package2 is the newer interface (introduced with SQL Server 2000), coding to the Package interface allows us to run on SQL Server 7.0.

Once the Package object is created, we load the specified package from its structured storage file. Each of the packages DTSDIAG uses is stored in COM's Structured Storage File format.

We next iterate through the tasks defined in the package and locate each Execute Process task by searching for CreateProcess in the task's name. We access each Execute Process task by assigning the CustomTask property of the generic task object in the Package.Tasks collection to the previously dimmed DTS.CreateProcessTask variable.

In case you're wondering, we iterate through the Execute Process tasks in each package in order to translate certain placeholders in the ProcessCommandLine property before executing the package. Because we need to execute complex scripts and retrieve their variable output in order to collect diagnostic data via DTSDIAG, we can't use a typical Execute SQL task to run much of the T-SQL DTSDIAG runs. Instead, we must shell to OSQL.EXE. Obviously, we want our calls to osql to be configurable—for example, we want to be able to specify the server and instance to connect to, the options for some of the diagnostic stored procedures we run, and so on. We could have used one of the custom task objects we built earlier in the book to make this a snap, but that would have required the custom task to be installed on the target machine when packages that contained it were executed. Because I didn't want to require COM objects to be registered before diagnostics could be collected, DTSDIAG doesn't use any custom tasks. Instead, it uses regular Execute Process tasks and placeholders in the ProcessCommandLine property in a manner similar to the ExecuteSQLScript and ExecuteScript custom tasks we built earlier in the book. Our VB code iterates through these tasks and replaces the placeholders with their appropriate values prior to executing a package.

Note the call to the TranslateVars function. TranslateVars is responsible for translating the variables in each ProcessCommandLine into their appropriate values. It's actually more complex than ExecutePackage, and we'll tour it in just a moment.

Once the ProcessCommandLine property for each Execute Process task has been properly translated, we write the translated package to the target package name and execute it. When the package finishes executing, we clean up the package object and return.

As I mentioned, the TranslateVars routine translates the placeholders in each Execute Process task's ProcessCommandLine property into their appropriate values. This means that, for example, it translates %server_instance% into the server and instance to which we want to connect. Similarly, it translates %auth_string% into the appropriate authentication string to be passed on the osql command line.

Some of the values we need to translate come from the DTSDIAG.INI configuration file. Therefore, our code contains a Declare Function DLL import for the GetPrivateProfileString API function, which is the Win32 function used to retrieve values from an INI file. Listing 25.4 shows the source code for TranslateVars and the GetPrivateProfileString import.

Listing 25.4

```
Private Declare Function GetPrivateProfileString Lib "KERNEL32" _
     Alias "GetPrivateProfileStringA" (ByVal AppName As String, _
     ByVal KeyName As String, ByVal keydefault As String, _
     ByVal ReturnString As String, ByVal NumBytes As Long, _
     ByVal FileName As String) As Long
```

```
Private Function TranslateVars(CmdLine As String) As String

   Dim strServer As String
   Dim strInstance As String
   Dim strProfilerParms As String
   Dim strBlockerParms As String
   Dim iBlockerPollingIntervalSeconds As Integer
   Dim iBlockerPollingIntervalMinutes As Integer
   Dim strWork As String

   ' Defaults for INI values
   strProfilerParms = ""
   strBlockerParms = ""
   iBlockerPollingIntervalSeconds = 0
   iBlockerPollingIntervalMinutes = 0

   Const BUFFSIZE = 1024

   strWork = Space(BUFFSIZE)

   ' Get Profiler Parms

   ' Events
   Res = GetPrivateProfileString("DTSDIAG", "ProfilerEvents", "", _
         strWork, BUFFSIZE, App.Path + "\dtsdiag.ini")

   If (0 <> Res) Then
     strProfilerParms = ", @Events=" + Chr(39) + Mid(strWork, 1, _
         Res) + Chr(39)
   End If


   ' MaxTraceFileSize
   strWork = Space(BUFFSIZE)
   Res = GetPrivateProfileString("DTSDIAG", "MaxTraceFileSize", "", _
         strWork, BUFFSIZE, App.Path + "\dtsdiag.ini")

   If (0 <> Res) Then
     strProfilerParms = strProfilerParms + ", @MaxFileSize=" + _
         Mid(strWork, 1, Res)
   End If

   ' Get Blocker Parms
```

```
' BlockerLatch
strWork = Space(BUFFSIZE)
Res = GetPrivateProfileString("DTSDIAG", "BlockerLatch", "", _
    strWork, BUFFSIZE, App.Path + "\dtsdiag.ini")

If (0 <> Res) Then
  strBlockerParms = "@latch=" + Mid(strWork, 1, Res)
End If

' BlockerFast
strWork = Space(BUFFSIZE)
Res = GetPrivateProfileString("DTSDIAG", "BlockerFast", "", _
    strWork, BUFFSIZE, App.Path + "\dtsdiag.ini")

If (0 <> Res) Then
  strBlockerParms = strBlockerParms + ", @fast=" + _
      Mid(strWork, 1, Res)
End If

' BlockingPollingInterval
strWork = Space(BUFFSIZE)
Res = GetPrivateProfileString("DTSDIAG", _
      "BlockingPollingInterval", "", _
      strWork, BUFFSIZE, App.Path + "\dtsdiag.ini")

If (0 <> Res) Then
  iBlockerPollingIntervalSeconds = Val(Mid(strWork, 1, Res))

  ' Since we are plugging the time part, max is 59
  If iBlockerPollingIntervalSeconds > 59 Then
    iBlockerPollingIntervalMinutes = _
        iBlockerPollingIntervalSeconds / 60
    iBlockerPollingIntervalSeconds = _
        iBlockerPollingIntervalSeconds Mod 60
  End If
End If

' Extract server and instance from ServerInstance TextBox
Dim iPos As Integer

iPos = InStr(1, tbServerInstance.Text, "\")

If 0 <> iPos Then
  strServer = Mid(tbServerInstance.Text, 1, iPos - 1)
  strInstance = Mid(tbServerInstance.Text, iPos + 1)
```

```
Else
  strServer = tbServerInstance.Text
  strInstance = ""
End If

' Replace tokens
CmdLine = Replace(CmdLine, "%auth_string%", strAuth)
CmdLine = Replace(CmdLine, "%ver%", strVer)
CmdLine = Replace(CmdLine, "%server_instance%", _
    tbServerInstance.Text)
If taVersion.SelectedItem.Index = 1 Then
  CmdLine = Replace(CmdLine, "%trace_output%", App.Path & _
      "\output\" & "sp_trace.trc")
Else    'Omit file extension for 80
  CmdLine = Replace(CmdLine, "%trace_output%", App.Path & _
      "\output\" & "sp_trace")
End If
CmdLine = Replace(CmdLine, "%server%", strServer)
CmdLine = Replace(CmdLine, "%instance%", strInstance)
CmdLine = Replace(CmdLine, "%profilerparms%", strProfilerParms)
CmdLine = Replace(CmdLine, "%blockerparms%", strBlockerParms)
CmdLine = Replace(CmdLine, "%bis%", _
    Str(iBlockerPollingIntervalSeconds))
CmdLine = Replace(CmdLine, "%bim%", _
    Str(iBlockerPollingIntervalMinutes))

TranslateVars = CmdLine
End Function
```

Once all the required configuration values are retrieved from DTS-DIAG.INI, TranslateVars uses the VB Replace function to translate each token into its appropriate value. It finishes by returning the translated process command line as its function result.

You may be wondering why we don't just use a Dynamic Properties task inside the relevant DTS packages since these INI values ultimately end up inside packages. After all, a Dynamic Properties task can retrieve values directly from an INI file without requiring any type of Automation code. Rather than coding an external app that modifies packages on the fly using COM Automation, wouldn't it be simpler just to use a Dynamic Properties task inside each package where we need to read INI configuration values? The answer is that we do use one when possible. However, many of the configuration values we need to supply must be inserted into the middle of task property values, so they can't readily be supplied by a Dynamic Properties task. Using a Dynamic Properties task to assign an INI configuration value to a property is tenable only when you are assigning the entire property. Assigning only a portion of the property requires a script or external Automation code.

So, now that we've toured the VB source code for DTSDIAG, let's talk about the DTS packages it uses. Open dtsdiag_template.dts (in the CH25\ dtsdiag subfolder on the CD accompanying this book) in the DTS Designer so that we can discuss a few of its high points.

The package begins by creating a folder under the startup folder named OUTPUT. If the folder already exists, it is deleted and recreated. This folder will contain all the files collected by DTSDIAG. Output files from tasks we execute to get set up for the collection process (e.g., creating stored procedures) will have ## prefixed to their names. This allows them to be easily distinguished from the actual diagnostic files we're interested in. Normally you can delete these ## files after the collection process is complete. You'll need them only if there is some problem with DTSDIAG.

Note the use of a Dynamic Properties task to load configuration values from DTSDIAG.INI. As I mentioned earlier, we load as many configuration values as we can using a Dynamic Properties task. Each type of diagnostic has a global variable associated with it that controls whether it gets collected. For example, the global variable sqldiag controls whether SQLDIAG.EXE is executed. The Dynamic Properties task sets the sqldiag global variable by reading DTSDIAG.INI and retrieving the value of the SQLDiag key.

The Blocker, Profiler, and SQLDIAG processes within the package begin by calling osql to create the stored procedures they will call to collect the required data. The blocker process creates two stored procedures: one named sp_code_runner, a stored procedure capable of running other procedures or T-SQL code on a schedule or until a logical condition becomes true, and one named either sp_blocker_pss70 or sp_blocker_pss80 (depending on the version of SQL Server you're connecting to), the blocking detection stored procedures provided in the Knowledge Base articles I mentioned earlier. Because the sp_blockerXXXX procedures belong to Microsoft, I have not included them on the CD accompanying this book. You will have to access the aforementioned Knowledge Base articles at http://www.microsoft.com and download them yourself if you want to use DTSDIAG to run them. Alternatively, you can supply your own blocking detection procedure(s)—there's nothing requiring the use of the Microsoft stored procedures in DTSDIAG.

Note that we don't execute SQLDIAG.EXE directly from our DTS package. SQLDIAG.EXE must be run on its host SQL Server; running it directly from the package would require that the package be run on the server, something you might not want to do. Instead, we call a stored procedure that shells to SQLDIAG.EXE on the server via xp_cmdshell. This allows you to collect a SQLDIAG report without physically being on the SQL Server machine. Note that this technique requires additional steps on a SQL Server 2000 cluster (see Knowledge Base article 233332).

The Perfmon task executes a custom utility I've written in C++ (also included on the CD) that collects a specified set of Perfmon counters and writes them to a Perfmon BLG-format log. PMC is similar to the LogMan utility included with Windows XP and later (see Knowledge Base article 303133) but works on Windows 9x and later as well. Note that, because of a header file change Microsoft made with the introduction of Windows XP, you will need the version of PDH.DLL (the Performance Data Helper library, the engine behind Perfmon/Sysmon) that ships with Windows 2000 in order to use PMC on Windows XP or later. For your convenience, I've included this file in the dtsdiag folder on the CD accompanying this book. If you decide to run PMC on Windows XP or later (as opposed to running LogMan), I recommend that you use the version of the PDH.DLL I've included with DTSDIAG. You shouldn't replace the version of PDH.DLL that comes with the operating system with the one I've included. Just leave it in the DTSDIAG startup folder, and PMC will find it when it starts.

PMC reads the INI file name passed into it as a parameter (DTSDIAG.INI, in this case), locates INI values named CounterN, and adds each one to a Perfmon BLG log. If it finds the string "%s" in a counter name, it translates this to the name of the specified SQL Server instance (optionally passed on its command line) before adding it to the Perfmon log. If no instance name is specified, but PMC encounters "%s" in a counter name, it assumes the default SQL Server instance is being specified and replaces the entire "MSSQL$%s" string with "SQLServer" in order to add the counter for the default instance.

The event logs are collected using the elogdmp.exe utility included with the Windows 2000 Resource Kit. Again, since this utility belongs to Microsoft, I haven't included it on the CD accompanying this book. You can actually use any event log dumper utility you want (e.g., dumpel.exe from the Windows NT 4 Resource Kit will also work)—you just need to configure the event log Execute Process tasks accordingly.

Note that the event logs are collected via an Execute Package task, which starts a separate package that collects all three of them in parallel. This is done because event logs are one of those tasks that can be collected at startup or shutdown or both. So, in order to allow for event log collection from dtsdiag_template.dts as well as dtsdiag_shutdown_template.dts, we've put the event log collection tasks off in their own package, which we execute as appropriate during startup or shutdown.

A final aspect of DTSDIAG that's worth exploring is the way we use ActiveX script workflow associations to enable/disable certain execution paths within packages. You'll recall that we discussed this technique earlier in the book. In DTSDIAG we use it, for example, to disable the Profiler task path when the DTSDIAG.INI Profiler value is set to 0 (false). Listing 25.5 presents the ActiveX script that's associated with the Create Profiler Proc Execute Process task.

Listing 25.5

```
Function Main()
  If DTSGlobalVariables("profiler") Then
    Main = DTSStepScriptResult_ExecuteTask
  Else
    Main = DTSStepScriptResult_DontExecuteTask
  End If
End Function
```

The global variable profiler is assigned by the Dynamic Properties task at the start of package processing. If this variable is nonzero, we execute the Profiler task path, otherwise, we skip it.

For tasks that can be executed at startup, shutdown, or both, we have to check a second global variable to determine whether to execute them. Listing 25.6 shows the ActiveX script associated with the SQLDIAG task line.

Listing 25.6

```
Function Main()
  If (DTSGlobalVariables("sqldiag")) And _
  (DTSGlobalVariables("sqldiagstartup")) Then
    Main = DTSStepScriptResult_ExecuteTask
  Else
    Main = DTSStepScriptResult_DontExecuteTask
  End If
End Function
```

So, we check not only the global variable sqldiag but also sqldiagstartup (or sqldiagshutdown) to be sure that we're supposed to collect the SQLDIAG report when this particular step is executed. In the dtsdiag_template.dts, we check sqldiagstartup; in dtsdiag_shutdown_template.dts, we check sqldiagshutdown.

That's DTSDIAG in a nutshell. You can run the utility to experiment with it further and load its various packages into the DTS Designer to see how they're constructed. You can play with the VB code to explore controlling DTS packages via Automation. The source code and support files for DTSDIAG are located in the CH25\dtsdiag subfolder on the CD accompanying this book.

A natural evolution to the DTSDIAG concept is the notion of loading the collected data into SQL Server for analysis. I will leave that as a reader exercise but will provide a few hints for the adventurous. The event log and SQLDIAG reports are plain text files and, with some massaging, can be easily imported into SQL Server tables. The blocking script output can also be processed as text and imported into a set of SQL Server tables, although it's a little more challenging because of the variability in the output format. A Profiler trace can be read as a rowset using the fn_trace_gettable T-SQL function, so importing it into a table is a snap. A Perfmon BLG log can be converted to a CSV format using the Relog tool included with Windows XP and later (see Knowledge Base article 303133), which can then be imported into SQL Server using DTS. Once you have all the data in a SQL Server database, you can dream up all sorts of sophisticated analysis for it. The trick is in coalescing the data in the first place.

PART V

Essays

Why I Really, Really Don't Like *Fish!*

Get people to have a positive attitude and like those they work with so that they'll be better workers? Gee, wish I'd thought of that. What a novel concept! You mean I can boost my effectiveness as a manager just by pumping people up with hokum? And to think all this time I've labored under the delusion that my people actually wanted substance from me. Now, after all these years, I learn that they just want me to stroke their egos, to blow smoke up the proverbial *derrière*.

Recently, I had the misfortune of being subjected to the latest surfacing of what has become a cyclic management fad: the positive-attitude triteness known as the Pike Place Market *Fish!* story. It's a fish story, alright.

I originally stumbled across this frivolity a few years ago in video form. While designing a new human resources system for the CIA, I arrived early for a meeting one day to discover the entire team I worked with crowded around a television set engrossed in the story of the Seattle fish market and how wonderful everything was simply because the employees had decided that it would be.

I had a bit of a revelation as I watched the poor saps eagerly eating up the stale *Fish!* claptrap: *I'm in the wrong business*. To paraphrase one of the best conmen of them all, if a man really wants to make a million dollars, all he needs to do is come up with a clichéd, banal self-help philosophy that has no substance or quantifiable means of measuring its effectiveness. Drum up a few anecdotal success stories, put the whole thing on video or turn it into a book, and you've got everything you need to make *your* company a happy place, regardless of what it does for anyone else. Making a million dollars would make almost anyone happy, even a cynic like me.

The reason that *Fish!* and similar fads are so vacuous is that many of the real problems of management and employee morale cannot be solved by simply changing one's attitude. If someone is grossly underpaid, all the positive thinking in the world won't put more money in her bank account each month. If an employee is working the graveyard shift, all the toy fish in the sea won't make him feel any better about being away from his family every night. And if management is truly inept, eagerly jumping from one fad to another on what seems like a monthly basis, no self-help video is going to fix that for the long term. In that situation, the employees' frame of mind isn't the problem; management is. Given that it is the root cause of the problem, only management can effect a long-term solution.

You might view *Fish!* and its ilk as harmless drivel. After all, what's wrong with getting someone to work at being happy, to try to keep a positive attitude regardless of the situation? There's no harm in that—if only it ended there. The problem with *Fish!* and similar nonsense is that it gives management an out, a way to shirk its responsibility to keep employee morale at a respectable level. It puts the onus of keeping the employees happy on the employees themselves, which works out nicely for management (I'm sure it improves *their* morale), but not so well for the employees, who are often powerless to address the real issues affecting their happiness: compensation, opportunities, job fulfillment, job security, and so on.

Subscribing to the *Fish!* mentality allows management to say, "So, you find stapling reports all day, every day boring? Well, just 'choose your attitude'! 'Learn to play'! Throw that stapler across the office every now and then!" When an employee says, "I haven't had a raise in five years, and my daughter starts college next month, and I can't help her financially," management can respond, "Learn to 'be present' for her. Learn to 'make her day.' She'll appreciate that more than any financial help you could give her." *Fish!* provides a convenient mechanism for substituting clichés and platitudes for substance. It allows management to address real-life problems with glib nonsolutions in a Dilbert-esque fashion. And it's a great cost-cutting move for the business—after all, talk is cheap.

Beyond giving management a way out of doing what it should instead want to do—namely, keeping its most valuable resource, its employees, happy—the thing that really peeves me about *Fish!* is that it encourages management to treat employees like children. In place of having a substantive discussion about real issues, *Fish!* makes it okay to hand people a child's toy and brand them as malcontents if they don't find that satisfactory. It makes it okay to twist someone's arm into going home at the end of a twelve-hour day and making cookies to bring in the next day so that he or she can remain a "team player." Beyond the inanity and emptiness of the hollow promises and nonsolutions *Fish!* encourages management to proffer, it actually adds insult to injury by making it acceptable to humiliate adults by treating them as though they had the emotional awareness of a two-year-old and expecting them to be pacified by trinkets, manager-speak, and token gestures. Amalgams of self-help management gobbledygook such as

Fish! are demeaning by their very existence because they presume that those who hear their pitch are naive enough and emotionally shallow enough to fall for it. Unfortunately, those subjected to their ploys often have little choice in the matter.

Management often displays an astonishing audacity and utter lack of empathy in embracing the type of thinking that *Fish!* encourages. In response to my complaints about being unchallenged and underutilized in a job I once had, management offered me a "promotion" to a position that involved working a graveyard shift and required me to be on call day-in and day-out. The new position didn't offer a raise or any level upgrade within the organization. It did, however, have a fancier title. On hearing this pitch, I countered, "Are you sure you couldn't throw a pay deduction in there somewhere? Maybe take away some of my benefits? I've really been wanting to move to that cube in the basement—any chance you could swing that?" That they could even propose such a thing with a straight face was downright amazing to me.

So, I'll offer you the same words of wisdom Ernest Hemingway gave Stanley Karnow in *Friendly Advice*: Develop a built-in baloney detector (only Hemingway didn't say "baloney"). Don't fall for such fluff. Insist on substantive discussions with management. Don't be a malcontent, and *do* work at being happy, but, to paraphrase Billy Crystal in the movie *Mr. Saturday Night*, don't let anyone defecate in your hat and then say, "Thank you, it fits much better now." When we acquiesce to lame management overtures, we make things worse for everyone. We give those in management who don't realize the value of their employees no reason to change their ways in the future. Stand up for your rights, your fellow employees, and your dignity. No job is worth losing your self-respect.

Pseudo-Techie Tactics 101

How to Make Yourself Appear to Be an Expert via Newsgroup Postings

1. Answer a different question than what was asked, with lots of superfluous detail, particularly if the detail is obscure or hard to verify.
2. Avoid answering questions directly. If a poster asks a direct question such as, "Will this work?" or "Will technique x perform better than y?" avoid actually answering the question at all costs. Never give a definitive answer to a question and never make definitive statements if you can avoid it. If you are forced to make a definitive statement, keep it safe—something along the lines of, "SQL Server is a Microsoft product" or "XML stands for eXtensible Markup Language" is a good place to start.
3. Answer simple questions with longwinded discourses that take the conversation into, again, superfluous detail, particularly if it's obscure or hard to verify.
4. Pick up answers from later responses in a thread, then go back to older postings and reply to them with those answers as though you didn't see the later posts.
5. Answer questions in general, vague terms, with lots of references to product documentation, Knowledge Base articles, books, and whitepapers even if you haven't actually read and/or don't understand any of them.
6. Whenever possible, work into a response extracurricular work you have done or plan to do that may or may not be related to the question at hand. For example, if the question is about how one might optimize a stored procedure they've written, refer them to the Web cast you're working on regarding .NET technologies.

7. Be hypercritical and sanctimonious about a feature that's off-limits, lacking, or doesn't work quite right in a product or technology when you know it is safe to do so, that is, when the actual experts on the topic have already spoken out about it. An example would be the limitations one encounters when storing XML documents in SQL Server tables. Given that there are well-known limitations here involving text columns and loop-back connections, it pays to get on your soapbox and preach to the converted about these limitations. This will convince newbies that you know what you're talking about and is especially impressive to managers, who like to encourage people to develop shallow expertise.

8. Troll FAQs and newsgroup archives for canned responses, then, when a newbie or other uninformed person asks a question, regurgitate what you found, even if it's not entirely on point. You get special bonus points for using responses from technical experts you want to impress. So, for example, if you want to impress Joe Celko, when you come across a response in an archive that he posted, use the response almost verbatim when posting a response to a similar question. Joe may have forgotten his original post and may infer that you think like he does, and the recipient will infer that you're cut from the same cloth as people like Joe, that you have similar technical depth. You get to appear to be an expert, while someone else did all the work—what a deal! Give credit for such nuggets only on a rare occasion, usually when you have some reason to throw the original poster a bone. If the original poster is someone you don't care about impressing or schmoozing with, never, ever give credit for the original post. If someone notices the similarity between your post and the original, feign ignorance, an area in which you are actually likely to have expert skills.

9. Without appearing to be a jerk, come as close as possible to flaming newbies and other posters who mention sacred cows such as using undocumented features or hacking system files or tables. Be sure to toe the company line in such situations as much as possible. Speak as though you are the resident expert on system hacks and undocumented features and the sole guardian of the vendor's interests in such matters. Without offending the folks you want to impress, be as sanctimonious and condescending as possible, especially if the actual experts on the technology have responded in kind recently. Actively seek out such bandwagons to jump on.

10. Embed as much code as possible in your postings, even if it's unnecessary or doesn't add materially to the point you're making, espe-

cially on newsgroups that have high vendor visibility. You get special bonus points for dropping into C++ or assembly language, even if you excerpted the code straight from source code owned by other people or a debugger and don't have a clue as to what it actually does. You get an additional bonus point if you drop into a lengthy code discussion and use the explanations by the actual experts on it as though you came up with them yourself. Good sources of information here are bug database entries, MVP mailing lists, books, vendor whitepapers, and private exchanges with developers or product support experts. Be careful to never, ever give credit to the original source of your information. People need to believe that you are an expert coder and that you did all the analysis yourself.

11. Along these lines, do as much as you can to portray yourself as a "bit head" even though you may not actually know what a bit is. One of my personal favorites is using Courier fonts for all your postings (the inference being that your postings typically consist of so much code and alignment-sensitive data such as stack dumps and the like that you're better off just using a fixed-pitch font in every post). Low-level details that are beyond the technical depth of the average manager are especially impressive—divulge these, even if they're not relevant to the discussion at hand and even if you don't understand them yourself, whenever possible.

12. When an actual expert responds to a post, be quick to jump on the bandwagon, especially if the post is regarding a technology in which you have nothing significant to contribute but would like people to form a general perception of you as having deep skills in the area. For example, if you want to convince people that you're a debugging expert, be quick to jump onto bandwagons regarding symbols server issues and debugger quirks. Be careful not to offer any substantive information in your posts; the idea is to create a perception, not to actually add any value or stick your neck out in any way.

13. Along these lines, never, ever be the first respondent when a new issue in a technology in which you want to appear to have expertise arises. Always let someone else make the first post. It's far better for another poster to stick his or her neck out while you hang back in the shadows and wait for someone else to come up with the right answer.

14. Avoid doing research to answer a posted question. If the question requires you to think, run a repro scenario, or otherwise do much of anything except get credit for other people's work, avoid it. Let someone else do the dirty work.

15. Attempt to answer as many questions as possible with other questions. Take the conversation off into irrelevant areas using such questions whenever possible.

16. Post responses to the entire newsgroup whenever it benefits you to do so, regardless of whether the ongoing conversation would be beneficial to the other members of the newsgroup and especially if it embarrasses the poster. This is particularly important if the newsgroup has high vendor visibility or if it has a large number of members. Never offer to take a conversation offline that would benefit you personally to discuss in a public forum (e.g., when discussing with a newbie the fine points of how to read a stack dump or how SQLXML is put together from an architectural standpoint).

17. Regularly forward information you receive on one newsgroup to another, even though you know most of the people on the second newsgroup are also on the first and have already received the information. So, for example, if an MVP posts something of interest to the SQL Server programming newsgroup, forward it to the SQL Server administration newsgroup, even though everyone on the administration group is very likely to already be on the programming newsgroup. This makes you appear to be the custodian of such information and links you by association with it, even though you had nothing to do with its creation.

18. Make a point of asking esoteric questions involving fringe technology elements on newsgroups with high vendor visibility and/or PYNTI (People You Need To Impress) membership. Attempt to work in enough techno-babble that people will infer that you're knee-deep in something of historical complexity. Be sure you ask these questions on newsgroups where they are least likely to be actually answered and most likely to impress the people you want to impress. For example, you might ask questions having to do with reading symbol files directly on a SQL Server newsgroup. A question like, "Has anyone implemented a fast Fourier transform algorithm in assembly language?" would be a big hit on a Visual Basic newsgroup. Similarly, "Has anyone successfully replaced the .NET Framework XML parser with MSXML using Pinvoke?" would be a great one for one of the Office newsgroups. Never actually say what you're doing or why—after all, you're just trying to attract attention to yourself, not actually get an answer. Never let anyone know that you barely understand enough about the fringe technology you're referencing to ask a question about it, let alone build anything with it.

19. Along these lines, attempt to work into your esoteric newsgroup questions superfluous detail that makes you look good. For example, if your question asks whether the order of the page frame array returned by AllocateUserPhysicalPages has changed in a particular release of Windows and possibly caused some code you're reviewing that sorts the array to take much longer to run, include detail on sorting algorithms in general and a long discourse about how the code you're reviewing uses the array. Provide a tutorial for the gullible on shell sorts, bubble sorts, memory access algorithms, and so on. Completely ignore more obvious potential causes of your issue, such as that you don't know what you're talking about and the length of the sort hasn't increased at all. Also, gloss right over the fact that a simple "Does anyone know whether the page frame array order for AllocateUserPhysicalPages changed for Windows nnn?" would have sufficed. Remember: You're not actually after a resolution to your issue—you are attempting to impress people.

20. Work as many buzzwords into your newsgroup posts as possible. Especially if these are esoteric or fringe terms, use them as though everyone already knows what you mean. Terms like "undetected distributed deadlock," "thread priority inversion," "scribbler," and "merge nonconvergence" are good candidates, especially on general-purpose newsgroups where lots of people are likely not to know what the terms mean. Throw these terms around like you were born knowing what they mean (heck, convince people that you actually *coined* the terms, if you can) and that people who don't know what you're talking about must be profoundly ignorant.

21. Regularly criticize technologies you don't understand, especially those you fear or those that people you consider rivals hold in esteem. Be sure to keep your criticisms general and above any sort of reason-based debate. Remember: Your job is to spread FUD—Fear, Uncertainty, and Doubt. Don't let anyone know that you've not actually used a technology you're criticizing to build anything of any significance and that you only "know" what you read. If dissing a language, be sure to keep secret the fact that you haven't written a line of production code with it. Those are all details that people who listen to you don't need to know. This type of criticism will establish you as having skills and knowledge that you don't in the eyes of some of the folks you want to impress. For example, if you say, "C# isn't a real language," some gullible people might actually believe you've written production code in C# and that you have enough experience

with languages in general to say which ones are and are not "real." This allows you to demean your rivals for espousing such poor technology and allows you to feign knowledge you don't have—two for the price of one!

22. Let as many people as possible know about anything of any significance that you do. For example, if you are forced to conduct what seems to you to be significant research into a particular issue, make sure lots of people know about your in-depth investigation. You get bonus points if you come to conclusions that actually required several hours to reach but you understate them and pretend to have arrived at an answer in a matter of minutes. This can make you look like a wizard to the gullible and can conceal how long it actually takes you to figure out even the simplest of problems. An effective means of doing this is the ubiquitous newsgroup "sanity check" post. It works like this: You identify an area in which you'd like to be perceived as having expertise (e.g., SQL Server LPE nuances). You then conduct some research into a particular issue within it (e.g., how determinism affects UDFs). Let's say the research takes, oh, twelve hours. Post a message to a newsgroup with PYNTI members outlining your research and asking for a "sanity check" of it. Don't actually ask any specific questions—that might betray that you actually don't know enough about the subject even to ask an intelligent question. Remember: You aren't actually wanting any sort of "check"—the purpose of your post is to inform the poor saps on the newsgroup of your latest grand achievement. Casually mention that you spent only about 15 minutes looking into the issue. This covers you in case your research is off in left field and also makes you look like a genius to the dimwitted on the newsgroup—again, another two-for-one bargain.

23. Characterize fringe and rarely used problem resolutions as being so commonplace that everyone except the hapless ignorant would know about them. Refer to unusually creative solutions as "the usual course of action" or something similar. Be especially dismissive of creative ideas from those you consider rivals. This does two things for you. First, it conceals the fact that you don't know commonplace solutions from truly innovative ones because you know next to nothing about the subject area. Second, it demeans the innovation and outside-the-box thinking of the people who come up with these unusual solutions in the first place. You get to one-up the more agile among your "peers" (which includes almost everyone) by pretending

their creative solutions are so commonplace as not to constitute anything really innovative. And you get to imply that you knew of the solution all along (as everyone does) because it is so pedestrian. To the truly dimwitted, you may even seem to be associated with the creative solution in some way—you may be able to appropriate it to some extent. And, if you do this well enough and long enough, you may actually succeed in discouraging your rivals from thinking outside the box in the first place, which would serve your ends just fine.

Index

From Ken Henderson and Addison-Wesley

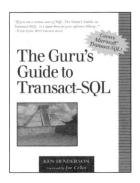

The Guru's Guide to Transact-SQL

Ken Henderson

0-201-61576-2

"If you are a serious user of SQL, *The Guru's Guide to Transact-SQL*, is a must have for your reference library."

—*Wayne Snyder, IKON Education Services*

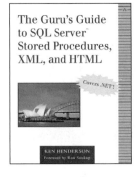

The Guru's Guide to SQL Server Stored Procedures, XML, and HTML

Ken Henderson

0-201-70046-8

"This is a book that deserves a prominent place by anyone who aspires to be a real professional developer of SQL Server applications."

—*from the Foreword by Ron Soukup*

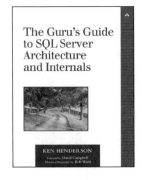

The Guru's Guide to SQL Server Architecture and Internals

Ken Henderson

0-201-70047-6

"I can pretty much guarantee that anyone who uses SQL Server on a regular basis, (even those located in Redmond working on SQL Server), can learn something new from reading this book."

—*from the Foreword by David Campbell*

For more information including sample chapters, go to **www.awprofessional.com**.

informIT

CD-ROM Warranty

Addison-Wesley warrants the enclosed disc to be free of defects in materials and faulty workmanship under normal use for a period of ninety days after purchase. If a defect is discovered in the disc during this warranty period, a replacement disc can be obtained at no charge by sending the defective disc, postage prepaid, with proof of purchase to:

Editorial Department
Addison-Wesley Professional
Pearson Technology Group
75 Arlington Street, Suite 300
Boston, MA 02116
Email: AWPro@awl.com

Addison-Wesley makes no warranty or representation, either expressed or implied, with respect to this software, its quality, performance, merchantability, or fitness for a particular purpose. In no event will Addison-Wesley, its distributors, or dealers be liable for direct, indirect, special, incidental, or consequential damages arising out of the use or inability to use the software. The exclusion of implied warranties is not permitted in some states. Therefore, the above exclusion may not apply to you. This warranty provides you with specific legal rights. There may be other rights that you may have that vary from state to state. The contents of this CD-ROM are intended for personal use only.

More information and updates are available at:

http://www.awprofessional.com/